DYNAMIC
OF
DESTRUCTION

CULTURE AND MASS KILLING
IN THE FIRST WORLD WAR

ALAN KRAMER

OXFORD
UNIVERSITY PRESS

OXFORD

UNIVERSITY PRESS

Great Clarendon Street, Oxford OX2 6DP

Oxford University Press is a department of the University of Oxford.
It furthers the University's objective of excellence in research, scholarship,
and education by publishing worldwide in

Oxford New York

Auckland Cape Town Dar es Salaam Hong Kong Karachi
Kuala Lumpur Madrid Melbourne Mexico City Nairobi
New Delhi Shanghai Taipei Toronto

With offices in

Argentina Austria Brazil Chile Czech Republic France Greece
Guatemala Hungary Italy Japan Poland Portugal Singapore
South Korea Switzerland Thailand Turkey Ukraine Vietnam

Oxford is a registered trade mark of Oxford University Press
in the UK and in certain other countries

Published in the United States
by Oxford University Press Inc., New York

© Alan Kramer 2007

The moral rights of the author have been asserted
Database right Oxford University Press (maker)

First published 2007

British Library Cataloguing in Publication Data

Data available

Library of Congress Cataloging in Publication Data

Data available

Typeset by SPI Publisher Services, Pondicherry, India
Printed in Great Britain
on acid-free paper by
Clays Ltd, St Ives plc

ISBN 978–0–19–280342–9

1 3 5 7 9 10 8 6 4 2

Acknowledgements

I should like to mention first of all the support of Trinity College Dublin. Like many other universities it has not been immune to the ruthless drive for rationalization, and the demands of teaching and administration compete for time with research, but fortunately the Department of History has continued to show its commitment to research, not least by preserving the essential system of sabbatical leave. I am grateful especially to the head of the School of Histories and Humanities, Jane Ohlmeyer, for her consistent support. During my research leave in 2002–3 I was able to complete one major project, and start research on two other projects, the fruit of one of which is the present book. I gratefully acknowledge the assistance of the Arts and Social Science Benefaction Fund of TCD.

A great intellectual debt is owed to several friends and colleagues. I want to thank John Horne for the many discussions over the years in the research seminar which we take turns to convene in Trinity College Dublin, for countless impromptu conversations about the writing of history which can only happen when one works in the same department, and for reading and commenting on the draft of this book. I should also like to thank the participants at the research seminar in modern European history at Trinity College, and at the Modern History Faculty, Oxford (and especially Nicholas Stargardt), where I presented papers based on the main ideas of the book. Gerhard Hirschfeld (Stuttgart) has been a stalwart friend and expert adviser on Germany in the First World War and beyond. Richard Evans (Cambridge) has been a major influence on my own writing; he has given generously of his time to discuss the ideas of this book and advise on the manuscript. Thanks are due also to the anonymous reader of the manuscript for his or her comments. I have benefited also from the incisive comments of Michael Wildt (Hamburg) and from our discussions during long walks by the beautiful Alster lake on the continuities and radical differences between the First and the Second World Wars.

Many others have provided helpful references and much-needed support in other ways; I particularly want to mention Heather Jones (Dublin), Ian Kershaw (Sheffield), Sophie de Schaepdrijver (Penn State), Irina Renz (Stuttgart), Lothar Kettenacker (Munich), Ute Schneider (Darmstadt), Daniele Ceschin (Venice), and Maria Pia Critelli (Rome). MacGregor Knox (London) spotted many errors, for which I am most grateful.

During my sabbatical year, spent mainly in Rome, I used the excellent library of the German Historical Institute. I wish to thank the Institute's director, Michael Matheus, and above all Lutz Klinkhammer for many hours of enlightening discussion on Italian history. The staffs at Trinity College Library Dublin; the Staats- und Universitätsbibliothek Carl von Ossietzky, the library of the Historisches Seminar of the University, the library of the Helmut-Schmidt-Universität, and the library of the Bernhard-Nocht-Institut für Tropenmedizin (all in Hamburg); and at the Biblioteca di Storia Moderna e Contemporanea in Rome all provided essential assistance, for which I am grateful. Matthew Stout drew the maps. My editors at Oxford University Press deserve thanks for their careful attention to the manuscript and their perseverance in the production of the book: Luciana O'Flaherty and Matthew Cotton, and the production editor Catherine Berry. Tom Chandler did a fine job of copy-editing, and Emmanuelle Péri succeeded admirably in tracking down the copyright-holders of the illustrations.

Most of all I should like to thank Renate Ahrens. Since both of us are authors, each reads the other's work before anyone else, and thus contributes to the creative process. Renate has enriched my work, and much else besides, through her love. However, readers who expect to find here the conventional dedication will be disappointed. This book is a story of unremitting violence, destruction, hatred, and misery; and it seems inappropriate to dedicate it to anyone.

A.K.

Trinity College Dublin
January 2007

Contents

List of Illustrations

List of Maps

Abbreviations

ACS	Archivio Centrale dello Stato, Rome
BA	Bundesarchiv, Berlin
BA–MA	Bundesarchiv-Militärarchiv, Freiburg
BEF	British Expeditionary Force
Cheka	All-Russian Extraordinary Commission for Combating Counter-Revolution and Sabotage
CPU	Committee for Progress and Union (radical nationalist faction of the CUP)
CUP	Committee for Union and Progress (the Young Turk party)
KPD	Communist Party of Germany (Kommunistische Partei Deutschlands)
KA	Kriegsarchiv, Munich
OHL	German Supreme Army Command (Oberste Heeresleitung)
PAAA	Politisches Archiv des Auswärtigen Amts
SPD	Social Democratic Party of Germany (Sozialdemokratische Partei Deutschlands)
USPD	Independent Social Democratic Party of Germany (Unabhängige Sozialdemokratische Partei Deutschlands)
WTB	semi-official German press bureau (Wolff'sches Telegraphen-Bureau)

Introduction

Let them come, the good firebrands with their singed fingers! There they
are! Yes, there they are!... Come, set fire to the bookshelves of the
libraries!... Divert the canals to flood the museums!... Oh, the joy of
seeing the glorious paintings, torn and discoloured, float away on these
waters!... Use pickaxes, hatchets, and sledgehammers! Demolish without
pity the venerated cities![1]

This text by one of Europe's avant-garde intellectuals was published in
1909. It reads like a prescription for the massive destruction of Europe's
cultural heritage and mass killing that ensued in the years 1914 to 1918. Its
author was an Italian poet and extreme nationalist, Filippo Tommaso
Marinetti, who proclaimed his ideas in the manifesto of Futurism from
which the quotation is taken. Marinetti's movement was part of a Europe-
wide revolt of a younger generation of intellectuals against the stuffy old
order; his own version of revolution was characterized by militarism,
nationalism, misogyny, and the worship of death and destructiveness.

Bizarre and deliberately provocative though some of his ideas were, the
outbreak of the First World War saw them put into practice. The burning of
the university library of Louvain in August 1914, which the Futurist
Manifesto calls to mind, stood as a symbol for warfare that not only
demolished cities like Ypres, Péronne, or Treviso, but also targeted the
culture of the enemy. This cultural war is one of the main themes in the
following chapters, and it is emphasized in a way that distinguishes this book
from most other histories of the First World War, whose extreme result,
cultural destruction, was both the incidental by-product of combat and
the consequence of deliberate policy. Writing about the destruction of
the cultural heritage of Europe in the Second World War, the historian
D. C. Watt noted: 'What Europe lost through the war was a great part of its
history and an immense treasury of delight and joy for all generations to
come. To destroy the relics of the past is, even in small things, a kind of

amputation, a self-mutilation not so much of limbs as of the memory and the imagination.'² Even though human lives lost could never be replaced, and although the medieval cathedral at Rheims and the Cloth Hall at Ypres were, in the end, rebuilt after their destruction in the First World War, cultural destruction is a particularly symbolic transgression—a 'self-mutilation' of humanity.

The other major theme is mass killing. An approximate definition of mass killing is the killing of a large proportion of a military formation, or a large number of civilians. Although the term 'mass' cannot be reduced to a simple formula, since military and political culture shaped people's responses to violence, the death of 12 per cent of United Kingdom soldiers, 15 per cent of German, and 16 per cent of French soldiers, constituted mass killing by any standard. What made the First World War appear to be so unprecedented in history was the mass nature of warfare and its industrialization. Yet in one way it did not differ greatly from previous wars: in the Franco-Prussian War of 1870–1 the annual death rate in the German army was 30 men per 1,000, while the rate was 34 per 1,000 in 1914–18. The First World War was therefore proportionately not very much more lethal. The essential difference, as the historian Michael Geyer has argued, lay in the fact that the war lasted 52 months instead of 12, and that 197 men per 1,000 population, instead of 36, participated in the war. Moreover, the enormous losses resulted not only from the increased destructive power of modern weapons, but also from the organizational power of modern states to coerce, and the willingness of the nation to be mobilized.³ That included the mobilization of all the resources of finance, industry, agriculture, science, and culture. Mass killing is distinguished from genocide by reciprocity, for both sides conduct it, while the victims of genocide are defenceless, and by its lack of discrimination: the victims are identified as enemies, but they are not targeted because of their membership of a people which the enemy intends to exterminate. Nevertheless, the intentional killing of ten or more civilians in a single incident was regarded as an atrocity, and the mass murder of the Armenians was described at the time as a 'crime against humanity'.

Naturally, the mass, industrialized killing of soldiers in trench warfare is the central topic of most books on the war. However, I intend to show how the war was seen by the belligerents as a war to defend their culture; for some, it was a war to export culture. In that sense there was a conceptual link between cultural destruction and mass killing. In addition, for all sides in the war, enemy civilians and other non-combatants came to be regarded to a greater or lesser degree as targets of war policy, even as legitimate objects of violence. That therefore raises the questions whether there were parallels between nations and whether distinctions can be drawn between different war cultures and war policies. This is therefore a comparative, transnational cultural and military history of Europe in the era of the First World War. The term 'transnational' is used in the sense that perceptions, events, and developments in the war were not purely national, but arose through interaction between nations.

The starting point of this book is the destruction of Louvain and the burning of its university library in August 1914, but the scope is rapidly widened to include the dynamic of destruction that compelled all belligerent nations to adopt ever more extreme war policies. Unlike most books on the war the focus is not exclusively on the western front, vitally important though that was. Cultural destruction and mass killing were the feature of all fronts in Europe and the Near East in the First World War.

Thus the crucial role of Italy is restored to its rightful place in European history, not only because of the vast scale of the fighting in that theatre, 1915 to 1918, but also because Italy's post-war development produced the world's first fascist state in 1922. Just how destabilizing the effects of the war could be was visible not only there, but also across all of central and eastern Europe. To say that the Russian Revolution of October 1917 and the nature of the Soviet Union were profoundly affected by Russia's experience in war would be an understatement: it was a seven-year catastrophe of war, political upheaval, and civil war, which shaped the entire political culture of the Bolshevik regime for the following decades.

In explaining how the First World War broke out I have attempted to avoid a 'Germanocentric' approach. Since the war began as a consequence of the assassination of the Austro-Hungarian heir to the Habsburg throne, it is vital to discuss the role of the initial parties in the conflict, Austria-Hungary and Serbia; the interests of each of the belligerents of 1914 are examined in the light of the motivations for war and what they expected to gain from it. The notion of German singularity, in view of Germany's enormously destructive policies in the First World War and the apparent continuity of total destructiveness in the Second World War, is tempting and attractive to many historians, but we have to exercise caution and not read history backwards. There can be no doubt that Germany did follow a *Sonderweg*, a 'special path' into modernity—but then so did every other nation. The idea of singular German destructiveness and its fateful turn to fascism and genocide as a result of its alleged political backwardness and domination by a feudal military caste since Bismarck is challenged in this book by examining also Italy, the Balkan Wars 1912 and 1913, and Turkish policy towards its Greek and Armenian minorities. In fact, in the seldom studied period 1911 to 1914 many of the ideas of a militant, sometimes racist, nationalism, were not only developed in theory but tried out in practice, starting with Italy's invasion of Libya and ending with the mass atrocities committed by all sides in the Balkan Wars. Another open question for this 'pre-war' period (often erroneously called the last years of peace) is whether collective mentalities affected the policies of individual decision-makers. Moreover, how the war was unleashed in summer 1914 had a great deal to do with how it was waged, with its several breaches of international law.

The invention of national cultures and the mobilization of national culture for war were important both for these 'pre-war' wars and the World War; without wartime cultural mobilization it would be impossible to explain the birth of fascism. In this book I therefore focus attention not only on the European cultural avant-garde (the term, tellingly, is military in origin), but in widening concentric circles also on culture in the broadest sense to include artists and intellectuals in general and popular mentalities, and thus the attitudes of European societies towards foreign peoples and foreign cultures, and finally also on mainstream political culture. For culture in fact was important for the prosecution of war: the mobilization of minds was essential for the resolve and resilience of home front and soldiers alike.

The effects of mass killing on the bodies and minds of participants are analysed in the broadest sense, for not only men at the front, but non-combatants of all kinds, including women, children, and prisoners of war, suffered the impact of war. The effects of the new technology of war on men under fire were dichotomous: in some, they produced an affirmation of the new culture of war; for (most) others they meant loss of innocence, disorientation, a challenge to masculine identity, and a decline in morale. Many former soldiers, including some of Europe's leading intellectuals, became lifelong pacifists.

The last section of the book analyses the end of the war and the political and cultural responses to the memory of war. It is sometimes argued that the war led to the brutalization of politics in Europe, and there is a good deal of evidence to support that contention. However, matters were not that straightforward everywhere. There was no single European political culture: divergent paths of the memory of war were apparent with the pacifist turn in Britain and France by the mid-1920s, and even in Germany there was a majority consensus to reject war for many years after 1918. In Italy and Russia, by contrast, the affirmation of the values of war became state policy in mass violence against the internal enemy, which included the destruction of the enemy's culture. That shift came ultimately in Germany, too, in 1933.

With all due acknowledgement of my debt to fellow-historians, whose work is discussed in the historiographical note at the end, the present book seeks to build on their arguments and findings in the light of my own research.[4] The thesis is that there was a 'dynamic of destruction' which produced the most extensive cultural devastation and mass killing in Europe since the Thirty Years War. However, it did not operate in a mechanical sense, or in the sense of a law of nature. At the centre of the analysis are the human beings, whether as ordinary soldiers who suffered violence and were agents of violence, as civilians, or as commanders and politicians, who were the decision-makers with the power to modify the process.

I

The Burning of Louvain

Louvain and the atrocities of 1914

In 1914 Louvain was a wealthy university town, with a rich architectural heritage of the late medieval and early modern periods. St Peter's church, the City Hall, and the University Library were examples of Brabant Gothic. The university, founded in 1425, had been the intellectual centre of the Low Countries; after having been closed in the eighteenth century it was re-founded in 1834 as a Catholic university. Its library was not the most significant in Europe: Oxford, Paris, and several other university and ducal libraries had greater collections. Nevertheless, it possessed valuable special collections, among them books and manuscripts from the golden age of humanism, the history of early book printing, the Latin classics, theological literature from the early Christian period down to the Jesuits in the eighteenth century, medieval manuscripts, and the entire university archive. The library was located in the cloth hall, a fourteenth-century building which had served as the main seat of the university until the modern era.[1]

The German troops arrived in the town in the morning of Wednesday, 19 August, to find a peaceful population frightened by the news of German cruelties perpetrated along their invasion route since 4 August.[2] In the area around Liège, closest to the German border, some 640 civilians had been killed by 12 August, but no precise numbers were known at the time. The town of Aarschot, only some ten miles north-east of Louvain, was the scene of mass killings on 19 August, with 156 dead; in Andenne, further south, 262 were killed the next day. The Louvain civic authorities had confiscated all weapons in private hands in early August, to prevent any spontaneous individual acts of resistance that might provoke reprisal, and published warnings that only the regular army was entitled to take military action. The population was in any case so scared that any idea of fighting the juggernaut would have been regarded as folly. After the Belgian army had left the town on 18 August, the Germans entered the next day without encountering resistance. For several hours, troops filed into the town in perfect order: first cyclists, followed by infantry marching to the sound of fifes and drums, singing songs such as *Die Wacht am Rhein* ('The Watch on the Rhine'). To the inhabitants it appeared to be a long, interminable column of masses, wearing their 'hateful pointed helmets', fringed by the 'elegant and haughty' cavalry. Then came the field guns, ammunition vehicles, ambulances, and the mobile field kitchens. Finally there were more infantry battalions, artillery batteries, squadrons of Uhlans (lancers), and mounted staff officers. From 19 to 22 August the town was the headquarters of the 1st Army, a sign that the security threat to the commanders of one of the most important attacking armies was judged to be minimal. Day by day more troops arrived, many of them continuing their march towards the front after a short rest, but some remaining to be billeted on the inhabitants, who were expected to supply food and drink. For several days there was an oppressive quiet, enforced by the presence of about 15,000 troops and the measures of the occupation: posters warned of ruthless measures if weapons were found or in case of the slightest resistance; the front doors of houses had to be kept open all night and windows lit. Heightening the anxiety of the citizens, hostages were taken from among the city's notables of the municipal administration, the magistrates, and the university, who would forfeit their lives if there were any hostile acts. The remaining cash in the city hall, three thousand francs, was requisitioned.[3]

In the late afternoon of Tuesday, 25 August, while many soldiers were in their quarters to change and wash their clothing, the alarm was sounded at about 6 p.m. The men rushed out into the streets to assembly points, often still wearing clothes lent to them by their hosts. Some two hours later, firing suddenly broke out at several points in the town, and wild shooting ensued, with troops breaking into houses and firing down into the streets from the upper windows, and others firing from the streets into the houses. The shooting bore all the signs of panic: troops were on high alert because the Belgian army had launched a counter-attack from the north, forcing the German forces to withdraw to Louvain. The retreating German units entered Louvain towards nightfall, provoking wild shouts of *die Engländer sind da!* ('the British have arrived!'); a German troop train entering the station from the south-east was taken to be carrying the enemy, and both arrivals unleashed hysterical shooting which the officers had great difficulty in stopping. On the pretext, or possibly the genuine misapprehension on the part of many soldiers, that they were being fired on by Belgian civilians, the hunt began for these presumed 'francs-tireurs', a term that recalled the French civilian volunteers in the war of 1870–1. This was a search for a chimera, for in reality no civilians had fired, the population having been disarmed, and in any case in a town teeming with enemy troops it would have been madness to start an insurrection. The inhabitants were dragged out of their homes, and the houses were set on fire. The fifteenth-century Collegiate Church of St Peter was badly damaged; the roof collapsed, but the vaulting remained intact.

The worst was yet to come. In front of their terrified families some men were beaten and shot on the spot. Hubert David-Fischbach, a man of eighty-three, who had had German officers quartered in his house, was tied up and made to watch his house burn, beaten with bayonets and finally shot, together with his son. Others were killed during the night as they fled from their burning houses. Three café-owners and a waiter were executed in the station square, and several other civilians who had taken refuge in their cellars when the firing started were dragged out and killed elsewhere in the town; several others died in the flames. The people thrown out of their houses were assembled at the station and the town hall. Soldiers executed several captives on the way, on the mere suspicion that they had fired, without waiting for orders from their officers. When some of the corpses were exhumed in January 1915 on German orders, it was found that there were not only bullet wounds, but also signs that the victims had been injured by bayonets, possibly tortured. This indicates that the 'executions' were carried out with extreme violence and emotions of great hatred. Many of the dead had not even been given a decent burial, but dumped pell-mell in ditches and construction trenches.

In the university library, the troops by contrast did a thorough job of destruction. The neighbouring houses were broken into and set alight, and at about 11.30 p.m., soldiers broke into the library. Using petrol and inflammable pastilles, they set it on fire. The library burned for several days, but within ten hours, little remained of the building and its collections apart from blackened walls, stone columns, and the glowing embers of books (see Figs. 1 and 2). The Rector of the American College, Monseigneur de Becker, was rescued from German captivity on Thursday night by Brand Whitlock, the US ambassador, who recorded his moving account:

Figure 1. Grand Hall of Louvain Library

He sat there at my table, a striking figure—the delicate face, dignified and sad, the silver hair, the long black soutane and the scarlet sash, in his hand a well-worn breviary ... Monseigneur described the experience. He told it calmly, logically, connectedly, his trained mind unfolding the events in orderly sequence: the sound of firing from Hérent, the sudden uprising of the German soldiers, the murder, the lust, the loot, the fires, the pillage, the evacuation and the destruction of the city, and all that.

The home of his father had been burned and the home of his brother; his friends and colleagues had been murdered before his eyes, and their bodies thrown into a cistern; long lines of his townspeople, confined in the railway-station, had been taken out and shot down; the church of St. Peter was destroyed, ... and the Halles of the University had been consumed. And he told it all calmly. But there in the Halles of the University was the Library; its hundreds of thousands of volumes, its rare and ancient manuscripts, its unique collection of *incunabula*—all had been burned deliberately, to the last scrap. Monseigneur had reached this point in his recital; he had begun to pronounce the word *bibliothèque*—he had said '*la biblio* ...' and he stopped suddenly and bit his quivering lip. '*La bib* ...' he went on—and then, spreading his arms on the table before him, he bowed his head upon them and wept aloud.[4]

The killings continued the next day and night, Wednesday 26 August. One can imagine the terror suffered by the people, many of whom were driven out of their homes into streets filled with smoke, rubble from destroyed

Figure 2. Grand Hall of Louvain Library after the destruction of 25 August 1914

buildings, and human and animal corpses. They were manhandled, insulted, and menaced by soldiers, and witnessed scenes of unprecedented brutality. In all, 248 citizens of Louvain were killed. Some 1,500 inhabitants were deported to Germany on a long journey in railway cattle-wagons, including over 100 women and children, and were forced to endure the harsh conditions in Munster camp until January 1915. Among them were four of the hostages, one of whom was suspended by the wrists from a ring in the ceiling of the cattle-wagon. One of the women later recounted:

> On Wednesday 26 August the people in our street were violently expelled from their homes. I was brutally separated from my husband and led to the station; a large number of women was already assembled there, among them a mother with her three small children, of whom the youngest was only one year old. We were forced to get into cattle-wagons, and we were told we were being taken to Aachen. When we got there, we were not allowed to get out. The population showed itself to be very hostile to us; they were using abusive language, and the soldiers fired salvos into the air to celebrate our capture. We were then taken to Cologne, where we were still not allowed to get out of the

cattle wagon . . . The train departed again and we did not arrive at Munster until Friday evening. During these 60 hours we had nothing to eat or drink but a little water and a little black bread passed to us by the soldiers. At Hanover the mother I referred to sent a request via a Red Cross intermediary for milk for her one-year old baby. He was told that milk was not given to prisoners of war. One compassionate soldier could not help crying out '*Unmensch!* (monster!)' and took the bottle himself and filled it with milk. On arrival at Munster we were . . . taken to a barn . . . where we stayed until Tuesday evening, sleeping on straw. The only food for us, adults and children, was a bad soup morning and evening. During the four days and four nights in the barn there were terrible scenes. Children fell ill; old women—one of them was 82 years old—collapsed from exhaustion. One of them went mad, and in the night clambered over those sleeping next to her, saying she was going to look for her house . . . They did not let us go free until 27 September.[5]

Meanwhile, several thousand other citizens of Louvain were forced from their homes and driven at gunpoint through the burning town on Wednesday, 26 August, forced to spend the night in the open without shelter or food, marched to Herent, then towards Mechelen (Malines), and through the village of Bueken, which had been utterly destroyed, and Campenhout, where they were forced to dig trenches. Next day they were marched back through the ruins of Herent, Windgat, and back to Louvain. On their way they passed the burned corpses of executed civilians, whose hands had been tied behind their backs, with gaping wounds to their heads, their faces contorted, their skin already turning green and their eyes still open, decomposition beginning to distend their bodies, and everywhere large flies.

Still the misery was not over. On Thursday, 27 August the German army announced that the town was to be bombarded, because its citizens were allegedly firing at the troops. Thousands fled into the surrounding countryside, some being maltreated by troops on their way. The bombardment commenced, but only about ten shells were fired before it was stopped. Most of the destruction had been caused by arson. In a town of 8,928 houses, 1,120 were destroyed, including many of the wealthiest properties, in addition many public buildings and commercial premises. Not only the university library and archive, also the personal libraries, research papers and professional documents of five notaries, 14 solicitors, 5 judges, 15 medical doctors, and 19 professors were lost.[6] Possibly the intention of the threatened bombardment was to empty the town in order to pillage it the more thoroughly. At any rate witnesses testified to pillage on a large scale. This account by Albert Lemaire, professor of internal medicine, was included in the Prussian war ministry's internal investigation, but edited out of the subsequent German publication, the '*White Book*' on the events in Belgium:

> On 25 August Landwehr soldiers (I do not know which regiment) were billeted in my house. The Germans were calm and behaved decently. Later on they were summoned by the alarm and left. Later in the evening, while I was eating supper with my family, I heard wild shooting in the street. We took refuge in the cellar. Between 11 and 12 o'clock (Belgian time) I went out into the garden. I was shot at several times, but in the darkness I could not tell by whom. I had just heard a German shout 'Louvain is burning'. I did not see civilians shooting from the houses or in the streets. Almost all the houses of doctors and professors in Leopold Street [where his house lay] were burned down.
>
> Next day I had my family taken to the hospital for safety, by two German soldiers. On Thursday, 27 August, the bombardment and destruction of the town was announced. I went with my family into the countryside. On my return I found my house had been burned down.[7]

Pillage was ubiquitous in the invasion. It went beyond the requisitioning of food for immediate use, which all armies engage in when their supply columns cannot keep up. In Louvain, where there were a well-established garrison and well-ordered supplies, it had nothing to do with military necessity. German soldiers were aware that pillage was widespread, and did not even disguise it in print. One described in a letter which was published in 1915 in a series of collected soldiers' letters: 'Homes are searched and whatever is left is just requisitioned, as it is called. In proper German this is called "taking away"; whether it pleases the owner or not is of no concern and does not bother anyone.'[8]

Soldiers evidently regarded the events of 25 to 28 August, in which the lives of the citizens of Louvain were turned upside-down, as an opportunity for personal enrichment. Professor of history Léon van der Essen wrote in a subsequent report: 'While they were being hustled along, the townspeople were searched by officers and soldiers, and their money was taken from them (some officers gave a receipt in return), as well as any objects of value. Those who did not understand an order, who did not raise their arms quick enough, or who were found carrying knives larger than a penknife, were at once shot.' On the next day, 26 August,

> the soldiers started again to fire at intervals, to plunder, and to burn. They could be seen strolling about the town, drunk, laden with bottles of wine, boxes of cigars, and objects of value. The officers let them do it, roared with laughter, or set the example themselves ... In several places soldiers were seen entering the houses and the gardens, firing shots, so as to prolong the mystifica-

tion and the looting. Some walked along firing phlegmatically into the air. If a house was of fairly good appearance, a group of soldiers would assail it with shouts of 'There was firing from here,' and at once began to loot. . . .

At 11 o'clock on this Thursday, August 27th, the town was as dead. Nothing could be heard to break the profound silence except the sinister crackle of houses on fire. Then, the inhabitants having disappeared, the regular sack began. There was no more talk of bombardment. The sack was organized methodically like the burning, which also continued at the same time. The doors of wardrobes and drawers of desks were smashed with rifle-butts. Safes were broken open with burglars' tools. Every soldier took his pick amid the heap of furniture spread over the floor. Silver-plate, linen, works of art, children's toys, mechanical instruments, pictures—everything was taken. Whatever could not be carried off was broken. The cellars were emptied. Then the looters finished up by depositing their filth in all the corners.

This lasted eight days. Every time fresh troops reached Louvain, they rushed on their prey. Recalling his entry and his stay at Louvain on August 29th, a Landsturm soldier from Halle wrote in his diary: 'The battalion . . . arrived dragging along with it all sorts of things, particularly bottles of wine, and many of the men were drunk . . . The battalion set off in close order for the town, to break into the first houses they met, to plunder—I beg pardon, I mean to requisition—wine and other things too. Like a pack let loose, each one went where he pleased. The officers led the way and set a good example.'

And Gaston Klein, the soldier in question, concludes: 'This day has inspired me with a contempt I could not describe.'[9]

Naturally, the symbolism of the destruction of a seat of culture was a gift to Allied propaganda, and newspapers were not slow to take up the story. 'The Oxford of Belgium burnt by the German "Huns"', as the *Illustrated War News* (London) put it on 2 September 1914. 'Holocaust of Louvain', as the *Daily Mail* wrote (see Fig. 3). Yet even in private, the shock was genuine.

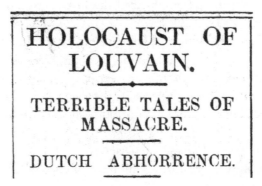

Figure 3. 'Holocaust of Louvain' (Headline, *Daily Mail*, Monday 31 August 1914)

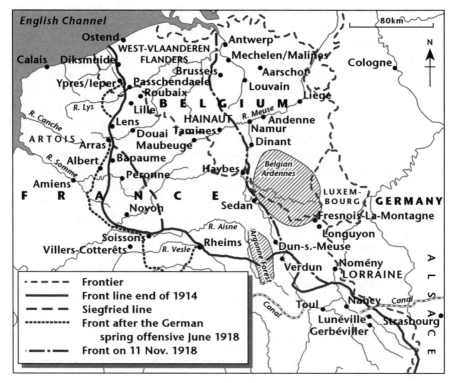

Map 1. The western front, 1914 to 1918

The Liberal prime minister, Asquith, for example, wrote in a letter at the end of August that 'the burning of Louvain is the worst thing [the Germans] have yet done. It reminds one of the Thirty Years' War...and the achievements of Tilly and Wallenstein.'[10] In Ireland, too, at a rally organized by the Nationalist John Redmond, the Irish voiced their condemnation of destruction of Louvain and emphasized the links between Irish Catholics and the University of Louvain.[11]

The news of the destruction of Louvain made an immediate, and deep, impact on neutral international opinion. In The Netherlands, the *Nieuwe Rotterdamsche Courant* contrasted the German with the Belgian/British accounts of events, and concluded that the true account might never be told. But: 'What difference does that make? The fact of the destruction of Louvain remains and this fact...is so terrible that the whole world must have taken note of it with the greatest sadness....It is a punishment which has affected all western culture.'[12] In Italy intellectuals condemned the 'cultural atrocities', and forty journalists protested with a public declaration against the 'barbarity' of Louvain.[13] This, and other German atrocities played a role in Italy's estrangement from its allies Germany and Austria; 'Belgio sventurato' (unfortunate Belgium) was a major theme in building Italy's sympathy with the Entente in 1914/15.

Less well known today, but just as prominent as Louvain in the international outcry over the German atrocities during the first year of the war, was the destruction of the small town of Dinant and the mass executions of its citizens. (See Map 1.)[14] As in Louvain, it was clear to the officers and the men that the victims of the killings could not have been involved in firing at the Germans, but there was an assumption that civilians had engaged in shooting. This helps to explain why many of the perpetrators were convinced of the justification of their procedure; it also explains, crucially, why the killings were driven by high emotion. German witnesses to one mass execution at the suburb of Les Rivages stated that the order was given by a major whose face was 'contorted with rage' after shots were fired at his troops, even though it was clear that the incriminated civilians were unarmed and had been in the custody of German soldiers when the firing started. More than half of the seventy-seven killed at Les Rivages were women and children: thirty-eight women and girls, and fifteen children under 14, of whom seven were babies; seven of the men were over 70 years old.

In another case, numerous civilians were taken from their houses in the town centre and from the prison, and the men and youths separated from their families. They were told that they had fired on German soldiers and were to receive exemplary punishment, lined up against a garden wall, and executed. The order for the execution was given by a battalion commander, and the testimony given by Captain von Loeben, who commanded the execution squad, shows how hearsay and an officer's word sufficed to condemn people to death. Neither Captain von Loeben nor his company witnessed any franc-tireur shooting, but he was told that his regiment continually came under fire from the houses.

> Finally [commander of 1st Battalion] Count Kielmannsegg decided to make an example and ordered me to have a large number of men of military age shot. The men were taken partly from the prison, partly they were brought in groups. I assumed they were people who had been firing or had otherwise behaved in hostile manner towards our troops. The people were arranged in several ranks by the garden wall. Women, children, and older men were

excluded . . . I had some difficulty separating the women and children. One woman clung to her husband and wanted to be shot together with him. I therefore decided to let her go free, together with her husband. One man had a child of about five in his arms, which was not his own, according to his own words. The child was taken away from him and sent to the women. The man was shot with the rest.

In this mass execution 137 civilians were killed; the survivors provided evidence for the published Belgian account, which matches in every respect Loeben's affidavit, which was given to an internal German investigation. These arbitrary killings were not committed to punish alleged francs-tireurs, for the soldiers knew the victims were 'innocent'; but they perceived the civilians as collectively culpable for the supposed actions of francs-tireurs.

Even after the massacres on 23 August, the destruction continued. After looting the town, troops completed the devastation by destroying all Dinant's public and historic buildings, including the post office, main banks, a convent, the collegial church, and the town hall with its archives and art treasures. The fires continued for days, lighting up the countryside at night. Smoke and the smell of corpses decomposing in the hot sun polluted the air. A total of 674 people, including many women and children, or one in ten of the population of Dinant, had perished in the executions.

These acts were not the 'collateral damage' of modern warfare. There was an intent to destroy, which the case of Andenne also reveals.[15] General von Gallwitz, commander of Guards Reserve Army Corps, issued orders on 16 August, before the corps embarked on the invasion, to respond to any act of resistance by destroying not only houses from which firing was suspected to come, but the entire village or town. The killing of 262 civilians in Andenne resulted from an order which has not survived in written form, but which an ordinary soldier recalled thus:

> I cannot say from my own experience whether any inhabitant of Andenne took part in the fighting against the German troops . . . An order was issued regarding the treatment of the inhabitants . . . which I remember clearly and which stated: 'An example has to be made; all captured men are to be shot', or words to that effect. There was certainly no qualification that only those men bearing weapons were to be shot. In one house I entered we found a man who . . . so far as I recall, had no weapon . . . He was fetched out, placed against the wall, and shot by one of those who captured him.[16]

Major Bronsart von Schellendorf, commander of Guards Reserve Rifle Battalion, and Major Scheunemann, commander of Pioneer Battalion 28, told the company commanders that 'all men capable of bearing arms were to be executed on the spot' and that they wanted 'an example to be made' of the town. The order was easily interpreted as a licence to execute any civilian.

During the night of 20–21 August there was random widespread violence, in which not only men, but also several women and children were killed. As from early morning on 21 August, civilians were dragged out of their houses, but an attempt was made to confine the violence to 'suspects', and the women and children were separated from the men. The men considered suspect had a white cross marked on their backs. At least 130 men, possibly 150 according to Belgian sources, were killed in the mass execution following a sham court-martial trial.

The killings in Andenne were not only the result of policy dictated by orders from above and applied systematically in cold blood, but as elsewhere were characterized by passionate hatred and anger. Burgomaster Camus was dragged from his home and hacked to death with an axe, almost certainly because he was suspected of having orchestrated the alleged resistance of the town; many other civilians were killed in their own homes during the house-to-house searches, and some were bayoneted on the forced march

Figure 4. The ruins of the Cathedral and Cloth Hall at Ypres

to the 'court martial'. But not all soldiers were infected by the destructive rage: at least three junior officers and two NCOs admitted at the time to Belgian survivors of the massacre or to the subsequent German inquiry that they had found no evidence of Belgian civilian resistance and that the executions had been arbitrary revenge on the innocent. Their testimony was vital in helping to deconstruct the web of propaganda and reconstruct what actually happened.

Finally, the shelling of Rheims cathedral illustrates how the German methods of warfare were soon seen so negatively in international and neutral public opinion that even a case in which causality was unclear and German culpability was at least debatable could be taken as a prime example of deliberate cultural destruction. Here, no civilians were executed at all; what counted was the supposedly wilful destruction of a pre-eminent French place of national memory. The magnificent Gothic cathedral had been the place of coronation of French kings. The German press and government claimed that the French were using the cathedral spire as an artillery observation post, but somewhat contradictorily also that it served as a first-aid facility for German soldiers, that it had not been targeted, and that it had been hit eight times, but

Figure 5. Rheims Cathedral under attack

had not been seriously damaged. According to a WTB (the semi-official German press bureau) report on 22 September, orders had even been given to spare the cathedral. Aware that the French had protested in neutral Switzerland at the destruction of the cathedral, the German press alleged that the French had stationed artillery batteries behind the cathedral, forcing the Germans to return fire. Only the facade had been damaged, which could be restored. As the shelling continued, on 23 September the German government again denied that the cathedral had been targeted. If the cathedral had been burned down by the bombardment, which was a military necessity, 'no-one would regret it more than we'. But only the French were to blame for making Rheims into a fortress. 'We protest energetically against the slander that German troops destroy historical and architectural monuments out of lust for destruction and without urgent necessity.'[17]

Yet the damage to Germany's image was done. Architects, artists, and other intellectuals from the USA and around the world showered the American president with protests at the German cultural atrocities, and the *New York Times* abandoned its Olympian detachment to condemn the 'Great Crime at Rheims'. The Italian ambassador in Berlin told the German government that the bombardment of Rheims cathedral had done more damage in the eyes of neutral Italy than a lost battle.[18]

A 'German way of war'? German self-justification and the international response

To the Belgians it appeared that the German actions in the invasion of their country in general and in Louvain in particular were premeditated: a systematic policy to inspire terror and provoke the flight of the population.[19] The German troops believed there had been an uprising by 'francs-tireurs'.[20] What is the evidence for these two contesting interpretations? In the evening of 25 August, when shooting in Louvain began, and in the dark of night, amid the confusion of gunfire and burning houses, panic-driven soldiers evidently fired on each other, inflicting serious losses. Premeditation, in the sense of a plan to destroy the town, devastate its symbolic intellectual centre, and kill a significant part of its civilian population, can thus be ruled out, even though there is some anecdotal evidence of German soldiers announcing their intention to destroy Louvain to its inhabitants in the days before the event. There would simply have been no military rationale for such wanton destruction, since the town was obviously more useful intact as an accommodation and supply base for the 1st Army. So far as one can tell, in the absence of the documents of the Prussian army, which were destroyed in the Allied bombing of Potsdam in 1945, the causation of the events is not to be sought on the level of military strategy, but was rooted rather in the mentalities, cultural assumptions, and fears of the troops.

It had a great deal to do with the anti-Catholic phobias in the German army and Louvain's status as the intellectual centre of Belgian Catholicism. Anti-Catholicism was a powerful element in German militarist nationalism's will to subjugate enemies, and the destruction of a rival cultural symbol featured as part of the missionary sense of German militarist nationalism. One German officer, Reserve Captain Rump from Hamburg, reaching Louvain twenty-four hours after the massacre began, saw the evening sky lit up by the burning town. He was told how under the leadership of the *Pfaffen* (the derogatory word for Catholic priests), hordes of Belgians had attacked the Germans, 'slit the throats of sixty ill soldiers, castrated them and committed other infamies'. The consequence, Rump was told, was the order for the destruction of Louvain.[21]

Once the violence began, the clergy were singled out for particular abuse. One young Jesuit, Pater Dupierreux, was executed because he was discovered to have a notebook in which he had written his private thoughts: 'Decidedly, I do not like the Germans. In my youth, I learned that centuries ago it was the barbarians who burned unfortified towns, pillaged houses, and assassinated innocent townsfolk. The Germans have done exactly the same thing. I was told that long ago Omar burned the library of Alexandria; the Germans have done the same thing at Louvain. This people can be proud of its *Kultur* [. . .].'[22] The parish priest of Herent was thrown over the balustrade into a square; before he was shot he shouted out: '*Bandieten! Lafaards! Brandstichters! Moordenaars!* (Bandits! Cowards! Arsonists! Murderers!)'[23] Paulin Ladeuze, rector of the university, stated in a report to the Vatican that the soldiers who set fire to the library mistakenly thought that it was the 'university', whereas the university in fact was spread throughout the town.[24] In other words, the German troops saw Belgian Catholicism and its intellectual institutions as an expression of cultural identity which was Germany's enemy. One of the notables taken hostage, Monsignor Coenraets, vice-rector of the university, was forced by General von Boehn to march through the streets of Louvain during the evening, at the height of the shooting and burning, to 'warn' the people not to fire on the troops. Next morning he and five other hostages were told they were going to be executed. One officer gripped Coenraets by the throat, and told him: 'We are Protestants ... and we are going to show that we know how to shoot dirty Jesuits like you!' In the end, Coenraets escaped execution.[25]

But what of the broader case put by the Belgian, British, and French governments, that the 'atrocities' were deliberate policy throughout the invasion zone, designed to strike terror into the civilian population to provide a short cut to quick victory?[26] Clearly, the destruction of Dinant was premeditated, prepared by orders issued at least by the two army corps concerned and probably by the 3rd Army commander, General von Hausen. Thus General d'Elsa issued an order to his 12th Army Corps on 15 August, several days before the assault on Dinant, to suppress franc-tireur resistance with mass death and destruction: 'Where the culprits cannot be found ... hostages and also villages will be held liable with life and property.' However, the atrocities at Louvain, Aarschot, and Lunéville in France had their origins in panic; even at Dinant General d'Elsa, whose order had prepared the violence of 23 August, intervened, late that day, to stop the executions. The evidence of ordinary soldiers illuminates the causal connection between orders and mass killing. One soldier, captured by the French who conducted a systematic enquiry on the events at Dinant, stated:

> We were given the order to kill all civilians shooting at us, but in reality the men of my regiment and I myself fired at all civilians we found in the houses from which we suspected there had been shots fired; in that way we killed women and even children. We did not do it light-heartedly, but we had received orders from our superior officers to act in this way, and not one single soldier in the active army would know to disobey an order from the senior command. My company did not kill more than about thirty civilians in the conditions I have just described.[27]

Many other soldiers told the enquiry that an order had been given simply to massacre civilians, not just the supposed francs-tireurs. But policy on the ground radicalized in response to the franc-tireur myth-complex. This consisted of the stress of battlefield conditions meeting the template of German military doctrine and training which, as we have seen, led the army to expect francs-tireurs. It was thus the genuinely held belief of many of the German troops that there had been franc-tireur uprisings in Belgium and France. The consequences far exceeded contemporary moral and legal norms protecting civilians against violence, whether measured by the standard of the German warfare in France in 1870–1 (when real francs-tireurs had to be combated) or the recent example of British warfare against the Boers in South Africa, 1899–1902.

The myth of the franc-tireur uprising soon became the standard German defence against the Allied charges against Germany for committing 'atrocities' against Belgian and French civilians in August–October 1914. German troops routinely accused the population of having engaged in fighting whenever civilians were executed, such as in the Belgian towns of Aarschot, Andenne, Dinant, and Tamines (where 383 were killed), and the French towns Nomény (55 killed), Fresnois-la-Montagne (51), Gerbéviller (60), Longuyon (60), Haybes (61), over a period of one week from 19 to 25 August 1914. In reply to the barrage of official and unofficial Belgian, French, and British publications, and a rising tide of criticism in the neutral countries, the German foreign ministry produced a book in May 1915 known as the White Book with the official title of *The Belgian People's War, a Violation of International Law*.[28] This argued that the German army had been treacherously attacked in Louvain (as elsewhere) by civilians in an uprising designed to coincide with the Belgian army offensive. Those who had raised arms against the German army enjoyed none of the rights of combatants, and it was absolutely essential to take the most drastic measures: francs-tireurs, including those taken captive, therefore had to be killed.[29] Remarkably, in the ninety-page chapter on Louvain, the *White Book* made no mention of the destruction of the library, merely a cryptic claim that the troops confined themselves to destroying only those parts of the town where they were fired on by the inhabitants, and whenever possible they protected the artistic treasures of Louvain, as of other towns.[30] None of the witness statements collected from soldiers and a few selected inhabitants mentioned the library, not even in passing. Even the cathedral was mentioned, which had 'caught fire' because it was 'impossible to prevent the fire from spreading'. The nearest the *White Book* came to speaking of the library was the acknowledgement that 'Louvain is a town famous on account of its time-honoured University, its rich architectural monuments and art treasures, the fate of which would interest wide circles'.[31] It is as if the German authorities, by making the world-notorious crime unmentionable, made an unwitting admission of guilt.

In 1958, a young German scholar, Peter Schöller, subjected the evidence of the *White Book* in relation to Louvain to a rigorous examination and compared it with the results of the unpublished war ministry internal investigation. Schöller showed that most of the evidence for a franc-tireur insurrection was hearsay or unreliable, and that important evidence had been altered for publication. Crucially, Major von Manteuffel, the town commander of Louvain, confessed to the Reich Supreme Court in 1921 that he had not personally witnessed any inhabitants of Louvain participating in the fighting, nor did he have any such evidence.[32]

There is therefore no credible evidence of a franc-tireur attack at Louvain, and only negligible evidence of any kind of civilian resistance anywhere in Belgium or France.

After the defeat in the battle of the Marne in early September 1914 and the growing realization that the policy of ruthlessness was just possibly not in Germany's best interest, the army sobered up. The international repercussions of the destruction and wanton violence against civilians during the invasion deprived Germany of support in important neutral countries like Italy and the USA. From autumn 1914 on, the German methods of warfare were taken to be characterized by wilful destruction and mass killing of everything and everyone who stood in the path of German war aims. There were two main responses in Germany. The first was to establish on 9 September 1914 a 'Military Investigation Department for Violations of the Laws of War' under the Prussian ministry of war, in order to seek information from the army to publish a rejoinder to the Belgian accusations.[33] The second was almost certainly an order, which has not survived in the archives, to stop the commission of acts that might be construed abroad as atrocities against civilians. While there were 119 incidents in which ten or more civilians were killed down to 6 September, there were only ten further incidents: two in September, and eight more from 19 to 21 October, after which no further French or Belgium civilians were executed in circumstances resembling those of the invasion. Mobile warfare, during which civilians were likely to be entangled in fighting, continued until 24 November, and it resumed with the German offensive in March 1918, followed by the Allied counter-offensive. Ending the targeting of civilians must have been a conscious decision, for the much-publicized atrocities were a heavy liability to Germany's reputation in the battle for international support in a long war. The opportunity to maltreat civilians was still present, since most of Belgium and a large part of north-east France were under German occupation for the rest of the war. Whatever the considerable degree of oppression during the occupation, including forced labour, forced prostitution, deportation, prison sentences for recalcitrance: mass killings of the type seen in August to October 1914 were not repeated.

Yet the fundamental principle of German warfare was not questioned by its practitioners. As Colonel Nicolai, chief of German military intelligence and propaganda, told the American journalist John Reed in early 1915, the goal of war was victory, above all else; there were no means a soldier did not have the right to use in the pursuit of victory. If it was a question of terrorizing the civilian population, or shelling undefended towns, to accomplish his aims, he would do it.[34]

International law in 1914

Why the victims of German military violence in the invasion should feel justified in their outrage can be understood against the context of the development of international law in the course of modern history. The Belgian government delegation which visited Washington to appeal for justice before 'international opinion' called the deliberate annihilation of an academic library, 'in the midst of these horrors', a 'crime of lèse-humanity', i.e. a crime against humanity.[35] Why should the Belgian government send a high-level delegation, led by Henry Carton de Wiart, the minister of justice, accompanied by three ministers of state, to the USA? It was not primarily the hope of military intervention, for the American army, with 108,000 men, was only half the size of the Belgian army and incapable of making a decisive difference at that stage. Rather, it was because the USA was seen as the leading force in the development of international law in the past fifty years, as a moral instance. In his address to President Wilson, Carton de Wiart cited the Swiss international lawyer Bluntschli:

> The present International Law denies entirely the right to dispose arbitrarily of the fate of individuals, and does not admit of ill-treatment or violence against them. Personal security, honor and liberty are private rights which the laws of war do not permit to be attacked. The enemy may take such steps only as are necessary for military operations or necessary for the safety of the State.

He went on:

> It falls to the honor of the United States to have been the first nation in history to inscribe its principles in a code, 'Instructions for the Army During the Campaign.' These principles have, since that time, been accepted by all the Powers at present engaged in the European war. Germany has subscribed to them; she has adopted the rules of The Hague. She has given before the

associated nations of the world the solemn promise not to infringe these rules.
She is responsible before international opinion for this promise.[36]

Carton de Wiart was referring to the 'Lieber Code', drafted by the German–
American international lawyer Francis Lieber during the American Civil
War, *Instructions for the Government of Armies of the United States in the Field*
(1863), which became the foundation for the subsequent codification of the
laws of war over the subsequent half-century. It might be objected that the
Belgian government was tilting at windmills in an anachronistic appeal for
'justice . . . for the honor of civilization and of humanity'. The nature of
modern industrial warfare, it has been argued, had utterly transformed the
'productivity of destruction' and reversed the trend since the seventeenth
century to 'tame' warfare and impose legal and political rules on it. Modern,
technological war tended towards total war, which not only meant that war
involved the mobilization of entire societies and all their resources, but also
that the new war recognized no other rules but its own.[37] Yet that did not
mean that the mass killings in Belgium and France in 1914 and the destruction of cultural monuments were the inevitable by-product of industrialized
war: they had been allowed to happen or were more often directly ordered
by responsible officers, and were carried out by soldiers imbued with
nationalist hatreds and stereotypical images of the enemy.

The difference between the victims' and the perpetrators' perspective was
rooted not only in the events but therefore also in irreconcilable views of
the laws of war. By 1914 a substantial body of law existed, consisting of
national laws and usages of war and more recent international conventions.
The attempts to 'humanize', if possible prevent war, were expressed in the
codification of existing laws at the Geneva Conventions of 1864 and 1906,
and the Hague Conventions of 1899 and 1907. The former were devoted to
improving the lot of wounded soldiers and by recognition of the Red Cross
also that of soldiers taken prisoner. The Hague Conventions referred to by
Carton de Wiart, in particular the convention 'Respecting the Laws and
Customs of War on Land' (the 4th appendix to the convention of 1907),
attempted to confine the effects of military violence to combatants, by
stressing the protection of civilians and their property and preventing wilful
destruction of cultural monuments and public buildings; it also allowed
civilian militias and volunteers to take up arms to resist invasion.

It was above all this last aspect that aroused the ire of the German military.
Although Germany signed the Hague Conventions, its military leaders

remained fundamentally opposed in spirit. If civilians resisted, the German delegate at the 1907 conference, Colonel Gross von Schwarzhoff, maintained, they forfeited any claim to be treated as combatants according to the laws of war.[38] The Prussian general staff had responded to the 1899 convention by publishing in 1902 the *Kriegsbrauch im Landkriege*, known in English as the *German War Book*.[39] This claimed that most attempts during the nineteenth century to codify warfare had 'completely failed'. The implication was that the German army should not rely on written international agreements, but reciprocity and custom. The Prussian General Staff felt that the principles of humanity in warfare conflicted with its own concept of war:

> But since the tendency of thought of the last century was dominated essentially by humanitarian considerations which not infrequently degenerated into sentimentality and flabby emotion there have not been wanting attempts to influence the development of the usages of war in a way which was in fundamental contradiction with the nature of war and its object.

The German officer therefore had to 'guard himself against excessive humanitarian notions', and to learn that 'certain severities are indispensable to war, nay more, that the only true humanity very often lies in a ruthless application of them'.[40]

The extract from Hague Convention IV reproduced in the Appendix illustrates how important the international community held the protection of non-combatants and cultural monuments to be, as well as recognizing the rights of civilian combatants. After the 1907 convention, Hague Convention IV was attached as an appendix to the German field service regulations in 1911.[41] But German officers were trained to expect civilian resistance in a coming war and treat it as criminal. At the war academy in Berlin, the elite officer college from which the top graduates joined the general staff, it was taught that Article 2 of the Convention 'did not comply with the German viewpoint, since it opened the door to franc-tireur war and permits the most impudent evasion of the previous article.'[42] In relation to occupation, too, the German understanding of international law conflicted with the Hague Convention which aimed to preserve the rights of civilians and their property; as Germany's 'Handbook of International Law' stated in 1915, 'war is in its essence violence, [and] the violent force of the conqueror in the conquered land is completely unlimited'.[43] In other words, the German army selectively interpreted the clauses of the Hague Convention to suit its own doctrine. Officer training manuals published before 1914 reiterated over and again the expectation that the civilian population of the enemy country (invariably seen as France) would rise up in franc-tireur resistance; ruthless reprisals for this supposedly illegal activity, also on the 'innocent', would be necessary.

The shock and outrage felt by contemporaries in the countries of Germany's victims and in neutral states can be explained not only by the breach of international law. It was also because the killing of civilians and the destruction of cultural monuments during the entire war did not, with the exception of aerial bombardment, even involve complex modern technology or long-range artillery fire, but unsophisticated weapons including bayonets, rifles, and simple incendiary materials. Most of such killing was done face to face, unlike the killing of military enemies which was done mainly by artillery and machine gun fire.[44] In this sense, too, German warfare was held at the time to represent a reversion to barbarism. In fact, it was an expression of something entirely modern: the logic of annihilation, and its roots are to be found in modern mentalities and modern culture.

The intellectuals' response to atrocities

Contrary to the image produced in Allied propaganda, German artists and intellectuals were a diverse group and by no means a bloc of warlike nationalists in the tradition of the nineteenth-century historian Treitschke or conservative worshippers of obedience to the state in the tradition of Luther and Hegel. German scientists, scholars, and artists not only enjoyed a prime international reputation, but were also intimately connected with the international academic and artistic community through frequent exchanges, correspondence, publications, and exhibitions. Yet the modern art expert Wilhelm Worringer, who was anything but a chauvinist and whose works were influential internationally, wrote about the destruction of Rheims cathedral:

> There is no foreign or domestic work of art, no matter how large and sublime, that we would not today sacrifice, filled with pain but without hesitation, if its sacrifice were the price to pay to save the life of only a handful of German soldiers. That may be barbarism, but then it is a piece of healthy barbarism for which we will never want to be ashamed.[45]

One might think this was a singular, perverse reaction, but understandable because Worringer himself had joined the army and seen action in 1914.

But when the Swiss artist Ferdinand Hodler, who had been working in Germany and who enjoyed great acclaim for his 1909 mural depicting the departure of the students of Jena for the war of 1813, added his signature to a public protest by Swiss artists at the destruction of historic monuments in Belgium and France, above all Rheims cathedral, the reaction of his German colleagues was swift, and vindictive. Hodler was expelled from the Munich Secession and the Berlin Secession, both of which were modernist, anti-establishment bodies, and from the German League of Artists. The editor of *Kunst und Künstler,* Karl Scheffler, a leading art critic, advocate of Impressionism, and an opponent of Kaiser Wilhelm's conservative taste in art, supported Hodler's expulsion in the journal.[46] The Hamburg artist Nölken, much more conservative and traditional in his artistic taste, wrote in a letter to his friend Captain Rump, who was serving in the artillery:

> This sanctimonious blather in the press and among sensitive people about the shot-up cathedrals like Rheims is dreadful. Just make sure you smash everything up; in the first place the French don't deserve any better, and secondly our good pieces will rise in value. The statues in Rheims are very nice, for sure, those in Bamberg, for example, are no worse; and would people be *so* outraged if they were shot to ruins?[47]

The destruction of Rheims cathedral prompted this poem, published in 1915 by the bestselling novelist Rudolf Herzog:

> Rheims
> Silent in the forest ... From tree and bush
> Quietly the mist drips,
> The sun parts the morning smoke.
> Just one more step to the edge ... how our hearts beat ...
> And the step is taken and the heartbeat stops,
> And the eye grows big and hot,
> And we watch and stare leaning over
> Onto the plain below at the prize of battle:
>   Rheims,
> There you lie, a brooding silence all around ...
> Like a dying man struggling for breath
> Who, with lead in his breast and his limbs heavy,
> Harks whether the death-bell tolls for him—
> And the bells in the double-tower cathedral
> Sing no song, the blessing is over,
> From the platform your hail of cannonballs cursed,

Then we shut with lead your house of idol-worship:
  Rheims

. . . .

Batteries—fire! And the thunder rolls and rumbles:
  Rheims[48]

German intellectuals' rejoicing in the destruction of cultural monuments was explicitly linked with their role as national signifiers, just as was the condemnation by French intellectuals. Reporting from the front at Soissons, a German journalist wrote: 'In the distance the mighty cathedral of Soissons rises up from the sea of houses. One tower is broken, the other still stretches towards the sky like an ominous emblem for France. Just wait, soon you will fall, too.'[49] German readers will have recognized the reference in the last sentence to Goethe's poem 'Wanderer's Song at Night II', no doubt intended in its sentimental way to convey a sense of the inevitable, because natural, fall of France, for the original implied the inevitability of night following day.

    Few German intellectuals went so far as Nölken or Herzog and revelled in the destruction of Europe's cultural heritage. More typical of the German intellectuals' attitude to cultural destruction was to declare their solidarity with the German military, most famously in the 'Appeal to the World of Culture!' of 4 October 1914, which was translated and published world-wide within a few days. This truculently rejected Allied claims that the German military had acted in barbarous manner; it denied that German soldiers had 'brutally devastated Louvain' and that German warfare 'flouts international law'. The Appeal, signed by ninety-three of Germany's inter-nationally most respected scientists, scholars, and artists, provoked condem-nation in the Allied and neutral countries, as was to be expected, but also particular disapprobation from the intellectuals there to whom the Appeal was directed. Many of them had close links with the German signatories as their students or research collaborators in the international republic of letters that thrived before the war. Throughout the world the German university system was renowned as the most progressive and innovative model, if possible to be emulated. Both in the universities and in the wider sphere of art and literature intellectuals enjoyed a position of cultural autonomy and freedom, and in many cases they used that freedom openly to criticize the status quo. Perhaps that explains the reaction of disbelief and outrage when intellectuals outside Germany read the 'Appeal'. The Académie Française formally denounced the 'Appeal', as did the entire academic staff of all French public universities; not only the Republican establishment in a culturally still divided nation, but also Catholic and royalist intellectuals condemned the German signatories.[50]

The 'Appeal' prompted also a stream of publications in France seeking to demonstrate that the German denials were untruthful. The most important of these was Joseph Bédier's pamphlet *Les Crimes allemands d'après les témoignages allemands*, which, as the title indicates, showed that German troops had massacred defenceless civilians, killed captive soldiers, and engaged in wanton destruction of houses and villages, by the ingenious means of citing German evidence in the form of captured soldiers' diaries. One or two German academics responded by quibbling with some of Bédier's translations, but no one alleged he had fabricated the evidence: it was impossible to deny the Germany testimony, some of which he reproduced in facsimile.[51]

The reaction in the USA, the most important neutral country, shows how cultural destruction and its defence by German intellectuals had a devastating effect on sympathy for the German cause, which had certainly existed in great parts of American society, not least among its university academics. The declarations by German intellectuals, above all the 'Appeal' of the ninety-three, were not well received by American academics, and the proposed German role as Europe's leader in the struggle against Russian despotism was rejected as arrogance. In 1919, Paul Clemen, the Bonn professor of history of art who had been charged with the protection of works of art in occupied Belgium and northern France in the war, and who had been guest professor at Harvard in 1907–8, wrote: 'Today we may say that the three names Louvain, Rheims, Lusitania, almost in equal measure, have wiped out sympathy with Germany in America.'[52]

2

The Radicalization of Warfare

The logic of annihilation

The twin symbols of the destruction of the university library of Louvain and the cathedral of Rheims pointed to the historic shift in the nature of war: this was no 'cabinet war' fought between small armies led by gentleman officers, for limited aims and with limited fire-power, with a limited impact on the belligerents involved. This was war waged with all the resources of modern, industrialized nations, fought for national aims for the survival or domination of nations. The enemy was not merely the enemy army, but the enemy nation and the culture through which it defined itself. Germany went to war in 1914 with a concept of the 'war of annihilation' that was based on the military doctrine developed by Alfred von Schlieffen, chief of the Prussian general staff from 1891 to 1905. Schlieffen's ideas, which dominated German military theory and practice in the era of the First World War, were based on an extreme reading of the great early nineteenth-century theorist of war, Carl von Clausewitz.

Schlieffen distilled the essence of Clausewitz's views thus: 'The "annihilation of the enemy armed forces [appeared to Clausewitz] always as the purpose that stood above all others pursued in war." '[1] This was correct, if grossly oversimplified. But the Schlieffen plan failed the test of reality in 1914, because the French and British armies evaded the envelopment battle with which Schlieffen and his successor Moltke had intended to annihilate them; when the Allies launched the counter-attack in September 1914, the German army was forced onto the defensive. All Moltke's successor, Falkenhayn, could offer was the attempt to continue the 'envelopment' strategy by moving the attack further north until he was stopped by the British near the English Channel in November, followed by attrition warfare. When the most extreme version of attrition, Falkenhayn's gruesome concept of 'bleeding the French white' by a massive attack on Verdun in 1916 in the hope of causing greater French losses than German, also failed, the new army leadership of Hindenburg and Ludendorff further radicalized military doctrine. Ludendorff claimed that Clausewitz taught that even when the enemy armed forces had been annihilated and the enemy country occupied, ' "the war cannot be regarded as ended so long as the will of the enemy has not been broken, i.e. its government and its allies have been compelled to sign the peace or the people compelled to subjection." '[2] This would have been the fate of France, Italy, or Poland, if Germany and its allies had won the war: 'annihilation' of the armed forces, occupation, and subjection of the people. Yet Ludendorff's 'will to annihilate' was based on a wilful misinterpretation of Clausewitz. In the first book of *On War* (1832–4, entitled 'On the nature of war'), Clausewitz wrote:

> If wars between civilized nations are far less cruel and destructive than wars between savages, the reason lies in the social conditions of the states themselves and in their relationships to one another . . .
>
> If, then, civilized nations do not put their prisoners to death or devastate cities and countries, it is because intelligence plays a larger part in their methods of warfare and has taught them more effective ways of using force than the crude expression of instinct.
>
> The invention of gunpowder and the constant improvement of firearms are enough in themselves to show that the advance of civilization has done nothing to alter or deflect the impulse to destroy the enemy, which is central to the very idea of war . . .

That looks like a tendency towards annihilation, but in fact Clausewitz reiterated that the aim was merely 'to disarm the enemy'.

> If the enemy is to be coerced you must put him in a situation that is even more unpleasant than the sacrifice you call on him to make . . . The worst of all conditions in which a belligerent can find himself is to be utterly defenceless. Consequently, if you are to force the enemy, by making war on him, to do your bidding, you must either make him literally defenceless or at least put him in a position that makes this danger probable.[3]

The sense of the above paragraph is that the degree of destruction of the enemy's country was to be limited to that necessary to force his submission. The destruction of cultural objects and mass killing of civilians were unnecessary, because they are not relevant to the main aim of obtaining the enemy's 'defencelessness'. This contention is supported by the following passage:

> Later, when we are dealing with the subject of war plans, we shall investigate in greater detail what is meant by *disarming* a country. But we should at

once distinguish between three things, three broad objectives, which between them cover everything.

The fighting forces must be *destroyed:* that is, they must be *put in such a condition that they can no longer carry on the fight.* Whenever we use the phrase 'destruction of the enemy's forces' this alone is what we mean.

The country must be occupied; otherwise the enemy could raise fresh military forces.

Yet both these things may be done and the war . . . cannot be considered to have ended so long as the enemy's *will* has not been broken: in other words, so long as the enemy government and its allies have not been driven to ask for peace, or the population made to submit.[4]

Thus even the word 'destruction' has a restricted sense with Clausewitz. It did not mean destruction of an entire nation, its people, and its wealth.

Thus it is evident that destruction of the enemy armed forces is always the superior, more effective means, with which others cannot compete.[5]

Nowhere in *On War* did Clausewitz recommend the destruction of civilian life and cultural objects as an object of warfare, although he did theorize on 'laying waste' an enemy's territory in order to put pressure on the enemy. That was intended as an extreme alternative, and the preferred course was to 'wear down the enemy' in a prolonged conflict 'to bring about a gradual exhaustion of his physical and moral resistance.'[6] There is no doubt that the main means to be employed, as he stressed over and again, was combat, 'the only effective force in war'.[7]

The 'war of annihilation' waged by Germany's leaders in 1914–18 thus went much further than the 'combat' envisaged by Clausewitz, or even Schlieffen. Partly, this was because of the demographic factor: armies were far larger than in 1870–1. Even more important was the prodigious increase in fire power: compared with 1866, as Schlieffen wrote in 1909, armies had lighter and more mobile quick-firing artillery with more powerful, smokeless shells, and superior rifles; each army corps thus had ten times the firepower of its equivalent in 1866.[8]

We think today of the massive destruction wrought by men and machines in the Great War as a feature of the major battles that involved artillery bombardment and the relentless throwing away of lives in near-suicidal assaults in 1916 and 1917: Verdun, the Somme, Third Ypres. Yet the opening battles of the war were significant in two ways that have hitherto usually been ignored in histories of the war. First, the destruction of cultural objects and the deliberate killing of civilians prefigured the mass destruction of later years of the war. Second, the initial two months of war were immensely costly in lives of soldiers, to a far greater extent than in popular imagination. The enormous losses in August and September 1914 were never equalled at any other time, not even by Verdun: the total number of French casualties (killed, wounded, and missing) was 329,000. At the height of Verdun, the three-month period February to April 1916, French casualties were 111,000. In fact, the three months April–June 1915, which included the failed Artois offensive, with 143,000 casualties, and the months June to August 1918, the checking of the massive final German onslaught and the victorious counter-offensive, with 157,000 casualties, were both bloodier than the height of the battle of Verdun, but still did not match the blood-letting of 1914. In general, French losses were higher than those of the Germans and the British, because French defensive positions and trenches were less efficient.[9]

The total German losses (killed, wounded, sick, and missing) at the start of war, as computed by the army medical service, were 159,929 in August and 213,440 in September 1914, amounting to 373,369 on the western front in just two months. They were significantly higher than French losses, though not as high as total Allied losses on the western front.[10]

Taking just one part of the casualty figures, the numbers killed, as reported by the medical service, confirm that the first three months of the war were by far the deadliest, with death rates of 1.43 per cent in August, 1.65 in September, and 1.04 per cent in October 1914. Such high rates were never again to be reached, the next highest being in November 1914 with 0.88 per cent, May 1915 with 0.81, September 1915 with 0.85, and July 1916 with 0.75 per cent, before the data series breaks off in July 1918. Not even in the great offensives of spring 1918, therefore, were such high rates reached (April 1918: 0.67 per cent).[11] Contrary to received wisdom, it was not trench warfare, but the mobile warfare of the first three months which was most destructive of lives. The death rate of September 1914 was at least ten times higher than those of December 1915, January 1916, and January–March 1917, and forty times higher than those of January and February 1918 (0.036 and 0.042 per cent).[12] The closer we approach smaller units, the more clearly we can imagine the impact of the devastating losses. In the last ten days of August alone the German army lost 2.93 per cent of its men killed and missing on the western front, and about 10 per cent including the sick and injured; the 18th Army Corps in the 4th Army lost 3,101 men killed and missing, out of a combat strength of 36,351, or 8.53 per cent; the 4th army's total losses (killed, missing, injured, and sick) amounted to 16.69 per cent.[13] On one day, 6 August, the 14th Brigade, repulsed by Belgian defenders at Liège, lost almost three-quarters of its men and many of its officers, including the brigade commander and a regimental commander killed.[14]

British losses in the early weeks of the war were little short of catastrophic. The original British Expeditionary Force was almost wiped out, although volunteers quickly filled the gaps. Down to 30 November 1914 the BEF had 89,964 casualties, which exceeded the establishment of the original seven divisions; 54,000 had been lost at Ypres.[15]

The great losses of the first two months of war resulted from the collision of million-strong armies, both sides attacking in a war of movement, without having built adequate defensive positions. Prime examples were the experience of the Germans at Liège in Belgium and in the area of Nancy and Toul in France, and of the French offensive into German Alsace and Lorraine and into the Belgian Ardennes. All involved high numbers killed, wounded, and taken captive; army units were decimated, officers and men alike were in a state of shock, and a crisis of leadership ensued. To take one example: Bavarian commander Crown Prince Rupprecht, eager to take advantage of repelling the French invasion of German Lorraine, insisted, against the advice of the OHL (the German Supreme Command), on pressing a counter-offensive into French territory from 19 to 25 August. The French retreated into the fortified area of Nancy and Toul and inflicted severe damage on the Sixth (Bavarian) Army. In retrospect, General Ludwig von Gebsattel, commander of the 3rd Bavarian Army Corps, realized that the entire idea was foolhardy.

> Downright incomprehensible, the crazy idea of allowing the 2nd [Bavarian] Army Corps to march southwards with Toul and Nancy on their flank. It is a miracle that the 2nd Bavarian Army Corps was not completely annihilated (OHL and the Sixth Army are arguing about copyright!).
> Another idea that was caused by underestimating the enemy was trying to 'overrun' the position of Nancy as Liège had been overrun, with completely inadequate means and forces. That cost me alone more than 10,000 men.[16]

Although another officer had a different opinion on who was responsible for the slaughter, he was even more emphatic in the privacy of his diary on the catastrophic effects of the doctrine of the offensive:

> (25 August) Yesterday the replacement divisions were already in a terrible state ['Schweinestall', literally pigsty], as a result of which Lengerke, poor chap with that inadequate formation, is said to have shot himself. These divisions came

under heavy fire today, which was murderous, and the same for the 3rd Army Corps, which despite the prohibition ran into the firing area of the heavy guns of Nancy, just because Gebsattel, who has not had any successes yet, wanted to have his battle. He also hounds the 5th Reserve Division into that fire at Lunéville.[17]

These terrible experiences of the new warfare forced men to go to ground: to dig in for protection. Trench warfare stabilized along a 450-mile (720-kilometre) front from Ostend to the Swiss frontier in which any further attack could only be launched with massive use of artillery preparation and yet would still be enormously costly of lives to attacker and defender alike. (See Map 1.) This is not to say that trench warfare was an innovation of the Great War, or that commanders had not anticipated its development, as the popular historical myth has it. Troops had dug in for protection in the South African War (1899–1902) and in the Russo-Japanese War (1904–5); foreign observers took careful note and Europe's armies trained before 1914 in the technique of digging in. But in the two recent wars trenches had only been a temporary expedient, before mobility was restored to deliver the decisive blow. The hugely destructive set-piece battles of 1915 to 1918, in which men, defensive positions, and entire landscapes were pulverized before attacks were launched, were part of a broader, considered strategy, but the process of massive destruction arose incrementally and developed out of the logic of the armaments stalemate of 1914. One officer on the staff of the 4th Bavarian Infantry Division described the transformation of warfare well in December 1914 in a private letter to the retired general Konstantin von Gebsattel:

> We were working on the breakthrough here [Comines, south of Ypres] from 20 October to 18 November. After six day-long forced marches we attacked the fortified positions 19 days on end with the same troops. At first with good success. Once a position was taken, behind it there was a second and a third. Barbed wire fences everywhere. The *good* men and the officers fell, and in the end everything came to a halt ... At the end of the 19 days the French were deserting in droves. With fresh troops we would have achieved a breakthrough, but our men were completely exhausted, and the officers had fallen or were injured. . . . For two days now the British have been attacking fiercely. They are brave men, far better than the French, better, I fear, than our old Landwehr men with whom we have to plug the gaps. . . . The fearful effects of modern artillery and infantry fire have to be combated with an even more threatening compulsion to obey the will of the leadership so that cowardly men are more afraid of what awaits them behind the lines than the fire from the front. Our entire tactical doctrine has been thrown overboard. Frontal

assaults can only be carried out by the best material, with quite enormous losses, but since the enemy has built a whole series of fortified positions one behind the next we would need fresh troops for each position, for after taking one position the storm troops ['Sturmtruppe'—a term which did not yet designate special units] are finished up. The long time spent lying in the trenches and shelters has damaged the morale of the men. They only care about staying under cover, and they forget that there are moments when that thought has to be dropped. The order comes from the top that officers are not to expose themselves unnecessarily. Result: down to the level of company commander they sit around in shelters. The men do the same, of course, as best they can, so when the time comes to go over the top their drive is not exactly overwhelming. That also comes from the nerve-wracking artillery fire. I have seen brave officers who were complete wrecks. I myself have only been under [artillery] fire three times and then not for very long, but I can well imagine that men who have to crouch in those holes for days and weeks and are just shot at are quite soon demoralized; after all, they see too often how their comrades next to them are torn to bits. Only very few people can withstand these impressions. In open combat we have always been far superior to the French. . . . But now the French no longer let it come to battle in open country. With the entire civilian population they build defences behind their advance lines. Only with colossally heavy artillery, which shoots everything to pulp, can an energetic advance be achieved. But we do not have enough heavy artillery.[18]

We can ignore the bragging about German superiority over the French: after all, the recipient of the letter was a leading Pan German, a rabid nationalist, who within fifteen months was forced to recognize the equality of French military prowess. The essence is the confession that morale had collapsed, the officers were perplexed, and traditional doctrine had failed. Now 'everything' had to be shot to pulp, by which the author meant not only the defensive positions, but also the bodies of the men. This was the logic of modern warfare given the state of military technology in 1914, and it was the same logic that governed the British preparation of the Somme offensive in 1916.

Before that point, however, the British contribution was small compared to the French, who withstood the brunt of the German onslaught. On 1 January 1915, the British held 50 kilometres of the western front, the Belgians 20, and the French the remaining 650 kilometres. When Kitchener launched his appeal for volunteers, 2.46 million British and Irish men signed up by the end of 1915, reflecting the high degree of popular consent to the war. But these citizen soldiers had to be trained, equipped, given uniforms, organized, and armed, and thus their deployment in battle proved to be slow and gradual.[19] In the meantime, it was the French who were on the offensive; from late 1914 to February 1916, this was the general pattern of warfare on the western front. As Ludwig von Gebsattel, commander of the 3rd Bavarian Army Corps, told his brother Konstantin, 'In the west we are absolutely in the defensive; we are the besieged, the attacked, and one cannot say that the French are inactive.'[20] By 1916, at the height of the battle of Verdun, Konstantin von Gebsattel was forced to admit that even though he still deemed the French to be a degenerate race, he held the French army in great admiration for its resilience and bravery, and its brilliantly led artillery; it was an opponent of equal rank.[21]

On both sides military doctrine had sought to adjust to the enormously increased power of defensive weapons by placing even greater emphasis on psychological preparation, on instilling in their men the spirit of the offensive, on the superiority of that army that had the morale of the offensive. This helps to explain the extravagant losses of August–October 1914. An ammunition supply officer wrote to Gebsattel:

> I am only aggrieved by the fact that I have so little to do . . . That is because against all expectation the corps have too many infantry ammunition supply columns. Only a few days ago I gave out all my ammunition from my column for the first time, and the 3rd and 4th columns behind us haven't issued a single bullet. Partly it is because our infantry shoot so little and in their excessive élan want to overrun everything. That explains the unprecedented losses. The 'Leibregiment' [Sovereign's own regiment], which has already been refilled twice over, is again 2,000 men short. Of the 60 officers in the 3rd Infantry Regiment who marched out, only 4 remain; when I saw the 15th Infantry Regiment in Metz, it only had 800 men left. At present, our corps therefore has no offensive strength, and this racing forwards has just ceased all by itself, much to the grief of the commanders.[22]

An infantry regiment had a full complement of 3,000 men.

A cavalry officer, downcast at the progress of the invasion in general and the experience of the cavalry in particular, wrote in early December 1914:

> The merry, fresh war which we were all looking forward to for years has turned out to be quite different from what we thought! It is murder of troops by machines, and the horse has become almost superfluous . . . The cavalry can do nothing in this territory, and we are deployed only as riflemen in the trenches . . . Artillery fire is inflicting enormous losses on our troops, and our best men have been laid to rest in the earth of Lorraine; those who replace them are worth nothing. Especially the Palatinate men, whom we always used

to call great soldiers in peacetime, simply cannot be brought to advance under fire. Some of the few remaining officers on the front are nervous wrecks... All the theories of decades have proved to be worthless, and now everything has to be done differently. We often have a shortage of artillery ammunition, and only the food supply is exemplary... We are all sick of the war; how long is it going to last?[23]

This signified more than the plaintive regret at the obsolescence of the cavalry: this was recognition of the revolution in warfare that produced strategic stalemate and industrialized mass killing—or 'murder', as he put it.

Were no other countries apart from Germany responsible for cultural destruction and mass killing? In Chapter 4 the notion of German singularity will be investigated. Suffice it to say at this point that the British and the French engaged in the same kind of war of attrition that was so destructive of men's lives, both of the enemy and their own armies, and Allied naval warfare amounted to the attempt to starve the civilian population of Germany, for there was at the time no strategic alternative in the face of the German war of conquest. This explains, for example, why the Basilica of Albert (Somme), an early twentieth-century edifice, ruined by German shellfire, was finally destroyed by British artillery after the Germans overran the town in April 1918.[24] The German concept of the 'war of annihilation' was no secret during the war. The French understood it in the sense Ludendorff intended: as an attempt to 'destroy the French "race" by waging total war'.[25] (The use of the term 'race' was ubiquitous in Europe at the time, for example among the medical profession in France: the war was seen as a struggle between two 'races' which were intrinsically opposed.[26]) In tendency, this propelled Allied warfare into the same logic of annihilation, although the scope of destruction was limited to the territory on which the war was fought, not enemy territory. Before the tank had proved its capacity to break through enemy lines—which did not happen on a significant scale until autumn 1917—the destruction of space was the only strategy, as expressed by the British general Robertson in September 1917: massive fire by heavy artillery to destroy the German machine guns, 'but unfortunately this entails the entire destruction of the surface of the ground and renders it almost impassable, especially in Flanders.'[27]

With their superior economic resources, access to world markets, and, from 1917, the support of the USA, the Allies gradually turned the tables of annihilation against their enemies in what was becoming total war. At first, this shift resulted from a position of relative weakness; in 1916, Verdun had shaken the confidence of the French. Their chief of staff General Joffre told General Haig, commander of the BEF, that the French were 'much disturbed by their diminishing manpower [and] the feeling of growing weakness'; they were now 'averse to undertaking any offensive themselves on a decisive scale ... they could not afford to risk great losses'.[28] The Nivelle offensive of April 1917 excepted, the pattern was of declining French involvement in offensive warfare until the end of the war: the total strength of French units on the western front fell from 2.23 million men on 1 July 1916 to 1.89 million in October 1917, and 1.67 million by 1 October 1918.

In the long run there was a fundamental shift in the nature of the French military effort. With vastly increased production of tanks, aircraft, and artillery, by 1918 French strategy was clearly to rely on technology and armaments, not manpower, or at least no longer French manpower. The French army had started the war with 156 aircraft, but by the end it had 2,639 first-line aircraft, and more than 3,000 tanks.[29] Initial German aerial superiority (German fighters being the first to be equipped with machine guns that fired along the axis, synchronized with the propeller) was soon challenged, and by 1918 the Allies had absolute air superiority. Aerial warfare had an impact also on the civilian population, as German bombers and airships attacked civilian targets, killing 1,400 civilians in Britain. The Allies flew 2,800 raids on Germany, mainly on armaments plants in industrial areas in Lorraine, the Moselle, and the Saar, and occasionally larger cities, in which 728 civilians were killed.[30]

By the standards of later wars in the twentieth century, aerial warfare was only at the beginning of its development towards total destructivity. But its potential to transform warfare was recognized by visionary thinkers, not only by novelists like H. G. Wells, but by those who had influence on military decision-makers. Giulio Douhet in Italy was one. A talented artillery officer on the Italian general staff before the war, he began to publish on the subject as early as 1910, predicting that large air forces would dominate in future war. He was an explicit admirer of Marinetti and the Futurists, and became a close friend of the Turin industrialist Caproni, together with whom he developed Italy's fleet of long-range heavy bombers during the war. In 1917 he drafted a plan for a vast Allied air offensive in which 1,000 Italian aircraft, 3,000 French, 4,000 British, and 12,000 American, would drop 1,000 tons of bombs on Hamburg, Essen, Berlin, and Vienna. This plan was not realized at the time, but his book of 1921, *The Command of the Air*, influenced an entire generation of military and civilian decision-makers in the inter-war years. It called for the construction of an independent air force which, rather than act as auxiliary to the land army in tactical support, would engage in ruthless strategic bombing of civilian targets, to destroy the enemy's industry, infrastructure, and government.[31]

Finally, it should be clear by now that the losses affected all sections of society. The notion, common throughout Europe, that a callous ruling class, seconded by middle-class patriots safe in their armchairs, wasted the lives of millions of the working class and peasantry in futile slaughter, does not bear closer examination. Almost half the primary and lycée teachers in France were called up, and of these, three-quarters were dead or wounded by late 1915. By 1919, 260 university professors had been killed in the fighting, more than one-quarter of the total. Of the 240 students who entered the elite *Ecole Normale Supérieure* between 1908 and 1913 and who served in the armed forces, exactly one half, 120 men, were killed. One quarter of British and German students who joined the military were killed. Between 23 and 29.3 per cent of those who entered Oxford between 1905 and 1914 and who served in the military died, compared with a death-rate of 12 per cent of all men mobilized.[32] The losses among Europe's future political and economic elite were thus even more catastrophic than among the working classes and peasantry.

Occupation, exploitation, destruction

Military destructiveness was not a reflection of some innate human (or male) tendency, but arose from strategic, political, and economic calculations. It extended also to the ruthless exploitation of occupied territories and the destruction of property, and industrial and agricultural capital.

Ruthless occupation policies caused hardship, disease, and death on a large scale. Requisitioning of food and other supplies began with the moment of the invasion, and continued in modified form for the duration of the occupation. This was not random foraging by hungry troops, but official policy: German military plans laid down before the war expected the troops to live off the land of enemy territory, indeed to requisition all available resources and production 'beyond the current needs of the army'. In early September 1914 the Prussian finance minister advised the chancellor: 'It's better that the Belgians starve than that we do.'[33] One German officer wrote home from a village near Péronne in the Somme:

> In November [1914] we village commandants were given the instruction to confiscate all grain, have it threshed, and send it to Germany in so far as it was not needed by the army. The population was to be left with nothing, and was to be provided with food by Switzerland. In December this was changed so that the population was allowed 200 grams of wheat per day until 1 May. Now, in January [1915], the order arrives for all troops to take over the task of tilling the fields with wheat, oats, etc. so that we get the benefit of the next harvest.[34]

Evidently the realization that the war would not be over soon caused a shift towards a policy of long-term exploitation: occupied France and Belgium had to be made productive for the needs of a long war. The effects on the population were soon felt. One civilian in the French occupied zone wrote:

> 25 December 1914. Sad, sad Christmas Day. Instead of Christmas brioches we eat detestable bread better suited for horses, and we are happy to have a loaf at all. The Germans have been celebrating Christmas in all ways. Christmas trees everywhere they are accommodated [Christmas trees were alien to French culture at that time], Christmas mass in the churches, and banquets, etc. . . . 2, 3, 4, 5 January 1915. Even bad bread is becoming more and more scarce . . . 10 January. Six bakeries have closed.

People grew weaker, illness and deaths became more frequent. Malnutrition made the civilians more susceptible to whooping cough, measles, scarlet fever, dysentery, and especially typhoid. A citizen of Roubaix noted over the months March 1916 to November 1917:

> Everyone is getting thinner . . . The death rate is high; in ordinary times two gravediggers were enough in Roubaix, and now there are six of them . . . Food is becoming ever more expensive . . . Since sugar, milk, meat, pasta, eggs, and wine have been taken off our diet, it is no wonder we are getting thin.[35]

However, Germany needed the population of the occupied territories, and did its best to keep it there. In a little-known (and today forgotten) operation of the Great War, in summer 1915 the German occupation of Belgium went to the length of erecting a barbed wire and electrified fence along the 300-kilometre Dutch border to prevent escapes. Thousands of Belgians, as well as Allied soldiers who had evaded capture, and German deserters, attempted to cross into the neutral Netherlands, and perhaps as many as 25,000 persons succeeded, using means such as wooden or rubber insulation materials and insulated wire-cutters. However, many were caught by the guards, warned by automatic alarm bells, and anyone touching the fence would receive a lethal shock from the high-tension charge, usually 2000 volts. It is estimated that between 300 and 500 were killed in the attempt to flee through Europe's first 'iron curtain', an extraordinary harbinger of later totalitarian methods.[36]

Destruction or removal of industrial capital in the occupied zones in the war sounds like a dry, abstract economic subject far away from the fierce emotions of hatred that accompanied cultural destruction and mass killing. Yet for the French textile entrepreneurs in the département du Nord the requisitioning of their stocks of material, beginning within weeks of the invasion in 1914, and later the confiscation of copper (pipes, taps, and boilers), meant more than the end of business activity. The removal of patterns, which were the irreplaceable basis of textile production, effectively deprived the industrialists of the instruments of recovery. The process culminated in the dismantling of the machines and the destruction of the factories at the end of the occupation. Not only did workers lose their employment and industrialists their factories, but also for the owners it meant the emotionally painful loss of their professional identity in family firms built up over several generations.[37] Probably the majority of machines in occupied France was dismantled.[38]

In Belgium, General von Bissing, the governor-general in Brussels, and his political adviser Baron von der Lancken, tried to moderate the policy, and stop the army high command from destroying 'superfluous' Belgian factories, but in vain. They argued that it would leave Germany open to the accusation that it was suppressing Belgian competition. Both the French and the Belgians claimed that Germany had deliberately destroyed the industry of the occupied territories order to favour German industry in the post-war period.[39] Baron von der Lancken commented in retrospect that the Allied charge that German policy was to do long-term damage to Belgian competition was 'not entirely without justification'.[40] Bissing's and von der Lancken's efforts were in vain. In 1916 the competence of the German War Raw Materials Office was extended to include the Belgian economy, and as from February 1917 Belgian industry was much more intensively exploited for German purposes. Almost every factory had to apply for a permit to continue producing. The result was the closing down of many plants, followed by the dismantling of their machines for transport to

Germany. What remained in Belgium were factories that had to produce purely for the German armaments economy, and any plant deemed 'superfluous' was scrapped. As factories closed, their plant and machines were systematically dismantled and sent to Germany. In particular, the entire engineering industry of the Walloon region from Charleroi to Liège was completely pillaged. Ten out of eleven steel rolling-mills of the Cockerill company and all iron-processing plants in the Liège and Charleroi regions were destroyed.[41] In Germany, the 'Weapons and Munitions Office' ('Wumba') and the 'Raw Materials Procurement Office' ('Rohma') organized the disposal of the assets for the profit of the military; they were deluged with bids from German companies eager to obtain the Belgian material.[42] Even private households were deprived of their essential items. In 1918 the German occupation requisitioned the mattresses from bedrooms, using the wool to manufacture warm clothing for five million soldiers. 'You have no idea of Belgium's wealth. New sources can always be found', the officer responsible for the requisitions said.[43] In 1921 the Belgian government calculated that the damage caused by the German occupation amounted to $2.22 billion (not including Belgium's own war costs of $1.5 billion and $500 million for pensions).[44]

Belgium and occupied France had become vast prisons for their inhabitants, who were affected also directly by two other drastic measures—deportations and destructions. During the invasion in 1914, at least 10,000 French and 13,000 Belgian civilians were deported to Germany and held under harsh conditions. The motivation of the German army is not entirely clear, but in some cases, as we saw with Louvain in Chapter 1, it may have been to deter resistance, so potential 'ringleaders', usually men of influence in the community, were deported. However, women, children, and old people were also deported, so the motivation was collective punishment for an alleged uprising.[45] Thus no fewer than 1,500 citizens of Amiens were arrested in September 1914 and incarcerated in camps in Germany for four years, until 1918.[46] This policy merged into deportation for economic exploitation. To meet the voracious demands of German industry for ever more labour, Belgian workers were forcibly deported to Germany to work in war production. In peremptory manner General Ludendorff stated that 'all social misgivings or reservations deriving from international law' must be ignored; the OHL warned that the 'fate of the war could under certain circumstances depend precisely on it'.[47] Altogether 58,432 Belgians were deported to Germany to work; another 62,155 Belgians were forced to work behind the front in France and Belgium, sometimes under fire from

Allied guns but forbidden to take shelter, and often beaten by the guards.[48] Countless thousands of Frenchmen and women were forced to work digging trenches, building other fortifications, roads, and railways for the German army. This was not only contrary to international law, it was deeply repugnant to the people forced to work against the interests of their own nation. 'We are forced to construct trenches to kill our fathers, our brothers, our cousins,' one wrote.[49]

The deportations provoked protests not only from those affected, but also from the Belgian church, the Vatican, and from neutral countries such as the USA. The American ambassador in Germany, James W. Gerard, was told on his visit home in autumn 1916 that the carrying of 'a great part of the male population of Belgium into virtual slavery had roused great indignation in America'. President Wilson took a great interest in the deportations from Belgium, and Cardinal Farley of New York told Gerard: 'You have to go back to the times of the Medes and the Persians to find a like example of a whole people carried into bondage.'[50] This was somewhat of an exaggeration. But even the German military governor, General von Bissing, warned against the policy, and Baron von der Lancken pointed out that it ran counter to the other intentions of German policy, to promote pro-German feelings in the Flemish community.[51] Conditions for the deportees were harsh: they were transported usually in cattle wagons, and their accommodation was in camps. A total of 2,614 of the civilians died during their time as forced labourers (2.17 per cent of those deported), which is a high figure, given that most of the deportees were men judged healthy enough to work.[52]

Some idea of the hatred caused by this radicalized exploitation is to be seen in the violent tone of a letter sent in October 1918 by five members of the French Academy of Science in the occupied zone, which had just been liberated:

> It is the tribunal of history which will have the duty of assessing the military utility of the methodical destruction of all our factories . . . the pillage of our private property, the forced requisition of our furniture, our mattresses, our clothing, our objects of art, our household utensils, the imprisonment or deportation of a multitude of our fellow citizens for the mere refusal to work for the German army. But we do not believe it can be excused or justified to inflict cruel and cold torture on the entire defenceless population, and we are of the opinion that those who issued such orders must be held to account morally and held liable for damages . . . What is to be said, above all,

about the atrocious cruelty with which almost all our children between 14 and 18 were torn away from their families and schools to go, together with a large number of old people from 60 to 65 years, to form labour battalions to work under fire? . . . The number of these poor children and poor old people whom we have not seen again is immense, or those whose health has been permanently compromised! . . .

In our century can one conceive of the leaders of an allegedly civilized people carrying out such shameful, ferociously cruel acts, without the least fear of the judgement of the other nations? How would it be possible for us to forget or to pardon such horrors? Those who have not suffered from them, in free France, cannot comprehend the deep grounds of our animosity. Some would willingly concede that the German people is not responsible for the foul deeds of their army leaders. We wish that were true. But when one has seen, as we have, the eagerness, the zeal of the soldiers, . . . the officers who are not professional military men, medical doctors, for example, in accomplishing the most odious acts without a word of apology, regret, or pity, one is obliged to recognize that . . . with very rare exceptions the German heart is not accessible to noble, generous, or merely human feelings . . . This people, which used to merit the esteem of the world both for its industriousness and for the work of intellectual and social progress achieved by its scientists, philosophers, and poets, cannot any longer inspire anything but feelings of disgust and terror for the crimes it is responsible for.[53]

The Allied perception that Germany intensified the use of illegal methods was even confirmed by the German government. In April 1916 the US ambassador, James W. Gerard, was called to German headquarters at Charleville-Mézières for discussions intended to prevent American intervention in the war, in view of increasing US protests at German attacks on neutral ships. On 1 May Gerard had a long conversation with the Kaiser and chancellor Bethmann Hollweg, in which the Kaiser complained at the tone of American notes, and said that 'as Emperor and head of the Church, he had wished to carry on the war in a knightly manner'.

He then referred to the efforts to starve out Germany and keep out milk and said that before he would allow his family and grandchildren to starve he would blow up Windsor Castle and the whole Royal family of England. We then had a long discussion in detail of the whole submarine question, in the course of which the Emperor said that the submarine had come to stay, that it was a weapon recognised by all countries . . . He stated that, anyway, there was no longer any international law. To this last statement the Chancellor agreed.[54]

It is hard to explain why some of these radical measures that flouted international law should have disappeared from historical memory; possibly the deportations and forced labour lacked the dramatic impact of the executions of civilians or U-boat warfare. At the time, the Allies considered the deportation question to be so important that in the list of Germans to be extradited for trial as alleged war criminals in 1920 it was second only to the killings of 1914 (by number of charges).[55]

In eastern Europe occupation policies were more radical still. In 1915 the German army first drove the remaining Russian troops out of East Prussia, and then in a series of victorious offensives with more than half a million men reconquered Galicia together with Habsburg forces, and took Warsaw, Kovno, Brest-Litovsk, and Vilna. Russian forces had been driven back 500 kilometres, losing a territory similar in size to France (See Map 2). The Germans found a landscape devastated by the war and by the Russian policy of 'scorched earth', impoverished, and left in chaos.[56] Under Ludendorff's command a military state known as 'Ober Ost' was set up stretching across most of present-day Lithuania, Latvia, Estonia, and parts of Poland and Belarus. Only recently has the history of this part of Europe during the First World War been researched, and Vejas Gabriel Liulevicius has shown in his powerfully argued book *War Land* how Ober Ost was a laboratory for the utopian war aims of the German occupation which enjoyed far-reaching powers to experiment and act autonomously, as a proto-colonial regime. The Lithuanians experienced the occupation as a system of violent, arbitrary rule. They were obliged to step off the pavement and salute the occupation officers; strict pass laws were introduced, with frequent identity checks in the streets, outside churches, and in trains. The economy was ruthlessly exploited. To achieve maximum efficiency every cow and chicken, every tree in the forests, and every fish in the lakes was to be statistically recorded. To feed the insatiable appetite of the war machine entire forests were cut down. The demand for workers was met through forced labour—in 1917 amounting to about 60,000 on Lithuanian territory. Potentially, all men and women were subject to forced labour as from 26 June 1916, so the true number might have been far higher. When instructions to report to labour camps were ignored, people were simply rounded up in raids. The conditions for the forced labour were harsh, and the rations amounted to only 250 grams of bread and a litre of soup—at most 700 calories, a starvation diet.[57] Public corporal punishment, also of women, and torture in the prisons, were routinely employed to force people to respect the occupiers.

Map 2. The eastern front

The consequences of the exploitation were impoverishment, famine, and epidemics in which thousands died in winter 1917–18.[58]

The German occupation in eastern Europe saw itself as a colonial regime with a civilizing mission, to transform savages into decent Europeans. Compulsory inoculation and disinfection programmes were carried out by German doctors, and the damaged infrastructure was to some extent rebuilt. In an ambitious cultural development campaign newspapers were published in the native languages and schools were founded in which the local language was the main language of instruction. German language was compulsory from class one, and people were encouraged to acquaint themselves with German culture. The authoritarian occupation tried to accustom the population to thinking in terms of ethnicity, which was for many a new concept, and in terms of space, by controlling their mobility and creating new administrative boundaries (*Volk* and *Raum*). Above all it was the German soldiers (of whom two or three million served in the East) who returned from the war with a new concept of space: the East they encountered was a desolate, partly depopulated, under-developed region ready to be colonized. They encountered a confusingly wide range of ethnic groups to whom they felt culturally superior. Yet this was not racism in the sense of race hatred; it was rather the common western European or north American sense of a natural differentiation between races. Antisemitic officers found confirmation of their prejudice, but most German soldiers rejected antisemitism, and Ober Ost issued guidelines for equal treatment of all ethnic groups.[59]

Two important conclusions can be drawn from the German occupation of eastern Europe. First, the brutality of the occupation, including a policy of deporting Polish civilians to work in Germany which was identical to the deportation of French and Belgian citizens, provoked far less international protest. This was another indication that west European victims of war were privileged in the international public sphere. Second, on the level of mentalities the occupation had long-term consequences, especially for right-wing German political culture which built on the experience of colonial-style occupation and racist stereotyping. Yet it would be mistaken to see the occupation as a pilot programme for the Third Reich: occupation in the First World War was colonial and authoritarian; in the Second World War it was devoted to a programme of brutal ethnic redistribution, enslavement, and genocide.

On the western front, when the Germans retreated to defensive positions on the Hindenburg line in 1917 the areas into which the Allies marched were deliberately devastated in a policy of 'scorched earth'. This policy was repeated in the great retreat of 1918: during both, the German high command ordered that everything should be destroyed, leaving behind only a waste-land for the enemy to take. At the end of October 1918 the political department of the German occupation in Belgium heard that the retreating army planned to flood a large number of the coalmines in Hainault, and even blow up some of them, as they had done to the French mines at Douai and Lens. The political department managed to inform the foreign ministry which obtained a royal order that only such measures of destruction were allowed that would stop production for at most a few months, but which would not lead to flooding or permanent disuse.[60] However, the army ignored this, and the removal of industrial plant, the dismantling of machines, the destruction of the coalmines, and theft from museums continued until the last days of the occupation in November 1918.[61] By no stretch of the imagination could these measures be justified as a military necessity: they were pillage and destruction without any military purpose, as the dynamic of destruction escaped from the control of its nominal commander in chief.

Italy in the Great War:
from the 'radiant days of May' to catastrophe

The closest Germany (and its Austrian ally) came to repeating 1914-style destruction of civilians and civilian targets was on the Italian front. Before we come to discuss these events which are scarcely ever mentioned in histories of the war, we should consider one aspect of the decision of the Italian government to go to war in May 1915, namely the prospect of huge losses in a lengthy war. The reasons for Italy's intervention will be explained in Chapter 4, and can be summarized here as the desire of Salandra's wing of the Liberal establishment to consolidate its rule through nationalist mobilization and defeat the previous prime minister Giolitti and his powerful following. This meant harnessing the demands of the nationalists for territorial expansion at the cost of the evidently weakened Austro-Hungarian empire and for imperialist expansion in Africa, and the revival of 'national aspirations' in the tradition of Mazzinian and Garibaldian nationalist mobilization in which this was a fourth war of unification.[62] At any rate, the prospect of immense loss of life and a stalemate war seems not to have featured at all in the deliberations. Amazingly, the Italian army had learned nothing from the experience of its allies over the previous ten months, according to the Italian historian Melograni. Five months after Italy's entry in the war, the chief of staff of the 13th army corps, General Grazioli, told a member of the supreme command in November 1915: 'We advance only metre by metre, with enormous losses out of proportion to the goal. All the generals are against Cadorna [the chief of the supreme command] . . . ; there is a lack of grenade-launchers, good artillery tubes, telephones, etc. Nothing is up to date, nothing has been learned from ten months of war of the others.'[63] It is hardly surprising that there were huge losses in the first four bitter battles of the Isonzo for very little gain in territory, and one Italian general called the campaign of 1915 'a war of madness': from 24 May to 30 November 62,000 men were killed and 170,000 wounded, out of an army of about one million.[64] These were in fact smaller losses in proportion to army size than in the first two months of war in 1914, but that was not apparent at the time.

The enthusiasm for war in the 'radiant days' of May 1915, expressed in the joyful nationalist demonstrations of the interventionists, soon dissolved upon contact with war. That sense of disillusion, but also the realistic appreciation of what the future held out, was best expressed not in the technical language of the generals, but by a young interventionist, a nationalist student called Napoleone Battaglia, who wrote to his professor after only 12 days of combat, on 10 September 1915:

> Oh, believe me, here, facing the terrible reality which desperately calls upon all the instincts of life, there can be no enthusiasm. It is the sense of duty. People in Italy should be under no illusion; they will have to extinguish their Garibaldian flames in the slow monotonous water of tenacity, patience, constancy. Our war will be long, hard, hard, ferocious. We have before us a formidable and brave enemy, well entrenched in a most formidable territory. We have before us a high, smooth wall, which offers no toeholds: to surmount it, we will need to pile high the corpses.[65]

In eleven great battles on the line of the Isonzo River from May 1915 to September 1917 the Italians tried to overcome the resistance of Austrians (See Map 3). A strip of territory was gained, but at the cost of great massacres. One factor was the inferior quality of Italian trenches: while the Austrian troops were behind well-constructed deep trenches with parapets and barbed-wire entanglements the Italians had shallow trenches little more than one metre deep with only sacks of earth and stones which afforded no protection from artillery fire. Not even that fundamental lesson had been learned from the western front. Italian military doctrine prescribed mass frontal attacks, but the army lacked sufficient artillery support. There were not enough field guns and heavy artillery; modern infantry weapons, machine guns, munitions, trench-building equipment, even uniforms were in short supply; the men were poorly trained for modern warfare, and the medical service was

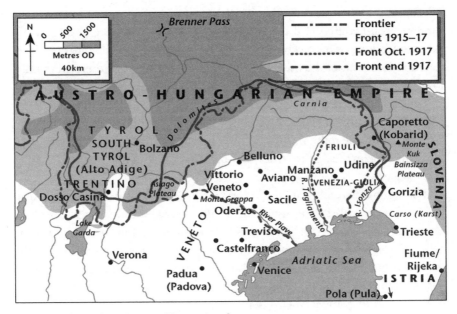

Map 3. The Italian-Austro-Hungarian front

patchy. The harsh terrain of the Carso, with its barren rock, windswept and cold in winter, lacking water in the summer and always without shelter, in contrast to the other Italian fronts the Trentino, the Carnia or High Friuli, caused immense suffering to the men and gave the defenders a great advantage. The attempt to advance by sending men to cut the wire often amounted to a suicide mission, and the frontal attacking waves of Italians were mown down by Austrian machine guns and artillery. Artillery support, when there was any, often rained down shells on the attackers instead of destroying the defences.[66]

In the tenth battle of the Isonzo (12 May to 6 June 1917), the Italians lost 36,000 killed, 96,000 wounded, and 27,000 men taken prisoner, for the gain of two miles of arid plateau. Habsburg losses were 52,300 casualties and 23,400 captured.[67] The eleventh battle of the Isonzo, in August 1917, brought a significant victory. Although the territorial gains were meagre—the plateau of Bainsizza and a few kilometres along a 20-kilometre front from Gorizia/Görz down to the sea in the attempt to advance towards Trieste—the political consequences were profound. Both the Entente and the Central Powers turned their attention to the Italian front as the 'most important in the entire European theatre'. In terms of morale, too, this was an important victory for the Italian army, because of the great obstacles to be overcome: the crossing of an Alpine river with large masses of troops, the throwing of 14 bridges under enemy fire, followed by the scaling of a steep mountain and crossing three lines of defence, without the benefit of good roads. However, the prestige of the *Comando supremo* was one matter, the morale of the front-line troops, who suffered murderous conditions and enormous losses, was another. The Italian army lost 160,000 men, the Austrians 85,000. Moreover, it prompted the Central Powers to organize a large counter-offensive to regain the lost territory and prestige.[68]

The horrendous losses in the tenth and eleventh Isonzo battles outnumbered even those suffered by the French during Verdun in a similar four-month period: *total* French losses on *all* fronts from February to May 1916 were 140,800.[69] Although its losses were lower, the Austrian army suffered so badly on the Carso that its morale was severely damaged, and the military and political leadership of the Austro-Hungarian Empire decided that it could not withstand a twelfth Isonzo battle. It appealed to Berlin for support, and the German high command agreed to help launch a counter-offensive 'in order to prevent the collapse of Austria-Hungary'. That was the origin of the Caporetto offensive, which was to prove such a disaster for Italy.[70]

Giulio Douhet, later to become the internationally influential theoretician of aerial warfare, wrote in his diary in 1915: 'In a war of machines we present ourselves naked, with our muscles and our heart, and, after the first steps, the machines, after having smashed many of us to atoms, bring us to a halt.'[71] Under these circumstances it is almost a mystery how the Italian troops fought with such tenacity for over two years. The collapse of Italian morale in autumn 1917 was occasioned by defeat at Caporetto, the twelfth Isonzo battle, but it was prefigured by a gradual decline in the spirit of the men at the front and the growth of disillusion and distrust of the leadership. Two letters illustrate this process:

> Oh, dear parents, to witness the tears and cries of the injured is something to make you weep with fear. I almost no longer count on going back home into your arms and to your beautiful eyes, oh, my dear parents and brothers, we will not see each other again. (1 July 1916)

> If you happen to receive a notice that I am dead, do not say I died for the nation, but that I died for the rulers, that is, for the rich who are to blame for the death of so many good young men. (15 April 1917)[72]

Caporetto and the consequences
of the invasion of Italy

Caporetto was well prepared by the Austrians, and the Germans, who lent several divisions. According to Cadorna, the enemy, now freed from the 'nightmare' of Russia, deployed 53 divisions (645 battalions), mainly on the Isonzo, supported by the German Alpine corps. Apparently the Austrians and Germans expected to repeat their success against Russia: they thought that the domestic political situation in Italy was so fraught that a military defeat would provoke a revolution and lead to a separate peace.[73] The offensive, directed by the German General von Below working to a plan by the Bavarian General Krafft von Dellmensingen, was carried out by elite German and Austrian formations. The Germans sent seven divisions experienced in mountain warfare plus artillery, trench mortar and air units; five Austro-Hungarian divisions were taken from the Tyrol front and Russia.[74] At the point of attack, the Central Powers concentrated twelve divisions with more than 1,800 artillery tubes, ranged against only eleven Italian brigades with 600 guns; the numerical superiority was about 180,000 against 66,000.[75] The German divisions were, moreover, up to complement, with 10 battalions and 15,400 men and officers each, and a total of 2,183 pieces of artillery, plus 1,000 gas grenade launchers. Each artillery battery (160 men, 136 horses, 6 cannons) and each of the 162 battalions took up half a kilometre of road.[76]

The artillery barrage that began the offensive at 2 a.m. on 24 October was unprecedented on the Italian front, with 1,182 tubes opening fire on 18 kilometres. At first the Italian artillery returned fire, but the attackers used gas grenades to paralyse the Italian gunners, whose masks were ineffective against phosgene, and their firing soon fell silent. A heavy bombardment of explosive shells commenced at dawn, and the infantry attacked at 8 a.m. A senior German officer noted:

> It seemed that all the Alps were collapsing. Not even the veterans of Verdun and the Somme had ever seen such an infernal pandemonium. In their hearts they were thinking: today I really would not want to be an Italian.[77]

The gas caused havoc among the Italians. While many units put up stout resistance, others were so rapidly overwhelmed they surrendered without a fight. Others fled, leaving behind valuable supplies. The result was a chaotic retreat that rapidly turned into a rout, a sudden collapse of morale in the army, and a political crisis. One million men withdrew behind the River Tagliamento and the Piave, only a few kilometres east of Venice. They left behind 40,000 dead and wounded, and 293,000 Italians were taken captive. In total 3,150 artillery guns were lost, including two-thirds of the large-calibre artillery and half the medium artillery. More than 400,000 civilians fled the war zone, becoming refugees in their own country.[78]

The German/Austro-Hungarian invasion of Italy involved the same kinds of deliberate cultural destruction, mass killing of non-combatants, and ruthless exploitation of occupied territory which had already been a feature of warfare on the western front, but which have remained largely obscured from popular memory in Anglophone countries. When the German–Austrian offensive, their troops exhausted, ground to a halt in November, coming under increased counter-attack from the Italians, now reinforced by French and British divisions, they began indiscriminate bombardment. General von Below noted that his air squadrons bombarded Padua, Castelfranco, and Treviso.[79] At the end of January 1917 Kaiser Wilhelm had declared in response to a Papal letter to Cardinal Hartmann, according to the *Kölnische Volkszeitung*, that he would make every effort to spare respected places dedicated to religion and monuments of art which he considered to be the property of all humanity.[80] In other words, the German government in theory recognized international law regarding the protection of cultural heritage. The practice, however, was different: the army and navy commands ordered the air and sea bombardment of undefended Italian cities, forbidden under articles 25 and 27 of Hague Convention IV.

As on the western front, the deliberate destruction of cultural objects and the targeting of civilians were not merely a by-product of modern warfare, but one of its characteristic features, and the result of policy. In that sense, the Italian royal commission's idea that the German army had raised 'brutality and violence to a principle' was undoubtedly correct. True, Italy had wantonly entered the war for manifestly selfish reasons of territorial conquest, but the Austrian government was well prepared. On the first day of hostilities, Austro-Hungarian aeroplanes had attacked Venice with ten bombs. The Italian royal commission saw this as a deliberate attempt to destroy or mutilate the 'incomparable beauty of Venice and its monuments', reflecting not only the envy of the glorious beauty of centuries, but also the hope, as the Germans had in destroying Rheims cathedral, of intimidating Italy with the fear of the mortal danger thus facing its 'città adorabile'.

Further bombing raids followed. When today's visitors arrive in Venice by train, the first church they see is Gli Scalzi, a few paces from the railway station, which was badly damaged in a bombing raid on 24 October 1915, an important mural by Tiepolo being destroyed. The royal commission recalled how the Austrian *Fremdenblatt* of 14 November 1915 declared that the sorrow with which it regarded the perishing of such marvels of art was mitigated by the joy of seeing the damage caused to Italy's national wealth and to its income from tourism, and that this thought would serve to guide pilots in the future. The commission commented that the allies and neutrals were indignant at the attack on 'fragile Venice', whose 'regal immunity was a common dogma of civilization. Is it not like a temple, without any offensive or defensive forces but those of morality?'[81] On 23 June 1916 San Francesco della Vigna was damaged by two bombs, and San Pietro in Castello, the former cathedral of Venice, was damaged by an incendiary bomb on 10 August 1916. Several other churches and hospitals were damaged, and many public and private buildings. Ultimately, the damage to Venice done in the war was limited, and did not rival that done under Napoleonic rule. However, the royal commission, publishing its report with the benefit of four years of the experience of war, was right in seeing in it a new enemy calculation.

Austrian and German forces flew 343 aerial bombing raids over Italy, causing the deaths of 984 people. Even cities as far from the front as Bari and Naples were bombed by airships. The royal commission concluded that in hoping to paralyse the resistance of Italy the enemies deployed brutal force, using aerial bombardment far more against the civilian population of un-defended cities, as 'weapon of terror', than as a means of warfare against military objectives. The commission denied that the Italian air force employed the same methods, stating that it almost only bombed military targets, and respected inhabited places. Incidents in which international law appeared to be violated by Italy only took place by exception as necessary reprisals.[82]

The 4th German bomber squadron, which was transferred to the Italian front in December 1917, bombed Padua nine times from December to February 1918, with a total of 718 bombs; Treviso was attacked 16 times in the same period with 517 bombs, Vicenza was bombed on 31 December 1917, and Venice was bombed in the night of 27–28 February 1918, with 281 bombs. The commission concluded that Germany was jointly responsible with Austria not only because of its alliance, but also because of its active participation in the criminal conduct of the war.[83]

The city that suffered from the heaviest bombing was Treviso, undefended, and only a short distance from enemy lines. The commission described it as a jewel of architecture and sculpture since the thirteenth century. Almost all the churches of Treviso were hit by bombs, some several times, as were many other public buildings, museums, libraries, and archives. Among the losses were again murals by Tiepolo, prompting the commission to comment that Tiepolo was the painter 'most often massacred' by this war. Further down the Adriatic coast, in the air raid on Ravenna in February 1916 a bomb was dropped on Sant'Apollinare Nuovo. This church was one of the most important buildings of early Christendom, erected in the early sixth century as a monument to the Ostrogoth king Theodorich, decorated in 560 with celebrated mosaics of the procession of the Virgin and the White Martyrs. The bomb damaged the roof, broke windows, damaged part of the ceiling and a corner stone and abutments of the portico, and caused mosaic stones in the main nave to fall.[84]

In the Italian view, Germany's war crimes were worse even than the Turkish crimes against the Armenians. This grossly distorted perspective is a revelation of how Italy perceived German policy. The royal commission accused Germany of breaking international law by participating in the war against Italy before Italy declared war on Germany in August 1916. This was confirmed by Bethmann Hollweg in a speech to the Reichstag on 28 September 1916: 'When our ambassador left Rome when Italy declared war on Austria-Hungary, we informed the Italian government that the Italian army would encounter German troops in the fighting with the Austro-Hungarian troops. German soldiers have in fact been fighting on the Italian front together with their Austro-Hungarian comrades.'[85] The Italians accused the Germans of providing the means and the instructions for the use of poison gas at S. Michele on 29 June 1916, before the state of war, and of bombarding undefended cities in January and February 1918, and wreaking havoc during their occupation of the Veneto.[86]

In addition to destruction, the Austrian and German occupation forces removed works of art on a grand scale. Various reasons were given to provide a justification, such as that the objects were removed from houses whose owners had fled. Many objects were removed without any kind of pretext. The Austrian government, apparently in order to put a good face on matters, resorted to the same expedient as the Germans had in Belgium and France: the formation of expert commissions for the libraries, archives, and the collections of public and private art. These managed to restore a small fraction of the works taken from the Municipal Library and the chapel Sant'Antonio in Udine, the Museo Civico in Belluno, and some other places. The Italian royal commission acknowledged that these expert commissions often did their best to protect what remained of the cultural heritage in occupied Italy from the rapacity of the occupiers, and it praised them even though their work was to little effect. The commission concluded by calculating the total loss in damage and cost of protecting art works and monuments at 79 million lire, and it appended a list of Italian paintings in the possession of Austrian, Hungarian, and German galleries which it regarded as being suitable as reparation demands.

Deliberate destruction was not the only expression of ruthless war policy. The ruthless exploitation of the resources—human and economic—during the German–Austrian occupation of 1917–18 flowed directly from the military policies of the invasion. It was as if the developments on the western front of invasion, occupation, and exploitation were compressed into a short space of time because the 'lessons' of 1914 could be simply transferred.

Occupied Italy was to be exploited for maximum gain, both for the troops and for the broader economies of the Central Powers. According to orders issued by the Austro-Hungarian Field-Marshall Boroevic on 5 December 1917 and 21 August 1918, German and Austrian occupation authorities expressly allowed each soldier to send home without any special licence 25 kg. of food, 80 kg. of other goods, 20 kg. of clothing, and in addition works of art and furniture. A conference was held at Baden on 16 December 1917 between the German and Austrian high commands to reach agreement on the 'economic exploitation and the administration of the occupied Italian territory'. According to the Italian royal commission, the Germans pursued a policy of ruthless spoliation in their sectors, without regard to the longer term, even for the purpose of occupation, unlike the Austrians.

> In regard to the provision of food and rations for the population the German administration was of such a nature that even in early February 1918 famine raged in the German-occupied zone. It is undeniable in the view of the testimony of the Austrian delegation, presented at the Paris Peace Conference by Perathoner on the activity of the joint economic group in the Veneto: this was forced to admit that the cause of the lack of food in the foothills zone was to be sought also in the especially intense exploitation of the region by the German troops![87]

It concluded:

> In general, all the evidence collected shows that the Germans proved them-
> selves to be the most violent during the occupation against the civilian
> population, the worst administrators, the first to initiate requisitions, pillage,
> and depredations. They removed the best, most useful, and most valuable part
> of the items requisitioned and were the most demanding, methodical, and
> brutal in the execution of their work of spoliation.[88]

In fact, although the Austrians also accused the Germans of looting Italy, they
behaved little better. The almost starved Habsburg soldiers fell upon the
abundant supplies left by the Italians, and a 'massive traffic jam ensued . . . as
10,000 wagons hauled away the captured booty'. The victors benefited for
months from the captured supplies of food.[89] The Austrian share of the booty
was six times greater than the German.[90] This vast programme of pillage,
which went on for the duration of the occupation, temporarily helped to
alleviate the acute food crisis in Austria, but there was precious little left over
after the large occupation force—at least as many soldiers as civilians—had
eaten their fill. Just as in Belgium, industrial machinery was dismantled to be
transported into the 'Fatherland'.[91]

Just as in Belgium and northern France, the Austro-Hungarian occupying
forces also deported many Italian citizens, especially in the last year of war.
The motivations may have differed from the deportations of 1916 in Belgium and France, which were mainly for forced labour, but the effects on
citizens who had committed no act of hostility other than to be found living
in the wrong place were similar. It began with the Italian-speaking subjects
of the Habsburg state, who were given the choice of being interned or
resettling in Italy. The police had prepared lists of people of Italian nationality
long before the war, and internment began on 20 May 1915, three days
before the declaration of war. The internees were kept as prisoners under
harsh conditions. The main 'concentration camp', as they were termed, was
at Katzenau near Linz; but there were others in Austria and Hungary,
including one at Steinklamm which Italians called the 'Campo della morte'
(Death Camp). There was humiliating treatment of men, women, and
children, and cruel punishments were inflicted, including tying prisoners
to a pole and beating them, which led to death in some cases. They were
forced to work with little payment and inadequate nutrition. In fact, the
Italian royal commission of investigation stated that the 'really tragic characteristic of these concentration camps was the hunger'.[92] So many died,

especially children, that the commission accused the Austrian authorities of wanting to 'destroy or reduce to a small number the Italian race on their territories'. The total number of Italian internees from Austro-Hungarian territory was 11,916, according to the list submitted by the Austrian Red Cross, but the commission held that this was an understatement.[93]

Italian families in Istria and Dalmatia were persuaded to let their children under 14 years to be sent into Croatia to be given better food. But they were sent to Croatian or German-language schools, and separated from their families. Workers at the arsenal of Pola were threatened with redundancy if they did not agree to send their children to German or Slav-language schools. The ostensible philanthropic intention, the Italian royal commission argued, disguised the real motivation which was to deprive the children of their Italian nationality. One deposition, by advocate Dr Wondrich, affirmed that at least 3,000 Italians from Trieste were interned by the Austrian authorities during the course of the war. He had occasion to visit the concentration camp at Feldbach near Graz, where he saw the prisoners in a miserable condition, suffering hunger, malnutrition, and tuberculosis, some of them no longer able to stand. The prisoners told him they received as food only boiled cabbage.[94]

During the year of the occupation after Caporetto civilians were deported as a measure of collective punishment. For example, in the township of Marsure (Aviano), shots were fired at a group of Hungarian soldiers on 24 March 1918. The occupation authorities deported the mayor, the priest, and all men between 15 and 50. Most were only released after several months. There were several cases of individual deportations as punishment for alleged opposition to the occupation.[95] Mass deportations took place that were not even described by the occupation as punishments, but exclusively for military reasons, directed at an enemy population capable of bearing arms.[96] In some cases they were sent to work in the locality, others to concentration camp. There were forced marches of several days, without food and drink, followed by long train journeys in cattle-wagons, where they were forbidden to descend even to relieve themselves. In the first days of the occupation about 2,000 were deported, of whom about 1,500 were sent to the camp at Katzenau. Their families pleaded in vain with the occupation authorities to tell them the whereabouts of their men. The deported were allowed to send Red Cross postcards, but these did not reach their destinations for months. Some of them were allowed to work, in order to earn a little money, in various factories across the empire, including in munitions production. The total number of deportees of all kinds was 16,000, including internees and deportees. At least 3,000 died as consequence of their maltreatment and privations. For example, from Manzano 30 were deported, of whom 15 died; of the 55 deported from Pradamano 30 died. The Commission calculated a death rate of 187 per thousand, compared to the average peacetime death rate of 20, and the mortality in the invaded provinces during the invasion of 50 per thousand.[97]

The relatively low total number of deportees indicates that the German and Austrian military authorities decided that mass deportations of civilian forced labourers would be counter-productive, given the chastening experience of the deportations of Belgian workers. However, the German supreme command did not give up the idea: in December 1917 Hindenburg, clearly expecting the imminent defeat of Italy and a separate peace, wrote to the German foreign ministry and sketched out the war aims of the OHL. These included Italian forced labour for the German economy, as well as reparations in money and kind, and the takeover of Italy's colonies in Africa.[98]

Perhaps the most extraordinary feature of this little-known occupation is that like the invasion of Belgium and France in 1914 it was accompanied by the killing of civilians. The Italian historian Daniele Ceschin has calculated that about 5,000 Italian civilians were killed during the invasion or died as a result of military violence during the occupation; the number of deaths caused directly or indirectly by war measures was 24,597, of which 12,649 were because of inadequate medical care, 9,797 from starvation, and 961 during the exodus.[99] The reason why this is unknown in Anglophone histories of the war is that the fate of these victims of military violence and other war measures remained almost totally obscured from the public sphere in Italy both at the time and in later memory of the war. This represents a complete contrast to the shock waves spreading locally, nationally, and internationally from the atrocities of 1914 on the western front. Such was the degree of amnesia about these victims that even the Italian royal commission of investigation arrived at a figure of only about 600 civilians killed by enemy troops. Still, it had no hesitation in identifying the main perpetrator: the German military. The royal commission argued that the Germans, who were primarily responsible for the success of the Caporetto offensive, were also the educators of the Austrians 'in the art of occupation, . . . raising brutality and violence to a principle of government and applying broadly the principles of the *Kriegsbrauch*, which was their guide in the occupation of Belgium'.[100] It stated that the violence was not random, nor was it perpetrated by isolated individuals, but that it was actively encouraged by the supreme commands of the enemy armies. The harsh treatment of the civilian population resulted from political aims pursued systematically by the Central Powers, to terrify the population in order to get the starving, demoralized population to beg the Italian government to make peace.[101] However, the Italian accusation of a German and Austrian policy of systematic killings as in France and Belgium in 1914 lacked credibility. There were no mass executions to magnify the horror: most killings were committed by individuals or small groups of soldiers, and took place in the context of requisitions or robbery, often in the first few weeks.[102] This may explain the amnesia and the underestimation of the total by the royal commission; in addition, official Italy made every effort to forget the defeat of Caporetto and its demoralizing consequences and remember instead Vittorio Veneto, the victorious counter-offensive at the end of the war.

The treatment of captured soldiers and prisoners of war

Until recently it has been assumed that the dynamic of destruction did not apply to prisoners of war, and that by and large, captured enemy soldiers were treated in conformity with international law by France, Britain, and Germany. Under the 1907 Hague Convention on the Laws and Customs of War on Land (articles 3–20) prisoners were afforded rights to humane treatment which were generally recognized. They were to be treated humanely, provided with safe and sanitary shelter, and given food equivalent to the rations given to the host nation's soldiers. For a range of reasons, neither the Central Powers nor Russia adhered to these standards, with the result that for some nationalities it was actually more dangerous to be in a prisoner-of-war camp than to be on the front line as an infantryman. Partly, this was because warfare with millions-strong armies produces millions of prisoners. One argument frequently advanced to explain poor conditions for prisoners was the sheer quantity involved: by October 1918 Germany had 2.4 million men in captivity, 2.25 million were in Russia, and Austria-Hungary had to accommodate 916,000 prisoners: army administrations were overwhelmed by and unprepared for such vast numbers.[103] They actually had no good reason to be surprised. Moltke, beginning to realize the failure of the Schlieffen plan on 4 September 1914, said: 'We should not deceive ourselves. We have had successes, but we have not yet gained victory. Victory means annihilation of the enemy's power of resistance. When million-strong armies confront each other, the victor takes prisoners. Where are our prisoners?'[104]

In fact, the poor conditions were not caused primarily by incompetence or lack of preparation: harsh treatment of prisoners was a matter of policy. As early as 31 August 1914 an order in the German 8th Army, on the transport of Russian prisoners from the eastern front, stated that 'feeding the prisoners is not possible as due to the uncertainty of the eastern army's supply lines, all food to hand must be reserved for the German troops... Prisoners must be treated strictly... They are not to be given water at first; while they are in the vicinity of the battlefield it is good for them to be in a broken physical condition.'[105] In other words, prisoners were to be 'broken', for reasons of military efficiency.

The most dangerous time for prisoners was the moment of surrender. The crime of killing soldiers at the moment of capture or during transfer into regularized forms of captivity occurred on all sides in the war. In some cases it was ordered by combat officers, in others it occurred 'in the heat of battle' on the initiative of ordinary men. We know it happened at the beginning, during the war of movement (for example, the case of the German Major-General Stenger, who issued orders to his 58th Brigade to kill all captured and wounded French soldiers on the battlefield at Thiaville in late August 1914).[106] It certainly occurred at critical moments during trench warfare, for some British officers issued such orders at the battle of the Somme,[107] and at the end of the war (there were reports of captured Austrian soldiers being killed by Italians in summer 1918).[108] The historian Joanna Bourke argues that the killing of German captives was routine, an 'important part of military expediency'.[109] This is an extreme judgement. Some of Bourke's own evidence suggests the crime was the exception to the general rule. One of the witnesses she cites confessed to finding the killing of captives horrifying, and another perpetrator noted that an officer 'was furious with me' for gunning down a defenceless German. New Zealand soldiers apparently shot at and killed several captured Germans on 15 September 1916, but were prevented by British officers from continuing. Other British soldiers, however, stole valuables from captured Germans and beat them up.[110] In the absence of any systematic investigation it must be considered an open question how widespread the killing of captured soldiers was. At any rate, there was evidently a hierarchy of hate according to nationality and race: Germans reserved a special hatred for the British (for having entered the war), and frequently maltreated British captives, but attempted to treat Irish prisoners well, in the hope of recruiting support. The Italians had a more successful policy of favoured treatment for those Habsburg nationalities considered to be potential allies, such as the Czechs. There are indications that the Germans often maltreated or even killed French African soldiers, out of sheer racist malice. Artillery Captain Rump wrote to his wife:

> We reserve our greatest hatred, just like you at home, for the lying English, whose true nature has now been revealed to even the most stupid recruit. Some men who beat up the English at Solesnes or St Quentin said they had been unable to deliver all the captured English, because they had died en route of heart attacks (!!!). That is of course just boasting, but it tells you something about the men's attitude. I have also seen the Zouaves, who according to the French proclamations are also fighting for culture, just like the Japanese, who have collected some very pretty bumps on their heads. The Bavarians, especially, have their own way of dealing with the dark-skinned sons of the desert.

In another letter he wrote, 'As an officer I protect every prisoner. But woe to any Englishman who falls into the hands of the men.'[111] Until we have more research, the best conclusion appears to be that such behaviour was episodic, not routine; opportunist, not systematic; with some well-documented cases and others more like apocryphal stories.

Once captured, the great majority of prisoners in captivity in Britain, France, Germany, and Italy survived. The known mortality figures show that of the British and French soldiers in German captivity about 3 per cent died. This figure is from German official calculations, however, which are today no longer held to be reliable, since the prisoner-of-war camps' administration and the system of registration of new captives broke down in the last three months of the war. Both sides sometimes illegally forced prisoners to work near the front, endangered by gunfire, often in retaliation for similar measures of the other side. The vast extent of exhausting prisoner labour under fire, especially, but not only on the German side of the western front, indicates that the concept of the prisoner of war as a protected non-combatant had collapsed by 1916, and this reveals a tendency towards brutalization in the First World War. Even for those in camps inside Germany, away from the front, conditions were often grim. Just how grim is still the subject of historical research, but with the deteriorating supply of food, prisoners evidently came a long way down the list of priorities, ranking after the civilian population. British and French prisoners survived mainly thanks to food parcels from home.[112]

The eastern and southern fronts presented an entirely different picture: in Russian camps men were often housed under harsh conditions with inadequate sanitation and medical care. Of the more than 2.11 million Habsburg prisoners 9.24 per cent died in Russian camps; another 9 per cent were missing.[113] Of the 158,000 German soldiers in Russian captivity, 9.97 per cent died, plus 33 per cent missing, of whom many managed to return home, so that the total mortality rate has recently been estimated to be 20 per cent.[114] There are as yet no reliable modern statistics for the number of Russian prisoners in the hands of the Central Powers and their mortality rate. The contemporary official German figure was 1,434,529, with 72,586 deaths in captivity, a mortality rate of 5.06 per cent, which was almost certainly an underestimate.[115]

The German army made massive use of Russian prisoners for labour in constructing the Siegfried Line (often also called the Hindenburg Line) in 1917, but the shift in policy had occurred in 1916, even before the OHL of Hindenburg and Falkenhayn. In early 1916, in order to bring up supplies to the German offensive at Verdun, a railway line was built by thousands of Russian prisoners. Their housing and sanitation facilities were so poor that they were plagued by lice, despite periodic treatment in delousing facilities. General von Einem, commander of the German 3rd Army, well known for his right-wing and racist views, took this as proof that the Russians were evidently an inferior people that did not belong to Europe.[116]

Italian prisoners in Austro-Hungarian captivity fared particularly badly: out of 468,000 men at least 92,451 (19.75 per cent), possibly 93,184 (19.91 per cent) died.[117] Another 7,549 Italians died in Germany on German official figures, out of 132,920 held there (5.68 per cent).[118] The Serbs suffered a higher death rate in German captivity (6.07 per cent), and by far the highest was that of the Romanians (almost 29 per cent). There were several reasons for the horrendous death rates of Italians in Austria-Hungary, Germans and Austro-Hungarians in Russia, and Romanians. The total number of prisoners and of deaths is difficult to calculate with any certainty in the case of captivity in Russia, but the three main reasons were administrative chaos and neglect, e.g. in allowing fatal epidemics of typhus to get out of control; harsh conditions, and lack of food. There did not appear to be an official policy to maltreat the prisoners, and the central government in principle attempted to respect the Hague Law of Land Warfare in relation to prisoners.[119]

The extraordinary dimension of the mass death of Italian prisoners has not yet been explained satisfactorily.[120] Most died from illness, directly related to hunger and cold. The Italian historian Giovanna Procacci has argued in her pioneering study that since Austria-Hungary suffered its own severe shortage of food, the starvation of the prisoners was not the responsibility of the Habsburg state, but the Italian state, for the Italian supreme command tried, at times with success, to prevent the sending of food parcels to Italian prisoners. Procacci argues that the mass death of the Italian prisoners 'was provoked, and frankly in large part willed, by the Italian government, and above all the supreme command. Thus Italy transformed the prisoner of war problem, which all the belligerent states had to deal with urgently, into a real case of collective extermination.'[121] The supreme command was trying to discourage soldiers from deserting by having the news published about the poor treatment of the prisoners by the Austrians. In line with General Cadorna's obsession with discipline, it was also punishing those soldiers who had fallen into enemy hands for their alleged cowardice or desertion.

This is certainly correct, but it is not the whole explanation. Although it is true that the civilian population in Austria suffered terrible hunger, the excess mortality rate was not 20 per cent, but under one per cent. The harsh conditions arose partly from objective circumstances in Austria and Germany, but may well have been due to intentionally poor treatment. The maltreatment of the Italians started at the moment of capture, when Habsburg soldiers stole all their valuables (money, wedding rings), and also—in the midst of the Alpine winter—their winter clothing and boots. A forced march with insufficient food for up to twelve days brought them to camps like Mauthausen, Theresienstadt, and Sigmundsherberg, where the men lived in almost unheated wooden barracks which were often wet, their beds wooden boards on the ground. Often the prisoners had no blankets or straw. The official ration was 350 grams of bread per day and meat five times a week, but in winter 1917–18 they often received less than 100 grams of bread per day, watery soup with a few slices of turnip or cabbage, and sometimes a small piece of meat or fish. This was a starvation diet: 100 grams of bread contain less than 200 calories, and turnips and cabbage have hardly any calorific value. Able-bodied prisoners were expected to work outside the camps, where food, particularly on farms, was sometimes more readily available, but the work was frequently exhausting and the guards often resorted to corporal punishment. To what extent was this part of a deliberate policy by the Habsburg state and society will be seen from further research, but it is clear that from the simplest soldier up to Field-Marshall Conrad and Kaiser Franz Josef open hatred of the Italians was expressed for their alleged betrayal of the Triple Alliance.

One letter written home by an Italian illustrates the conditions and the resulting loathing of the enemy:

> Despite the severe cold and snow we are forced to work by this German [i.e. German-Austrian] rabble. If I had only known what they are like I would have taken my life ten times rather than be taken prisoner. Curse Austria and its allies! The Hungarians especially are real brutes. Every day they beat us with iron bars, and force us to work day and night. Almost nothing to eat, 150 grams of bread per day of poor and bitter quality. The dried fish stinks, and just to mention the other food makes you retch with disgust. We are treated like animals; with our tattered shoes we resemble tramps. I hope this damned war is over soon, or else we will die in Austria. If I could get to the front again, I don't know how much I would pay to take vengeance on these barbarians. Today I was tied to the pole for an hour, for no reason. I would rather be shot. During the hour I was tied to the pole I suffered such pain I will remember it forever.[122]

While the Italians were treated miserably in Habsburg captivity, the worst treatment was reserved for the Serbs. The Italian high command received reports that the Serbs received no food parcels, and those who did not work and were often ill were kept like animals in cages. The only nutrition they had were the remnants of inedible bread, carrots, and uncooked turnips which the Austrians threw through the bars. The high command concluded that 'Austria intends to destroy the [Serb] race'; at least 30,000 to 40,000 had died of starvation by January 1918.[123]

Given the harsh conditions and the brutal maltreatment, it is hardly surprising that the prisoners were soon locked in a mentality of hatred that did not bode well for the peace. One French soldier, a teacher who was taken captive at the end of the war, described the hunger and its effects in his diary:

> The morale of the prisoners is detestable: all suffer from hunger and have become unapproachable, usually refusing all duties, regarding each other as wild animals and replying acrimoniously to the most delicate words. It's really a case of: 'starving belly has no ears.' As soon as the occasion arises of obtaining food, whether given to them by civilians or by a German offering the remains

of a meal, they all rush for it without the slightest consideration for anyone they might knock down and devour the food without even thinking of comrades who are just as unfortunate as them . . . Among us there are those who steal bread and it is extraordinary how skilfully they operate. I suffer greatly at the sight of Frenchmen who have arrived at this point where they present such a spectacle to our enemies. However, I excuse them: is it not our enemies who are responsible? . . . [M]y hatred of Germany grows day by day.[124]

An Italian soldier in Austro-Hungarian captivity wrote home in a letter from Katzenau prisoner-of-war camp:

[I]t is better if the war lasts a long time, so that this cruel, barbarian race is completely exterminated.

Have you ever heard of people in the civilized states of Europe being threatened with a club to force them to work? But that is what goes on here. Beating men with clubs and starving them to death is regarded here as heroism and a virtue. But one day this will all come to an end; the new generations will have to imbibe hatred of this vile race with their mother's milk and . . . swear by the ashes of their ancestors to hate this disgraceful race and wipe them out in every corner of Italy, wherever they find them.[125]

In conclusion, we can identify a radicalization of war with a tendency towards systematic, total exploitation of enemy civilians and the resources of the conquered territory. From cultural destruction, in the sense of the deliberate targeting of cultural objects the war moved to a 'culture of destruction'—the acceptance of the destruction, consumption, and exploitation of whatever it took to wage the war (including the lives of one's own soldiers, as well as the enemy's) in unprecedented numbers. In occupied lands the logic of annihilation stopped before it reached the stage of mass murder of entire populations—the exception, to be discussed later, in the genocide of the Armenians, took place on home territory. In combat, Germany's 'war of annihilation', enormously destructive and self-destructive in the first three months of the war, forced on the Allies a dynamic which was no less destructive. How the nations of Europe descended into this nightmare is discussed in the next chapter; and whether Germany was unique in its 'culture of destruction' is considered in Chapter 4.

3

The Warriors

What activated the dynamic of destruction? How the war was un-leashed, and the assumptions and expectations behind the decisions for war, were intimately connected with how the war was fought. Popular explanations for the war range from the notion that the 'rigidification of the alliance system' made war inevitable once the successor to the Habsburg throne was assassinated, to 'the irrevocability of military timetables', from imperialist rivalry between capitalist states to the arms build-up.[1] Some explanations focus mainly on Germany, taking the Allied judgement in the peace treaty of 1919 as the starting point, with Article 231 ascribing the war to the 'aggression of Germany and her allies'. Others spread responsibility more widely. The German governments after the war consistently rejected 'war guilt', and found willing supporters, above all in English-speaking countries. Lloyd George, the British wartime prime minister, wrote in his war memoirs in 1933 that in July 1914 nobody in Europe had wanted war, and that 'the nations slithered over the brink'. The idea that 'all the powers were more or less responsible' has been an influential interpretation ever since the Harvard historian Sidney B. Fay advanced it in 1928, with American foreign policy adviser Henry Kissinger arguing as recently as the 1990s that 'nation after nation slid into a war whose causes they did not understand but from which they could not extricate themselves'.[2]

As will be made clear in this chapter, the idea that no one was in control of their actions is absurd. It is possible to show who wanted war, or who the warriors were, by asking two key questions. In whose interest was it to go war? And why did the decision-makers of some states see benefits to be gained through war, despite the risks of defeat and destruction? By dividing the question into long-range causes, pre-war imaginings of war, and the decision-making processes of states in the July crisis of 1914, we can perhaps provide some answers.

Long-range causes of the war

One of the most popular interpretations of the First World War is that it resulted from imperialism. This originated in the Marxist view that capitalist economic rivalries in the age of imperialism caused war, in which workers, who had no fatherland, should have no part. Popularized by the anti-imperialism of Lenin, the idea is still common on the Left as well as among respected historians.[3] According to this theory the root of the war was the fundamental conflict between imperialist powers competing for markets, resources, prestige, and ultimately world domination. Not one single power was thus 'guilty', but the imperialist 'system'. In fact, colonial tensions between France, Britain, and Germany had been resolved peacefully, on the basis of a division of the booty, the only losers being the native peoples. France and Britain did not covet Germany's colonies—these were too poor in resources, and strategically unimportant. Imperialism was thus not the cause of the war in the sense of conflicting imperialist interests, and it certainly did not indicate the direction of future war: Japan, which had fought against Russia for colonial domination in Manchuria in 1904, fought alongside Russia ten years later. Certainly, Lenin's analysis that the states involved in unleashing the war had capitalist economies, even politically conservative Russia, was not incorrect; in a general sense the conflicts between them indisputably formed the background of rising tension. Yet nothing especially predisposes capitalist states, compared with feudal states in history or today's developing states, to wage war on each other; nor has the continued advance of capitalism and imperialism since 1918 produced any greater propensity to wage war. The only historical rule that can be derived is that democracies tend not to wage war on each other.

Imperialist rivalry, in the sense of economic tensions, too, did not cause war. Britain was by far the most important market for German exports.[4] Russian–German trade was colossal, and it was continuing to grow in the ten years down to 1914. Germany was easily Russia's most important market, and Russia was Germany's third most important trading partner. In fact, Russia was a more important trading partner for Germany than her ally Austria-Hungary. The main European powers therefore all had a vast stake in each other's prosperity.[5] In less tangible ways, however, economic rivalry, as will be seen, became part of the popular discourse of nationalism and thus contributed to the tensions already existing, such as that between Britain and Germany.

It was not trade rivalry, but the growing commercial interchange between states which characterized pre-war international relations. This was paralleled by the improvement of diplomacy which succeeded in managing conflicts and even major crises by means of ambassadors' conferences. The London ambassadors' conferences of 1912 and 1913 in connection with the Balkan Wars showed how concerted diplomacy was still capable of achieving results, as it had been in the international crises of 1905 (over Morocco), 1908–9 (over the Austro-Hungarian annexation of Bosnia), and 1911 (Morocco again).[6] Lenin's idea in 1914 that just as Germany was waging an imperialist war, the British and the French bourgeoisie were aiming for 'the seizure of the German colonies, and the ruining of a rival nation',[7] was good socialist polemic, but it does not withstand close scrutiny. German business leaders and high finance had no wish for a European war: Germany's unbounded economic development was holding out the prospect of ascendancy in Europe. In 1911 the Ruhr iron and steel magnate Hugo Stinnes told Heinrich Class, chairman of the extreme right-wing Pan-German League, who was advocating a preventive war: 'Another 3–4 years of peaceful development, and Germany will be the undisputed economic master in Europe.'[8] While German commercial competition was keenly felt in some circles in Britain, rational business sense counselled peace, not war. Financial and trading interests in the City and the governor of the Bank of England, along with liberal newspapers, were totally opposed to British intervention in European war in July 1914.[9] After the German ultimatum to Belgium, however, the mood changed, and public opinion, especially of the capital's bourgeoisie, turned firmly to support the declaration of war.

Another line of interpretation sees the arms race as a major cause of the war.[10] The argument is that the piling up of more and more expensive military hardware and the expansion of armies until they recruited almost all able-bodied young men of each nation created the explosive potential which only needed to be ignited by a small spark. Yet this mechanistic argument ignores logic and history: at what point exactly does an arms race cause conflict? When arms spending reaches a certain proportion of state revenue or total economic output? When particularly destructive weapon systems are developed, such as heavy artillery, bomber aircraft, or nuclear weapons? Arms spending during the Cold War rose to far higher levels than the period before 1914, but did not lead to the outbreak of war between the

main protagonists. Associated with this is the idea that the division of
Europe into two blocs (the Triple Entente of France, Britain, and Russia;
and the Triple Alliance of Germany, Austria-Hungary, and Italy) meant that
an incident causing a local conflict would automatically be converted into a
major continental war. This argument takes little account of real historical
developments: the Entente was only an informal set of bilateral understand-
ings, not a binding triangular contract. That the alliance system was not an
automatic cause of war can be seen in the Triple Alliance which broke up
when Italy remained neutral in 1914.

Nevertheless, it is possible to identify predispositions to go to war in
certain countries. A predisposition does not just mean the principled recognition that war is one of the options of state policy of any sovereign
country, but a mental framework of a government and nation prepared to
go to war. Yet the existence of such predispositions does not explain why
war broke out in 1914, rather than 1910 or 1918, or why it became a
European and world war.

The answer is to be sought in Europe's unstable region, the Balkans. Why
that region had such explosive potential will be shown in Chapter 4; at this
point I want to focus on the fears and ambitions of Germany and Austria-
Hungary. Germany had begun to develop an appetite for world policy just
as the age of imperial expansion was coming to an end (for lack of un-
claimed territories), and its successes in gaining new territories or zones of
influence were modest. Yet Germany's new policy began to raise fears
among the other powers, and its openly sceptical attitude towards initiatives
in international law to maintain or secure peace, for example the Hague
peace conferences, did little to allay these fears.[11] Germany's brash attempts
to stake imperial claims, e.g. in Morocco in 1905–6 and again in 1911–12,
Austria's annexation of Bosnia and Herzegovina in 1908 which nearly led to
war with Russia, the Balkan wars in 1912 and 1913, and German military
assistance to Turkey in 1913, all raised international tension. Increasingly, it
was not a matter of Germany being 'encircled' by hostile powers, as its
leaders claimed, but of manoeuvring itself into isolation. When France and
Britain reached agreement over colonial issues, the result, contrary to
intention, was to increase suspicion in Germany of 'encirclement'. German
diplomacy at the conference of Algeciras, held in 1906 to resolve its claims
to Morocco, appeared at once bristling and chaotic, being poorly coordinated between the chancellor, foreign policy advisers, and the delegation.[12]
Germany's decision not to back the Austro-Hungarian desire to go to war in

November 1912 to stop Serbian expansion, on the other hand, caused great anger in Vienna, with talk of being 'stabbed in the back' by one's ally.[13]

Although these crises were solved without a general European war, the result was the race to increase arms spending. Cause and effect are difficult to disentangle, and it was not merely a question of international relations, but also of the interdependence of foreign and domestic politics. Germany's *Weltpolitik* (world policy) before the turn of the century had provoked the Anglo-German naval arms race, which itself concentrated the minds of the British admiralty on planning for a war in European waters. As one member of the British admiralty said after the war, 'This sea service in the years prior to the outbreak of hostilities was one long preparation for war. We expected war, we were ready for it, and almost wished for it.'[14] Yet 'almost' was an important word. To British decision-makers it was self-evident that Britain's vital interests had to be protected: over half its food supplies came from overseas; British prosperity depended on overseas trade.[15] The navy was the instrument for the protection of that trade. Germany's attempt to build a battle fleet to challenge British supremacy at sea inevitably raised hackles, but it proved ultimately to be an expensive failure; its abrupt end in 1912 came too late to resolve tensions, all the more since resources were switched to expanding the army. This was partly in response to international developments (such as the growing realization that Austria-Hungary was preparing for war against Serbia and Russia), partly because the aggressive rhetoric of the new German foreign policy had aroused demands for real action by the vociferous nationalists. In 1911, after Germany had made the dramatic gesture of sending a gunboat to Agadir in the second Moroccan crisis and been forced again to back away, the Kaiser was mocked as '*Guillaume le timide*' by the radical German nationalists who regarded him and his government as lacking the guts to go to war. This handed the initiative to the army leadership which was pushing for war.

In order to avoid a repeat of such accusations, chancellor Bethmann Hollweg followed up the decision not to support an Austrian war against Serbia in November 1912 with a speech in the Reichstag that amounted to a public warning to Russia that Germany would stand by its alliance with Austria if the latter were attacked 'by a third party while enforcing its interests'. This was a provocative move, since it hinted that a future Austrian attack on Serbia would be backed by Germany, and it forced Russia to renounce support for its protégé. Bethmann's speech was welcomed by the right-wing parties (and the pro-Austrian Centre) as a return to an aggressive policy backed by the threat of war, while the social democrats criticized the government for issuing a 'blank cheque' for whatever dangerous Balkan adventures the Habsburg empire might undertake. The reaction in London, not unnaturally, was deep disquiet at the prospect of an Austrian attack on Serbia which might yet cause Russian intervention and an inevitable European war; Lord Haldane, the war minister, gave the German ambassador a formal warning on 3 December that Britain could not afford to remain neutral in such a conflict and would not tolerate the defeat of France.[16]

On 'discovering' that Britain would come to the aid of France in the case of European war, the outraged Kaiser called a meeting of his top naval and military men on 8 December. In fact, Lloyd George's well-publicized Mansion House speech in July 1911 had been a signal of Britain's determination if necessary to fight to safeguard its great power status and stand by France in the Moroccan crisis; Bethmann Hollweg knew that Haldane had merely restated to the German ambassador in December 1912 'what we have known for a long time: that England still advocates the policy of balance of power and that she will therefore support France'.[17] The so-called 'war council' of 8 December was less significant for its results, for it did not actually decide on war, than for its indication of military thinking at the time. Moltke (army chief of staff) took the opportunity to press for an increase in size, and found support in the Kaiser and the chancellor. Moltke advocated war now rather than later, a demand he had made in 1908 and now insistently repeated in the coming eighteen months. He argued that Germany was losing its superiority in view of Russian and French rearmament, and promised that 'at present we can contemplate a war with tranquillity' and demanded a campaign in the press to prepare public support for a war against Russia. Moltke's confidence in its military situation in the present was coupled with a sense of insecurity and alarm about the medium-term future.[18] Rearmament was driven not so much by the monarchy and the conservative elite (and still less by 'the people'), but by the new militarist nationalism of the bourgeois pressure groups, above all the Army League (founded in January 1912), and the 'modern militarists' in the army. An echo of their fears and ambitions was clearly audible in the deliberations of the 'war council', revealing a mix of social Darwinist pessimism about Germany's future survival and an aggressive imperialist nationalism.

This ideology or rather world-view of social Darwinism was one of the most powerful 'unspoken assumptions' which the historian James Joll identified throughout Europe in this era, but its link 'with militarism and imperialism was probably closest in Germany'.[19] Not only influential military theorists like Friedrich von Bernhardi, best known today for his bellicose *Germany and the Next War* (1912), used crude social Darwinist assumptions to justify Germany's drive for 'domination of the earth' and in asserting that 'strength is the highest right and the legal dispute will be decided by the measure of strength, war, which always decides biologically, and therefore fairly'.[20] Also many intellectuals who regarded themselves as politically progressive and were critics of the conservative German political system, such as the liberal Max Weber, and a great part of the educated bourgeoisie, saw contemporary politics as a struggle between those nations which were destined to rise and those doomed to fall in a global struggle for the survival of the fittest. Certainly, the ideas were not unknown among intellectuals and politicians in Britain, France, and the USA before 1914, but in Germany they had become part of the mental furniture of decision-makers including chancellor Bethmann Hollweg, his influential political adviser Kurt Riezler, war minister Erich von Falkenhayn, and chief of the general staff Helmut von Moltke; in Austria, where the fear of decline had a particular resonance, Moltke's colleague Franz Conrad von Hötzendorf was particularly prone to using the language of social Darwinism.[21] Riezler had published a book that appeared just before the war which provided the intellectual underpinning of '*Weltpolitik*'. There could be no such thing as peaceful coexistence of nations; rather the opposite: it was a kind of natural law that the aim of all nations was eternal struggle for nothing less than world domination. The Germans (like the Russians) were a 'young' people, destined to grow, while 'old' peoples (like the French) were doomed to perish. 'The demands of the German nation for power and prestige, not only in Europe, but throughout the world, have increased rapidly... Hemmed in by unfavourable frontiers it needs to display great power, so long as it is obstructed... from freely pursuing its *Weltpolitik*.'[22] The German and Austrian social Darwinists were by turns fatalist (because what was inevitable could hardly be decided by human agency, thus reducing personal responsibility for war) and voluntarist (in that an unfavourable tendency could be reversed by intervening at the right historic moment). They therefore believed in an inevitable racial struggle in which the idea of preventive war was a perfectly legitimate option.[23]

In this sense Moltke wrote to Conrad soon after the First Balkan War about the need to find a suitable *casus belli*: a war which was fought for the existence of a state needed the 'enthusiasm of the people'. Austria should therefore not provoke a war over a minor local matter, which the German people would find little reason to support. With a statement betraying his clumsy ignorance of the realities of his main ally, Moltke continued that a European war was 'bound to come sooner or later, in which the issue will be one of a struggle between Germandom and Slavdom. To prepare themselves for that contingency is the duty of all states which are the standard-bearers of Germanic ideas and culture.'[24] Almost half the population of the Habsburg empire was Slavic, as Conrad reminded Moltke in his reply, and would hardly be enthused by a 'racial war' against 'their fellow-tribesmen'.[25] Conrad and the Habsburg political leadership were nevertheless convinced that with German support the joint Austrian and Magyar hegemony over the empire would be strengthened through a war, especially given the perceived threat posed by Serbia.

Russian leaders were likewise inclined to pronounce on the allegedly inevitable 'struggle of Slavdom not only with Islam but also with Germanism' which dictated that one 'must prepare for a great and decisive general European war', as the Russian ambassador in Paris, Izvol'sky, warned in October 1912.[26] The difference was this was a prediction rather than a prescription for preventive war, which not even the Russian military were demanding. French political and military leaders, even when using some of the language of race, had an essentially defensive concept so far as France in Europe was concerned. In the birthplace of Darwinian thought some intellectuals (who subscribed to a diversity of conservative and liberal political views), some army officers such as the young infantry officer J. F. C. Fuller (later to become an influential military writer), empire propagandists like Baden Powell, and the Conservative prime minister at the time of the South African War, Lord Salisbury, employed social Darwinist clichés. Unlike in Germany, however, it is not possible to find a strong link between Darwinism as an ideology of biological determinism justifying war and the decision-makers in London in July 1914.[27]

Imagining and preparing the future war

How, in an age when the last war between major European powers was a distant memory (forty-three years, to be precise, since the Franco-Prussian War), did general staffs envisage future war? Did they take into account the rapid modernization of weapons technology and the industrialization of economies? The most incisive theoretical enquiry into the shape of war to come was the work of an outsider, *The War of the Future* by Jean de Bloch, the Polish railway entrepreneur and banker, published in Russian in 1899 and soon translated into the major European languages. Bloch argued that developments such as precise breech-loading rifles, smokeless powder, and the reduction of weapon calibre, had enormously increased the firepower of infantry weapons which would force troops to dig in for defence. Between the trenches a fire-swept zone would be created which could be crossed only at the cost of devastating losses. Professional military theorists responded by arguing that as a civilian he understood nothing of the topic and ignored the importance of troop morale. French military theorists emphasized the superiority of the attack, the *offensive à l'outrance* (outright offensive). For General Foch, from 1907 to 1911 the director of the French military academy, the doctrine of the offensive was an unquestionable principle.[28] In Britain, even a modernizer like General Ian Hamilton rejected Bloch, in particular the thesis that the offensive would need an eight-to-one superiority to succeed against entrenched defence. He actually accepted Bloch's point about the defensive advantages of magazine rifles and smokeless powder, but stressed that these could be overcome by the 'human factor': enthusiasm, *esprit de corps*, and clever tactics like using cover of darkness to cross the fire zone.[29] Majority opinion in the British army stressed the offensive and the moral qualities of officers and men, not despite, but precisely because of the lessons in firepower in the South African and Russo-Japanese wars. Hamilton wrote in 1910:

> Blindness to moral forces and worship of material forces inevitably lead in war to destruction. All that exaggerated reliance placed upon chassepots and mitrailleuses by France before 1870; all that trash written by M. Bloch before 1904 about zones of fire across which no living being could pass, heralded nothing but disaster [i.e., Manchuria]. War is essentially the triumph, . . . not of a line of men entrenched behind wire entanglements and fire swept zones over men exposing themselves in the open, but of one will over another weaker will.[30]

This was expressed even more drastically by Friedrich von Bernhardi, co-author of the field service regulations of 1908 which were in force during the Great War. In 1910 he wrote in his book on modern infantry tactics:

> [Effective, realistic training and patriotic instruction of the infantry] is the means by which we *can* and *must* trump all our opponents, compensate for the numerical and possibly also technical superiority of our enemies and which

must lead us to victory. For in the battle of today the mental and moral strength of the individual, despite all advances in technology, is the best and most successful weapon.[31]

Bernhardi saw the task as one which concerned more than just the military. Although many older men had experienced the wars of unification, and younger officers had gone through 'an excellent schooling' in the colonies, the long period of peace meant that the 'people in arms' had to be maintained in physical and mental health and a warlike state of mind.[32] In concluding the book he wrote:

> Blood and iron. Our infantry will only remain a sharp weapon of German policy if it is determined, just as in the glorious days of the past, to shed streams of blood, and if it is possessed of the iron will to beat the enemy, cost what may.[33]

In a sense the conclusions drawn by the general staffs across Europe—and in this there was no fundamental difference between them—amounted to a reaction against the logic of Bloch. Bloch had written that it would be 'nonsensical and crazy' to start a war. He asked: 'Is there not an inner contradiction in the piling up of ever greater means of destruction and the calling of almost the entire population to the colours, and the spirit of the time which in many states is in rebellion against militarism?!'[34] The general staffs instinctively sensed that Bloch was right, and that the human, social, and economic cost of modern war was catastrophic. In place of his logic they put the irrational obsession with the offensive. When that failed, the logic of attrition and annihilation was all that was left.

As from 1912 the German army regarded itself as well prepared for war. (The German navy, by contrast, was less confident in its capability to wage war; moreover, there had been virtually no coordination of army and navy policy.) Moltke succeeded in securing an increase in army size of 29,000 in 1912 and 136,000 men in 1913, taking the peacetime strength in 1914 to 800,675; on mobilization some of the reserves and volunteers joined up at once. Reasonable estimates of the size of the German army in August 1914 range between 1.3 and 1.6 million men.[35] The infantry were equipped with modern rifles, with a range of up to 1.8 kilometres, accurate at up to 600 metres; French and British rifles were of equal quality.[36] All three armies had introduced machine guns which could fire between 400 and 600 rounds per minute. The German army had 4,500 to 5,000 machine guns when it went to war in 1914, but the Maxim MG 08 was a heavy weapon that weighed between 62 and 66.5 kg. and required at least six men to carry it and its ammunition. The French and British machine guns of 1914 were not much better: the French Hotchkiss weighed 47 kg. and the British Vickers-Maxim 54 kg. The French had 2,500 machine guns in 1914. The Russian army was equipped with a relatively high number of Maxim guns similar to the British model.[37] The problem for the British army was the shortage of men trained in their use; one expert later found that 'practically no records of machine gun achievement during 1914 can be traced'.[38] While the French had a light machine gun which was used to great effect at Verdun, the light German machine gun, 08/15, was not generally available until 1917; even then, at 21 kg. it could only just be carried by one man. The German army had more heavy artillery than all its enemies put together, and the first trench mortars. In terms of training and morale, too, the German leadership had good grounds to be confident in the superiority of its army. Tactics had been revised to take into account the use of modern firearms and large formations of men.[39]

No one in Europe could have been unaware of the effect of these modern weapons of mass destruction. The German field service regulations published in 1908, widely available and still in force in 1914, stated clearly the devastating impact of machine guns: 'The high rate of fire concentration of the bullet-sheaf, and the possibility of bringing several machine guns into action on a narrow front, enable great effect to be produced in a short time, even at long ranges...Dense lines of skirmishers standing suffer severe losses at ranges of 1550 metres and under.'[40]

By 1914, the French army, too, was well prepared for war: it was better equipped and more confident than at any time since 1870. France's introduction of the three-year military service in March 1913 and the much higher proportion of men of military age who were drafted compared with Germany indicate how the French army had recovered its prestige and popular acceptance after it had been discredited during the Dreyfus period. France drafted 82 per cent of men of military age, while the German army took only 52 to 54 per cent.[41] Defence expenditure as a proportion of net national product was 4.3 per cent in France versus 4.9 per cent in Germany (3.5 per cent in Austria-Hungary, 3.4 per cent in Britain, and 5.1 per cent in both Russia and Italy).[42] In terms of crude military spending, France was spending more per capita of the population than Germany on the military, but France had far higher military costs in its colonial empire, its spending was met out of a much smaller economy, and the higher proportion of men was drawn from a smaller population. While Germany could afford to draft the best young men, the French army had to accept men of lower physical quality.[43]

Neither French rearmament nor its alliances with Britain and Russia amounted to a policy to bring about war. No French documents have emerged which resemble Moltke's or Conrad's incessant goading of their governments to seek an early occasion for war. Nor did the doctrine of the outright offensive, that much-abused notion, imply French belligerence; plan XVII, which had been adopted in spring 1914, was not a design for offensive operations, but a plan for the mobilization and initial distribution of the French armies.[44] Certainly, French policy had shifted to a more confident mode, especially under the impact of the growing German threat which emerged with the second Moroccan crisis of 1911. France began to give assurances of support to Russia over its Balkan policies, and in September 1912 Poincaré told the Russian ambassador that if an Austrian invasion of Serbia (or another Balkan crisis) caused a war between Russia and the Central Powers, France would regard this as sufficient grounds to fulfil its treaty obligations to come to the assistance of Russia.[45] The French government and military continually urged Russia to speed up its pace of rearmament and linked the approval of loans to the commitment to build strategic railway lines.[46] Nevertheless, this was a policy designed to defend the status quo: France was equally concerned to restrain Russia from taking any aggressive action in the Balkans or against Turkey.[47] France had no reason to provoke a military conflict in Europe.

Britain, too, had no interest in starting a war. It was satisfied with the status quo, and stood only to lose if Europe descended into war. The obsessive belief in German nationalist circles that Britain, for reasons of envy and commercial rivalry, had long been planning a war to destroy Germany, was a delusion.[48] Almost half its regular army of fewer than 250,000 men was stationed overseas to police the empire. For decades, British military planners had regarded Russia as the greater threat to the security of Britain and its empire. Planning for the deployment of the British Expeditionary Force (BEF) assumed as late as 1911 that its most likely theatre of operations would be Central Asia, to defend India, with the option of launching a naval offensive against Russia. As from August 1911, however, strategy shifted. If war broke out in Europe, it was now envisaged that the BEF would in the short term come to the assistance of France to prevent a quick German victory and German hegemony on the Continent. Ultimate victory would be obtained through naval strategy: economic warfare and blockade.

The BEF, comprising six divisions plus a cavalry division, was far too small to contemplate a war of conquest against Germany.[49]

In Germany, by contrast, the fatalist view gained ground that the 'Gordian knot of German "*Weltpolitik*" could only be cut by a European war', as the late Wolfgang Mommsen put it.[50] The military leadership (as well as militarist writers) increasingly warned that war was inevitable and that Germany ought to seize the opportunity to launch a preventive war. When the heir to the Habsburg throne was assassinated on 28 June 1914, the government of Austria-Hungary saw it as the chance to wipe out the troublemakers in Bosnia by invading Serbia. The German government and military leadership concurred, seeing the opportunity for preventive war against France and Russia while it could still be waged with the prospect of victory. The German government was under pressure from two sides: the military leadership was urging war sooner rather than later, when France and Russia would be in a stronger position because their plans for army expansion would come to fruition in 1916 or 1917, and nationalist public opinion wanted to see tangible successes for *Weltpolitik* and would not forgive the government if it shrank back from seizing the opportunity offered by the 'third Balkan crisis'.[51]

Whether German leaders were expecting a long war or a short war in 1914 has been a matter of sharp disagreement among historians. It has generally been assumed that since Germany went to war on the basis of the Schlieffen plan, which laid down a schedule for the defeat of France within six weeks before the German armies would turn east to defeat Russia, a war of lengthy duration was not envisaged.[52] Recently, this view has been questioned. There is considerable evidence to show that leading thinkers had warned of the changed nature of warfare. Helmuth von Moltke the elder, the commander of the German armies in the wars of unification, gave a noteworthy speech in the Reichstag in 1890 in which he said:

> The time of cabinet wars is now behind us—we now have only popular war (*Volkskrieg*) . . . Gentlemen, if the war . . . breaks out, its duration and end cannot be predicted. It will be the greatest powers of Europe, more heavily armed than ever, which will enter battle with each other; none of them can be so completely defeated in one or two campaigns that they would declare defeat, that they would make peace and accept harsh conditions, that they would not recover again, if only after years, and resume the struggle. Gentlemen, it can be a seven years war, it can be a thirty years war—woe betide him who sets Europe alight, who first casts the lighted match into the powder-barrel![53]

While the message Moltke wished to convey near the end of his life was that war should be avoided altogether, by a moderate policy of deterrence, the conclusion drawn by the general staff was to make plans to mobilize the entire cohort of young men and prepare the mental mobilization of the whole nation. The Schlieffen plan was conceived precisely in order to avoid a long war. It was designed to make war feasible and winnable. As Isabel Hull has shown, Schlieffen's assumptions were shared throughout the army leadership. General von der Goltz wrote in 1908 that rapid victory was necessary on both the western and the eastern fronts. 'Germany could only hope for success if it succeeded in opening the war with an effective blow, which it could do by virtue of its lead in mobilization and initial assembly, and if it managed to defeat both of its enemies one after the other by exploiting the inner line.'[54]

The ministries of the interior and finance warned in January and April 1914 that if Germany were to be involved in war on three fronts, it would be cut off from world markets, and would have to be self-sufficient in wartime. Yet neither the general staff nor the key civilian ministries made any strategic plans for a long war; Moltke, nephew of the victor of three wars, in the words of his biographer Annika Mombauer, 'was willing to implement a strategic plan based on the premise that Germany's only chance of victory lay in a short, decisive initial campaign'.[55] Yet when Austria declared war on Serbia on 28 July, he wrote a curious memorandum for the Kaiser and Bethmann in which he predicted a 'frightful war . . . which will annihilate for decades the civilization of almost all Europe', a war which Germany did not want, but in which it was bound to support its ally.[56] Perhaps Moltke, who was so resolute in wanting war, was hedging his bets as to the consequences, with an eye to the later historical record. The mood among the staff in the war ministry at any rate, when the state of emergency which was the precondition for mobilization was announced on 31 July, was one of relief and happiness: 'Everywhere beaming faces, handshakes in the corridors, congratulations on having taken the hurdle.' Moltke's real feelings were revealed on 1 August, a day of high drama, when German mobilization was announced and war was declared on Russia: that evening, when the Kaiser ordered the cancellation of the advance into Luxemburg because of a false report promising British and French neutrality, Moltke 'wept tears of despair'—out of frustration at the Kaiser that his war plan, which depended on rapid invasion of France, would be thwarted.[57]

In terms of predisposition, in sum, international research has essentially confirmed the assessment made by American diplomats in Europe in 1914 who identified a war spirit in Germany, which was ready to go to war, while Britain, France, and Russia were all seen essentially as having pacific intentions: France had given up all idea of revenge and the recovery of Alsace-Lorraine, and Russia was anxious to avoid war.[58] The key, however, was Austria-Hungary, which must also have had an interest in going to war.

The Austro-Hungarian Empire: the innocent abroad?

The question of Austro-Hungarian responsibility for the outbreak of war in 1914 still has the capacity to divide historians. One of Austria's foremost historians, Manfred Rauchensteiner, writes that the Habsburg monarchy, compared with other European great powers, had no foreign policy goals worth naming: it did not want to gain any territory, and for decades it had just been fighting to survive. Indeed, it was other nations—Italy, Serbia, and Russia—that coveted parts of its empire. For this backward, pre-democratic state preserving the multinational empire meant the containment of Serbian expansionism, the Great Serbian dream of uniting all Serbs, including those of Bosnia-Herzegovina which had been under Austrian occupation since 1878. The Austro-Hungarian government, Rauchensteiner states, had no idea that an attack on Serbia would lead to a general European war; Vienna did not want to unleash a great war, and was surprised when the rival alliances entered the war.[59]

At the beginning and the end of the long crisis was a flashpoint: Bosnia-Herzegovina, a small, ethnically mixed region of the Balkans, that Russia had helped to liberate from Ottoman rule in 1877 and which contained a large Serb minority. As from 1908, when Austria-Hungary announced it would formally annex Bosnia and Herzegovina, policy in Vienna took on an increasingly high-risk profile. Confident in the knowledge of German support and Russian weakness after defeat in war and a revolution that almost toppled the tsar, the Habsburg government demanded Serbian and Russian recognition of the annexation, failing which it would invade Serbia. On this occasion, Russia had to back down, to the fury of its political class; and a legacy of the Bosnian annexation was Russian resolve to act differently once its temporary weakness and isolation had been overcome. In Russian perception, the death of the old Habsburg emperor Franz Joseph or the collapse of the Ottoman empire, which were both expected in the near future, were certain to mean an increase in the aggressive nature of Austro-Hungarian policy. Russian leaders were not lacking in expansionist ambitions of their own: in addition to the long-standing goal of control over the Straits, some, such as the chief of the naval general staff, argued in 1912 that it would be essential to wield power also over the hinterland in Turkey and the Balkans. This helps explain the potential for rivalry between two weak empires which could ill afford the risks of war.[60]

Conrad von Hötzendorf, chief of the Austro-Hungarian general staff, was notorious for demanding war at every opportunity, calling for war against Serbia in 1906, 1908–9, and 1912; in 1913 he called for war no fewer than twenty-five times.[61] But Serbia was not Vienna's only bugbear. Conrad pressed for a war on Italy while it was fighting against the Ottoman empire in Libya in 1911, suspecting it of harbouring expansionist aims in the Balkans. He advocated a policy of 'defensive imperialism', which included a definitive reckoning with Serbia; but since war was in his view inevitable, the best solution was preventive war. Conrad therefore endorsed the Schlieffen plan which entailed pre-emptive war against France and Russia, and as from 1909 he and Moltke conducted conversations that resulted in dangerous commitments for mutual support.[62] Yet Conrad's opinion was not decisive: the civil government, especially Count Berchtold, the foreign minister, had decision-making power, and the Emperor had the last word. Why did Berchtold change his mind and tell the German government on 30 June 1914 that it was necessary to have a 'final and fundamental reckoning' with Serbia?[63]

In the period 1912–14 Conrad took all reports from Russia about army exercises as evidence of aggression, and suspected that with its 'test mobilization' of April 1914 Russia was aiming to promote its sponsorship of south Slav unification and to intimidate the Habsburg empire. Even to the cautious Berchtold this appeared to be 'dangerous'. These developments coincided with reports in German newspapers about Russian military preparations that threatened East Prussia, although German military intelligence reported that there were no Russian measures that could be interpreted as preparations for war. Nevertheless, the mood grew increasingly tense, with mutual suspicions voiced in the press in Germany and Russia in early 1914. One Austrian military journal warned that another crisis without a war 'would be worse than a defeat; it would demoralize army and people'.[64]

War, in other words, to 'save the nerves' of the army and the 'people'?
'The people' was code for the establishment and the political elite, and so
this amounts to an argument to save a few men in uniform the embarrassment of not going to war. Today this archaic reasoning for a decision of
such momentous importance appears ridiculous to us. Yet the rulers of the
empire thought in the terms of their society and their time, and feared that a
loss of prestige incurred in *not* fighting would destroy their state. For a state
used to conducting diplomacy with the threat of military force this was not
an unreasonable argument; but by any standard it was a high-risk strategy
because defeat would bring certain destruction of the state.

The mood in Vienna swung wildly between fears of powerlessness and
delusions of potency. The general staff underestimated the strength and quality
of the Russian army, and it was reported to Berlin that the Austro-Hungarian
army was willing to risk a war against Russia on its own.[65] In late 1912 Conrad,
temporarily out of office, presented the government with an essay on the
Balkans, putting forward the notion of a Balkan League under Habsburg
domination. There would be a customs union, a common currency, and a
joint foreign and military policy. If not attained by peaceful means, then
by war, above all against Serbia. Conrad's reappointment in December 1912
was a signal to public opinion at home and abroad that Austria-Hungary was
determined to pursue its interests in the Balkans with all means.[66]

Conrad's continual demands for war may have been rejected time and
again by the political leadership, but his concept of a preventive war was
accepted. The predisposition for war, the dissemination of enemy stereotypes such as 'the Slavic tide' and the unreliability of Italy, and of the cliché
self-image of the heroic nature of the Habsburg army, raised the tempera-
ture further. The chief medical officer of the 12th army corps, Wenzel
Schuller, addressed the makers of foreign policy in a poem (December
1912): 'Oh, utter finally the word of redemption! | It must be war, we
want joyfully to bleed.'[67] The governor of Bosnia-Herzegovina, General
Potiorek, consistently demanded the reinforcement of troops in his territory, and was convinced that Serbia was bound to launch an attack on the
empire sooner or later. In December 1912 he announced that the morale of
the troops in Bosnia-Herzegovina would suffer irreparable damage if the
crisis were not solved by a clear victory for Austro-Hungarian diplomacy or
a war. So persuasive were the arguments of the military that the empire
nearly went to war there and then: at a meeting between senior ministers
and Conrad just before Christmas 1912, almost all those present supported a

preventive war. Only Berchtold's superior political instinct stopped the
terrible logic of the military solution: he told his colleagues it was impossible
'to attack Serbia without a tangible reason that will be understood by public
opinion in Europe'; Austria-Hungary would be left isolated, without even
German support. The implications are clear: the political leadership, Berchtold included, was not opposed to war on principle, but decided to wait for
the most propitious political occasion. The threat of war was a constant
factor in Habsburg foreign policy: 'militant diplomacy', as Samuel Williamson calls it. But the threat was a wasting asset, and its use progressively
reduced the political room to manoeuvre. Another Serb 'provocation', real
or imagined, would suffice to unleash the catastrophe. The emperor and his
heir apparent thought likewise, albeit with differing war aims. Franz Ferdinand did not want to wage war on Serbia to gain territory, he told Conrad
in February 1913, but to 'chastise' it, whereas in a war with Italy the aim
would be to regain Venetia and Lombardy, which had been under Habsburg rule until Italy's unification, 1859–66. Conrad called for the annexation of Serbia, which the civilian ministers rejected.[68]

The Second Balkan War, in which Serbia again increased its territory,
drove Berchtold's 'militant diplomacy' to the brink of war. Serbia's conquest of northern Albania, achieving its goal of access to the Adriatic, was
unacceptable to Vienna. Berchtold rejected the general staff's fresh demands
for immediate war, but was aware that 'it would be impossible to impose a
third mobilization upon our public opinion without adequate success'.
Conrad, who resented the use of the military threat as a diplomatic counter,
demanded 'Ultimatum, short deadline. If ignored, war. Therefore mob[il-
ization] B[alkans] and execution of the operation regardless of any subsequent Serbian concessions.' When Serbia rebuffed the Austro-Hungarian
demand for the evacuation of northern Albania, the response was indeed an
ultimatum. Two days after its receipt, on 20 October, the Serbian prime
minister Pašić announced that all Serb forces would be withdrawn immediately from northern Albania. 'Militant diplomacy' had succeeded, but at
the cost of raising the stakes, making the use of the military option all the
more likely in future conflict. Moreover, avoiding war at the last minute
was felt by the army leadership to be a cruel blow to their hopes.[69]

In early 1914 intelligence reports about the Russian army exercises
planned for the autumn caused deep unrest in Vienna, and prompting the
semi-official *Militärische Rundschau* to write that Russia was 'the arch-enemy
of our monarchy, which consciously and constantly menaces us and the

peace of the continent'.[70] By this time the empire was in an unenviable geo-strategic situation, facing the possibility of hostilities on three, or even four, fronts: Serbia, Romania, Russia, and its nominal ally Italy.

In spring 1914 the military intelligence department estimated that Russia could put 92 divisions into the field, the Serbs $16\frac{1}{2}$, Montenegro 5, and Romania $16\frac{1}{2}$, a total of 130 divisions against 48 Austro-Hungarian divisions, while Germany could only be expected to place 14 divisions on the eastern front. Despite this crushing numerical superiority of enemy forces, at their last meeting before the war, on 12 May 1914 at Karlsbad, the Austro-Hungarian and German general staffs encouraged each other to think in terms of a surprise offensive against Russia in Galicia and a simultaneous attack on Serbia, although Moltke had his doubts that Conrad was capable of carrying out his intention, since the Habsburg chief of staff was impor-tuning him for the immediate deployment of German troops in the east as soon as war started. Conrad and Moltke were in agreement that because Russian rearmament and the lengthening of army service had not yet taken effect 'as matters stand favourably for us at the moment, one should not hesitate to take energetic action in the appropriate circumstances and, if necessary, begin war. From year to year the chances will deteriorate.'[71]

Only a few weeks later the 'appropriate circumstances' arrived. Was the assassination at Sarajevo a suitable *casus belli*? That was not immediately appar-ent. On 1 July the Hungarian prime minister Tisza, a powerful figure in the imperial government, warned emperor Franz Joseph of the extraordinary risk that foreign minister Berchtold's policy would unleash 'a great war'.

> I did not have the opportunity to speak to Count Berchtold until after my audience, and only then heard about his intention to use the atrocity in Sarajevo as the occasion to settle accounts with Serbia. I made no secret of my opinion that this would be a fateful error and that I would not under any circumstances share the responsibility. First, we do not have sufficient evi-dence to hold Serbia responsible and . . . provoke a war with this state. We would have the worst conceivable legal standing (*locus standi*); we would appear before the world as disturbers of the peace and ignite *a great war* in the most unfavourable circumstances. Second, I consider this moment, where we have practically lost Romania without having gained anything in return, and when the only state we can count on, Bulgaria, is exhausted, to be really most unfavourable.[72]

Two aspects are crucial. First, Tisza wrote that it would be mistaken to use the assassination as 'occasion' for war; he thus distinguished it from a 'reason';

he was by no means opposed to war on principle and wrote in the same paper that a suitable *casus belli*, given the tense situation in the Balkans, would be easy to find. Second, he was absolutely clear that if war were started, it would mean a 'great war', that is, no localized conflict between Austria-Hungary and Serbia, no police-type action, but a general European war.[73] So much for the notion of Austrian innocence. By 7 July, Count Berchtold was also aware that action against Serbia would mean war with Russia, as he told the council of ministers.[74] All the ministers present except Tisza wanted war on Serbia as soon as possible, while Tisza now suggested that it would be best not to start war without first having presented Serbia with an ultimatum. This should contain 'very tough demands', but 'not of such a kind that our intention to make unacceptable demands could be clearly recognized'. The chief of the general staff and the representative of the navy joined the council of ministers, and following Conrad's explanations of the military plans there was a debate 'about the probable course of a European war, which because of its secret character was not suitable to be reported in the minutes'.[75] Tisza did not finally accept war against Serbia until 14 July, and the ultimatum was not sent until 23 July, but the Austro-Hungarian minister in Belgrade was already instructed on 7 July: 'However the Serbs react to the ultimatum, you must break off relations and it must come to war.'[76] Notwithstanding Tisza's and Berchtold's compunctions about launching war, of the result of any 'localized' war there could be no doubt: war with Serbia would mean war with Russia. The previous year, when the First Balkan War brought Austria-Hungary to the brink of intervention, in an audience with the emperor in January 1913 Conrad demanded 'as often before' a 'reckoning' with Serbia; Franz Joseph 'repeated his old concerns, above all fear of the Russians and that it would lead to a world war'.[77] The Moltke–Conrad correspondence of February 1913 had shown that both chiefs of staff were working on the assumption that the coming war would be at least a European if not a world war. As Moltke said to the Habsburg military attaché: 'The starting of a world war is to be considered carefully.'[78]

A more convincing argument than the idea of localized war is Williamson's thesis that 'the Habsburg monarchy went to war not for territory or glory but to save itself. How war would achieve that goal the policy-makers never really examined.'[79] If we understand this as the intention to save the empire, the calculation was not entirely without logic. If they had succeeded in destroying Serbia (i.e. destroying its army and reducing its territory or even ending its independent existence), and if Russia had been defeated, the threat of south Slav expansion would have been stopped at least for the medium term. And in fact by 1917 the calculation had proved correct. The Serb army was virtually destroyed and driven off its home territory, and Russia was defeated. The problem, as Franz Joseph feared in 1913, was that it really had become a world war. Moreover, the strains of war stretched the multinational empire beyond its limit: rather than extinguishing the smouldering nationalist aspirations, the war did the opposite of what the Habsburg state intended. It exacerbated existing national and social tensions, and fanned the flames of separatist nationalism.

Hoyos, Berchtold's *chef de cabinet*, revealed the usually unspoken war aim of the destruction of Serbia in his endeavour to gain the support of Germany. In his meetings with the German emperor and Bethmann Hollweg on 5 and 6 July 1914 Hoyos termed the annexation of Serbia a war aim of Austria-Hungary.[80] Despite Tisza's insistence on an official announcement that no annexation of Serbia was sought, that was precisely was what was being discussed in Habsburg military and political circles. There was consensus among the leading civilian policy-makers (with the exception of Tisza) that the aim was 'the total annihilation of Serbia'.[81] A young general staff officer noted in his diary on 24 July: 'Only if Serbia and Montenegro cease to exist as independent states will the question be solved; to enter war with Serbia without the firm decision to erase it from the map would be without purpose, a so-called "punishment expedition" would be pointless . . . ; the south Slav question must be solved radically in such a way that all south Slavs are united under the Habsburg banner.'[82]

After Tisza had given his approval on 14 July, the decision was clear. The Common Ministerial Council of the empire met on 19 July to agree the terms of the ultimatum. As the ultimatum made demands which no Serbian government could meet, the meeting concentrated on what was to happen after the inevitable rejection.[83] Austria-Hungary, in other words, was determined to go to war against Serbia, come what may, while the rest of the world was in a state of unsuspecting innocence. Even before Serbia had received the ultimatum, professors and lecturers in medicine at Austro-Hungarian universities were secretly called up for army duty.[84] As Baron Giesl, the Austro-Hungarian ambassador to Belgrade, told his Italian colleague in an unguarded moment, 'if the Austro-Hungarian government adopts a menacing attitude towards Serbia, the investigation in Sarajevo [i.e. the interrogation of Gavrilo Princip and his co-plotters] can provide the pretext for any kind of action'.[85]

In Austro-Hungarian eyes Serbia was virtually an outlaw state which had to be destroyed, and the normal rules of law would no longer apply.[86] Expressing the ideas of the Habsburg military and civilian leadership, General von Appel, the commander of the 15th Army Corps in Sarajevo, wrote on 10 August 1914:

> We not only have to win here but also shatter and destroy the Serbo-Montenegrin army—this is the carrier of Russian ideas and propaganda. Above all we must thoroughly wean them of their megalomania and arrogance . . . I have forbidden my officers under pain of punishment with loss of honour to treat with Serbian officers on an equal footing . . . If they are captured . . . they are to be treated like common soldiers . . . for an officer corps that takes into its midst foreign deserters like comrades, tolerates regicides, conspires, and [includes] members of secret societies deserves no other treatment than captured soldiers.[87]

Thus the mentalities of the Austro-Hungarian elite—its fear of decline, the contempt for the Serbian state, the criminalization of the Serbian officer corps—affected the decision for and nature of the war: the invasion and occupation of Serbia turned into a brutal war of annihilation, a theme taken up in Chapter 4.

Ever since 1919, the 'war guilt' debate has centred on Germany's role, largely ignoring the responsibility of Austria-Hungary. Would the Habsburg state have gone to war without firm assurances from Berlin? In the aftermath of the war, Leopold Baron von Andrian-Werburg, one of the inner circle of Habsburg diplomats, confessed: '*We* started the war, not the Germans and even less the Entente—that I know.'[88] Certainly, it is true that it was Vienna that requested the blank cheque, and Vienna that cashed it. Yet Germany had the decisive role in the July crisis: to use another metaphor, it had the power to accelerate the engine and send the locomotive towards the abyss, or apply the brakes and bring the train to a halt.[89] Before we examine the dénouement of the crisis, therefore, the role of Germany should be explained.

Germany and the July crisis

Ever since 1914 the role of the German government has been at the centre of the attention of those seeking to understand the causes of the catastrophe.[90] German responsibility, and that of its allies, was the moral justification cited by the victors in 1919 as the legal basis for the demand for compensation, or 'reparation', for the loss and damage they suffered in the war. Yet ever since 1914 successive German governments, military leaders, and, until the 1960s, the historical profession, sought to proclaim German innocence. In the 1920s the German state launched a mammoth historical research project in which German and even foreign scholars, notably in France and the USA, were paid secret funds by the foreign ministry to 'prove' that Germany was not to blame. Some maintained the idea that the war had somehow begun like an uncontrollable natural phenomenon in which all the major belligerents were to a degree co-responsible. Some held the other powers responsible for escalating the crisis into war: Russia, because it had ordered mobilization in the interest of pan-Slavist expansion; Serbia, because it had orchestrated the assassination of the Austrian Crown Prince to provoke a war for territorial gain; France, out of a long-held desire for revenge and to recover Alsace-Lorraine; Britain, because of a desire to destroy its more successful commercial rival.

Scholars who in no sense seek to re-create national myths have recently made more plausible arguments. Volker Berghahn puts forward the thesis of risk miscalculation. He argues that the idea of the limited war prevailed in Berlin at the beginning of the July crisis, in other words, a localized Austro-Hungarian conflict with Serbia. This only proved to be an illusion later, and it was then converted into a world war by the hawks. The 'civilian doves', who at the start believed Russia and France would stay out of the conflict, therefore left it to the government in Vienna for two weeks to work out the ultimatum to Serbia, which would be followed by an international conference to consolidate the Habsburg position.[91] However, this evidently does not apply to the Austro-Hungarian government, which accepted the probability of war with Russia, and in any case Conrad knew Moltke's plans for a European war on two fronts. The awareness of the high risk of a general European war was widespread in the German leadership, too, well before the crisis. In January 1913 Prince Heinrich, Kaiser Wilhelm's brother, told the Austro-Hungarian naval attaché in Berlin that Germany regarded war at the present time as 'extremely undesirable', because of Britain's unmistakable readiness to defend France and Russia against the Triple Alliance. Heinrich's reasoning, as a navy man, was that until the Kiel Canal had been completed the British navy was superior to the German. Over the course of the next eighteen months most German decision-makers reached the opinion that the time was now fast approaching to launch a war.

In November 1913 the Kaiser told the Belgian King Albert that war with France was now 'inevitable and imminent'; Moltke warned Albert that in this 'inevitable' war 'the smaller states would be well advised to side with us, for the consequences of the war will be severe for those that are against us'.[92]

For several months before the assassination in Sarajevo, Moltke had been calling for 'preventive war', most notably in a conversation with Jagow on 20 May 1914, in which he suggested that the foreign secretary 'might consider shifting our policy with the aim of engineering a war in the near future'.[93] In fact, Jagow answered that he was not prepared to 'bring about a preventive war', although he was not opposed to one in principle. Politically, in other words, the occasion was still not opportune. The details of the shift in policy after the assassination on 28 June need not concern us here; suffice it to say that after several days' reflection, Bethmann Hollweg and the foreign ministry concluded that the occasion should be used to provoke a general European war. On 5 July, the most fateful day of the July crisis, under-secretary Zimmermann, standing in for Jagow, told Hoyos that there was a 90 per cent likelihood of a European war.[94]

In any case, the idea that Bethmann Hollweg and his close advisers in the government were 'doves' can be rejected. Bethmann and the foreign ministry were perfectly aware of the 'calculated risk' of European war, indeed goaded the Habsburg government into this far-reaching decision. Moltke had played a crucial role in chivvying his own government, and given the prestige and the unusually strong constitutional position of the army in the German state, his advice carried great weight. All that was necessary, before issuing the famous 'blank cheque' to guarantee support to Austria-Hungary on 5 July, was for the Kaiser to ask the minister for war, General von Falkenhayn, whether the army was ready. Falkenhayn merely replied in the affirmative.[95] After that date, the Austro-Hungarian government could concentrate on persuading the waverers in its ranks, then draft the ultimatum to Serbia in suitably unacceptable terms, and choose the propitious moment to send it when the French president and prime minister were unable to take decisions, having left St Petersburg for the long sea voyage back to Paris.

There remains the question of whether Germany brought about war (or at least provided essential impetus for it) in pursuit of particular aims. Were German war aims the *cause* of war? Or was it after all German desire for world power? In his seminal work of 1961 the Hamburg historian Fritz Fischer argued the former, and made a strong case for the latter.[96] Before the outbreak of war, however, none of the powers had concrete territorial aims, and Germany was no exception. Not until September 1914 did the German government formulate a programme of desirable objectives for the forth-coming peace (it was drafted at the height of euphoric expectation of victory during the battle of the Marne): annexation of territory in western Europe, Belgium to become a vassal state, degrading France to the status of a second-class power, and the construction of a large German colonial empire in central Africa.[97] Fischer argued that economic interest groups, especially those of heavy industry, long before the war had been eager to secure markets and sources of raw materials by conquest, and that they had influenced the decision to go to war. There is a certain danger in such retrospective reasoning, and this element of Fischer's argument is uncon-vincing. German business had no input into the decisions of the government to go to war in July 1914; many business men, including those who were the staunchest supporters of the government during the war, such as Stinnes, the Ruhr industrialist mentioned above, Walther Rathenau, director of the giant electrical company AEG, and influential bankers like Arthur von Gwinner (Deutsche Bank) and Max Warburg regarded the prospect of war as a disaster for the economy, which needed peaceful development. Yet almost *en passant* Fischer had succeeded in shattering the myth of German innocence, for there could be no doubt that whatever the war aims, the German leadership had wilfully pushed for war in July 1914 on the assumption that victory would produce hegemony in Europe. As Bethmann Hollweg wrote in late 1914 in a private letter: 'The aim of this war is not to restore the European balance of power, but precisely to eliminate for all time that which has been termed the European balance of power and to lay the foundations for German predominance in Europe.'[98] The government attempted to keep the war aims discussion secret, for fear of alienating neutral countries and disturbing the *Burgfrieden* consensus that Germany was fighting a defensive war. That did not stop a very public debate in which nationalist intellectuals and interest groups demanded annexations of enemy territory after victory. Thus the historian Johannes Haller, influential and popular among fellow academics and students alike, announced in 1914: 'Thus we are all agreed that we desire nothing less than world rule.'[99]

Bethmann Hollweg and the civilian government took the advice of the military experts and shared their view that the moment offered a 'window of opportunity'. When no longer in office, in 1917, he admitted to a leading liberal member of parliament, Conrad Haussmann:

Yes, by God, in a certain sense it was a preventive war. But if war was in any case hovering above us, if it would have come in two years' time, but even more dangerously and even more unavoidably, and the military men say now it is still possible without being defeated, in two years time no longer! Yes, the military![100]

Bethmann was nevertheless troubled by what he had done, describing the decision as a 'leap into the dark'. Moltke, too, wrestled with his conscience and showed he had scruples. Erich von Falkenhayn, soon to be Moltke's successor as chief of staff, had none. He revelled gleefully in the outbreak of war, saying to Bethmann on 4 August: 'Even if we perish as a result of this, it was beautiful.'[101] This aestheticization of destruction, even self-destruction, was a leitmotif throughout the war; the gross irresponsibility of leadership which he revealed was unusual only for its candour. The private doubts of Bethmann and Moltke were revealed only to close confidants, and outwardly the mood in the general staff was optimism, pride in the German military machine, and relief, satisfaction, and even elation that the long-prepared wish had at last come true.[102]

Britain, the prospect of war, and war aims

Deliberately misinformed by the Austrian and German decision-makers for most of July 1914, the British government had the impression that Germany was exercising a moderating influence on Austria. Sir Edward Grey, the foreign secretary, was not concerned at the first signs of Austrian belligerence, and on 20 July was even optimistic at the prospect of a peaceful resolution of the tension between Austria and Serbia. Nevertheless, at the latest on 27 July the German government was warned by Grey that Britain would not stand aside as a neutral if Austria invaded Serbia.[103] Haldane, the lord chancellor who as war minister had created the British Expeditionary Force, was not opposed to intervention if it was absolutely essential, but also hoped that Britain would 'not be dragged in'.[104]

The decision-making process in Britain was in the tradition of civilian cabinet government; the military played no role in British intervention. Field Marshal Sir John French, due to become the commander-in-chief of the BEF, only found out about the decision by telephoning Lord Riddell, of the Newspaper Proprietors' Association, on 2 August, to ask: 'Can you tell me, old chap, whether we are going to be in this war?'[105] Why Britain entered the war had nothing to do with military (or naval) staff demands, or popular jingoism. Nor was Britain forced into war by a plot of anti-German diplomats in the Foreign Office, pro-French militarists, or any other conspiracy. The decision was taken in order to defend British interests, which were identified at the time as the security and integrity of the empire.[106]

Had Britain stood aside, as some in the ruling Liberal party were proposing, the result would have been the near-certain defeat of France, and German hegemony on the Continent. Unquestionably, that was an unacceptable risk for Britain which had for centuries been concerned to ensure a balance of power in Europe, on the principle that no state should become so dominant over the Continent that it would pose a strategic threat. The German policy of starting war on France by breaching the neutrality of Belgium thus came as a welcome gift to Asquith and Grey, enabling them to depict intervention in the war as the defence of the rights of small nations, not merely as the fulfilment of alliance obligations: a morally just cause, not diplomacy and power politics, as their liberal critics alleged. At the time, British decision-makers could only sense intuitively what we know today— this was far more than a conservative defence of the status quo: had Germany succeeded at the Marne in September 1914, which it almost did, the defeat of France and a separate peace would have been followed by a defeat of Russia and, after a pause to build up the German navy, the invasion of Britain from a position of towering strength on the Continent.

The mood of the British cabinet at the time of the decision to intervene could hardly have been more different from the overflowing confidence and joy in Berlin. Herbert Samuel (the postmaster-general) viewed the prospect of war with dread; it would be 'the most horrible catastrophe since the abominations of the Napoleonic time, and in many respects worse'. He described the cabinet meeting of 3 August, which discussed the German demand for free passage through Belgium, thus: 'Most of us could hardly speak at all for emotion . . . The world is on the verge of a great catastrophe.'[107]

Paradoxically, most politicians and military leaders had a limited concept of the war. The extensive empire was defended by a relatively small army that was dispersed around the globe, plus the Indian army staffed by British officers, and the Royal Navy. Recent experience of colonial warfare had not been encouraging: although it was easy to defeat primitive tribes in the Sudan, faced with the Boers, who were equipped with modern weapons, it was a very different matter. The shock of the South African War prompted a process of army reforms, however, which helped the British army adjust to modern warfare, and persuaded London gradually to reduce its 'imperial overstretch' and seek alliances.[108] Standing aside from the conflict, as some recent historians have suggested would have been preferable (and argued almost happened because of the strength of Liberal pacifism), was not an option: a victory of the Franco-Russian entente over Germany would have posed its own threat to the security of the empire if Britain had remained neutral.[109]

Expecting a short war, in which the navy would give full support to France and wage economic warfare with a blockade of Germany, military men and politicians planned only a limited commitment. Grey, despite his gloomy and much-quoted prediction that the lamps were going out all over Europe, was not anticipating a major role for the British army; even after the declaration of war he did not want to send troops to the Continent.[110] Kitchener, appointed secretary of state for war on 4 August, was almost alone in expecting a long war; Churchill, the first lord of the admiralty, almost alone in welcoming it. Kitchener, predicting a three-year conflict, immediately acted to 'raise, train and equip a continental-scale army', in order to increase it from six regular and fourteen territorial divisions to seventy divisions by mid-1916.[111] Meanwhile, Britain was able to send only five divisions with 90,000 men in August 1914. This was very small by comparison with the millions-strong armies of the Continent, but it was a well-prepared force, with recent war experience.[112] An army of conquest it was not. But it might just be enough to tip the balance in the defence of France.

Self-defence of the integrity of the United Kingdom and the empire, and thus defence of the status quo in Europe, was what was stressed by the large lobby of those urging intervention before the declarations of war. That included most of the Conservative opposition and most of the conservative press led by *The Times*: 'We dare not stand aside . . . our strongest interest is the law of self-preservation.'[113] Bellicosity, even the lust for destruction, were not precluded. Admiral Fisher, first sea lord 1906–10 and again 1914–15, professed a dismissive attitude to the laws of war: 'humanity in war' was humbug. It was better to 'hit your enemy in the belly and kick him when he is down, and boil your prisoners in oil (if you take any!), and torture his women and children, then people will keep clear of you'. Yet this went together with a genuine aversion to war: he regarded massive deterrence as the best security, but also viewed conflict with Germany to be inevitable.

The best way to conduct such a war would not be through the commitment of the British army in a land war on the Continent, but economic warfare through blockade. In 1912 Fisher wrote:

> Perhaps I went a little too far when I said I would boil the prisoners in oil and murder the innocent in cold blood, etc., etc. But it's quite silly not to make war damnable to the whole mass of your enemy's population, which of course is the secret of maintaining the right of capture of private property at sea ... [114]

In other words the rhetoric of cruelty was employed, but it was economic warfare which was meant. It would be the threat of hardship, rather than physical violence and mass death which was Fisher's—and the British navy's—strategy in war.

Unlike in Germany the radical right wing remained politically isolated; their calls for drastic punitive measures such as the dismemberment of Germany, the occupation of Berlin until all British demands were fulfilled, the permanent annexation of a coastal strip from Bremen to Kiel, and the extension of British imperial interests in Europe, did not find popular support or establishment approval. On the other hand, in secret diplomacy in 1915 the British 'offered' Russia control of the Dardanelles while hoping to grab for themselves the oil wealth of Mesopotamia.[115] The Russian revolutions of 1917, coinciding with mounting war weariness and workers' protests and strikes throughout Britain, reawakened the debate about war aims and utterly changed its terms of reference. Britain had gone to war in defence of the rights of small nations; the Bolshevik demand for the self-determination of nations had the potential to subvert the liberal concept since the British government intended self-determination only for existing nation-states, not necessarily for nationalities contesting imperial rule such as Ireland. In order to find a new legitimation for its war aims the British government decided to maintain the loyalty of the labour movement by echoing the Left's call for the self-determination of nations.

Both sides in the war attempted to use the demand for national liberation, with 'an inextricably tangled mix of tactics and idealism', trying to foment national uprisings in Austria-Hungary, Poland, Ireland, the Ottoman empire, and India. The British government thus supported the national movements in the Habsburg empire in the belief that they would shatter its fragile unity.[116] In relation to Germany, British policy aimed for a complete transformation of its political system. Lord Kitchener, secretary of state for war, told the American government in March 1916, 'The only really satisfactory termination of the war would be brought about by an internal revolution in Germany.'[117] Robertson, chief of the imperial general staff, tried to persuade the government to adopt tactics to start a revolution in Germany. However, Haig was opposed, and the government did not follow Robertson's suggestion. The political and military leaders were agreed on the need to obtain military dominance over Germany in order to dictate peace terms, but that did not mean the revolutionizing, still less the destruction, of Germany.[118] Prime minister Lloyd George's war aims speech of 5 January 1918 held out the prospect of new European order involving the self-determination of nations that would include a democratic Germany.[119] By that stage British policy was therefore no longer conservative, but in effect it did amount to revolutionizing the old state system in Europe and the Near East, a liberal agenda which came close to the left-wing belief that the oppression of nationalities had been the cause of the war; the new order would be a democratic world in which the need for war had become obsolete. Yet Britain did not aim for the destruction of the German state or the German economy; the Treasury resisted calls from lobby groups who called for Germany's export trade to be strangled.

France, the prospect of war, and war aims

France, a nation that had seen severe political division over the Dreyfus affair at the turn of the century and further strains over the social question and army expansion since then, rapidly united with the looming prospect of war. Although there had been a 'nationalist revival' since 1905, French nationalism remained defensive. J.-J. Becker has shown in his classic study of public opinion that while the Parisian bourgeoisie was nationalist and believed war would soon become a reality, the majority of the population was 'apatriotic'.[120] In foreign policy under Poincaré (prime minister and foreign minister from 1912, and president from 1913) France wished to maintain the alliance with Russia, but also preserve the status quo in the Balkans, since war in that region might threaten French interests in the Near East. Indeed, before July 1914, its main concern was not the Balkans, but Syria; Poincaré, denounced after the war by the Left as 'Poincaré-la-guerre' and depicted as violently germanophobic, was in fact anxious to reach agreement with Germany over the future of the Ottoman empire. On the other hand, the government and the military had quietly gained confidence in the strength of the Triple Entente and the French army: a report of the war ministry of September 1912 had predicted a victory for the Entente in a war against the Triple Alliance.[121]

Naturally, there were some French nationalist extremists calling for a belligerent policy. Albert de Mun, the leader of the Catholic workers' association, told the diplomat Maurice Paléologue in April 1913: 'Don't you understand, my dear friend, that France, which has fallen so low, can only rehabilitate itself before God through war? Do you not understand that this war which is taking shape on the horizon, inevitable and imminent, is one we must wish for?'[122] But his was a relatively isolated voice.

In July 1914, the majority of the French people neither wanted war nor believed it to be inevitable. Public opinion was preoccupied with the Caillaux trial, not Sarajevo and Austro–Serb relations. (Madame Caillaux had shot the editor of Le Figaro for publishing her love letters to finance minister Joseph Caillaux, written while he was still married to his first wife; on 29 July she was acquitted of the charge of murder.) In the last five days of the crisis, as Germany's aggressive intentions were revealed, the mood switched, and most French people, even the anti-militarist labour move-ment, rallied to the idea of fighting a just war of defence. No one doubted that France was the victim of German aggression; contrary to the long-held myth there were no calls for 'revanche' (revenge for defeat in the Franco-Prussian War), and not even Alsace-Lorraine, the territories annexed by Germany, figured as an important issue.[123] Once war started, it was seen as something that threatened the cultural and political existence of the na-tion.[124] This was no chauvinist hysteria: the values for which France fought were those of patriotism, certainly, but also, in republican and left-wing opinion, the universal values of the Rights of Man and democracy. The Right in French politics could still find plenty of common ground with the Republic to join in the *union sacrée* in order to defend the nation. Ultimately France had been forced to enter war by the German declaration of war; the skilful crisis management of President Poincaré helped to ensure that France not only appeared to be, but was the injured party, deriving a powerful moral advantage from German belligerence. Yet at a deeper level, even if Germany had had no immediate aggressive designs on it, France, like Britain, could not have afforded the security risk of standing aside while Germany defeated Russia and gained a position of overwhelming domin-ation on the Continent.[125]

The execution of the Schlieffen plan made the issue simple: Germany declared war on France on the evening of 3 August, citing unsubstantiated rumours that French aeroplanes had bombed Nuremberg. The invasion of Belgium signalled the obvious intention of invading France. Once war commenced, the objectives for France were plain: the restoration of the territorial integrity of France and Belgium, the return of Alsace and Lorraine, and the imposition of terms on a defeated Germany that would ensure permanent security.[126] Other aims were discussed at various points during the war, such as the idea of annexing the Saarland and even the dismemberment of Germany, but it would be unhistorical to view these war aims as the causes of French entry to the war. Even at the end of the war, little had changed. Although President Poincaré, most of the French Right, and some radicals, wanted a total German surrender—and on 5 October 1918 Poincaré even tried to stop prime minister Clemenceau from discussing an armistice while the enemy occupied any part of France or Belgium—the course taken was to secure an immediate armistice on the basis of the return of Alsace-Lorraine to France and a temporary disarmament of Germany. French public opinion, as revealed by postal control records, was evenly divided between those who wanted acceptance of such a quick end to the fighting and those who wanted to take the war into German territory.[127]

Russia

The matter is more complex with Russia. Did Russia go to war for reasons of imperialist expansion, as was argued at the time (and subsequently) by socialists? Or in order to stabilize tsarist rule through a kind of social imperialism, to divert internal political opposition to patriotic goals? The American historian Peter Holquist remarks that the political and educated elite regarded the prospect of war in July 1914 as 'an opportunity to . . . build an "all-nation struggle," . . . and seal the rift between society and the regime'.[128] This, however, is only part of the story, for it reflects elite hope for national unity as a consequence of war, to transform Russian society and the regime, but not why it was felt war was necessary in the first place.

Russia's defeat in the war against Japan in 1905 had two consequences in this regard. First, Russian foreign policy interests were redirected towards Europe. It was not the first time the Balkans aroused public as well as political support: in 1876, as Serbia was facing near defeat in its struggle against the Ottoman empire, several thousand Russian volunteers served in the Serbian army which was placed under the command of a retired Russian general. Although the tsar disapproved of the adventure, the ministry of war lent tacit support, since the idea of solidarity with the Balkan Slavs enjoyed a substantial following in the pan-Slavic movement, the nationalist press, the urban public, and the clergy. Despite the Serb victory, the extravagant expectations of the Slavophiles were disappointed when Britain and Austria-Hungary forced Russia to back down in the Treaty of Berlin of 1878. This was a humiliation for the regime, causing a crisis of confidence in the autocracy, which turned to internal repression for fear of revolution.[129]

Second, 1905 was a reminder to Russia's rulers that moderation had to be exercised in foreign policy. Soon the regime came under pressure at home: not so much from 'public opinion', the existence of which was severely limited by the repressive state, or even the Duma (parliament) with its restricted franchise and limited powers, but rather from the press and political groupings on the fringes of the system which were attempting to prove themselves more patriotic than the government. One such group was the Slavic League, whose leader General Kireyev wrote in 1909: 'We have become a second-rate power'. It is this fear of losing power status which in the long term motivated Russia's entry into the Great War. Although 'public opinion' (in the sense of fringes of the elite) was one factor in Russian foreign policy, it was not the most important determinant; the tsar, with his close advisers, was the active arbiter, and he was virtually isolated from and immune to the weak pressure exerted by anyone outside his small entourage. The government could thus virtually ignore the agitation of nationalists and militarists who were becoming more influential in the Duma and among the right-wing intelligentsia. By temperament Nicholas II was not easily swayed—either by public opinion or even by the council of ministers. Thus Russian foreign policy goals in the period before 1914 were in general defensive, not aggressive. Despite the alliance with France, dating from the years 1891–4, St Petersburg made it clear to Paris that it had no interest in supporting any potentially aggressive foreign policy, such as in Africa.[130]

Nevertheless, Russian decision-makers were convinced that war was inevitable. No sooner had Russia suffered a crushing defeat by Japan than the chiefs of staff of the army and navy were making plans to construct a new fleet of modern dreadnoughts and rebuild the army in order to seize the Straits and establish a dominant position in the eastern Mediterranean. Russia's 'historic mission' would be achieved 'solely by means of the

struggle and the presence of well-armed forces'.[131] After Austria annexed
Bosnia and Herzegovina, Sazonov (the deputy foreign minister, who became foreign minister in 1910) concluded that Austria was 'hostile to Balkan
Slavdom and to Russia'; the annexation had 'displayed with indisputable
clarity the aims of Austro-German policy in the Balkans and laid the bases
for an inevitable conflict between Germanism and Slavism'.[132] Yet this did
not mean that the regime was eager for war. On the contrary, tsar Nicholas
and his government were notably cautious. Until 1911 the finance ministry
successfully resisted the armed forces' ambitious spending plans for rearmament, because priority was given to restoring budgetary stability.[133] 'Do not
for one instant lose sight of the fact that we cannot go to war . . . It would be
out of the question for us to face a war for five or six years,' Nicholas told his
new ambassador to Sofia in early 1911. Russian intentions were to 'guarantee the free development of those Balkan peoples whose independent
political existence Russia had called forth', and to help them prevent
German penetration and Austrian invasion of the area. While this was not
necessarily connected with an aggressive aim against the Austro-Hungarian
Empire, events in the Balkans, with the rapid growth of local nationalisms,
proved to be impossible to control from St Petersburg.

The Russian government itself was surprised at the autonomous mo-
mentum that developed from the new alliance, created by Serbia and
Bulgaria, from which emerged the Balkan League that was ready to go
to war. When the war between the Balkan alliance and the Ottoman
empire broke out in October 1912, events threatened to run dangerously
out of the control of the great powers. The unexpectedly rapid victories of
the Balkan states against the Ottoman forces, which caused dismay to the
Habsburg government and general staff, were heartily welcomed in the
Russian press. Yet the Russian government was careful not to go beyond
diplomacy. Armed intervention in support of the Balkan gains was expressly ruled out, and Serbia's demand for territory on the Adriatic coast
was not supported.[134]

Still, Russian foreign policy was gradually shifting to a more active line
that stressed deterrence rather than the preservation of peace at all cost.[135] In
October 1912, trial mobilizations near the border in Galicia caused deep
concern to the Habsburg general staff; according to Austro-Hungarian
intelligence the number of troops in the Warsaw district alone was raised
to 320,000 in autumn 1912, more than double the usual number.[136] In turn,
Russian suspicions about German intentions were heightened by the Liman

von Sanders affair as from October 1913. The German general Liman von Sanders was appointed as commander of the 1st Corps of the Ottoman army, with instructions from the Kaiser to 'Germanize' the Turkish army and secretly prepare Turkey for its role as Germany's ally in a war against Russia; German officers were appointed to positions on the Ottoman general staff and in the war ministry, and Liman led the work to reinforce defences on the Straits, including laying mines and strengthening the artillery. The news soon leaked out, provoking fears in Russia for its important seaborne trade through the Straits, and the Russian government protested in Berlin. British and French refusal to back a joint Entente protest (so much for the 'rigidity' of the alliance system!) meant that Russia had to climb down.[137] Inflammatory articles in the German and the Russian press in spring 1914 mutually heightened the tension by urging preparation for war. Neither government had inspired the articles, and the Russian foreign minister and the German ambassador met to reassure each other of their peaceful intentions.[138] But Russian intelligence reports in spring 1914 strongly suggested there was a widespread expectation in Germany that a preventive war on Russia would soon be launched.[139]

So how real were Russia's belligerent intentions? Clearly, nationalist forces in Germany had an interest in portraying Russia as an immediate threat, and between 1912 and 1914 even mainstream German politicians became convinced that Russia was planning to attack in the near future. Privately, however, the German chancellor Bethmann Hollweg himself did not believe in Russia's aggressive intentions.[140] This was a correct assessment, and although the Russian government prepared to match the rearmament of its rivals, it was 'unwilling to take the calculated risk of a preventive first strike', and even in July 1914 it had no such strategy.[141] The Austro-Hungarian government also did not believe that Russia was preparing war, even at the time of the trial mobilizations in autumn 1912 or at the turn of the year 1913–14; at the height of the German–Russian tensions in spring 1914 nothing fundamental had changed. Rather than concrete news (for example, about mobilizations or troop concentrations on the border) there were vague assumptions: Vienna expected the Russian threat to materialize if Austria-Hungary intervened in another Balkan war; there were unsubstantiated fears that the Balkan conflicts were part of a secret plan by the Entente to isolate Germany and Austria-Hungary; and there was the prediction that Russia would go to war when its rearmament was complete in 1916–17. The military authorities took the propaganda of pro-Russian,

Polish, or Ukrainian nationalist groups on Habsburg territory as evidence of dangerous subversion by Russian pan-Slavism.[142]

Inside Russia, however, pro-Slav feelings did not run very deep: one leading campaigner, Kovalevsky, recorded that interest in pan-Slavism or the Balkans was not very substantial in St Petersburg: whereas he could get 2,000 people to a public lecture on Rousseau, barely 150 attended talks on south Slav contemporary politics in 1912. Certainly, in the years 1912 to 1914 the Octobrists and Nationalists, the Duma parties usually loyal to the government, began to criticize Sazonov for his hesitation and not support-ing Slav interests. This parallel with the increasing pan-German and extreme nationalist influence on German government policy in the same period is more apparent than real, however. The paramount figure, the tsar, was no pan-Slav, for all his support for Balkan nationalism. His favoured foreign policy adviser, Prince Meshchersky, was a conservative newspaper editor who counselled friendship with Berlin and published scathing criticism of pan-Slav opinion, arguing that Russia should keep out of Balkan entangle-ments. The decisive shift in Russian policy only came in the July crisis. Even then, policy was not consistent, for Russian decision-making lay in a series of miscalculations and false perceptions of enemy intention. Nicholas be-lieved in his ability to preserve the peace, backed by the power of the Russian military which inspired respect in its neighbours. He ignored, or chose not to see, the fear aroused in Germany and Austria at the prospect of future Russian superiority or by its current actions in the Balkans; and he took at face value the frequent assurances of his cousin Wilhelm of Ger-many's pacific intentions.[143]

Russia neither encouraged the Serbian government to provoke Austria-Hungary, nor did it know of the assassination plans, as shown by the documents published by the Bolshevik government, which had no grounds to exculpate the tsar's regime. The Russian diplomats were unsympathetic to the Serb radical nationalists around 'Apis' and their plotting against prime minister Pašić, and would not have supported a dangerous scheme which would provoke war.[144]

The order for general mobilization, issued on 30 July, resulted from the following considerations. First, the Russian government knew that refusal to support Serbia again after the failure to do so in 1913 would mean the end of Russian prestige.[145] In other words, pan-Slavism as an ideology was not important; the dominant factor was fears about Russia's geopolitical position and hence also the prestige of the regime at home. Second, the government realized that it had been deceived by Germany: Berlin was not, after all, exercising a moderating influence on Austria-Hungary, which had commenced bombarding Belgrade on 29 July. Finally, the partial mobilization in the districts facing Austria-Hungary on 28 July placed in jeopardy the army's schedule for mobilization against Germany which had evidently begun secretly to mobilize. Any further delay would thus mean falling further behind in the race to mobilize, concentrate, and deploy troops.[146]

The Russian military and political leadership expected a short war, as did the other powers. Only a few predicted a long war, which would destabilize the rule of the tsar and possibly lead to revolution; in February former minister of the interior Durnovo warned the tsar precisely of this danger to his throne. On receiving news of the Austro-Hungarian ultimatum, the tsar recalled this prediction at a meeting of the council of ministers on 24 July, saying that war 'would be disastrous for the world and once it had broken out it would be difficult to stop'. However, the great majority of the press, the liberal and conservative parties, and ministers and military leaders demanded military action in order to prevent any further loss of prestige and power; the new interior minister, Maklakov, thought there was little risk of revolution, and argued that war would on the contrary unify the nation.[147]

Yet Russian military leaders were not blind to the risks of another war. In fact, a debate was being conducted on the general staff: several leading officers had drawn perceptive conclusions from recent modern wars, especially the war against Japan. In 1911–12 General A. A. Neznamov, the leading 'Young Turk' on the general staff, argued that war would no longer be decided by a single great battle, but rather, by a series of operations. Drawing partly on German military doctrine, including von der Goltz's concept of the 'nation in arms', Neznamov put forward the idea of a war plan based on total involvement of the nation. Modern armaments technology meant that contemporary armies had to prepare for lengthy war. In 1913, Lieutenant-Colonel Svechin assessed the demographic and strategic balance of forces in Europe, and while he did not openly challenge the doctrine of the superiority of the offensive, warned that one 'must be prepared for protracted conflict'.[148]

The ideas of the 'Young Turks' provoked controversy which raged until late summer 1912, when the tsar ended the debate by declaring, 'Military doctrine consists of doing everything which I order.'[149] On the eve of the Great War, the assumption on which the ministry of war had been planning was that war would last between two and six months.[150] The army had a

peacetime strength of 1,423,000, enlarged through the reforms of 1910 by
13 per cent. Although a 'Large Programme' had just been approved in June
1914, which was to see expansion by almost half a million men over three
years, an increase in the air force, and an increase in artillery capacity to
match that of Germany, little was done (and even less could have been done
by the outbreak of war) to construct strategic railway lines or build stocks of
munitions and supplies. Despite great improvements since 1890, Russia's
railway system still lagged a long way behind that of its central European
enemies: it was inferior in terms of density of railway track, locomotives,
and wagons. In artillery, too, although rapid progress had been made in
supplying the modern 76 mm gun, there were still fewer guns in relation to
infantry numbers than in Germany or Austria-Hungary. By comparison
with the enemy armies the Russian officer corps and NCOs were woefully
inferior in quantity and quality.[151] Still, the assurance by the ministers of war
and navy, that the armed forces were ready for war, was crucial for the
government's decision to go to war in July 1914.[152]

Yet despite Russian hostility to Austro-Hungarian designs, and increasing
fears of Germany, Russia did not possess the expansionist, aggressive dynamic that characterized Germany. Berlin knew Russia was not pushing for
war. In March 1914 Moltke had written to Conrad:

> None of the intelligence we have from Russia indicates at present any
> intentionally aggressive position. I do not believe that Russia will seek in the
> near future an opportunity for war against Austria or against ourselves, which
> amounts to the same thing, nor will it try to produce one . . . Still less is an
> aggressive position to be anticipated from France. France is at the moment in a
> very unfavourable military situation. The introduction of the three-year
> service and the training of two years' recruits within a short space of time
> have revealed difficulties which cannot be overcome so easily. Thus France is
> doing everything to strengthen its ally Russia, but for the foreseeable future it
> will hardly exhort it to war against the Triple Alliance.[153]

The Prussian military attaché at the Russian court reported to Berlin on 30
July: 'I have the impression that here one has mobilized for fear of imminent
events, without aggressive intentions'; on which Wilhelm commented:
'correct, exactly so'. This key sentence was suppressed in the official
documents published in Germany's inter-war campaign to prove its innocence in causing war.[154]

Yet when it became clear there would be war, alliance considerations and
military doctrine dictated a strategy of the offensive: mobilization according

to 'Schedule 19A' which envisaged simultaneous invasions of Austro-Hungarian territory in Galicia and of East Prussia to destroy the German forces there.[155] Even in political development there was a parallel: Russia had its own version of the 'Burgfrieden' (peace within the fortress) or 'union sacrée' (sacred union), or national unity in war. In the Duma (parliament) the leader of the extreme right wing embraced his political enemy Miliukov, the spokesman of Constitutional Democrats, in a demonstrative gesture of national unity. Politicians of all parties hastened to add their support, including the socialists who had been fundamentally opposed to the tsarist system. Only the Bolsheviks opposed the war.[156]

Serbia

Did Serbia have an interest in provoking war with Austria? If so, was the Serb government behind the plot to assassinate Archduke Franz Ferdinand? The answer to these questions is made up of three elements. First, the context of political development in the Balkans before 1914; second, the background in Serbia itself; and third, the role of the Serb government during the unfolding of the crisis after the assassination.

The Balkans were in a sense a historic crucible: the meeting point of three great empires and three world faiths. Yet this was not a recipe for permanent warfare: for centuries Ottoman and Habsburg rule had ensured a modicum of stability, albeit by means of illiberal regimes, repression, and fostering social, religious, and ethnic divisions. Only the relatively recent importation of nationalism from western Europe had introduced a powerful ideological challenge to imperial rule.

The two Balkan wars, 1912 and 1913 (discussed in Chapter 4), ended with victory for Serbia which encouraged Serbs on Austro-Hungarian territory to look forward to the creation of a Yugoslav state or possibly a Greater Serbia. However, although many Croats looked forward to a time when there would be unity with other south Slavs within the Habsburg empire, there were also some romantic nationalists, especially students, who looked to Serbia for leadership, and a few who turned to terrorism and tyrannicide. This pattern was even more pronounced in Bosnia-Herzegovina.[157]

The assassination of Archduke Franz Ferdinand should be seen against the background of a social and cultural revolt in Bosnia and Herzegovina. There were already signs of modern social unrest in the 1900s, with a

general strike of industrial workers in 1906 and fatal clashes between demon-
strating workers and the army in Sarajevo and many other towns. The peasants
and serfs, who suffered under the system of servitude continued from the
period of Ottoman rule, engaged in open rebellion in 1910, when more than
13,500 peasants were evicted from their land for not paying tribute to feudal
lords and taxes. The army was deployed to stop the peasant strikes and the
burning of feudal estates. Concessions to Bosnia and Herzegovina were only
partial and late: the parliament envisaged for the future would have had no
power to choose or control the executive, which was run by a governor
appointed in Vienna. However, Franz Ferdinand found even such a policy
of limited concessions too liberal, and demanded measures to 'end the Serbs'
obstruction'.[158]

The Young Bosnia movement, part of a revolutionary movement among
south Slav youth in Austria-Hungary and Serbia, had the goal of the
destruction of the Habsburg empire. Their ideology went beyond nationalism. Composed of Bosnian Serbs, Croats, Herzegovinians, and Muslims,
the target of their rebellion was the entire old order, not just Habsburg rule;
they wanted to destroy with bombs the Serbian bourgeoisie in Bosnia-
Herzegovina and the pious Orthodox acquiescence in annexation. As
young intellectuals they regarded themselves as modernists, opposed to
academism. Their political model was that of the Italian struggle for unification of Garibaldi and Mazzini; their name 'Young Bosnia' derived from
Mazzini's *Giovine Italia*, and their ideas were shaped by the Mazzinian idea
that the youth should become men of a new type, 'self-denying crusaders
prepared for sacrifice'. When the First Balkan War broke out, several members crossed into Serbia and fought as volunteers. The young assassin,
Gavrilo Princip, rejected because he was 'too small and weak', felt the
humiliation for long thereafter. He was a sensitive boy who read widely
and fancied himself as a poet. He despised the new Serbian bourgeoisie in
Sarajevo as money-grubbing exploiters and said shortly before 28 June 1914
about the Serb business district in Sarajevo, the *carsija:* 'If I could force the
whole of *carsija* into a box of matches, I would set it alight.'[159] He was fond
of reciting the verse by Nietzsche: 'Yes, I know where I spring from! |
Unsated like the flame | I glow and consume myself. | Everything I grasp
turns to light, | everything I leave turns to cinder. | Flame am I, surely!'[160]

The context of social unrest and cultural–national revolt helps explain the
fanaticism of the Austro-Hungarian subjects who were plotting against their
overlords. Nevertheless, the idea that the 19-year-old Bosnian schoolboy

Gavrilo Princip and his juvenile fellow-conspirators aimed to provoke a war between Austria-Hungary and Serbia can be consigned to the realm of legend. Certainly, the plotters received help from radical nationalist pan-Serbs, and, it emerged much later, from the head of Serbian military intelligence Dragutin Dimitrijević ('Apis'), although the degree of his involvement has been questioned. According to some versions Apis tried to warn the inexperienced youths not to carry out the assassination or perhaps wanted to use them for his own purposes.[161] Recent research has shown that Apis gave instructions to Serbian border officials in early June to allow two young students to cross the border into Bosnia carrying arms. However, the prime minister, Pašić, on hearing of rumours about an impending assassination attempt on Franz Ferdinand, issued instructions to stop such cross-border arms smuggling and to start an investigation into the revolutionary activities of Apis, aware that these 'could provoke a war between Serbia and Austria-Hungary, which in the present circumstances would be very dangerous'.[162] The Austro-Hungarian government tried to find evidence linking the Serb government and the Russian military attaché to the plot, and searched the archives during the occupation in the First World War, as did the Nazi occupation in the Second World War, to no avail. In summer 1914 it was unable even to find the connection between the terrorists and Apis.[163]

Indeed, Serbia could have little interest in another war so soon after the last. True, the Balkan wars of 1912 and 1913 had ended with victory for Serbia, doubling its territory. The victories had charged Serb nationalism with fresh energy. Above all, the battle of Kumanovo (24 October 1912), in which the Turks were defeated, was integrated into the new national mythology: it was held to have effaced the defeat at the Field of Blackbirds in June 1389 in Kosovo. Briefly to explain this apparently bizarre anachronism: in the course of Turkish expansion in Europe, the Ottoman forces defeated the Serbs at the battle of Kosovo, leading ultimately to Ottoman domination in the Balkans. The fierce resistance of the Orthodox Christian Serbs against the Muslim Turks to maintain their autonomy was not as such a myth, but what was probably an inconclusive battle was reworked in Serb popular culture over the centuries, and especially in the nineteenth century, to become a powerful symbol of Serb national identity.[164] With victory over the Ottoman empire in the First Balkan War, vengeance for 1389, in the newly invented tradition of Serb national culture, marked the beginning of a new epoch in Serb history. Serbia's culture had proved itself to be

superior, and the superior 'Serbian race' was destined to unite all the south
Slavs. On the other hand, Serbia was exhausted and could not contemplate
waging another war immediately. In the two Balkan wars it lost 14,000
killed, 57,000 who died as a result of injuries or disease, and 54,000 injured,
out of an army of 350,000 to 400,000 men. The death rate of about 18
per cent was even higher than that suffered by most nations in the First
World War. Although Serbia could be satisfied with the successes, it had to
share the coveted territory of Macedonia with Greece, and it had not
obtained access to either the Adriatic or the Aegean Sea. Pašić's goal of
uniting the entire Serb nation, of Serbia playing the role Piedmont had in
the unification of Italy, had not yet been fulfilled. The national debt had
risen from 660 million dinars in 1912 to 900 million in 1914; state revenues
were not sufficient to service the debt, and in January 1914 Serbia received a
credit from France of 250 million dinars.[165]

Even the Austrian military attaché in Belgrade, Gellinek, did not ascribe
belligerent intentions to the Serbian government. At the beginning of
1914 he reported that Serbia was in a state of chaos and internal difficulties.
Prime minister Pašić feared that tension between Greece and Turkey
would disturb the badly needed peace in the Balkans, and that Serbia
was under threat from marauding Bulgarian bands, although it had an
'absolute need for undisturbed peace for the next few years . . . warlike
complications would have a completely catastrophic effect, above all on
the economy'. Nevertheless, Gellinek concluded his report by saying that
a 'radical rehabilitation of our relations with Serbia will only be attained by
the destruction of the present kingdom as independent state'.[166] He left no
doubt that Serbia remained a danger for the Habsburg empire in the
medium term, as shown by the Serb interest in fusion with Montenegro,
the policy of 'eliminating' ethnic minorities, and the 'brutal struggle
against the Albanians' and their state. He also feared an ever-closer
relationship between Serbia and Russia, and warned that any Austro-
Hungarian attack on Serbia would almost certainly lead to war with
Russia. In mid-June 1914 Gellinek recorded increased readiness in the
Serbian army, which now had 100,000 men; however, he still did not
believe that Serbia presented a short-term military threat. By contrast, the
Austro-Hungarian general staff estimated in July 1914 that the Serbian
army had 400,000 men and 260,000 rifles, presumably in order to bloat the
perceived threat, probably counting the reserves together with the active
servicemen.[167]

While estimates of the number of active troops varied, the general picture was clear: the regular army had been seriously depleted in two wars; infantry weapons, ammunition, artillery, transport, and medical facilities were all grossly deficient.[168] A power struggle was taking place, in which a group of officers associated with Apis and the parliamentary opposition were demanding a greater role for the military in decision-making and in the control of Serbia's newly won territories. Pašić enjoyed the support of the aging King Peter and Crown Prince Alexander, as well as the Russian minister Hartwig. While Pašić and his government had not relinquished their aims of creating a Serb-dominated Yugoslavia, their perspective was that Serbia needed a long period of peace, 'a generation or more', to recover from the devastation and integrate the new territories. However, elections were scheduled for 14 August, in which Pašić could ill afford to be seen as conciliatory towards Austria-Hungary, lest he lose ground to the more nationalist forces.

Aware of the grave risk that the assassination might injure relations between Austria-Hungary and Serbia, the Serb government took care to order official mourning, send condolences to Vienna, and condemn the killings. Secretly, Pašić also took the precaution of soliciting support from friendly powers, above all Russia. But for almost three weeks, official Vienna was silent, giving no hint of the storm to come. Count Pallavicini, the Austro-Hungarian ambassador to Turkey, even assured his Serbian counterpart that his government did not link the assassination to Serbia, and wanted to maintain good relations. However, by 7 July Pašić knew that the Habsburg monarchy might adopt the course of demanding an Austrian enquiry in Belgrade, which he was determined to consider an unacceptable interference in internal Serbian affairs. Meanwhile, on both sides inflammatory comments in the press intensified the crisis and restricted the politicians' room to manoeuvre. The Austro-Hungarian press accused Belgrade of complicity in the crime, alleging a pan-Serb conspiracy, while some opposition newspapers in Belgrade, to the embarrassment of Pašić, rejoiced openly in the elimination of the Archduke. Optimism that war might be averted gave way to pessimism on 17–18 July, as Pašić pieced together the warning signs from Vienna, Budapest, and Berlin that the Habsburg government was preparing a severe diplomatic move. Still, because he was receiving mixed signals, with the Russian foreign minister Sazonov saying on 18 July he thought Austria-Hungary would not take any action, and with his own election campaign making increasing demands on his attention, Pašić assumed that the situation was under control. Had he not assured the

Austrian envoy Baron Giesl that if Vienna made a request, Serbia would certainly comply with any measures 'compatible with the dignity and independence of a state'?[169] The cabinet decided on 19 July not to dissolve the pan-Serbian societies, as the Italian government had proposed in the interest of conciliation, but it told the Italian ambassador it 'would not hesitate for one instant to dissolve them and punish the guilty if the Austro-Hungarian government furnished evidence of their complicity in the assassination'. However, it feared that to do so now would 'provoke a popular revolution'.[170]

Pašić left to go campaigning in the north-east of the country on 19 July (or early in the morning of the 20th), and returned on the 22nd; next day he travelled to the newly acquired territory in southern Serbia. It was thus the minister of finance, left in charge by Pašić, who received the note of 23 July from Vienna containing severe demands including a Habsburg investigation on Serbian soil, and a 48-hour ultimatum. The Serbian government replied on 25 July with a note that was so conciliatory it amazed the Austro-Hungarian government: it granted all demands except for that which infringed Serbian sovereignty, namely an Austro-Hungarian investigation in Serbia.[171] With the prospect of an Austrian attack beginning to worry it after the ultimatum, the Serbian government had begun to redeploy the army, 80 per cent of which was still in the new territories, to the north to meet a possible invasion, and made plans to evacuate the government from Belgrade on the northern border to Niš. Pašić was nevertheless surprised at the swift brutality of the reply from Austria-Hungary: the severing of diplomatic relations was the prelude to imminent war.[172]

Now more confident of support from Russia, where opinion had finally shifted in favour of intervention on 26 July, the Serb government was still hopeful that the diplomatic intervention of Britain for a four-power conference might force Austria and Germany to back down.[173] Not until the Austro-Hungarian declaration of war on 28 July was the uncertainty resolved. In other words, although Serbia had been forced to seek international support and make preparations to defend itself, in no way can its conduct before or during the July crisis be construed as a policy to bring about war. Nor can Serbian policy in the July crisis be interpreted as a series of cocky rebuffs to Vienna, confident in the knowledge of a Russian 'blank cheque':[174] the Russian government did not (and could not) make its position clear until the long-prepared Austrian ultimatum was published, and only then could Serbia count on Russian support.

The Russian announcement of mobilization was the cue the German government was waiting for. The German ultimatum to Belgium was drafted on 26 July by Moltke (rather than the foreign ministry), determined to follow Schlieffen's prescription to breach Belgian neutrality. This opened the door to military predominance in most important aspects of war policy. Germany declared war on Russia on 1 August and demanded free passage for its army through Belgium the next day. As further declarations followed, Bethmann Hollweg received the British ambassador to tell him that the international guarantee of Belgium's neutrality was a mere 'scrap of paper'; in a speech to the Reichstag on 4 August he admitted that the invasion of Belgium broke international law, but that 'necessity knows no law'. The dynamic of destruction thus began with two deliberate violations of international law. The other violation, almost a week earlier, the Austro-Hungarian bombardment of Belgrade on 29 July, although destined to be almost entirely forgotten in the western world, was equally the prelude to further breaches of international law, culminating in the utter devastation of Serbia.[175]

4

German Singularity?

German history, according to an influential interpretation, developed in
the nineteenth and twentieth centuries along a fateful 'special path'. In
this view, advanced by German scholars (notably Hans-Ulrich Wehler), but
also in related form by Anglo-American historians (such as A. J. P. Taylor),
Germany diverged from the normal path of western societies which
proceeded from feudalism to capitalism and liberal democracy. Instead,
authoritarian, militarist regimes, dating back to the rise of Prussia as a
European power, dominated Germany; Bismarck's unification of the German states through war consolidated the political rule of the pre-industrial
elite, the Junkers (the landowning nobility). After the turn of the twentieth
century, when the working class and its political representation, the Marxist
Social Democratic Party appeared to make the land ungovernable, the
ruling elites launched Germany into a high-risk war to pre-empt democratization and revolution. When it became clear that quick victory was not
going to materialize, they turned to a policy of brutal, radicalized warfare
against the external enemies, and racism and brutal suppression of the
internal political opposition. After defeat, the pre-industrial elites, in alliance
with reactionary capitalism, lashed out against both liberal democrats and
socialists of all hues, for allegedly having betrayed the nation in 1918. The
emerging Nazi Party represented the distilled essence of all the right-wing
ideologies, and the advent of the Nazi dictatorship, the new war, and
the Holocaust marked the logical conclusion of Germany's 'special path'.[1]
The experience of mass industrialized death in the trenches of the First
World War, mass killing, and victimhood, had led Germans to become the
perpetrators of mass murder in the Second World War.

It has recently been argued (cf. Historiographical Note) that German
warfare in the First World War represented a policy of 'absolute destruction', the result of a unique military culture that left a legacy in National

Socialism with its cult of violence and the mass destruction of the Second World War.[2] However, it cannot be said there was a direct path from the policies of 1914–18 to those of 1939, except for the continuity of territorial war aims. The relationship is more complex, and outcomes more contingent, than the 'special path' would lead us to expect. The defining feature of the Nazi regime was violent antisemitism leading to genocide. Yet there was no straight path in this regard from the First to the Second World War. During the First World War the German state came under great pressure from racists and xenophobes. Its response was the 'Jewish census' of 1916, a count of Jews in the army carried out after a persistent campaign by the antisemitic Right alleging that Jews were shirking their patriotic duty. The war ministry had actually not intended to lend support to antisemitism by organizing the 'census', but the result was inadvertently to lend great impetus to the spread of antisemitism in the army. Nevertheless, the state succeeded in containing antisemitism (and also anti-Catholicism, which early in the war had threatened to destabilize national unity). The poor results of the antisemites and the conservative nationalists in the 1919 elections show that racism had not yet entered mainstream politics. The war regime and the very idea of war were so thoroughly discredited that the vast majority voted for a fresh start, for democratic, republican parties; at least until the mid-1920s, arguably even until 1939, the prevailing mood of the German people was 'never again war'. However, militarist nationalism fought a grim rearguard action, initially to preserve its existence in a Faustian pact to lend the new republic a dubious security, and soon to prepare the coming war of revenge. The coming of the Third Reich supercharged militarist nationalism and fused it with the previously half-hidden undercurrent of racism.

However, Germany had no monopoly on militarist nationalism, and neither mass death nor mass destruction was the experience or the prerogative of any single state. In Italy, the forces of militarist nationalism came to power as early as 1922, and in Turkey the ethno-nationalists carried out in wartime a policy of genocide as a part of a nation-building project.

Italy's imperialism: a forgotten crusade

The prevailing image of the Italian character is replete with clichés about their generosity, charm, and civilization; at worst they are seen as bumbling, possibly corrupt, and hopeless at military matters. Yet in the *belle époque* the

Italian state eagerly emulated the other powers' imperialism with its concomitant brutality and racism. Italy's militarism did not have the same influence in political decision-making as in Germany, but the nonchalance with which war was contemplated was easily the match of other European powers.

The history of the origins of the First World War is often told as a story of the tensions in the Balkans and the war aims of Germany and Austria-Hungary providing the background to the assassination at Sarajevo and the decision to launch a war. The Balkan wars of 1912–13 occasionally feature in the explanation, but Italy's invasion of Tripolitania and Cyrenaica (the area known today as Libya) features at best as a footnote to the grand narrative. The war in Libya in 1911 was not a cause of the world war, for there were no direct repercussions among the powers of Europe. Yet it had fateful consequences in the Balkans, and in a way it was also a vision of future warfare.

Not only the small nationalist groups, but also larger Catholic interests pushed for action: the Banco di Roma, whose director was Ernesto Pacelli, uncle of the later Pope Pius XII, had invested in Libya and egged on the government, although the degree of its political influence was probably quite limited. Don Luigi Sturzo, the priest and founding leader of political Catholicism, also supported the colonial enterprise.[3] The Bishop of Cremona welcomed the invasion of Libya as a 'crusade' against the Muslims and barbarian Africans. In the twenty years since 1896, when the Italian bourgeoisie had opposed the ill-fated invasion of Ethiopia, the constellation of forces changed: new industrial and financial companies saw opportunities in an aggressive foreign policy. The idea gained currency that only a strong, aggressive policy would restore Italy's status as a Great Power and give the state the authority and prestige it lacked. 'Public opinion', meaning almost all the influential non-socialist newspapers owned by private business, urged the government to 'go to Tripoli'.[4]

Luigi Albertini, the editor of the liberal-conservative *Corriere della Sera*, argued that the occupation of Libya would not be useful in terms of Italy's economy or its military position; he argued there were more worthwhile objects to spend state funds on, such as the Mezzogiorno, or making preparations for defence in what he saw as the inevitable war against Austria.[5] But his newspaper printed odes to war by the nationalist poet D'Annunzio, and ultimately Albertini supported the colonial enterprise. He wrote later: 'Although the Libyan war deprived the army of material force that could have been more useful in 1914–15, it gave back more in moral force and prestige.'

Popular novelists, such as Alfredo Oriani, depicted grand historical tableaux showing the global role of Italian civilization. A collective effort would be necessary to restore the Italian nation to its former glory. Bizarrely, he rejected industrialization, but ascribed an imperialist mission to Italy which would conquer barbarous Africa and become a dominating nation, ruled by superior Nietzschean heroes. Mussolini later recognized Oriani as one of his spiritual masters who influenced his thinking about a vast Latin empire and the kind of manipulation of the masses that required.[6]

Such ideas were common currency when prime minister Giolitti decided on war in Libya, seizing the opportunity of the weakening of the Ottoman empire presented by the 1909 revolution and the distraction in international relations caused by the second Moroccan crisis. The war was preceded by an ultimatum issued during the night of 26–27 September, demanding Turkey's consent within 24 hours to Italian military occupation of Libya, on the flimsy pretext that Turkey had neglected the territory. Giolitti promised a short war, and within three weeks Italy had seized most ports and coastal towns.

Soon, however, the imperial venture turned sour. The Arab population, rather than welcoming the Italians as their liberators from Ottoman despotism, began a long guerrilla war conducted by tenacious hill tribesmen. There was fierce fighting at Sciara Sciat on 23 October, in which Turkish soldiers were supported by Arab cavalry and rebels fighting from houses and gardens in the oasis. The Italians suffered over 400 killed, and alleged many were 'horribly maltreated' by the Arabs. There were over 500 Italian casualties in fighting at Sidi Bilal in September 1912, before peace was signed in October. The response was a brutal policy that targeted also civilians. The original expeditionary corps of 34,000 was increased to 100,000 troops.[7] On the orders of Giolitti hundreds of Libyan families were driven from their homes and shipped to the barren Tremiti islands in the Adriatic, without sufficient shelter. Many were housed in buildings without glass in the windows, some in caves and stables; they slept on a thin layer of straw on the bare ground, which offered no protection against the damp and the cold. Blankets were provided only to those in the infirmary. The accommodation, lacking in basic sanitation, was deemed in one inspector's report to be 'unfit even for animals'.[8] Food supplies were insufficient, and usually declined as soon as the inspectors left the islands.

There was no supply of clean drinking water. Ravaged by illness, 437 people died, almost one in three of the deportees; in addition, 'many' had died during the voyage to the islands, and their corpses were dumped overboard, to be washed up on the beaches of Apulia.[9] The evidence of contemporary inquiries reveals that the maltreatment of the Arab deportees was the result not only of neglect, inefficient administration, and corruption, but also of a deliberate government policy to treat the detainees harshly.

Giolitti had intended the war to be a piece of his usual technique of rule: *trasformismo*. He hoped to 'absorb' his opponents. But the war strengthened the forces of nationalism which unjustly claimed the credit for forcing the government into war and then accused it of betraying the army by depriving it of sufficient resources. On the Left, although it divided the Socialist Party, it strengthened the majority's rejection of imperialism and war. Some even urged militant strikes to stop the war, such as the radical editor of *Avanti!*, Mussolini. A few reformist Socialists on the other hand, such as Bissolati, supported the war out of patriotic loyalty. The extreme syndicalists welcomed it as a short cut to revolution. Arturo Labriola thus called the Libyan war 'an act of national defence', a way 'to break out of our customary stinking laziness'. This anticipated the later convergence of syndicalism and nationalism in the frenzy of the intervention campaign, 1914–15.[10] In another consequence, Italy's bourgeois feminist movement renounced its pacifism, sending it on a path towards nationalism and support for Italian intervention in 1915 in a 'just war' against the 'Teutonic barbarians'.[11]

After victory, the historian Pasquale Villari published an article in *Corriere della Sera* in which he expressed the nationalist longing for Italy to take its place among the great powers. He recalled how Italy had achieved unification in the 1860s only with the help of France, and that the defeats of Custoza, Lissa, and Aduwa still rankled. Italy did not have sufficient confidence in itself, and sensed that other countries did not have confidence in it. The war on Libya was to show Italy was a great power, a question of 'to be or not to be'.

> This was the reason for the great enthusiasm which worked miracles with us; even if it was not greater, it was more universal than that shown in the wars of national independence. The latter were supported by the most cultivated classes, but the peasantry hardly participated in them if at all. Garibaldi himself deplored many times the fact that the peasants did not join his army, and attributed that to the adverse influence of the clergy. Undoubtedly, the present war was the first time enthusiasm was shown by the entire

nation. All social orders participated in it: aristocracy and bourgeoisie, the urban and the rural population, the south no less, perhaps even more than the north. Even the clergy, so often opposed to any national feeling, blessed from the altar our soldiers, wishing them victory. The enthusiasm of the clergy was probably due to the idea of the war against the infidels. It is a certain fact that the deep conviction has formed in the country that this war was destined definitively to constitute the nation; Great Italy was becoming a reality recognized by everyone. Our soldiers departed like new crusaders, acclaimed by the people . . . Every hostile voice was drowned out; all opposition to the government disappeared . . . Unity, cemented with the blood shed in community for the fatherland, has truly become indissoluble.[12]

Villari had certainly overestimated the political effects of the war on Italy, Albertini commented, but they indicated 'the state of mind of Italy during the Libyan enterprise'.[13] Villari's nationalist idealism held out the promise of what a government might achieve through war; but this was a social imperialism whose fragility would become apparent as soon as setbacks revealed the weaknesses and tensions in Italian society. The high cost of war, concealed at the time, forced the state into deficit. The illusion that Libya had sponsored social harmony was soon shattered by the two general strikes in Milan in 1913; in the elections that year the Liberals suffered a serious haemorrhage of support, while the Socialists, Catholics, Nationalists, and anti-Giolittian Liberals increased their vote. Giolitti's system of *trasformismo*, clientelism, and attempted consensus with the Socialists, collapsed about his ears, and he resigned in March 1914. Libya continued to strain Italy's resources, and even after August 1914 Italy faced guerrilla warfare which was only contained with the presence of 60,000 troops.[14]

The long delay before Italy entered the war in 1915 thus had little to do with moral compunctions or a pacifist rejection of war. As King Vittorio Emanuele III said to the American ambassador in the context of the Bosnian annexation crisis of 1908, which strained Italy's relations with its ally, Austria: 'I am more than ever convinced of the utter worthlessness of treaties or any agreements written on paper. They are worth the value of paper. The only strength lies in bayonets and cannon.'[15] Had a German statesman said this, as Bethmann Hollweg did in August 1914, it would have been taken as further evidence of German perfidy. Of course, alliances and treaties could be changed if conditions warranted; cynicism was mutual, Conrad von Hötzendorff, as we saw in Chapter 3, demanding war on Italy during the Libyan war. But General Pollio, the chief of staff, astounded his German and Austrian colleagues in the Triple Alliance in April 1914 by demanding preventive war. Pointing to the risk that French and Russian rearmament would pose by 1917, he asked: 'Why don't we begin now this inevitable conflict?'[16]

'Sacred egoism': Italy's decision to intervene

Although the outbreak of European war in summer 1914 was not influenced by Italy, its eventual entry into the war in 1915 had serious repercussions, both for Italy and for European history. In the decision-making for war, two strands must be distinguished: the governmental process, and the pro-war campaign of certain parties and social groups, and above all intellectuals.

The war was willed, uniquely in Europe, by those at opposite ends of the political and cultural spectrum. Prime minister Salandra and his Liberal friends were confident of two things: first, a swift victory—and to believe this after nine months of war was a triumph of self-delusion, in the face of explicit warnings. Second, they believed despite the chronic instability of Liberal governments, the rivalry with Giolitti, and the unpredictability of the nationalist and revolutionary forces they had aroused, that they would be able to stabilize the existing political order. This was precisely the opposite of what a large part of the interventionist movement intended.

The major obstacle was that the prospect of war aroused no mass enthusiasm in Italy, and although the Vatican press consistently argued Austria's case, the prevailing sympathy was for Serbia. Some Italian newspapers were already receiving subsidies from Germany and Austria before the outbreak of war, such as the pro-Austrian *Popolo Romano*, but in July 1914 almost all were opposed to war. The anti-war mood was so strong that foreign minister Di San Giuliano was told by the ministry of the interior that a general mobilization 'might itself provoke revolt'.[17] Italy's decision to remain neutral did not surprise Germany and Austria-Hungary: their alliance with Italy provided for mutual defence against attack, and after their ultimatums and invasions Germany and Austria were unable to convince anyone that they were the victims of aggression. In any case, they had not involved Italy in their planning for war during the July crisis; Pollio's assurances of support would have been just as meaningless even if he had not died suddenly in early July 1914.

By the winter of 1914–15, however, several groups were pressing for war against Austria: the moderate Socialists, a majority of the Radical Party, the

Republican Party, the Nationalists led by Enrico Corradini, the small elite group of Futurists, and small extreme right-wing parties. These groups were supported by students, a considerable proportion of the urban middle class, and some of the industrial elite. There were also the irredentists, who wished to complete Italian unification by 'redeeming' the territories held with dubious justification to be ethnically Italian, mainly the port city of Trieste and its Dalmatian hinterland, and Trento and the Trentino. By now these groups were joined by the Italian press: some thirty newspapers, many of them subsidized by the iron and steel industry, were in favour of intervention on the side of the Entente.[18] Albertini called in the *Corriere della Sera* for war against the 'Violator of Belgium and the Oppressor of Small Peoples'.[19] Still, the war party was in a minority. The prefects' reports show that the 'popular classes', i.e. the peasants and workers, were opposed to war, while the upper classes were in favour of intervention, especially the educated bourgeoisie. However, the classic Marxist interpretation of the war as the product of capitalist machinations does not do justice to the case of Italy. A large part of the commercial, financial, and small industrial bourgeoisie was at the start in favour of neutrality, fearing the effects of war on business.[20] The Turin industrialist Gino Olivetti denounced the war as 'a monstrous phenomenon' which caused the 'brutal destruction of men and wealth'; in May 1915 he even toyed with the idea of supporting a workers' general strike to stop Italian intervention.[21]

The majority of parliament and the major political forces were opposed to war (the Catholic People's Party, the Socialists, and the Giolittian Liberals). But the king chose war on the advice of the government of the Liberal Salandra, utilizing the interventionist mobilization of the piazza, supported by the vast majority of intellectuals, the important newspapers, like *Corriere della Sera*, and some powerful economic enterprises like FIAT and Ansaldo.[22] While ordinary Italians rejected violence for the sake of violence, Salandra embraced it, deliberately flouting the will of the majority as a show of decisiveness. He aimed to destroy the Giolittian system, split and defeat the Socialists, and integrate political Catholicism through war.[23] With a candour that was as brutal as it was irresponsible, Salandra defined his war diplomacy as 'sacro egoismo', sacred egoism.[24]

Italy entered the war on the side of the Entente, yet unlike Britain and France, its motivation was not defensive. On the contrary, the Italian government had concrete territorial goals, secretly agreed by the Entente at the Treaty of London, 26 April 1915: Trieste, South Tyrol, the Trentino,

Istria, and Dalmatia, at the cost of the Austro-Hungarian empire. Italy's imperialist appetite was further whetted by the Gallipoli landings which excited expectation of an early Allied victory over Turkey, and it laid claim also to territory in western Anatolia.

Italy entered the war ultimately because 'not to do so would have been to admit that her pretensions to being a Great Power were false, and therefore, by implication, that her pretensions to liberalism, parliamentarism and a constitutional centralised monarchy were equally false'.[25] This absence of a 'real' motive to justify intervention was one of the main elements of hostility to war in popular opinion. People knew that the country was not threatened with invasion by anyone, the prefect of Chieti (Abruzzo) reported, and no one had attacked its dignity. They also realized that a new order would result from the conflagration, and that Italy would not be able to take the territories which 'geographically and ethnically belong to it', thus compromising forever Italy's future and the 'right to consider ourselves a Great Nation'. Yet the overwhelming sentiment was fear: fear of the immense loss of life and suffering of the countries at war, and fear of the dangers facing their own loved ones.[26] This mature political assessment on the part of the people and prefect of Chieti reveals that nationalism was simply not a dominating political force in pre-war Italy; nor was the thought of conquest. Nor, too, was race the priority, although an 'ethnic' definition of the nation was already in use.

Conventional wisdom has it that the Italian government, like most of the belligerents of 1914, expected a short war. In March 1915 the US ambassador to Rome told his government that 'there is a prevailing conviction that if and when she [Italy] enters . . . it will be with the hope that the war will be of short duration'. At the time of the Treaty of London, Salandra and foreign minister Sonnino predicted that the war would end with an Entente victory by the autumn of 1915.[27] The army, too, is believed to have expected a short war.[28] Did nine months' observation of the stalemate of industrialized war really have no effect on Italy's decision-makers? Outwardly the Italian government projected confidence in its armed forces and their capacity to achieve victory relatively soon. In private, however, doubts were discussed which could not be published at the time. Di San Giuliano predicted a long war, and was anxious not to let Italy join the war before it was clear which side was going to win.[29] His successor Sidney Sonnino privately told the newspaper editor Olindo Malagodi in December 1914: 'The war will be long—he repeats—it will be necessary to enter it as late as possible; however, we must not be too late.'[30] Salandra, by contrast, when his political friend Nitti asked him one hot evening in Rome in August 1915 whether he had made provision for winter clothing for the army in view of the cold winter in the Alps, was surprised. Salandra replied: 'Your pessimism is truly inexhaustible. Do you think the war can last beyond the winter?'[31]

General Cadorna, the army commander, claimed in his memoirs that he had not been consulted by the government in the decision to enter the war. His transparently self-exculpating memoirs have to be read with due scepticism, but that much was true.[32] Yet it is implausible that he offered no counsel to the government. On his own evidence he gave conflicting advice: when the war broke out the government refused to meet his demands for greater allocations for the armed forces; he therefore stated on 22 September 1914 that the army could not expect a favourable result if it were to confront a major enemy such as Austria. However, since both Austria and Germany faced several enemies in several theatres, Cadorna encouraged the hope of favourable results, especially since the national spirit in Italy had been aroused in the army and, he misled himself into believing, among the population at large. Only a few days later, 24 September, he was informed by the war ministry of the severe shortage of army uniforms and equipment needed for mobilization. Moreover, there was no provision for a winter campaign or for operations in the Alps. Cadorna thus replied that the army was not in a position to enter the war.[33]

On 21 December 1914 Cadorna asked the chief of the Mobilization Office to evaluate how to utilize all resources, human and natural, for war: he evidently did not believe it would be a short war. Certainly, preparations were made during the nine months of neutrality: weapons production was increased, officers and men were recruited and trained, and Cadorna warned of the necessity to increase industrial capacity for the production of armaments. On 4 March 1915 he wrote to the ministry of war, referring to the necessity to supply armament materials of all kinds, including explosives, metals, arms, munitions, boots, animals, etc. in sufficient quantities, and the limited potential of Italian industry to produce goods, 'especially if the war were to be of long duration'.[34]

Arms production was improved, but starting from a low level. In March 1915 Italy's two small-arms factories could only produce 14,400 rifles per month, quite insufficient for the enormous needs of the war. Cadorna therefore demanded increased production by all means, and proposed also using private industry, thus anticipating the industrial mobilization that began two months after Italian intervention. He made repeated demands before the ministry of war would supply wire-cutters, and even then the ministry delayed distributing them to the army. As from 9 July 1915, when the Supreme Munitions and Armaments Committee was founded, as part of the government's response to Cadorna's demands, 'industrial mobilization produced excellent results'. But at the time of entry the army possessed only 700 machine guns, despite his 'lively interest'. The mobile militia had no machine guns at all. Even the Alpine battalions only had 2 machine gun detachments, of which the second was often incomplete. The infantry had only 618 machine guns, on average two per regiment. The mountain guns were inferior to the Austro-Hungarian mountain artillery, and although the Italians had 192 heavy guns (modern Krupp 149 mm howitzers), these were too few for the tasks.[35]

On being informed of the intention to go to war Cadorna warned the government on 21 May that it would be mistaken to believe it would be a short war. On 1 July he demanded the recruitment of approximately 200,000 fresh troops to be equipped and ready for battle in spring 1916, together with as large a quantity as possible of all kinds of artillery.[36] However, Salandra told him in September 1915 that the state could not afford this vast expansion.

Cadorna's protestations about the government's failure to meet his demands have to be seen in their context. During the early years of the Fascist regime, Cadorna and Salandra, among others, pointed to the weaknesses of Italian military preparation in order to absolve themselves of responsibility for the disasters of the war. Yet the Italian army before 1915 was not as weak as portrayed by its post-war critics, Liberal or Fascist. On mobilization in 1915 it had 900,000 men, a force at least nine times that of the British Expeditionary Force of 1914, plus 350,000 in the territorial militia in the interior. Despite some shortcomings in weaponry, after 1907 the artillery had adopted the French 75 mm gun, the best in its class, and the fortifications on the border with Austria had been strengthened.[37]

Cadorna was not the ingénu he later portrayed himself to be, innocent of all political involvement. As the intervention crisis developed, power shifted increasingly towards the chief of the general staff. In August 1914 he had demanded mobilization, and in September active intervention, both of which were refused by the government, just as his demand for immediate war on Austria had been in 1912. It is true that Salandra, because of fears about the weakness of his parliamentary support, did not discuss his plans with Cadorna, but the latter nevertheless began planning an offensive war against Austria, because it was clearly becoming the most likely option.[38] Anticipating his disastrous and counter-productive wartime policy, Cadorna issued a circular to all officers on the eve of the declaration of war, on 19 May 1915, which stressed the importance of iron discipline and threatened immediate and severe punishments in case of infringement. It gave commanders the right to take the initiative and apply 'extreme measures of coercion and repression'. Punishment was to be immediate and was to serve as 'salutary example'.[39]

Mobilization itself began to reveal weaknesses in Italian preparations. The army was not assembled and ready at the front until six weeks after the declaration of war, mid-July. Cadorna's measures had brought the army up to a state of preparation suited to August 1914, but not that of July 1915. The Austro-Hungarian army was thought to have lost almost as many men as its establishment of 1914, or one and a quarter million casualties and missing out of 1.5 million, but by summer 1915 it had managed to fill the ranks with one million fresh recruits, and it was more accustomed to trench warfare and was better equipped in machine guns and artillery than the Italian army.[40]

Italy's contradictory war: from the 'holocaust of the volunteers' to millenarian visions of future consolation

The Italian war experience preceding Caporetto, the succession of twelve immensely bloody battles along the line of the river Isonzo, in the harsh conditions of the Carso plateau and in the Alps, has been discussed in Chapter 2. (See Map 3.) The near-catastrophe of the collapse in morale at Caporetto has often been read backwards in historical accounts to explain the entire Italian war effort from 1915 to 1917 as a prelude of inefficiency, miserable performance, and inevitable demoralization. But that was not how the Italian troops experienced war until then. Morale was surprisingly high at the beginning. One former member of the special assault units, the *arditi,* wrote after the war that the 'spirit of the *arditi*' was not confined to these units, but in the year 1915–16 was widespread in the army, even though he called it the 'year of the holocaust of the volunteers'.[41] The spirit of heroism, which was a reality as much as a construction, had its roots in the more or less willing self-sacrifice of thousands of ordinary soldiers.

But morale was slowly eroding after the countless human losses for little strategic gain, and suffered a knock in spring 1916. The Austro-Hungarian offensive in the Trentino Alps, May 1916, was called the '*Strafexpedition*' (punishment expedition): the troops had been incited to hatred of Italy for its 'betrayal', and told there would be rich booty to claim in wealthy Venetia.[42] Its real aim was to reach the Venetian plain and knock Italy out of the war. After initial Austrian gains, the Italian forces rallied and counter-attacked; the territorial loss was compensated to some extent by the conquest of Gorizia on the Isonzo front. Both sides registered a loss of morale, but when the disaster of Caporetto occurred the following year, the Italian military was actually on the upward portion of the learning curve. While Italian losses in the first six battles of the Isonzo had been far higher than Habsburg army losses, sometimes almost twice as numerous, the number of casualties in the seventh, eighth, and ninth battles were roughly equal on both sides. There had been vast improvements in weaponry: starting with only 700 machine guns in 1915, there were 12,000 available by October 1917; in addition, in the course of 1917 many infantrymen were equipped with the new light machine guns which could be carried by one man. There was a substantial increase in the number of artillery guns and the supply of shells was adequate. However, the Habsburg army had also made improvements and had benefited from the collapse of the Russian army. Italian losses in the eleventh battle of the Isonzo were once again almost double those of the Austrians.[43] The Italian air force, which was rapidly built up into superiority over the Austrian air force by 1918, was used mainly for reconnaissance; there was less bombing of civilian populations compared with the Austrian and German air forces (cf. Chapter 2).

Italian strategy was no more enlightened than that of the British, French, or Germans; its goal was to massacre the greatest possible number of Austro-Hungarians in a war of attrition on the enemy's human, economic, and moral resources.[44] That was a negative sum game until 1918. Yet Italy's war aims—the conquest of Habsburg territory—made an offensive war a military imperative. One result, as with the German offensive in 1914, was to convince the Italian commanders of the hostility of the population in the areas they invaded on both sides of the Isonzo in 1915. Everywhere they spotted spies and saboteurs, and reacted by taking hostages, arresting priests, and executing suspect civilians. The Slovene population was indeed predominantly pro-Habsburg in sympathies, but in fact passive in the face of the invasion. The echo of the (mainly invented) stories of the Belgian resistance produced a harsh policy of repression, and 70,000 people were interned. Italian propaganda for the troops stressed not only the moral necessity of the nation's cause, but also the need to 'execrate the enemy' and for a 'spirit of aggression'. In contrast to French and especially German propaganda, there was little sign of an Italian imputation that the enemy aimed to destroy Italy, still less of a will to annihilate the enemy. Propaganda proclaiming 'Delenda Austria!' was more a mimicry of Mazzinian rhetoric rather than a call to anything beyond normal military action. On the contrary, the army leadership despaired because Italian troops were notably lacking in aggressive spirit, were of a 'gentle disposition, disinclined to violence, and prepared to live and let live'.[45]

The Italian high command's solution was to impose ruthless discipline. As from the start, the 'Department of Discipline, Promotions and Justice' in the high command was given extensive powers by Cadorna. It urged the military tribunals to develop 'rigid and rapid action in support of the dual aim of severe repression and setting salutary examples'. In 1916 the supreme command further tightened the penal regime. Judges were exhorted to apply extensively the charge of 'desertion in the face of the enemy', which carried the death penalty. The increase in cases of collective indiscipline and especially of desertions in 1917 caused Cadorna to demand stern measures also against the domestic opposition, which he blamed for seditious propaganda. If the government failed to respond, Cadorna threatened to extend the army's own measures to include the death penalty 'applied immediately in an exemplary manner to a large number of soldiers'. The Italian army duly executed some 750 soldiers after court martial trials. In addition, a policy known as 'decimation' was used. The idea came from the stern punishment meted out by the Roman army in the period of the Republic when all the soldiers of a unit were alleged to be guilty of grave acts of indiscipline or cowardice: one man in ten (or in some cases one in 20 or 100) was selected for exemplary punishment, usually the death sentence. In 1915–18, some 250 men were executed under this policy, unique to Italy in the First World War.[46] The entire system of military discipline was condemned by the secret parliamentary sessions that debated Caporetto, and the practice was condemned by one witness in the Commission of Inquiry as 'savage, not justified by anything'. But Cadorna refused to abandon the measure, and his successor applied it throughout the army, also for less grave offences. In addition, a large but unknown number of soldiers were killed in summary punishments in the field, and others were killed by machine guns posted behind the attacking soldiers for refusing to advance.[47]

The vast extent of Italian military discipline can be seen in the figures. The total army size was 4.2 million men serving at the front; a total 356,188 men and officers were court-martialled. In other words, one in twelve was subjected to court martial proceedings, and one man in 24 was convicted. The 750 executions (plus the 250 killed in decimations) may be compared with military discipline in France, Britain, and Germany: despite the greater length of their participation in the war and larger armies, they implemented fewer death sentences: France 500–600, Britain 346, and Germany 48.[48]

Caporetto nevertheless forced a major rethink. The reorganization of the armed forces, the massive rearmament, and the remobilization of the nation, produced a significant increase in destructive capacity over the course of 1918. Despite the loss of many guns in the retreat, by June 1918 every aspect of the artillery had been improved. In 1915 a total of 3.3 million shells were fired, 7.9 in 1916, 16.5 million in 1917, and 14 million in 1918, but given there were only two major battles, the intensity of fire was greatly increased.[49]

In another respect, too, Italy's capacity for violence was greatly enhanced. The formation of special assault units, the *arditi*, in summer 1917, actually predated Caporetto. After reorganization in 1918 there were 39 assault units with a total of about 24,000 men in autumn; if the casualties since August 1917 are added, a total of 30,000 or 35,000 men served as *arditi*. The *arditi* were modelled on the storm troops of the Austro-Hungarian army. The difference was that while the *Sturmtruppen* remained a part of the larger infantry units from which they were formed, in order to lead and encourage the demoralized masses, the *arditi* were separate units, since the morale of the Italian infantry had generally remained intact. Even the rout of Caporetto did not change the policy: the *arditi* had an autonomous role in battle. Special assault units had a marginal role in the countries and armies which remained strong, while in Italy and Austria-Hungary, which showed greater signs of internal weakness, they played a more important role.[50]

The *arditi* were given intensive training, especially with their weapons, of which the mainstays were automatic rifles, hand-grenades, and daggers. In order to overcome the immobility of trench warfare, they engaged in face-to-face combat. The dagger, which underlined the intimate nature of their killing, its danger, and its bloodiness, became their symbol. Their privileges, prestige, and successes meant that their morale was far superior to that of other troops, and they departed for each battle 'in the highest corporate spirits and with exceptional aggressivity'. As one veteran wrote, 'The *arditi* of the 2nd Army departed for action each time not with the resigned calm of those who do a duty, . . . but with explosions of barbaric joy [they] spread the smell of a carnevalesque orgy before the imminent battle.'[51]

Yet praise was mingled with misgivings. Colonel Gatti, historian and propagandist of the *Comando supremo*, wrote in his diary on 6 September 1917:

> [The *arditi*] go into battle without rifles, but with hand-grenades and knives: each company has a machine gun section. Wherever there is an enemy machine gun or a trench to be taken, the grenade-throwers, who always work in pairs (one hands up the grenades, the other throws), throw a smoke bomb, then the squad smothers the machine gun with grenades . . . After the grenade squads the flame-thrower squads advance, . . . who launch burning liquid over everyone. Both units operate without harming each other.
>
> . . . When they return from action the soldiers say to each other: I killed six of them, eight, ten. Each one is proud of his stabbing, and experiments in the best way of clearing out the adversary. All this is very good for the war, but for the peace? Alas, I can imagine already what these men will do who no longer know the value of human life.[52]

Gatti was acknowledging the danger presented by the transformation of young men into fanatical killers, who lack the psychological protection of killing at a distance, as with most infantry and artillerymen who seldom see their victims at close quarters. Even the professional officer had cause for concern for the subsequent peace.

Gatti's fear was not misplaced. Rather than the memory of the industrial production of death, whether of the enemy or the heartless slaughter of Italy's own infantry, it was the myth of the fierce, young, efficient, modern, but individual fighter of the *arditi* which emerged as the predominant model for nationalist and fascist Italy after the war. Yet this image veiled the contradiction that the First World War brought modernity to the masses, to the peasant masses above all who were the majority of the Italian army and had not previously known modernity—electricity, cinema, aircraft, mass communications, and the destructivity of modern weapons.[53]

The Italian civilians' experience of war was a contradictory mix of forced modernization with ruthless treatment by the state and employers. Civilian

mortality rose owing to the hardships caused by war: consumption of
food was restricted to provide the soldiers with good rations; there were
shortages of essential medicine, causing increases in death from malaria and
other diseases; and dangerous conditions in industry (e.g. in explosives
production) also caused illness and accidents. It was calculated that there
was an excess civilian mortality of 546,450 during the war, or 1.5 per cent, a
far higher rate than that in Germany.[54] This was due to the incompetence of
the Italian state and its political priorities. Although Italy's maritime imports
were curtailed by submarine warfare, Italy was not as dependent on imports
as Britain, nor did submarine warfare pose such a grave threat. Yet the
mortality rate of the civilian population was higher than in France or
Britain. In Britain the poor actually improved their standard of provisions,
which helped to ensure their loyalty; pay rates for unskilled workers were
considerably increased, and progressive taxation helped to create a system of
redistribution of collective burdens. These political choices enabled France
and Britain to consolidate popular support for democracy, even in the face
of growing wartime and post-war tensions. As the social historian Giovanna
Procacci has shown, in Italy, instead, 'growing hardship, accompanied by
the conviction of inefficiency and social partiality on the part of the state,
exacerbated the pre-existing sentiments of hostility'.[55]

The key shift in Italian war politics came in autumn 1917. Every wartime
state faced tensions, especially in the crisis year 1917: in Germany they were
resolved with the army leadership forcing the resignation of chancellor
Bethmann Hollweg and imposing a civilian government that was under
their control; in France the crisis over the mutinies of 1917 was resolved by
a flexible mix of repression of soldiers' dissent and improvements in conditions and a change in offensive strategy, above all by the civilian government under Clemenceau asserting overall control over conduct of the war.
In Italy, by contrast, Generalissimo Cadorna denied the government any
input into military policy, to the extent that even war minister Bissolati was
prevented from entering the war zone.[56] After anti-war agitation in May
1917 and the suspension of the tenth battle of the Isonzo, General Cadorna
sent four letters to prime minister Boselli, in which he laid the blame for the
indiscipline in the army and its failures upon the Socialists, and demanded of
the government exceptional measures to deal with the 'internal enemies'.
With the internal situation close to collapse and the cohesion of the army
beginning to disintegrate, the Socialists and the Giolittian Liberals might
have come to power to sue for immediate peace. The interventionist press

thus began to emphasize the similarity between the Italian Socialists and the Russian Bolsheviks (for example, *Popolo d'Italia*, 17 June 1917).[57] The interventionists, whether Liberals, nationalists, or followers of Mussolini, called for violent repression of 'internal enemies', especially the Socialist Party.

The pro-war movement was then rent by disagreement over how to deal with dissent. Cadorna toyed with the idea of a coup to install a military dictatorship, which would have to be preceded by a kind of interventionist mass mobilization in the piazze like that of 1915, but foreign minister Sidney Sonnino, who was regarded by the militarists as their last hope, denounced it in a secret session of the Chamber in June as a danger to the country, and interior minister Orlando condemned the 'comitati di irresponsabili' who wished to unleash civil war. Cadorna himself came under criticism for his failed military leadership, as he was attacked by General Marazzi. The anti-war movement of the Socialists and Giolittians appeared to be unstoppable. Workers in the industrial triangle of northern Italy increasingly voiced their protest at poor wages and lack of food, demanding bread and peace. In August 1917 a spontaneous strike of 100,000 workers in Turin turned into massive demonstration that threatened to take over the city, conjuring up for the ruling elites the nightmare vision of a popular rebellion against the war and the state itself. The uprising was ruthlessly suppressed as elite units of *Alpini* killed dozens of workers.

In a crisis session of the Chamber of 16 October, a few days before Caporetto, which began on 24 October, the army and the government came under severe criticism from Socialists, Giolittians, and also the left-interventionists, to which Bissolati gave a notorious, over-excited reply: 'To defend the army I would also give orders to open fire on you.'[58] The news of Caporetto plunged the government into a crisis, and finance minister Nitti wrote in a telegram to the new prime minister Orlando that Italy was already in 'a revolutionary phase'. The king talked of abdication, and there were rumours of an impending declaration of the republic. Cadorna raged at 'treachery' by internal enemies, and Bissolati claimed, somewhat more accurately, that the cause of the defeat was a 'military strike', a term he coined. With their anti-socialist campaign and demands for a strong government the interventionists had succeeded in creating a state of paranoia; an 'insane and noxious ferment', as the Socialist Anna Kuliscioff wrote, spread throughout the country. Even the news of the Bolshevik Revolution was overshadowed by Caporetto, but fears that the collapse of the Russian front would mean increased pressure on Italy were allayed by news that the French were sending troops to the Italian front, and that the USA had finally declared war against Austria-Hungary. The Italian Socialists' support of the Bolsheviks made it easier for them to be isolated by their enemies, lending credence to the idea that Caporetto was the work of defeatist Socialists, which the Socialists denied. Even Giolitti and his followers supported the newly formed group of interventionists in parliament, which was powerful enough to control government policy for a time.[59]

As the military situation improved after Caporetto, the internal political climate relaxed again somewhat, and the mood of paranoia receded. However, in this period millenarian visions of future consolation increasingly took hold, offering an escape from the horrors of the present. Frequently, these visions were closely connected with the notion of the apocalypse in which the 'other'—evil in whatever form—would be destroyed. Even the government participated in the spiralling competition, making rash promises that raised inordinately the hopes of the peasant soldiers for the post-war period. The enormous sacrifice had to be worthwhile: about 650,000 Italian soldiers died in the war (including prisoners of war, those who died of illnesses, and from injuries shortly after the war).[60] The proportion of mobilized soldiers who died was 11.6 per cent, somewhat lower than that of Germany and Austria, but similar to that of the UK. Italy's own logic of annihilation, which was above all enormously self-destructive, produced a regime of internal repression and also supercharged the pressure of utopian expectations—whether in the guise of socialism, or nationalism, or, as soon became apparent, of an entirely new form of mass politics that combined internal war and a state form that expressly continued the wartime regime of national mobilization (see Chapter 8).

The Balkan Wars, 1912 and 1913: wars of culture or prelude to genocide?

The two Balkan wars resulted essentially from the decline of the Ottoman and Habsburg empires confronted by national independence movements in the region. (See Map 4.) Seen in the historical long term, the process of nation-state formation in the Balkans threatened the integrity of both great multinational empires. Serbia had achieved autonomy within the Ottoman

Map 4. The Balkans

empire in 1830, and became fully sovereign in 1878, as did Montenegro and Romania; Bulgaria gained independence in 1886. All the Balkan nations had rulers or would-be rulers who discovered that nationalism was a useful tool to legitimate their own authority and who voiced ambitions to extend the national territory to include not only areas in which their ethnic group was the majority, but also mixed areas where they could stake some historical or cultural claim.[61] In addition, by the turn of the century each country had a nationalist movement consisting of the younger generation of intellectuals which aimed for social revolution to break up traditional power structures.

An additional factor in the equation was greater Serb nationalism, the movement for south Slav unity under Serb leadership.

Long before they engaged in a military campaign, the Balkan nations were waging a cultural war against both the Ottoman and Habsburg empires. A survey of Serbian schoolbooks conducted by the Habsburg legation in Belgrade before the July crisis of 1914 concluded that they were brimming with nationalist ideas: there were many references to the oppression of Serbian people living in the Habsburg empire and to the idea that Bosnia, Herzegovina, and Croatia all belonged to the Serb nation. They stressed that Croats and Serbs were one people; the population of Bosnia allegedly consisted only of Serbs divided into three religious confessions.[62] Serbia was not alone in playing with the fire of nationalist myth-making. Thus an intermittent struggle for the possession of Macedonia, one of the last remaining Ottoman territories in Europe, began in 1878, lasting until 1913, and is not fully resolved to this day. Macedonia was a territory of geostrategic importance for Serbia, Bulgaria, and Greece, as well as for the Great Powers. Serbia, Bulgaria, and Greece engaged in a 'regular battle for predominance' with the weapons of the churches, education, and national societies. One such Bulgarian national society engaged in terror attacks on villagers and assassinations of Turks, hoping to call down reprisals on the population which would force it to revolt. The Greeks and Serbs joined in with more violence; foreign observers reported that all sides committed atrocities.[63]

There was also acute competition between Croatian and Serb nationalisms in Bosnia-Herzegovina, occupied by Austria-Hungary since 1878, with a population of 20 per cent Croats, 43 per cent Serbs, and the remaining third Muslims. In the period of strong antagonism between Serbs and Croats from 1878 to 1903 the Serbian governments worked closely with Vienna; in Croatia, ruled by a Hungarian governor, the empire successfully increased hostility through a policy of divide and rule—by favouring Serbs in employment and education. Violence between Serbs and Croats in Croatia prompted some Serbs in Belgrade to 'demand a war of extermination between the two South Slav peoples'. Although King Peter, who had been brought to power by the army in 1903, was sympathetic to the idea of 'Yugoslavism', the dominant forces in army and government directed their attention instead towards the goal of creating a great Serbian state to unite lands that were ethnically or historically Serbian. However, the army differed from the government by its willingness to risk war, while the government was wary of the dangers of an expansionist foreign policy.

After Austria-Hungary's formal annexation of Bosnia-Herzegovina in 1908 the Serb government realized it had to back down, while the army drew the opposite conclusion and decided to prepare for military action in the next crisis in order to expand Serbia.[64]

The Austro-Hungarian government also pursued policies of abrasive nationalism, though usually without the violent edge of the Balkan states. The policy combined colonial-type rule with cultural imperialism, which proved to be counter-productive to the end of stabilizing Habsburg hegemony. In 1886 there were 16,275 Austro-Hungarian subjects in Bosnia and Herzegovina, and by 1910 there were 108,000. The number of German schools was increased. General Potiorek advocated a policy of favouring the Roman Catholic church, and called for the construction of many new churches, in order to reduce the influence of the Eastern Orthodox Serbs and Muslims. Archduke Franz Ferdinand also demanded priority for Catholics and the conversion of Serbs to Catholicism.[65]

The First Balkan War was triggered by the attempt of the Young Turk rulers to reconstruct and modernize the Ottoman empire, by abolishing the rights and privileges of the Christian nationalities—a programme of 'Ottomanization'.[66] Prompted by the apparent ease with which Italy triumphed in Libya, in October 1912 Serbia, Greece, Montenegro, and Bulgaria launched a war on the Ottoman empire, jointly conquering Macedonia and Thrace. Austria-Hungary, which ruled over Slovenia, Croatia, and Bosnia-Herzegovina and feared Serbia's increasing influence in the region, insisted that Albania should be set up as sovereign state, thus blocking Serbia's access to the sea. The Balkan allies began to quarrel over the territory they had gained, and in a second war in 1913 Bulgaria attacked Serbia and Greece over Macedonia, but was defeated. Romania then attacked Bulgaria, gaining the Dobrudja, and Turkey reconquered some of Thrace.

The Balkan wars truly prefigured twentieth-century warfare, combining the attributes of modern technology, national liberation, war on the enemy's culture, and war on civilians. Soldiers and civilians alike suffered all the horrendous effects of modern warfare, but without the protection offered by modern infrastructure like sanitation and adequate medical treatment. State-of-the-art warfare meant the first use in the history of war of wireless telegraphy and aerial reconnaissance (for example, the deployment of Bulgarian aircraft in the fighting at Catalca).[67] Austro-Hungarian medical officers observed for the first time the terrible injuries caused by shells from the Serbian artillery, the modern guns recently purchased from the French company Schneider-Creusot, but they also reported that the medical orderlies in the Bulgarian army in 1913 had no bandages, there were no chemicals to combat lice, and that no latrines were dug. There were outbreaks of malaria and cholera, and the injuries caused by modern weapons were often left untreated or were badly treated.[68]

It might be thought that the Balkan wars, with the flagrant contrast of lethal modernity and backward squalor, aircraft and no latrines, mass military casualties combined with terrible consequences for civilian populations, were exceptional in the era of the Great War. In fact, the western front was the exception, but only in that it combined industrialized mass killing with excellent medical care and sanitation, while the eastern front and fighting in the Balkans and the Near East closely resembled warfare in the Balkans in 1912 and 1913, with endemic disease and mass fatalities among civilians. During the Balkan wars, all sides committed atrocities on enemy civilians. Propaganda claims exaggerated the extent, and the investigation of the validity of the competing allegations still awaits its modern scholarly researcher. According to a Greek publication of 1913, the Bulgarian army massacred 220,000 to 250,000 civilians in Macedonia and Thrace.[69] This figure was greatly overstated, but there is no doubt that significant massacres occurred. Austro-Hungarian medical officers were told by the wounded that injured men left behind on the battlefield had been massacred by the Greeks. Civilians, mainly Muslim Bulgarians, fled before the advancing Greeks.[70]

The atrocities were not merely a discrete phenomenon, a short-term by-product of war. They were part of a longer-term project of nation-state construction on the basis of the chimera of 'ethnic' purity. The south Slav peoples were indeed mainly of the same ethnic origin, but divided by historical development: many Muslims in the region were, historically speaking, recent converts and not ethnically different from their neighbours; Croatians and Serbs speak essentially the same language. The differences in religion and culture between Eastern Orthodox Serbs, Catholic Croatians, and Muslims had been exploited by the Habsburg and Ottoman rulers in the spirit of *divide et impera*. Yet for all their rhetoric of south Slav unity, the Serbs treated the populations in the 'liberated' territories harshly in the aftermath of the Balkan wars, especially Muslims and those suspected of having sympathized with Bulgaria. There were frequent rapes, including rapes of Muslim women.[71] Of the thirty-two mosques in Prizren (Kosovo), only two were used for worship in early 1914. The rest were being used as stables, hay stores, and barracks. Serb soldiers made it difficult for Muslims to observe their religion, mocking with laughter the muezzins' calls to prayer. Villages were destroyed, and others were preserved from destruction only by the payment of bribes to the new masters.[72] The Austro-Hungarian envoy in Belgrade, Giesl, reported that the violent acts of the Serbian authorities in the new territories, including pillage, arson, and executions, were terrorizing the population, causing many non-Serbian people to flee the country.[73] Under the impact of the world war, the miseries of the Balkan wars and the atrocities were soon forgotten, at least in the western public sphere and in historical memory. For that reason, they remain under-researched to this day.

Yet the atrocities figured prominently in the international public sphere at the time. Newspapers across Europe, such as *The Times* and the *Frankfurter Zeitung*, carried on 14 July the protest addressed by King Constantine of Greece 'to the whole civilized world' condemning the Bulgarian 'outrages'; he warned that he was 'compelled to take vengeance in order to inspire terror into these monsters'.[74] A few days later King Ferdinand of Bulgaria issued an appeal to Europe against the Turkish invasion and massacres in Thrace, which *The Times* held to be 'fully justified by the facts of the case'.[75] Both the British and the German press reported extensively, even-handedly condemning the perpetrators where the evidence appeared convincing. *The Times* noted in a tone of resignation the 'flood of charges and coun-ter-charges of atrocities on the part of the belligerents', which it would be impossible to investigate. For *The Times* it was self-evident that Europe was a superior, more civilized place than the Balkans: 'The lower instincts of human nature have prevailed, and the Balkan Peninsula is threatened with a return of the conditions which prevailed in the Middle Ages. The horrors which have taken place at Kukush, Nigrita, and elsewhere recall the most hideous features of medieval warfare, and civilized Europe witnesses unmoved the triumph of lawlessness and barbarity.'[76] The *Frankfurter Zeitung* stated that it had received plausible reports, confirmed by impartial European observers, that Serbs, Greeks, and Bulgarians had all committed massacres in Macedonia and Albania. The worst, it said, were the Serbs, who had declared that the Albanians 'must be eradicated'. The Bulgarians had been guilty of 'the most terrible atrocities' against the Muslim popula-tion; the Greeks had committed serious crimes against the Muslim and Jewish inhabitants of Saloniki. There was a report on the massacre of over 200 Bulgarian and Turkish civilians and wounded soldiers by Greek soldiers at Seres in the *Frankfurter Zeitung* of 15 July, and another on 'Bulgarian

Atrocities' alleged by the Greek government on 16 July. The German satirical weekly *Simplicissimus* published a cartoon entitled 'The Greeks in Epirus', which depicted against a background of burning, destroyed houses and corpses of civilians a Greek soldier, wearing headgear with long tassel, kilt, shoes with pompoms, nonchalantly lighting a cigarette, saying to a photo-journalist who might be American, British, or German: 'Of course we kill the women and children—the men might defend themselves!'[77]

The international public condemnation of the atrocities culminated in the publication in early 1914 of the *Report of the International Commission to Inquire into the Causes and Conduct of the Balkan Wars* under the auspices of the Carnegie Endowment for International Peace, an American philanthropic foundation which engaged the voluntary services of men such as Baron d'Estournelles de Constant, who had represented France at the Hague conferences of 1899 and 1907; Professor Walther Schücking from Germany; from Britain Francis Hirst, editor of *The Economist*; and the Russian Constitutional Democrat leader and history professor Pavel Miliukov. This remarkably well-documented and impartial investigation, coolly sceptical of exaggerated claims, reached conclusions that have not been improved upon to this day.[78] The Muslim population of Macedonia had endured 'lawless vengeance and unmeasured suffering' at the hands of Greek, Serbian, and Bulgarian troops and irregulars in the first war; in many cases entire villages were burned by their Christian neighbours. It estimated that 700 to 800 were killed in and around Strumnica. In the Second Balkan War, it acknowledged that Greek civilians had been the victims of Bulgarian violence, but found the original Greek accusations to be untrustworthy. Probably 500 Greeks were killed at Doxato, 200 Bulgarians at Seres/Serres, and there were mutual killings of Greeks and Bulgarians at Demir-Hissar.[79] Muslims and Greeks were forced to abandon their homes in the part of Macedonia occupied by Bulgaria under threat of massacre, and there were forced conversions to Bulgarian nationality and from Islam to Christianity. There were massacres of Greeks, Bulgarians, Turks, and Armenians in Adrianople (today Edirne) and elsewhere in Thrace in the period March to July 1913, with 'many thousands' killed.[80] Serbian and Montenegrin troops committed mass violence 'with a view to the entire transformation of the ethnic character of regions inhabited exclusively by Albanians'. At Ohrid 150 Bulgarians and 500 Turks and Albanians were killed by Serb forces, and throughout Serbian Macedonia the new regime attempted to impose its culture and Orthodox religion.[81] If the rape of women and girls was 'widespread and almost universal' in the Balkan wars, as the Carnegie Commission found,[82] we can assume it was a systematic policy of ethnic warfare: this form of extreme dehumanizing behaviour is often the prelude to genocide.[83]

The killing stopped somewhere short of genocide, but the Carnegie Commission found that all the belligerents had violated the laws and customs of land warfare, in particular the Hague Convention of 1907, which had been signed by all the powers but 'remained unknown to the Balkan armies generally'. Yet even the Geneva Convention, which established the principle that wounded prisoners should be given the same treatment as the wounded of one's own side and was generally made known, was often broken. In one case, out of 1,200 Bulgarian prisoners taken by Greek soldiers, only forty-one survived.[84] Apart from destruction necessitated by military requirements, such as bridges blown up, there was widespread wanton pillage and destruction, with hundreds of villages burned. The cost of the wars was immense. The commission estimated that Bulgaria lost 52,716 military killed and missing, Serbia approximately 30,000 (as we saw in Chapter 3, the total in Serbia was probably over 70,000, including deaths from disease). As a result of expulsion and flight, about 156,000 people took refuge in Greece, 104,000 in Bulgaria, and more than 200,000 Turks were driven out by the Greeks and Bulgarians.[85]

More prophetically than it can have imaged, the Carnegie Commission concluded that the Second Balkan War 'was only the beginning of other wars, or rather of a continuous war, the worst of all, a war of religion, of reprisals, of race, a war of one people against another, of man against man and brother against brother. It has become a competition, as to who can best dispossess and "denationalize" his neighbor.'[86]

In another more or less forgotten corner of the Balkans and Asia Minor, there were mass population expulsions which presaged the events of 1915 to 1923. In early 1914 terror bands under the direction of the later president of the Turkish republic, Celal Bayar, expelled 130,000 people, mainly Greeks but also Armenians, from the Izmir region, Thrace, and the Aegean coastline into Greece. This was part of a cultural war in the period 1912–14: 'Turkification' of the Greek population, restrictions on instruction in Greek language, compulsory enlistment of Christians in labour battalions, and forced labour under harsh conditions. Turkish ethnic nationalism and Islamism were to replace the multi-ethnic and multi-confessional character of the Ottoman empire. In secret meetings of the Young Turk central committee

with the so-called 'Special Organization' in spring and summer 1914 'popu-
lation-technical' measures were called for, with the aim of the 'liquidation of
non-Turkish settlements in strategically important positions which are in
contact with foreign interests'. By the end of 1914, 1,150,000 people, mainly
Greeks, had been deported.[87] The fears of the Carnegie Commission, then,
were being confirmed in the continuation of the cultural war, mass killing,
and population transfer, even before the World War broke out. Why the
Balkan wars and also the other wars in this immediate era (Italy's invasion of
Libya, the population expulsions in Turkey) took on the character of such
extreme brutality and systematic violence against non-combatants cannot
be explained by the backwardness of these regions. It is the very modernity
of these developments which is their striking hallmark. Just as in the First
World War, and still more in the Second, modern (and modernizing)
ideologies of nationalism, race, and the pseudo-scientific discourses of hygiene
and purity, combined with the revolution in fire power and communications
to draw in ever broader swathes of society as victims—and as perpetrators.
Moreover, in states where traditions of civil society, democracy, and the
discourse of the rights of man were weak, the thin veneer of protection
afforded by international humanitarian law was easily broken.

The Balkans in the Great War

The pattern in the Great War in the Balkans remained unchanged from the
wars of 1912–13, except for the intervention of much larger powers. (See
Map 4.) The Austro-Hungarian war on Serbia was accompanied by mass
violence against civilians on its own territory in Bosnia, especially those
suspected of having been involved in conspiracy to destabilize the empire.
Members of the secret Young Bosnian organization were arrested in Sarajevo
and elsewhere in Bosnia-Herzegovina, including forty schoolboys in Tuzla
and sixty-five members in Sarajevo. Auxiliary units made up of Muslims and
Croats took revenge on the Serb population, in one case hanging Serb civilians
from the bridge over the Drina at Višegrad (the event features in the last part of
the epic historical novel by the Nobel laureate Ivo Andrić, *The Bridge over
the Drina*).[88] By the end of July 1914, 5,000 Serbs were in jail, and within a
few months 150 had been executed. This turned into a war on Serbian culture
in Bosnia, in which Cyrillic script was officially banned and denomin-
ational schools were closed. In 1915 156 Bosnian Serb intellectuals, including

professors, teachers, priests, and students, were put on trial. Concentration camps were set up in which tens of thousands of Serbs were interned, among them Andrić; many suffered under starvation conditions, and few survived.[89]

In Berchtold's 'final and fundamental reckoning' with Serbia, the Austro-Hungarian army devastated Serbia, but it was a disaster for the Habsburg forces, too. The invasion at the end of July 1914 went badly wrong, and the Serbs repelled them, even invading Bosnia. The success prompted the Serb government to revive its plans for a Greater Serbia, aiming to extend its rule to all regions where Serbian was spoken, to Bosnia, Herzegovina, Dalmatia, Croatia, and Slavonia.[90]

In November, however, the Serbs were forced to retreat, mainly owing to lack of ammunition. The Austro-Hungarian armies captured Belgrade on 1 December, and occupied a large part of the country. With the aid of fresh supplies of artillery ammunition from France, the Serb forces launched a counter-offensive which imposed heavy losses on the invaders, and succeeded in ejecting them by mid-December.[91] They even conquered a part of central Albania. But at great cost: by the end of 1914 between 125,000 and 175,000 Serbian troops had been killed, wounded, or taken prisoner; lethal epidemics, including cholera, smallpox, and four forms of typhus, ravaged the country, and by February 1915 the strength of the army was no greater than 270,000.[92]

In the Austro-Hungarian army rumours abounded of atrocities committed by civilians and civilian irregulars on soldiers: mutilations of the wounded and attacks from ambush by civilians, including women. In turn, the troops committed atrocities on injured and captured Serb soldiers, and on civilians. On one hand, it was clear that some atrocity accusations were invented: the writer and war reporter Egon Erwin Kisch described the Austro-Hungarian retreat across the Drina in September 1914 as a 'witches' sabbath', in which hundreds of injured and sick men were left by the river bank, some fighting to get across on pontoons, hundreds drowning. His regiment covered up the news of the disaster by accusing the Serbs of having shot captives and wounded.[93] On the other hand, with their recent history of brutality against non-combatants, it was unlikely the Serbs had begun to respect international law in the meantime. But between 3,500 and 4,000 Serb civilians were killed in executions and random violence by marauding troops, mainly in 1914. In 1915 Austria-Hungary made a renewed attempt at invasion, supported this time by German and Bulgarian forces. Their massive superiority in numbers and equipment forced the Serbs to withdraw from

Belgrade and Niš in October/November, and the remnant of the army retreated across the mountains of Albania to the Adriatic Sea, taking with them civilians and more than 20,000 Austro-Hungarian prisoners of war. This epic, well known in Serb national narrative, was a hunger march under terrible conditions, and many fell ill and died from exhaustion and sickness. The Allies shipped the Serbs to Corfu, which the French cleared of its inhabitants, to enable the Serb army to recuperate. The Italians took over the majority of Habsburg prisoners, and transferred them to the uninhabited island of Asinara (off the coast of Sardinia). Cholera and typhus broke out already during the sea crossing from Albania (or were already present), and between 1,500 and 7,000 died. The hospital consisted of tents, the men lacked water, and there were no proper stone-made buildings.[94] This letter by an Austro-Hungarian prisoner medical officer writing from Asinara illustrates the conditions of the death march across Serbia and Albania to Valona (today Vlorë):

[October 1915] . . . Then we Austro-Hungarian medical officers went by train to Čačak where we stayed for a week . . . One day we received orders to prepare to depart . . . We loaded the wagons and left for Kraljevo, and from there to Kaska, and then to Mitrovica. Until here everything went well; above all, we had enough to eat and were treated well considering the circumstances. We stayed several days at Mitrovica . . . From then on things got much worse; we had to march on foot, although the baggage was transported, and so we marched two days to Prizrend [sic: probably Prizren in Kosovo]. Here the conditions deteriorated; we were assigned to the combat officer prisoners. Each of the officers had to carry his own baggage, and we received something to eat plus bread only once a day, and that only in principle, and it got worse. From Prizrend to Dobra we marched across Albania; the weather was terrible: wind and rain, we were soaked every day, and were unable to sleep for cold. Sometimes we stayed around the fire to sleep in a sitting position. Many officers' boots wore out, and they had to continue walking barefoot. At Dobra there was nothing to buy but dried chestnuts, which was all we had to eat one day. From Dobra to Struga we had to march towards Monastir; we were happy because we were looking forward to a calm stage. But there was another misfortune! At half way we had to turn round and go back via Struga to Elbassan: it was snowing and terribly cold, there was no bread, nothing to eat: we ate uncooked maize, and we were content to be able to buy at high price this horrid food. From Elbassan we went to Cavaja [Kavajë] and from there to Valona. The march between Cavaja and Valona was indescribable: marshes, peat bogs. For hours we trudged through water and then slept in the open on the wet ground; of course, nothing to eat. In Valona we received food in abundance; we wanted nothing but to eat and sleep: we were saved.

That is where the story of our Albanian voyage ends. You can imagine that if our officers suffered like this, how badly the poor soldier prisoners fared. The route was strewn with the bodies of prisoners who died of cold and hunger...We have nothing left, everything is ruined...We are now prisoners of Italy and Italy treats the prisoners of war very well—as human beings, and that says everything.[95]

Serbia was almost completely occupied, and it was divided up between the Habsburg empire and Bulgaria. Uprisings against the military regime were crushed with severity, in which thousands of Serbs lost their lives, many again in executions. (See Fig. 6. According to the caption on the photograph, in 1917 partisans renewed the attack on the occupation, destroying railway lines and reaching within four kilometres of Niš.) Bulgarian troops, too, committed widespread atrocities in their invasion of Serbia.[96] The Serb army returned in 1918 to find a land devastated by war and exploitation; Serbia had suffered proportionately the highest military losses and the highest total losses of any belligerent country (250,000 soldiers and 300,000 civilians out of 3.1 million). Yet the Austro-Hungarian forces had fared no better.[97] Austro-Hungarian losses amounted to 273,000 men out of

Figure 6. Public execution of alleged Serb partisans by Habsburg troops

450,000 troops deployed in Serbia during the war.[98] Such extraordinary losses, and the harsh treatment of non-combatants on both sides, indicates a variation of the pattern on the western front. Not only was war on the south-eastern front by intention a war of annihilation to destroy the Serb state, but also in fact, largely because of the opportunities offered by a war of movement and anti-partisan warfare. Moreover, warfare in the Balkans meant modern destructiveness in a region with a weak infrastructure that had already been heavily damaged in previous wars, where the reserves of the economy and the population were already depleted.

Turkey and the expulsion of the Greek community

Why did the Ottoman empire enter the war? This was a state that had suffered defeats at the hands of Italy in Libya in 1911 and had been forced to give up most of its remaining European possessions in the Balkan wars of 1912 and 1913. In the years before 1914 the empire was racked by rebellions: by Kurds in Anatolia, Druses in Syria, and Arabs in Yemen, which were all put down by military intervention.[99] Its army was in a parlous condition, and there were massive internal tensions in Anatolian society, especially between the majority Turks and the large minority groups. The empire, with its ancient ways and Byzantine administration, was visibly disintegrating in the face of modern national movements. These were perceived by the Ottoman Turkish elite as a conspiracy by the European powers to break up the empire and snatch the booty.[100]

Several factors played a role in the decision to enter the war, taken in late October 1914. For one, the Young Turks feared that neutrality would tempt the victors at the end of the war to dismember the tottering empire. For another, they regarded war as the opportunity to enhance their domination within the empire, accelerate the pace of Turkification under way since their revolution in 1908, redraw the ethnic map and attain the nationalist utopia of an ethnically 'pure' Turkish state. (See Map 5.) Victory alongside Germany would remove the threat of Russian invasion and shatter the Russian imperialist dream of control over the Straits. Collaboration with Germany would enable the empire to rebuff Anglo-French influence in the Middle East.[101]

Turkification meant that the anti-Greek policy was continued into the war. In the region of Kerasounda, for example, 88 Greek villages were

Map 5. Ottoman Turkey

burned in the months December 1916 to February 1917, according to the Greek government:

> [Their 30,000 inhabitants] . . . , mostly women, children and old men, were taken by force to the district of Ancyra (Angora) [i.e. Ankara], in the harshest winter weather, and at a time when epidemics were rife, without their being permitted to take even their clothing with them. Of this population one-fourth perished on the road in consequence of the hardships, starvation and exposure.

The ethnic war was part of a campaign for the modernization of the Turks. Not only were food and other goods requisitioned from the Greeks, contributions were exacted in money for the purpose of erecting barracks, installing telephones, building Muslim schools, or buying farm equipment. Greeks who refused to pay were flogged and imprisoned. Turks were forbidden to repay their debts to Christians and were no longer to pay rent to Christian owners of farms. By these, and other means, the material prosperity of the Greek population was ruined. Greek boys who had become orphans because their parents were killed, or who were taken away from their families, were placed in the 'Orphan Institutions' at Panormo, funded by exactions from the Greek community. Here the boys were converted to Islam. Girls were 'abducted' and placed in Muslim families.[102]

The Greek government alleged a policy of rape of women and girls, torturing men, and committing 'scattered murders', especially of prominent members of the Greek community, in order to terrorize the population and

force them to leave their homes.[103] In 1913, negotiations were started with
the Greek government for the 'voluntary' exchange of Greeks from the
Aegean coast of Turkey for Turks from Greece. The war prevented the
population transfer; instead, the hundreds of thousands of Greeks were
deported to the interior of Anatolia, the islands, and Cilicia, and used as
forced labour in agriculture and for the transport of army supplies. Was it
true, as the Carnegie Commission contributor Ahmed Emin wrote, that
'the Greeks suffered relatively little by the World War'? Emin admitted
there had been deportations, but these were 'more or less a matter of
military necessity'.[104] Certainly, in contrast with the Armenian deportations
the Greeks were not intended to be eliminated, but no doubt 'many
thousands' died in the process.[105]

After the war, the Greeks established a harsh occupation of the Aegean
littoral. In pursuit of the goal of the return to Greece of Constantinople
and an Anatolian Greek empire, Greek forces invaded Anatolia, and committed atrocities upon the Turks, burning and looting villages; according
to a report to the British parliament, they carried out a 'systematic plan
of destruction and extinction of the Moslem population'. The Turkish
remobilization under the modernizing regime of Mustafa Kemal created a
new national movement which, combined with a military offensive, forced
the Greek army back to the coast. Greek refugees fled, out of fear of Turkish
revenge, or many because they were ordered to flee by the Hellenic Greek
commanders who burned Greek villages and homes. The culmination of
the terror was reached in September 1922, when tens of thousands of
refugees crowded into Smyrna, in addition to the resident Greek, Armenian, and Turkish population. When fires broke out (probably laid by the
Turks), the panic-stricken population was driven to the harbour, and
robbed and beaten on the way by Turkish soldiers. Armenian men and
boys were hunted down and killed. Greek estimates ran to 125,000 people
killed, but a more realistic total given by the American historian Norman
Naimark is 10,000 to 15,000, or fewer. At any rate, the burning of Smyrna
marked the end of the nearly 3,000-year history of the Greek presence
on the Aegean coast of Anatolia. Eventually the Treaty of Lausanne of
July 1923 provided for the compulsory population transfer of some 1.2 to
1.5 million Greeks from Anatolia and 356,000 Turks from Greece. In fact,
by the time of the treaty, more than 1 million Greeks had already fled
Anatolia.[106]

Turkey and the Armenian genocide

Initially, Armenian radicals had supported the revolutionary Young Turks in their struggle for power, in the hope of a departure from the repressive and increasingly Pan-Islamic policies of Sultan Abdul Hamid. In the massacres of 1894–6, at least 100,000 Armenians had been killed, apparently at his instigation.[107] The autocratic regime of Sultan Abdul Hamid was overthrown in the revolution of 1908, but the hopes of the Armenians for a tolerant regime were disappointed. In 1909 Muslims massacred thousands of Armenians in Cilicia, although the involvement of the government is not proved.[108] The Ottoman empire came under the influence of the Young Turks, whose 'Committee for Union and Progress' (CUP), founded in 1889 in a military medical school, infiltrated the government and civil service. It was a modernizing movement with constitutional and Pan-Islamic aims; it fought against the 'miserable Byzantine influences' of Constantinople, and published bellicose organs with titles such as *The Weapon*, *The Bullet*, and *The Sword*.[109] Successive defeats in the Balkans and Libya since 1908 strengthened the radical ethno-nationalists in the CUP, and after violent unrest Enver Pasha came to power in a putsch in 1913; he radicalized the repressive policies against minorities and carried out a purge of liberal political opponents in the army: 1,100 officers were sacked in January 1914, and several were arrested.[110]

Once in power, the Young Turks showed no further interest in autonomy for the Armenian regions. In fact, the Young Turk movement subscribed to ethnic Turkish nationalism, rather than Ottomanism, which held out the promise of equal rights in a multinational empire. Schools had to teach Ottoman Turkish and promote Turkish and Islamic values. Radicals began to project utopian visions that called for the union of all Turks and Turkic peoples, from Anatolia through Central Asia ('Pan-Turanism' or 'Pan-Turkism').[111] Having lost Libya to Italy in 1912, the new Ottoman Turkey supported the local guerrilla fighters who continued resistance to Italian rule, and helped to convert resistance against imperialism into a Muslim war against Christians. Funds were collected from Muslims from Afghanistan to Tunisia to assist Libyan Arabs, and on 14 November 1914 the Sultan of Constantinople issued a call for Islamic holy war, as demanded by the German government.[112]

Under the influence of Dr Bahaeddin Sakir (who led a faction confusingly named the Committee for Progress and Union—CPU) the CUP was turned into a conspiratorial, anti-democratic, and centralist organization. Sakir managed to present several images of the CUP simultaneously: progressive, patriotic-Islamist, or Pan-Turkish, depending on the nature of his audience. The alliance with the Armenian Dashnak party in 1907 was portrayed in the western press as a campaign of Ottoman unity, but soon after he wrote to a friend that he regarded the alliance with the 'mortal enemy' as tactical and provisional. The 'Turkism' of Sakir and his followers was characterized by envy and hatred of Europe, which they perceived as a monolithic bloc. One of the CPU's publications, the newspaper *Türk*, called since 1902 for a social and economic boycott of the Armenians, using the language of Darwinist racialism.[113] It was Dr Sakir who directed the 'Special Organization' which set up hundreds of armed groups, with some 12,000 men, many recruited from the refugees from the Balkans. As from late August 1914 the 'Special Organization' acted to terrorize the Armenians in eastern Anatolia and provoke conflict with Russia by cross-border attacks before Turkey's entry into the war.

Before a genocide is committed, the state constructs its victims as the 'enemy'. Frequently, the internal enemy is associated with (real or fictitious) foreign enemies, and the thesis of provocation used to justify eradication. Thus the CUP considered the rights guaranteed by the 'Armenian Reform Agreement' imposed on Turkey by the Great Powers in February 1914 and the presence of international observers to be a humiliation, even a part of a Russian plot for the annexation of eastern Anatolia, and it alleged Armenian betrayal.[114] It did not help that the Dashnak party hoped for the victory of the Entente, and organized volunteers to join the Russian army.[115] To this day some writers imply that Armenian 'subversion and espionage', desertions, and uprisings fomented by Russia, caused or provoked the genocide.[116] In the context of the Young Turk aim predating the war to create a racially 'pure' state in Turkey, the actual conduct of the Armenians in the war was practically irrelevant. In any case, the great majority of Armenians were not disloyal, as German officers in Turkey confirmed.[117]

Naimark argues there is insufficient evidence of the Turkish government's intention to carry out genocide.[118] Yet although specific orders by the government have not been discovered—mainly because incriminating records were destroyed after Turkey's defeat and because the Turkish archives remain closed to this day—sufficient evidence is available to demonstrate intention. The decisions appear to have been taken in March 1915 by the central committee of the CUP, in which Bahaeddin Sakir was authorized to 'eliminate the internal danger'.[119] German theologian and philanthropist Johannes Lepsius was told in an interview with war minister Enver Pasha in Constantinople in August 1915 that the Ottoman government would continue its campaign against the Armenians; Enver admitted that the government intended to 'make an end of the Armenians now'.[120] Similar statements were made to the American ambassador, Henry Morgenthau. Some members of the CUP were reported to have said that 'all foreigners would have to disappear from Turkey; first the Armenians, then the Greeks, then the Jews, and finally the Europeans'.[121]

The genocide began in Constantinople with the closing of an Armenian newspaper in March 1915 and the arrest in April of 600 Armenian intellectuals, ostensibly because of the threat of a putsch. Only eight of them were released; the rest disappeared without trace. News of the uprising of Armenians in Van on 20 April served to end the debate inside the Young Turk leadership with a victory of the radical faction over the moderates. The government claimed Russian infiltration had instigated the rising. Lepsius concluded there was no connection with Russia; rather, arbitrary arrests and killings by Djevdet Bey, a brother-in-law of Enver Pasha, had provoked the Armenians into defending themselves against the feared impending massacre. The defence lasted four weeks, after which the Russians liberated Van, to the surprise of the Armenians.[122] The rising in Van was (and is) taken by the Turkish government to be the origin of the deportations, but in fact the first deportations, leading to the mass death of Armenians, took place in February in the region of Adana in southern Turkey. The Armenian population of Zeitun was deported following a series of arrests and the disarming of the population by 'Islamic gendarmes' (probably Sakir's 'Special Organization') starting in March. Armenian members of the Ottoman army were disarmed on the orders of Enver Pasha as from 25 February, and Armenian members of labour battalions were being executed probably as from March.[123] The Allied landing at Gallipoli on 25 April confirmed and heightened the Young Turk regime's fears for its existence, but had no causal connection with the genocide.

With these events began the systematic destruction of the Armenian people as from May 1915: the disarming and arrest of men and boys, the beatings, torture, rape, and deportation of the remaining men, women,

and children from eastern Anatolia, and after July from western Anatolia and
Thrace, to the deserts of Syria beyond the Euphrates. Some were killed on
the spot—burned in their houses or drowned in the Black Sea. Most died
during the deportation. During the forced marches many were shot
or hacked to death, others died from exhaustion, starvation, or disease.
Plentiful testimony was provided by Armenian survivors, American and
German diplomats, and by Turkish witnesses at the Istanbul trials held after
the war.[124] One of the officials who was centrally involved in the genocide
proudly wrote that he 'sought to exterminate the Armenian nation to the
last person . . . 300,000 Armenians . . . more or less, I did not count them.
Wherever they rebelled against my state, I crushed and punished them
with reserve forces.'[125] Estimates of the total number of deaths range
from 150,000 (the figure given by the Turkish Historical Society) to 1.5
million (Armenian estimate). In March 1919 the Turkish minister of the
interior produced the figure of 800,000.[126] At least one million (out of the
Ottoman Armenian population of 1.8 million) is the consensus among international scholars.

The war on culture stood at the beginning and the end of the Armenian
genocide. The Young Turks, led by intellectuals, many of whom were
themselves not 'ethnic' Turks, attacked Christian Armenians in order to
create a modernized, Turkified nation, which was intolerant of religious
pluralism. The policy of deportation and annihilation 1914 to 1916 was
succeeded by the confiscation of the land and property of the deportees and
the assimilation of those who remained, especially of children. 'Economic
Turkism' sought to replace non-Turks with Turks in companies, and,
through the 'Language Law' of 1916, insisted on the use of Turkish in
business correspondence. Cultural Turkism meant the compulsory teaching
of Turkish in all schools. In the following decades there was a policy to
eradicate Armenian culture, especially its churches, and to suppress even the
memory of Armenia. The 'transformation of human landscapes' is how one
historical geographer has termed the expulsions of Greeks and Turks.[127]
This applies equally to the eradication of the Armenians from Anatolia. An
official history of denial has been created which reveals the refusal to cope
with international scholarly criticism.[128] Two books published in 2002 and
2004 by the Turkish Historical Society denied there was any intention to
exterminate the Armenians and reiterated the thesis of the Armenian 'stab in
the back': 'Armenian wickedness', 'treason', 'desertion', and 'rebellion' had
made deportations a military necessity.[129]

Civilians as expendable beings

Official Turkish denials notwithstanding, the mass death of the Armenians was clearly caused by a deliberate policy of genocide. But in other states too, the politics of war entailed callous neglect and resulted in hunger for many hundreds of thousands of civilians who were regarded as expendable. During its retreat in 1915 the Russian army carried out an immensely destructive scorched earth policy that deliberately emulated that of 1812. Suspected hostile populations in the western regions of the empire were deported to the east: at least 300,000 Lithuanians, 250,000 Latvians, at least 500,000 Jews, and 743,000 Poles.[130] The motivation was fear of betrayal by spies and deserters, and to leave no resources behind for the enemy. The death toll is impossible to establish, but in the administrative chaos and harsh conditions of Russia during the war it must have been considerable.

Paranoid Great Russian chauvinism especially targeted Jews and Germans. Some 200,000 ethic Germans from Russian Poland were deported to Siberia. In Habsburg Galicia, occupied by the Russian army, there was a vicious antisemitic campaign, in which almost all Jews were suspected of espionage or betrayal, and subjected to arrest and deportation. The wave of antisemitism soon spread to the rest of the Russian army and society, with orders issued to scrutinize the conduct of Jews in the army; soon some officers were refusing to accept Jewish soldiers in their units. During the course of Russia's participation in the war, at least half a million Jews, possibly as many as one million, were driven from their homes. The point about the various deportations was not just their enormous scale. These violent disruptions of entire communities reflected the destructive potential of modern ideologies of ethno-nationalism, backed by the resources of a modern state with modern communications (telegraph and railways). Moreover, this was army policy, not necessarily that of the civilian authorities. The army gained the power to carry out policy in wartime in a way that was impossible in peacetime. The army's policy, ostensibly based on the fear that the Jews (and other ethnic minorities) might conduct espionage and betray secrets to the Germans, was a part of the shift in the nature of warfare between the French Revolution and the First World War from war between small professional armies and war between mobilized nations, in which some ethnic groups were defined as the nation and others defined as 'foreign'; it thus contributed to the emergence of antisemitic violence among soldiers and the local populations.[131]

The occupation of Galicia was accompanied by harsh suppression of the Ukrainian separatist movement and the attempt to unify Galicia with the Russian empire. Thousands of Ukrainians were arrested and deported, and a cultural war was waged to impose the Russian language and the 'Russian spirit', and to convert the Catholic and Uniate believers to Orthodoxy.[132] Inside Russia proper, subjects of German descent were the victims of violence, in pogroms orchestrated by the pamphlets and propaganda of the extreme right wing, using the language of xenophobia and the rhetoric of annihilation. Mobs from the poor districts of Moscow pillaged shops and houses thought to belong to anyone with a German name, in an orgy of violence tolerated by the state.[133] The Russian measures were chaotic and ultimately counterproductive because alienating the various national minorities cost the state valuable potential support; anti-German sentiment turned against the many high-ranking army officers of German descent, and against the tsarina herself.

By contrast, food supply policy in Germany and Austria showed a ruthless logic of the sacrifice of the expendable. Germany introduced rationing of bread in January 1915, and soon other measures restricted the availability of food. Prices rose rapidly, putting many products beyond the reach of many normal consumers. The example of Hamburg was typical of most urban areas (the peasant population was mostly self-sufficient, even well-supplied in food). The social-democratic *Hamburger Echo* reported in summer 1915 that it was 'a naked, sad fact that . . . countless families cannot afford a piece of meat, eggs, or butter for weeks on end, while their men are spilling their life-blood for the Fatherland'. In March 1916 potatoes, a staple food in Germany, were rationed to 2 kg. per week, and the supply dried up completely in June and July, and again as from mid-August. The quality of food declined drastically, soup kitchens having to resort to all kinds of substitute foods. Consumers complained the meals were 'disgusting', and that it 'made them sick' to eat the 'pigswill' on offer: 'stinking barley broth, salt-water rice soup without seasoning, or sour plums with watery noodles without sugar'. A poor harvest and unusually cold weather impeded the transport of food, and the potato ration was reduced to 1.75 kg. from January to mid-May 1917 the supply of potatoes was only sporadic, and they were replaced in people's diets with turnips. The 'turnip winter' 1916–17 was the low point: turnips were served as soup, vegetable, even as dessert. At their best they do not have the energy value of potatoes, and often they had been frozen in the cold, and were semi-rotten. Bread was restricted to 1,800 grams per week, and often the bread flour was 'stretched' with turnips. Milk was only available for children, pregnant women, and the sick; the meat ration was reduced in December 1916 to 200 grams per week. Hunger riots broke out in Hamburg and other cities in August 1916, and again in January and February 1917, at first in working-class districts, but soon spreading to middle-class quarters as well. Police, supported by the army, quelled the protests. Infantry and cavalry were deployed against their own people, and the military made plans for future civil war scenarios.[134]

Workers in armaments plants received wage rises and rations of up to 3,270 calories per day, including some meat, but this did not compensate for the intensity of work and the increasing length of shifts. In the armaments industries the 15 or 16-hour day, including Sundays, was the norm. In July 1918, according to a police report, shipyard workers who had been reclaimed from the army said they would prefer to be sent back to the front, 'because . . . they would rather be killed in battle than slowly starve at home doing heavy labour'.[135] Although food supply improved somewhat in spring 1917, it remained at a low level, and in winter 1917–18 the average nutritional value of rations for civilians was less than 1,000 calories, about half the daily requirement. By giving munitions workers extra rations, and by ensuring these were not shared with the workers' families, the military authorities displayed cold disregard for the survival of working-class women and children.[136] Clearly, the German war leadership established priorities in the distribution of dwindling food resources: first came soldiers at the front, who were usually given sufficient food and plenty of meat; in general, only local difficulties caused temporary shortages, for example during heavy fighting. Next came troops in the rear area, in administration, and in the occupation armies, who did not face such a tough physical challenge. The army took 70 per cent of all officially available food.[137] Then came armaments industry workers, followed by various categories of 'normal' civilians who needed extra food, and then civilians who had to make do with official rations. Finally, there were the populations of the German-occupied Europe, who were deprived of their own resources in order to feed Germany; the story of their suffering has yet to be integrated into mainstream accounts of the First World War. An extra category was German civilians deemed to be unworthy of survival, as will be seen in relation to patients in psychiatric hospitals (Chapter 8).

According to German calculations published after the war, over 700,000 civilians died directly from malnutrition.[138] German nationalist claims, blaming

the British 'hunger blockade' for these deaths, should be re-examined crit-
ically. However, it is going too far to argue, as the historian Avner Offer
does, that while the German people suffered sometimes from hunger, Germany
did not starve.[139] The evidence is clear: from winter 1916/17 to summer
1917, and again in winter 1917/18 average rations for civilians dropped below
1,000 calories per day; meat, fats, milk, leather, wool, and clothing were in short
supply; and on average adults lost 20 per cent of their body weight during the
war.[140] A more realistic estimate has been made by the demographic historian
and First World War expert Jay Winter, who calculates that there were 478,500
'excess civilian war-related deaths in Germany'.[141]

What were the causes of the hunger in Germany? Some authors argue
that the blockade caused these shortages directly, or indirectly through
preventing the import of fertilizers, which had an immediate effect on
harvest yields.[142] However, it is time to challenge such assumptions, which
have usually been taken over unquestioned from German writings of the
time. In fact, at the start of the war German nutritionists had stated that
Germany could produce 90 per cent of its calorie needs by itself.[143] Some
of the reasons for shortages were those common to all belligerent countries
that suffered a decline in food supply: the most productive part of the
agrarian work-force was drafted into the army, to be replaced by women,
children, and old men. Draft animals (horses, oxen) were requisitioned by
the army. German imports of food, fodder, and fertilizers inevitably
declined, but not only because of the blockade: Germany was at war
with several countries that had been its main suppliers of grain, above all
Russia. Even without a blockade, Germany's enemies were not likely to
continue sending it food. Switching away from a meat-based diet could
have made up the shortfall in food imports: it takes eight times more
calories to produce meat than would be available from grain. These are
factors affecting supply, but distribution was just as important. Food requisitioning by the authorities alienated the peasantry both from normal exchange
and from the state, distorting the pattern of distribution and even affecting
production. Inefficiencies, favouritism, and corruption in the rationing
system did not affect overall supply, but further distorted distribution and
angered working-class consumers. Finally, the German state diverted food
away from civilians who were deemed expendable in the war effort.

Looking at food supply in terms of geopolitics, the Allied blockade
obviously played a role (but not the only role) in stopping imports, in so
far as they were seaborne: 74 per cent of Germany's imports came by sea,

directly or indirectly.[144] Just as important, Allied naval superiority prevented Germany from obtaining food from alternative neutral sources, such as in south America, while enabling the Allies to draw on global agrarian resources. Germany could strive to make good the shortfall through ruthless exploitation of occupied territories, which helps to explain its radical war aims for vast annexations in eastern Europe.[145]

The illogicality of the hunger-blockade thesis is shown by the comparison with Russia and Austria-Hungary. In Russia, there were food shortages as early as August 1915; by 1916 the energy value of the diet of unskilled workers had fallen by a quarter and infant mortality doubled.[146] The prime reasons were the shortage of labour in the countryside owing to the draft and the collapse of the transport system under the impact of the war. Yet Russia had a grain surplus before the war, and was a major exporter of food.

The hunger crisis was far worse in the Austro-Hungarian empire than in Germany. Austria-Hungary's mass hunger did not result from the naval blockade. Before the war the empire was almost entirely self-sufficient in food production, and boasted of its independence of food imports.[147] It exported as much grain as it imported in the decade before the war, and in any case 80 per cent of its imports arrived by land transport, not sea.[148] In the war Austria went hungry because of Hungary: the 'granary of the empire' refused to send supplies. Military service deprived Hungarian agriculture of 50 per cent of its male labour, and the Hungarian government stopped Austrian access to its produce as a sign of the intensifying separatist tendencies in the empire. To make matters worse, the Russian invasion of Austrian Galicia stopped supplies from this region which contained one-third of Austrian arable land.[149] Unlike in Germany, the government was unable to carry out food requisitioning from the farms. To a great degree the starvation of the civilians resulted from the privileged supply of food to the army. A senior commander told chief of general staff Arz von Straussenburg in early 1918: ' "The army must eat, it has to receive what it needs ... It is a matter of indifference whether a few more old people in the hinterland die or not." '[150] In January 1918 Vienna and the Austrian industrial regions were on the verge of famine. Only a few days' supply of bread was left, and hunger protests turned into major strikes.[151]

Soldiers as expendable beings

Even the Habsburg army suffered hunger, although it enjoyed top priority. By early 1918 the famished Austro-Hungarian soldiers who had devoured the food reserves of occupied north-eastern Italy were once again hungry, and by summer the men were receiving 100 grams of meat on 5 days a week, a mere pound of potatoes per week, and fresh vegetables were a rarity. Malnutrition and disease, even lack of trousers and underwear, were reducing the imperial army to a demoralized rabble.[152]

The Habsburg empire was incapable of meeting the enormous demands of modern warfare on three fronts, and was fortunate that two of its enemies were knocked out of the war with German assistance. Mass production of the means of destruction was something only highly industrialized societies could manage. The contrast with Germany makes this clear: by summer 1916 Germany manufactured 160 heavy artillery guns per month, 5,500 trench mortars, and 29,000 tons of barbed wire. In Austria-Hungary 43 heavy artillery guns, 45 trench mortars, and 3,000 tons of barbed wire were being turned out. Every day German factories produced the enormous quantity of 250,000 artillery shells, Austrian factories 60,000. The Habsburg empire was producing at best 27 per cent, in some cases less than one per cent, of essential items of armaments production. The Austro-Hungarian army was not so much smaller than its German ally, but the manpower demands of the war were disastrously high: by the end of 1916, 7.5 million men, or 67 per cent of men of military age between 18 and 50 years, had been called up to serve in the armed forces.[153] By 1918 nine million men had been mobilized, five million of whom became casualties, with 1.46 million men killed. This was 16 per cent—a higher proportion of mobilized men killed than in Germany (15 per cent), as well as a higher proportion of men of military age (13 and 12 per cent respectively), and was thus exactly the same proportion as in France.[154]

On the eastern front, both the Russian and the Austro-Hungarian armies treated their men as an infinite resource. With the partial exception of Brusilov in summer 1916, most Russian generals had not progressed beyond nineteenth-century military doctrine, with massed frontal assaults at great loss and over-reliance on the vulnerable, ineffective cavalry which consumed huge resources of supplies and transport; they showed contempt for modern techniques of defensive warfare with their obsession with fortresses and their refusal to construct trenches, exposing the infantry to the murderous artillery fire of the enemy. The Russian army was notorious for saving its guns in retreats at the cost of abandoning the infantry, leaving 'the cattle', as they were known, in the lurch.[155] In the Austro-Hungarian offensive in the Carpathians, Conrad chose the month of January 1915 for his inadequately equipped men to cross icy mountains. Rifles had to be heated over fires before they could be used; supplies had to be brought across icy passes or became stuck in mud; entire units of men froze to death at night; one night a Croat regiment suffered 1,800 cases of frostbite; and in early March the 2nd Army lost 40,000 men through frostbite. One senior Habsburg officer later recalled: 'Every day hundreds froze to death; the wounded who could not drag themselves off were bound to die; . . . and there was no combating the apathy and indifference that gripped the men.' The Carpathians offensive cost the army 800,000 men, three-quarters of them from illness, a sure sign that the supplies of winter clothing, fuel, shelter, and medical treatment were inadequate to the point of gross irresponsibility.[156]

The Habsburg soldiers were not the only ones to be treated with evident callousness. The Ottoman army was also badly clothed and badly fed. Ahmed Emin recorded that

> There were instances where soldiers, equipped for a hot climate, were suddenly sent to the Caucasus front in wintertime. As only a one-third ration could be issued, the death rate due to exposure, hunger, and resulting disease was great. On the Syrian front, soldiers had often not only to live on half rations, but they were given the same flour soup for months and months, and at last became incapable of touching a spoonful of it.

A former officer described the situation before the third battle of Gaza (November 1917):

> The Turkish soldiers concentrated at that time in Palestine had not enough bread to maintain their strength. They received almost no meat, no butter, no sugar, no vegetables, no fruits. Only a thin tent gave a semblance of protection from the hot sun by day, and from the cold of the night. They were wretchedly clothed. They had no boots at all, or what they had were so bad that they meant injury to the feet of many who wore them. Soldiers had been without word from home for years and years. Owing to the bad communications no leave was ever given.[157]

Turkish losses in war were vast, and to this day have not been reliably calculated. Of the 3 million men enrolled in the army during the course of the war, 325,000 were killed; owing to the high rate of sickness (with 461,799 cases of malaria alone), another 466,759 died. Thus the true total was probably around 800,000 deaths, in excess of one-quarter of mobilized men, a higher rate than any belligerent after Serbia and Romania.[158]

Mass death on the western front was therefore not a singular experience, or rather, it was singular only in that mass death on that front mainly resulted from enemy action, not neglect and ruthless treatment by one's own leaders. Despite similarities between the three main belligerents on the western front, nations involved in the First World War differed greatly in their methods of waging war and in their war policies. Mortality rates would suggest that the deliberate neglect of civilian welfare was at least as pronounced in Russia, Italy, and Austria-Hungary as in Germany. Military discipline, contrary to common assumptions about Prussian militarism, was significantly harsher in Italy than in Germany. It would be quite incorrect to speak of a German singularity of destructiveness, although it is clear that the German military doctrine and practice of annihilation tended to radicalize warfare on all sides. The German state did not, however, turn against putative internal enemies beyond the degree of repression necessary to continue prosecution of the war; racism was more or less kept in check. Military self-destructiveness, which Isabel Hull imputes to the German army, was far more evident in the Austro-Hungarian, Italian, Russian, and Ottoman armies. No state pushed the dynamic of destruction further than the Ottoman empire, which waged a campaign of eradication against a section of its own people. A tentative answer can be given here to the question why Ottoman Turkey was the only state to embark on a pro- gramme of genocide. The Young Turk version of ethno-nationalism was more murderous than that of the radical nationalists in the Balkans from 1912 to 1918, where mass killing and cultural war had moved further along the path towards total destruction than in western and central Europe. In Turkey the forces of ethno-nationalism had come to power in an unstable, post-imperial, revolutionary state in which the ruling elite was uncertain of its hold on power and determined to expunge the humiliation of successive defeats, and in which fears of external enemies coincided with the existence of large ethnic minorities with international connections. This distinguished Turkey from the other states in the First World War.

5

Culture and War

Cultural destruction was not merely an incidental phenomenon of the Great War, but intrinsic to it. Intellectuals anticipated and welcomed the war, and played the leading role in the mobilization of culture and minds. They popularized the idea of the war to defend civilization, as the Allies saw it, or a war to defend culture, as Germany saw it. It is practically a cliché of Great War historiography that intellectuals, even those regarded as the cultural 'avant garde', everywhere reacted in parallel fashion in rallying to their nation, only to be gradually disillusioned by the reality of industrialized mass killing in a long war of attrition. This was especially the case with those who witnessed the war at first hand, as will be seen in Chapter 7. However, there were many intellectuals, including those who played a role in the dissemination of cultural values such as clergymen and academics, who resolutely maintained the patriotic certainties of wartime mobilization. Moreover, there were national differences. While Britain and France went to war to preserve the status quo, Germany was fighting to change it, as we saw in Chapter 3. German intellectuals believed their nation had a cultural mission to export German values. By implication this could—and sometimes did—mean a war on the enemy's culture which should be replaced, even destroyed.

Militarists, intellectuals, and the anticipation of war

Why professional militarists—whether active officers or not—wanted war was relatively straightforward. It is the task of general staffs to plan for war and they generally look forward to the day when they can test their ideas in reality. For retired general Colmar von der Goltz (reactivated in the war), author of popular military works such as *The Nation in Arms* and founder of the mass-member Young-Germany League, Germany needed war in order to purge society, especially the lower orders, of their addiction to personal possessions, pleasure-seeking, and their demand for rights. British militarists argued in very similar terms that modern urban society was decadent, and that military service would be healthy for the body politic. One officer wrote in the *United Services Magazine* in 1904: 'The British nation has stepped far along the road to ruin in a wild debauch of so-called freedom. It is time to call a halt . . . to inculcate the value of discipline . . . ' Another wrote that the working-class masses in the cities were nervous, restless, and excitable. There was a general consensus among officers that there was a decline in the virility of the nation: military and masculine virtues were being replaced by feminine and unpatriotic qualities. The solution was to impose discipline and moral reform through education. Lieutenant-General R. S. S. Baden-Powell shared these fears, and, as the founder of the scout movement, strongly supported the idea of military preparation for boys which would eradicate 'vice' and make them 'manly, good citizens'.[1] In other words, militarization of society for war in order to turn the clock back, restore traditional gender roles, and reverse urbanization and modernization.

The question of how boys and young men were socialized in the pre-war period is crucial for an understanding of soldiers' expectation of war and how they interpreted it. The ideas of the scout movement were imported into Germany in 1909, very soon after its creation by Baden-Powell in Britain; it soon had 90,000 members. Although several of its basic ideas were held in common—youth welfare, outdoor activity, the promotion of a healthy lifestyle, and the inculcation of patriotic values—Baden-Powell's recognition of boys' need for activities suited to their age such as games, symbols, and rituals, as well as a degree of self-organization, was absent in the German movement; instead the emphasis was on pre-military training, with war games, strict discipline, and military-style authority.[2] Defence of the empire was, naturally, the basic assumption of the British scout movement, but its German counterpart had an aggressive edge to its imperialism, with undertones of an imminent war of expansion. As *Der Feldmeister,* the 'leadership newspaper' of the German scout movement, directed at the 5,000 scout leaders who disseminated these values, wrote in 1914, before the outbreak of the war:

> The rapid victory of the idea of scouting can only be explained by the fact that national moods and undercurrents resonate with it. It is the growing insight into the necessity of German *Weltpolitik* which has seized more and more

circles of the people since the campaign in China, the war years in South-West Africa and the Morocco crisis. The push for expansion by a people of 65 million is becoming day by day more tangible. Today our imagination is fired by the colourful thought of distant coasts and lands; we have a dark and secret inkling that we are approaching new fields of war and work; and our yearning beholds over the seas a sun-drenched, shining heritage in the future. Not Baden-Powell and Boer War, but the colonial army and South-West Africa have made scouting popular, for we are arming ourselves for the same tasks. We are tired of our youth spoiling their bodies in factories and poisoning their minds to produce guns and textiles for foreign nations; we want to clear forests and settle villages ourselves in order to find a *Heimat* as free Germans on our own piece of land. Germans, listen: the storm wind whistles![3]

(The word *Heimat* means not only home, but also home region, and has strong connotations of emotional bonds with that region and its culture.) In another article in *Der Feldmeister* the target was not only far-away places in the sun, but pacifists at home and above all Germany's European neighbours. Militarist nationalism was suitably camouflaged with the rhetoric of defence, alleging that France was preparing to invade.[4]

The Young-Germany League, of which the scouts were a part, was directly involved in the burgeoning national festivals in the years before 1914. Important occasions and sites of popularizing militarism were the various festivals connected with anniversaries of historic events. The centenary of the 'Battle of the Peoples' at Leipzig, significantly commemorating victory over France in the War of Liberation, with the mass participation of veterans' and gymnastic associations on 18 October 1913, was only the most notable in a series of such festivals in the last few years before the outbreak of the war. State-sponsored youth welfare programmes were intended to deflect young males from the dangers of social democracy and inculcate military values in organized leisure activities. The state involved the Young-Germany movement directly in its youth welfare work, as did the army veterans' associations, which with their 2.8 million members played a central role in militarizing society and in nationalizing the public space, by lending financial and organizational support.[5]

The enthusiastic anticipation of war was often a motif of official culture, attempting to mobilize the nationalist idealism of youth. One of the most powerful images to capture the mood in the educated bourgeoisie in the immediate pre-war years was the fresco painted by Ferdinand Hodler for the University of Jena in 1909, *Departure of the Jena Students 1813* (Fig. 7), to commemorate the War of Liberation.[6] The naturalistic style served to make

Figure 7. *Departure of the Jena Students,* fresco by Ferdinand Hodler

the historical subject appear contemporary and of immediate relevance, placing German preparation for war in the context of a new war of liberation.

None of this is particularly surprising. Why not only militarists, but also so many intellectuals wanted war, or rallied enthusiastically to support the nation once war started, is more difficult to explain. Why did many intellectuals in Europe feel society was so rotten that the only solution was a 'purifying' war? Was their concept of war a realistic vision of industrialized slaughter, or a more traditional, chivalrous, and romantic picture? A wartime publication by the noted economist Werner Sombart throws some light on the pre-war desire for war on the part of intellectuals, at least so far as Germany was concerned. Sombart was one of those many intellectuals who expressed the sense of deep dissatisfaction with pre-war German culture. He was a prime example of a leading intellectual, well respected internationally, who helped to turn the war into an ideological crusade. In a chapter entitled 'Das Leben vor dem Kriege' (Life before the war) in his book *Händler und Helden*—'Traders and Heroes', the anti-British import of which is discussed later, he wrote:

All life appeared senseless and without purpose ... One saw humanity decaying in a life of luxury, copulating, stuffing their stomachs and emptying their bowels, and in senseless rushing to and fro ...

We heaped riches upon riches and yet we knew that they would bring no blessing; we created wonders of technology and knew not wherefore. We played at politics, quarrelled with each other, threw dirt at each other: why?

We wrote and read newspapers; mountains of paper towered up before us every day and suffocated us with worthless news and even more worthless commentaries: no one knew what for.

We wrote books and plays, and hordes of critics did nothing else their whole lives but criticize, and cliques were formed and fought each other, and no-one knew what for.

We worshipped 'progress' in order to intensify our senseless lives: more riches, more records, more advertising, more newspapers, more books, more plays, more education, more comfort. And he who was thoughtful asked again and again: wherefore, wherefore?

Life, as one of its best describers has said, had really become a slippery slope. A life without ideals, which means eternal dying, putrefaction, a stink, since all human life turns into decomposition, from which idealism has disappeared like a body from which the soul escapes.[7]

The point of all this is that culture was expendable, according to this view of the world. Politics, by which Sombart meant the parliamentary political culture that was becoming quite highly developed in Germany before 1914, was also expendable. Sombart thus provided the justification for the destruction of elements of German culture, so long as they did not serve the war; this could just as well be extended to contempt of the enemy's culture. Parliament and a free press were an unnecessary luxury. He attempted to explain why he and 'many, many others, not the worst sort' had become addicted to this 'cultural pessimism', as he correctly called it, by saying that they became convinced that mankind was doomed, that the human race was becoming a mob, an anthill, that the spirit of commerce was taking root everywhere.[8]

In November 1914 Thomas Mann, already a famous writer, expressed similar feelings about 'purification, liberation' from the 'toxic comfort of peace'. Of the old world before August 1914 he asked: 'Did not vermin of the mind swarm about in it like maggots? Did it not ferment and stink of the decaying matter of civilization? ... How could the artist, the soldier within the artist, not praise God for the collapse of a world of peace of which he was so utterly sick?'[9]

How to make sense of this? The key is in Sombart's words 'mob' and 'anthill'. This was a profoundly middle-class view, an expression of bourgeois pessimism in the face of the 'masses' who certainly did not live a 'life of luxury': the working class whose living standards were still objectively low, with poor housing, a lower life expectancy, far lower incomes, and insecurity of existence in the face of unemployment, old age, or illness. Yet their real wages had actually doubled between 1871 and 1914, their Social Democratic Party had become the largest force in parliament, and their demands were beginning to pose a threat to the privileges of the bourgeoisie and expose deep divisions in the nation. His cultural pessimism derived from a Lutheran tradition of asceticism and rejection of luxury. At the same time Nietzsche's idea of the 'will to power' had come increasingly to influence German writers since the 1880s, with the idea of the creation of a 'Superman' (*Übermensch*) who had the power to transform reality.[10] It therefore made perfect sense for Sombart to interpret the outbreak of war not merely as a 'miracle' that offered redemption and the possibility of reversing that slide into decay, but as the 'ideas of 1914' that united all Germans once again in a single cause: national unity. It made perfect sense for Thomas Mann, the Nietzschean and self-declared enemy of western democracy, to state that the war revealed Germany's true inner being: 'Germany's whole virtue and beauty, as we have seen, reveals itself only in war.'[11] The myth of war enthusiasm was thus the logical counterpart to cultural pessimism.

Italian culture and war: nationalism and Futurism

In pre-war Italy, too, intellectuals and the ruling Liberal establishment struggled to come to terms with the age of mass politics. Faced with the growing threat of socialism from the Left, political Catholicism, and extreme nationalism on the Right, the Liberal governments extended the franchise to almost all men. The *Belle Époque* in Italy was a period of ten years which were punctuated by ever more frenzied calls from nationalist intellectuals welcoming war. In 1904 Enrico Corradini wrote in his journal *Il Regno*:

> The war, at last, has broken out. At this moment it is the Russians who do not enjoy perfect health and the Japanese who have attained their Nirvana. The gun that thunders over Port Arthur has confirmed with its gruff and

decisive voice the ideas and passions which are dear to us. This is truly a great war, just made for us.

Vilfredo Pareto, the anti-democratic economist and sociologist, writing about the Socialist International's opposition to the Russo-Japanese War (1904–5), warned that to prevent the working class from taking over as the new ruling elite a long war was necessary. Papini and Prezzolini, founders of the journal *Leonardo* in 1903, and then of *La Voce* in 1908, became closely allied with Futurism and advocated a bellicose nationalism. Each successive war was welcomed by nationalist intellectuals: 1911 (Libya), 1912, 1913 (the Balkan wars), 1914, and 1915, with works such as the 'Ode to Violence' of the Futurists (Enrico Cardile in 1912), the 'hot bath of black blood' by Giovanni Papini in the journal *Lacerba,* and Giuseppe Prezzolini's calls to war in the influential *La Voce*, 'Let us make war', and 'Welcome to the New World!' in 1914. Nationalist intellectuals were already advancing the idea of war as panacea to all the ills of the nation at the time of the invasion of Libya, and in 1914/15 they eagerly reasserted it in the intervention campaign.[12]

The Italian government's decision to go to war in 1915 was too transparently for selfish reasons (*sacro egoismo*) to rally broad popular support, however. Its aim was to stabilize the Liberal system, or more precisely Salandra's rule against his Liberal rival Giolitti, by holding out the prospect of territorial conquests from Austria-Hungary. The problem was that the support of the interventionist street campaign, a numerically small but rapidly growing and vociferous assortment, was a dangerous thing: many of the interventionists were hoping to shatter the Liberal system. Mussolini, speaking at the founding meeting of the *Fasci di Combattimento* in 1919, thus saw Italy's entry into war as the beginning of a revolution: 'We started off that May, which was exquisitely and divinely revolutionary, because it overturned a shameful situation at home . . . '[13] Not for nothing did Mussolini state at the founding meeting that Italian intervention had represented the 'first phase of a revolution' that was '*not finished*'.[14] Mussolini's newspaper *Il Popolo d'Italia* had urged Italy to go to war with the headline on 21 January 1915: 'For socialism and for the war: against the fossils!'[15]

Mussolini broke with socialism in autumn 1914 to become a 'left-interventionist'. He was only one among many rabble-rousers along with other ex-socialists and revolutionary syndicalists who saw war as a short cut to revolution. The running in the intervention campaign was made on the right, by the nationalists, where the best-known figure of interventionist mobilization was the poet Gabriele D'Annunzio. In common with many other right-wing intellectuals and later fascists he was a Darwinist and a Nietzschean, and was contemptuous of the masses. However, he believed that the 'barbarian' masses could be manipulated and mobilized for the support of nationalist aims by charismatic leadership. He hailed modernity and modern technology, and the potential that the machine age offered to create a new society out of war, ruled by a technocratic aristocracy.[16] His extravagant, florid speeches, replete with classical references and myths, fascinated crowds. The climax of the interventionist campaign was reached with the arrival of D'Annunzio from France in May 1915.[17] Speaking in Genoa on 5 May at the opening of the monument to the 'Thousand' (Garibaldi's volunteers of 1860, the redshirts who set out to conquer Sicily and ultimately unify Italy), D'Annunzio said: 'Blessed are those young men who hunger and thirst for glory, for they shall be sated . . . Blessed are the pure of heart, blessed those who return from the victories for they shall see the new face of Rome, the recrowned head of Dante, the triumphant beauty of Italy.'[18] No doubt the echo of the Sermon on the Mount was entirely intentional, with the provocative inversion of its message of peace. From the moment he crossed the border he was welcomed almost as a second Messiah by his many admirers (for whom legendary stories of his love affairs were a part of his charisma), and he embarked on a speaking tour of Italy, addressing interventionist crowds. D'Annunzio's campaign, using religious imagery and invoking the idea of a nation reborn as a united soul, explicitly provoked violence, encouraging his supporters to launch riots. On 13 May 1915 he announced in Rome, 'If inciting citizens to violence is a crime, I will boast of this crime, assuming sole responsibility for it.'[19] There was also an echo of the idea of palingenesis, which goes back to the Greek philosopher Heraclitus, the renewal of all being through fire, later to become a central trope of fascism.

Once war was declared, the war poet turned war hero. D'Annunzio joined up and served as a lieutenant. Absolved of normal military duties by his fame, he resided in a hotel in Venice and busied himself with inventing his persona as the Nietzschean Superman. In August 1915 he flew on a well-publicized and dangerous mission to Trieste to drop irredentist propaganda leaflets; later he took part in risky naval missions against the Austro-Hungarian fleet. After recovery from an eye injury suffered in a crash landing, he turned to land war, fighting on the Isonzo and Carso fronts, and was promoted to captain, later to major, and in 1919 to lieutenant-colonel. He redoubled his speaking campaign after Caporetto to remobilize the troops and revive their spirits. His most spectacular exploit was the air raid on Vienna on 9 August 1918; instead of bombs thousands of leaflets were dropped containing the message that the Italian air force could rain tons of bombs on the city, but preferred to send them greetings with the message of the tricolour, 'the colours of liberty'. Italy's victory on 4 November left him cold, and he denounced it as incomplete, 'mutilated'. For him the war was not over; according to an acquaintance he said: 'I smell the stink of peace.' He was looking forward to new battles, and while the peace conference was still discussing the new order of Europe, D'Annunzio, in anticipation of his symbolic occupation of Fiume, was demanding the complete fulfilment of the Treaty of London for territorial expansion in Istria.[20]

Although the government had calculated that going to war would deflate the interventionist street campaign and allow the state to suppress the unrest, the explosive potential of this mixture of left-interventionists and nationalists posed a long-term threat. In an article published under the title 'Down with parliament!' on 11 May 1915 Mussolini demanded that 'for the health of Italy a few dozen deputies should be shot: I repeat *shot* in the back'.[21]

Not all Italy's intellectuals were in favour of war, and the war increased the divisions between them. The two most famous philosophers, Benedetto Croce and Giovanni Gentile, took opposing views during the intervention crisis, 1914–15, despite their friendship. Both wrote for the journals *Leonardo* and *La Voce*, both were laicists, realists in politics, and patriotic, being convinced of the necessity to create Italian national identity. Croce was against Italian entry into the war, and believed it should maintain its alliance with Austria and Germany; Gentile saw the war as a positive opportunity for Italy. Croce was opposed to war not only because he sympathized with German philosophy and with the German cause, but also because the revolutionary socialists and republicans wanted Italian intervention to bring about a revolution in Italy. Gentile, who was neither a warmonger nor a fanatical nationalist, feared that if Italy remained neutral and the Central Powers won the war, they would seek the first opportunity to attack Italy. Without any allies, Italy would be crushed, and Germany and Austria would dominate southern Europe. If Italy, by remaining neutral, wanted to become one big museum, fossilized in contemplation of its ancient past, its past glories and beauties, then the sacrifice of the patriots of the Risorgimento would have been in vain. War, for Gentile, was the opportunity for Italians to show they had really become a people ready to defend itself, not merely an unformed mass: it would be a test of nationhood. Citing Heraclitus, he wrote that war was the mother of all things; war was inevitable in history as a principle of nature, and peoples were in a continual struggle for existence.[22] The striking resemblance of Gentile's thought to Max Weber's call in 1895 for newly united Germany to embark on imperialist expansion does not indicate lineage or influence, but rather that such ideas were common parlance among the most influential intellectuals in certain cultures where nationalism was soon to become an explosive force.

Marinetti's ideas were therefore not merely those of an eccentric, flamboyant individual, but were part of a broader stream of nationalist thought. He was looking forward to war with fierce joy as early as 1909, as we saw in the Introduction to this book. The 'Futurist Manifesto', published in 1909 in the French newspaper Le Figaro, announced his intention clearly:

> We will glorify war—the world's only hygiene—militarism, patriotism, the destructive gesture of freedom-bringers, beautiful ideas worth dying for, and scorn for woman. We will destroy the museums, libraries, academies of every kind, will fight moralism, feminism . . .

The destruction of past culture would make space for the modern:

> We declare that the splendour of the world has been enriched by a new beauty: the beauty of speed. A racing car with its bonnet adorned with great tubes like serpents with explosive breath . . . a roaring motor car which seems to run on machine-gun fire, is more beautiful than the Nike of Samothrace.[23]

This would be the key to a glorious future of modern technology, fast cars, air travel, violence, and authoritarianism. Marinetti soon acquired a reputation as poet and initiator of Futurism that reached beyond the salons of Florence and Milan before 1914. Because he and his movement became so closely associated with fascism, his anticipatory justification and cultural affirmation of war illuminate the dynamics of cultural destruction, mass killing, and the political development of Europe in the period from before the First World War to the age of fascism. He was an agitator for war throughout the four years before Italy's intervention. He travelled Italy speaking in favour of the war in Libya in 1911, supporting the Bulgarian siege of Adrianople in 1912–13, and throughout the highly-charged debate on intervention as from August 1914.

Marinetti loathed the Italy of his day as the land of museums, professors, tour guides, which he denounced as 'il passatismo', the obsession with the past. The 'Manifesto of the Futurist Painters' (11 February 1910), signed by

Umberto Boccioni, Carlo Carrà, Luigi Russolo, Giacomo Balla, and Gino Severini, called on Italy's young artists to 'destroy the cult of the past, the obsession with the ancients, pedantry and academic formalism'. It ended with the words: 'The dead shall be buried in the earth's deepest bowels! The threshold of the future will be swept free of mummies! Make room for youth, for violence, for daring!'

Why this revolt against the cultural heritage in Italy, of all places? The Futurists railed against liberal Italy which they saw as incapable of action; they saw through the new nation-state's clumsy attempts to appropriate the past with its invention of national symbols, the monuments of bad taste of King Vittorio Emanuele. The Liberal political establishment, despite its name and its shift to mass politics, was conservative, notorious for corruption, electoral fraud, and even intimidation. There were plenty of grounds for dissatisfaction with the system, and while working-class and to some extent peasant discontent was mobilized by the Socialist Party, secular middle-class intellectuals found a ready outlet for their anger in nationalism and militarism. The violent rhetoric of the Futurists, and of the entire interventionist campaign, would soon be turned not only outwards, against the enemy abroad, but by 1917 also against the internal enemy, foreshadowing the violence that destroyed liberal Italy and its infant democracy.

Futurism outside Italy

In Italy the Futurists were joined by nationalists and revolutionary syndicalists to become a powerful force in the intervention crisis, 1914–15, and were given further impulse by the war. After the war, Futurism fused with the fascist movement. In Britain, Germany, and Russia Futurism took a different trajectory. In Britain the writer and artist Wyndham Lewis and the Anglo-American writer Ezra Pound founded the journal *Blast* in June 1914; 'Vorticism', as Pound called the movement of avant-garde intellectuals in London, shared many of the aesthetic and political aims of Futurism. They too attacked what they perceived as the decay of established society, academicism, rigid aestheticism, half-hearted flabbiness. They wanted to purge Britain of its lassitude and apathy with energy and violence. Although the Vorticists stressed their independence of Italian Futurism, Marinetti, who had addressed audiences in London and staged an exhibition of Futurist art, clearly exerted decisive influence on it; Lewis called him the 'Cromwell of our time'.[24] A certain short-term influence of Vorticism can be traced in the works of T. E. Hulme and Ford Madox Ford; however, apart from Lewis himself, who expressed admiration of Fascism and Hitler, the post-war political impact of Vorticism in Britain was negligible.

Christopher Nevinson was the only English painter to espouse the cause of Futurism, enthusiastically banging a drum at Marinetti's performances in pre-war London. Yet although his early war paintings of 1914–15 show a strong influence of Futurist style, for example in the strong dynamism of *Returning to the Trenches* (1914–15), they do not pretend that war is glamorous. His *Flooded Trench on the Yser* (1915, Fig. 8) evokes a sense of desolation. *La Mitrailleuse* (1915, Fig. 9), despite the Futurism of the geometric lines and the subject-matter of the machine gun, conveys no radiant joy in violence; with the dead soldier in the picture Nevinson broke the usual taboo on depicting one's own war dead, and the machine-gunner and his team are grim-faced, dehumanized beings. Partly owing to his experience as an ambulance driver in France and partly to his rejection of patriotically sanitized versions of the war, Nevinson dropped his allegiance to Futurism. Lewis wrote that 'Marinetti's solitary disciple has discovered that War is not Magnifique, or that Marinetti's Guerre is not la Guerre.' Still, even his Futurist comrades in France, Severini and Guillaume Apollinaire, praised Nevinson's work. Apollinaire published an essay to say that

> people are talking a lot about an Englishman who has been painting the present war: C. R. W. Nevinson. The secret of his art, and of his success, lies in his way of rendering and making palpable the soldiers' sufferings, and of communicating to others the feelings of pity and horror which have driven him to paint. He has set down on canvas the mechanistic aspect of the present war: the way in which man and machine are fused in a single force of nature. His picture, *La Mitrailleuse*, makes this point ideally well.[25]

Lewis himself abandoned his Vorticist theories by 1917, replacing near-abstraction with representation. But early on he had rejected the Futurist affirmation of war. He wrote in *Blast No. 2*, published in 1915: 'As to Desirability, nobody but Marinetti, the Kaiser, and professional soldiers WANT War.' Nevinson, even as an official war artist, could not summon up the hypocrisy required to depict patriotic glory, and ran into trouble with the War Office for his unheroic depiction of two dead British soldiers lying in the mud, tangled in barbed wire (*Paths of Glory*, 1917, Fig. 10).[26]

Figure 8. *Flooded Trench on the Yser* (1915), painting by Christopher Nevinson

The exhibition of Futurist art in Berlin in 1912 organized by Herwarth Walden, art critic and editor of the avant-garde journal *Der Sturm*, provoked controversy and succeeded in making the movement well known in Germany. The Expressionist painter Franz Marc and the writer Alfred Döblin praised the works of Boccioni, Carrà, Russolo, and Severini, while the editor of the leading art journal *Kunst und Künstler*, Karl Scheffler, denounced the Futurists as mere sensationalists 'totally lacking in talent'. Raoul Hausmann, later to become an anti-war Dadaist and anarchist, defended the Futurists and demanded that Scheffler should resign as editor. Arthur Moeller van den Bruck, writer and journalist, revolutionary conservative and best known as the author of *Das dritte Reich* (1923), was impressed by their paintings but above all by their political ideas. He especially endorsed the ideas of imperialism, expansionism, and the rejection of liberalism and socialism; he connected the affirmation of war to a prediction of victory for the 'victory-accustomed nation' in the coming 'immense

Figure 9. *La Mitrailleuse* (1915), painting by Christopher Nevinson

conflict', and added his own view of the social Darwinist superiority of 'young nations' over others.[27]

Ideas similar to those of the Futurists were expressed by Georg Heym in his poem 'The War', written during the apocalyptic mood at the time of the 'panther-leap to Agadir' in 1911. His expectation was that the destructive violence of war would cleanse the ossified old civilization and replace it with vitality. If Marinetti found pre-war Italy decrepit in its 'passatism',

Figure 10. *Paths of Glory* (1917), painting by Christopher Nevinson

Heym, in a diary entry in 1910, held Germany at peace to be 'foul, greasy, and sordid ... What a pitiful government we have, a Kaiser who could just as well be a harlequin in any circus, statesmen who would do better as spittoon-holders than as men who are supposed to inspire the trust of the people.'[28] Johannes R. Becher, later to become a communist and minister in the East German government, emulated Futurism in both the style and content of his poetry of the war period, including the ode 'To a machine gun' and 'Brothel' (both 1916), which rival Marinetti in his obsession with killing, brutality, and the pornographic linking of violence and sexual exploitation of women.[29] But even the admirers of Futurism did not automatically follow its principles. Alfred Döblin, who was to become one of Germany's great modernist writers, intensively studied and reviewed Marinetti's prose work between 1910 and 1924, and was evidently fascinated

by his 'hardness, coldness, and fire', his violence and his scorn for women, but
went his own way in his novels, and was not necessarily influenced by
Futurism.[30] For others it was not the aesthetics of Futurism that made war
attractive: to the later anti-war writer and revolutionary Ernst Toller and his
extreme right-wing pro-war counterpart Ernst Jünger, war held out
the prospect of adventure, exoticism, and quite simply an early escape from
school.[31]

Not every anticipation of war in German avant-garde culture was posi-
tively connoted. In painting Ludwig Meidner's arresting apocalyptic visions
(*Apocalyptic Landscape*, 1913, and *Burning City*, 1913) appear to draw on
Futurism, and indeed in Berlin Meidner associated with Heym. However,
his work belongs clearly in the context of German Expressionism, and by no
means expressed enthusiastic anticipation of war, rather dread and horror.
This was especially clear in *Apocalyptic Landscape*, (1913; Fig. 11). The
nakedness of the dreamer emphasizes the vulnerability of man before
the devastation being unleashed around him.

Figure 11. *Apocalyptic Landscape* (1913), painting by Ludwig Meidner

In Russia, the Futurist artist Natalia Goncharova produced in 1914 a series of fourteen patriotic lithographs, 'Mystical Images of War', which draw on traditional Russian folk myth and Orthodox religious symbols.[32] Her Futurist (to be precise 'Cubofuturist') colleague Kasimir Malevich produced posters showing images such as a giant Russian peasant woman smiling as she skewers a tiny Austrian soldier on a pitchfork.[33] Goncharova emigrated in 1915 to France, where she stayed after the Revolution. Malevich turned against the war and welcomed the Revolution in 1917, eventually becoming director of the art academy in Vitebsk and of the Art Institute in Petrograd in 1923. His work underwent an aesthetic revolution in 1915 with the shift to radically abstract geometric forms (Suprematism), and in his theoretical writings he associated the future international socialist revolution with the victory of abstract Suprematism over the decadent art of the previous epoch.[34] Remarkably, Malevich produced no work directly condemning the war, unlike so many members of the artistic avant-garde in Germany.

Only Italian Futurism thus showed a clear link between aesthetic glorification of war and fascism.

Holy war and visions of the apocalypse

With the outbreak of war conventional, dominant culture rallied swiftly to the cause of nationalist mobilization everywhere in Europe. German Protestant Christianity, which since the time of Luther saw itself as servant of the state, contributed powerful ideological support. The 'League of Free Church Preachers' of Berlin and Brandenburg declared:

> The members of the Evangelical Free Churches serve the Kaiser and the Reich as do all other patriots. They are second to no one in love of their dear fatherland. Their knowledge, gained from the bible and history, teaches them that bloody wars between peoples are a natural necessity until the end of all time.[35]

Other pastors spoke of Germany's 'holy war', and that it was a 'crusade';[36] another wrote that this war was a war of defence, a 'moral duty and thus a work pleasing to God'. Theology professor Dr Titius wrote:

> He who is ready as a Christian not only to give his life to the fatherland but also, if it must be, also to kill or to throw the flaming torch, in short, to do what is alien and loathsome to his innermost desire, does not stand far from the warm love of the Apostle . . . not far from the sense of the great sufferer who was ready to bear the sins of his people and of all the world and to atone for them.[37]

A sermon by pastor Wilhelm Lueken (Frankfurt am Main) in 1915 stressed rather the expansionist, imperialist aspect of German policy: this was a war for 'freedom of movement and development, in order to have space for us and our children, to be able to act freely on the entire planet, . . . [for our] place in the sun'.[38]

Many others stressed the sense of the war as the mission of German Protestantism to spread the gospel throughout the world; it was only logical that they saw Germans as the 'Chosen People'.[39] Pastor Wilhelm Herrmann published an article arguing that Germans were closer to the Turks in a religious sense than to the utilitarian and individualist British. The purpose of the war was thus to excise the Anglo-Saxon mentality from the world, 'this cancerous growth on mankind', in order to 'free the world from the fantastic nonsense that one nation wants to rule over all others'.[40] (The latter remark appears to be a condemnation of the British empire.) The Russians were a 'savage, semi-barbaric race, led by a godless, immoral party of masters who were lacking in conscience and greedy for booty, aiming to turn our blossoming, orderly people and land into a wilderness'; the French were immoral atheists who hated Germany and wanted to ruin Germany. Protestant sermons declared the enemy nations to be the personification of 'sin', 'evil', the 'forces of darkness', the 'Antichrist', and the 'devil'. One pastor went a step further and saw a hidden meaning in the war, which was to serve to transform and rejuvenate mankind with the aim that 'peoples that have had their day will be eliminated' and 'peoples suitable for the future' would rise—a novel addition of vulgar Darwinism to Christian theology. It was more common to see in the war a sign of the coming day of judgement, an apocalyptic and chiliastic vision, i.e. the expectation that the end of the world war would bring the second coming of the Messiah and a new historical epoch of world peace.[41]

Even the 'bloody trade' of hangman was justified: 'The soldier has been given cold iron; he shall use it without awe; he shall thrust the bayonet between the enemy's ribs; he shall smash his rifle on their skulls; that is his holy duty, that is his service to God.'[42] At the same time Protestant theology could provide a kind of moral absolution: the war was often seen as a 'judgement of God', for Germany as well as its enemies. One pastor saw the war as proof of the power of God, and quoted God in his sermon: 'You do not hold peace in your hands; *I* hold the thought of peace. You have been cast down into the vortex and shall not boast of your power; *I* have the power.' Human beings, in other words, could do nothing to stop the war: it was an 'act of God'. This was just as well, since the war brought 'salvation': the death of soldiers was interpreted as martyrdom, and the blood of the fallen fertilized the field from which the new Germany would arise; the fallen and even the injured were 'precious seeds', and they wove their 'dying with our living'.[43] In this way the obscene mass death of young men was given a positive meaning; we can trace here one of the theological roots of the fascist idea of palingenesis.

The Catholic church in Germany was less extreme in its statements supporting the war effort, although Catholics as a whole were no less loyal than their Protestant fellow-countrymen. Its main emphasis was placed on religious welfare and care of the wounded, rather than on theological justification of war.[44]

Each of the churches in the belligerent nations declared their solidarity with their respective armies. Despite the well-known 'impartiality' of the Vatican, and the repeated condemnations of the war by Pope Benedict XV, the Italian church and its priests saw no incompatibility between their faith and the bearing of arms. Italian military chaplains were informed that the doctrine of Saint Augustine, whose teaching on the fundamental distinction between just and unjust war was the highest authority in Christian theology, was not being violated. Although Italian intervention in the war did not exactly match Augustine's definition of just war, the subjects owed loyalty to the state, even if they did not understand the necessity of the war, since it could not be proved clearly that the war was unjust.[45] In France the Catholic poet Charles Péguy, who was to die as a volunteer on the Marne in August 1914, had written in 1913: 'Happy are those who die in a just war. | Happy the ripened grain, the harvested wheat.[46] Above all through the intervention of the extreme nationalist Barrès, the figure of Péguy as martyr came to symbolize France in this 'just war'. The French church transformed its attitude towards the state with which it had been engaged in a bitter struggle only a few years previously, over the Dreyfus affair, control of education, and its entire relationship with the Republic. In the *Union sacrée* both the Republic, with its universal values of the Rights of Man, and the Catholic church adopted a form of messianic belief which was not far removed from that of the German Protestant church. Both parts of French culture could agree on the notion of the war for the defence of civilization: the defeat of France would mean the decline of civilization; victory would mean progress for all mankind. French Catholics saw France as 'the eldest daughter of the Church', and the war would prepare the redemption of the nation.[47] Like the German Protestant theologians, French Catholics saw the French war dead as martyrs who had died in the crusade and for Christ.[48]

Naturally, for the French Catholics the German nation became 'the collective embodiment of evil'. Conflating mass killing of soldiers, atrocities against civilians, and cultural destruction, the Catholic poet Paul Claudel wrote 'La Nuit de Noël 1914', in which fallen soldiers and civilian victims of German atrocities celebrate Christmas Mass in heaven, while the Germans shell Rheims cathedral. Indeed, not only Catholics, but also Protestants and Jews expressed particular outrage at the destruction of churches by the Germans. 'Our city bears forever the stigmata of their hideous "Kultur"'...Everything has been swept away, crushed, burned by Teutonic iron. Ruins everywhere, everywhere the silence of the tomb', wrote Abbé E. Foulon of Arras. The burning of the university library of Louvain was seen as a deliberate attack on culture and Christianity, and the Chief Rabbi of France denounced the destruction of Rheims cathedral: 'The destruction of the Rheims basilica is an odious blasphemy against God, the Father of all, and reveals the absence of all religious and human feeling in its perpetrators.'[49]

Some Christian intellectuals in France went beyond outrage and condemnation of the enemy. Joséphin Péladan, a right-wing neo-Catholic who revived the Rosicrucian movement, and author of numerous books of popular cultural history, published in 1916 *L'Allemagne devant L'humanité et Le Devoir des Civilisés* (Germany before humanity and the duty of civilized peoples). This was written 'to expose how the Germanic race had become inhuman, that is, opposed to the universal principles and conditions of the progress of the species'.[50] His argument was that Germany had adopted a perverted ideology; by 1914 it had become 'the incarnation of evil' and was aiming to shape the universe in its image. For one hundred years the German spirit had corrupted a France which was fascinated by its *Kultur* (as he was himself). Even Kant, who was defended by so many French professors, was 'the enemy of the classical spirit' and the 'poisoner'; people had embraced Wagner: France had become by 1914 a 'spiritual and moral colony of Germany'. In other words, this was a call to extirpate all signs of German culture from France. Half his battle, in fact, was to cleanse decadence from France: 'Stop seeing nothing but the German army. It is in Noyon, but German thought is in the Sorbonne.'[51]

Péladan concluded that after two years of warfare in which 'three million Germans' had been killed, there was only one solution. The Germans were 'too numerous to exterminate; [they therefore] have to be *removed*, reliably, completely, and permanently'. This would require the unity of nations after the victory, new armaments, and a new campaign that would mobilize those who had not fought; and he warned not to heed the pacifists: 'The pope bleats for peace and so does Romain Rolland: they will preach disarmament in the name of Christ or humanitarianism.' By 'removal' he meant that the entire world should expel all Germans to Germany, eradicate all German ideas, cease trade with Germany, and isolate Germany totally.[52]

The importance of these ravings of an eccentric leader of a small sect, which Péladan was, should not be overstated. But although his proposals were not taken up by any responsible French leaders, the fact that he made them indicates how the shock at the immense destructivity of the war had deformed thinking and made possible the notion that an entire nation could, or should, be 'removed'. Moreover, his narrow-minded critique of French intellectuals and his denunciation of the Sorbonne as a pacifist bulwark of pan-Germanism echoed the more influential Charles Péguy.[53]

The Church of England occupied an analogous position to that of the Evangelical church in Germany, as the established church. It seldom went beyond identifying with the nation and acting to provide chaplains and spiritual support for the troops. However, the Bishop of London, A. F. Winnington-Ingram, soon became well known for making blood-curdling speeches. He announced that this was a holy war, and the soldiers who died fighting for the cause would go to heaven.[54] Yet his views were those of an extremist, and the established church tended to moderation; in any case, unlike in France and Germany, there was no revival of formal religion of any major confession in Britain. Since Britain was not waging a war to overturn the balance of power, neither the church nor lay intellectuals engaged by and large in the kind of violent rhetoric of cultural superiority that was characteristic of German intellectuals.

Naturally, the apocalyptic vision was not unknown outside Germany. It was present in the French Catholic interpretation of the war, although it did not occupy a central place.[55] There was also a secular hope that 'this struggle will be the last of all wars . . . for a century at least! The last war! Terrible and magnificent phrase!'[56] The British idea of the 'war to end wars' was thus by no means unique in expressing this hope for eternal peace. The phrase was in fact secular in origin, although one of its authors was making use of religious language. It was the editor of *The Observer*, J. L. Garvin, who wrote: 'And after Armageddon war, indeed, may be no more'; H. G. Wells popularized the idea and wrote in August 1914 of 'The War that Will End War'; and added that when victory came, Britain would 'save the liberated Germans from vindictive treatment'.[57]

Russian nationalist culture was perhaps more closely identified with religion than any other, as testified by the frequent use of images from Orthodox popular religion in Russian propaganda posters, postcards, and film. Posters depicted an unlikely holy trinity of France, Britain, and Russia as females, with the Russian figure carrying a crucifix; the dragon-slaying St George; and various allegorical angels. In propaganda films the Kaiser was depicted as Satan or as the Antichrist, responsible for all the atrocities committed by his soldiers. There was even a film called *The Horrors of Rheims*, in which a German officer attempts to rape a nurse on the altar of the cathedral. He is stopped by a priest holding a cross, just in time for the German artillery to shell the cathedral.[58]

The mobilization of academics

Mainstream intellectuals lent their support to the war, often using conventional images drawn from religion and national culture. Ulrich von Wilamowitz-Moellendorff, Germany's leading classical philologist and internationally respected among classicists to this day, justified the war as a 'holy struggle . . . for a just cause'. Unlike the Protestant theologians Wilamowitz did not stress the idea of the natural loyalty owed by a subject to the state, but rather the idea that the war revealed the inner unity of the German people which no longer knew party, class, or confessional differences. He went on to list the objectionable features of Germany's enemies, and wrote that the war had revealed the true soul of the Belgians, who were cowardly murderers whose weapons were the dagger and the flaming torch. The British were the real driving evil spirit which had unleashed this war, with their envy of German freedom, industriousness, order, and of the goodness of German work. Wilamowitz announced that Britain was striving to destroy German inventiveness, German strength, hard work (*Fleiß*), and the achievements of German merchants, whose products and whose ships were rivalling the British on all the high seas.[59] The charges laid against Belgium and Britain amounted to a projection of the German militarists' own aims and methods. The term *vernichten*, to destroy or annihilate, used by Wilamowitz, is ambivalent, and here it means defeat rather than physical elimination. Yet it could imply also the latter, and the philosopher Adolf

Lasson made this explicit: 'This war is terrible above all because of the number and the kind of enemies who waylay us and seek to destroy [*vernichten*] us without mercy. If they were to succeed, they would like best to exterminate us [*ausrotten*].'[60]

Gustav Roethe, professor of medieval German language and literature, spoke of the 'flame of holy belief in the world-historical mission of the German people against barbarity and over-culture'. Unwittingly—or perhaps wittingly?—he accepted the French accusation that the German army was acting like the barbarian hordes destroying Roman civilization: 'If today the Germans, to the horror of our enemies, surge over them like storm waves . . . , we recognize the strength of our Germanic ancestors who once inundated the Roman Empire in a tremendous tidal wave.'[61] Otto von Gierke, professor of law and like Roethe a member of the Prussian Academy of Science, on the one hand stressed that Germany respected and valued all foreign cultures; other peoples should not fear that the 'supremacy of Germanness' would endanger their own particular culture. Yet on the other hand he referred approvingly to Fichte's 'Speeches to the German Nation' of 1808 claiming that the Germans were the only people in Europe which had retained its original authenticity and thus its capacity for intellectual development, and quoted the unforgettable lines of otherwise justly forgotten mid-century poet Emanuel Geibel:

> Und es mag am deutschen Wesen
> Einmal noch die Welt genesen.
>
> And one day by the German soul
> Shall the world be made whole.[62]

Adolf Lasson compared the German nation and its culture and education with those of its enemies, and wrote:

> No, thanks be to God, today [i.e. in contrast to Fichte in 1808] we should show rather on what a proud height Germany stands today, and how this height arouses the envy, anger, frustration, and thus the implacable hatred of the others. What excites the others against us is the feeling that 'we cannot match these Germans—they are superior to us'. We may joyfully confess it here: the consciousness of German superiority, intellectual and moral, is well founded; this consciousness lives in us and makes us strong. Our moral institutions are superior; the entire state of our culture is superior. That is why they are fighting us, out of common envy and base profit-seeking . . . [63]

France's foremost public historian, Ernest Lavisse, did indeed argue that 'arrogance' (*orgeuil*) was the basic trait of the German national character and directly compared Hermann the Cherusker's ambition to free Europe from the yoke of Rome in the first century AD with contemporary Germany's unscrupulous destruction of cultural monuments such as the library of Louvain and the cathedral of Rheims.[64] Lavisse was wrong in his reductionist argument about German 'national character', but the effusions of some German intellectuals made it easy for him and others to claim that 'arrogance' was a common thread running through the German intellectuals' praise of the German war effort. The neo-Kantian philosopher Émile Boutroux argued in essays for the *Revue des deux mondes* that German culture had turned away from the classical tradition and the humanism of Kant and was now fundamentally antagonistic to Graeco-Roman civilization, for Germany had chosen to repudiate its principles—morality, compassion, justice, virtue. This argument had the greater weight, coming from one who knew Germany well and had worked to promote fruitful relations between German and French academics, and who had taught and influenced Bergson, Delbos, and Andler.[65]

Artists and intellectuals between humanism and hubris

Yet although Boutroux attacked German culture as 'une barbarie savante', he called on France not to pay Germany back in the same coin, but to uphold the values of humanism.[66] Lavisse and his collaborators did not respond in kind to the German concept of cultural imperialism, and did not argue for French hegemony to supplant German hegemonial ambition. In his 'Appel aux Français', addressed to mayors of all *département* capitals and returned by most of them with their signatures, thus signifying a national statement about the war, Lavisse warned that France must win the war in order to have Germany punished and force it to repair all the damage suffered by France. However, Germany would continue to fight for as long as it could, and there could therefore be no compromise peace. France, in defending itself, was 'protecting humanity from the hateful yoke' of barbarous Germany.[67] In earlier times France had made the 'regrettable error' of pursuing hegemonic aims, such as under Louis XIV and Napoleon, but today France was fighting only in self-defence and for the preservation of humanity and civilization.[68]

The French imputation of German 'barbarity' in fact preceded the German intellectuals' statement of cultural superiority, and even preceded German acts of war that might be interpreted as 'atrocities'. From the very outset of the war the French press, government, and intellectuals depicted the conflict with Germany as the struggle of '*civilisation*' against German '*Kultur*'. As the philosopher Henri Bergson, president of the Académie des Sciences Morales, announced on 8 August 1914: 'The struggle embarked on against Germany is the struggle of civilization against barbarism.'[69] It was Germany's act of war itself, the violation of international law and what the French saw as a long-planned thrust for domination in Europe which prompted immediate recourse to the images dating back to 1870. All parties from left to extreme right, from Socialists to Action Française, united in a war to 'defend civilization'; *Le Matin* on 4 August 1914 called it a 'holy war of civilization against barbarity'.[70]

Yet there were differences: for the Socialist *L'Humanité* it was not 'the Germans', but the Kaiser and the military leadership who were the true barbarians. The right and the Catholics condemned the Germans without further distinction as barbarians. Soon the French press and many intellectuals were ascribing racial characteristics to the Germans, such as congenital dissatisfaction, ill-humour, envy, greed, selfishness, and vanity, which could all be traced back to their physiognomy: their square heads and sack-like bodies. The psychologist Professor Edgar Bérillon published a scholarly article which argued that Germans had a particular body odour, a 'racial smell' that resembled that of a rabbit-hutch, rancid fat, stale beer, or curdled milk; it was caused by the fact that German intestines were abnormally long and had an extra loop.[71] This racism, from which *L'Humanité* in general remained honourably distant, culminated in the denunciation of the German in 1917 as the 'entirely vile and evil sub-human . . . the degenerate boche' in the popular weekly *L'Illustration*.[72] It symbolized the radicalization of war culture which was shifting to the right; it was paralleled in domestic developments in a certain 'brutalization of French politics' in which perceived enemies of the state were severely punished, in some cases by execution.[73]

As the war dragged on, the idea of 'civilization', which would be identical with the victory of France, proved impossible to sustain. When the end was in sight, it tended to be replaced by ideas of vengeance, justice, and punishment. The 'barbarians' had lost the war, but no one could claim that 'civilization' had won it. As from September 1918 newspapers debated the punishment Germany would soon have to face. Germany, German products, and German influence were to be excluded from France forever.[74] There was consensus that war criminals would be punished in formal prosecutions and reparations would have to be paid in order to reconstruct the devastated French economy; Marshall Foch and prime minister Clemenceau wanted for reasons of strategic security to shift France's borders as far as possible to the east and detach the Rhineland from Germany. Germany would be kept permanently weaker than France. Yet the disappearance of 'civilization' from the French discourse about the war did not produce a vision of destruction, nor even an imperialist 'civilizing mission', rather an inward-looking desire for protection, coupled with the rhetoric of 'liberty', which expressed the hope of US support for the common goal. The theme of destroying the enemy certainly featured in French war posters, but usually in the stylized form of the tough *poilu* (the ordinary soldier; the term means the 'hairy one') strangling the vicious German eagle, or Marianne as a flying angel leading the heavenly host of Allied troops into battle. The depiction of France as victim of devastation figured in several posters. One, *Journée de l'Oise. Pour les éprouvés de guerre* ('The day of the Oise. For the victims of war', Valentine Reyre, 1916; Fig. 12), shows the destruction of Senlis and the civilian victims to commemorate the atrocity of 2 September 1914 and collect money for the refugees. In another, *Par deux fois j'ai vaincu* ('I have vanquished twice', Maurice Neumont, 1918), a battle-worn but steadfast French soldier stands before a devastated landscape, warning the home front not to succumb to the 'boche' propaganda which was calling for a negotiated peace.[75]

When war came, Russian intellectuals did not differ greatly from their German or French counterparts in rallying to the national cause. This was an unexpected development, since by comparison with France, Germany, or even Britain, most Russian people and above all the intelligentsia were 'peculiarly inhospitable to military values and virtues'; nationalism and imperialist expansion simply were not popular issues.[76] A large part of the intelligentsia, down to the level of primary school teachers (who in France were the backbone of the Republic), fundamentally opposed the Tsarist regime. Nevertheless, most writers and artists rallied to support the nation at war, and even the Futurist writer Vladimir Mayakovsky, who had joined the Bolsheviks in 1907 while still at school and was later a supporter of the Bolshevik revolution, wrote to condemn the Germans for trampling upon 'centuries of Europe's cultural achievements': 'The rings from the treasures of Liège are on the fat, beer-sodden fingers of Prussian Uhlans, and

Figure 12. French poster: 'The day of the Oise. For the victims of war', Valentine Reyre, 1916

candy-filled bakers' wives sweep the streets of Berlin with petticoats of Brussels lace.'[77] There had always been a desire of Russian intellectuals to overcome their isolation from 'the people', and many artists turned to the production of patriotic propaganda posters based on Russian national folklore images. This 'patriotic culture' was developed by the intelligentsia and even by avant-garde artists (a small minority of the latter) without government direction. Primitive images depicted the Germans as beer-swilling, sausage-eating rapists of Belgium, and Kaiser Wilhelm with his distinctive moustache as a brutal buffoon; Russian soldiers as invariably more courageous and faster than the enemy, and always victorious.[78] With the disastrous military setbacks of 1915, the self-mobilized patriotic culture retreated and weakened, and patriotic themes no longer featured often in iconography. In the theatre, too, patriotic plays soon disappeared from the schedules. Both avant-garde and popular culture fractured, with some artists and intellectuals maintaining a devotion to traditional nationalist values of tsar and church, some engaging in satire and criticism against the regime, and others escaping reality into abstraction.

To turn back to German intellectuals, the remarks of Lavisse and Boutroux applied perfectly to Werner Sombart, who wrote that Kant's *Perpetual Peace* (1795) was a dishonourable exception in German writing. Pacifist utterances were for Sombart 'always a sin against the holy spirit of German-ness'.[79] Without a shadow of intellectual doubt Sombart termed the war 'the holy war which Germany is now waging against a world of enemies'. This was a 'Glaubenskrieg', a war of beliefs. In many ways Sombart was right: he pointed correctly to the fact that the war was for France also a war for Alsace-Lorraine, and for the allies it was a war for 'west European civilization', 'the ideas of 1789', against 'German militarism' or 'German barbarism'. Naturally, this ignored the question of the origins of the war and the fact that France and Britain had reacted in defence. But for Sombart the main battle was that between 'merchants' and 'heroes'. 'Merchants' symbolized British mentality, the British empire, and western capitalist domination of the world; 'heroes' were a symbol of German dedication to duty, service of the individual to the nation, striving for freedom, obedience, sacrifice.[80] The idea of sacrifice is contained in Sombart's quotation from Nietzsche's *Thus Spoke Zarathustra*:

> The living creature values many things higher than life itself . . .
>   So the greatest, too, surrenders and for the sake of power stakes—life.
>   The devotion of the greatest is to encounter risk and danger and play dice for death . . .
>   And life itself told me this secret: 'Behold', it said, 'I am that which must overcome itself again and again . . . '
>   Go apart and be alone with my tears, my brother. I love him who wants to create beyond himself, and thus perishes.[81]

Given the outstanding importance of Nietzsche in German culture in the era of the First World War, the ideas of the sacrifice of the individual to a great cause, the overcoming of danger and risk, and contempt for life, were very familiar to well-educated Germans, even if they were derived from second-hand readings or distortions of Nietzsche. In Sombart's argument only the Germans possessed the word 'Aufgabe', which means both task and self-sacrifice, and thus only they possessed the capacity for 'union with the deity in this world' through action which made Germans heroes, while the British remained merchants in spirit.[82] As did the ninety-three intellectuals who signed the 'Appeal to the world of culture' in October 1914 (see Chapter 1), Sombart identified 'German militarism' with German culture:

Militarism is the heroic spirit which has risen up to become the spirit of war. It is the highest unity of Potsdam and Weimar. It is 'Faust' and 'Zarathustra' and Beethoven scores in the trenches. For the Eroica and the Egmont Overture are also truest militarism.[83]

It is hard to imagine Beethoven, Goethe (or even Nietzsche, for whom culture was the highest value, standing above the state), endorsing such militarist nationalism.[84] But it was entirely consistent of Sombart's caricature of German society to claim that Germany was 'a warrior people'. He was right to claim that Germany gave the highest state honours to warriors, that from the Kaiser down its officials often appeared in military uniform, and that the militarist spirit held war in high esteem. But he went too far in claiming that 'all other branches of social life serve the military interest, and in particular economic life is subjected to it'.[85] French propaganda only needed to translate Sombart for a perfect condemnation of German culture at war, but not many German capitalist entrepreneurs would recognize this as a true picture; still less would the working class, a great part of which was anti-militarist and anti-state in its political affiliations.

There was, naturally, something in common between Sombart's excogitations on the nature of patriotic sacrifice and the rhetoric used in every nation to mobilize men and the home front. Yet it is the particular formula of the compound which made German militarist nationalism so violently explosive. In Sombart's view, a commonly held opinion among German intellectuals, duty and sacrifice of the individual were necessary because the existence of the state stood above the life of the individual; indeed, the fate of the individual was to sacrifice himself for this higher life: 'With this belief, indeed only with this belief, the painful dying of thousands gains sense and meaning. The heroic philosophy of life finds its highest consecration in heroic death.' Sombart went on to quote a poem by Richard Dehmel, one of Germany's best-known contemporary writers, who volunteered for the army in August 1914 at the age of 51:

> What are goods and chattels in life?
> All things that pass away!
> That we tremble with rapture
> When we rise up in battle,
> That will survive forever,
> That is God's will!
>
> God is courage in adversity,
> Is the noble spirit that drives us:

> Honour, loyalty, discipline, conscience!
> Nation, thus be enraptured,
> That your spirit may stay immortal,
> Spirit of God![86]

In traditional societies still dominated by Christianity, death in war had a transcendental meaning: it lent purpose to mundane existences, a kind of short cut to the metaphysical state only achieved otherwise through years of tedious devotion to obedience to social, moral, and religious norms. But more still, the idea that worldly possessions were purely temporal, and could be lightly discarded, could serve not only to render one's own sacrifice easier, but make the property of anyone else liable to easy destruction. At once, therefore, German soldiers had a passport to paradise and a licence to pillage.

Does this mean Sombart endorsed the will to destroy the enemy's culture? He does not go so far as to state this explicitly, but his aim for the peace that would follow German victory was that Germany would become more or less autonomous, in economic and cultural terms, relying mainly on its own resources:

> Basically we Germans need nobody so far as intellectual and cultural matters are concerned. No nation on earth can give us anything worth mentioning in science, technology, art, or literature that we cannot comfortably do without.

Breathtaking arrogance of this kind could be found among British, French, or Italian chauvinists, although arguably among the more marginal figures; contempt for foreign culture could be one step towards its wilful destruction. In a passage that seems bizarre today but was common belief at the time, Sombart expressed the idea that like the Greeks and the Jews of history, the German people 'of these centuries' was the Chosen People.[87]

Such exalted rhetoric was perhaps necessary for a middle-aged professor who unlike his students was not exposed to danger and death, as a kind of compensatory act. Sombart dedicated *Händler und Helden*—'Traders and Heroes', his tirade of hate against Britain, to the 'young heroes out there facing the enemy' and intended his book to be his contribution to the struggle 'which will have to continue when you return home' as a 'battle of the minds'. He was not only trying to ingratiate himself with the younger generation: Sombart actually expected a revolution from the war, to be led by the young generation returning from it victorious, in a vision that resembled the chiliastic expectations of the Protestant theologians:

A new, a German life shall begin after the war, and you shall create it. You, who return home with a free and pure spirit and whose fresh strength of youth will shatter the thousand barriers and prejudices and established opinions which until now have weighed so heavily upon our people. You are our hope and our trust. Like a mighty plough the war cuts its furrows through the fallow land of the German spirit.[88]

There was a connection between the intellectual mobilization of nationalist hate and the broader trend of anti-democratic thought on which Nazism fed, and the fear of proletarianization. This fear runs like a thread through German right-wing thought, becoming stronger in the 1920s as it was given more sustenance by the spread of mass media such as radio and cinema, the relative decline in living standards of a significant part of the middle class, and university expansion and graduate unemployment. For some the road ended in cultural pessimism, while for the 'revolutionary conservatives' the response to the perceived threat was a campaign for culture, such as that which was the concern of Eugen Diederichs, the publisher with a broad network of contacts among German intellectuals dating from before the war. During the war he attempted to remobilize intellectuals, e.g. through the Burg Lauenstein meeting of 1917. After the war he published the journal *Die Tat* ('The Deed'), which aimed to establish the cultural hegemony of the educated bourgeois elite.[89] He increasingly associated his publishing house with the radical right, and published *völkisch* (i.e. racist) and national conservative writers; the 'young conservative' intellectual Hans Zehrer was the editor of *Die Tat*; and Diederichs himself gave a lecture to the 'League for the Struggle for German Culture', the organization led by the Nazi 'intellectual' Alfred Rosenberg.[90]

Tracing connections with later Nazi figures, however intriguing, is not the essential point. It was mainstream German nationalism that welcomed the destruction of the enemy's culture. Wilhelm Kahl, professor of law at Berlin University, announced from the lectern in 1914 that 'the bones of a German soldier, with the breast of a hero and his immortal soul, are worth more than a cathedral'.[91] Kahl was later to become a leading parliamentarian of the DVP, one of the liberal parties in the Weimar Republic, the party of Stresemann, the 'good European'.

Although our image of German artists during the war is dominated by the devastatingly graphic depictions of destruction, bloodshed, filth, and ugliness by artists such as Grosz, Beckmann, or Dix, at the start most artists welcomed the war. The editor of the leading modernist art journal *Kunst und Künstler*, Karl Scheffler, wrote that it would bring liberation and a 'regeneration of idealism'. Convinced of German intellectual superiority, Scheffler wrote that the issue was 'world rule' which would fall to Germany in due course. 'We must become a master race not just in politics, but also in the spiritual realm.'[92] Thus leadership in art would pass to Germany, which would take the form of the further development of Impressionism. In doing so, 'all the recent foolery . . . of Expressionism, Cubism, and Futurism' would disappear.[93] In the meantime, he hoped that artists would produce war pictures which would combine blood and beauty, devastation and cruelty. Yet in aesthetics he was no narrow-minded chauvinist: Impressionism was dominated by French painters, and Expressionism mainly a German movement (although influenced by the French *Fauves* and the Norwegian Munch); Scheffler continued to voice respect for French art.

The German artists who had been at the forefront of the modernist movement and had therefore been rejected by the conservative art establishment before 1914, such as the Expressionists, likewise rallied to the support of the war. We have seen in Chapter 1 how they too could justify the destruction of cultural monuments. The initial reaction of some artists was indeed patriotism mixed with delight at the potential for new motifs and new aesthetic experiences. Ernst Ludwig Kirchner and Max Beckmann, to take two well-known artists, both welcomed the war and initially participated with enthusiasm, as will be discussed below. Beckmann contributed to *Kunst und Künstler* a sketch of the conquest of Liège, depicting the commanding officer in heroic-aggressive pose.[94]

How do we explain this outburst of pleasure at the outbreak of violence and hate, of hypertrophic chauvinism among men who were known for their refinement and cosmopolitanism? Even someone so detached as the writer Stefan George, who felt himself to be above war, was not immune. It is true that in his poem 'The War' he wrote: 'I will not take part in the quarrel that you perceive' (addressed probably to his circle of followers, talented young intellectuals). Stefan George saw the war in the first instance as a 'penance for the transgressions of humanity, which had led to a gigantic decline of culture'. George confessed in his poem he could not 'rave about national virtue and foreign perfidy'. Yet he welcomed the coming of the war for its purifying powers, because it would bring 'redemption'. From his great distance from the bloodshed he saw war in the sense of Nietzsche as something that would bring about a new man, a new culture—a recurrent thought in Germany's cultural elites. His circle of followers was by no means so detached: they saw it as their task to mobilize culture for war.

Friedrich Gundolf, the literary scholar, wrote on 11 October 1914 in the *Frankfurter Zeitung* of his yearning for the unification of the German mind with the German nation, to be achieved by the 'unlosable victory', and that the future world of culture was to be 'a new Reich of European values' which would be determined by the 'German mind'.[95] The German-Austrian writers Rilke and Hofmannsthal also welcomed the war as catharsis and as an opportunity for a fresh start in a unified community.[96]

Before the war the weekly *Simplicissimus* was best known for its anti-establishment satires and trenchant anti-militarism, in general poking fun at the authoritarianism of Imperial Germany. Within days of the outbreak of war it had switched to supporting the idea of the *Burgfrieden*, national unity. One drawing showed the ghosts of Bismarck and Bebel, the latter in Landwehr uniform with a rifle, and below their cloud a column of marching German soldiers. Bismarck says to the veteran leader of the pre-war SPD: 'Well, Bebel, now we are getting to know each other properly at last!'[97] Soon *Simplicissimus* was publishing special editions with titles like 'Gott strafe England' ('May God punish England'—a phrase so popular it replaced for a time common greetings), pictures and drawings illustrating the thesis that the Belgians were illegally engaging in 'franc-tireur' warfare, and racist cartoons accusing French colonial soldiers of cannibalism—of not bringing in German prisoners because they had eaten them.[98]

The writer Gerhart Hauptmann, famous for his social criticism such as in his plays *Vor Sonnenaufgang* ('Before Sunrise') and *Die Weber* ('The Weavers'), who had for that reason as well as his pacifism encountered hostility from the establishment and the Kaiser before 1914, moved to the front ranks of the literary mobilization. Co-signatory to the 'Appeal to the World of Culture', Hauptmann also wrote in a famous open letter in September 1914 to the French pacifist Romain Rolland that 'Russia, Britain, and France had forced the war' on Germany, which was fighting a defensive war. He denounced the 'mendacious French press' and its 'criminal attacks on the life of healthy and industrious people'; this was a war to defend German culture and German liberty which were under threat.[99]

The chiliastic element expressed by many of the intellectuals involved in the war effort made German militarist nationalism a different phenomenon to British or French nationalism. It became fashionable to give the war the same meaning for German national identity as the French Revolution for France. From the social-democratic movement to conservative intellectuals 1914 was seen against the background of 1789 and 1848.[100] In 1915 cultural historian

Professor Ernst Borkowsky published *Unser Heiliger Krieg* ('Our Holy War')
in which he tried to anticipate the judgement of future generations:

> The struggle between Germany and the world was a struggle of political beliefs;
> from the time of the French Revolution the world had subscribed to the dogma
> of democratic liberty, but when this line of thought ran its course Germany
> advanced the demand for the organized state and put forward the duty of one
> for all in place of individual egoism, integration into humanity in place of
> isolation, discipline instead of unrestraint, refinement instead of paralysis.[101]

Konrad Haenisch, later SPD Minister of Education in Prussia, interpreted
the war as a 'revolution'. Even in 1919 Haenisch was still invoking the
'thoughts of 1914' to prepare for the victory of organizational socialism.[102]

The interest in the war as theme and as source of inspiration was receding
by 1916. Ever fewer war paintings were reproduced in the two leading art
journals, although the more conservative and populist *Die Kunst* went on
producing war propaganda into 1917. By that time, one art critic wrote that
'people had undeniably become tired of war art (and of the war itself)'.
The end of the war and the revolution of November 1918 were hardly
mentioned.[103] Most leading writers, who had voiced their enthusiasm in
1914, had fallen silent so far as the war was concerned (e.g. Hauptmann,
Rilke, George).[104] Dehmel, who had written several poems welcoming war
in 1914 and glorifying the *Volksgemeinschaft* (people's community),[105] had
changed his attitude. His poem of 1917, 'Hymnus barbaricus', was a grim
satire on all nations who rejoiced each time heroic deeds were reported,
involving the killing of masses. Many other poems published over the
course of the war marked the gradual shift in mood, and in the later years
of the war, as Julius Bab, the compiler of a multi-volume collection, noted
in 1919, the emotion expressed was ever more frequently horror, no longer
pride; poets expressed a sense of human solidarity more strongly than the
national unity of 1914, and began to point to the antagonism between rulers
and ruled.[106]

Others gradually distanced themselves from the heady emotional views of
1914. By 1916 the great German historian Friedrich Meinecke had adopted a
more moderate position than that of most intellectuals in 1914, and he
criticized the position of his more extreme colleagues in the universities.
He rejected the view that saw the war as a struggle between good and evil,
and wrote that it was wrong for Germans to explain the war as a conflict
between races and cultures, because the character of nations was not some-

thing that was fixed for all eternity, but had developed out of cultural communities which were subject to a process of continual change. 'Of course, a rigid, stupid, dogmatic nationalism is not able to tear itself away from the notion that the spirits of the nations are unchanging gods or idols which command an exclusive cult of worship and unconditional obedience.'[107] Meinecke, the most important German historian in the first half of the twentieth century, was a heavyweight counter-balance to the strong militarist-nationalist culture among German intellectuals who paved the way to a racist world view and the Third Reich.

Some intellectuals held out until the end, like Thomas Mann, although in private he expressed doubts in 1915 as to whether a German victory would be desirable: 'I for my part would find little pleasure in belonging to a nation that places its boot on the neck of Europe'; for the German spirit it would be 'unbearable' for a victorious Germany to occupy northern France for decades, which would 'demoralize and brutalize our people'.[108] In public, however, he stood by his words of 1914, and in an angry, polemical book he completed in 1918, *Confessions of a Non-Political Man,* restated his solidarity with the nation and rejection of western democracy and civilization. Repeating the encirclement paranoia, he argued the war was started by 'international freemasonry as a war of "civilization" against Germany'.[109]

There were many German scholars who rejected militarist nationalism, but few who dared to go public at a time of patriotic fervour: the medical professor Georg Nicolai responded to the appeal of the ninety-three with an 'Appeal to the Europeans', drafted in October 1914 together with the astronomer and veteran pacifist Wilhelm Foerster. This was sent to a large number of professors, and called on them to defend the principles of 'common world culture'. The 'Appeal' warned that fratricidal war ('this barbarity') would exhaust and destroy Europe, and it called for European unity, for which 'good Europeans' would provide the leaders. Apart from the physicist Albert Einstein and a graduate in philosophy from Marburg, nobody else was prepared to lend their signature, and the 'Appeal' would have remained unpublished had Nicolai not reproduced it in his anti-war book published in Switzerland in 1917, *Die Biologie des Krieges* ('The Biology of the War').[110] Einstein wrote to the French pacifist Romain Rolland in March 1915: 'When posterity recounts the achievements of Europe, shall we let men say that three centuries of painstaking effort carried us no farther than from religious insanity to the insanity of nationalism? In both camps today even scholars behave as though eight months ago they suddenly lost their heads.'[111] He frequently condemned the war in his private correspondence and expressed his loathing of German imperialism. He told Romain Rolland that a German victory would be 'a misfortune for all of Europe, but especially for that country itself'[112]) and wrote to Ernst Weisbach, an art history lecturer who was a pacifist, that the victory of 'Bismarck and Treitschke', as he put it, would mean the 'moral pollution of the world', bringing an 'endless chain of... dreadful acts of violence'.[113] However, when he went public Einstein published a more general critique: patriotism was the source of evil, and in time of war it allowed the 'aggressive instincts of the male creature' to commit mass murder.[114]

Some indication of the balance of opinion among German academics can be seen in the relative success of further manifestos. On 6 October 1917, eighty-one professors, among them Einstein, published a declaration calling on the government to adopt the resolution passed by the three parties forming a majority in the Reichstag (SPD, left liberals, and Centre) which advocated a 'peace of reconciliation', renouncing all territorial acquisitions. However, some 1,100 professors signed declarations against the peace initiative, almost fourteen times as many.[115]

Nevertheless, some other noteworthy German and Austrian intellectuals refused cultural mobilization in their own way: some of the signatories to the 'Appeal to the World of Culture' (such as Paul Ehrlich, August von Wassermann, and Lujo Brentano) withdrew their assent or (like Max Planck) openly questioned the objectivity of the 'Appeal' during the war.[116] The writers Heinrich Mann, the brother of Thomas, Arthur Schnitzler, Ricarda Huch, and Karl Kraus, among others, voiced criticism of the war from the start or remained pointedly silent. Hermann Hesse stayed in Switzerland and made no secret of his pacifism, or rather, his distance from national mobilization, for which he was frequently attacked in Germany. The younger generation of Expressionist writers, who had welcomed war in 1914, had almost all turned against war by 1916, and many of them were to become associated with the Revolution in 1918 and the Weimar Republic.[117]

Perhaps the most spectacular trajectory was that of the writer and performer Hugo Ball. Before 1914 he was involved in avant-garde theatre and associated with the modernist journals *Die Aktion* and *Der Sturm*. He admired Expressionist painters and Walden's exhibition of Futurists, the latter in an ecstatic review. When the war broke out he attempted to volunteer, was turned away, but travelled to the front at his own expense in order to get as close as possible to the fighting. What he saw he found so shocking that his early patriotic enthusiasm evaporated. Before fleeing into Swiss exile he spent New Year's Eve 1914/15 together with Marinetti's translator, Else Hadwiger, declaiming from her balcony 'À bas la guerre' into the Berlin night. In Zürich Ball was one of the founders of the Dada movement in 1916 together with anti-war exiles from all over Europe, but was still in contact with Marinetti, from whom he recited texts and exhibited works at Dada soirées, at least until 1917. In the first Dada manifesto (July 1916) Ball's asyntactic use of language, humorous puns, and rejection of convention ('I do not want any words which others have invented') show that he was acknowledging a debt to Futurism and Marinetti's concept of 'words in liberty' while attempting to build something new. Dadaism, which became an international movement with branches from Paris and Berlin to New York, rejected all previous art and culture and expressed contempt for the old bourgeois order which was responsible for the catastrophe of the war.[118]

In these varied careers we can observe how avant-garde art and the desire for a radical break with the past could be refracted by the war experience into Futurism, affirmation of war, lust for physical destruction, and ultimately fascism; or Dadaism, rejection of war, lust for metaphorical destruction, and ultimately (in the case of Ball) Christian mysticism, or (in Becher's case) communism.

Finally, if we turn from the cultural avant-garde to moderate establishment intellectuals, we find developments that are less spectacular, but nevertheless provide a telling characterization of the relationship between culture and the politics of war. The sociologist Max Weber, possibly the most influential German intellectual figure of the twentieth century, supported the national cause and volunteered for military service in 1914, but never engaged in the extremist rhetoric of a Sombart. He maintained a realistic assessment of the potential of German power, argued against extreme annexation demands, and called for the democratization of the Reich.[119] Hans Delbrück, liberal-conservative military historian who held a chair in history at Berlin University and was well connected with Bethmann Hollweg, developed from a pre-war supporter of *Weltpolitik* to an opponent of extreme annexationist demands. In his articles for the *Preußische Jahrbücher* he argued that the German army would not be able to win victory by military means alone, given the superiority in resources of the enemies. It had 'staked everything on a strategy of destruction in 1914 and failed', and must now turn to politics to divide its enemies through a policy of moderation and the offer of a negotiated peace. This would convince at least some members of the world coalition ranged against Germany that their 'fear of German world hegemony' (Delbrück) was unjustified.[120] Nevertheless, the realism of Delbrück, and that of his collaborators, the Protestant theologians Adolf Harnack and Friedrich Naumann, was not capable of persuading the military who controlled high policy since the fall of Bethmann Hollweg in 1917 that a pragmatic approach would be more effective than the hubris of maximum hegemony.

War art and war politics in Italy: from Futurism to Fascism

Many of Italy's artists welcomed the war from the start, and were unflagging in their efforts to support the national cause. Futurist painters were inspired by the war they were longing for, and Carlo Carrà greeted Italian intervention with a sketch in 1915 calling for the bombing of Vienna. Marinetti greeted war with a sketch entitled *Words in Liberty (Irredentism)*, in which spear-like arrows point north-eastward on a map from Italy into Austro-Hungarian territory, over key goals like Trento, Trieste, Fiume, Zara, and even Vienna. In *Armoured Train* (1915; Fig. 13) Gino Severini, who was in France, based his painting of stylized soldiers and artillery firing on a photograph of an armoured train deployed by the Belgian army between Liège and Antwerp in 1914, and lent it Futurist dynamism and the image of the violence of gunfire.[121] Another Futurist, Giacomo Balla, depicted the *Arditi Coat of Arms*, a skull with the *arditi* dagger between its teeth (Fig. 14).[122] War propaganda posters ranged in style and content from the conventional, using romantic-heroic motifs or stylized symbols of the nation and the enemy, through the realistic, to semi-abstract Futurism. The most famous war-loan poster, by Achille Mauzan, depicted an athletic infantry soldier pausing on his way to the attack to make a direct appeal to the civilian, looking deep into his or her eyes in the manner of the Kitchener recruitment poster. This was reproduced everywhere, including in giant format: thirty square metres, the largest in Europe.[123] Gaetano Previati left a memorable anti-war painting, *Gli orrori della guerra (L'esodo)* ('The Horrors of War—The exodus', 1917–18), which shows women and children fleeing, Munch-like terror in their faces. But since the civilians are

Figure 13. *Armoured Train* (1915), painting by Gino Severini

evidently fleeing from Austrian and German soldiers, Previati, who was known for his pacifism before the war, was not condemning war as such.

Similarly, the work of Giulio Aristide Sartorio ranged from objectivist, emotionally neutral depiction of the everyday business of war (for example

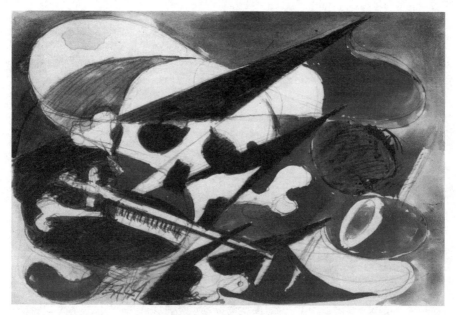

Figure 14. *Arditi Coat of Arms*, painting by Giacomo Balla

of troops and horses crossing a river estuary) to the utterly drastic scene of a battlefield strewn with corpses, without a living soul in sight (*Sacile*, 31 October 1917; Fig. 15) The interesting thing about Sartorio is how the war changed him. Before the war a symbolist influenced by the English Pre-Raphaelites and by D'Annunzio, with whom he collaborated, during the war Sartorio made systematic use of modern technology—the camera— producing paintings based on photographs. Not only his style but also his subject-matter changed from the allegorical to the realistic, or rather the objectivist or Verist. His *L'Isola dei morti. Fagaré* ('The island of the dead. Fagaré'; Fig. 16) depicts mass death, corpses lined up in a desolate landscape. These paintings have a painful intimacy with death, corporality, and the obscenity of contamination which is completely absent in Futurism.[124] Yet Sartorio was no subversive pacifist: he had been an interventionist who volunteered for military service, and was an official war artist. His *Attacco aereo di Venezia* ('Air attack on Venice'; Fig. 17) is a powerful work of geometric shapes, apparently abstract, but on closer inspection objectivist, the viewer's attention being directed towards the visual effects of modern war technology: searchlights and anti-aircraft fire, which totally dwarf the distant shore-line of Venice.

Figure 15. *Sacile,* 31 October 1917, painting by Giulio Aristide Sartorio

With Italy's entry into war the Futurist poet and publicist Marinetti volunteered immediately and joined the Lombard battalion Volontari Ciclisti Automobilisti; he first saw action in October 1915 at Malcesine, then in an attack on Dosso Casina. He was given leave in December 1915. During the course of 1916 he toured Italy, giving speeches, making a Futurist film, and putting on experimental theatre shows described by him as 'violently patriotic anti-neutral and anti-German'. He returned to active service in December 1916 after being promoted to sub-lieutenant and being trained in artillery, joining the 73rd Battery at Gorizia in February 1917. He became ill and went into hospital in March–April, returned to the front in the 161st battery, and was injured in the attack on Monte Kuk; he was in convalescence until September, promoted to full lieutenant, and returned to the Isonzo front. His book *Come si seducono le donne* ('How to Seduce Women') was published in September 1917, and in November *Noi Futuristi* ('We Futurists'). He took part in the retreat of Caporetto, returned to the front at

Figure 16. *L'Isola dei morti. Fagaré*, painting by Giulio Aristide Sartorio

the Piave as a company commander, and participated in the final battles in 1918. He was widely acknowledged to be a brave and competent officer, and to judge by his diary, much in demand from fellow officers as a patriotic speaker.[125]

Four months into the Great War, in a 'Manifesto to the Students' in Milan, on 29 November 1914, Marinetti explained that Italy urgently needed Futurism as a medicine against 'passatism':

> Our programme is one of bitter combat against Italian *passatismo* in all its repugnant forms: archaeology, academicism, senilism, quietism, cowardice, pacifism, pessimism, nostalgia, sentimentalism, erotic obsession, the tourist industry, etc. Our ultra-violent, anti-clerical, anti-socialist, and anti-traditional nationalism is based on the inexhaustible vigour of Italian blood and the struggle against ancestor worship which, far from reinforcing the race, is making it anaemic and causing it to decay...In every question, in the parliaments, in the public squares, men are divided into *passatists and Futurists*.

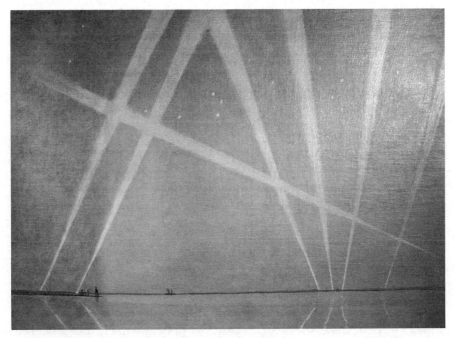

Figure 17. *Attaceo aereo di Venezia*, painting by Giulio Aristide Sartorio

(Today, in Italy, *passatists* are synonymous with *neutralists, pacifists, and eunuchs*, while *Futurists* are synonymous with *violent anti-neutralists*.)

. . .

The present war is the finest Futurist poem that has yet appeared . . . Today, we are witnessing an immense Futurist spectacle of dynamic and aggressive pictures, which we want to enter soon and exhibit our works.

. . . War cannot die, for it is a law of life. Life = aggression. Universal peace = decrepitude and the slow death of the race. War = bloody and necessary consent of the force of a people.[126]

The rambling 'Manifesto to the Students' ended with the menacing words:

We will settle accounts later with the pacifists, anti-militarists, and internationalists who have been more or less converted to the War. Down with discussions! All in agreement and en masse against Austria! Our war of hygiene is not from the hands of [prime minister] Salandra, but is ours! You want it, and we will wage it![127]

Together with other Futurist soldiers Marinetti issued in December 1915 a manifesto from the front entitled 'Italian Pride', which contains a lengthy eulogy to the qualities of the Italian soldiers, who had already shown themselves superior to the Austrians. Marinetti then praises war, and calls on the army to carry out acts of violence on the perceived internal enemy:

> Italians!
> ...Slaps, punches and shootings in the back for any Italian who is not arrogantly proud of being Italian and convinced that Italy is destined to rule the world with the creative genius of her art and the power of her incomparable Army. Anyone who betrays the slightest trace of the old imbecilic, denigratory boorish pessimism which has characterized old funereal Italy hitherto deserves slaps, punches and shootings in the back: the old Italy of the medieval Christian anti-militarists (of the type of Giolitti), of pacifist professors (of the type of Benedetto Croce, Claudio Treves, Enrico Ferri, Filippo Turati), of archaeologists, the erudite, the restorers, the museums, the hoteliers, the bookworms in the libraries and the dead cities, all neutralists and cowards, whom we, the first and the only in Italy, have denounced, vilified as enemies of the nation and as empty frustrated beings, with abundant and continuous showers of spit...[128]

Respect of international law played no part in Marinetti's world view, even though he denounced the German atrocities in Belgium. He told soldiers in a speech on 29 April 1917:

> I speak...to 3 companies at their base barracks. About 1,000 soldiers. Very attentive. I know that my speech went down well. Clear simple extremely violent—I invite them to put it into action outside with the loathsome enemy massacring him and making a definitive breakthrough.[129]

A speech Marinetti gave to a group of 300 *arditi* officers, published in September 1918, was not only an attempt to instil hatred of the enemy in the field, which could be expected of any officer of any nation, but also an incendiary call to violence against fellow-Italians, and an incitement to rape. He started by declaring how he felt honoured to be a part of the glorious *arditi* corps, as an officer fighting in the front line. He complimented the men by saying there was no need to teach the *arditi* courage, for they had that already. He described himself as a Futurist, which he explained as a patriotic revolutionary, but not a revolutionary who had anything to do with Lenin, or the Italian socialists Serrati, Lazzari, or Treves. His revolution wanted to rejuvenate Italy (*svecchiarla*, which means also modernize), 'cleanse it, sweep it clean of pedants, priests, cowards, and make it younger, stronger, greater, faster, more intelligent, more modern'.[130] This was followed by an attack on the German national character: the cretinous German people were inferior, lacking in inspiration and mental flexibility, and had no claim to hegemony. He told the *arditi* officers they were the elite of the Italian race, who loved 'our heavenly Italy'.

> Be proud to feel Italian, born precisely in this period of history of Italy and destined to resolve by blood, at a stroke, all the enormous problems of our Italian future. Sole privilege: to save Italy, to make it enormous.
>
> . . .
>
> You have become Arditi out of unfettered love of freedom, which you temper with the discipline necessary for any army that wants to conquer.
>
> . . .
>
> You have become Arditi out of love of violence, of war and the fine heroic gesture.
>
> . . .
>
> The triumphant military slang of the Arditi is beautiful; they love beautiful women whom they conquer like trenches with a heroic gesture. They do not hold themselves up with coaxing smiles and the conceits of the shirkers and those wrecks who mock you from the sidelines in the cafés . . . They fear you, they do not have the strength to hate you, but try to devalue you. They will not succeed . . .
>
> You are the first, the most worthy. You must be the masters of the new Italy. I love your insolent simplicity of manners. You have every right when you cut the throat of an Austrian!

Marinetti praised the *arditi* for their audacity in attack, despising artillery preparation, but using surprise and speed. This also amounted to an incitement to break the laws of war: 'Few prisoners, many stabbed and the rest kicked down from the conquered summit.' He reminded them of their claim to be the new elite:

> You are not only the best infantry of Italy. You are the new Garibaldians . . .
> You are the new generation of Italy, reckless and brilliant, preparing the magnificent future of Italy.[131]

In a matter-of-fact manner Marinetti wrote in his diary how an Austrian attack was 'violently repulsed'; 27 prisoners taken, 'big massacre of the enemy'.[132] And at the end of the war, during the final Italian offensive, Marinetti noted (with evident joy at the speed of his armoured car) at Aviano on 1 November 1918: 'We have to massacre them these swine these thieves these rotters!'[133]

In his war diary there is constant aestheticization of combat, in which he attempted to portray onomatopoeically the sound of artillery fire. For

example, just after witnessing two inhabitants of Gorizia badly injured by
Austrian artillery fire he wrote:

> PUM-PUM-PUM PTAAAA
> *PA-PA-PA VIIIIA*
> (la pallottola che passa) [the bullet passing]
> iiiiiiiiiiiiiiiiuuuu
>
> .   .   .   .
>
> PUTUUU PUTUUU 75 nostri [i.e. the Italian 75 mm artillery gun].[134]

His friend Boccioni, the Futurist painter who was killed in a cavalry exercise
in 1916, aestheticized war in a more conventional way, with the vitalism
common to many European avant-garde intellectuals. Describing the capture
of Dosso Casina in October 1915, Boccioni wrote:

> ... I am at rest with the battalion after unspeakably exhausting effort. My body
> suffers. I have marched up to twenty hours without eating without drinking
> without sleeping. Terrible! A tempest of shellfire and shrapnel rained down on us
> without respite. *Bellissimo!* The fallen were dragged away on all fours, without a
> word, and we advance, always slowly, with ruthless leaps ... Ten days of march in
> the high mountains, in the cold, hunger, thirst! ... Sleeping in the open, in the
> rain at 1400 [metres] ... Very significant booty, necessary and immediately
> used ... My unit has suffered 240 hits from shrapnel shells! ... The war is a
> beautiful thing, marvellous, terrible! ... Grandiosity, immensity, life and death!
> I am happy![135]

Marinetti's aesthetics of war, his interpretation of the war as a grand Futurist
festival, and his vision of the new Italy which will be inspired by Futurism,
were intimately linked with his notions of gender. His prediction:

> The conflagration synthesis of ruthless patriotism of methodical militarism of
> improvised Garibaldinism of ferocious revolutionism of proud imperialism
> and of democratic spirit disavows all political parties smashes all the passatists
> and renews the world. The conflagration develops all the sciences and all the
> sports lends velocity and multiplies hundred-fold terrestrial marine aerial
> communications; disembowels and ploughs up the cemeteries with artillery
> fire overturns and unravels the cities destroys and massacres good taste and
> delicatessen foods nostalgias and sentimentalisms degrades and devalues love
> (all the soldiers at the front know they are betrayed by their women) *but they
> are indifferent to it* ... The conflagration ... has extinguished with gunfire the
> lamps of the philosophers and made the ground tremble under the feet of the
> men of order in the museum and the library. The conflagration ... has started
> well has done a great deal and will do everything. We alone, Futurists, we are
> truly at the place at the conflagration we understand it we predict its progress and

we receive its secret messages. The conflagration was contained in this phrase of our first manifesto. Let us glorify the War the sole hygiene of the world, patriotism militarism, beautiful ideas, for which it is worth dying and contempt for woman.[136]

Clearly, Marinetti's Futurism went far beyond Italian nationalism: it was a millenarian mission for total renewal. His political and aesthetic mission was inextricably linked with his personal outlook. His attitude to women was that of a sex-obsessed adolescent. His diary has frequent references to his need for sex, his visits to brothels, and his contempt for women. He also admitted he could not spend more than one day with a woman, and that his preference was for 'fast, violent sexual intercourse'.[137] His image of women corresponds to that sketched by Klaus Theweleit in his study of extreme right-wing German war veterans, *Male Fantasies*.[138] While the peasant women he encountered in occupied Slav territories were treated little better than prostitutes and objects for his sexual gratification, the Red Cross women and nurses he encountered were from the Italian middle and upper classes, and many of them were sisters of friends and comrades. They are termed 'dama', and one is typically described as 'dolce e bella creatura intelligente', the sister of his officer neighbour in the hospital. She was, of course, 'veramente graziosa con me'; hardly surprising since she was from a family of cotton mill-owners. Conspicuous by their absence are any remarks by Marinetti on the sexual availability of such women.[139] In his novel about the last weeks of the war, *L'alcova d'acciaio* ('The Steel Alcove') Marinetti identified the reconquest of territory with sexual reconquest; Italian men 'with the healthy virility of their race' were to repossess 'their women and their mountains'.[140]

The private and the political were quite deliberately intertwined by Marinetti. In July 1918 he was called to give evidence at a court martial trial in defence of *arditi* accused of being drunk and disorderly at Verona. Marinetti considered that the *carabinieri*, the civil police, showed a lack of the proper psychology, or, as we could say, war psychology: there was a difference between war morals and peace morals. It was not to be forgotten, he said, that 'the great victory of the Piave was owed mainly to this *Holy revolutionary Mob*'. Afterwards, the members of the court invited him to dine with them and speak about Futurism. He said:

I explain the origins and the aim of Futurism new Italian religion force virility violence health originality prestige superiority creative force youthful and aeroplanic agility against cultural pedantic nostalgic passatism exploiter of past glories, dispiriting castrating complainer etc.[141]

The words 'virility' and 'castrating' indicate his notion that true masculinity was inherent in the modern, violent soldier; the ruling Italian elite was not only outdated, but also no longer manly. Futurism was no marginal phenomenon. Marinetti was well regarded among elite troops and officers, and was often invited by officers to address their men with violently aggressive speeches. General Capello, commander of the 2nd army in the zone of Gorizia, asked him for example to speak to the troops on the eve of the forthcoming attack, which was to be the tenth battle of the Isonzo.[142] Capello, one of the few generals who was prepared to try out new ideas, rather than sticking with the rigid doctrines of General Cadorna, politically progressive, rather than Catholic-conservative, was at the time initiating a programme of propaganda to remobilize the troops, to be staffed by about forty trustworthy officers who were to give lectures.[143] Another of Marinetti's admirers was General Enrico Caviglia, commander of the 29th Division at the plateau of Asiago and then of the 24th Army Corps at the battle of Bainsizza, and finally at the end of the war in command of the 7th Army with a decisive role in the battle of Vittorio Veneto. Caviglia met Marinetti several times before, during, and after the war, and at one meeting on 20 April 1918 said he had great sympathy with the Futurists for their courage and heroism and 'the example they gave in the face of the imbecilic masses'.[144]

Futurism and fascism were closely linked after the war, even if the affinity between them was not always perfect, but the connections went back some time. Between 1910 and 1914 Mussolini did not show much sympathy with Futurism, and sometimes openly criticized it. The shift in attitude came in 1918, when the Futurist party was founded and merged with the *arditi* in the first 'fasci di combattimento'. The periodical *Roma Futurista*, founded on 20 September 1918, adopted political positions similar to that of Mussolini. Mussolini wanted to meet Marinetti in Genoa in July 1918, when he visited that city at the invitation of a local committee of war invalids on 14 July to commemorate the anniversary of the French Revolution.[145] They duly met, to mutual admiration, on 18 July, and again the following day. Mussolini gave him news of the latest French victory, told him of his contempt for the (Italian) government, and his lack of understanding for a strike of munitions workers, which he explained as financed by German money and by Fiat which wanted to see the value of Ansaldo's shares go down. He spoke with scorn of Italy's intellectuals, described as 'bookworms'; Marinetti commented that he was full of Futurist ideas.[146] Mussolini met Marinetti again on 20 July, when they celebrated the Allied victory on the Marne by eating well, and ruminating on a post-war Italy ruled by ex-combatants.

The war on the internal enemy which the Futurists promised was already becoming a reality in wartime, as we saw in Chapter 4. In the frenetic campaign against the Socialist party, Mussolini's 'left-interventionists' were joined by the democratic press. As from mid-May 'all the press organs of the left-interventionists, including the democrats, made a distinct shift to the right', and their language and content became similar to that of the nationalists.[147]

After the shock of Caporetto and the stabilization of the defence along a front that ran from close to Venice to the top of Lake Garda, there was a sustained patriotic revival in internal politics. This was not merely a product of propaganda from the state, or manipulation of public opinion by the establishment. Its main social basis was the middle class. Private people and associations sent telegrams of support to Orlando from rallies in cities throughout the country. At the forefront was the 'borghesia umanistica', the educated bourgeoisie, which participated in the patriotic rallies, headed the cultural associations, newspapers, and educational institutions, and which disseminated the propaganda among the people. This unprecedented consensus was due to the new dimension created by Caporetto. The millenarian vision of future consolation (cf. Chapter 4) went together with something quite vindictive. It was a national mobilization of war culture that turned the war onto the perceived internal enemy. As Procacci writes, 'The war had for the first time become the defence of the national territory, for the enemy invasion posed the danger of wiping out the moral and territorial conquests of the Risorgimento, and it was thus an attack on the national and cultural identity of the country'. In the new mood of paranoid suspicion Jews and, more frequently in Italy, freemasons were targeted for disloyalty. A climate of witch-hunting arose, and for example the 'Anti-German League' offered a reward of 30 Lire for a defeatist, and 20 Lire for a presumed spy. The government encouraged denunciations to the authorities, with rewards offered to the most zealous officials.[148]

Many roads led to fascist Rome. One common feature was the radical rejection of Liberal Italy and the affirmation of violence and war. Consistent with this rule, the philosopher Gentile ended up after the war supporting the Fascist regime; even the anti-war Croce at first greeted the advent of Fascism as a necessary temporary measure to stamp out the threat of socialism. But by the mid-1920s Croce had realized that Fascism was not going to restore the liberal state; reasserting the values of rationalism, he became an important inspirer of anti-Fascism. When Gentile published a 'Manifesto of Fascist Intellectuals', signed, among others, by Marinetti and the playwright Pirandello, Croce responded with a 'Manifesto of Anti-Fascist Intellectuals', and soon became a beacon to almost the entire younger generation of Italian intellectuals, whose influence is felt down to the present.[149]

Another intellectual whose militant nationalism and wartime role took him into the orbit of fascism was Gabriele D'Annunzio. His charismatic role as soldier and poet, war hero, and propagandist culminated in his spectacular post-war action as leader of a band of ex-combatants who occupied the Istrian port of Fiume (Rijeka), defying the Italian government. However, his brand of aestheticized politics, for all its similarities with Futurism and fascism, proved to be too elitist and his movement was soon eclipsed by Mussolini who was more effective at mass mobilization.

A part of the old establishment was itself dissatisfied with the old order, and thus the Liberal party made common cause with fascism in 1922. General Cadorna was another example of how conservative politics converged with fascism after the war. In his memoirs written immediately after the war, he invoked the myth of the Roman empire as a quintessential part of modern Italian identity, underlining the need for strong state discipline in order to reach expansionist goals. He approvingly quoted from an essay published in January 1919 by Alfredo Rocco, professor of political science, who described old Italy, i.e. pre-war Italy, as a state lacking in cohesion and national discipline. The weakness of the state, Rocco wrote, was caused by hypertrophic individualism and class egoism, economic inefficiency, incapable bureaucracy, parliamentary degeneration, and the inflation of political doctrines including 'liberalism, democracy, [and] socialism'. Cadorna approved of a political philosophy that engaged in a critique not only of the contemporary Italian political system, but of its entire culture. This amounted to a will to destroy liberalism and individual liberty, socialism and the idea of collective solidarity of the working class, and even democracy, which was identified with electoral suffrage and majority rule. Rocco was a leading nationalist who published several works before 1914 on the need for an authoritarian, protectionist, corporative state; and criticism of parliament and liberalism. He was an interventionist, and after the war he aimed to create a corporative state in which the 'consequences of socialist classism and liberal individualism would be liquidated'. He entered Mussolini's first government, joined the Fascist Party in 1923, and became justice minister in 1925, introducing a programme of laws that helped to construct the totalitarian state, e.g. gagging the press, changing the labour laws, instituting the corporations; and he helped to draft the treaties for the Concordat with the Vatican.[150] In other words, Cadorna, a key figure of the old regime, approved the political concepts of an intellectual who was a central figure in the construction of the fascist regime. Moreover, Cadorna was not writing this in order to gain retrospective approval from the fascist regime—he published the memoirs as early as 1921, and thus probably wrote them in 1919–20, when the shape of Italy's post-war political system was not yet decided.

Mussolini himself, despite his admiration for Marinetti, and the close organizational bonds between Futurism and Fascism, was no Futurist. There is nothing in Mussolini's published war diary that resembled a Futurist attitude: he respected culture, literature, and religion, even if he was not religious, and claimed to have visited noteworthy churches and occasionally church services. There is no worship of speed, technology, and modernism. His mentality was that of modern soldierly nationalism, certainly tailored to the political needs of the fascist regime, but showing none of the radical, revolutionary sides of the movement. However, certain key ideas of fascism can certainly be found. Mussolini continued to publish articles in his newspaper *Il Popolo d'Italia* during the war, including extracts from his war diary. His thinking developed during the war through his actions, and he invented for himself the persona of heroic combatant and warrior politician. At Christmas 1916 he noted: 'Today our hearts are as hard as rocks . . . Modern civilization has "mechanized" us. The war has driven the process of mechanization of European society to the extreme.'[151] As Paul O'Brien has convincingly argued in his book on Mussolini at war, Mussolini's interventionism was anti-socialist and anti-democratic from the start. Mussolini had fully absorbed a 'war culture' before Caporetto, which was related to an authoritarian vision of post-war Italy. This was to be a state of permanent mobilization under a charismatic leader. After Caporetto, Mussolini portrayed the nation in biological terms, as a being which had suffered 'the most ferocious torture'. Now 'the Nation must be the army, just as the army is the Nation'; on 9 November 1917 he demanded: '*The whole Nation must be militarized*'.[152] After the victory, the war would be turned on the internal enemy.

The distinctions between the cultures, as expressed in the wartime mobilization of theologians, artists, academics, and writers, are indicative of
broader differences between Britain, France, Germany, Russia, and Italy.
It is simply not the case, as is implied in the writings of George Mosse, that
there was a common 'myth of the war experience' that was valid everywhere. Beyond certain similarities in the cultural and mental responses to
war one cannot extrapolate from the German war experience to draw
conclusions for other nations at war. At the same time, Eksteins's thesis
of German exceptionalism, that the modern sense of alienation affected
German society more than any other, can be rejected, at least so far as Italian
and Russian culture are concerned, which in their own way revealed at least
as deep a sense of alienation.[153]

6

Trench Warfare
and its Consequences

The Somme

Trench warfare has been described many times, so we may focus on the main developments, the essential differences between the belligerents, and the effects on the men. As explained in Chapter 2, it was not an innovation of the Great War; European armies made trench digging a part of their training before 1914, although all the belligerents shared the assumption that only a strategy of the offensive could win a war. Two battles above all others stand for the horrors of trench warfare and the vain attempt to restore mobility through massive frontal attack: the Somme and Verdun. (See Map 1.)

The battle of the Somme, in Picardy, northern France, from late June to late November 1916, saw 2.5 million Allied soldiers launch a series of massive assaults on 1.5 million German defenders. Losses on both sides were enormous: a total of 1.1 million men were killed, injured, or taken prisoner. On what is generally known as the 'first day of the Somme', 1 July, the British lost 19,240 men killed and a total of 57,470 casualties. The territory gained, a strip of land 6 kilometres long and 1.5 kilometres in depth, was insignificant. By any standards this was an unmitigated disaster. A German machine gunner described the scene:

> When the English started advancing we were very worried; they looked as though they must overrun our trenches. We were very surprised to see them walking, we had never seen that before . . . The officers were in front. I noticed one of them walked calmly, carrying a walking stick. When we started firing we just had to load and reload. They went down in their hundreds. You didn't have to aim, we just fired into them.

Many British accounts confirm this retrospective interpretation. General Jack recorded: 'The enemy's machine guns, some 1,400 yards from my position, now swept the crest like a hurricane and with such accuracy that many of the poor fellows were shot at once. This battalion had 280 casualties in traversing the 600 yards from our front line.'[1]

So many were killed in a confined area in such a short time that the British army ordered that burials were to be in trenches rather than graves, the corpses in layers covered with quicklime. Even so, grisly scenes of the mass destruction were still visible four months after the end of the battle, when the poet John Masefield was at the Somme:

> The first thing I saw in High Wood [i.e. Foureaux] were two German legs sticking out of the ground. Just inside the wood, there was a skull high up in a tree and helmets with bits of head in them and legs galore. From there I walked to Delville Wood, which is nothing to High Wood, it has been so nicely tidied up. Still, the north west corner must have had more shells on to it. The dead lay three or four deep and the bluebottles made their faces black there.[2]

Why did the British suffer the appalling losses? Why did the men advance ponderously in thick lines, offering such easy targets? The Somme is often described as useless slaughter, in which inept generals, above all General Haig, sent brave British, Irish, and Dominion men to certain death. Commanders are described as unimaginative and inflexible in their tactics, continuing to send men in even when it was obvious they would be killed—as today's press cliché puts it, 'lions led by donkeys'. In popular imagination in the English-speaking world the Somme is reduced to that first day of battle, and it remains a symbol of the futility of the First World War. In fact the orders for slow linear advance with full equipment represented 'best practice' as seen at the time by both the British and the French army. A free-for-all, it was feared, could turn an advance into a panic, 'with units intermixed and becoming exhausted'. The French general Foch also taught that 'Go as you please' brought disaster.[3] Recent research by the Australian historians Robin Prior and Trevor Wilson has shown that in any case only a minority of the British troops advanced walking at a steady pace in straight lines—of the total of 80 battalions only 12 or at most 17 did so. Already engaged in a learning process, the other battalions had used the cover of dark to emerge from their trenches and advance to the German front line, and others decided on their own to form small, flexible groups using different tactics. Yet whatever the alternative tactics, the result was the same, for wherever German machine gun nests and artillery guns were intact, the British were subjected to devastating fire as soon as they were exposed in the open.[4]

The nature of the defensive systems the Allies had to overcome in July 1916 was formidable. By late 1916 Germany had constructed over 10,000 miles (16,000 kilometres) of trenches (the British and French had constructed just over 12,000 miles). The German system allowed for 'defence in depth', with a front line up to 1,000 metres from the enemy trenches, but often as close as 100 or 200 metres. German front line trenches at the time of the Somme were protected by two barbed-wire belts, and by mid-1916 Germany was bringing 7,000 tons of barbed wire up to the front every week. The second line, 2,000 or 3,000 metres from the front, consisted of support trenches where the men could rest from fighting and where support troops were held in readiness to reinforce the front line. Another 2,000 metres back was the third line, the reserve trenches. All were connected with communication trenches for the supply of rations, ammunition, and men. At regular intervals of 600 metres machine guns, emplaced in concrete bunkers about 800 metres behind the front trenches, could pour deadly fire on the entire 'no-man's land' between the front lines.[5] The trenches were up to 9 metres (30 feet) deep, with roofs protected by 4 metres of timber beams, earth, and stone, sometimes reinforced with concrete. Steel doors protected the soldiers from infantry incursions or trench mortars.

The Allied artillery onslaught that preceded the Somme offensive of July 1916 turned these massive defensive works into rubble, burying the infantry and destroying the artillery. The British fired 1.5 million shells in the seven days of artillery preparation before the infantry attacked on 1 July 1916.[6] However, even this weight of shellfire turned out to have been insufficient to destroy German defences (failing especially to cut the barbed wire). Most German machine gunners and other infantrymen survived to emerge from the deep trenches and shoot down the waves of heavily laden soldiers, lumbering slowly across open ground. The British had not yet learned to coordinate artillery and infantry.[7] Over the entire campaign, July to November 1916, the British lost 420,000, the French 204,000, and the Germans 465,000 to 500,000 men. The first British tanks, deployed in September, were not yet sufficiently advanced in motorization or armour to achieve a decisive breakthrough, nor did the British use of poison gas, something that has been edited out of popular memory.[8]

Yet on 1 July the French achieved all their objectives in the southern sector of the Somme, for comparatively light losses (some 7,000 men).[9] This suggests that the 'first day of the Somme' has become a kind of trauma in British national memory that has obscured the real history of the battle, as Gary Sheffield and other historians have recently argued. The entire course of the four and a half-month battle should be considered, not only the first day, as part of a steep learning curve for the British army, at the end of which it had become a highly trained, well-equipped, and effective fighting force which succeeded in taking the initiative away from Germany and restoring mobility to warfare in 1917 and 1918. Despite Haig's notorious rigidity, at operational and tactical level there were substantial improvements. Flexible, more agile formations of infantry carried out limited offensives, backed by heavier, more accurate artillery fire which was learning how to lay down a 'creeping barrage', in other words devastating shell-fire which proceeded 100 yards or less in front of the advancing infantry to destroy enemy defences. This was how the French had operated on 1 July, benefiting from their far greater experience and superior artillery.[10]

Some idea of the conditions for men on both sides may be gained from eyewitness accounts. However, it is vital to distinguish between contemporary sources and later interpretations, even by participants. The Somme, as Malcolm Brown has put it, is 'almost universally seen as a symbol of . . . futility'. It prompted ringing denunciations of the war by participants, most memorably the British war poets. Any description of the horrific conditions evokes compassion, and Sassoon's cry 'Oh Jesus, make it stop!' (in his 1917 poem *Attack*) is still unanswerable. However, unlike the later accounts written with the knowledge of hindsight, sources written by men at the time show that they saw no alternative but to go on fighting.[11] General Haig, known to many as the 'Butcher of the Somme', was not the only soldier to believe the strategy had been correct. Morale among the British troops remained high, while it declined among the Germans.[12] Despite the carnage, ordinary British soldiers continued to believe in victory: 'If things go on as they are at present', wrote one in October 1916, 'the War will soon be over . . . At the bottom of our hearts we are elated at the success of the work done during the past few months.'[13]

The cumulative effect of the bombardment on the Germans was devastating. One gunner described his impressions with the words: 'Simply horrendous. With God's help I shall also get out of this hellhole unhurt. But even if you have nerves of iron and steel you will be shaken.' The soldiers waiting in their bunkers were worn down even more by their fear of their unknown fate than by the direct impact. The destruction of shelters, burying soldiers alive, could likewise drive men to insanity. German soldiers, who had already begun to express in their private letters home the desire for peace, now for the first time wrote of the 'revolution' which would have to follow the end of the war.[14]

The Somme gave the German military leaders a profound shock. By 4 July they realized that the French had won a victory, as one army commander admitted in a letter to his wife.[15] On 7 August, Lieutenant-Colonel Albrecht von Thaer, chief of staff of the 9th Reserve Army Corps, wrote in a letter:

> These are *horrendous* days. We have lost some territory, although not very much. Our good 9th Reserve Corps is now 'finished up' after fourteen days of fighting uninterrupted. The infantry have lost about half their men, if not more. Some of those who have survived are no longer human beings, but creatures who are at the end of their tether, no longer *compos mentis*, incapable of any energetic action, let alone attack. Officers whom I know to be *particularly* strong men are reduced to sobbing.[16]

In a secret report to the German high command on 27 September 1916, Crown Prince Rupprecht, who commanded an army group, described the Allies' overwhelming superiority in artillery, ammunition, and air power, which made a devastating impact on the German troops:

> The enemy's almost complete air superiority until recently, the superiority of their artillery in accuracy and number, and the extraordinary quantity of ammunition they have, allow them utterly to pulverize our defensive positions and cause us heavy losses, and they prevent us from rebuilding them. Our men can only lie in shell-holes, without barriers or shelters. All communications have been ruptured, movement between the front lines and the rear area is costly of lives, and it is extremely difficult even to bring food up to the front. Also, the men often cannot eat in the forward lines because of the smell of corpses, and they cannot sleep either.[17]

The fighting on the Somme was so exhausting for the Germans that the army decided that no unit could be left in the front line for more than fourteen days before being allowed to rest. The Allied artillery fire continued to be so intense, even after the first days, that German soldiers were unable to leave their shelters to bring in their injured comrades, normally a self-evident duty. Fresh soldiers were told by men coming out of the line how terrifying the shellfire was.[18]

By the end of September, the weather had changed, and the battlefield turned into a vast 'primeval mud landscape', an open-air sewer, in which men, horses, and vehicles got stuck fast. A German medical officer described the Somme battlefield in autumn in his diary:

> Everywhere deep shell holes, usually filled to the top with water. One feels one's way past the edge, wading through mud. Then there are tree-trunks, shot to pieces and lying across the ground, which one has to climb over. Then a group of corpses, [the sight of] which makes your flesh creep, about six of them, their bodies torn apart, covered with blood and mud. The head of one of them has been half shot away, and some distance away there is a severed leg, and some of the bodies have been so intertwined in the mud that one can no longer distinguish the individual corpses.[19]

While the German army probably suffered fewer casualties in the course of the campaign than the attackers (although this is no longer clear), it never recovered from the serious losses. As the German official war history later put it, at the Somme 'The old kernel of the German infantry, which had been trained in peacetime, so far as it was still extant, bled to death on this battlefield.'[20] The Allied offensive revealed German weaknesses in artillery, shell supply, and air support. Falkenhayn, chief of the army command, already under pressure from his subordinates to rethink his costly offensive at Verdun, launched a few last, desperate attacks there, deploying a new poison gas, but to no avail. He was forced to order a return to 'strict defensive' as from 11 July, and diverted several divisions to the Somme, and by the end of August 42 additional divisions were transferred to the Somme, 35 of them to face the British.[21] After British success on the Somme on 14 July, 'Falkenhayn's nerves were shot', war minister Wild von Hohenborn recorded next day; 'he was about to throw in the towel completely.'[22]

Verdun

The Somme itself was the Allied response to the vast German assault on Verdun ordered by Falkenhayn. To the French and the Germans, Verdun is the 'blood mill' that symbolizes the Great War in the same way as the Somme in the Anglophone world: months of unrelenting shellfire, devastated landscape, mass death in industrialized war for minimal territorial or strategic gain. Along a front of 13 kilometres, 1,225 German artillery pieces opened up fire on 21 February 1916, the greatest ever concentration in one place. The intention, after German victories against the Russians in 1915, was to wear down the French. The French, it was thought, had lost more than 600,000 men killed by the end of 1915, and the German high command calculated that they could no longer sustain losses. In the logic of 'attrition' all that was needed was to keep killing French soldiers at a place they could not afford to retreat from, for reasons of prestige.[23]

Falkenhayn's internal explanation of his strategy shows that his plan for the attack on Verdun was the result of weakness, not strength:

> Certainly the enemy would have to concentrate strong reserves against such a push. But it is just as certain that with his surplus of strength he would despite that be in a position to press against us with great superiority at another, necessarily weak, section of the front.... *Our problem is therefore to cause serious damage to the enemy at a decisive point, but with relatively modest expenditure on our part.* We also cannot ignore the fact that the experience of war with mass deployments of men does not really invite repetition.[24]

Used correctly, Falkenhayn argued, relatively weak forces could achieve better results in attacks than mass assaults which the French had tried the previous autumn. The strategy marked a shift from mass assaults by human bodies towards the machine war. The intention was not to break through, but to force the French to commit their entire army to defend Verdun. This would 'bleed the French dry'.[25] His cynical calculation was that the French would lose at least three men for each German casualty. During the early days of the battle he appeared to be proved right, as initial French losses were high. However, he consistently concealed the rising German losses from the government, and exaggerated French losses in his reports. Falkenhayn informed the chancellor on 20 May that German losses amounted to 134,000 men; on 1 June the OHL claimed that the French had suffered 800,000 casualties, and the imminent fall of Verdun would cause revolution to break out in France.[26] In fact, French casualties were not 3:1 or 6:1, but almost equal; the total from February to September 1916 was 380,000 French killed, injured, and captured, against 340,000 Germans.[27]

The German experience of Verdun was no less bloody. The French responded with unexpected resilience, rushing almost 2,000 artillery guns into battle, and rotating almost every French division through Verdun for short periods. Verdun thus became the symbolic site of the struggle for the liberation of France for almost all French soldiers, becoming a 'sacred place, a place of sacrifice and consecration'.[28]

One young German described Verdun thus. Walter Pechtold was sent to the front as a 17-year-old in April 1916. His 4th company (in Reserve Regiment 94) had lost 60 per cent of its men in its last tour of front duty, and there were only 120 in it, now refilled with fresh young recruits. His perspective as he gradually neared the zone is worth noting. From the train approaching Dun he was puzzled to hear the unceasing, monotonous growl coming from the south, which increased in volume as they drew closer.[29]

From Hardaumont, near which the army HQ of the Crown Prince was located, one had a view of the entire north front of Verdun. The rumble of the firing and the impact of the shells had not ceased for a single minute; the old hands said that it was always like this here. At night-time the game offered a picture of countless flares in all colours, the groping traces of the searchlights, and the red fire clouds of shrapnel—its grandeur underlined by the heavy thuds shaking the earth and the constant artillery fire.... [He described the exhausting march to the front, carrying 35 kilos, 'a great deal for my body-weight of 50 kilos'; his new boots rubbed the skin off his feet, and he only managed to creep from milestone to milestone.]

It had turned dark, and the company marched along the edge of the road in file, one after another. The pace had increased. I had to take care not to fall behind. I was not aware of being in any particular danger . . . I now no longer felt the heavy burden so badly . . . Barely had we passed Forges when there were several flashes of light right in front of us followed by a loud detonation. Everyone hit the ground to take cover. After a while I heard Heinrich [an experienced soldier or NCO] shout: 'They are aiming at the road!' and I realized that we were in the line of fire . . . The firing must have lasted three-quarters of an hour. Then we went on, now back on the road, running, although it was uphill. I managed to keep going.

. . . On 8 [April] iron rations and hand-grenades were brought up and distributed. We are to storm the right-hand section next to us near R[egiment] 82 and 71. The 9th [artillery battery?] takes it under heavy fire. The village Cumières, which was still more or less intact, is completely shot to pieces and disappears in smoke and dust.[30]

In a letter to his father on 1 May 1916 he wrote:

Dear Father,

Through the kindness of a comrade who is going on leave and can take this letter I hope to write a few things for you which will not harm anyone but which might nevertheless be taken amiss by the censors. Our position is still the same one, directly in front of Cumières on the slope of Raven Wood where we have dugouts that are not too bad. We are relieved about every seven days . . . Conditions are quite tolerable. The most unpleasant thing is just the dirt. . . . The attacks are often carried out with fewer men (and almost without reserves) than the enemy himself has. So the artillery just has to do a good job of preparation. I have seen sections of our trench near the enemy, several hundred metres long, defended by only 8 to 10 sentries and 2 machine guns. However, the sentries have hand-grenades which have the same effect as a 10.5 cm shell. Nobody talks or has talked about a breakthrough here. Every day we expect an offensive on another part of the front which will give us a breathing space.[31]

That was the 'sanitized' version for his father. What he confided to his personal diary was less complacent. He was still capable of shock at the sight of mass death, but his senses were beginning to be dulled:

On 13 May we returned to the front . . . In the tangle of tree-trunks lie many dead men, shown in the bright daylight more unsparingly than during our usual night-time marches; I often avert my gaze from these scenes.

In other words, this young boy had already seen more dead than most people see in an entire lifetime, a disturbing sight to be avoided if possible. He charted also how artillery fire had a devastating mental effect on men.

[24 or 25 May 1916] The air pressure of the heavy 28 cm shells has the effect of body blows . . . The emotion of the first period fades and a dull apathy sets in, waiting for the next heavy impact. The lighter ones are hardly noticed any more. Every 40 seconds a 28-cm shell lands, all close in a line, and in fact all the firing is concentrated on the platoon . . . One group is completely shot to pieces by a direct hit. Then it's the turn of the machine gun. Soon a fresh [machine?] gun gets through the fire to the front. They are selected soldiers. But by midday they, too, are finished. One of them, bleeding, comes to us. The men are so apathetic that they cannot bring themselves to bandage the man. I am glad to escape from the depressing inactivity and be able to do something, and I bandage him as best I can . . . The air in the dugout is so foul that I sit by the entrance. Walter Mayer and Hendrich from my squad sit next to me. Hendrich has completely lost his composure. He is a devout Catholic, and is down on his knees and prays. Mayer loses all patience. He has nerves of steel and tells him off for his unsoldierly behaviour. In this situation a prayer is senseless. Now it's the turn of our group. Our roof is blown apart by a 28 cm shell. Because I am sitting by the entrance, I am left unscathed, just shoved aside. Most of the men are dead.

. . .

About 10 pm, in the dark, the French come. The machine gunners were the first to notice and start firing. Sergeant Bek emerges from some hole or other . . . and tells me to give the signal for an artillery barrage, and I fire red signal flares. I see with satisfaction that . . . immediately afterwards one layer of shrapnel shells after the next explodes above our heads and scatters in front of us. The firing is accurate. All we see of the enemy are the flashes of their rifle fire right close in front, about 15–20 metres away. I fire wherever I see the flashes. Next to me an older man has completely lost his nerve. He wants to desert and loudly urges us to do so. Then he aims his rifle at my ear and squeezes the trigger, without hitting me. The sharp report makes me lose consciousness for a moment. Then I berate him, but I do not have time to concern myself with him. The enemy is pressing the attack on our left flank, where our men have been wiped out. I am ordered over there with a few others. We all shoot standing and freehanded . . . From hill 265 the searchlight is trained on the battlefield, dazzling the attackers. The coordination of all weapons is good and lends a sense of security. Since holding my rifle by my cheek all feeling of fear has disappeared. This regained freedom of action makes us unable to feel the danger we are in . . . [32]

Pechtold's unit was not relieved until 30 May. He had not slept or eaten for four days. But on 2 June he had to go back into the front line. Despite the danger and exhaustion, he found a certain satisfaction in his role, proudly boasting to his father that his regiment had held four French regiments at bay.[33]

The French experience was parallel. The soldiers experienced Verdun as an unspeakable horror. Infantry captain Charles Delvert, history teacher, who was defending the approach to Douaumont on 1 June, wrote:

> The appearance of the trench is atrocious. Everywhere stones are dotted with red splashes. In places pools of blood. On the protective wall, in the communication trench, stiff corpses covered with tent canvas . . . An unbearable stench poisons the air. To crown it all, the Germans send us tear-gas shells . . . [2 June:] I have not slept for almost 72 hours. It is raining. One gets sucked in to the mire.

Another soldier, Thellier de Poncheville, wrote in his memoir:

> Some injured men who are able to drag themselves to the rear, the one supporting the other, some using their rifles as crutches. Stretcher-bearers follow them in single file, carrying their burdens of suffering . . . Oh! The terrible explosion! With infernal violence, a 150 [i.e. 15 cm shell] bursts right amongst this mob and hideously tears it to pieces.[34]

The response by one French painter stands for the mood of a great many soldiers who experienced Verdun. In March 1916 Félix Valloton had written in his diary that 'out of all this horror there emerges something perfectly noble; one feels truly proud to be standing on this side of humanity, and whatever happens, the notion "French" is once more young and resplendent as never before'. A year later, in his painting *Verdun, an Interpreted Picture of War* (1917), the sense of 'horror' is dominant, and nothing was left of noble patriotism. In a landscape devoid of humans the earth itself burns blood red, the dark sky is riven by searchlights and explosions. Dehumanized technical destruction leaves as the only signs of nature whitened tree-stumps and rain which fails to extinguish the fires. Valloton began to doubt, as did many French people in spring 1917, whether France could survive, and whether the sacrifice of life was worthwhile.[35]

Consequences

The result of Verdun and the Somme was for both France and Germany a crisis of authority. Nowhere in Europe was the old order left entirely intact, even if Britain and France did not witness revolution. France had warded off defeat, Verdun was never captured, and the French retook the fort of Douamont, but the effect was demoralizing. One French officer who was to die at Verdun wrote: 'They will not be able to make us do it again another day: that would be to misconstrue the price of our effort.'[36] France's crisis was expressed through the soldiers' mutinies of spring 1917, which were not aiming to end the war, as has sometimes been argued, nor were they the result of revolutionary subversion, as the generals claimed at the time. Rather, they were a protest at a pointless and lethal offensive at the Chemin des Dames and at bad conditions at the front and especially in the rear areas.[37] The military crisis was overcome by replacing General Nivelle as army commander with the more defensive General Pétain, and a shrewd mix of exemplary punishment of alleged ringleaders of the mutinies and concessions to the soldiers to improve conditions. In a broader sense the political crises of 1917, the strikes and the growth of anti-war sentiment, were also a long-term consequence of the depleted reserves of authority because of the bloodshed at Verdun and the Somme.

For Germany, five main consequences ensued from the combined Allied offensives of summer 1916—the Russians routing the Austro-Hungarian army in Galicia, and the heavy battering delivered on the Somme.

1. The first was a crisis in the German leadership. Until early June 1916 Falkenhayn and the German leadership had believed they were close to victory. Coming on top of the German failure at Verdun and the Brusilov offensive, the Somme shattered that belief. Falkenhayn was heavily criticized by senior army commanders in particular for miscalculating the effects of attrition on the French at Verdun, for his rigidity in holding fast to his strategic concept despite its evident failure and the terrible losses, and for

refusing to believe the Allies would attack on the Somme. By mid-August he had 'lost the confidence of the army', according to Crown Prince Rupprecht of Bavaria (commander of the 6th Army).[38] The victim of intrigues by senior commanders and chancellor Bethmann Hollweg, Falkenhayn was sacked on 28 August (for failing to prevent Romania joining the war on the Allied side), to be replaced by the dual leadership of Hindenburg and Ludendorff. They did not differ fundamentally in their strategic concept of a war of attrition, but their shift of emphasis promised to win the war by defeating the weakest enemy first, Russia, while vastly increasing armaments production in order to out-gun the Entente in a machine war. This amounted to a radicalization of the war of annihilation at all costs, including the ruthless exploitation of Germany's civilian population, other non-combatants, and the occupied territories.

2. A direct result of the Somme was a radical transformation of armaments production to match the shift of gear by the Allies in industrial, mechanized warfare. This took the form of the Hindenburg Programme of August 1916 to increase vastly the production of munitions, artillery, and other essentials of war.[39] The underlying idea, as summarized by war minister Wild von Hohenborn speaking to industrialists, was this: 'The further we fall behind with our human material, the more the machine, the artillery piece, the machine gun, the shell, etc. have to replace men. That means we not only at least have to keep up with our enemies, but overtake them.' Within a year the production of ammunition and trench mortars was to be doubled, artillery guns and machine guns trebled, and the extraction of iron ore and the mining of coal considerably increased. The programme entailed the militarization of labour, curtailing workers' freedom to change their place of work, and the deportation of foreign labour, especially from Belgium, to work in German industry.

The systematic exploitation of civilian labour in occupied territory was a part of the radicalization of warfare discussed in Chapter 2. Everywhere in Europe under German control, from France to Lithuania to Italy, civilians were forced to feed the German war machine, construct its defences, and see to the everyday needs of the army. It began with the invasion, sporadically, cleaning up debris, but soon labour camps were established where men, but as from 1916 even women and girls, were separated from their families and forced to do hard labour under harsh conditions, with poor nutrition. The most notorious case, well publicized in Allied propaganda published worldwide, was the deportation of 20,000 women and girls from the city of Lille at Easter 1916. The round-up was followed by compulsory gynaecological examinations, even of young girls.

The humiliation was intended to demonstrate that Germany was absolute master; targeting women (and children) showed it was making no distinctions any longer between enemy civilians and enemy soldiers; women were conscripted to the same kind of heavy physical work as men.[40] The scale of this use of forced labour is still under-researched, although recent scholarship has begun to tackle this question. After the war French civilians lodged 305,000 claims for compensation for damages in relation to low-paid or unpaid work, but the true extent was greater still.[41]

3. The OHL decided upon a new strategy of defence in depth. It noted that the heaviest losses had been incurred by the infantry assembled in the front-line trenches, and that artillery and machine guns had a better chance of surviving if placed well behind the lines. The rethink entailed withdrawing men so far as possible from the front line, leaving only a light force behind. Enemy artillery was to be combated by artillery fire. The enemy was to be allowed 'to exhaust itself and to bleed itself'; no longer was the object 'the deployment of the greatest number of live bodies,' but rather 'preponderantly machines (artillery, trench mortars, machine guns)'. The old trench system of two miles in depth was to be extended to six miles, with machine guns now located in 'steel-reinforced concrete bunkers that could withstand 15 cm shells' (i.e. much of the light and medium artillery). The rigid system of defence of every inch of ground down to the last man was abandoned in favour of elasticity in which the infantry would resist and then evade frontal assault which would be crushed by machine gun fire.[42]

The new strategy produced a tactical retreat which saw 'the greatest feat of engineering' of the war. The soldiers of Army Group Crown Prince Rupprecht (1st, 6th, and 7th Armies) were reported to be 'exhausted' and 'used up'. The prospect of an Allied offensive in spring 1917, spearheaded by a force of 2,000 tanks, prompted a withdrawal from exposed flanks to well-prepared defensive positions on a shorter defensive line. Best known as the Siegfried Line, this was in fact the name given to just one of five defensive positions, the only one finished on schedule. This vast construction effort was carried out over four months by 370,000 German reservists, civilian workers, and 150,000 (mainly Russian) prisoners of war; 170,000 construction workers, in addition, laboured well behind the front. In breach of international law the Germans forced civilians from the 500 French communities in the area as well as Belgians to work on the project, digging trenches, building shelters, gun emplacements, munitions depots, and railways; those who refused the ostensibly 'voluntary' work were imprisoned and often beaten. Some worked within range of Allied guns, and were injured and killed. It is no exaggeration to see in the system of forced labour, with camps, armed guards, brutal punishment of the 'recalcitrant', an omen of future totalitarianism as the prerequisite for total war, as the Chicago historian Michael Geyer argues.[43]

The fortifications consisted of anti-tank trenches, barbed-wire barriers, steel and concrete bunkers for machine guns, for the first line, followed by a system of zigzag trenches to prevent enfilading fire in the second line, with roofs 6 to 7 metres thick that were capable of withstanding the heaviest shells and bombs. While the troops, equipment, and food were moved in March 1917, the territory abandoned was deliberately devastated on the instructions of Ludendorff: a scorched-earth policy which he adopted from the Russian model of 1915. In the words of Ernst Jünger:

> Right up to the Siegfried Line, every village was reduced to rubble, every tree chopped down, every road mined, every well poisoned, every stream dammed up, every cellar blown up or booby-trapped, all metals and supplies taken back to our lines, every rail tie unscrewed, all telephone wire rolled up, all combustible material burned; in short, we were turning the country that our advancing opponents would occupy into a wasteland...
>
> Among the surprises we'd prepared for our successors were some truly malicious inventions. Very fine wires, almost invisible, were stretched across the entrances of buildings and shelters, which set off explosive charges at the faintest touch.[44]

All movable property, including furniture from the houses and livestock from the farms, was transported east, and what could not be moved was blown up; all factories and any form of productive machinery were removed or destroyed; fruit trees were chopped down, and even the infrastructure was destroyed: bridges, railways, roads, electricity cables. The entire population was forcibly deported—about 150,000 people. The aim was to ensure that when the German army retreated to the safety of the Siegfried Line, the enemy would take over a wilderness. Destruction became a matter of scientific study and industrial-style mass production. Houses were not only destroyed, but walls were broken down so that no shelter could be found; all plumbing and water supply infrastructure was destroyed, since no army can survive without fresh water. Bapaume, for example, was destroyed in 45 minutes by five simultaneous explosions in the town centre, then more detonations, after which the town went up in flames in 400 places.[45]

4. Offensive tactics were also changed. German counterattacks on the Somme had been no less crude and bloody than the British, and they

regained less ground. The war correspondent Philip Gibbs reported how they marched towards the British lines 'shoulder to shoulder'. It was 'sheer suicide . . . I saw our men get their machine-guns into action, and the right side of the living bar frittered away, and then the whole line fell into the scorched grass. Another line followed. They were tall men, and did not falter as they came forward, but it seemed to me they walked like men conscious of going to death.'[46] Now, instead, small groups of specially-trained 'storm battalions' would seize the initiative to counter-attack weak spots in the enemy's lines. Drawing on initial experiments with storm battalions by his predecessor Falkenhayn in May–June 1916, Ludendorff, with Lieutenant-Colonel Bauer, stressed how the infantry had to abandon entrenched notions of combat and learn to fight with the new 'machines of war'. The storm battalions were given special training and equipped with hand-grenades, bread sacks, daggers, and light machine guns. Training courses began in January 1917.[47]

5. Finally, the shock of the Somme prompted also a fundamental shift in German strategy which had world historical significance. Ever since the first attempt at unrestricted submarine warfare against merchant ships in British waters was called off in August 1915 for fear of American retaliation over the loss of American lives, the German navy had been chafing at the leash, frustrated over the enforced inactivity of its surface fleet. Now, with the army committed firmly to the defensive, the OHL, too, was persuaded by calculations of the naval experts that Britain's backbone could be broken by a campaign of 'unrestricted submarine warfare', i.e. in which the laws of war at sea would be ignored. U-boats would now be allowed to attack all ships on routes to the British Isles, without warning and without attempting to rescue crews and passengers. In a crucial meeting in January 1917, Ludendorff announced that the army 'needed to be spared a second battle of the Somme'. Bethmann Hollweg allowed himself to be convinced that the high risk of provoking American entry into the war was worth taking, for the prize was that so many ships would be sunk that Britain would starve by August 1917, and be forced to sue for peace.[48] This decision was another costly disaster. In military terms the campaign failed to sink enough ships to stop British maritime supplies, and in political terms it brought the USA into the conflict, with all the military consequences that implied for the Central Powers. Yet the threat was very potent: the U-boats destroyed the almost unbelievable number of 6,394 ships, 11.9 million tons of shipping, and killed 14,722 merchant (i.e. civilian) seamen.[49] The cost in human lives was very

great among the German submarine crews, too: 3,226 men perished at sea, and another 1,908 men went 'missing' or died in Allied camps.[50]

Verdun and the Somme were in a sense harbingers of the immense destructiveness of warfare yet to come in 1917 and 1918. The balance shifted even further in favour of the artillery, which aimed to obliterate everything and everyone in its target areas, and in favour of the Allies. Germany and Austria had deployed 15 guns per kilometre to prepare the breakthrough at Gorlice-Tarnów against Russia in 1915, but already in September that year the French used 49 guns per kilometre in the failed offensive in the Champagne; the modest gains at the Somme in 1916 required 70. At La Malmaison/Laffaux in 1917 160 guns were used per kilometre, enabling the French to conquer a strip of land 10 by 6 kilometres, firing 80,000 tons of shells over six days, or 8 tons per metre of front line, transforming French countryside into a landscape of utter devastation.[51]

One example of this shift, which at great cost in lives eventually brought a return to mobile warfare in 1918, was Third Ypres (July to November 1917). Known also as Passchendaele, it is the 'symbol for all that is most awful about war in general, and the First World War in particular'; for Britain, Australia, New Zealand, and Canada its name came to stand for the suffering of biblical quality, with bloody attacks through waist-high mud. The losses were horrendous, Allied and German casualties in the end being equal, with about 260,000 each. As with the Somme, the contemporary perception on the German side was quite different to the British 'futile slaughter' cliché. The Allies had this time launched a well-prepared action in which artillery was carefully coordinated with the infantry to reach limited goals: the 'bite-and-hold' tactic.[52] The British artillery superiority was beginning to yield results, and there were the first hints that mobile warfare was once again becoming possible. 'We are living through truly horrid days', confessed Albrecht von Thaer, chief of staff of the 'Messines group command' in the German 4th Army, later to become a member of the OHL.

> I just don't know what can be done to counter the English. They set themselves a fairly limited goal, an advance of only 500 to 1,000 metres, albeit on quite a lengthy stretch [of the front]. In front of this space, deep into our own zone, such devastating British shellfire is laid down that in fact no being is left alive. Under cover of this fire they then simply advance without many losses into this field of corposes, swiftly establish themselves, and our counterattacks first have to cross the raging fire wave, only to find a solid phalanx of machine guns behind it, and they are smashed to pieces. In the last few days here we have had the most

appalling losses of men. The day before yesterday, when one of our divisions was attacked in the morning, I immediately deployed a fresh new division to launch a relief counterattack. It lost many men even while coming up to the front because of the terrible shelling and then could not advance a single step. Naturally, the British also have losses, but with this procedure probably not so many. After all, it is mainly an artillery battle. The British have three times as many guns and six times as much ammunition . . . Tomorrow Ludendorff is coming to speak to us, but he also won't have a panacea to offer. If we had tanks, and in large numbers, they could help, but we Germans don't have any.[53]

Some idea of the utter destruction caused by the British artillery can be seen in the photograph of Passchendaele (probably taken in October 1917; Fig. 18). Another indication of the total destruction, caused mainly by Allied shelling, can be seen in these photographs of Dixmuide; the second photo shows the main square of the town. (see Figs. 19 and 20) The conclusion is inescapable: 'absolute destruction' was not the monopoly of Germany, for in order to defeat Germany, the Allies had to emulate the doctrine, backed with the superior global resources at their disposal. Such was the logic of annihilation.

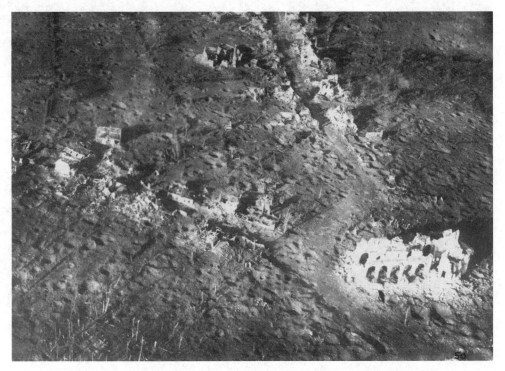

Figure 18. Destruction caused by British artillery at Passchendaele

Figure 19. Dixmuide after Allied shelling

Figure 20. Dixmuide, the main square

7

War, Bodies, and Minds

Glorious death, heroic combat: the aestheticization of destruction

> No more blissful death in all the world,
> Than he who is killed by the foe,
> On the green heath, in the wide field
> He will not hear great cries of woe.

Thus began one of the poems most often quoted by soldiers in their letters and diaries in the First World War. The evocation of heroic death in a green and pleasant land could be from a contemporary English poem, but it was in fact by the German poet Jacob Vogel, who served as a medical officer in the Thirty Years War (1618–48), and whose verse was often found in students' song-books in the nineteenth century. It went on:

> In a narrow bed where one has to go
> Alone to the ranks of the dead.
> But here he will find fine company,
> Falling with him like blossoms in May.
> I say without scorn:
> No more blissful death
> Is in the world,
> Than to fall
> On the green heath
> Without song and sorrow!
> With beating drums
> And fifes whistling
> One is buried.
> Many a brave hero
> Will thus have
> Immortal glory.
> Body and blood has he
> Sacrificed for the sake of the Fatherland.[1]

Motivating men to fight, once the initial excitement and passion of national defence had cooled, was a problem that beset all nations in the Great War. Promoting military and patriotic values was standard state practice; on another, less official, level the aestheticization of violence and death had a broad appeal extending throughout the highly literate European societies of 1914 which constructed their image of war with reference to war stories in classical antiquity and national history.

The diaries and letters of the better educated in the German army in the Great War thus often echoed with Jacob Vogel's verse. Two medical orderlies from Darmstadt, who published a book on their experience serving in France and Belgium in 1915–16, chose the poem to preface their description of the battlefield at Bertoncourt by the river Aisne, which they visited as tourists two years after the battle there in 1914. The terrain was covered with shell-holes and debris of war matériel (army supplies, munitions, and equipment) and rows of graves. These men had been close enough to war to see its destructive effects on the bodies of men, but resorted to euphemisms and aesthetic stylizations of death to give it a particular meaning. The mass graves at Gozée near Charleroi, where 600 German and over 100 French soldiers were buried, prompted the two men to write: 'Here, too, friend and enemy sleep in a common resting-place.' Death is reconfigured as peaceful sleep, the violence and hatred of battle interpreted not as result of hostility between nations but as a symbol of reconciliation and unity.[2] War was thus seen as a natural phenomenon, destruction and mass death as a thing of beauty.

Ernst Jünger, a self-avowed elitist who stylized himself as hero, carried the aestheticization of war to a high art in his publications which appeared after the war. He, too, quoted Vogel's verse on the first page of his *Storm of Steel* (1920), which was based on his war diary; we can imagine that Jünger, as lieutenant and company commander, tried to inspire his men in similar terms. In another book based on the war, *Der Kampf als Inneres Erlebnis* ('The Struggle as Inner Experience'), Jünger rejoiced in the lust for violence, which represented a mix of the desire to kill and the death wish.

> We have known one another for a long time as bold adventurers, have met on many a hot day beneath the smoke-filled sky of a battlefield where it is simply the spirit of the hour that always brings those similar together. We know we are the select embodiments of a powerful masculinity and take pride in this awareness. Just yesterday we sat together following the old tradition of a final drink and felt how the will to battle, that peculiar lust to cross the front again and again, to leap where volunteers are needed, would not have lost its

familiar intensity and this time, too, would cast us into danger. Yes, if only it were time; we are a race that rises to the challenge.[3]

Delight at killing runs through Jünger's entire war literature. It is especially evident in the passage in *Storm of Steel* describing an action near Cambrai in early December 1917:

> And these soldiers we were pursuing gradually felt the Siegfried Line becoming too hot for them. They tried to disappear down a communications trench that led off to the right. We jumped up on to the sentry steps, and saw something that made us shout with wild glee: the trench they were trying to escape down doubled back on itself towards ours, like the curved frame of a lyre, and, at the narrowest point, they were only ten paces apart! So they had to pass us again. From our elevated position, we were able to look down on the British helmets as they stumbled in their haste and excitement. I tossed a hand-grenade in front of the first lot, bringing them up short, and after them all the others. Then they were stuck in a frightful jam; hand-grenades flew through the air like snowballs, covering everything in milk-white smoke. Fresh bombs were handed up to us from below. Lightnings flashed between the huddled British, hurling up rags of flesh and uniforms and helmets. There were mingled cries of rage and fear. With fire in our eyes, we jumped on to the very lip of the trench.[4]

The reference to the lyre, the musical instrument of the ancient Greeks, played to accompany poetry, was no chance simile; it was designed to aestheticize, even though no gory details are spared ('rags of flesh'). The elevated position, in mortal danger, indicated the victor's pose.

A British counterpart to such writers was Julian Grenfell, a young officer in the cavalry and amateur poet, educated at Eton and Oxford, who took delight in everything about war, especially in killing. He wrote in a letter to his parents: 'The war just suits my stolid health, and stolid nerves, and barbaric disposition. The fighting excitement vitalises everything, every sight and word and action . . . One loves one's fellow-man so much more when one is bent on killing him.'[5] His poem 'Into Battle' (1915), although it does not mention the enemy, rejoices in the excitement of battle in terms which are quite similar to the passages from Jünger waiting for battle with his storm troop.

> The naked earth is warm with spring,
> And with green grass and bursting trees
> Leans to the sun's gaze glorying,
> And quivers in the sunny breeze;
> And life is colour and warmth and light,
> And a striving evermore for these;

> And he is dead who will not fight;
> And who dies fighting has increase.
>
> .   .   .   .
>
> And when the burning moment breaks,
> And all things else are out of mind,
> And only joy of battle takes
> Him by the throat, and makes him blind...

Rupert Brooke, educated at Rugby and Cambridge, expressed in his first sonnet 'Peace' sentiments that paralleled those of German and Italian intellectuals welcoming war:

> Now, God be thanked Who has matched us with His hour,
> And caught our youth, and wakened us from sleeping.
> With hand made sure, clear eye, and sharpened power,
> To turn, as swimmers into cleanness leaping,
> Glad from a world grown old and cold and weary,
> Leave the sick hearts that honour could not move,
> And half-men, and their dirty songs and dreary,
> And all the little emptiness of love![6]

Although Brooke's 'War Sonnets' immediately became popular in Britain, reflecting the mood of the many enthusiastic volunteers of 1914/15, (the fifth sonnet 'The Soldier' was often quoted, and later often reviled, as an example of celebration of patriotic sacrifice: 'If I should die, think only this of me: | That there's some corner of a foreign field | That is for ever England'), we should be careful not to ascribe his views to the majority of men. Brooke had particular reasons to welcome danger and the prospect of death: he had been unlucky in love, and fell into a deep and suicidal depression in 1912 from which he suffered recurring bouts in 1914. Yet on the way to Gallipoli, with the knowledge of the 75 per cent casualty rate there, he wrote he had 'never been quite so pervasively happy' faced with the prospect of battle.[7] He died, unheroically, from septicaemia after a mosquito bite, en route. Ernst Jünger was injured several times, but survived the war to build a literary career around the aestheticization of his war experience. He died, aged 102, in 1998.

A 'barbaric disposition' was not the sole origin of the desire for extreme violence: it could emerge also from the yearning for revenge. The British navy's defensive strategy condemned it to inactivity, much to the dissatisfaction of its commanding admirals. Admiral Beatty, commander of the battle cruiser squadron, wrote to his wife in May 1915: 'I heard rumours of terrific casualties [on the Western Front]...I don't think, dear heart, you will ever realize the effect these terrible happenings have upon me. It seems to turn everything upside down in my mind and leave only the one desire to do something, to destroy, to inflict punishment upon the German head.'[8] Joy in vengeance for the victims of impersonal warfare could emerge at any time in combat, as this French soldier's experience at Verdun showed. Having endured the terrible artillery bombardment for days, he described a German infantry attack which they were prepared for, tipped off by a prisoner:

> It is like a relief to us soldiers, a cry of deliverance. Against the colossal shells, they were disarmed. Now, they want to measure themselves, man against man . . . Only two or three machine guns are still in a good state . . . In a few minutes, rows of Germans line up on the ground, like lead soldiers overturned by a ruler. Thanks to this first slaughter, our men take delight in the game. Several of them jump on to the parapet to see better and to aim better . . . They hurl defiance at the enemy, addressing them in the manner of Homeric heroes . . . Come over here, Fritz![9]

The two medical orderlies from Darmstadt whose impressions of mass graves we have already encountered visited the ruins of the forts of Maubeuge, destroyed by German heavy artillery in September 1914. They were horrified and at the same time also proud at the extent of the destruction, exclaiming 'Who knows how many corpses rest under the rubble!' Their pride in the destructive power of German artillery which had penetrated concrete walls five or six metres thick was a common expression of enthusiasm for the armaments technology of one's nation. Aesthetic pleasure at massive destruction—caused by one's own side—clearly outweighed the feelings of sympathy with the victims.[10]

With a mixture of pride in the destructive power of their weapons, belief in the coming victory, but also awareness of the shocking nature of their daily activity, German soldiers took innumerable photos of houses and infrastructure. Damaged and destroyed churches were a favourite motif.[11] One pro-war collection of photographs, published in 1928, reproduces a photograph of a church being deliberately blown up, presumably because it was serving the enemy as a target-marker (Fig. 21).[12] Naturally, some of the buildings had been destroyed by enemy fire; thousands of such photos were published in German newspapers as part of the historic record of war, and some could be used in propaganda against the Entente, in articles and books arguing that it was not the Germans who were guilty of destroying churches and other places of culture, but the British and the French.[13] Thus pictures of the cathedral at Soissons, which (some) Germans rejoiced at destroying in 1914 (cf. Chapter 1),

Figure 21. The deliberate demolition of a church by German forces—probably because it was being used as a target marker

were used to demonstrate that French artillery had later targeted it. With the destruction of churches, there was perhaps also a residual sense of regret at cultural loss. There were no compunctions, however, about the destruction of military or infrastructural installations, as shown in the photograph of officers posing by the fort of Loncin near Liège, destroyed in the heavy bombardment of August 1914, and in that of the fort of Marchovelette, near Namur later that month (Figs. 22 and 23). The common element of such photos was fascination at the fact that everything in civilization was capable of being destroyed.

There was a strange symmetry in this. The French army photographic department published picture albums on each battle which sold for one franc; the Marne album, for example, showed destroyed houses.[14] In the campaign highlighting German atrocities many books and pamphlets, both official and commercially published, showed houses and churches destroyed by the Germans.

Apart from their use in propaganda, the taking of photographs also helped soldiers to make sense not only of the scenes of destruction, but also of their own feelings of disorientation and helplessness in the face of violence and chaos.[15] Contrary to George Mosse's argument in his influential book *Fallen*

Figure 22. Officers posing next to the destroyed fort of Loncin, near Liège

Figure 23. Officers posing next to the destroyed fort of Marchovelette, near Namur

Soldiers, German soldiers were not alone in their fascination with the visual aspect of war.[16] Marc Bloch, the French historian who fought as a junior officer, not only kept a diary, as is well known, but also took many photographs.[17] Henri Barbusse, the author of the internationally famed anti-war novel *Le Feu* (*Under Fire*), also took many pictures and had no compunction about photographing the decaying, maggoty corpses of German soldiers in a captured trench.[18] Jean Cocteau, later to become known as avant-garde writer and designer associated with Dadaism and Surrealism, took photographs of his war experience as medical orderly which are notable for their realism and humanity in the face of suffering.[19]

Patriotism, consensus, or coercion?

French soldiers were not motivated by the idea of conquest or destruction. As one *poilu* wrote, 'the soldier of 1916 does not fight for Alsace, neither to ruin Germany, neither for the *patrie*. He fights out of honesty, out of habit, and because he has to.'[20] Ordinary French soldiers had no need of overt patriotism, for the geography of the conflict made national defence so self-evident it hardly needed explicit mention. Were German soldiers motivated by similar defensive principles, as some have argued? In strategic terms it had been a war of defence for Germany on French territory ever since September 1914. Yet a German victory could only be attained through successful invasion and occupation of the rest of France, and thus even if the ordinary German soldier did not read the writings of the patriotic intellectuals calling for a war to bring German culture to the world, he could hardly claim to be defending his own soil in the way a Frenchman could. French soldiers 'understood trench warfare as digging into the ground and defending the land centimetre by centimetre'; the national territory was thus 'sacralized'. The stories of atrocities committed on the civilians of occupied France, which continued to circulate until the end of the war (and beyond), generated hatred of the invader. For the men 'defending the home' literally meant just that, and protecting wives and children from the horrors of war. The soldiers from the occupied regions, as postal control found, separated from their families, had a strong personal motivation for a war of liberation.[21] The theme of defence of the national territory, depicted as a fertile land in which the women have taken on the work while the men, urged on by Marianne, the symbol of the French Revolution, launch an attack in the imagined background, is captured perfectly in the poster for a war loan in 1918 (Fig. 24). The caption reads, significantly, 'To restore to wholeness the pleasant land of France'.

Nor did ordinary British and German soldiers make a habit of expressing nationalist views in their private letters; concepts such as 'nation', 'Vaterland', 'Deutschland', or 'England' simply did not figure in their language.[22] So what motivated the men to keep fighting?

Why men on almost all sides continued to accept suffering, mostly without resistance, is explained by several factors. Military training to obey orders and fear of punishment by officers goes a long way to explain why men stayed at the front. Command authority was based on a panoply of formal and informal instruments ranging through humiliation, imprisonment, beatings, to the death sentence. Solidarity in a community of suffering, peer pressure, commitment to men who had become comrades who depended on each other, were also powerful forces that operated on the level of small fighting units (companies or platoons). Gender expectations, too, made men conform. The Italian army, which suffered from a catastrophic loss of cohesion in 1917, but

Figure 24. Poster for a war loan (*Emprunt national*) by Chavanaz, 1918

unlike the Russian army managed to recover, illustrates well many of these factors. Mussolini, who published his war diary in 1923, had some interesting things to say about morale and motivation:

> The state of mind which is summed up in the word 'morale' is the basic coefficient of victory. It is decisive in comparison with the technical and mechanical factors. The man who *wants* victory will win, he who disposes of greater reserves of mental energy and more will power . . . The morale of the front-line troops is different to those of the rear area, and it varies between older and younger classes of men. There is a vast difference between those who came from the land and those who were born in the cities and lived there. The 'morale' of those soldiers who have seen some of the world is higher than that of those who have never set foot outside their home village. . . .
>
> The war establishment of a company is about 250 men. They can be divided into the following groups from the point of view of morale. There are about 25 soldiers—workers, professional men, and Italian volunteers—who understand the causes of the war and fight with enthusiasm. Then there are 25 who have returned home from other European countries and overseas, who have lived and have acquired certain social experience. They are excellent soldiers

in every respect. Another 50, mainly young men, enjoy the war. The largest part of the company, about 100 men, consists of those who half submit to their fate, and half willingly take part... They would rather have stayed at home, but now it is wartime and they do not fail to do their duty. In every company there are in addition another 40 indefinable individuals who can be brave or cowardly, according to circumstances. The rest of them [i.e. ten] consists of recalcitrants, those lacking in conscience, a few rogues, who hide behind a mask for fear of the court martial.[23]

He was right about the absence of a sense of national identity among peasant soldiers. As even Mussolini recognized, few Italian soldiers were primarily motivated by patriotism. Traditional society conditioned men to the discipline of the family and work. Most Italians regarded the war as a natural catastrophe like an epidemic or an earthquake. Peasant Catholic society was 'an extraordinary school of obedience and acceptance of destiny', and peasant Catholic culture was still a strong force in the cities, despite the atomizing effects of modernity and the spread of socialism.[24] This is true not only of Catholic Italy, but also of Protestant Germany and Orthodox Russia. Less authoritarian societies with a culture of individual freedom and rights, notably France and Britain, proved ultimately to produce more resilient soldiers. Admittedly, this also had something to do with the fact that British and French soldiers were better fed than German and Austrian soldiers, but morale is a complex thing in which the importance of politics and constitutions should not be underrated. Russian soldiers rebelled in 1917, even though their rations (at 4,000 calories, with 400 grammes of meat per day, 1 kg. of bread, and plenty of sugar) were normally more than adequate.[25] Despite the victory of the Brusilov offensive of summer 1916, the Russian army suffered a crisis of confidence, as the realization of the great losses needed for final victory set in. Yet despite the deepening despair at ever achieving final victory and the food crisis in winter 1916–17, the front troops held out and were prepared to continue defending Russia; their most frequent demand to the Soviet during the February Revolution was that the workers should resume production to keep them supplied with armaments. The level of desertions from the Russian army actually fell during 1916, and it only increased dramatically *after* the February Revolution 1917.[26] Throughout that winter, however, troop morale was being eroded by the knowledge that their families were suffering severe shortages of food, and the collapse of the old regime deprived the Tsarist army commanders of their legitimation. By mid–April 1917 the authority of the commanders had collapsed, and even among the front troops a widespread desire for peace developed.[27]

For many Frenchmen traditional Catholic faith, especially the idea of 'sacrifice', had a real meaning, as Annette Becker has shown. But Catholic intellectuals went further, raising this to the level of a positive spiritual experience. Henri Massis wrote in January 1915:

> What monastery, what enclosure can offer such a spectacle of nakedness and abandonment, a deeper, more intense vision of death, such depths of solitude, such a society of fraternal souls sustained by such fervour?[28]

The Jesuit writer Pierre Teilhard de Chardin even found that

> The front casts a spell on me . . . The unforgettable experience of the front, to my mind, is an immense freedom . . . There is a world of feelings I would never have known or suspected, were it not for the war. Only those who were there can ever experience the memory charged with wonder of the Ypres plain in April 1915, when the Flanders air smelled of chlorine, and shells were cutting down the poplars . . . or the scorched slopes of Souville, in July 1916, with their smell of death. Those more than earthly hours instil into life a tenacious, unsurpassable essence of exaltation and initiation, as if they were part of the absolute. All the enchantments of the Orient, all the spiritual warmth of Paris, are not worth the experience of the mud of Douaumont [i.e. at Verdun] . . . Those men are fortunate, perhaps, who were taken by death in the very act and atmosphere of war, when they were robed and animated by a responsibility, an awareness, a freedom greater than their own, when they were exalted to the very edge of the world, and close to God![29]

This fascination with suffering, this longing for the appalling sight of horrors and the sickening smell of death, cannot be regarded as representative or even typical of religious believers. Instead, it should be seen as a reaction by one man whose world-view was dominated by a fixation on torture and death. The secular viewpoint was more down-to-earth. Blaise Cendrars (the Swiss poet and novelist who volunteered for the French Foreign Legion) wrote: 'God is absent from the battlefields and the dead of the war's beginning, those poor little *pioupioux* [young soldiers] in their red trousers, lying forgotten in the grass, splashes as numerous as cow-pats in a meadow, and scarcely more important.' Not all men would have expressed their feelings with such apparent impiety, but there is no doubt that the majority of the men in the French army were indifferent to or rejected the church. Even among devout Catholics it was more usual to pray for an end to 'this terrible carnage', this 'damned' war.[30] As we have seen, most British and German soldiers, too, differed from the intellectuals among them, whether religious or secular, in rejecting the hyperbole of patriotism; most ordinary men reacted to industrialized warfare and mass death with fatalism; soldiers' letters expressed variously the hope for survival, a sense of duty, or an acceptance of death: 'One can only hope for the best; the worst will come in any case, and no one can do anything against Fate, the best thing is to submit to it, happy is he who forgets what cannot be changed', wrote a German soldier in 1915.[31]

Motivation beyond fatalistic acquiescence could also be provided by commemoration of the dead, which expressed a sense of community with fallen soldiers. Commemoration, which was not only a state-driven manipulation of sentiment designed to aestheticize mass slaughter, but also reflected real emotional needs of surviving comrades and relatives, was a universal need that took on national differences. In the churchyard of Bazeilles near Sedan there was an ossuary, in which the skeletons of those killed in the battle of Sedan in 1870 were on public display. To the Germans who invaded in 1914 this showed the 'unparalleled irreverent coarseness of feeling of the French government', and they reburied the remains of the Germans under a large cement sarcophagus.[32] Each confession has its own culture of remembrance, as does each nation. Protestants—which the two men from Darmstadt evidently were—could easily react with surprise, even shock, at seeing evidence of Catholic religiosity, whether it was roadside calvaries or graphic depictions of Christian martyrdom in churches.

The particular version of Christianity that was prevalent in France perhaps explains the rapid spread of the story of a lieutenant, Jacques Péricard, in spring 1915. He reported that on hearing the cry 'Debout les Morts!' (Rise up ye dead!), wounded men rose up and fought off the Germans who were surrounding their trench. In the version that the right-wing intellectual Barrès published in his newspaper, it was not the wounded, but the dead themselves who rose up to fight. By the end of the year the story was known throughout France;[33] it evidently embodied the dream of both the individual and the nation to overcome mortal injury and survive. It was in other words a myth of resurrection. That is not to say that resurrection was unknown elsewhere: Ernst Jünger made use of the image in a famous passage in *Storm of Steel*:

I especially remember the picture of the emplacement, torn apart and still smoking, as I reached it just after the attack.... Here and there the sentry post stands were covered with the fallen, and between them, as if they had grown out of their bodies, the new relief sentries stood, rifles at the ready. The sight of these groups made me feel strangely numb—as if for a moment the difference between life and death had been extinguished.[34]

But Jünger's aestheticization of war, although he claimed it to be a war diary, was in fact a carefully worked post-war construction. It should thus be read as a contribution to a proto-fascist mobilization in which we can identify the central myth of palingenesis, i.e. the notion of rebirth after death and renewal of the people after decay and near-destruction (cf. Chapter 5).[35] This palingenetic myth featured also in Italian fascism, where the idea of vengeance for the dead, not uncommon in any soldierly community, took on a particular form. Mussolini noted that the following words were inscribed at the entrance to a soldiers' cemetery he visited in 1916: 'Exoriare aliquis ex ossibus nostris ultor' (may an avenger arise from our bones).[36]

The idea of resurrection was not unknown in the British army, where it took on a more prosaic form of a belief held by common soldiers. Vera Brittain, an Oxford student working as voluntary nurse, related a story of three injured men in her ward at Étaples who were convinced they had seen comrades during the retreat in March 1918 who had been killed in action on the Somme in 1916. The vision figured as a symbol of encouragement to hold out. The sceptical Brittain asked a sergeant:

'Do you really mean that in the middle of the battle you met those men again whom you'd thought were dead?'

The sergeant's reply was insistent.

'Aye, Sister, they're dead right enough. They're our mates as was knocked out on the Somme in '16. And it's our belief they're fightin' with us still.'[37]

Naturally, it is impossible to distinguish between a no doubt common desire to brag with tall tales and a genuinely held belief; the sergeant's response nicely expressed the awareness that it was 'belief' and therefore not 'reality', but also not a pathological hallucination. It was, as Brittain put it, a 'consolation of superstition'.

While death and destruction were given a transcendental meaning, at least by patriotic intellectuals and clergymen, ordinary soldiers often registered their horror, and expressed the desire to spare their families the same experience. After participating in the destruction of Dinant on 23 August

1914, during which one in ten of the population was massacred, one German soldier wrote home to his parents: 'Dinant has fallen, everything burnt down. French have fled . . . We press on further. The men are shot, the houses plundered and burned down . . . Don't be afraid for me. It will all turn out well and we will see each other soon—I look forward to it! . . . Germany cannot thank God enough that it has been spared the atrocity of war.'[38] Another German wrote in 1916: 'You cannot imagine the devastation there, where whole villages are devastated, whoever hasn't seen it cannot possibly imagine the terrors of the war.' A British man wrote: 'It eases my mind to know there is to be only one of the family in this awful bloody ordeal. I can stand it, and prefer to be the one in it, my eyes have opened.'[39]

Straightforward fear and hatred of the enemy were an important factor, sometimes ignored by historians who stress the community of suffering of men at war. The enemy was often unseen, or seen only fleetingly, at a distance. He seemed to inhabit another land, as one British soldier recalled in 1935, 'the strange land that we could not enter . . . the garden over the wall'. This other world was 'peopled by men whose way of thinking was totally and absolutely different from our own'. As the literary historian Paul Fussell concluded from his survey of British writing, the Germans were frequently seen as vile animals, grotesque, and inhuman.[40]

Gender, sexuality, and national defence

Implicit in the discourse of enemy stereotypes was the knowledge of what conquering armies can do to conquered women. Above and beyond the real extent of rape during the invasions and occupations was the lurid propaganda which suggested that the enemy was routinely violating women. German propaganda expected Russian soldiers (or often 'the Cossacks') to commit rape if they were allowed to invade East Prussia, and soon after the real invasion the newspapers were filled with stories of wanton cruelty and rape of women and children. Not even Social Democratic newspapers were immune from the clichés: the *Rheinische Zeitung* wrote on 5 August 1914 that tsarism, with its bear's paws, 'wants to crush the culture of all of Western Europe and incite its barbaric hordes to attack our women and children'.[41] When refugees from East Prussia arrived in Berlin in late August, bringing unconfirmed rumours of Russian cruelties, of

'heads...cut off, children burned, women raped', the newspapers were
quick to spread the news.[42] The relatively brief Russian invasion served to
create a genre of German propaganda focused on defence against barbarism
and alleging atrocities, especially against women, that lasted almost the
length of the war. Likewise, in British propaganda, alleged German sexual
crimes against Belgian and French women at times overshadowed the real
and well-documented violence against civilians. One Church of England
minister, addressing a recruiting rally, said:

> To be shot dead is bad, but there is a worse fate for them. Our mothers and
> grandmothers would have gone crazy at the thought of their men tamely
> submitting to the imposition of a mixed race in England. Yet that would, we
> know, be the result of a German invasion. Half the children born next year in
> a town occupied by German troops would have a German soldier for a
> father...I cannot speak plainer than I do.[43]

Governments did not necessarily encourage such exaggerations, but sensation sells newspapers; by the end of the war the burgeoning film industry
also specialized in suggesting that German invasion would mean violation of
the nation's women.[44]

War led to extreme versions of gendered society. Italy's war was transformed by the threat of invasion which loomed in autumn 1917 into a war
of defence. Addressing artillerymen at the funeral of three of their comrades,
their colonel said:

> Hate, hate! It is necessary to arm yourselves with hatred to avenge your
> comrades who died for Italy. Today we are no longer Calabrese, Milanese,
> Sardinians, Sicilians, or Tuscans. Today we are all Italians ready to fight the
> vile enemy who butchers the Belgian people, cuts off the hands of children,
> rapes children, and would like to invade your conjugal beds. The enemy who
> denigrated us, but whom we have already beaten. But not completely.
> Therefore hate, hate, and we shall have complete Victory.[45]

Hatred of the enemy, the reinvention of national identity, and moral superiority over an atrocious enemy were thus invoked here, but also a gender fear.
Italian men had to protect their wives from the enemy who would invade their
conjugal beds. Major Zappalà spoke to his battalion on 23 April 1918, saying
that now the Austrians had captured several doors to the home, it was vital not
to let go of the stairs, because they must not be allowed to enter the bedroom.
'Over there lies the beautiful plain and the beds of your wives. If you let them

through they will enter your beds and take your wives . . . It must not happen. You will resist! They shall not pass beyond here.'[46]

A part of the extreme gendered vision was the insinuation that those who did not fight properly were not proper men: General Caviglia, an admirer of Marinetti, told one brigade which had been somewhat slow in action at the battle of Bainsizza: 'I thought you were a bunch of passive pederasts. Now I know you are contented cuckolds.'[47]

However, women were not only there to be defended. Sexual violence committed by soldiers, whether direct rape or forced prostitution in occupied territories or even the state-regulated prostitution of women in 'friendly' territory, was related to men's feelings of impotence in the face of the dual threat to masculinity posed by one's own commanders and the lethal and arbitrary violence of the enemy; it was also the product of the experience of destruction and breakdown of normal gender relations. Rape was probably committed by soldiers during every invasion in the Great War. The absence of systematically collected data makes comparison difficult; the shame felt by victims in an age of prudery undoubtedly meant that the incidence of the crime was understated. The bulk of the testimony in archive sources rather than published reports suggests it was a random crime, committed by individual soldiers, although in one case strong evidence suggests there were mass rapes of women and girls in conjunction with the mass killing of civilians in the Belgian town of Aarschot over several days in August 1914.[48] In France, there was an intense debate during the war about the 'child of the barbarian', the children conceived through rape by German soldiers. Some women demanded the right to abort the foetus, supported by doctors, lawyers, and eugenicists who argued that the 'child of the Boche' would be the 'enemy within'.[49]

During the invasion of Italy men of both the German and Austro-Hungarian armies committed rapes. Approximately 735 rapes were reported to the post-war royal commission of investigation on the violations of human rights; there is little doubt that the true figure was far higher, since many cases went unreported. Most incidents of sexual violence occurred during the invasion of November 1917, rather than during the occupation of the next twelve months. Those who were most at risk were girls and single women in isolated houses in country districts; rape was often preceded by extreme violence or the threat of violence: shots fired into the air or at walls to intimidate, robbery of food, the threat of killing the males, rape committed in front of children or male members of the household. Some fifty-three women were killed after the rape, and about forty women died later from their injuries. During the occupation, as conditions for the civilian population became progressively harsher, with widespread hunger because of the ruthless exploitation of the resources of the region, many women, deprived of their men and deprived of their stocks of food, were forced to beg the occupation troops for sustenance. The result was prostitution, probably on an informal and occasional level, rather than with established brothels. Nevertheless, it must have been quite widespread. Overall figures for the number of children born as a result of rapes or of such war prostitution are not available, but in one small town alone, Oderzo, there were no fewer than forty infants termed 'children of the enemy'. Daniele Ceschin, who has pioneered research in this area, concludes that there was no systematic policy or a pre-ordained plan of the army commanders for sexual violence as an instrument of war. Rather, he ascribes it to the lack of discipline over troops in the field, and he sees it as indivisible from other violence towards civilians in the invasion and occupation.[50]

Rape and war prostitution were not simply private sexual violence, which faded from collective memory because of a sense of shame on the part of the victims: the occupation troops were given explicit orders to live off the territories of Friuli and the Veneto and exploit thoroughly the stocks of food and drink; men evidently extended this policy to the exploitation of women, which the commanders must have known about and tolerated. On the other hand, there was widespread war prostitution in Italy itself, indicating that poverty and the devastations of war had forced women to sell their bodies.[51] Along with military brothels, there was a great increase in promiscuity among the many women in the war zone whose husbands were absent for long periods.[52]

On both sides of the western front the armies, with varying degrees of toleration and regulation, allowed their men to visit brothels. These were at the base camps and in the towns where soldiers congregated on leave from the front or for training on home territory, in Germany, France, and England. In occupied France and Belgium, German soldiers made frequent use of prostitutes, who worked in brothels or informally in 'estaminets' (small café bars). Men in the mud and misery of the trenches would pass the time, when they were not fighting, talking idly, cursing the war, and complaining, but would also try to lift their spirits by talking about their plans for the next rest days—a proper night's sleep, a visit to an estaminet, and a girl who would offer her services for as little as a loaf of bread.[53]

The men might laugh and joke about the widespread availability of sex, and they were 'amazed at this mass supply of women and girls prostituting themselves', as Heinrich Wandt wrote in his bestselling revelations about army life behind the lines in occupied Belgium. But

> [t]hey did not stop to think about the degree of systematic cruelty of the militarism which cast these unfortunates into shame, and that these pitiable women, deprived of every other way of earning their living, simply had no other choice if they did not want to die of hunger. Great and terrible was the suffering of the men who had to risk their lives for the mad carnage at the front, or who sacrificed their lives or ended up crippled. Greater still and more terrible was the mental suffering of the women and girls, and the greatest and most terrible was the suffering of the realm of women reduced to penury in the occupied territories.[54]

The German occupation tolerated prostitution, and soon soldiers regarded Brussels as a debauched city of cheap entertainment and sex (see Fig. 25). The military governor of Belgium, the venerable General von Bissing, defended the existence of brothels and prostitution, writing to the German government that front officers found it necessary to enjoy some relaxation in Brussels to recuperate from the 'serious mental and physical strains' of

Figure 25. German brothel in Belgium, from Ernst Friedrich, *War against War!*

combat. It is difficult to tell how many prostitutes there were, because some probably escaped detection by the German 'morals police', but by July 1917 there were 3,855 officially recorded by the German authorities in Brussels and Louvain (the latter with very few). This was probably at least four times more than before the war. Women and girls (with many 14- and 15-year-old girls, and some as young as ten) were forced into prostitution by the material poverty, as the cost of living rose and unemployment became widespread.[55]

Prostitution was illegal in Britain, and to prevent the spread of venereal disease among the men the army officially counselled abstinence; however, there was little the army could do to stop men visiting prostitutes in France, where brothels were legally allowed. In March 1918 it emerged that the British army was running at least two brothels in France.[56] Casual relationships and casual prostitution merged into each other, and were widespread, even close to the fighting zone. William Orpen captured the transient nature of such relationships and the men's urgent desire for sex in *Changing Billets, Picardy* (Fig. 26). In his war memoir he recalled seeing three young prostitutes plying their trade among the bodies of men about to be buried, 'death all around and they themselves might be blown into eternity at any moment'.[57]

On the eastern front, years of occupation, the devastation of war, and the impoverishment of the civilian population likewise forced many women to turn to prostitution. For the population, prostitution underlined the humiliating exploitation under German rule which dissolved the fabric of east European societies. For the German army everywhere in occupied Europe, east and west, there was a regulated system, with separate brothels for officers and men, and compulsory medical examination of the women. The main concern of the army was to prevent the men from contracting venereal disease, so there were weekly medical inspections in the army (which the men promptly dubbed the 'prick parade'), and soldiers who wished were given an ointment which was supposed to protect against infection. Soldiers were encouraged to buy and use condoms.[58]

Even the German civilian population was affected. Prostitution, which was illegal in Imperial Germany but tolerated and regulated by the authorities in certain large cities, increased to a vast extent in the war. Not only Berlin, therefore, but even small villages—wherever there was a military presence—witnessed what was described euphemistically as 'loose morals' on the part of women.[59] Naturally, this shaded over into changing sexual mores, a historic shift which was not only caused by sheer economic

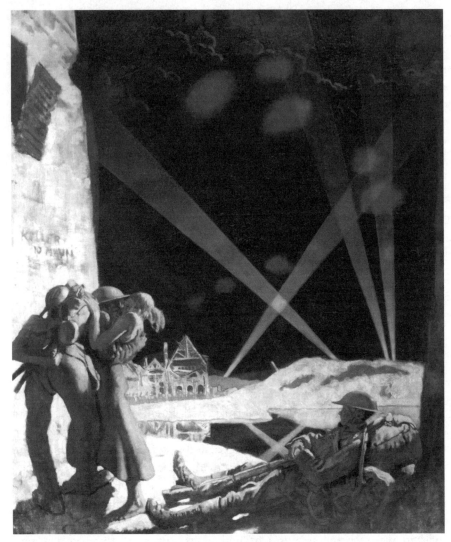

Figure 26. *Changing Billets, Picardy*, painting by William Orpen, 1918

necessity of the immediate wartime circumstances. This helps to explain the rise in illegitimacy rates in London (a 35 per cent increase between 1913 and 1917), and Paris (a 28.6 per cent increase).[60] For a variety of reasons, there was an increase in promiscuity, not only because of separation from partners, but also because traditional religious and patriarchal society was breaking down under the impact of the war. As early as the end of August 1914 the suffragist journal *Common Cause* denounced what it viewed as sexual misconduct by women, who were hanging around the training centres, as a 'national shame', and called for 'the protection of our young soldiers, many of them only nineteen, from the solicitations of women'. Women drinking and loitering near the camps was 'a real scandal'.[61]

Knowledge about methods of birth control spread even to rural districts such as Catholic Upper Bavaria.[62] The First World War marked the definitive end of the Victorian era for British society and its bourgeois sensibilities. The notion that a loved one might be absent for months or years, or killed in an instant of bad luck, was difficult to square with the conventions of eternal faithfulness and chastity outside marriage. For many men and women the yearning for sexual fulfilment was separated from moral codes, at least for the duration of war.[63] This worried the moralists, as did the increase in 'illegitimate' births, but a real danger emerged with the rise in venereal disease, calculated by the British Army to be incapacitating the equivalent of one division (10,000 to 15,000 men) by 1918.[64] In the German 6th Army about one per cent of the men were being treated in hospital for venereal disease in February–March 1917, which made it the third most common sickness after influenza and pneumonia.[65]

Bodies

Almost 9 million men were killed in military action, and almost 6 million civilians died as a result of war. The daily accompaniment of battlefield death were the myriad injuries to the human body. A total of 20 million men suffered injury. Of the 8.4 million Frenchmen mobilized during the war, 40 per cent were wounded at least once; the proportion among the infantry was far higher since they were in the front line of defence and attack. By 1918, about 300,000 men were counted as war disabled.[66] Most injuries were caused by artillery fire—during trench warfare 76 per cent of injuries in the French army were caused by artillery. The British army recorded that 59 per cent of the deaths were due to artillery fire, a figure that relates to the entire war and thus included mobile warfare at the beginning and end of the war; 39 per cent were due to infantry fire.[67] The German medical corps calculated that 85 per cent of the injuries were caused by artillery fire down to July 1918.[68] The higher proportion is probably explained by the Allies' proportionately greater deployment of artillery, especially in 1917–18. Out of the 13.2 million men who served in the German army, 4.2 million were injured.[69] The shell fired by the most common artillery gun (the German 77 mm, the French 75 mm, the British 18-pounder) was typically a shrapnel charge that exploded into 300 to 500 fragments, each of them potentially fatal.[70] A shell explosion at close range caused unprecedented damage to the human body, at worst obliterating it so that nothing recognizable remained. A British medical officer recalled: 'A signaller had just stepped out, when a shell burst on him, leaving not a vestige that could be seen anywhere near.'[71] Hand-to-hand combat between men, characterized by frenzied fear and hatred, which has led some historians to write of the intimate nature of killing, was in fact extremely rare in the First World War. Only 1 per cent of injuries were caused by bayonet or knife, according to French calculations, or 0.1 per cent according to a German estimate.[72]

Injuries to the bladder, kidney, and lungs could cause such excruciating pain that the injured were sometimes found biting into the earth. Injuries in the abdominal region often led to peritonitis which was fatal if not treated early. Both bullets and shellfire could cause extensive destruction of tissue, and by carrying bits of filthy uniform cloth into the wound raise the likelihood of infection. Although antibiotics were not to become available until the Second World War, war medicine, including surgery and hygiene, had made considerable advances by 1914, and the standard of treatment was generally high. Operations were normally carried out under general anaesthesia (ether and chloroform) or local anaesthesia (Novocain and adrenaline), but shell splinters were often removed without anaesthesia, which was very painful.[73]

In early 1918 a travelling exhibition was to be seen in German cities, showing war injuries. Wax figures realistically depicted fresh wounds and scars, trepanations, before and after surgical resections, skin transplants, plastic surgery. The intention was to show how modern medicine was able to help invalids, but did it impress visitors? One, Victor Klemperer, who had himself served at the front, was particularly upset at the sight of facial injuries: 'Half-covered by veils lay the worst heads, without jaws, raw red flesh, hacked into pieces, cut open, grossly swollen. They were in glass cases with the notice: "For doctors only".'[74] 'Terribly depressed' by the exhibition, Klemperer was haunted for a long time afterwards by the images of mutilation. The men with mutilated faces themselves, however, mainly kept out of public view, often not even daring to go home for fear of shocking their families, and remained in institutional homes.[75] A disturbing collection of photographs showing the horrors of war was exhibited by the pacifist Ernst Friedrich in his Anti-War Museum in Berlin and published in his internationally known book *Krieg dem Krieg* ('War Against War') in 1924.[76] (It was not possible to obtain permission to reproduce images from Friedrich's book, but Figure 27 is an example of the kind of material he exhibited.)

Other war invalids, with severe injuries such as arm or leg amputations, had a more public presence, both during and after the war. Official German policy, encouraged by the medical profession, was to try to reintegrate these men into society as far as possible, by giving them work, preferably their old jobs. Yet the 89,760 'mutilated', or severely handicapped men, according to incomplete figures that did not go beyond 1 August 1918, were only a small proportion of the total: there were 503,713 men who were recognized as disabled and entitled to claim (mostly inadequate) benefit payments. In wartime they were given the 'good news' by leading orthopaedist Professor Konrad Biesalski that no one need be a 'cripple' any longer, since medical

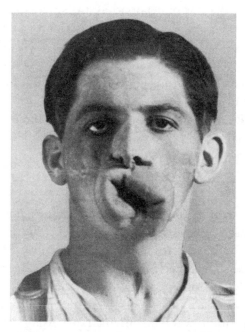

Figure 27. Railwayman, mouth torn away and lower jaw gone

progress and the 'iron will' of the patients would ensure they could return to useful employment. Newspapers were encouraged to reinforce the message about integration, showing the rapid advances made in prosthetics, for example.[77] This was, in one sense, a positive policy, which formed the context of the exhibition Klemperer visited. The reality was different, for the intention to show war as a phenomenon that could be efficiently managed by modern science and technology was a delusion that afflicted only inhuman militarists and their medical henchmen; the aim of reintegration failed in the real world of factories, workshops, and offices that refused to employ invalids. Weimar social policy was more generous, and recognized 1.5 million men as permanently disabled.

Some form of collective trauma, physical and mental, could equally affect civilians. In the case of women in occupied northern France, there was a specific complaint: amenorrhea, the absence of menstruation, which was virtually unknown outside the occupied territories.[78] This affected no fewer than 45 per cent of women in the occupied zone of France. Amenorrhea may have had physiological or psychological causes: the lack of nutrition could have produced it, but so, too, could the trauma of the invasion of the private sphere that came with military invasion, the terror of the occupation, the fear of deportation, the strict separation from loved ones, the lack of news about husbands, brothers, and fathers at the front.[79] Conditions in Germany, Austria, and Italy, as discussed in Chapter 4, deteriorated in 1916–18 to such an extent that hundreds of thousands of civilians died prematurely from hunger and malnutrition. However, this death rate of about 1 per cent, grim though it was, cannot compare with the suffering endured, as we saw in Chapter 2, by the prisoners of war.

Mental responses to war

From bodies we turn to the effects of war on the mind. How did men experience combat, in particular going into attack? The situation of extreme peril produced extreme emotions, which many men were afterwards unable to express in words. The experience of waiting in dread before climbing out of the trench to 'go over the top' (a Great War expression that has entered the English language in a notable anti-war shift of meaning to denote an emotional exaggeration) was quite international. Many accounts by French soldiers simply stopped at that point, because the overwhelming sensation of danger, the deafening noise, and the immediacy of injury and death produced a sensory overload. Those who continued their narration often noted the disappearance of fear while feeling quite defenceless, and mere survival was itself ground for jubilation.[80] Wilfred Owen wrote:

> The sensations of going over the top are about as exhilarating as those dreams of falling over a precipice, when you see the rocks at the bottom surging up at you ... There was an extraordinary exultation in the act of slowly walking forward, showing ourselves openly.... When I looked back and saw the ground all crawling and wormy with wounded bodies, I felt no horror at all but only an immense exultation at having got through the barrage.[81]

However, the euphoria did not last for long, and fear and horror were certainly more common. One young British officer, Captain Edwin Campion Vaughan, captured these feelings in an engagement in Third Ypres in August 1917:

> Feeling icy cold from head to foot I took my troops out and through the ominous silence of the bright midday we advanced in line to the Steenbeck Stream ... An instant later, with one mighty crash, every gun spoke, dozens of machine guns burst into action and the barrage was laid. Instantaneously the enemy barrage crashed upon us, and even as I rose, signalling my men to advance, I realized that the Germans must have known of our attack and waited at their guns. Shells were pouring on to the St Julien-Triangle Road as we advanced, and through the clouds of smoke and fountains of water I saw ahead the lines of figures struggling forward through the mud ... I saw, with a sinking heart, that the lines had wavered, broken, and almost disappeared. Over our heads there poured a ceaseless stream of bullets from 16 machine guns behind, and all around us spat the terrifying crackle of enemy fire ... I was dazed, and straining my eyes through the murk of battle I tried to distinguish our fellows, but only here and there was a figure moving.[82]

The aftermath of battle was grim. The two Darmstadt medical orderlies did not conceal even the most gruesome descriptions of the severely injured, describing how, in the aftermath of the Somme, owing to the lack of medical staff some men's bandages had evidently not been changed for days, with the result that the festering wounds were the home for lice and even maggots. Assisting badly injured men must have been disturbing enough for medical orderlies, but witnessing them act out the horror of their traumas could tip their balance. The two men described in all frankness a journey home in the hospital train:

When 12 severely wounded men lie in the narrow space of a railway carriage, with pus soaking the bandages of injuries to the abdomen, chest, and pelvis, it is only natural that even by day the smell is not pleasant . . . If one or more of the patients lets go of everything beneath himself, the air becomes breathtakingly dreadful and even spoils the sleep of the other patients. The orderly has to put up with this atmosphere . . . In addition, there is the terrible pain caused by artillery shells and hand-grenades which makes even the most patient man whimper and moan, often just when the morphine injection loses its beneficial effect after a few hours. Then there is no sleep for the orderly. He is often startled by the men shouting out in their dreams . . . Many of them dream they are still in the trench among their comrades in an attack; they call out words such as 'Let them have it, the dogs!', or 'Watch out, watch out, they're coming! Bring out the machine guns!', or 'Out of my way, I'm going to shoot!' . . . It is no wonder that many orderlies are exhausted at the end of a long trip . . . Quite a few have realized that they were not up to the tasks and have asked to be relieved.[83]

Even men who remained outwardly stable had been deeply affected. Ernst Rump, a wealthy Hamburg import–export businessman who volunteered and fought as a captain in the artillery, revealed in his private letters to a friend, the artist Nölken, how witnessing death at first hand, hearing stories about death, and finding that his business was facing potential ruin, led him into a kind of fatalistic death-wish which he could not discuss even with his wife.

Now I want to tell you something about me which you ought to keep to yourself, for I can only send my wife, who is suffering to an extraordinary degree from the war, reports which do not deepen her unease. I want to write about mental processes which I noticed in myself under enemy fire. I am leaving out the general dangers, such as when I was without military cover alone with my men [i.e. without infantry to protect his battery] for days and nights on end in Belgium or on the march . . . [In the letters to his family he did not mention the slightest dangers during the march through Belgium; instead, he stressed how healthy he felt, even after camping at night in the rain.] The first time was when I came under intense enemy infantry fire at close range while taking a horse-ride between Cuy and Dives west of Noyon. [He described riding, despite the warning of his commanding general, into artillery fire, where he narrowly escaped being hit.] . . . Then I transferred into the 18th Reserve Field Artillery Regiment, where I took over temporarily from an officer who had been killed; the tremendously sad effects this death must have caused the family of the deceased, the sight of burning, shelled villages which were once prosperous, inhabitants tied up about to be shot, the boundless misery of innocent women and children, the sight of many terrible injuries, carts heaped high with naked corpses and body parts, but above all the lack of success on our side despite gigantic losses . . . , lying in trenches for days and nights . . . , hardly any sleep: all this made such demands on my nerves and those of my comrades that we all had the same need for rest. Since that time I feel the need—keep this to yourself—to expose myself to greater danger. Thus I rode out yesterday afternoon with one of my lieutenants to a small farm . . . where a battery . . . was emplaced . . . [Despite a warning from his lieutenant that he would attract enemy artillery fire, he rode towards the enemy positions.] I could see from my map that . . . the further I rode, the more likely I would come into enemy fire . . . If I had received the order to ride straight into the enemy lines, which were no more than 700 metres away, I would have done it and calmly ridden on.[84]

Not only soldiers' minds, but also the theory and practice of psychiatry were profoundly affected by the war. Sigmund Freud, the founder of psychoanalysis, like most intellectuals in Europe, was at first carried away with enthusiasm for the national cause; his 'entire libido', he wrote, belonged to Austria-Hungary. That soon gave way to a growing sense of horror, and to disillusion about human nature. In November 1915 he wrote in his essay 'On Transience':

One year later the war broke out and robbed the world of its beauties. It destroyed not only the beauty of the countrysides through which it passed and works of art which it met with on its path but it also shattered our pride in the achievements of our culture, our admiration for many philosophers and artists and our hopes of a final triumph over the differences between nations and races. It tarnished the lofty impartiality of our science, it revealed our instincts in all their nakedness and let loose the evil spirits within us which we thought had been tamed for ever by centuries of continuous education by the noblest minds. It made our country small again and made the rest of the world far remote. It robbed us of very much that we had loved, and showed us how ephemeral were many things that we had regarded as changeless.[85]

In other words, Freud saw war as a return to something primitive in human nature; violence was something which had been kept under control by the thin veneer of civilization, and he regretted the passing of the international community of western culture and science. War was a 'disappointment', as he wrote in *Thoughts for the Times on War and Death* (1915):

We cannot but feel that no event has ever destroyed so much that is precious in the common possessions of humanity, confused so many of the clearest intelligences, or so thoroughly debased what is highest. Science herself has lost her passionless impartiality; her deeply embittered servants seek for weapons from her with which to contribute towards the struggle with the enemy. Anthropologists feel driven to declare that enemy inferior and degenerate, psychiatrists issue a diagnosis of his disease of mind or spirit.[86]

The Europeans, to his disillusionment, were conducting themselves like barbarians. Not only did the war disregard 'all the restrictions known as International Law', it also threatened to 'cut all the common bonds between the contending peoples, and threatens to leave a legacy of embitterment that will make any renewal of those bonds impossible for a long time to come'.[87]

Freud drew the conclusion which was to influence the subsequent development of psychoanalytic thinking that human life was not entirely dominated by the sexual drive, but by the conflict between that and the death instinct. Judged by our unconscious wishes, he wrote, we are 'like primitive peoples a horde of murderers'.[88] Yet Freud's fundamentally pessimistic world view is too narrow, and does not function as a general rule. Captain Rump succumbed to the same 'hate and loathing' of Belgian civilians who had allegedly fired on German troops, he repeated the same lurid rumours of Catholic priests as ringleaders of brutal Belgian hordes who cut the throats and castrated German injured men at Louvain, that elsewhere had led to the commission of atrocities on civilians. However, he also attempted to keep his men under control, did not allow them to plunder, tried to stop drunkenness, and in one case prevented the execution of hostages. His own mental disturbance amounted to a case of suicidal depression, not a wild destructive urge. In fact, Freud himself after the war overcame his resignative pessimism, and ended the 1929 edition of his *Civilization and its Discontents* with the cautiously optimistic words: 'Eternal Eros will make an effort to reassert himself in the struggle with his equally immortal adversary.'[89]

Siegfried Sassoon experienced a similar suicidal depression to that of Ernst Rump when he was in charge of a small unit that had to occupy a captured trench on the Somme in July 1916 and attack the retreating Germans. Having taken the trench, the unit was ordered to withdraw. Sassoon sent his men back, but advanced on his own into the next trench, where he saw the German troops retreating. He then returned to the British lines, earning a reprimand from his colonel.[90] This went beyond bravery to foolhardiness. Unnecessarily courting danger represented a form of mental disturbance caused by war, and was perhaps a prelude to the mental breakdown Sassoon suffered in 1917.

No other language has quite such a pithy term as the English 'shell-shock', invented by the Cambridge military doctor Charles Myers in an article in *The Lancet* in February 1915.[91] Known elsewhere as 'traumatisme de guerre', 'Kriegshysterie', or 'neurosi di guerra', the symptoms were the same everywhere, and it could incapacitate a man as surely as severe physical injury. Robert Gaupp, one of Germany's leading psychiatrists, registered the illness at about the same time as the British army:

> From [December 1914] on, the number of these cases grew ever more quickly.... The main causes are terror and anxiety in the face of exploding enemy shells and mines, at the sight of dead and maimed comrades, wounds, or bodily injury on one's own person. The results are the now familiar symptoms—sudden muteness, deafness, general trembling, the inability to stand and walk, fainting spells, and cramping.[92]

Sources created by the victims of mental breakdown are rare. One French doctor reported the following cases of amnesia:

> [First patient]: I was buried by [the explosion of] a mine, I freed myself and I left without knowing where I was going. I didn't know where I was... [Second patient:] I am restless, and I am sick of everything... my life is now ruined... I have no memory left, I can't remember anything... I don't know whether I am dead or another man.[93]

A German patient wrote in a letter from a military hospital:

> Particularly during the last three days our shelter was smashed and literally uprooted by enemy artillery fire. Because of this overexertion I caught a nervous disease. Two days before the general assault, I was taken behind the lines... I'm on my feet only a few hours a day now. This bloody illness has settled in my innocent legs, so I can't move on account of the pain and paralysis in my legs and my right arm.[94]

The self-diagnosis of the physiological cause of his mental illness was no more naïve than that of medical doctors who tried to treat shell-shock with electro-convulsive therapy or other such brutal methods. But at least they began to recognize that traumatic events such as being buried alive could have devastating consequences for the psyche. One medical report published in a journal of neurology in 1918 may serve as an example:

> Case 421. 25-year old officer. Upper arm injury 1915. In 1917 his shelter was buried in a direct hit. Tried to dig his way out together with his comrades. The latter gradually lost strength, and probably died of asphyxiation; the patient is unable to say anything about it. He also feels that air is running out. A second shell hits the buried shelter, which enables him to climb free. Ever since repeated panic attacks, sleeplessness, nightmares, nervousness. Frequently feels difficulty in breathing, imagines he is about to suffocate. Three months' treatment without success, therefore transferred to psychiatric hospital. A strong man, previously always healthy, intelligent, and ambitious.[95]

The injured men in the train, the orderlies, Rump, Sassoon, these unnamed French and German patients, were all witnesses to the destructive effect of modern warfare on the mind, on the human personality. It would be mistaken, however, to see these as exceptional cases suitable only for medical treatment. The Great War had a long-term effect on societies which has been described as collective trauma in the recent cultural history of the war.[96]

Collective trauma was expressed in intellectuals' responses. Annette Becker argues that the French avant-garde after the war, such as the literary surrealists, never made the connection between war and madness; the trauma of war did not interest them once the war was over. Like the scientific establishment they were afflicted by amnesia concerning the war.[97] Further research is needed to compare the former belligerent nations, but this clearly did not apply in Germany.

The cultural avant-garde in Germany was interested in trauma both during and after the war. Max Beckmann is a case in point, for all his ambivalence. One of the leading German painters of the age of classical modernity, he is well known for his social criticism and his pictures depicting the horrors of war with drastic openness. Yet in 1914 Beckmann welcomed the war, joined the army, and wrote from Belgium in February 1915: 'It is impressive when you see what our country achieves, as it spreads out with elemental force, like a river bursting its banks.'[98] Often uncritical of the war, he was sometimes almost in a state of ecstasy about the inspiration it provided and the aesthetic experience it offered him as material for his creativity. However, nothing was straightforward about Beckmann. Among his first works at the beginning of the war was a drawing based on the news of the first week of war, *Aufbrechender Mars und trauernde Frau 1914* ('Mars departing and woman mourning', Fig. 28), in which Mars, whose skull-like face wears a helmet that resembles that of the Death's-Head Hussars, grins at the weeping, crouched woman. Another was an etching, *Die Kriegserklärung* ('The declaration of war', 1914), which flatly contradicted the official consensus of war enthusiasm, showing solemn, troubled faces. He sensed the great human cost of war. Not wanting to kill, he volunteered for service as a medical auxiliary. Even though he was appalled by witnessing the pain and horror of the wounded victims, and deeply affected by the loss of his brother-in-law who died from his injuries, (as can be seen in his *Portrait of my Wounded Brother-in-law Martin Tube*), Beckmann wrote in a letter in May 1915 that he was seeing a type of beauty that he had hardly ever seen before, because it was beauty in suffering, especially on the

Figure 28. *Aufbrechender Mars und trauernde Frau 1914* ('Mars departing and woman mourning, 1914'), drawing by Max Beckmann

verge of death: 'I saw fabulous things. In the dim light of the shelter I saw half-undressed men covered in blood who were being bandaged in white. Great and painful expression.'[99] Compassion with his subjects, even though their suffering contorted their features, is evident in much of his work, and he did not glorify destruction. His drawing *Die Granate* ('Shell', 1914; Fig. 29) depicts war as apocalypse, to which he himself was witness. In another letter he wrote: 'For me the war is a miracle, albeit a rather uncomfortable one. My art finds fodder here.'[100]

Beckmann suffered a mental and physical breakdown in summer 1915, and was given a temporary discharge to recuperate; however, it did not fundamentally change his attitude to the war, and he was soon back. In 1917 he still wrote in a letter from the front: 'The times suit me.'[101] Yet the memories of the

Figure 29. *Die Granate* ('Shell', 1914), drawing by Max Beckmann

Figure 30. Spielende Kinder ('Children Playing', 1918), by Max Beckmann

horrific injuries and the corpses haunted him for the rest of his life. He had little hope for the younger generation, as *Spielende Kinder* ('Children Playing', 1918; Fig. 30) shows: the children are fighting in a savage game of face-to-face combat, using vicious-looking spears and swords. Of course, children have always played at war, and this picture recalls Pieter Brueghel's famous *Children's Games*, but it has an uncanny echo of the scene witnessed by the American journalist Irvin S. Cobb, and hints at the mental injuries to war children. Cobb saw children playing in the street in Liège in September 1914:

In the gloomy, wet Sunday street two bands of boys playing at being soldiers. Being soldiers is the game all the children in Northern Europe have played since the first of last August.

From doorways and window sills their lounging elders watched these Liège urchins as they waged their mimic fight with wooden guns and wooden swords; but, while we looked on, one boy...proceeded to organize an

execution against a handy wall, with one small person to enact the role of the
condemned culprit and half a dozen others to make up the firing squad.

As the older spectators realized what was afoot a growl of dissent rolled up
and down the street; and a stout, red-faced matron, shrilly protesting, ran out
into the road and cuffed the boys until they broke and scattered. There was
one game in Liège the boys might not play.[102]

Beckmann's unfinished painting *Auferstehung* ('Resurrection', 1918; Fig. 31)
also hints at the erasing of distinction between civilians and soldiers in the
war. It holds out no prospect of the Messiah ascending to heaven; equally,
there is no sense of the second meaning of 'resurrection', the idea that at the
end of the world all the dead will rise up to enjoy everlasting life in a
kingdom of peace. It is a vision of despair, in which living civilians and
almost naked soldiers risen from the dead confront a world of devastation
under a black sun. The work he produced in the Weimar period reached an
intensity of condemnation of the violence of man that was unsurpassed in its
unsparing portrayal of modern suffering.

Figure 31. *Auferstehung* ('Resurrection', 1918), unfinished painting by Max Beckmann

Even Otto Dix, who painted the war and its horrors more explicitly and consistently than any other artist, wrote of war as a 'natural phenomenon' which one could not resist, although he fervently wished for peace. He was the only one to see action throughout the war, and fought as machine gun unit commander at the front. He was interested above all in how war 'changes human matter in a demonic way'. His focus on violent acts showed the perspectives of both victim and perpetrator: the dying could be German, French, or British; the victim of a direct hit could be his imagined self or an enemy.[103] His fifty etchings of 1924, *Der Krieg* ('The War'), and the painting *Schützengraben* ('Trench') are drastic depictions of the consequences of war, showing injuries, corpses, destroyed landscapes, civilian victims, which aimed to scandalize and provoke a post-war society that wished to forget the horror of war. *Mahlzeit in der Sappe* ('Meal in the Sap', i.e. forward trench; Fig. 32) shows a soldier devouring his meal out of a can, seated next to the skeletal remains of another soldier. Life and death are intimately close, the smell of putrefaction easy to imagine, as well as the danger. The Nazis imposed their terrible certainty on the ambivalence of Dix: all fifty etchings

Figure 32. *Mahlzeit in der Sappe* ('Meal in the Sap' [i.e. forward trench], 1924), etching by Otto Dix

Figure 33. *Dead Germans in a Trench*, painting by William Orpen, 1918

'Der Krieg', the oil painting 'Schützengraben', and thirty-four other works by Dix were shown in the Nazi exhibition of 'degenerate art' in 1937 (along with many works by Beckmann, Chagall, Feininger, Grosz, Kandinsky, Kirchner, Klee, Kokoschka, Marc, Meidner, Nolde, Schlemmer, and Schmidt-Rottluff); thereafter, many vanished forever.[104]

If German avant-garde artists did not shrink away from depicting German war dead, for British war artists it seems to have remained a taboo to depict one's own fallen. Establishment artists, at any rate, did not do so. Muirhead Bone, appointed as Britain's first official war artist by the War Propaganda Bureau in 1916, produced hundreds of realistic sketches, drawings, and paintings, yet even when he depicted wounded soldiers never showed anything unseemly, unsettling, disgusting, or dead. Even his pictures of ruined villages and churches in France have the quality of picturesque landscapes. The title of his series 'The Great War. Britain's Efforts and Ideals' indicates his uncritical attitude to war, and since his work was conventional but very accomplished it is not surprising that he was the most frequently exhibited war artist in Britain.[105] He used his influence to have his colleague William Orpen, who was a successful and wealthy society painter before the war, appointed official war artist. Orpen was profoundly affected by the war, and despite his official status his work underwent an aesthetic and even political transformation. His *Dead Germans in a Trench* (1918; Fig. 33) is free of any sense of triumph or beauty. The first corpse shows signs of rigor mortis, but also the agony of his death. Orpen deliberately transgressed the contemporary aesthetic norms of war painting, for there is no comforting feature here, and even the bright blue sky does not radiate warmth, but an unmerciful glare.[106]

Orpen, Dix, Beckmann, and Valloton had in common a vision of despair and of horror at the mass killing and destruction of war. The doubt whether the sacrifice had been worthwhile gnawed at the consciences of millions of Europeans. Yet some intellectuals and some soldiers ended the war still affirming the values of violence. Jünger was not alone in this, nor was Germany the only nation to produce such bellicose culture after the war, as we will see in the final chapter.

8

Victory, Trauma, and Post-War Disorder

The end of the war

The end of the war came in several stages in 1918. The first stage was German victory in the east, crowned by the Treaty of Brest-Litovsk of 3 March 1918. This harsh peace deprived Soviet Russia of territories containing one-third of its population (Finland, Estonia, Livonia, Poland, the Ukraine, and part of the Caucasus), and the greater part of its natural resources and industry. For Germany it held out the promise of rich supplies from occupied eastern Europe, of grain, cotton, and oil, and above all of releasing troops to launch the final offensive to win the war in the west before the Americans arrived in significant numbers. The next stage, the Spring Offensive in the west, starting on 21 March, was a desperate effort to divide the Allied armies, push the British to the Channel and force them to retreat from the Continent, and defeat the French. German soldiers were motivated as much by the thought of 'peace' as they were by 'victory': it was to be a 'Siegfrieden'. Impressive initial successes, driving back the Allies tens of kilometres, were followed by gradual depression when the advance stuttered, then swift demoralization when the Allies recovered from the shock of the surprise attack and launched their own counter-offensives. Yet throughout several months of retreats, declining fighting effectiveness, and sinking morale, German commanders were still revelling in the utopian fantasies of victory and expansion. Plans were made to shift German troops across the Alps for another assault on Italy, and there was talk of the ambition to take Tiflis and oil-rich Baku, the cotton-fields of Turkestan, and then 'knock on the gates of India'.[1] As late as the end of August 1918 Lieutenant-General Groener, who was soon to succeed Ludendorff as quartermaster-general, stated that: 'The Ukraine is at present nothing other than an extended German economic region', and that Germany had to conquer Baku as soon as possible because its oil was essential to run the German railways, ships, U-boats, and lorries, and likewise Turkestan for its cotton. These territorial goals were not only to feed the war machine in the short term; they were long-term ambitions for imperialist expansion. He went on, in a perversion of Clausewitzian doctrine: 'Therefore it is non-sense to speak nowadays of peace. Think about it: peace is the continuation of war with other means. Everything is struggle, and this struggle will be eternal, so long as the earth exists.'[2]

The final stage, the German reverses on the western front in July, August, and September, gradually forced the OHL to realize the impending defeat, possibly even the destruction of the German army. Events gathered pace with the British breakthrough in Palestine (20 September), Bulgaria's capitulation to the French (29 September), the British–Arab advance into Damascus (1 October), the start of revolution in Austria-Hungary (21 October), and the Ottoman empire's capitulation on 31 October. The Italian army, now recovered from Caporetto, launched twin attacks on the Monte Grappa and across the Piave at Vittorio Veneto on 24 October, and within five days the Habsburg army was in dissolution; entire divisions retreated as fast as they could to their home countries, and at least 300,000 men and twenty-four generals were taken captive. (See Map 3.) Austria-Hungary's armistice on 4 November saved the empire from invasion, but not from disintegration along national lines.[3] Germany's call for armistice, which Ludendorff had been insistently demanding since 29 September, was designed to preserve the army; he initiated internal democratization to prevent revolution from below, maintain the monarchy, and to bring the Reichstag majority parties into office to incur the odium of signing the defeat. Finally, after five weeks of protracted negotiations, Germany signed an armistice whose conditions made clear it was a capitulation that ensured it would not be in a position to resume warfare, and the guns fell silent on 11 November.

Only that spring, Germany's prospects for victory had looked bright. The offensive of 21 March was meticulously prepared. A total of 192 divisions with 1,386,177 men were assembled on the western front against 178 Allied divisions. The main target was the British 5th and 3rd Armies in the Somme–Arras sector, where only twelve divisions faced forty-three German divisions on a 42-mile front. For weeks the divisions selected for the assault, which had proved their success in battle, were trained on the basis of the successful Caporetto offensive in mixed arms tactics; they were well equipped, especially with light machine guns and trench mortars, and their food supply was improved. The offensive opened with a short bombardment of unparalleled intensity, followed five hours later by the infantry attack. Innovative use was made of the creeping barrage and swift penetration by the infantry. But the barrage crept too fast for the men, who were soon lost in the dense fog of that day, and choked by smoke and gas. Communications between the artillery and the infantry were cut by the intense shell-fire. German losses on the first day, 78,000 killed and wounded, far exceeded the British losses of 38,000, or those on the first day of the Somme in 1916. (Why this terrible slaughter of 1918 should so completely be forgotten, while that of 1916 is so vividly present in modern British memory, is a telling paradox.) Nevertheless, the Germans overran the first line of British defences held by the 5th Army, and after fierce battle on the second line, the British retreated to the third line. Within a week, the British were pushed back beyond their positions before the battle of the Somme, the 5th Army retreating in confusion. Plans were made to evacuate the British army from the Channel ports, and the French government left Paris for Bordeaux. It was the worst setback suffered by the British in the entire war: 160,000 men and 1,000 guns were lost.[4]

However, it was not a defeat. In this first phase of the offensive, in two weeks the Germans had driven into a large bulge up to sixty kilometres deep and wide, which proved to be difficult to defend, at the cost of 239,000 casualties (on German figures), including many of the best stormtroops. (See Map 1.) No strategic objectives had been gained, for there were none. Asked about the operational objectives, Ludendorff replied: 'I forbid the word "operation". We will simply punch a hole [in the line]. For the rest, we shall see.' A second attack, launched after the offensive ground to a halt on the Somme, had met well-prepared defences of the British 3rd Army and was a complete failure. The real aim of driving apart the French and British had not been realized. On 5 April Ludendorff suspended the attack. Morale among the ninety exhausted divisions thrown into the struggle started to decline, a process that began on 27 March, when the troops were ordered to dig trenches in view of stiffening Allied resistance. A regimental history recorded: 'These orders have a nightmarish effect on officers and men. *Trench warfare again?*'[5] Subsequent phases of the offensive were wild thrashing about to seize tactical opportunities as they arose, although still dangerous to the Allies: an offensive along the Lys in Flanders on 9 April made initial gains of a few miles, but British counter-attacks there and further south stopped the advance and prevented the Germans reaching the important railway junction at Amiens (24 April). The Aisne offensive against the French in late May, preceded by the heaviest German artillery effort of the war, with 2 million shells fired in 4.5 hours, brought an advance to within 70 kilometres of Paris, and a modified 21 cm. naval gun with a range of 120 kilometres fired several shells at the city, destroying a church, killing civilians and reviving the Allied charges of German barbarity. Yet neither this offensive nor another in June gained a strategic breakthrough.

The apparent success of the German army created more problems than it solved. Communication lines were longer, and it was difficult to bring supplies and reserves up to the front across the shattered landscape of the Somme, without roads or railways. Advancing soldiers, who soon went hungry, fell upon Allied stores of food and drink with a delight that soon turned to dismay. Crown Prince Rupprecht noted that his thirsty troops had stopped their attack on discovering the plentiful stocks of wine; Colonel von Thaer recorded that 'entire divisions had *totally* gorged themselves on *food* and *liquor*', and refused to continue the attack.[6] Ludendorff admitted nothing could stop the men pillaging.[7] The discovery of the Allied supplies of white bread, corned beef, biscuits, jam, rum, wine, boots, fur jackets, fresh underwear—everything Germans had been deprived of for years— made the men realize the incomparable economic superiority of the enemy. Moreover, the cost in men was immense, more than at any other time apart from the first two months of the war: 235,544 in March and 257,176 in April, and a total of 915,000 casualties by the end of June.[8] Casualties of such a magnitude indicate the recklessness of Ludendorff's gamble, the wager on victory without the means to hold on to tactical gains, without a concept of warfare that integrated strategy, politics, and economics. While German losses, often of the best and most experienced fighters, could not be made good, the Allies were more than replenishing their ranks with the 250,000 Americans now arriving every month.

The sudden drop in German morale is explained finally by the huge expectations attached to the offensive. According to a report by Italian soldiers who escaped from captivity in north-eastern Italy in February 1918, the German soldiers were well clothed and had better food than the Austrians. Their morale was high, and the men were 'as fresh as at the start of the war'. Leaving Italy to prepare for 'one final grand offensive', they said they were 'ready to sacrifice one million men in order to succeed'. Not only does this show a mood of high expectation. More importantly, it reveals more starkly than elsewhere the fundamental power relationship of armies at war: 'sacrifice', a religious term for the acceptance of mass death, including one's own, was not something submitted to on the orders of the generals, the ruling class, or militarist pressure-groups, but rested on consensus. The terms of that sacrifice were negotiable, not unconditional. The German soldiers ended by saying: 'But if we do not succeed we will have to make peace three months later.'[9] By 27 April Colonel von Thaer, chief of staff of the Second Quartermaster-General, found that all the troops involved in the Lys offensive were suffering from the 'depression of a very great disappointment'.[10]

Stiffening Allied resistance turned retreats, temporary confusion, and demoralization into their opposite: a decisive defensive victory. The French general Foch was promoted to marshal and made commander-in-chief of all Allied forces. Having learned how to combat the new German tactics with more flexible defence, Foch successfully coordinated counter-offensives of mounting intensity in which the French infantry (which by and large had been spared since early 1917) and soon also the fresh American forces, participated, supported by masses of French and British tanks. Which particular battle was the turning point depended on the observer. On 18 July the Allies unleashed their superiority in matériel on the overextended German positions on the Marne: thirteen French and three American divisions, spearheaded with 1,000 tanks and 2,100 guns, and the massive air power of over 1,000 airplanes. The entire German army had no more than twenty tanks. Caught by surprise at the forest of Villers-Cotterêts, the Germans retreated beyond the river Vesle to the Aisne. For the first time, Ludendorff panicked, and wanted to order withdrawal to the Siegfried line, the starting point of the offensive. General Groener described him later as physically and morally broken. Ludendorff himself saw the British attack at Amiens on 8 August as the true turning point, the 'black day of the German army'. The British 4th Army deployed devastating fire power in an all-weapons onslaught. One hundred thousand infantrymen, including elite Canadian and Australian troops, followed 552 tanks into the assault. Even more important was the accuracy and weight of the shell fire, in which 700 guns laid down a short, intense barrage that destroyed most of the German guns or allowed them to be captured: 450 out of the 530 German guns. Of the 27,000 German men lost, 12,000, significantly, were taken prisoner: a sign that men were surrendering in large numbers. Ludendorff's nerve broke, and he offered his resignation; the Kaiser refused.[11]

None of the following Allied attacks brought a real breakthrough, but that was not the intention. Rather, it was a continuous push at every sector of the front where weakness was discovered, in which the pattern was generally the deployment of massive fire power of machines followed by men to reappropriate territory: the annihilation of space and men to conquer space. German morale was ebbing away, albeit at varying speeds in each unit, a phenomenon the German historian Wilhelm Deist aptly called a 'covert military strike'. Men retreating on 8 August, seeing a fresh division going up to the front, called out 'war prolongers!' and 'strikebreakers!'[12] The horrendous losses, the physical and mental exhaustion, the loss of hope of victory and peace, and the ebbing authority of the commanders, produced a mass movement that broke the cohesion of the German army.

For those with direct knowledge of the front, the inevitability of defeat was clear. Participants at various levels of the army hierarchy recorded the destructive effects of the Allied onslaught on German morale. A divisional surgeon noted on 23 May 1918 the rapidly declining physical and above all mental state of men and officers, caused by exhaustion, 'general nervousness', and lack of sleep. 'The men were unable to recuperate during their entire deployment, even when at rest, since they were under fire everywhere, and since all houses were systematically shelled, they preferred to seek shelter in ditches along the hedges.'[13]

The remarks of a soldier in the reserve army hospital, Bremerhaven, were recorded secretly as he talked with another soldier a few days after the 'black day' of the German army, 8 August:

> You see, comrade, we're finished up, no-one believes in victory any more; what the newspapers write is all lies ... If we make an end of it now, we can salvage a great deal—money and human lives. Why should we allow our bones to be shot to pieces, just because the chiefs up there still take pleasure in this lunatic butchery? In Wilhelmshaven the U-boat men also want to stop everything; I am informed about everything. And if we all stick together, we can do it: we'll simply stop obeying orders, and either we cross over to the other side, or we desert. But first we'll have to work on the comrades at the front, only we have to take care. They also do not want to go on. . . .
>
> We'll bring our comrades round so that they'll all join in, like in Russia; we've nothing more to lose . . . [14]

The young soldier Pechtold, whom we encountered at Verdun, was involved in heavy fighting and gradual retreats in mid-August. He saw a British advance of 600 metres on 17 August, and then gaps suddenly appeared in the German lines of 2–3 km., at one point of 5–10 km. The British advanced with tanks and captured entire units. All the men and officers were exhausted by the heat, the constant combat, the lice, and the poor food supply. On 26 August his brigade retreated, destroying with explosives whatever was left behind, but harvesting the French grain. After retreating through Péronne in early September Pechtold witnessed British artillery shelling the nearby villages and barracks; Estrées-en-Chaussee, hitherto almost unscathed, was burned down. In Tincourt, German pioneers burned down everything combustible, leaving only the building housing the regiment staff.[15] Right across northern France the devastations of the 1917 retreat were repeated, but this time in haste and therefore not as systematically. Nevertheless, they were just as vindictive, and the long-term losses were vast: forty of the 111 coalmines were completely destroyed and flooded, and the surface machinery destroyed in all the remainder. As they retreated, hungry men pillaged whatever food and livestock the civilians still possessed.[16]

On 20 August General von Einem, commander of the 3rd Army in the Champagne, wrote in his diary that divisions that had been sent to the rear to recuperate were being called back suddenly and thrown into the battle, and the OHL had either 'lost its sense of orientation, or things have declined to the point where we have to live from hand to mouth'. 'None of the troops', he went on, 'have time to rest, recover, and get reorganized.'[17] He blamed the OHL for having disregarded the development of tanks, which were now the war-winning weapon of the enemy, creating terror among the German troops who were surrendering 'en masse'; another general complained that the troops were 'paralysed with fright' by the tanks. Although some attacks were being repulsed, others were pushing the Germans back; the mood on the home front had turned, and civilians no longer believed in the possibility of victory. A few days later von Einem realized the war had 'reached a very critical stage; the British and French are attacking ceaselessly'. He wished the OHL could take the decision to end the fighting. The defenders were 'suffering almost more than the attackers'; on 29 August 'the British, Canadians, and Australians attack with gigantic force and push us back'. He feared the Allies, under the leadership of the 'energetic' and 'resolute' Foch, would not give the Germans respite but continue the offensive into November.[18] Defeat stared him in the face, and he expected the Allies to impose the same kind of destruction on Germany which had devastated the occupied territories:

In my opinion we cannot count on a victory any longer, and therefore the
future does not look too good . . . May God let our grandchildren experience a
flourishing Germany at the end of their lifetime. Certainly, that sounds very
pessimistic, but I can only see the gravity of the situation, and I do not believe
in miracles any more. Hatred of us unites our enemies ever more firmly, and
their will to annihilate has grown stronger than ever.[19]

Kurt Riezler, the former political adviser to chancellor Bethmann Hollweg,
had an equally apocalyptic vision of the future: 'Slavery for 100 years. The
dream of world power gone forever. The end of all hubris. The scattering of
Germans throughout the world. Fate of the Jews.'[20]

After the Germans retreated behind the massive defences of the Siegfried
line in early September 1918, their mood picked up again; they felt reassured
because the Allies had not achieved a breakthrough; while the Germans
could rest in a land spared devastation, the attackers had arrived in a completely desolate zone, destroyed by the previous German retreat of 1917,
deprived of all places of habitation, without wells, roads, or even trees. But
this time there was no respite. On 9 September the French attacked the
German 3rd and 1st armies:

The French heavy artillery are now shelling all the villages behind us, turning
them into flames and rubble, in order to rob us of accommodation for our
troops. They are completely indifferent whether the population is still there or
not. Vouziers was also under heavy fire. Masses of unfortunate people, the sick
and elderly, on the roads, fleeing with their few belongings. I regret not
having evacuated the village of its population, but we assumed the French
would spare it.[21]

General von Einem's 3rd Army was the target of a major assault on 25
September between Rheims and the Argonne forest. Several of his divisions
parried the attack, but one simply ran away. Even elite units in the Guards
Infantry Division could not withstand the tanks. As they retreated, the Germans resumed the destruction of entire villages. By 28 September two more of
his divisions (202 and 103) were in such a state they could not carry out orders
to advance, because 'they have been burned down to cinders'.[22] It was said that
the 2nd Army had been 'completely beaten'.[23] Colonel Bauer, a close adviser
to Ludendorff, recalled that at this time 'not many more than $\frac{3}{4}$ million
infantrymen stood in the combat line'; in August there were one million
'shirkers and deserters', and by the end of September $1\frac{1}{2}$ million. Those still at
the front were exhausted, often hungry, and without the means of defence
against tanks and aircraft. Some regiments had been reduced to 200 men; one

consisted of only eight officers, eight NCOs and sixty-nine men.[24] The 5th Army broke and retreated on 1 and 2 November, opening the possibility for the Allies to surround it and cut it off from the rest of the army; entire divisions panicked, with communications breaking down in the rush to cross the Meuse. To the disgust of General von Einem, the disintegrating 5th Army was unable to prevent the Allies from crossing the Meuse into Belgium.[25]

The German army was fighting to self-destruction. Some historians have argued that it could have continued to fight into the winter and spring of 1919, and that the end of the war came as a surprise to the Allies in November 1918.[26] Only one part of this is true: British intelligence was not well informed on the state of German morale and fighting capacity. By coincidence the last meeting of the Supreme War Council to decide the armistice terms took place on 4 November; one day later news came that the German state was disintegrating, as a workers' and sailors' soviet formed in Kiel, and revolution spread to Hamburg and Lübeck on 6 November. Concerned not to repeat the misplaced optimism of 1916 and 1917, the British refused to realize the seriousness of the collapse for several days. Such was the confusion that Sir Henry Wilson, chief of the Imperial General Staff, told the war cabinet as late as 7 November that 'there did not appear to be any actual need yet for the Germans to accept the terms'.[27] This was a failure of intelligence at one of the few moments in history when it could have made a real difference. The other part of the argument is perverse, for if the fighting had continued, one German division after another would have crumbled as more men surrendered to the enemy, fled the war zone, or disobeyed orders. That was the nightmare scenario for the OHL: a high command without men was no longer an army, and cessation of the war before defeat became essential to preserve the army's remaining cohesion. The German high command thus halted the dynamic of destruction before it became total self-destruction— quite unlike the last consequences of Nazi warfare in 1945.

That is precisely what the Habsburg leadership failed to do. In every way the Austro-Hungarian army, economy, and society had proved unequal to the strains of modern, industrial war, as we have seen. But the problems went deeper than those of organization or strategy: in an age of nationalism and the mobilization of nations, a multi-ethnic state (at least in the way the Habsburg state was constituted) found it increasingly difficult to sustain loyalty among its many different peoples. This should not be exaggerated, for contrary to the expectation of many observers at the time, friendly and hostile, Austro-Hungarian mobilization proceeded in 1914 without the breakdown or mass desertions often feared; for two years, Czechs, Slovaks,

Hungarians, Slovenes, Ruthenes, and Poles, even Italians, fought loyally alongside German-speaking Austrians. Under the terrible conditions of the eastern front, however, and especially with the hammer-blow of the Brusilov offensive in summer 1916, morale had dropped and ethnic groups were singled out for blame. The Russian offensive, unlike all its predecessors, had been meticulously prepared, and although the Russian forces had only a small superiority in men and artillery, they were well supplied with shells, the artillery cooperated well with the infantry, and the attack took place on many broad fronts simultaneously. Austro-Hungarian troops were routed along a great line from the Pripyat Marshes near Pinsk to Czernovitz in the Bukovina, and thousands of prisoners fell into Russian hands. (See Map 2.) Demoralized gunners fled, leaving their artillery behind. Within little more than a week after the opening of the offensive on 4 June, the Russians had virtually destroyed two Austro-Hungarian armies, taken 193,000 prisoners, and captured 216 guns. Further Russian victories followed in July. With casualties, total losses were over half the Austro-Hungarian forces on the eastern front. Even the victory at Caporetto the following year could not make good the shattering of morale, and the resultant subservience to German command.[28]

The creeping loss of sovereignty to the Germans magnified the problem of the legitimation of the state; disaffection had already been growing on the home front and in the army. Czechs, Slovaks, Ruthenes, or Poles were usually commanded by German-speaking Austrian officers, or sometimes by Hungarians, who often did not speak the language of the men. Orders had to be translated, sometimes into three languages in a single regiment. The loyalty of Ruthenes, who understood Russian and shared their religion, was sorely tested, and during the Brusilov offensive large numbers of them deserted to the Russians near Czernovitz. There were desertions of Czechs and other Slavs, although not on the scale suspected by the military leaders, but above all the suspicion of disloyalty became corrosive.[29] Slav soldiers increasingly failed to obey their Habsburg officers, and there was widespread Austrian resentment at Hungarian protectionism and refusal to send food supplies. When the Russian army launched its last offensive at the behest of Kerensky's provisional government in July 1917, the only point at which it succeeded was where it used Czech legions formed from captured soldiers, prompting the mainly Czech infantry regiments 35 and 75 to desert to the Russians. The Central Powers managed to stabilize the front, however, and Czernovitz was recaptured, so the widening cracks in the Austro-Hungarian army were concealed by the even greater demoralization and collapse of the Russian army.

Yet the victories over Russia (and Romania) came too late to save the Austro-Hungarian empire. At the same time as the negotiations in Brest-Litovsk, strikes broke out in Hungary, Poland, Transylvania, followed by Moravia, Bohemia, and Vienna itself. The strikers were not only motivated by the lack of food, but also the desire for immediate peace. In addition, the national question became ever more urgent, with Czech and south Slav politicians demanding independent representation at the peace talks. Austrian politicians, with the support of Kaiser Karl and the right-wing German-Radical party, began to call for the protection of the justified interests of the German people, and by July 1918 to plan the separation on national lines of Germans and Czechs in Bohemia. The offer by Kaiser Karl on 16 October to consider equal rights for the various peoples of the empire inside a federation came too late to placate anyone, since the demand was now for full independence. The Czechoslovak Republic was declared in Prague on 28 October, and by the time Austria-Hungary signed the armistice with the Allies in Italy on 3 November, the empire had ceased to exist. The war to save the empire ended with its self-destruction.[30]

The failure of the tsarist empire to mobilize its human resources effectively for war was also linked with its inability to come to terms with its multi-ethnic identity. If Russia had mobilized as effectively as the French, it would have had an army of 60 million. But entire ethnic groups were excluded from the draft, for fear of rebellion or disobedience. When the army was forced by the great losses of Russian soldiers to conscript men from other nationalities, this reduced even further the cohesion of the empire. For example, in central Asia massive riots against conscription broke out in 1916; tens of thousands of lives were lost when the army restored order.[31] Although not to the same extent as with the Habsburg empire, the revolutionary breakdown of Russia in 1917 was thus partly caused by the destabilizing effects of war in an authoritarian multinational state.

Coping with collective trauma: one war, multiple memories

Nations, and different cultures within nations, responded in different ways to the collective trauma of war and its outcome. This affected the post-war history of violence. Systematic comparison across Europe shows that the demarcation lines in political violence did not run between victorious and defeated nations, nor even between revolutionary and non-revolutionary states. The pattern corresponds broadly to a typology of nation-state formation sketched by the German historian Theodor Schieder: west European nation-states created by internal revolution, central European states founded by movements of national unification, and east European states formed by secession movements. In western Europe violence after the First World War was kept under control, in the states founded by unification nationalism the democratic order was destroyed by paramilitary groups, and extensive, unlimited violence characterized the secession states of eastern Europe.[32] Such distinctions are arguably more useful than the thesis of a general 'brutalization of politics' following the war or the reductionist model according to which fascism was a response to the Bolshevik Revolution.[33] The different reactions to war had as much to do with culture, including the creation of myth and political interpretation, as with the actual tally of death, destruction, and economic dislocation.

In Germany, the talk of its army's brave, skilled defence, remaining intact until it was treacherously 'stabbed in the back' by the civilians who fomented revolution, rests on the accretion of individual anecdotes of heroism (of which there were undoubtedly many), an edifice constructed to hide the reality of collapse and the shameful memory of mass disobedience to create the post-war nationalist myth of the undefeated army. The legend of the 'stab in the back', which did so much to delegitimize the Weimar republic, and is discussed later in this chapter, was actually created during the war. Among militarists it was a common cliché well before the end of the war. General von Einem voiced his fear at various points in summer and autumn 1918 that the home front would not stand firm. On being informed by Ludendorff on 30 September that chancellor Hertling had resigned (but not aware that Ludendorff himself had ordered the formation of a new government made up of democrats to sue for peace), von Einem raged: 'The Fatherland is in greatest danger, and despite that there is no unity; everyone is just pursuing his own purposes. Parliament is an invention of the devil! Every German ought to be a soldier and obey orders, then everything would be possible!' When the Social Democrats entered the government a few days later, he wrote: 'This means the introduction of the parliamentary system and the downfall of Prussia and Germany... How is it possible for a Prussian king and German emperor to yield his power to the Social Democrats, the democrats, and the Roman Centre!'[34] These were subversive forces which were collaborating with the foreign powers to 'destroy

Germany', after which Germany would sink to the level of a fourth-rate power.[35]

Naturally, the legend could not have found ready listeners if it had been entirely without foundation. In some divisions or smaller units morale was still high enough to mount effective rearguard defence and retreat in good order rather than flee. The artillery had not suffered the same attrition as the infantry and were still in a position to return fire. There were generational differences, too. Young soldiers, recently drafted, were often still keen to prove themselves to be 'real men', while older, married men had stronger emotional bonds with home, and had no desire to be the last man killed in a lost cause.[36] In the most revealing inquiry, when Groener assembled the thirty-nine most senior army commanders at Spa on 9 November to ask them whether they would march back into Germany behind Kaiser Wilhelm to 'reconquer' the home front and crush the revolution, twenty-three said they would not. With regard to deployment against the revolution, eight said there was no hope of using the army against unrest at home, and all the rest expressed doubt or said that order had to be restored first in the army. The summary was: 'The troops are fully exhausted at the moment; only the ruins [of an army] are on hand.'[37] That put an end to all the utopian hopes of a desperate final struggle, the *Endkampf*, using hundreds of thousands of boys as new recruits and combing through the garrisons for older men who were not complete invalids. Equally suicidal schemes like that of Walther Rathenau for a *levée en masse* had previously been rejected, for fear that the army might be infected with revolutionary ideas.[38] Finally, it is important to recall the order of events: first came the OHL admission that it was at the end of its tether, which became public knowledge in early October; only after the breakdown of military authority in the fleet at the end of October did the home front show signs of revolution.

Equally pernicious was the associated myth of the Jews as shirkers and traitors. Why should this myth have spread in Germany, rather than Britain or France? Also preceding the end of the war, it was created by right-wing and antisemitic associations such as the Pan-German League which were influential both among army officers and outside the army. Already in 1914 the antisemites were demanding 'investigations' into the war participation of Jews, and attempted to obtain harsh measures of racial discrimination. Despite the fact that Jews had faced discrimination in the army and were prohibited before 1914 from becoming officers in the Prussian army, they served in approximately the same proportion as the rest of the population (taking their different age structure into account), and 12,000 of them were killed, almost the same proportion as national losses. One demand of the antisemites was met in October 1916, when the war ministry ordered a census of Jews in the army. This had the effect of singling out Jews, and Jewish men felt humiliated at evidently being considered untrustworthy or unpatriotic. It lent wings to antisemitic hatred at a time when there was no end in sight to the terrible slaughter and the inhuman conditions at the front. The 'Jew census' thus marked a turning point in the development of antisemitism in Germany.[39] Meanwhile the antisemitic forces moved from the margin of German politics towards the centre. The Pan-German League had become influential in mainstream militarist nationalism, above all through the Fatherland Party, and in October 1918 the League chairman, Class, called for the formation of a 'resolute national party' which would conduct a 'ruthless struggle against Jews' in order 'to divert the people's anger' at the impending defeat.[40]

If the war thus produced a rise in antisemitism in Germany, the position of Jews in France and Britain actually became more secure. Even in phases of low morale in the war, antisemitism in France and Britain, apart from sporadic incidents, remained marginal. Defeat would have produced a different trajectory in which the French Third Republic might have collapsed, to be replaced by its political enemies who were notoriously of the anti-Dreyfusard, antisemitic tradition. In Germany the antisemites, who were obsessed by their stereotypes, lit upon the notion of the Jewish–Bolshevist conspiracy, a new idea which proved to be so attractive to the extreme right that it henceforth became a fixed part of Nazi rhetoric. Although most German Jews were solid liberals who supported parties like the German Democratic Party (DDP), the German People's Party (DVP), and some would have supported the nationalist-conservative German National People's Party (DNVP) but for its antisemitism, the participation of Jews in some leading roles in the Russian Revolution and in the short-lived revolution in 1919 in Bavaria lent a spurious rationale to the ideas of racism. Revenge for 'betrayal' in the war was therefore closely linked with the destruction of the internal racial and political enemy, and the 'Jewish–Bolshevist conspiracy' was one hinge that joined the mass destruction of the First World War with the Holocaust of the Second World War.

Germany's cultural trauma of defeat was compounded by the collapse of the imperial regime. For conservative nationalists the abdication of the Kaiser (on 9 November) was an unbearable emotional blow, worse, in fact, than defeat. General von Einem, who had been imperturbable during war despite experiencing the loss of countless men and also close friends, broke down and wept when given the news that Wilhelm II had abdicated:

> At 6.15 pm Klewitz [his chief of staff] entered my room. I could tell at once from his deep solemnity that something very grave must have happened. By now we were accustomed to receiving bad news, but what now emerged was the most distressing report a Prussian officer could receive. Klewitz told me that the Kaiser had abdicated. I was so terribly shocked that I had to sit down, and covered my face with both hands . . . Later I informed the gentlemen on my staff of the terrible tidings, before we sat down for our dinner. I was hardly able to utter the words; my voice almost failed me.[41]

Following defeat the army demobilized, or rather the soldiers self-demobilized as soon as they reached home, and the peace treaty of June 1919 banned conscription and restricted the army to 100,000 men. While official and militarist Germany responded to defeat by creating myths about betrayal, and refused mentally to demobilize, Britain and France demobilized, but at different speeds. Britain, unlike Germany or Italy, did not have to invent myths about betrayal. Instead, it faced the reality of the Irish independence movement which launched an uprising in Dublin in the middle of the war, at Easter 1916. Appealing to their 'gallant Allies in Europe', but knowing they were hopelessly inferior in numbers and weapons, Irish nationalists led by Patrick Pearse attempted to seize power by attacking strategic points in the city, centred on the General Post Office. The British army reacted with overwhelming and incommensurate force, deploying artillery in city streets, to crush the rising. No fewer than 450 were killed on the nationalist side, with 2,614 wounded, including many uninvolved civilians, and 116 soldiers and sixteen policemen. In the aftermath of draconian repression the British executed fifteen leaders of the rising, which was legally uncontentious in view of treason, but politically inept. The result was that public sympathy, initially hostile to the 'physical force' nationalists, shifted inexorably and permanently against British rule. In the subsequent War of Independence (1919–21), the millenarian vision of Pearse's 'blood sacrifice' which would allow the creation of a free Ireland inspired thousands of fighters in a grim campaign starting with the assassination of policemen (who were usually Irish Catholics). Britain recruited ex-army men into police reinforcement units, the 'Black and Tans' and the 'Auxiliaries', which carried out reprisals and committed brutal atrocities. Yet the British government disengaged before it became an outright war—which the IRA acknowledged it could not win—and conceded independence in autumn 1921.[42] This is not the place to discuss the traumatic and even bloodier Civil War that followed in Ireland; but Britain had in a sense exported its post-war violence, and political conflict henceforth was characterized by its relatively peaceful nature.[43] Post-war Britain was characterized not by the 'brutalization of politics' and the legitimation of violence, but rather the fear of brutalization and the rejection of violence in politics.[44] Even in colonial rule British political culture became less tolerant of violence. The massacre by British troops of unarmed Indian demonstrators at Amritsar in 1919 outraged public opinion, and government and parliament censured the commanding General Dyer.[45] Britain ended conscription, which it had introduced only after controversial debates in wartime, in 1919, seeing little need in peacetime to maintain a standing army.

France was in a different position. It kept conscription throughout the inter-war period, ending it only in 2001. The different pace of mental demobilization is highlighted by the year 1923: the French occupation of the Ruhr to enforce payment of German reparations was seen as a kind of continuation of the war, to preserve the French victory and ensure German compliance with the terms of its defeat. Without directly breaking the alliance with France, the British government made plain its disapproval of the venture, and restated its policy of reconciliation with Germany which was already apparent over the Allied concession to Germany in the ending of the attempt to have German war criminals extradited, which Britain pushed through against a reluctant French government in 1920. By 1925, however, both nations were ready to readmit Germany to the comity of nations, and treat with it on the basis of the assumption that mental demobilization, in the sense of a weakening resolve for military revenge, was proceeding in Germany as fast as in France and Britain.

In France after 1918 political violence was comparatively rare. Certainly, the left wing of the French labour movement felt that the time had arrived for revolutionary change. The syndicalist Pierre Monatte wrote in June 1919: 'There are and there will be more and more men and women with us who will never pardon capitalist society for having begun the world war which has devoured our children. We will neither pardon nor forget.'[46] Disappointment with the peace treaty mixed with disillusion at the trade union and socialist leaders for their failure to advance the cause of the working class during the war, to produce the unrest of 1919–20: on May

Day 1919 one demonstrator was killed and several wounded, and that summer there was a mass strike of metalworkers in Paris. More mass strikes followed in 1920. Yet even with the formation of the French Communist Party in 1920 the Third Republic neither faced a serious threat to its existence from the Left, nor did it respond with the extensive repression applied by the Italian state, where the police and army killed 26 persons in 1919 and 92 in 1920.[47] Even such a central feature of the 'brutalization' thesis, namely the ideal of camaraderie which Mosse regarded as one of the most important parts of the 'myth of the war experience' in post-war Germany, worked in France in the opposite sense, promoting a growing anti-war consensus.[48]

The greatest distinction in collective trauma and the cultural memory of war was between France and Britain on one side, and Germany on the other. Italy and Russia, as will be seen, were again different, the one with an internally contested victory, the other with defeat overshadowed entirely by revolution and civil war. France and Britain commemorated the 'unknown soldier', with monuments at the Arc de Triomphe and Westminster Abbey (and also the Cenotaph in Whitehall, literally 'empty tomb'). The unknown soldier allowed the anonymous masses to enter public memory, rather than the hero, the ordinary man who embodied the nation. He provided 'a means to come to terms with the trauma of war', to 'return to normality, . . . to bury the dead and then go on with life'.[49] Italy, too, constructed a memorial to the 'unknown soldier' in the *Vittoriano*, the monument to Vittorio Emanuele II and Italian unification. The Liberal state, caught in the crossfire between left-wing social protest and Fascist violence, sought to use it to underline its legitimation as the rightful owners of Italian unity, but the Socialist newspaper *Avanti* claimed the Unknown Soldier as one of its own, a proletarian, and urged its readers: 'Honour him in silence and curse the war!'[50] Germany's path led in a different direction: there was no monument to the unknown soldier. The proposal was debated in Germany, but the nationalists and the veterans' association (the Stahlhelm) rejected it as a pacifist idea invented by the enemy. Theodor Wolff, liberal newspaper editor, commented that the unknown soldier could only exist in nations that recognized the principles of equality and democracy, which was why the Nazis could never bury an unknown soldier: they would risk honouring a Jew or a Social Democrat.[51] In Britain and France the unknown soldier was a symbol of the past; in Germany, memory of the dead was contested between the personal and the political sphere of the present. The fallen were at first commemorated in countless local war memorials across Germany, which were often modest and on a small scale, and usually made no explicit political statement about the war. Significantly, in the divided political culture of Weimar the use of natural stone and abstract forms indicated death in war as a fate to be submitted to, as did the use of Christian iconography which made death sacred, while in others victory symbols such as oak leaves and laurel crowns were quite common. About eight to ten years after the end of the war, heroicizing monuments began to appear, much larger than previous ones, and especially in the Nazi period, glorifying death in war and pointing to the future.[52]

Another distinction has sometimes been seen in a preoccupation with violence in German culture, with even the anti-war artists, such as Dix, Grosz, or Beckmann, revealing a 'fascination with depravity, mutilation, and inhumanity generally absent from representations of war in France' or, we might add, Britain,[53] or with the frankness and brutality of the descriptions of destruction in anti-war writers like Remarque. It might be argued that this was due to the German anti-war artists' desire to bring home the effects of war to the civilians who had mainly seen no violence or devastation; but that would not explain the relative absence of violence in British cultural representations of war. The explanation might therefore be in the German anti-war artists' need to cut through the official lies about war, which they sensed disguised preparations for a further war; a motivation that was mainly absent in France and Britain because of the consensus that war, however victorious, was a catastrophe.

Russia: defeat and new war

After the end of its participation in the world war Russia followed a different trajectory to western Europe. Russian history, traditionally seen from the perspective of the discontinuity of the 1917 revolution, should rather be seen in a continuum from 1914 to 1921. The most important point is that Russia's post-war history began while the rest of Europe was still at war; immediately after the Bolshevik seizure of power in the large cities a struggle for control of the rest of the territory broke out, while under threat of continued German invasion from the west. The Treaty of Brest-Litovsk of March 1918 brought peace in the external war, but the political and social violence in the Revolution, then the Civil War, brought far greater devastation than had been caused by the world war.

The Great War itself had created the conditions for revolution in 1917, not only through the demoralization of defeat, but also through the legitimation of violence and the build-up of utopian expectations. The external enemy was internalized: as one peasant said in March 1916: 'When we return to Courland, we'll hang the barons and colonists.'[54] Even the education of the peasant soldiers contributed; 60 per cent of the students attending officer schools between 1914 and 1917 were from the peasantry, and these were the men who led the soldiers in the revolution. Now they had won prestige and seen the world, they found it impossible to return to the idiocy of rural life. Joining the Bolshevik Party and the Red Army was the way to enter the new world of the big city. For many Bolshevik workers, it was a self-evident duty to join the Red Army (or the Cheka, the secret police) to defend the revolution, and 60 per cent of party members did so during the Civil War (1918–21). The party organizations they left behind in the cities fell under the control of the careerists and the corrupt. In turn, the Red Army militarized the Bolshevik Party and the Soviets. The need for ruthless military discipline spilled over into the entire Soviet state, and success at war reinforced the prestige of the military. 'Even the language of the Bolshevik regime', Orlando Figes has written, 'with its constant talk of "campaigns", "battles", and "Fronts", of its "vanguards" and "fighters" for Socialism, bore the traces of this militarism.'[55] The Civil War thus 'militarized the revolutionary political culture of the Bolshevik movement', bringing military language and fashion into the party, and producing a 'readiness to resort to coercion... [and] summary justice'.[56] Not only the members of the Cheka, but Bolshevik party members were entitled to carry a pistol as status symbol, removed from the latter only in 1937.[57]

The unique feature of Russian development was the extent to which the practice of violence towards external enemies was turned inwards and applied mutually as coercive measures against enemies in the Civil War.[58] Yet even in the appalling chaos of the breakdown of society in 1917 distinctions can be made. Revolutionary violence in 1917 emanated mainly from the soldiers, and even more so from the sailors. There were countless incidents of violence against officers, including many murders, as from February 1917. The soldiers' violent hatred of the commanders and the rulers, who in the opinion of the soldiers were profiteering from the war and prolonging it, was an essential component in the Bolsheviks' success in mobilizing mass support, and it thus influenced the political culture of Bolshevism. Paradoxically, it was the willingness of the Bolsheviks to mobilize this violent potential for their peace campaign that lent legitimacy to popular social and even criminal violence. The murder of officers, merchants, landowners, priests, and politicians after October 1917, along with pillage, land expropriation, and drunken orgies, resulted from the discrediting of the entire old order, above all from the collapse of the old army. By contrast, the political actions of industrial workers and even of the peasantry were usually restricted to symbolic forms of violence or the threat of violence; in the countryside murder remained relatively rare until October 1917.

The repercussions of Brest-Litovsk changed this. The peace treaty was bitterly resented by the Left Social-Revolutionaries (the coalition partner of the Bolsheviks), who wanted the war to continue as a revolutionary war. Their turn to violence and assassination (they succeeded in killing the German ambassador Count Mirbach to provoke resumption of war) removed the Bolsheviks' last remaining inhibitions to unleash the 'Red Terror' on their political opponents.[59]

With the outbreak of open civil war, in the desperate struggle to save the existence of the revolution, the Bolsheviks turned their violent rhetoric not only against the bourgeoisie, but, even though the bulk of the Red Army was recruited from the peasantry, also against the 'kulaks', i.e. the allegedly wealthier peasants, who hoarded food supplies. Lenin made an extraordinarily explicit call to violence in summer 1918:

> The kulaks are the rabid foes of the Soviet government . . . These bloodsuckers have grown rich on the hunger of the people . . . [They] have grown fat at the expense of the peasants ruined by the war, at the expense of the workers. These leeches have sucked the blood of the working people and grown richer as the workers in the cities and factories starved . . . Ruthless war on the kulaks! Death to all of them.[60]

The 'battle for grain' led to widespread terrorizing of peasants, rich and poor, and sparked a wave of peasant revolts, in which local Bolsheviks were lynched. The political enemies of the new state faced the repression of the Cheka—884 people were executed in the first months of its existence until July 1918. That was a moderate death-toll compared to the mass executions under Stalin, but worse was to come with the outbreak of open civil war.

After an assassination attempt by a Social-Revolutionary seriously injured Lenin in August 1918, the Bolshevik Party began to issue blood-curdling hate propaganda. One newspaper wrote:

> Without mercy we will kill our enemies in scores of hundreds. Let them be thousands, let them drown themselves in their own blood. For the blood of Lenin and Uritsky [Bolshevik leader assassinated on 30 August] let there be floods of bourgeois blood—more blood, as much as possible.[61]

The Bolsheviks turned to a policy of terror, explicitly derived from the terror of the French Revolution. The Red Terror now became a deliberate instrument of policy. Counter-revolutionaries, hostages from the bourgeoisie, and former tsarist officials were executed without trial, among them the former tsar, Nicholas II and his family. During the first year of the Terror up to mid-1919 at least 8,389 people were thus executed. Countless prisoners, many arbitrarily arrested, were the victims of unspeakable torture. The Terror was 'a war by the regime against the whole of society—a means of terrorizing it into submission', carried out by a paranoid government that saw real and imagined enemies on all fronts.[62]

However, Bolshevik repression and the Terror should not be understood purely as a planned process directed from the top. The political and social violence had started well before the Civil War, and even the institutions created by the Bolsheviks, the Cheka, for example, were shaped in response to the pressure from below. In other words, the Bolshevik government was presiding over a society in breakdown, a society at war with itself. There was an orgy of robbery and violence in the months after October 1917 in which churches, museums, palaces, warehouses were plundered. The Bolshevik government's Decree on Land of October 1917 sanctioned the spontaneous peasant seizures of land. The mob trials and lynchings which had taken place because the police and the criminal courts of the old regime had disappeared were lent legitimation by the new People's Courts set up by the Bolsheviks.[63] This was thus not only a political but also a social war, fought by desperate forces on both sides. For example, in the Don territory, the Cossacks, a martial estate that held the majority of the land and had enjoyed privileges under the tsar, launched insurgency against Soviet rule in spring 1918. Although there had been wild rumours about 'Bolshevik atrocities', the insurgents themselves had not witnessed any and admitted that the Bolsheviks in the territory had behaved 'properly'. German military intervention, reflecting the war aims of territorial expansion, was crucial in fomenting the Cossack uprisings, by aiding and arming the insurgents and engaging in military operations against Soviet forces. What caused the Cossack uprising, however, was their fear of losing their privileged position under the new revolutionary order, in particular the decree on socialization of land and the prospect of land redistribution; but it also resulted from fears similar to the 'Great Fear' of the French Revolution: the fear of brigandage, fear of revenge by workers and miners who had suffered under Cossack terror after the Bolshevik Revolution. The 'Great Fear' operated on both sides: Soviet supporters in the Don territory 'assumed that Cossacks were inveterate counterrevolutionaries who took pleasure in tormenting workers; Cossacks came to believe that all workers were Bolsheviks out to exterminate them'.[64]

A powerful mobilizing dynamic gripped the Don territory, as each side attempted to rally forces. Many Cossacks attempted to remain neutral and stay out of the looming confrontation, but those resisting mobilization were tried before courts-martial. In one district, where the Cossacks had preferred to remain neutral, a punitive detachment presented the community with the choice and threatened to open fire, saying 'either you are for the Cossacks, or against them'. In the period from May 1918 to February 1919 courts martial and other organs sentenced nearly 25,000 people to death. This was partly the inevitable result of revolution and civil war, but partly also a radicalized legacy of wartime methods. This extended to inventing and reinventing a social group identity: anyone who fought with the Cossacks was declared to be a Cossack; anyone who fought against them, whether peasant, worker, or Cossack, was automatically a Bolshevik, even if, as was more usual in the Don, they were politically affiliated to the Left Social Revolutionaries. Cossacks who were neutral or sided with the Soviets were 'traitors'.[65] On the Soviet side, some were beginning to speak of 'extermination' of the Cossacks, and an express policy of 'de-Cossackization' was declared in January 1919. At its height, the policy meant 'mass terror against wealthy Cossacks, exterminating them totally', and 'mass terror' also against all those who resisted Soviet rule. Although policy on the ground was often interpreted more cautiously by local military officers, as many as ten or twelve thousand Cossacks were the victims of executions.[66] In March, the policy of physical destruction was abandoned, and instead the goal was 'eliminating the Cossacks as a socio-economic class'. By May Cossacks were granted the right to bear arms 'in defence of the republic', and they were to be 'considered equal to the rest of the population'; by September to be 'potential allies'.[67] Nevertheless, returning Cossack soldiers were kept under the surveillance of the Cheka, and all officers and some soldiers were interned in 'concentration camps', set up on the model used by several powers during the Great War.

Soviet policies to force the rural producers to supply grain succeeded in the end in maintaining the Revolution in power, and by 1922 resistance had ended, partly owing to the repression and partly to the famine that resulted from Soviet policies; 85 per cent of the population of the formerly grain-rich Don territory was close to starvation.[68]

Yet it would be mistaken to see the roots of political violence merely in the Civil War or the Great War. The tsarist state attempted to quell the revolution in 1905 with violence, and in suppressing social protest after 1905 thousands of people were executed. Especially in the countryside, peasants in turn had resorted to brutal violence against landowners and state agents. Bolshevik violence thus took place not only in the context of the greatly magnified role of state violence against external and internal enemies during the World War, but also with the assumption that the Russian state could only overcome potential disintegration by measures of extreme violence. It also had something to do with the simultaneity of modernity in a predominantly backward and illiterate rural society. The violence took place largely in a mobile war, and in contrast to the World War it was not impersonal, technical violence at a distance, but direct, intimate violence between persons. The Bolshevik state used not only older instruments of violence such as cavalry, and brutal torture, but also modern communications; the political section of the Red Army had a train equipped to carry out political education among soldiers and civilians, with a printing press, editorial office, a radio station, and a film projector. Even mass executions, which were carried out as 'punishment' or revenge, such as the mass execution of officers and men of the captured Wrangel army in Crimea in November 1920, were transformed into something more sinister still: 'social surgery', or 'cleansing' of society.[69] True, the experience of civil war was also fundamental to this dynamic of violence, and the American historian Peter Holquist rightly argues against the German political scientist Ernst Nolte that it was 'not simply Bolshevik measures that summoned forth violence from the Soviet state's opponents'. Red and White (that is, counter-revolutionary) violence were 'twin strands ... emerging out of the 1914–1921 maelstrom of war, revolution, and civil wars'. The additional feature for revolutionary violence was the millenarian utopia of social justice and modernization, which appeared to justify all measures as a historic necessity.[70]

That explosive mix, but also the ambivalence it provoked in one astute observer, is illustrated well by the experience of the young writer Isaac Babel who accompanied the Bolshevik Cossacks as correspondent of the army newspaper the *Red Cavalryman*. His *1920 Diary* shows that much of the violence perpetrated by the Bolshevik Cossacks in the ill-fated attempt to invade Poland was not politically motivated: brutality towards civilians while requisitioning food and accommodation, rapes, antisemitic and anti-Catholic violence, massacre of prisoners: these were the hallmarks of a professional soldiery that had customarily behaved that way for generations under tsarist rule, a way of life that guaranteed them respect based on fear and privilege as landowners.[71] Although the Red Army issued orders to treat the population of invaded Galicia well, General Apanasenko, a division commander during the unsuccessful attempt to capture Lvov, declared that he would massacre the defenders, who consisted of 'professors, women, adolescents': 'Apanasenko . . . hates the intelligentsia, and it goes deep, he wants a state of peasants and Cossacks, aristocratic in its own peculiar way.'[72] Babel and the Bolshevik political commissars attached to the Cossacks also tried to exercise a moderating influence, endeavouring to prevent the massacres and looting.[73]

The violence inflicted on the Red Army soldiers by the war and by their own ruthless commanders was at least as brutal as that suffered in the World War. In one battle in July 1920 the 2nd Brigade 'bleeds profusely.' Babel recorded: 'the whole infantry battalion wounded, nearly all killed'. The reason: 'The Poles in old, screened trenches.' In other words, the commander General Budyonny had sent his men with scant cover into a suicidal attack on a well-defended position. A few days later, after a retreat and counter-attack in which the town of Brody was recaptured and devastated, Babel described the battlefield in terms that showed his own horror: 'The dreadful field, sown with mangled men, inhuman cruelty, unbelievable wounds, fractured skulls, naked young bodies gleaming white in the sun, jettisoned notebooks, leaflets, soldiers' books, Bibles, bodies amid the wheat.'[74]

It is difficult to imagine that Babel felt anything but scepticism about the Bolsheviks' declared intention to export their revolution by military means. He summarized thus the reports on the opening of the Second Congress of the Communist International:

> Unification of the peoples finally realized, now all is clear: there are two worlds, and war between them is declared. We will fight on endlessly. Russia

has thrown down the gauntlet. We shall advance into Europe and conquer the world. The Red Army has become a factor of world significance.[75]

But the Bolsheviks' rhetoric of world revolution was deadly serious, and although the Soviet state no longer posed a military threat to the world after its defeat in Poland, the political threat remained.

White Terror also made an ominous contribution to the history of mass killing in twentieth-century Europe: antisemitic violence. The tsarist regime had frequently resorted to fomenting pogroms at times of political crisis, before 1914 and during the war. White propaganda depicted the Bolshevik regime as a Jewish conspiracy and encouraged the antisemitism already widespread in the peasant population. The antisemitic White Russian leader Shulgin later justified the pogroms as revenge: 'We reacted to the "Yids" just as the Bolsheviks reacted to the *burzhoois* [i.e. bourgeois]. They shouted, "Death to the Burzhoois!" And we replied "Death to the Yids!" ' The racists denounced and victimized Jews both as wealthy exploiters and as 'the chosen people of the Bolsheviks'. White commanders encouraged their soldiers and local peasants to loot and steal the property of Jews. Thousands of Jews were tortured and mutilated, thousands of women and children were raped and killed. Previous estimates of the death toll ran to 50,000 or 60,000; recent research using a report of 1920 that surfaced in the archives after the fall of communism concludes there were more than 150,000 deaths.[76] Especially in the contested borderlands of the former empire, where power was weak and regions changed hands several times, nationalisms sought hegemony through exclusion and violence against what was redefined as foreign. Kiev had sixteen changes of control within two years, 1918 to 1920, between Germans, Poles, Ukrainians, the White Army under Denikin, and the Red Army; in Zhitomir (Ukraine), where the population consisted of 39.2 per cent Jews, 37.1 per cent Ukrainians, 13.7 per cent Russians, and 7.4 per cent Poles, the Jews suffered two large pogroms in early 1919 when it was held by Ukrainian nationalist troops, and another in June when it was under Polish and then Soviet occupation. Jews were not the only victims of ethno-nationalism, but they were particularly endangered by the accusation that they were behind Bolshevism. Increasingly, nationalists called, as did the Ukrainian dictator Grigoriev in May 1919, for 'the overthrow of the foreigners from Moscow and the country where they crucified Christ'.[77]

The Russian intelligentsia (a term that encompasses a somewhat broader spectrum than 'intellectuals' and implies also a distance from the state and the people) were to be found on both sides of the barricades in the Revolution. Those who identified themselves with the Revolution often worshipped the proletariat with missionary zeal, looking forward to an absolute utopia which would emerge from the catastrophe. But even supporters of the Bolsheviks, such as the writer Maxim Gorki, regarded the common people in the Revolution as a 'raging beast'; the historian Iurii Got'e (Gautier) wrote in his diary in 1920 that the new egalitarian but despotic popular culture was destroying all the enlightened 'European' values of the intelligentsia. The number of academics and intellectuals who were members of the Bolshevik party was negligible, many of them having fled the country or retreated into the 'White' regions out of fear for their personal safety. Universities remained largely hostile to the Revolution, until in autumn 1922 several hundred academics in the humanities and social sciences were expelled from the country, probably on instructions from Lenin.[78]

The background to the cultural history of the early Soviet period is the dissolution or the destruction of the old tsarist structures, traditions, and institutions, the values of the Orthodox church and the traditional family, and the fundamental shift in property relationships. In addition, there was the experience of mass death in the World War, the Civil War, and also during the terrible famine of 1921. The theme of death, however, was suppressed in propaganda and in art the topic was also absent, except when it was related to 'class enemies'. All this, as well as the mass exodus of the intelligentsia, was constitutive for the formation of culture in the early Soviet period. The new regime defined and consciously 'made' the new culture by force. Persons identified as representatives of the old regime were defined as 'pests', 'traitors', 'saboteurs', and became cultural debris.[79]

The marginalization of the Russian intellectuals was a part of the Bolsheviks' destruction of the old culture in their attempt to build their utopian new culture. The dynamism of this cultural destruction resulted not only from the revolutionary theories of Marxism but also from the destructivity of the First World War. Among the few writers and artists who supported the Bolshevik regime, apart from the 'Proletkult' movement, were, perhaps not surprisingly, the Futurists. There is a certain irony in the fact that Italian Futurism's aims of the destruction of all previous culture were not realized in the slightest in Italy, while they came closest to realization in Russia in the groundswell of social revolutionary violence against churches, palaces, and museums. But even for the rebellious Vladimir Mayakovsky, Futurist poet and designer of revolutionary posters, being an intellectual who supported the revolution was one matter, being a free-thinking writer under the increasingly stuffy and repressive regime was another. By the mid-1920s censorship in the arts was severe, and the remaining intellectuals felt the pressure to conform and serve the regime; as the historian Dietrich Beyrau has said, 'Mayakovsky's mutation from a poet of revolution into a poet of resolutions was typical'.[80]

Seven years of war, revolution, and civil war devastated Russia. Ten million died in the Civil War, including deaths caused by the terror, famine, and disease: at least five times more than the number of Russian military deaths in the World War.[81] In the period 1914 to the early 1920s the peoples of former tsarist empire suffered in a forgotten cataclysm on a scale that is still hardly comprehended in western Europe. The reduction of the value of individual human life, ethnic violence including deeply politicized anti-semitism, the Manichean image of friend or foe of the state, and the multifaceted legacies of the Soviet Gulag system, were to haunt Europe for the rest of the twentieth century.

Millenarian expectations and the end of the war

It is difficult to imagine today how the Bolshevik model gained a powerful hold on the imaginations of revolutionary movements all over the world after 1917. This was to some extent because news of the extent of the violence of the Civil War hardly filtered through to the west, and admiration for revolutionaries who had dismantled the notorious tsarist state made criticism inaudible; in addition, the counter-revolutionary Whites, with their antisemitism and promise of a return to tsarist despotism allowed the Bolshevik case to win by default. Finally, it derived also from the moral force of the anti-war message, familiar to the entire international socialist movement, with which the Bolsheviks had so successfully mobilized. In September 1915 anti-war socialists from France, Germany, Russia, and elsewhere meeting at Zimmerwald in Switzerland had adopted a resolution drafted by Trotsky which described the war as the product of imperialism. It stated:

> Millions of corpses cover the battlefields. Millions of men will remain mutilated for the rest of their days. Europe has become a gigantic slaughter-house for men. All the civilization created by the labour of previous generations is destined to be destroyed. Savage barbarism is today triumphing over everything that heretofore constituted the pride of humanity.[82]

The Russian February Revolution inspired Italian socialist workers in Turin in their uprising of August 1917, which had started as a protest at food shortages and military-style discipline in the factories but soon took on the demand for peace and revolution. In France, the anti-war deputy Pierre Brizon welcomed the Russian Revolution, echoing the Bolsheviks: 'The Russian Revolution has occurred just when the peoples are weary of spilling their blood to satisfy the appetites of the Tsar, the Kaiser, and Poincaré . . . The revolutionaries will impose peace, which will bring the regeneration of humankind and abolish all frontiers.' Even in Britain, opposition socialists called for the establishment of workers' and soldiers' councils.[83] The October Revolution of 1917 brought the Bolsheviks to power, and, consistent with their anti-war rhetoric, Lenin took Russia out of the war. True, this was not out of love of peace, but in the hope that a respite would provide the Bolsheviks with the opportunity to ignite world revolution.

Millenarian expectations were not confined to the Left. In Italy, from summer 1918 all state organs, military and civilian, launched propaganda campaigns making promises that raised inordinately the hopes of the peasant soldiers for the post-war period. This nourished the utopian expectations raised by the war. Opening the first session of parliament after the war, prime minister Orlando said the war had been 'the greatest socio-political revolution recorded in history, greater even than the French Revolution'. His rival Salandra wrote of the profound changes to come: 'The war has a profound significance for the renewal of the world . . . Grand and daring reforms will be enacted . . . laws and institutions will change; old habits of life and social relations will be transformed; old and venerated idols will collapse into rubble and dust.'[84] Yet why did violence arise here, and not in France or Britain?

In Italy, even victory was not sufficient to resolve the enormous tensions between militarist nationalism and the desire for peace and social reform. The Liberal ruling class proved to be incapable of integrating the masses into the state after the war, meeting the demands raised by all social strata, and dealing with the violent forms of expression of political conflict. It failed to respond with reforms, and instead reapplied wartime methods of authoritarian repression, justifying this, as in the years of war, with a presumed threat to the state.[85] Partly because the expansionist goals of the Italian government conflicted with Allied interests, the peace settlement was regarded by extreme nationalists as 'mutilated'. (See Map 3.) Partly, Liberal politicians were themselves responsible: on 30 October 1918, with Italian troops having seized the Dalmatian port of Rijeka (called Fiume by the Italians), Orlando irresponsibly announced that 'Fiume is more Italian than Rome', staking a territorial claim that had not even been mentioned in the 1915 Treaty of London; and the presence of Italian forces in Albania and Turkey led to more daydreaming about a great Italian empire.[86] At the Paris Peace Conference Italy was in fact given substantial territorial rewards: South Tyrol up to the Brenner Pass, despite its large German-speaking population, the Trentino, Venezia-Giulia, and Friuli. However, the conference refused Italy's claim, which had been promised in the Treaty of London, to Istria and the Dalmatian coastline, where there was only a minority of Italians in some towns, and the new claim to Fiume, which had a population of 25,000 Italian-speakers and 26,000 Slavs.

In another politically irresponsible move, Orlando, ostensibly or perhaps genuinely outraged, left for Italy in the middle of the conference in order to obtain a popular mandate for his hardline demands. He received massive backing in parliament, and returned to Paris only to find that in his absence the Allies had decided to present the treaties without conceding the Italian demands. Was there popular anger in Italy? Humiliation? Certainly, but resentment was expressed by some political groups and not others, and had been compounded by the mistakes of inept diplomacy and the resort to mass politics which further reduced the government's room for manoeuvre. The substantial gains were quickly forgotten: the destruction of its hereditary enemy, complete fulfilment of *Italia irredenta*, and an enlarged sphere of influence in the eastern Mediterranean. Socialists and conservative Catholics and some Democrats were satisfied with the result, but a vocal minority of zealous nationalists were indignant, and if Orlando and foreign minister Sonnino had not overplayed their hand they would not have faced such derision from their fellow-negotiators at Paris or at home, and the myth of the 'mutilated peace' would not have arisen.[87]

If nationalist expectations of a great Italian empire were potentially explosive, socialist expectations of revolution were no less so. Socialism was growing rapidly among peasants and workers, and the Socialists trebled their representation in the elections of November 1919, with 32.5 per cent of the votes, and gained a majority in many communes and provinces. Amadeo Bordiga and Antonio Gramsci, soon to transfer from revolutionary socialism to communism, talked openly about the need for the working class to seize power from the ruling class, and the inevitability of violent class struggle. One popular socialist song contained the lines: 'If Lenin comes,

we'll have a great party and go to the bosses and cut off their heads. Hi, ho
and the union will grow. The Royal Guards we'll put in a pot and turn into
soup, the *carabinieri* we'll steam and their sergeant-major we'll roast.' Its
crudeness probably made socialist leaders wince, and moderate socialists like
Turati rejected irresponsible talk about imminent revolution, but the great
surge of strikes, not only by industrial workers in northern cities, but also by
peasants, encouraged the belief that the utopia of revolution was nigh.
Landowners and the bourgeoisie were understandably concerned for their
existence when workers' councils were set up in Turin, calling for Soviet-
ization of industry, and when the 'largest agricultural strike in Italian history'
broke out in summer 1920 in Tuscany, with 500,000 peasants forcing
landowners to concede co-determination and new welfare provisions.
Even in the far south, where one would least expect radical social protest,
at Nardò on the heel of Italy, peasants seized power in a local revolution,
and kept the authorities at bay for three weeks.[88] Yet it is important to recall
that although strike activity in the *bienno rosso*, the two 'red years' 1919 and
1920, was intense, and although revolutionary rhetoric sounded fearful to
the employers, the actual level of violence among striking industrial workers
was low, and the socialists' paramilitary units were mainly defensive in
function, to ward off attacks by nationalist organizations.[89]

Italy from war to Fascism

Before Fascism became an overwhelming threat in 1922 Italian political
culture was thus a battleground between old and new ideologies, between
the Liberal establishment and social protest expressed through militant
socialism, and between these and those who sought to extend war politics
into peacetime. This latter thought was expressed in the trench newspaper
Volontà as early as 20 November 1918, in an article tellingly entitled
'Towards the Risorgimento' (a reference to the popular movement for
national unity in the mid-nineteenth century):

> We are approaching today our true national resurgence. The Sicilian, the
> Sardinian, the Friulian have fought for the first time with the same spirit, the
> same aim: defence of the land of his own comrade, his home and his honour,
> just as if it were his own land, his own home, his own honour. He shared with
> his brothers torn from their homes by the enemy invasion their emotion, their
> tears, and his bread. Such generosity of sentiment must not be lost; if we do

not know how to do that today, the basis of the reconstruction of Italy, we shall never again resurge. It is the task of Italy's leaders who have emerged from the war to reinforce the common sentiment with a common conscious-ness—whether this is history, ideals, faith—to perpetuate and perfect the fusion of these days in an exalted union.[90]

However, this Italian version of *Volksgemeinschaft* (people's community) was not shared by all. Militarists, expecting a privileged position for ex-combatants after the war, refused to demobilize, but rather turned against the perceived internal enemies. Mario Carli, a former *arditi* captain, gave a speech at an *arditi* meeting in Milan on 23 March 1919. The audience was largely the same as that at the founding meeting of Fascism the same day. Carli was one of the co-founders of the *Associazione fra gli arditi d'Italia* which was closely linked to Fascism, Futurism, and 'Dannunzianism'. Contacts between Mussolini and the *arditi* had been growing in intensity since autumn 1918. On 10 November 1918 Mussolini gave a public speech before a group of *arditi* in Milan, who gave him an enthusiastic reception, especially for his celebration of their admirable warlike youth and his declaration of solidarity with them against those 'cowardly philistines' who defamed them. And next day, some *arditi* declared they stood by Mussolini's side to 'fight the civil battles for the greatness of the fatherland'. The *Popolo d'Italia* began to publish frequent articles exalting the *arditi*, receiving many letters of gratitude from *arditi* units in return. The Futurists were also still closely involved: the address of the Milan section of the Association of *arditi* was Marinetti's home, and the president of the provisional committee was Captain Ferruccio Vecchi, a Futurist. In return for providing an armed security service for the offices of the *Popolo d'Italia* Mussolini channelled donations from industrialists to the Milan association.[91]

In a symbolic demonstration of the link between war, cultural destruc-tion, and Fascism, the political mobilization of the *arditi* expressed itself a few weeks after Fascism's founding meeting. The *arditi*, led by Captain Vecchi, organized a 'patriotic counter-demonstration' to a large demon-stration of striking workers protesting in Milan on 15 April at the police killing of a Socialist. About 300 men, of whom about 40 were armed *arditi,* attacked the Socialist procession when it reached the Piazza Duomo, throwing hand-grenades and firing revolvers, causing the Socialists to flee. The *arditi* then attacked and burned down the editorial office of the Socialist newspaper *Avanti!*, killing one of the soldiers protecting it. Vecchi and Marinetti, who organized the mob, disappeared from view for a few days, but soon the minister of war, General Caviglia, wartime sympathizer of Futurism, received them on a visit to Milan and told them they had 'saved the nation'. Amazingly, although some of the victims of the proto-fascist violence were policemen and troops—representatives of state power—the political and military authorities of the state welcomed the aggression against the perceived threat from Socialists. This incident represented a qualitative leap in the history of Italian politics: for the first time pistols and grenades were used by a handful of well-trained men, organized in a military fashion to get the better of many thousands of strikers. The flow of donations from business grew, to such an extent that in May Vecchi and Carli were able to found the weekly *L'ardito*. However, after this violent incident, the *arditi* renounced the use of force, restricting themselves to violent rhetoric. The reason was the rapid growth of the workers' movement and the social protest of workers and peasants during the period summer 1919 to summer 1920.[92] The place of the *arditi* was taken by the Fascists and the D'Annunzio followers, the latter coming to prominence with the occupation of Fiume.

If one compares political violence after the war in Germany and Italy, the attack on the Socialist demonstration and the *Avanti!* office shows that the *arditi* and their Fascist associates were privately funded, and publicly tolerated by the state. In Germany, the *Freikorps* (volunteer units commanded by army officers, used in the brutal suppression of socialist uprisings) were mainly state-funded, and acted directly under state control, until they overplayed their hand in the Kapp Putsch of March 1920. Although they were again used in suppressing the Red Army of the Ruhr in April 1920, their role was over, and they were disbanded or integrated into the regular army. The Nazi Party played no real role until the beer-hall putsch in Munich in 1923. In Italy the Fascists continued to be privately funded, but although they were obviously tolerated by the state, they despised it and took it over in 1922, more than ten years before the German fascists were able to destroy the Republican state. The forces who suppressed the radical socialist uprisings in Germany in the years 1918 to 1923 were under state control, and that partly explains why the democratic state survived longer.

It is important to differentiate between the *arditi* and other ex-combatants in post-war politics. Even the founding of the *arditi* association was a provocation: all the other ex-servicemen were catered for by two organizations, one for the mutilated and war invalids, and the national combatants' association. Both were patriotic, but liberal-democratic in their political orientation, demanding a programme of reform, but not revolution, aiming for greater social justice and democratic participation in the administration of the state. It would therefore be inaccurate to claim that Fascism was the progeny of Italy's war veterans. Moreover, the *arditi* themselves, despite their early contribution to Fascist violence, were soon eclipsed by the Fascist Party—first drawn into its orbit, then declining to negligence in 1920, and after reconstituting the movement in 1921 and supporting Fascist rule in 1922, losing their autonomy by 1924.[93] Crucially, although the Fascist squads had copied the *arditi* black shirts as a political fashion statement, Mussolini developed the flattering concept of the *trincerocrazia*, the idea that all those who had fought in the trenches should become Italy's ruling class, which had a broader appeal than the elite *arditi*.[94]

Fascism, communist, and anarchist critics wrote, was the continuation of the war. Fascism agreed. In early 1919 Mussolini swore to 'defend the dead . . . , even if it means digging trenches in the squares and streets of our cities'. It was a 'last war for independence and national unity', as the Fascist Corradini put it, against 'traitors' and the 'enemy within'. Fascism viewed its struggle for power as a revolutionary civil war, with the Fascist victims of violence as the heroes. It saw its violence as 'counter-violence', using the Austrian wartime concept of '*Strafexpedition*' to defend Italy against 'red barbarism'. The enemy stereotype of Bolshevism was thus closely connected with war propaganda.[95] Violence was the 'actual substance of fascism'; fascism 'did not want to convince its opponents or overcome them', the comparative historian of fascism Wolfgang Schieder has rightly argued, 'but destroy them. The will to *destroy its opponents* is the constituent element of fascist rule'. Fascism was the realization of the principle of war in peacetime, a continuation of war by other means.[96]

For decades, Marxist and non-Marxist scholars have debated the social basis of Italian Fascism, the former arguing that it was a mainly petit bourgeois movement acting on behalf of capitalism, the latter that it drew support from all classes in Italy, including the working class. Clearly, Fascism acted as a politically autonomous force, despite significant support from some wealthy businessmen. It is also just as clear that the bulk of the membership of the Fascist Party came indeed from the middle classes, especially of northern Italy. But the most significant feature of its social composition was its domination by ex-combatants: of the 151,644 members of the *fasci* in late 1921, almost three-fifths (57.5 per cent) were returned soldiers. Almost all leading Fascists proudly proclaimed their formative war experience. Dino Grandi and Achille Starace had been captains, Italo Balbo and Giuseppe Bottai lieutenants, Giacomo Acerbo a decorated officer, Mussolini and Farinacci non-commissioned officers.[97] Fascist squads were invariably far better armed and equipped than their Socialist victims, not only with small-arms, but with heavy weapons: police raids during the period summer 1920 to summer 1921 uncovered six cannons, forty-four machine guns, three flamethrowers, and 2,373 hand grenades. The war had bequeathed not only a political, but a very tangible physical legacy.[98]

Not that war led automatically to Mussolini's Fascism. Several political strands—Futurism, syndicalism, nationalism, competed to represent the new, warlike Italy, before Fascism eventually absorbed the others, and several leaders with charismatic appeal were in contention before Mussolini triumphed. To the Futurists the war appeared to justify extreme measures: extreme violence, 'total' mobilization, and the repressive apparatus of a modern state deployed against pacifists, socialists, and anyone regarded as internal enemies. Marinetti had deepened his loathing for the old system, and the war supplied oxygen to his political movement. He rejoiced at the results of the war which had caused the downfall of the religious concept of providence, divine intervention, and logical systems of philosophy. The conflagration had instead 'produced the glorification of brutal force', and had taught the victorious powers that only brute force and violence counted, not international law. In the victorious countries of the Entente he saw the birth of a new mankind, truly Futurist, composed of revolutionary violence, resilient, heroic, muscular, and steely. The war had made the ground tremble underneath the 'heavy, gouty feet of those sedentary pen-pushers who wished to misgovern Italy from the depths of their libraries and museums'. Among his other post-war effusions was the insight that the war meant the end of marital faithfulness and traditional marriage, for it compelled mankind to 'free and rapid love' and polygamy.[99] Possibly an avant-garde art movement and its self-consciously elitist leader were just too provocative to attract mass support.[100]

A more serious contender for right-wing leadership was D'Annunzio. His focus on irredentism brought both his early success at political theatre, with the occupation of Fiume, but circumscribed also his limitation as a national politician. In protest at the 'mutilated victory', D'Annunzio occupied Fiume at the head of a force of 2,000 *arditi* and syndicalists, with the aim of mobilizing for the future Italian state which would result from the overthrow of the old regime through a kind of private-enterprise imperialism. The army was incapable of restoring order against the Right, because so many of its

officers and men themselves supported extreme nationalist ideas. D'Annunzio's style of political ritual anticipated the later Fascist state in the structure
of charismatic rule, with stage-managed, theatrical politics, the commitment
to violence, and a corporative state to replace liberal democracy. The
occupation lasted one year, in which D'Annunzio hurled abuse at the Liberal
prime minister Nitti and his successor Giolitti. Finally Giolitti sent in the
navy at Christmas 1920 and D'Annunzio surrendered. Cleverly, Mussolini
gave no active support to D'Annunzio because he was not very interested in
irredentism, and because he was a realist who knew that Italy did not have the
forces available to wage another war.[101] Moreover, he did not like to be
upstaged by potential rivals in a future authoritarian regime.

Notwithstanding Mussolini's apparent lack of commitment to Fiume, the
borderlands were significant. It was not merely symbolic that the Fascist Party
in Trieste, the major port city on the Adriatic conquered from the Habsburg
empire, with an ethnically mixed population and Slovene hinterland, was led
by one Francesco Giunta, a lawyer and former machine gun captain, and his
deputy Piero Bolzon, *arditi* officer from a wealthy Genoa family. This had real
consequences for Fascist practice. Fascism in the 'redeemed' borderlands was
about ethnic struggle. As the Australian historian of modern Italy, Richard
Bosworth, puts it, 'For Bolzon, "Slavs" constituted a "barbarous" and menacing "flood", people who were...utterly supine, primordially given to
mysticism and murder.' Giunta claimed to be waging a battle against both
Communism and Slavs, and since the weak Liberal state had proved to be
'non-existent', a strong new state must replace it. Mussolini endorsed their
demand for drastic action against the ethnic minority in June 1920: 'We must
energetically cleanse Trieste.' Giunta and his paramilitary squads needed no
further encouragement, and proceeded to threaten and beat up ethnic enemies, torture Slovene priests, and burn down the headquarters of the Slovene
movement. This ethnic cleansing went hand in hand with the assault on the
political enemy, the Socialists and the unions, which were suppressed after a
strike in September 1920, and a war on the enemy culture by closing down
Slovene schools and banning the use of the Slovene language in official life.[102]

Aside from the north-east corner of Italy, the ethnic question was less
important than the main target of the Fascists: the labour movement, especially the trade unions of land labourers and poor peasants in northern and
central Italy. Typically, Fascist violence was well organized and highly
mobile. Squads were transported by trucks from Fascist strongholds to
carry out so-called *spedizioni punitive*, a term that consciously recalled the

World War, in far-flung villages and towns. Thus the Fascists of Pisa launched over one hundred punitive expeditions around Tuscany. The local large farmers or landlords selected the victims and often paid for the squads, and the vehicles and fuel were provided either by the farmers or the local army units. As well as assaulting persons the Fascists attacked the cultural institutions of the labour movement, destroying newspaper offices and printshops, trade union offices, workers' libraries and theatres, and labour welfare homes. In the first half of 1921 alone, there were 726 Fascist attacks on these labour movement institutions. The state turned a blind eye on Fascist violence, and the army, police, and courts often lent tacit support. Yet the function of Fascist violence was not only to intimidate and silence political enemies: it was highly symbolic, aiming to occupy public spaces and challenge the state's monopoly of force, and thus to usurp state power.[103] It was therefore not war against all previous culture, Futurist-style, but war against the culture of the political enemy.

Fascist violence was not without precedent: the state suppressed the hunger protests in Turin of August 1917 with massive force, the army deploying tanks and machine guns against workers, killing fifty and arresting over 800.[104] Social protest in pre-war Italy, especially by land labourers and poor peasants, had often turned violent; violent riots in 'Red Week' in June 1914, culminated in a full insurrection in Romagna province.[105] In rural unrest in 1920, violence extended from barn burning and the mutilation of animals to killings, in which 161 died, and 289 were injured.[106] Rather, Fascism promised to be a more ruthless agent than the old Liberal state in protecting the interests of those who felt threatened by the aspirations of Socialists and workers' and peasants' unions for social reform. Post-war violence thus did not erupt suddenly like a previously dormant volcano, but peaked as part of a continuum of social and political violence dating back at least to the 1890s and pointing forward to the explosion of 1943–5. The actual extent of the post-war violence was not as great as either anti-fascist or fascist myth-making depicted it. Mussolini spoke of 3,000 martyrs to the cause, anti-fascists claimed that tens of thousands were killed (including in the early years of the regime). In fact, 463 Fascists were killed in the period 1919–22 (on their own figures), and probably rather more Socialists (whose victims were never officially counted). Yet the violence was certainly widespread: during 1921, in the province of Bologna alone, 1,936 agricultural and industrial workers were beaten or shot, with nineteen killed. It was also clearly the result of the Fascist offensive against the labour

movement and other political and ethnic enemies.[107] Violence and intimidation were thus intense in large areas of Italy.

Curiously, although political violence affected everyday life in large parts
of Italy, the government practically avoided the topic in its declarations,
even at its height in 1922. While the Socialist deputy Turati warned in
parliament in 1922 that Italy stood on the edge between civilization and a
return to barbarism, and was in a state of outright civil war, prime minister
Facta rejoindered that the violence was mostly 'limited and isolated'. Liberals,
conservatives, and the bourgeois press played it down, relegating it to the
status of ordinary criminal activity. In a sense, Facta was right, because the
victims were not the respectable urban bourgeoisie. But others were sensitive
to its deeper meaning, as the correspondence of Anna Kuliscioff and her
partner Turati reveals: they realized the extraordinary nature of the new
situation, the destructive will and verbal aggression in Italian society.[108]

Liberal Italy, by contrast, turned a blind eye to Fascism, and eventually
supported it. Charles Maier rightly argued in his influential comparative
history: 'Nowhere else did the traditional "establishment" conceive of itself
both as so rightfully influential and as so threatened. Its sense of crisis led to the
destruction of the liberal state precisely because its members could not regain
security through mastery of parliament as in France, or manipulation of the
economic arena as in Germany.'[109] Already in 1921, Giolitti, the old survivor
of Liberal politics, brought the Fascist party into a 'national bloc' to contest the
elections. The 'march on Rome' of 28 October 1922 was therefore not really a
military conquest of power: many cities and entire regions had already been
'cleansed' by local Fascist groups before that, and Mussolini was called into
power by the Liberal politicians Giolitti, Nitti, and Salvemini, supported by
the king, the pope, the army, and the business elite, with a mundane telephone
call to Milan. But it was clearly no usual change of government. *L'Alpino*, the
war veterans' newspaper, welcomed it as the government that '*gives the nation
back its soul, the soul of the war, the soul of victory*'.[110]

Revolution, peacemaking, and political violence in the post-war era

The peacemakers of 1918–19 were aware of the magnitude of the task of
redrawing the political and military map of Europe. Peacemaking, Americans were told, would be an enormous undertaking in 'a Europe devastated,

bled white, convulsed, and impoverished by the war'.[111] According to
The Nation, 'the statesmen were charged not simply with closing a war
but with fully recasting the inherited world order', and for the *Philadelphia
Ledger* the Peace Conference had to balance 'the accounts of a whole epoch,
the deeds and misdeeds of an exhausted civilization'.[112] The prospect of
the spread of Bolshevism to central Europe in the chaos of collapse caused
alarm among the Allies, who took preventive measures, giving military
and economic assistance to the countries bordering the new revolutionary
state. Yet the major issue at the conference was not Bolshevism, but
Germany. Captain Charles de Gaulle, taken prisoner at Verdun in 1916,
wrote with uncanny prescience while still in prisoner camp in Germany
in October 1918:

> Will France be quick to forget, if she ever can forget, her 1,500,000 dead, her
> 1,000,000 mutilated, Lille, Dunkerque, Cambrai, Douai, Arras, Saint-Quen-
> tin, Laon, Soissons, Rheims, Verdun—destroyed from top to bottom? Will
> the weeping mothers suddenly dry their tears? Will the orphans stop being
> orphans, widows being widows? For generations to come, surely every family
> will inherit intense memories of the greatest of wars, sowing in the hearts of
> children those indestructible seeds of hatred? . . . Everyone knows, everyone
> feels that this peace is only a poor covering thrown over ambitions unsatisfied,
> hatreds more vigorous than ever, national anger still smouldering.[113]

German workers and soldiers associated the end of the war with the chance
for a completely new political order. Their concepts mixed the practical
with the utopian, the desire for immediate peace with millenarian visions of
a cleansing revolution that would need revolutionary violence. The bourgeoisie at once feared and exaggerated the risk of Bolshevism. One Hamburg
lawyer reported to the senator (minister) for police on 4 November 1918
about the mood in the city:

> Returning to Volksdorf by train yesterday my seventeen-year old son over-
> heard workers talking about the revolution which was about to break out.
> One of the workers declared he would of course also wield the axe.
>   When my daughter Ina, working as a voluntary nurse in Barmbek Hospital,
> was bandaging an injured soldier, he showered her with the most obscene threats
> of revolution . . . None of the other men, who until recently could not have been
> more grateful to my daughter for her comforting, self-sacrificing, and humorous
> treatment, raised a word in protest at the filthy utterances of this Bolshevist.
>   When the artist Merker tried to talk some good sense to some excited men
> at the station who were openly toying with the thought of revolution, he was

interrupted and threatened with the words, 'in Germany the guillotine will soon have a great deal of work to do'.[114]

News of the sailors' mutiny and the revolution in Kiel, the Baltic Sea port only 85 kilometres away, was regarded in Hamburg's city government as just a local disturbance, but soon mass meetings of workers were held at which radical demands were raised. At a meeting of 10,000 workers in the trade union headquarters on 5 November, the Independent (i.e. anti-war) Social Democratic member of parliament Wilhelm Dittmann, called on Hamburg to follow the example of revolutionary Kiel:

> Workers, soldiers, and sailors have seized power in Kiel and in the Baltic Sea fleet and are now the masters of the situation. This fraternization of workers in their overalls and in uniform is the most edifying spectacle of this war; it manifested itself first in Russia and now, at last, it is appearing in Germany . . . The example of Kiel will have the effect of igniting and inspiring people. Kiel has become the German Kronstadt . . . [a reference to the revolutionary sailors near Petrograd in 1917.]
>
> We stand at a decisive point. The war has brought to maturity what otherwise would have taken decades. The old regime is falling, and overnight the proletariat is faced with the task of seizing political power.

The revolution in Hamburg broke out that night; by daybreak workers were on general strike, revolutionary sailors and soldiers had taken over warships in the harbour, and set up barricades and machine gun posts around the trade union headquarters. Revolutionaries patrolled the streets in commandeered vehicles, waving red flags. An attempt by the regional army command to crush the rising with force failed when the artillerymen refused orders, and by the end of 6 November power was held effectively by a provisional council of workers and soldiers.[115]

In fact, violence was conspicuous in the German revolution by its absence, even when it reached the centre of power on 9 November: the old order collapsed in Berlin with hardly a murmur, and the new took its place with an overwhelming demonstration of strength, but without violence. The occasional incidents in which officers' epaulettes or other insignia of power were stripped went no further than that; they were symbolic gestures to show where power now resided. But that was the unsettling question for the new government: the collapse of the old army and police meant that it was powerless, and left without physical protection.

That day Prince Max von Baden, the last chancellor of imperial Germany, handed over government to the representatives of the workers' movement, the SPD, led by Friedrich Ebert. In order to integrate the popular movement of the workers and soldiers, the formerly Marxist but now merely pragmatic SPD, which had loyally supported the Imperial state in the war, brought in the anti-war Independent Social Democrats, the USPD. The Independents gave expression to the revolutionary aspirations of more radical members of the working class. Hugo Haase, USPD deputy and former chairman of the SPD parliamentary group, speaking in the Reichstag on 23 October 1918, had predicted a 'dark future with regard to the severe suffering of the people and because of the burdens of war'. But 'if we overcome the present social system we can be saved from poverty, misery, and oppression... [In] the end from all this misery will result the complete liberation of humanity!'[116]

Returning soldiers, contrary to common assumption, did not find it impossible to reintegrate into civilian life. Most men wanted to return to a normal life as soon as possible. At the end of the war German workers were filled with hatred of all things military. Noske described in his memoirs of the Revolution how 'no man in uniform could be tolerated in the factories'. The workers in arms factories wanted to convert them to the production of useful, peacetime commodities. Albrecht Mendelssohn-Bartholdy, the liberal professor of international law who wrote his history of German society at war in exile from the Third Reich, commented that it was a common dream of the period immediately after the war ('except for the few monarchists who had remained true to the old order and had begun to denounce the peace enthusiasts as traitors') that the American president would dictate the peace.

> The central idea of this peace dream was that the hundreds of thousands or even millions of men who were now to be dismissed from the ranks of war should enter the service of peace; and they would rebuild the towns they had been forced to destroy, restore the devastated regions to fertility, and generally turn swords into plowshares. It was partly a sincere feeling of commiseration for the victims of war devastation which was uppermost in the mind of the simple soldiers returning from France and Belgium, and even a real wave of pacifist idealism which created this desire to make good what the War had destroyed.[117]

Unlike in Russia, war-weariness in Germany meant that the mass of soldiers remained immune to left-wing revolutionary temptation, but they also could not be used as a counter-revolutionary force because they did not want to continue the external war as a civil war. That task was delegated to the *Freikorps*. For a variety of personal and ideological reasons these men had become addicted to violence, or found it impossible to reintegrate into civilian life, or genuinely believed it was necessary to defend Germany against Bolshevism; some, in fact, were young (usually middle-class) men who had just left school or university and had missed their chance for glory by serving in the real war.[118] Some of the *Freikorps*, between 20,000 and 40,000 men, also participated in the hidden war in the Baltic region in 1918–19 after the peace treaty of Brest-Litovsk. They fought against the advancing Red Army, but without any real political goals, rather as an unofficial continuation of the World War. One former *Freikorps* volunteer later wrote: 'The fighting in the Baltic was more savage and desperate than anything else in all the *Freikorps* fighting I saw before or afterwards. There was no real front to speak of: the enemy was everywhere. And whenever there was a clash, it turned into butchery to the extent of total annihilation.'[119] The author was Rudolf Höß, the later commandant of Auschwitz. Alongside the state-sanctioned brutal suppression of revolutionary uprisings in 1919 and 1920, it was members (or former members) of the *Freikorps* who committed the political assassinations of Centre Party leader Matthias Erzberger and foreign minister Walther Rathenau. No doubt some of these men had in some way been 'brutalized' by their experience in the war or in the Baltic fighting; however, it is more likely that they were *attracted* to killing as a way of life, and unlike the social misfits who exist in most societies found that their violent behaviour was given official approval or (later) approval as a tolerated part of political culture.

Yet most former soldiers were not a 'lost generation' of dehumanized misfits who glorified war and hated democracy. The largest veterans' association was not the notorious Stahlhelm ('Steel Helmet'), a right-wing, anti-democratic veterans' group, but the Reich Association of War Disabled, War Veterans, and War Dependants. Founded by Social Democrats, at its peak in 1922 this anti-war association had 830,000 members, far more than any right-wing association.[120]

Despite the unpopularity of war among the great majority of veterans, the public sphere—official memory, memorials, official histories, published memoirs, and so on—was dominated by the discourse of militarist nationalism for which the war was justified and the army remained undefeated. One reason why the myth of the 'unvanquished' army could take hold of the imagination was not only the obvious fact that the truce was signed before the German army was pushed back on to German territory, but also the awareness of what devastation lay in store. As the Prussian war ministry stated in its instructions for preparing a 'festive welcome' for the returning troops: 'Our field-grey heroes return to the *Heimat* undefeated, having protected the native soil from the horrors of war for four years.'[121] Hundreds of regimental histories with a total circulation of millions and the popular 36-volume series 'Battles of the World War', published by the Reichsarchiv from 1921 to 1930, reiterated the idea of the German soldier as victor.[122] As the radical nationalist historian Johannes Haller, who had called in 1914 for Germany to rule the world (cf. Chapter 3), now rector of the University of Tübingen, put it when he welcomed the students returning from the war in 1919, the war was 'not yet over'. The soldiers had been victorious against the far stronger enemy

> until the political poison gas from home reached the front and paralysed the hearts and bodies. But even then we could have avoided the worst if at the most dangerous moment the home front had not stabbed the warriors in the back...It was the people back home who lost the war, covered themselves with shame, and in the end pulled the army down with them into the abyss.[123]

This was tantamount to a call to civil war. The 'stab in the back' legend, launched on the public by Field Marshall Hindenburg at the Reichstag investigation committee in November 1919, was thus already the common battle-cry of the right-wing opponents of democracy.

The post-war period in Germany can indeed be characterized as a 'selective civil war' within a political culture in which violence became acceptable.[124] This has been obscured from history by the preoccupation with the revolution and the long shadow cast by the rise of the Nazis. Undoubtedly, the brutalizing effects of the war had an impact—German politics before 1914 had been almost entirely peaceful, apart from low-level police repression.[125] Signs of the shift from war against the external to violence against the internal enemy were already becoming visible in the war. Victor Klemperer, a patriotic academic soon to become professor of Romance philology, a Jew who had converted to Protestantism, witnessing striking workers in Leipzig in summer 1917, wrote: 'In August I saw for the first time a march of strikers. Several hundred young girls, some very young, and even younger boys, came past in unruly groups, singing, shouting, playing the harmonica, in high spirits as if at an amusement park. "Give them a thrashing!" I said angrily, "or if that doesn't help, use a machine gun." '[126] If such was the view of a cultured and essentially humane man, one can imagine the violent fantasies of the militarists.

In fact, most Germans were content with a shift to democracy, as reflected in the overwhelming majority gained by democratic parties in the elections of January 1919. But the bourgeoisie and the remnants of the old state were in a panic about the potential threat to their property and status, and searched desperately for protection and ultimately, when the time was right, revenge. As from October–November 1918 bankers and industrialists were prepared secretly to donate any sum of money to the army.[127] They were unsettled by the fact that workers, impatient for improvements in their living conditions, embarked on a series of protests and strikes. The demands focused mainly on concrete issues, such as the 8-hour day and improved pay, but anti-capitalist sentiment was widespread as workers demanded also 'socialization' of important industries like coal, iron, and steel. This did not amount to a call for a socialist revolution, as in Russia, but rather a re-balancing of power in society to share prosperity and opportunity more equitably. Nor did this movement, it is important to stress, employ violence. However, in many cities there were attempts by the peace and social protest movement to remove from power those identified with imperial Germany's catastrophic war, led by socialists of various hues, including a small minority of radicals who judged the moment ripe for revolution.

The real threat was small. The Communist Party (KPD) had no more than a few thousand members, and was easily and mercilessly crushed two weeks before the election when radical Berlin workers launched the mis-named 'Spartakus' Rising in January 1919. The two leaders of the KPD, Rosa Luxemburg and Karl Liebknecht, who were opposed to the rising, were caught by the *Freikorps* and brutally murdered. Despite the evident weakness of the Left, the SPD-led government continued to view any political or social protest movement as a Bolshevik-inspired threat to its authority, invoked the myth of the dangerous internal enemy, and reacted with astoundingly ruthless force. The 'Spartakus Rising' was a turning point in two ways: for the first (significant) time, radical workers defied the revolutionary government with armed force. It was a challenge to Ebert's authority which could not be ignored. Second, the incommensurate response of the government forces left a legacy of division and bitterness in the population which alienated a growing part of the working class, without consolidating bourgeois support for the new state.

The growing alienation of the working class can be seen in the course of social and political unrest from January to May 1919. Despite the millenarian rhetoric of socialism, working-class protest was usually non-violent, but the violent repression by the state provoked workers to anger. Thus during a general strike in Berlin unarmed demonstrators were shot down on the Alexanderplatz on 4 March 1919. Workers who gathered at various points in the city to protest at the shooting were confronted by troops who had been provided by defence minister Noske (SPD) on 9 March with a 'shoot to kill' order; in its written form it contained instructions to 'shoot immediately every armed person who is found fighting against the government troops'. Noske had been deliberately misinformed by Captain Pabst, First General Staff Officer of the Guards Cavalry Rifle Division, who had given the order for the murder of Luxemburg and Liebknecht. Noske was told that the Spartacists had killed in cold blood sixty captured policemen and other captives in Berlin–Lichtenberg. A sensationalist report in the SPD newspaper *Vorwärts* portrayed this as a 'mass murder and foul assassination' and butchery. For several days Pabst had been trying to persuade Noske to sign the 'shoot to kill' order he had drafted, and now this atrocity report swung the balance. Noske justified the order by citing the 'increasing cruelty and bestiality of the Spartacists fighting against us'. General von Lüttwitz, in command of 31,400 men of the Guards Cavalry Rifle Division and other units, remembered the order thus: 'Whoever is found with a weapon will be given a summary trial and where necessary shot.' The Guards Cavalry Rifle Division intensified it: 'Whoever puts up armed resistance or pillages will immediately be put up against the wall . . . All inhabitants of houses from which shots are fired at the troops are to be brought out into the street, no matter whether they protest their innocence or not, and the houses are to be searched for weapons in their absence; suspicious persons in the possession of weapons are to be shot.'[128]

Altogether 1,200 people were killed in the March fighting in Berlin, including many women and children. The government forces lost only 75 men. Two days after the initial reports about the 'Lichtenberg massacre' the story was revealed as a hoax, the only truth of which was that one policeman had been killed during the fighting.[129] Whether Noske had been manipulated by the military with their deliberate lies about Spartacist atrocities is not clear; he probably chose not to verify the reports with independent sources. It is clear, however, from the language of Lüttwitz and Pabst, and from the actions of the troops, that the Reichswehr was fighting a civil war against a German enemy using the same language and tactics that had been employed for combating the *francs-tireurs* in France and Belgium in 1914, legitimated also by its institutional memory of the instructions on fighting insurgency in cities dating back to 1907. The evident satisfaction of Lüttwitz at the ruthlessness of the operation suggests also a grim vengeance on the civilian population which was doubly guilty of causing defeat in the war and daring to defy military authority.

Violence in the early Weimar Republic was thus not really an anti-Bolshevik reaction; it was pre-emptive violent repression by the bourgeoisie and the uncertain new state, conducted by state-directed military forces against non-combatants (occasionally against armed but not militarized civilians) in the 'selective civil war'.[130]

The war on the internal enemy in Germany was intimately connected with foreign policy. Count Brockdorff-Rantzau, the imperial ambassador who was recalled by the SPD-led government from Denmark to become foreign minister in December 1918, made it a condition of his appointment that he should be empowered to refuse to accept the peace treaty yet to be presented, thus precipitating resumption of war. He also insisted that he would have the right to participate in domestic policy, on which foreign policy depended. That meant concretely that the army would carry out violent repression of 'Bolshevik activities and their leaders down to the final consequences'; the government should not shy away from spilling blood, for otherwise 'the government itself and with it the entire country will be drowned in a bloodbath'.[131] The history of the violent repression of social and political unrest, with unlimited force against revolutionaries who mostly posed only a limited threat, as well as indiscriminate and disproportionate force against striking workers and other civilians, reads like the precise execution of Brockdorff-Rantzau's programme before the peace was signed in June 1919.

Yet after the initial repression of the protest movement, the collapse of democracy and the rise of fascism were by no means inevitable, although the repression undeniably bequeathed a legacy of bitterness on the Left and a long-term division between moderate Social-Democrats and radical Communists. Political violence was made more likely by the manipulation of language and culture by the Right, which remained unreconciled to defeat. From the start, nationalist politicians and intellectuals portrayed the future as apocalypse: the destruction of Germany, and cataclysmic events like strikes and revolutions which would also bring down the Allies. Walther Rathenau, industrialist and talented war economy organizer, wrote in an open letter to US President Wilson's adviser Colonel House in December 1918: 'What we are threatened with, what hatred proposes to do to us, is destruction, the destruction of German life, now and for all times . . . [He predicted twenty years after the peace treaty:] The cities . . . half dead blocks of stone, still partly inhabited by wretched people, the roads are run down, the forests cut down, a miserable harvest growing in the fields. Harbours, railways, canals in ruins, and everywhere the sad reminders standing, the high, weather-worn buildings from the time of greatness.' Thomas Mann continued his wartime diatribe against western civilization, furiously condemning the Allies, accusing Clemenceau, 'that poisonous old man . . . with oval eyes' of aiming to create 'Kirghizian conditions' in Germany, or a 'Slavic Mongolia'.[132]

These outlandish utterances (by men who both later returned to reality and embraced reasoned, democratic politics), were characteristic of the curious period before Versailles. Between the armistice and June 1919, when the Peace Treaty was signed, German policy-makers (and public opinion) found themselves in a vacuum. Not admitted to the Paris Peace Conference, the German leadership lived in a dream world of its own, creating illusions about their ability to make Wilson's Fourteen Points the sole basis of the peace negotiations, to exclusion of the interests of France, Britain, or Belgium. Time and again Brockdorff-Rantzau expressed expectation of revolutionary uprisings in the enemy countries if Germany rejected the treaty, which would depose governments and lead to fresh negotiations and a moderate peace.[133]

For the French government, which hosted and chaired the Peace Conference, imposing a hard peace on Germany was about justice and security. The French people did not demand the destruction of Germany, as nationalist German politicians alleged, but 'wish and hope for strict conditions of peace which will make it impossible for Germany to dream of new aggression', as an army report on public opinion put it in April 1919.[134] French policy reflected a visceral hatred of the 'German race' which was not only barbarous in wartime, but even in defeat was superior to France in demographic and economic terms.

Certainly, Clemenceau intended punishment of Germany, including major territorial adjustments, drastic disarmament, war crimes trials, and the occupation of a broad swathe of western Germany. However, his British and American negotiating partners, Lloyd George and Woodrow Wilson, reined him back from extreme measures, and Clemenceau himself resisted domestic pressure to disarm Germany completely. Despite intermittent encouragement of Rhineland and Bavarian separatism, Clemenceau, supported by the majority of public opinion, did not want to break Germany up or annex the Rhineland.[135] But he pushed hard for the Allied occupation of the Rhineland for years to come, and the establishment of a Rhenish republic.

While the surrender of the German navy essentially removed the security threat to Britain and the US, France still faced the security nightmare of a revived German army. This explains why peace-making was so difficult, and why Clemenceau had to balance his harsh policy towards Germany with the need to keep his allies committed to French security.

Yet economic aid was an equally pressing need, given the vast destruction. In France alone, 42,000 square kilometres of land had been occupied or fought over, an area more than twice the size of Wales or Massachusetts. More than 600,000 hectares of forest were damaged, of which 166,000 hectares, or an area larger than Greater London, was so utterly destroyed and contaminated by residues it could not be restored to commercial use until the 1980s. After the loss of livestock and the requisitioning of harvests, there was damage to farmland, rivers, and fisheries to be made good. More than 480,000 houses, including 750 historic buildings, had been damaged or destroyed, along with their furniture and fittings, as well as objects of artistic and cultural value. The industry of the occupied zone had also been devastated, not by combat, but through requisitions for the German war machine and deliberate destruction in the retreats. In Belgium, all of which was either occupied or combat zone, the economic effect was even more catastrophic than in France. More than 70,000 houses were destroyed, and 12,000 partly destroyed, and 200,000 damaged. The city of Ypres, with its medieval Cloth Hall, was so completely destroyed that the government considered never rebuilding it; its citizens demanded reconstruction, which was only finished in the 1960s. The city of Louvain, much of which had been destroyed in August 1914, was rebuilt. The university library was rebuilt with American aid in the inter-war years, and Germany carried out its promise under the Treaty of Versailles to make restitution for the collection of books burned in 1914. In 1940, German artillery destroyed the library again.

Less is known about the extent of damage in eastern Europe, but in the war zones of eastern Poland and western Russia it was clearly very extensive, and the poverty of the region must have made reconstruction more difficult than in the west. In Galicia and the Bukovina alone 344,000 houses were destroyed.[136]

Germany, by contrast, had suffered (virtually) no invasion or occupation, and virtually no physical damage to its economy.

British policy at the Paris Peace Conference was in the end more moderate than would have been suspected from the violent anti-German mood of the general election campaign of November–December 1918.

Public hostility to Germany had been reinforced by the sinking of the *Leinster* in October 1918, during the armistice talks, prompting Arthur Balfour to say of the Germans, 'Brutes they were, and brutes they remain.'[137] On Armistice Day, Admiral Fisher, whose intemperate outbursts we have already encountered, vented his fury and frustration at the ending of the war before a conclusive battlefield defeat of Germany; he wanted to 'hang the Kaiser and sack Berlin'. A large part of public opinion, even Liberal supporters, and Lord Northcliffe's newspaper empire, including *The Times* and the *Daily Mail*, demanded harsh measures, and election candidates felt compelled to bow to the pressure. However, there were also influential voices of moderation on the Left, and both outside and inside government circles, especially within the Foreign Office. The mercurial Lloyd George, who initially wanted a moderate policy, was quick to respond to the public mood, and soon began to promise that 'Germany must pay the cost of the war up to the limit of her capacity to do so', and called for the Kaiser to be prosecuted. Yet he was careful not to commit himself to utopian goals, and although he mentioned an estimate of war damage of £24,000 million, he stated this exceeded German capacity to pay.[138]

Article 231 of the treaty, as is well known, required Germany and her Allies to accept responsibility 'for causing all the loss and damage to which the Allied and Associated Governments and their nationals have been subjected as a consequence of the war imposed on them by the aggression of Germany and her allies'. This clause, expressing merely what was self-evident for the Allies, and not intended as a moral condemnation of Germany, was inserted to provide a legal basis for reparation. It was followed by Article 232, the clause limiting reparations to Germany's capacity to pay, and no sum was mentioned. Reparations would not be based on total damage, still less on the total cost of the war (which would have included the cost of soldiers' wages and armaments), but on civilian damages, plus Belgium's war costs which Germany had already agreed to reimburse. The sum announced after lengthy inter-Allied negotiation in May 1921 was 132 billion gold marks, or about £6.25 billion sterling, but this nominal figure was an illusion, mainly designed to placate domestic public opinion in the Allied countries. The real capital sum was 50 billion marks, equivalent to about £2.5 billion or $12.5 billion, the rest being a notional amount consigned to a never-never land in the future. The real sum meant a considerable burden, but it could be paid once Germany's financial system was restored to normality, and if it possessed the political will to pay. Britain and France had war debts of a comparable scale, in addition to internal war debt. The reparations burden, measured in terms of debt, was nothing out of the ordinary by international comparison, especially since the Reich had virtually wiped out its internal debts in the inflation.[139] The best consensus internationally is that it was within German capacity to pay, and neither destroyed nor 'enslaved' Germany.[140]

The treaty of June 1919 was no 'Carthaginian' peace, contrary to Keynes' eloquent but misleading denunciation, glibly repeated ever since by generations of textbook authors. (It refers to Cato's constant demand for the destruction of Carthage after its defeat in the Third Punic War, 'Delenda est Carthago'. Carthage was evacuated and razed to the ground in 146 BC.) Versailles was a compromise peace far more moderate than German leaders expected in 1918 with their talk of the coming 'annihilation' of Germany and enslavement. The treaty maintained Germany's economic potential; after the territorial revisions, Germany was more highly industrialized than before, and after a transitional phase it would be able to resume international trade on the basis of equality.[141] German politicians nonetheless condemned it as a document which intended 'to destroy Germany as a world people', 'destroy German economic life', and 'deny its people the right to existence'.[142] Recalling the moment when the Allies presented the draft treaty, Brockdorff-Rantzau said that the German people 'would not allow its body to be torn to pieces', and he accused Clemenceau of treating the German people like a dog under vivisection.[143]

This extreme language was not empty rhetoric. Powerless now to resist the French, the Germans were whipped by such hyperbole into a state of hatred, sharpened by the humiliating knowledge of military impotence, that probably exceeded the wartime hatred of the French. The policy was to demonstrate that fulfilment of the treaty terms meant economic collapse, and the government provoked international conflict in the hope of dividing the Allies and ending reparations. Four years later, in the attempt to ensure the continued flow of reparation deliveries, on which Germany had deliberately defaulted several times, the French (and Belgians) occupied the Ruhr. The 'Ruhr struggle', as it was called on both sides, meant the forcible attempt to extract reparations and the German response with a government-sponsored general strike known as 'passive resistance'. Governments on both sides tried to prevent the conflict from spilling over from peaceful protest into a war, but were faced with the attempt of German extreme nationalists to sabotage the occupation by planting bombs and orchestrating riots. Escalating French repression of unrest and (suspected) sabotage led to the death of probably 130 to 140 German civilians, while twenty soldiers were killed;[144] the relatively low total over a period of some eighteen months belies the harshness of the measures that included mass expulsions of recalcitrant civil servants and others, the collective punishment of families and communities, court martial judgements and death penalties. Moreover, the economic hardships led to widespread famine. The occupation was not really a war; nevertheless, while it lasted, it bore the characteristics of what Gerd Krumeich has described as a 'replay of a war, a partly very violent mimicry of war' which had the purpose of 'making Germany too feel what war was really like'; in fact, the astonishing harshness of the occupation troops can only be explained by the memory of the brutality and destruction of the German invasion and subsequent occupation, 1914–18.[145]

Poincaré intended using the occupation to dismember Germany (above all by encouraging the Rhineland separatist movement), and shift France's borders eastward. Yet even in his most radical phase, Poincaré stressed that his aim was not 'to strangle Germany'. In the face of popular 'passive resistance' but also in the face of disapproval and non-participation in the occupation of the British and Americans, Poincaré gave up these aims, and by January 1924 he recognized the necessity of maintaining a democratic, unified Germany.[146]

The significance of the Ruhr occupation was in fact not the extent of violence of French troops, who were far more solicitous of German civilian lives than German troops had been in Berlin in 1919, but the deep-seated refusal on the part of responsible German authorities (political parties, the national and regional governments, employers, and unions) to recognize the legitimacy of the Allied claim to reparations. Yet ultimately, neither the French nor the Germans opted for a policy of unlimited destruction. The occupation was a turning point in European history, allowing recon-ciliation and the resumption of peaceful international relations. Germany had to acknowledge its commitment to make reparation payments, and was now enabled to do so through an Anglo-American loan to restart the economy after it ended passive resistance and stopped hyperinflation with a currency reform. France's reparation victory had come at high cost: the franc had to be devalued, and the realization filtered through that it could not recover from the war by forcibly exploiting Germany, but only through international cooperation. The same recognition was at the root of the policies pursued by Stresemann both in his 100-day term as German chancellor in 1923 and in his towering role as foreign minister until 1929. Despite the attempts of extreme right-wing groups (with some support from Krupp and the army) to unleash a terrorist campaign in 1923, most Germans had not wanted a violent confrontation with France. The Communists welcomed passive resistance as a prelude to revolution, made an unconvincing turn towards nationalism, and launched a botched attempt at an uprising in October 1923; their moment passed, and the KPD never again had a serious chance or the mass basis for a seizure of power.

The extreme right of German politics and culture saw the 'Ruhr struggle' as a real continuation of war, as a permanent conflict. The nationalist saboteur Schlageter, executed by the French, was celebrated first by the Communists and then by the Nazis as heroic martyr to the national cause, and he became the subject of numerous poems, songs, novels, and plays. The most famous of these, Hanns Johst's play *Schlageter*, written in 1933 and dedicated to Hitler, has the protagonist speak the apocalyptic final words before being executed:

> Germany!
> One last word! One wish!
> Order!!
> Germany!!!
> Arise! In flames!!
> Blaze up! Burn monstrously!!![147]

The nationalist mobilization accompanying the Ruhr occupation allowed the Nazis to claim to be the only consistent, radical force to combat foreign and internal enemies, and prompted Hitler to overestimate the potential of his Nazi Party, encouraged by the seizure of power by the relatively small Italian Fascist Party in October 1922. Hitler regarded the March on Rome as his political model, and Mussolini as 'sacrosanct'. The existence of Fascism in Italy was a significant factor in the 'making possible of Hitler'.[148] In no other country was so much written and published about Italian Fascism as in Germany: about 150 books, and thousands of articles in newspapers and periodicals appeared before 1933, not counting daily news reports by correspondents. In October 1923 Hitler gave an interview to an Italian paper, in which he admired Mussolini for his nationalism and for being 'the only one in Europe to have crushed Marxism and purged his nation'. Asked about the rumours in Italy that he was planning a march on Berlin, Hitler smiled, and then responded: 'I am like a spider who awaits the day that must come.' Regarding the form of the future state of Germany, whether it would be republican or monarchical, he said the form of the state was not essential, only its content; in the near future there could be but one form for Germany: 'a brutal national dictatorship'.[149] There is no doubt the March on Rome inspired Hitler's attempted putsch in Munich, only three weeks after this interview. Had it succeeded, it is clear that Hitler's next step would have been to install a dictatorship in Berlin. Its defeat meant that the Nazi Party was temporarily weakened, its leader imprisoned, but it did not mean, as is often thought, that Hitler decided to come to power by constitutional or democratic means. Until 1929 the Nazi Party remained on the fringe of German politics, where it took up the most extreme nationalist stance, and with its martial affectation, uniforms, and culture of violence pretended to be the true incarnation of the soldier's experience of war.

The appropriation of the war was by no means the monopoly of the Nazis, however. This was a central task of the ministries of foreign affairs and defence. In the Reichswehr ministry a plan was drafted to produce the 'German historiography of the world war as national task'. As part of this programme in March 1924 the ministry prepared an internal 'memorandum on the psychological preparation of the people for war', which stated:

> 1. Germany is in a situation of continuously growing danger. 2. Defence establishment and military capacity are needed to ward off danger. 3. The will for defence has nothing to do with political attitude. All circles of the people must and may participate in it without becoming warmongers. 4. Traitors and informers are enemies of the people.[150]

The memory of the war was used in Germany to prepare the next war, even though the majority of the people wanted nothing more to do with war. General von Seeckt, army chief of command, complained in 1922: 'It has to be admitted that the spirit which affected the delegation at Versailles has not yet disappeared and that the foolish call, "Never again war!" finds a widespread echo . . . Certainly, there is in the German people a widespread and explicable desire for peace.'[151] The great success of Remarque's anti-war novel, *All Quiet on the Western Front*, first serialized in the liberal *Vossische Zeitung* before its publication in 1929, shows that a very large part of the German public still identified with the rejection of the war which had destroyed a generation, and with the transnationality of the experience of victimhood. It sold one million copies in Germany in its first year of publication alone, before going on to become an international bestseller with a total of some 30 to 40 million copies. Yet the political culture of the establishment, including most political parties, continued to defend the memory of the imperial regime and the 'honour' of the German army; the nationalist Right and the Nazis launched furious attacks on Remarque's book and on Lewis Milestone's Hollywood film, released in 1930. When the Nazis came to power they banned both, naturally. The trenches of the Great War ran through German society, and for the Right the mass destruction of the war justified the call for revenge.

In France, by contrast, veterans' memory of the war and their antimilitarism gradually became the dominant force in political culture, as Antoine Prost has shown.[152] The culture of war lasted only long enough to help the Bloc National, the centre-right alliance, win the elections of November 1919. Most socialists were unable to see any positive meaning in the war, but the Right were able to mobilize the prestige of military victory and transmute it into political victory.[153] In the election campaign, when one would expect France to be suffused with the golden afterglow from the peace treaty, the Union Républicaine, a part of the Bloc National, referred to the 'appalling war of five years', and the need still to win the peace. In their election statement of 3 November 1919 the leading candidates Millerand, Barrès, and others began with an attack on Bolshevism, mentioned a number of pressing social problems, and finally stated the need to force Germany to meet its obligations. This was reiterated in a speech given by Millerand in Paris on 7 November. The election campaign was a nasty affair, in which the Right condemned the socialists as associates of the wartime enemy. In the Millerand papers there is a collection of wall posters and leaflets, among which is a leaflet entitled 'The Crime of German Social-Democracy. The Complicity of the [French] Unified Socialists'. It condemned the SPD for supporting the war, for pulling the wool over the eyes of the gullible French socialists on the eve of war, and for betraying the International. It condemned French socialists who were now fraternizing with 'les camarades boches'. 'Our heroic *poilus* fought in the trenches against these Social Democrats who distinguished themselves, just like their compatriots, by their bestiality and ferocity.' There are also small red labels (still sticky today): 'Poster paid by German agents', no doubt intended to be plastered over the election posters of the Socialist Party.[154] In the patriotic surge the Bloc National won a resounding election victory, the legislature becoming known as the *Chambre bleu horizon*; Millerand was the first premier, and he became president of the Republic from September 1920 to June

1924. His hard-line policy towards Germany ended in failure, and the Bloc national was defeated by the Left in the elections of 1924, signalling a turn towards a policy of reconciliation. Remarkably, France disproved de Gaulle's prediction of 'indestructible seeds of hatred', and the hardliner Poincaré was defeated and replaced by the more conciliatory Briand.

The French experience of the war was 'in some critical ways fundamentally different' from that of Britain, the historian Martha Hanna has shown.[155] In Britain, when the pacifist reaction to the immense losses began after the war, disillusionment with patriotic poets, propagandists, and traditional military values set in, and the literature of disenchantment of Sassoon, Owen, and Graves rose in popularity. The Great War is seen in the prevailing consensus in the English-speaking world as the product of incompetent, cynical leadership by British generals who sent their men into futile slaughter. This is mainly because the outcome of the war was for Britain apparently inconclusive: its territory had not been invaded, and it had therefore not succeeded in repelling the invader. It did not seek territorial expansion, and the eventual gain in colonial territory was virtually ignored in public opinion. The immense loss of life had brought no tangible reward or booty; Britain's position as creditor to the world was reversed, it had had to sell its investments in America, and London relinquished to New York the position as the capital of world finance. France had recovered the lost territories of Alsace and Lorraine, but far more important: it had successfully driven the invader from its soil and liberated the nation.

While France and Britain mentally demobilized, a significant part of German culture was determined to do the opposite. The 'war guilt' clause of the Treaty of Versailles is renowned until this day for the way it focused the hatred of German nationalists and militarists on the post-war world order and on Germany's democratic politicians who, to prevent invasion, had agreed to sign the treaty. Exactly why German politicians professed outrage at or genuinely loathed the treaty is seldom analysed. The elaborate campaign waged by the nationalist Right was crucial, but it was the German foreign ministry which secretly coordinated and funded it. (The struggle against Versailles was one of Hitler's main obsessions, but his role must not be retrospectively exaggerated because of his later career; until 1930, the Nazi Party led a precarious existence with little significance outside Bavaria.) Ostensibly the campaign was about the restoration of the 'honour' of the imperial regime, but the real agenda was the 'moral rebirth' of the German nation through rebuttal of the perceived moral judgement of Versailles in order to prepare another war. A document discovered by Fritz Fischer in the 1960s reveals how systematically the campaign was conceived. Bethmann Hollweg, Jagow (the foreign secretary in 1914), and Stumm, (director of the political department in the foreign ministry) agreed to conceal essential evidence about Germany's driving role in the July crisis from the post-war commission of investigation. A friend wrote to Jagow in July 1919:

> I agree with you in seeing the means for a campaign which has some prospect of success essentially in a well-guided press ... [The public needs in these difficult times] stronger stimuli ... to awake from its lethargic sleep in matters of foreign policy. Today I think it is absolutely vital to draw the German people's attention by means of repeated publications written in trenchant and provocative form to the fact that Britain, Russia, and France absolutely wanted and consciously prepared the war.[156]

Hermann Kantorowicz, the lawyer who was asked by the Reichstag in 1923 to write an official report for the investigation on the causes of the war, and who discovered in the files of the foreign ministry the documents showing the responsibility of Germany and Austria-Hungary in unleashing the war, was deeply concerned at the long-term political implications of the 'innocence campaign'. Publication of his report, which he completed in 1923, was repeatedly delayed and ultimately suppressed. Protesting at the delay and fearing that the foreign ministry would demand revision of the manuscript or even the publication of a dissenting report, Kantorowicz wrote in 1929:

> I am convinced that ... the entire official, semi-official, and private innocence propaganda ultimately has no other object but to prepare the morale of the German people for the moment when, as soon as the 'war guilt lie' is refuted, the entire Treaty of Versailles on which it is based and all the financial burdens linked with it, become void ... He who sows the wind, which the foreign ministry has been doing for ten years, will harvest the storm. I consider it to be my inexorable duty ... to work with the weak forces at my disposal to prevent such a catastrophe, which would mean nothing other than the automatic resumption of the world war.[157]

Kantorowicz was even more direct in a letter to Hermann Lutz, another member of the Reichstag investigation: 'The entire guilt propaganda campaign is nothing but a vast confidence trick played on the people, for the purpose of the moral mobilization for the next war.'[158] The Kantorowicz report was not published until 1967.

It was this deeper significance of articles 227 to 231 that explains why the German government accepted the drastic measures of disarmament, territorial loss, and harsh economic burdens, even the principle of paying substantial reparations, and concretely offered (as is usually forgotten in most textbooks that denounce Versailles) 100 billion gold marks (£5 billion sterling) in reparations, but refused to accept the so-called 'war guilt' articles of the peace treaty.[159] These concerned intangible questions of the 'honour' of the old army and Germany's responsibility (although not, as the German government depicted it, 'sole war guilt': the parallel treaties with Austria, Hungary, and Turkey contained similar clauses about their responsibility for making good the damage caused by their aggression), and it was thus a matter of preserving the prestige of the army in order to rebuild it for a new war.

For all the similarity between Italy and Germany in the development of fascism, there was a distinction in the public acceptance of political violence. Certainly, the seeds of political violence were being sown in the German army, which, while transforming itself into a small professional army, absorbed some of the *Freikorps* fighters and acquired much experience in the violent suppression of workers' uprisings and left-wing movements in 1919 and 1920. However, the army proved to be the loyal defender of the Republic in the crisis year 1923, even when General von Seeckt was given dictatorial power. The German militant nationalists were unable to threaten the Republic for another nine years. The Italian Fascist movement derived much of its dynamism from the transfer of the glorification of violence directed against the external enemy to the internal enemy over the short period, 1919 to 1922, fighting a political battle that would liberate and redeem Italy. While Liberal Italy gave tacit approval of Fascist violence and brought Mussolini into power, the German bourgeoisie approved only of selective violence: against the working class, but not against bourgeois politicians or the state. The assassinations in 1921 and 1922 of the Catholic politician Erzberger and the Jewish foreign minister Rathenau, hated by the extreme Right for their religious/racial origin, but above all because they were identified with acceptance of the Peace Treaty, provoked widespread public anger and large demonstrations. In particular the Rathenau murder caused chancellor Wirth to announce 'The enemy stands on the right!', and parliament passed a law for the protection of the Republic.

The shift in opinion towards the acceptance of political violence and mass murder came on different levels: most obviously, of course, with the arrival of the Nazis as a mass party some twelve years after the war, when millions voted for a movement that promised to silence all political rivals, that glorified and practised violence, and threatened to kill those it regarded as national traitors once it came to power; less obvious were the subterranean shifts in mentality.

One such shift was the crucial effect of the war experience not only on those who became Nazi party members and supporters, but on Adolf Hitler himself. Hitler was fond of recalling his service in the First World War, 'the most unforgettable and greatest time of my mortal life', as he wrote in *Mein Kampf* in 1925. His war experience was in every way constitutive for his entire subsequent career. He had volunteered to join up in August 1914, and served as a messenger and orderly for four years. Although he received medals for bravery, he was promoted only once, in November 1914, to lance corporal. He was regarded by his comrades as a humourless loner and by his commanders as lacking in leadership quality. In the final weeks of the war he was blinded in a British gas grenade attack near Ypres on 14 October. He was treated in hospital, and was gradually recovering when he heard about the Revolution and Germany's defeat.[160] In a scene he described in *Mein Kampf*, he felt his world had collapsed:

> I could stand it no longer... Again everything went black before my eyes; I tottered and groped my way back to the dormitory, threw myself on my bunk, and dug my burning head into my blanket and pillow... And so it had all been in vain... Did all this happen only so that a gang of wretched criminals could lay hands on the fatherland?[161]

However, Hitler had not suffered physical injury, but psychosomatic blindness. This is an extraordinary story that the Nazis succeeded in covering up, until its recent rediscovery. Hitler was transferred from field hospital in Belgium to the psychiatric department—not, significantly, the opththalmological department—of the military hospital at Pasewalk north of Berlin, where consultant neurologist Professor Edmund Forster diagnosed 'hysterical blindness'. Forster was an authoritarian figure who commanded respect; he regarded hysterical behaviour as sham acting, and treated patients with 'war hysteria' as malingerers. Hitler was released as cured on 19 November, and never complained subsequently about his eyesight and did not seek further medical treatment. In summer 1933, a few months after Hitler came to power, Forster travelled to France, and gave transcripts of the Pasewalk hospital records to anti-Nazi exiles in Paris. In September 1933 Forster was suspended from his professorship at Greifswald University. Fearing the Gestapo was about to arrest him for making defamatory remarks about leading personnel of the Reich, he committed suicide a few days later.

Colonel Ferdinand Eduard von Bredow, who had ordered the seizure of the Pasewalk hospital records, and knew and spoke about their compromising contents, including the diagnosis of Hitler's hysterical blindness, was arrested by the Gestapo and shot on 1 July 1934, while 'trying to escape'. Former chancellor and general Kurt von Schleicher, who also knew about the Pasewalk records, was executed along with his wife the day before.[162]

Hitler's response to his 'blindness' had been to deny anything but a heroic physical injury, for hysteria was a feminine disease, a confession of weakness. Thus ruthless eradication of those who knew Hitler's secret was one result of his shell-shock; the other was his decision, taken while at Pasewalk, he claimed, to go into politics. Hitler was thus one of a small minority of soldiers who were never able to overcome their war experience, who had continually to reassert their masculinity which had been questioned by the war. Everything he subsequently did in politics was in some way connected to the war: recovering that experience of 'front-line solidarity', ensuring the home front never again 'stabbed the army in the back', and taking revenge for the 'treachery' of 1918 on socialists, democrats, and Jews. The lesson Hitler drew from the war was its absolute affirmation, and absolute hatred of enemies. Naturally, Hitler's subsequent rise to power cannot be explained solely by his concealed war hysteria, just as Mussolini's career cannot be explained solely by his equally shameful syphilis which he successfully disguised as a heroic war injury.[163] But the uncanny parallels in these two pathological careers indicate that they represented a broader collective trauma among a minority of men, and they confirm the formative role of the First World War in the catastrophic rise of fascism.

Another subterranean shift in mentalities was in the world of medicine and law. In the existential struggle to renew the world, radical, even extreme measures could be considered that were previously unthinkable. One such mental consequence of war was the discussion of what to do about the great number of incurably ill and mentally handicapped patients, against the background of mass death in the war, and the shortage of resources. In 1920 the lawyer Karl Binding and the psychiatrist Alfred Hoche published a book called 'Permission for the Destruction of Life Unworthy of Life', in which they discussed what to do with human beings whose lives were 'not worthy of life'. Current law, Binding wrote, must be reformed, because it failed to 'distinguish between the destruction of life worthy of life and life unworthy of life'. He referred to the 'pointless waste of labour power . . . and wealth' to prolong 'for years and decades' the lives of those 'unworthy of life'. Binding and Hoche could see no legal or moral grounds to disallow involuntary euthanasia—the killing of such people who were the 'opposite of real humans'.[164]

German psychiatry was at a crossroads in its historical development. Binding and Hoche's tract appears ominously to foretell the history of euthanasia in the Third Reich, in which 70,273 people were killed in the 'T–4' programme of extermination of psychiatric patients and the mentally handicapped, mainly in gas chambers, in the period 1939–41.[165] Yet in many ways the treatment of the mentally ill before the First World War had represented a major step towards modernity—in both a positive and a negative sense. In the course of the nineteenth century formal institutions for the mentally ill were created, as older patterns of dealing with such sufferers within the family and the rural community were disappearing; the growth of cities and the modern state led to categorization and incarceration in mental institutions. The medical profession's humanitarian intention to care for patients increasingly came under pressure from those who saw psychiatric institutions as an instrument of social discipline and a financial burden. During the war, German psychiatry took a step towards the negative, destructive potential of modernity, and psychiatric patients became the first intentional victims of hunger. In the mental institutions of Saxony, for example, 8.3 per cent died during the year 1914, but in 1917 30.4 and in 1918 26 per cent died.[166] Even without an explicit ideology, the First World War provided a gruesome field for experimentation with the theory and practice of eugenics. Some 70,000 psychiatric patients in Germany died of malnutrition, disease, or neglect, in excess of any normal peacetime mortality. Most doctors callously deprived their patients of food for the benefit of 'the strong' and for national mobilization.[167]

In fact, in the Weimar Republic, the arguments of Binding and Hoche encountered stiff resistance, and the medical profession rejected their radically utilitarian ideas, restating the need for humanitarian care of the mentally handicapped. Once the crude ideas of utilitarian eugenics were implanted, however, the Third Reich offered the conditions and means to carry them out. Hitler made no secret of Nazi policy in this regard, too. At the party congress in Nuremberg in 1929, Hitler declared: 'If Germany receives one million children every year and eliminates seven hundred thousand to eight hundred thousand of the weakest, then the result would perhaps be an increase in strength.'[168]

Another subterranean shift in mentality was the new antisemitism, radicalized through the prism of modern, industrialized killing in the Great War. It was linked with the idea of imperialist expansion. Hitler developed views that were already common on the racist Right (above all in the imperialist ideology of the Pan-German League since the 1890s). His views, as expressed in countless speeches and in his book *Mein Kampf*, made the genocidal intention clear. The Jews, he wrote, were 'planning the enslavement and with it the destruction of all non-Jewish peoples'.[169] Hitler linked space with race in the goal of *Lebensraum*, or 'living space', in eastern Europe for the allegedly over-populated Germany. In an extreme, violent synthesis of ideas Jews were now linked with 'Marxism' and 'Bolshevism': the 'Jewish–Bolshevik world conspiracy' which was plotting to destroy Germany. What he envisaged was first a cultural war within Germany to purify it of 'Marxism', by which he meant not only the Communists but also the SPD and trade unions, followed by a war of annihilation against the external enemy to become a world power. 'The nationalization of the masses', Hitler wrote, 'will succeed only when, aside from all the positive struggle for the soul of our people, their international poisoners are exterminated.'[170] Once Germany had been saved, the next step was the elimination of the Jews in Russia and eastern Europe and a war of conquest to acquire 'living-space' in Russia:

> The right to possess soil can become a duty if without extension of its soil a great nation seems doomed to destruction . . . Germany will either be a world power or there will be no Germany. And for world power she needs that magnitude which will give her the position she needs in the present period, and life to her citizens . . .
>
> If we speak of soil in Europe today, we can primarily have in mind only Russia and her vassal border states . . . For centuries Russia drew nourishment from [the] Germanic nucleus of its upper leading strata. Today it can be regarded as almost totally exterminated and extinguished. It has been replaced by the Jew . . . He himself is no element of organization, but a ferment of decomposition. The giant empire in the east is ripe for collapse. And the end of Jewish rule in Russia will also be the end of Russia as a state.[171]

It was the total radicalization of these crucial elements deriving from Germany's First World War experience as well as long-term racist and imperialist ideas which formed the essence of Nazi warfare in the Second World War: cultural war on the internal enemy, the link between space and race, and the intention of carrying out a policy of mass destruction.

Conclusion

The further we are removed by the passage of time from the end of the Second World War, the more the two world wars appear as a single period, as a 'Second Thirty Years War', or as an 'age of catastrophe' as Eric Hobsbawm called the first part of his book *Age of Extremes*.[1] The problem with these concepts is that they imply a continuum, as if Nazi Germany were the linear extension of imperial Germany with virtually the same constellation of interests as in 1914, facing the same coalition of enemies, or as if Europe spent the inter-war years preparing the next war. While there were some obvious lines of continuity (such as Germany's initial territorial war aims in 1939 and the desire to change the verdict of the First World War), the discontinuities in international politics and in warfare were even stronger. Nazi Germany, Fascist Italy, and Communist Russia really were quite different regimes from their predecessors. For the victims of the 'age of catastrophe', whether the 'poor bloody infantry' on the Somme, the forgotten prisoners of war left to starve in both wars, the civilians caught in the bombing of Hamburg, Dresden, or Nagasaki, or the Jews transported across Europe to death camps, it must indeed have seemed as if the war machine had developed a terrifying, unstoppable dynamic beyond the control of human agency. But there is a problem with such a concept that implies that the dynamic of destruction was unstoppable, even that history was determined by impersonal forces of destiny.

As we have seen, war, cultural destruction and mass killing in the era of the First World War had identifiable causes. The destruction of Louvain, the mass killings of civilians on the western front in 1914, the genocide of the Armenians in 1915, the mutual mass slaughter of the trenches, the collective political violence in Russia after the Revolution, all had long-term causes in the history of mentalities, in military culture, or racism; but they were also clearly the result of orders issued by individual commanders and political leaders. Commanders could have decided otherwise, and sometimes did so, as we know from cases of avoided atrocities in the German army in 1914, or the cautious advance of the Allies in 1918 to spare the lives of infantrymen. Historical developments were contingent, not inevitable. This is not to make a case for banal counter-factual speculation, such as the idea that if Archduke Franz Ferdinand's driver had not taken a wrong turning on 28 June 1914, there would have been no world war. The dynamic of destruction was not a law of nature; rather, despite the tremendous pressure of nature, technology, and mentalities, it was man-made, capable of infinite variation, and as we saw with the German decision to end the war, capable of being stopped before ultimate self-destruction. The era of the First World War nevertheless witnessed a decisive step towards total war, as the tendency towards the erosion of the distinction between combatants and civilians, or to be more precise, between combatants and non-combatants, became more and more visible.

It was fascist warfare that totally eradicated that distinction. Mussolini's war against Abyssinia (today Ethiopia), which was both the last war of colonial conquest and the first fascist war in history, was waged with ruthless brutality against the entire population. Between 350,000 and 760,000 Ethiopians were killed in the course of a six-year war, most of them civilians, in which the technologically superior Italian forces terrorized the population with air power, bombing, poison gas, and collective punishments for guerrilla resistance.[2] Three important points relate to the argument of this book. First, the strategy derived directly from the lessons of the First World War. The Fascist regime based its war in Ethiopia on the theoretical concept of the 'guerra integrale' developed in the 1920s by the Italian military writer Giulio Douhet (cf. Chapter 2), above all that massive aerial bombardment was to be used to cause maximum damage to the enemy in the shortest possible time, even if it contravened international law. Second, it was explicitly conceived as a racial war, to demonstrate the racial superiority of the conquerors, to 'improve the race', and to prepare the Italian army for a future war in Europe. Even if the decimation of the population was not conceived as a genocidal war, the vast dimension of the killing pointed in that direction. Third, it directly challenges the thesis of German singularity, of a uniquely German development from a policy of total war (or 'absolute destruction') in the First World War to total war and genocide in the Second World War.

The fascist regimes, as I have argued, arose from their appropriation of the experience of the First World War; the Fascist war on Ethiopia thus showed continuities and conscious learning processes from that war, but also the new character of total warfare. The triad of continuity, learning process, and radical discontinuity applies all the more to the Second World War. Nazi policies towards the German civilian population at war were characterized by the attempt to put into practice the *Volksgemeinschaft,* the 'people's community' derived from the concept of equality of sacrifice in the First World War, but this time racially defined. There was the phobia of the 1918 phenomenon, in other words the Nazi reading of the defeat of Germany by internal revolution, which produced the desire to maintain a high level of food supply. The concomitant of that policy was to attempt to eliminate all those from the German population who were described in 1921 by Binding and Hoche as 'lives unworthy of life' or in Nazi jargon 'useless mouths', through the policy of involuntary euthanasia of the mentally ill, as well as those who were defined as racial enemies. Industrialized warfare in the First World War, ruthless occupation policies, and the radical dynamic of destruction were not invented by Germany's pre-industrial elites or Junker officers. This was the war culture of the modern militarists, who put forward the most extreme ideas for the reorganization of society around the goal of warfare and the most limitless aims for a new European order: Ludendorff, Groener, Bauer, and Jünger were middle-class men, not nobles. There is thus a certain historical logic in the fact that a petit-bourgeois dictator backed by an all-class mass movement and the old establishment should take up these extreme ideas, radically transform, and then implement them.

In some areas there were totally new departures without continuities. The first contrast is between the mood of August 1914 and the mood of September 1939. Notwithstanding all the qualifications with which we have described the mood in Europe in August 1914, there is no doubt that in Germany, at any rate, there was enthusiasm in large sections of society. Despite six years of Nazi propaganda and extreme militarism, that mood was absent in Germany in 1939, to a large extent because of the memory of the First World War as a catastrophe.[3] Even in a totalitarian state (if we may use the term here without a lengthy critical discussion) it was not possible totally to manipulate the mass of the population. Among leading army officers, too, the mood was at first cautious and sceptical. That changed with the unexpectedly quick defeat of France in 1940. However, the nature of warfare had begun to change, too, and even traditional officers who were not fanatical Nazis took an active part in the shift to a new type of warfare. This process was not confined to Nazi Germany: even the democratic nations waged a new type of war that approached even more closely to an 'ideal type' of total war.

Germany's cultural elite had welcomed the war in 1914 and self-mobilized to lend intellectual support to the army, and many saw a cultural mission to export German values, even an international post-war order under German leadership; by contrast, philosophers, artists, professors, writers, and theologians were conspicuous mainly by their silence in the period 1939 to 1945. Centralized leadership of intellectuals in the humanities along with total state control of propaganda left little space for free expression; even intellectuals who identified closely with Nazism, such as the philosopher Martin Heidegger, did nothing to create anything resembling the 'ideas of 1914'. Virtually the same can be said about the Protestant theologians.[4] Here more transnational research needs to be done, but matters were different for intellectuals in the Second World War in Britain and France, at any rate. Many writers and other intellectuals willingly engaged there in the cultural war against the enemy, in the case of France also in the infinitely more dangerous Resistance.

Since we have used the term 'total war' it is appropriate here to provide a brief definition of its main characteristics. According to the historian Stig Förster, they can be summarized thus:

1. Total war aims, which can include the demand for unconditional capitulation, or the goal of the complete destruction of the enemy.
2. Total methods of warfare: this amounts to the unrestricted violation of international law and all principles of morality.
3. Total mobilization, in which all human and material resources are exploited for the purpose of warfare.
4. Total control: central organization and control of all aspects of private and public life for the purpose of warfare.[5]

To deal with points 3 and 4 first: there was a pronounced tendency towards total mobilization and total control in Britain, Germany, and the Soviet Union in the Second World War which went further than in the First World War, but this was a difference of degree rather than a completely new quality. In relation to methods of warfare, the Nazi war machine violated virtually every part of international law, the only exceptions being the choice not to use lethal poison gas in combat and not to maltreat western Allied prisoners of war, both for fear of retaliation. In regard to the aim of complete destruction, Nazi warfare fully met this criterion, limited only by the physical restrictions on its destructive capacity. Allied aerial warfare was the near-total response.

In relation to genocide, Nazi policy was almost perfectly 'total'. A full treatment of the Holocaust is beyond the scope of this book. However, two main aspects are directly related to the question of the continuity of the dynamic of destruction and the themes of cultural destruction and mass killing. One is antisemitism, and the other is the genocidal process.

The history of antisemitism appears to reveal obvious continuities. The growing tensions during the First World War produced the first spike in the history of antisemitism in twentieth-century Germany, marked by the 'Jew census' in the army in 1916 and the spread of antisemitic ideology in right-wing parties after 1918. The election successes of the Nazi Party in the years 1930 to 1933 showed that one-third of the German electorate supported a party which stood for extreme, even violent, racism, although several other political issues were more important in mobilizing voters than Nazi anti-semitic ideology. The American author Daniel J. Goldhagen attempted to explain the Holocaust by reference to long-standing 'eliminatory antisemit-ism' widespread in German society and politics even before 1933.[6] On the level of ideology, it is true that the Nazis' ideas were not original: most of them can be traced back to Pan-German ideas current on the extreme right in Germany and Austria before 1914. Yet when we examine the decisions leading to the genocide and its implementation, it is not the continuities between the First and the Second World Wars, but the discontinuities which are most striking.[7] In the First World War and in the Weimar Republic the state actually attempted to prevent the spread of antisemitism; acts of antisemitic violence during the Republic were the work of extremists opposed to the state; by contrast, in the Third Reich antisemitism was raised to the status of official doctrine. Before 1933, Jews, like any other citizens, were afforded the protection of the law from arbitrary attack on their lives and property. Under the Nazi regime, they were gradually excluded from the civil service, public life, the private economy, and deprived of their civil rights, before being deported and murdered. The state actively encouraged theft, violence, and extreme brutality, overthrowing in the process the fundamentals of a state based on the rule of law as well as common humanity. Above all, the intention of genocide (in the sense of the aim of murdering all Europe's Jews) was not part of traditional antisemitism, nor even of the policy of the Third Reich, until late 1941.

In some ways the genocidal process of the Nazi regime resembled that of the Armenian genocide, but the similarities are due more to common patterns of political pathology than conscious emulation. It was certainly the case that the Nazi regime, like the Turkish CUP regime in 1915, constructed its victims as the 'enemy', associated them with perceived foreign enemies (the 'Jewish–Bolshevik world conspiracy'), and used provocation to justify eradication (the murder by a Jew of a German diplomat in Paris in 1938 which was the occasion for the pogroms known as 'Crystal Night'; and Hitler's rhetorical 'prophecy' of January 1939 that if the Jews were to unleash another world war, it would end with their destruction). It has never been properly resolved whether Hitler spoke the words ascribed to him: 'Who, after all, speaks today of the annihilation of the Armenians?' (22 August 1939, shortly before the start of the Second World War). In fact, the genocide of the Armenians was widely known in inter-war Europe, but the important issue is that Hitler was preparing his closest followers and commanders to carry out ruthless extermination (in the first instance of the Polish elites) by pointing out that the Allies in the end had done little to punish the Turkish organizers of the genocide.[8]

One strong similarity in the genocidal process on the eastern front, 1914 to 1920, the Armenian genocide, 1915, and the genocide in the Second World War, was the causal relationship between military setbacks, racism/ antisemitism, and a tendency towards genocidal 'reprisals' evident in the conduct of the Tsarist army in the First World War, in the Turkish genocide of the Armenians in 1915, during the Civil War in Russia, and in late 1941 in the German invasion of the Soviet Union.[9] Yet there was a difference between the degree of intentionality between the vicious, but largely sporadic and unplanned genocidal violence against Jews in eastern Europe, 1914 to 1921, and the Nazi policy of genocide. After three decades of discussion between historians who argued that the Holocaust was the result purely of Hitler's will and his long-held plan (the intentionalist view), and those who argued that it arose incrementally out of the progressive radic- alization of antisemitic policies in the competing power centres of the Nazi apparatus (the functionalist view), there can be no doubt that the mass murder was intended by Hitler and the Nazi elite, planned down to the last detail, and implemented by large staff of collaborators, administrators, and perpetrators of various degrees of direct complicity and responsibility. The genocide was not a natural catastrophe, but mass murder willed by human beings; the process was not run by machines, nor was it unstoppable.

This raises questions of the relationship between the dynamic of destruction and genocide and the distinction between combatants and non-
combatants. Total war, which tends towards annihilation, bears within it
the potential for genocide. Yet genocide was not an inevitable consequence
of total war; nor, as we now know from the experience of Rwanda in the
1990s, is total war even a necessary precondition for genocide.

In the First World War, not only with respect to genocide, but to war
policy in general, in making the distinction between combatants and non-
combatants, and in relation to the targeting of the cultural heritage, the
decisions were taken by the military. (The exception to this rule was the
genocide in Turkey, which was decided upon by the central committee of
the CUP, not the army.) In the Second World War, decisions were taken
by civilian leaders: Churchill, Stalin, Hitler, Roosevelt, Truman. One
important legacy of the First World War was therefore not the militarization
of society in the sense that governments and the decision-making process
were taken over by the military, but rather that civilian politicians, following the success of Clemenceau and Lloyd George, decided that war was too
important to be left to the generals. That process went furthest in Germany,
where the military was almost totally deprived of autonomy and totally
integrated into the Nazi state, and correspondingly made complicit in its
crimes.

From the First to the Second World War, in general, then, there was an
immense progression in the dynamic of destruction, with a terrible increase
in combatant and non-combatant loss of life. Whereas civilians amounted to
between one-sixth and one-third of the war dead in the First World War
(depending on whether one counts deaths from the global influenza epidemic which was unrelated to the war), the proportion in the Second
World War was around two-thirds. There were two main causes for this
dramatic shift: the revolution in the technology of war, primarily aerial
warfare, and the revolution in ideology, primarily racial warfare. Together
they totally removed the distinction between civilians and soldiers, between
'home' and 'front'; as the historian Ian Kershaw has written, the Second
World War was 'a *popular* war in the sense of the full involvement of the
peoples of Europe in the fighting, and the suffering'.[10]

The relatively low level of civilian casualties from aerial bombardment
during the First World War was due less to the observance of the laws of war
than to the fact that the technology of aerial warfare was in its infancy. By
the end of the war, however, the potential of aerial warfare for mass

destruction was recognized by thinkers such as Douhet, and it was realized in almost every war since then. During the Second World War, German and then British air strategy targeted enemy civilians. This distinguished it from Allied economic warfare during the First World War, which could achieve its objectives practically without bloodshed. The Germans, applying the lessons of Douhet, bombed Warsaw in 1939 and Rotterdam in 1940 to terrorize the population and succeeded in gaining quick surrender. However, it was the democratic states which took the logic of annihilation through air war to its extreme. The British bombing of German cities, starting in 1941, culminated in the obliteration of half of Hamburg in August 1943 and of the historic heart of Dresden in February 1945. While German bombs killed some 60,000 British civilians, British and American bombing killed ten times as many German civilians. It is difficult to escape the conclusion that aerial warfare on civilians was neither effective nor lawful. The American strategic air war against civilian targets culminated in the burning of Tokyo and the destruction of Hiroshima and Nagasaki with nuclear weapons. The same judgement as to its legality applies to the USA.

While the Anglo-American bombing campaign was a strategy embarked on only in response to attack, Nazi warfare was criminal from start to finish. It was a war of racial-biological annihilation to allow the German 'race' to dominate Europe by exploiting the inferior races and exterminating those deemed vermin. On 22 August 1939, Adolf Hitler explained to army commanders how the forthcoming war against Poland was to be started: 'I shall give a propagandist reason for starting the war, no matter whether it is plausible or not. The victor will not be asked afterwards whether he told the truth or not. When starting and waging a war it is not right that matters, but victory.' This is how it was to be waged: 'Close your hearts to pity. Act brutally. Eighty million people must obtain what is their right. Their existence must be made secure. The stronger man is right. The greatest harshness... The wholesale destruction of Poland is the military objective.'[11] The contrast with Bethmann Hollweg's public admission in 1914 that the invasion of Belgium broke international law, and that Belgium would be compensated, could hardly be greater. In the First World War Ludendorff (and others) drafted plans for the creation of a large strip of Polish border territory which would be settled by German colonists, and the Polish and Jewish population would be resettled further east. Yet these radical plans, which were discussed at highest level in the government and the

OHL, were never implemented, because the military leaders feared that such a violation of international law would have repercussions in international public opinion.[12] The Nazi policy of 'ethnic redistribution', which appears to be rooted in these proposals, was no continuation, but a radical break: for all the harshness of the occupations of 1914–18, the German state did not carry out brutal mass population expulsions which were the order of the day from 1939 to 1945. Nazi warfare represented the ultimate radicalization of the war on enemy culture: ideological warfare for total subjugation, exploitation, and ultimately removal.

While there was clearly a relationship between modern weapons of mass destruction and mass killing, it was thus the incursion of violence based on political ideologies, rather than weapons of mass destruction, which explains the highest death toll in the war. Poland and Yugoslavia suffered the greatest number of casualties in proportion to their population: Poland about 6 million, including 3 million Jews, and Yugoslavia about 1.2 million out of a population of approximately 16 million. From the first day of the invasion of Poland in September 1939, the German army acted with extreme violence against the population and prisoners of war. This meant not only the brutal treatment of individuals, but the predisposition to commit murder against large groups. The soldiers, frequently nervous, feared 'francs-tireurs', or Polish resistance fighters, who, according to the troops' pre-war training, would attack 'treacherously'; although there was no guerrilla resistance entire villages were burned down on suspicion, and thousands of civilians were murdered. There was widespread violence against Jews, not only because they were thought to be the ringleaders of subversion, but also because of soldiers' general antisemitic prejudice, drummed into them by years of Nazi propaganda. Fully two years before the decision for genocide was taken, in other words, there was a consensus in principle that a genocidal war was to be conducted.[13]

Soviet policy towards Poland, although it was not genocidal, was not much less destructive. With the intention of eliminating its military and political elite, the Soviets executed 4,000 Polish officers at Katyn in 1940, killed at least another 33,000 officers, political leaders, and intellectuals, and arrested 100,000 civilians.

The Yugoslav casualties resulted not only from the German invasion and the savage repression of the Yugoslav guerrilla resistance, but above all from what we could call the first Yugoslav civil war, in which Serbs were the victims of mass murder at the hands of the Croatian fascists, the Ustaša. In fact, violence was omnidirectional in the several overlapping wars in the Balkans. The Ustaša regime aimed to create an 'ethnically pure' state by expelling a third of the Serbs, forcibly converting one-third, and killing the rest. This amounted to a policy of genocide. But nationalist Serb Cetniks also targeted Croatians, Bosnian Muslims, and Albanians; civil war broke out between the Cetniks and the Communist partisans; Croatian fascists killed Roma and Jews and handed them over to the Nazis for deportation to the death camps; and at the end of the war the victorious Communist partisans killed between 33,000 and 38,000 (actual or real) collaborators and political enemies. The ugly euphemism 'ethnic cleansing' (etničko čišćenje), which entered the political vocabulary of the world during the wars of Yugoslav succession in the 1990s, was in fact invented in 1941 or 1942, when it was used by both Croatian and Serb nationalists to designate their programme to deport or kill the 'other' people and create 'ethnically cleansed' territories.

The treatment of prisoners of war by the Nazi and Communist regimes was also marked by a descent into barbarity. While about 5 per cent of the Russian prisoners of war in German captivity died in the First World War, in the Second World War, approximately 3.2 million Soviet prisoners out of a total of 5.2 million lost their lives in German captivity, a death rate of 61.5 per cent, because of a deliberate policy to starve them and work them to death. About 34 per cent of the 3 million German prisoners died in Soviet captivity. Yet it was mainly harsh conditions and administrative chaos that caused the high mortality of German prisoners, not deliberate violation of international law or a policy of annihilation; in that sense Soviet and Nazi treatment of prisoners diverged. Nazi racial ideology, the idea that the Soviet soldiers were 'sub-humans', drove the dynamic of destruction in Germany to its extreme.[14]

Finally, the spatial dimension had a new quality in the Second World War. The control of territory was determined partly by air power which— notwithstanding all its legal and moral problems—in the end did make a crucial difference: Allied aerial superiority ensured the success of the Normandy invasion in 1944 and paralysed the German war economy by destroying its infrastructure. By late 1944, lack of oil and other essential supplies reduced the German army to near-immobility in a fast shrinking space confined to German territory. Occupation policy, too, marked a radical shift from the First World War, and not only was it designed for maximum exploitation of resources in order to avoid a repeat of the food shortages that caused civilian unrest. Its crucial feature was not even the vast territorial extent of the German occupation from North Africa to Norway and deep inside Russia; rather, it was a part of racial policy for the total reorganization of Europe. The dystopia of vast population transfers and the targeting of civilians had thus not only become thinkable, but was implemented, not only by the Nazi state, but to varying degrees by all the powers in the Second World War.

Historiographical Note

The intention of this essay is to discuss those works which deal comparatively with culture and war culture, without surveying the entire range of First World War historiography, which would be far beyond the scope of this work and would sorely test the patience of my publisher.[1] Several major books have identified connections between modern culture and mass violence in Europe in the age of the First World War. Richard Cork hints at the connections in his book *A Bitter Truth*. The emphasis is on the powerful effect of participation in the war on avant-garde artists; the war forced them 'to forge a form-language capable of conveying their response to the suffering'. His implicit thesis is that most avant-garde artists, whether they experienced war as soldiers or not, turned towards more representational art as a way of expressing their horror of war and their rejection of it. Even official war artists like Nevinson (and, we might add, Orpen) in Britain and Slevogt in Germany produced work that directly opposed their governments' affirmation of war.[2] The Futurists, too, had lost their enthusiasm for war by 1916, he argues.[3] Cork's book is a rich and lavishly illustrated compendium of information about avant-garde artists and their works which are skilfully analysed, invaluable to anyone who wishes to study the subject, but it lacks a systematic reflection on the relationship between war and culture, and tends to blur the distinction between the nations and their art. Moreover, we might ask whether the distinction is always so clear between avant-garde and conventional art, and whether establishment and popular art does not also reveal something important about the relationship between culture and warfare.

The best-known book to make explicit connections between culture and war is that of Modris Eksteins, *Rites of Spring*. By turns exhilarating and exasperating, it starts with a discussion of the scandal created by the first performance of the Stravinsky ballet *Rite of Spring/Le Sacre du Printemps* in Paris in 1913, with choreography by Diaghilev, danced by Nijinsky and the Ballet russe. The music was revolutionary, the stage set radical, and the dance was designed to affront every good conservative ballet lover.

Eksteins uses this as a metaphor to show the shock of modernity, and how war brought modernity in the form of industrialized violence and even the aesthetics of modernity into everyday life and popular imagination. These are striking images, yet the connection between ballet and war is not made entirely clear: are we to understand that Stravinsky, Diaghilev, and Nijinsky caused the war? There are some extremely powerful descriptions of the different kinds of warfare on the western front, in which Eksteins rightly makes a distinction between the routine boredom and grim conditions faced by most troops during their time in the trenches, and the horror of the mass slaughter during the great battles of the Somme, Verdun, or Ypres. These descriptions, however, hardly tell us anything new about the war, and as a military history the book is impressionistic rather than analytical. Moreover, in calling the section that contains graphic description of attritional warfare 'Battle Ballet', Eksteins unfortunately echoes the aestheticization of violence favoured by Ernst Jünger and other militarist intellectuals. However, he provides a cogent answer to the question why men kept fighting so long: he argues that duty was a supreme virtue of the bourgeois age, whether this was patriotism or the more immediate sense of duty towards one's comrades in combat. This is not a complete explanation, but it is more convincing than Niall Ferguson's flippant, sensation-seeking answer to that question, 'because fighting was fun'.[4]

The main point Eksteins makes is that the country that embraced modernity in all its aspects most firmly and adapted to it best was Germany: it was the only country to recognize the importance of the defensive in industrialized war, and therefore to adopt attritional warfare. This overturned traditional military wisdom, which dictated that the offensive was the only way to win a war. Why? Because 'Germany had been the country most willing to question western social, cultural, and political norms before the war, most willing to promote the breakdown of old certainties...' The idea of attrition was not only the short-term response to the failure of the Schlieffen plan, but also the attempt to translate the emotional involvement of the nation into 'total war', in which 'the soldier and the civilian would no longer be distinguishable'.[5] Such ideas had their roots in the pre-war radical nationalist movements which wanted to revitalize German society through war. They were taken up not by the feudal-military elite, the Junkers, as the *Sonderweg* thesis would lead us to expect, but by the modern militarists like Ludendorff.[6] As I have argued in this book, it was the ascendancy of the modern militarists combined with a radical, limitless mission of Germany's political, cultural, and military elites, which produced the radicalization of warfare, eroding the distinction between soldiers and non-combatants in warfare and producing the application of terror.

The modern sense of alienation affected German society more deeply than any other nation, Eksteins argues, because of the swiftness of its transition from pre-industrial to urban society.[7] But was this so? And if so, why did Germany 'best represent the revolt' in culture? Yet although Eksteins intimates German exceptionalism, he also generalizes about all the European belligerent societies. He describes the war as 'the first middle-class war in history . . . , the first great war of the bourgeoisie'. Ultimately the argument thus remains unclear, if stimulating.

More recently, Isabel Hull has presented a powerful argument that restates the old *Sonderweg* thesis in a new form. According to Hull, the German military caste, its prestige rooted in the successful nineteenth-century wars, continued to dominate over the state, both before 1914 and during the First World War. She argues that because of the economic and demographic superiority of Germany's enemies, the military planners gambled on a ruthless strategy of the offensive—'absolute destruction'—to win rapid victory in a war on two fronts. This consciously involved brutal treatment of enemy civilians, and a policy of 'military extremism' that aimed for the 'utter annihilation of the enemy's armed forces'. Occupied territory was to be subject to 'total instrumentalization of all resources', and Europeans 'were instrumentalized . . . in ways astonishingly similar to those used against rebellious Africans'.[8] To some degree this was true during the first weeks of the war in 1914, but the argument ignores three weighty pieces of counter-evidence. The first is that even during the invasion in August–September 1914 there was no policy of complete annihilation, either of civilians or captured enemy soldiers. Nothing in German-occupied Europe resembled the policy of genocide of the Herero people in South-West Africa that Hull describes so impressively in the first section of her book. The second is that after the defeat on the Marne in early September, and at the latest after the failure to break through the British lines at Ypres in November 1914, the German army found itself mainly on the defensive on the western front, not the offensive, until spring 1918. The great operational strength, indeed superiority, of the German army for much of the war, which goes a long way to explaining its lower casualty level (which Niall Ferguson provocatively described as German killing superiority[9]) was its success in pioneering massive, and by 1916 flexible, defence in depth. The third major flaw in Hull's argument is that the French and British doctrine of the offensive as the best strategy was in principle no different to the German.[10] In fact, the nature of warfare in 1914–18 forced the Allies to adopt the same logic of annihilation, even on Allied territory. In this respect there is thus little that can be described as German singularity. Yet it is important to keep a sense of perspective: neither German nor Allied warfare went to the extreme of 'complete annihilation' of life. The vast majority of soldiers taken prisoner survived captivity, despite grim conditions and a tendency towards violent treatment and exploitation of their labour. Civilian labourers, whether forced and deported labour in German-occupied territory, or 'voluntary' and indentured colonial labour working for the Allies, generally had to be kept alive in the interest of war production, if not of humanity.

Nevertheless, there were real differences in military and political culture between the main belligerent nations. One, as Hull and several other historians have shown, was in the degree of control exercised by the civilian governments over the military: it was virtually absent in Germany; and while it was contested between military and civilian leaders in France and Britain to various degrees, ultimately civilian oversight, resting on national consent, won the day. In Russia it was precisely the power vacuum, where there should have been political control over the military, and the failure of the military leadership, that produced destabilization and revolution. Italy's uneasy balance between civilian decision-making at the start of the war and the increasing militarization of internal and military policy was also the precursor to the post-war catastrophe of destabilization and Fascism.

Hull's thesis on the continuity of the tendency to extreme destructiveness from Germany's colonial wars (notably in the genocide of the Herero in South-West Africa, 1904–7) to absolute destruction in the First World War rests on the idea of a long-term military culture which contained a 'dynamic towards extremes'.[11] Although only a few paragraphs in the conclusion discuss German development from the First World War to Nazism, Hull makes a strong case that military culture is just as important for the explanation of genocide in the Second World War as racist ideology and political culture. This is a compelling argument. Using sociological theories of bureaucratic organizations, Hull explains how 'basic assumptions that remain hidden from the actors' and that 'coalesce into a pattern' influenced the German military to at least as great a degree as explicit military doctrine.[12] However, it is not at all clear that 'a disproportionate, dysfunctional level of death and destruction produced routinely by the [German] military institution' and 'seemingly irrational acts of (self-) destruction' in the First World War were the monopoly of Germany.[13] The Italian supreme command's enormously wasteful attacks for little territorial and no strategic gain, its ruthless attempts to discipline army and civilian population alike, and the Russian army's profligate waste of lives, spring readily to mind. *Absolute Destruction*, in other words, offers a great deal to the attentive reader interested in German military culture, but does not fulfil its promise as a comparative work.

Some writers on war go to the opposite extreme. It was not German exceptionalism that caused the explosion of violence of the era of the First World War, some argue, but human nature itself. The First World War thus showed that once the veneer of civilization was removed, men were ultimately barbarians who rejoice in violence and killing. Sigmund Freud, whose psychoanalytic theories have had a profound influence on modern cultural theory, powerfully expressed the view writing in November 1914 that the human race had developed culture to the highest point, but had proved unworthy of it; the human race had to make way for a new species which would repeat the experiment of culture. Wolfgang Sofsky, a German sociologist who has written disturbing analyses of violence, war, and the system of concentration camps, shares Freud's gloomy view and further develops it:

> Violence is itself a product of human culture, a result of this experiment of culture. It is deployed according to the state of destructive forces as developed. Only those who believe in progress talk of regression. From time immemorial people have enjoyed destroying and murdering as if it were a matter of course. Their culture assists them to give form and shape to this potency. The problem does not lie in the gulf between the dark forces of instinct and the promises of the world of culture, but in the correspondence between violence and culture. By no means is culture pacifist. Rather, it counts as part of the disaster. In truth, humans are well suited to their cultures.[14]

This is not merely pessimism, which was entirely explicable in Freud's case in 1914 because of the shock of war, but an unhistorical and ultimately misanthropic view which ignores the role of political decision-makers. Without the decisions taken by some thirty or forty men in cabinets in European capitals in summer 1914, would violent cultures or primeval instincts have prevailed upon millions of men to hurl themselves into mortal danger and embark on a killing spree? Moreover, Sofsky's refusal to analyse the causes of war and violence and his anthropological focus on the forms of violence as social process mean that wartime violence is separated from any cultural and historical context. Development and systematic comparison fall by the wayside. Sofsky is an extreme example who stands for a broader trend among some writers to see the war as a juggernaut or a machine outside human control. Thus the French cultural theorist Paul Virilio wrote:

> Battle is now nothing more than the autonomy, or automation, of the war machine, with its virtually undetectable 'smart' weapons such as the Exocet missile, the Beluga bomb, the Tigerfish tornado, the 'Raygun Project' of lightning nuclear attack being studied by the Pentagon, the Doomsday machine . . . [15]

The influential Austrian-American economist Joseph Schumpeter (writing, notably, just after the war in 1919) traced a drive to belligerence and war back to the beginning of civilization in ancient Egypt, Assyria, and Persia, in which a 'war machine' was the essence of social and political organization. The cultural historian Daniel Pick takes this as the theme of his book, and writes of the relationship between modernity and military conflict, 'between political control and a violent machine that moves of its own accord'.[16] In other words, 'The "unstoppable engine of war" has become something of a modern truism.'[17] Even the Holocaust has been viewed by some commentators as the product of a modern 'murdering machine', 'a mundane extension of the modern factory system'.[18] As has been argued throughout this book, the present author finds that no matter how complex the arms technology, no matter how deep the cultural mobilization of hatred, no matter how impersonal the dynamic of destruction, it was ultimately identifiable human beings who had choices to make.

Another interpretation linking war and the culture of modern society is the influential book by George Mosse, *Fallen Soldiers*. Despite its misleadingly narrow title this is a fundamentally important text on the culture of the First World War. Discussing not only elite but also popular culture, Mosse showed how the cultural representation of war, especially its depiction as heroic, chivalrous combat in literature and iconography, the affirmation of the individual, and the worship of nature, served to deflect attention away from the horror and sordid reality of war and ultimately fed into the fascist appropriation of the memory of war. Germany was central to his analysis, but there are many comparative remarks on Britain, France, and Italy. Indeed, the trend of his argument was that there was a common 'Myth of the War Experience', which despite variation from nation to nation was valid everywhere. Over the course of the nineteenth century, Mosse argued, 'the nation absorbed the impulse of Christianity and of the French Revolution . . . War was made sacred, an expression of the general will of the people.'[19] Mosse had argued on similar lines in his earlier *The Nationalization of the Masses*: 'The general will became a secular religion, the people worshipping themselves, and the new politics sought to guide and formalize this worship.'[20] Formulations like these leave little space for variation between nations or political and social differentiation within nations, and place the working class and peasantry into the same category as bourgeois nationalists. Thus the discussion in *Fallen Soldiers* of the 'indescribable enthusiasm' for war in 1914 blithely extrapolates from the writings of (some) volunteers to the entire German army and nation.[21] This ignores the fact that volunteers were a small minority, and that those who were most likely to publish their patriotic sensibilities were from the educated bourgeoisie, who thus belonged to that relatively small class which was the most predisposed to aggressive nationalism. Perhaps the most influential part of *Fallen Soldiers* is the chapter devoted to the 'brutalization of German politics' after the war. Mosse located this process on the extreme right of German politics, but implied also a general drift in Germany towards 'a brutal tone of post-war politics' and 'indifference to the fate of others'.[22] In the final chapter of the present book I have attempted a European comparison of the 'brutalization' of politics after the war, and also a deconstruction of the concept to test its validity.

In writing this book I have greatly benefited from the work of several scholars in particular. Jay Winter, who has been a pioneering historian of the 'new cultural history of war', turned in the late 1980s (partly influenced by George Mosse) from demographic history and Britain in the First World War to a series of rigorously comparative studies of the war. *The Experience of World War I* (1988) is an all-round introduction to the war, with many excellent photographs, colour maps, and graphs. It is in many ways a model of comparative history, above all on the experience of war in Britain, France, and Germany, integrating military with social and cultural history. Because it remains a useful work of reference for anyone beginning study of the topic, three of its interpretations should be mentioned which recent research has modified: the tendency to deride military planning as unrealistic, to term operations (such as the Somme or Passchendaele) as futile slaughter that 'led nowhere', and to equate the war experience of each nation with those of others (e.g. in the idea that the war led to the 'militarization' of politics across post-war Europe).[23] Winter's subsequent work on the cultural memory of war and the collaborative project on London, Berlin, and Paris during the war are major contributions which have been equally stimulating for all those studying and writing about the First World War (*Sites of Memory, Sites of Mourning*; and *Capital Cities at War*).

Hew Strachan's authoritative work *To Arms*, the first of a three-volume series, is not only genuinely international, but also combines military, diplomatic, and economic history with a useful survey of the culture of war. However, the time-frame is essentially restricted to the pre-war years and the first year of war. The subsequent volumes are eagerly awaited. Holger Herwig's thoroughly researched book *The First World War*, as its subtitle indicates, is essential reading for Germany and Austria at war, with a particularly welcome emphasis on the latter, and also on the relationship between the two. Culture and mentalities are not part of Herwig's remit, but there are some unsurpassed passages on the reality of combat and the social and medical effects of war. The prolific team Gerhard Hirschfeld, Gerd Krumeich, and Irina Renz have been at the forefront of Great War historiography since the early 1990s, producing (and stimulating others to produce) high-quality work at the interface between military and cultural history; their influence can be traced throughout the present book. Their counterpart in France is the equally productive and innovative team Stéphane Audoin-Rouzeau and Annette Becker. I have found the most valuable introduction to the history of Italy during the war that by Mario Isnenghi and Giorgio Rochat, *La Grande Guerra*; the pre-war period was covered well by Richard Bosworth in *Italy and the Approach of War*, and Giovanna Procacci's books *Dalla Rassegnazione alla Rivolta* and *Soldati e prigionieri italiani* provide essential insights into the social history and mentalities of the period.

APPENDIX

Hague Convention (IV) Respecting the Laws and Customs of War on Land (1907)

Section I On Belligerents

ARTICLE 1

The laws, rights, and duties of war apply not only to armies, but also to militia and volunteer corps fulfilling the following conditions:

1. To be commanded by a person responsible for his subordinates;
2. To have a fixed distinctive emblem recognizable at a distance;
3. To carry arms openly; and
4. To conduct their operations in accordance with the laws and customs of war.

In countries where militia or volunteer corps constitute the army, or form part of it, they are included under the denomination 'army'.

ARTICLE 2

The inhabitants of a territory which has not been occupied, who, on the approach of the enemy, spontaneously take up arms to resist the invading troops without having had time to organize themselves in accordance with article 1, shall be regarded as belligerents if they carry arms openly and if they respect the laws and customs of war ...

Section II Hostilities

ARTICLE 25

The attack or bombardment, by whatever means, of towns, villages, dwellings, or buildings which are undefended is prohibited ...

ARTICLE 27

In sieges and bombardments all necessary steps must be taken to spare, as far as possible, buildings dedicated to religion, art, science, or charitable purposes,

historic monuments, hospitals, and places where the sick and wounded are collected, provided they are not being used at the time for military purposes.

It is the duty of the besieged to indicate the presence of such buildings or places
by distinctive and visible signs, which shall be notified to the enemy beforehand.

ARTICLE 28

The pillage of a town or place, even when taken by assault, is prohibited. . . .

Section III Military Authority over the Territory of the Hostile State

ARTICLE 46

Family honor and rights, the lives of persons, and private property, as well as
religious convictions and practice, must be respected.

Private property can not be confiscated.

ARTICLE 47

Pillage is formally forbidden. . . .

ARTICLE 50

No general penalty, pecuniary or otherwise, shall be inflicted upon the population
on account of the acts of individuals for which they can not be regarded as jointly
and severally responsible . . .

ARTICLE 52

Requisitions in kind and services shall not be demanded from municipalities or
inhabitants except for the needs of the army of occupation. They shall be in
proportion to the resources of the country, and of such a nature as not to involve
the inhabitants in the obligation of taking part in military operations against their
own country.

Such requisitions and services shall only be demanded on the authority of the
commander in the locality occupied.
. . .

ARTICLE 56

The property of municipalities, that of institutions dedicated to religion, charity
and education, the arts and sciences, even when state property, shall be treated as
private property.

All seizure of, destruction or wilful damage done to institutions of this character,
historic monuments, works of art and science, is forbidden, and should be made the
subject of legal proceedings.

Source: James Brown Scott (ed.), *Texts of the Peace Conferences at The Hague, 1899
and 1907* (Boston and London, 1908), pp. 209–29.

Notes

INTRODUCTION

1. 'Manifesto del futurismo' (first published in *Le Figaro,* 20 February 1909), in Marinetti, *Teoria e invenzione futurista,* ed. Luciano De Maria, pp. 7–14, here pp. 12–13. All translations from French, German, and Italian are by the author, unless otherwise indicated.

2. Donald Cameron Watt, *How War Came. The Immediate Origins of the Second World War, 1938–1939,* New York: Pantheon, 1989, pp. 5–8. I am grateful to Lothar Kettenacker for this reference.

3. Michael Geyer, 'Vom massenhaften Tötungshandeln', p. 115.

4. Cf. Horne and Kramer, *German Atrocities 1914*; Kramer, 'The War of Atrocities. Murderous scares and extreme combat'; id., 'War crimes'.

I THE BURNING OF LOUVAIN

1. Schivelbusch, *Eine Ruine im Krieg der Geister,* pp. 19–22. After the destruction, the university librarian Paul Delannoy estimated the number of books to be almost 300,000, and almost two thousand early printed books and medieval manuscripts—ibid., p. 23.—'Louvain' is the name used in the English-speaking world. It is in the Flemish part of Belgium, and should more properly be called 'Leuven'; however, for the sake of easy recognition, 'Louvain' is used in this book, without the intention of expressing a preference for one language or another.

2. This account of the destruction of Louvain is based on that in Horne and Kramer, *German Atrocities 1914,* esp. pp. 38–42, with further references to contemporary sources.

3. One American journalist who spent three days in Louvain before 25 August thought that as many as 200,000 Germans passed through the town. Cobb, *The Red Glutton,* p. 72. It is possible that a large part of the 1st Army, such as one army corps, passed through the town, which would be about 40,000 soldiers, but very unlikely that any more did so, and impossible for all of them to have been billeted there. Cobb's impression, at any rate, was that 'grey masses' of German troops completely filled every street, every shop, and every house in the town, and squares were 'jammed with horses and packed baggage trains and

supply wagons.' Ibid., pp. 70–1. This indicates that the town was an important transit base. Professor of history Léon van der Essen estimated in his report to the Belgian government that there were about 10,000 troops in the town.

4. Whitlock, *Belgium under the German Occupation* vol. 1, pp. 104–5.

5. Cuvelier, *L'Invasion allemande*, p. 291.

6. Ibid., pp. 293–301.

7. Bundesarchiv-Militärarchiv (BA-MA) Freiburg, PHD 6/145, ministry of war, bureau for the investigation of breaches of the laws of war: memorandum on the events in Louvain, submitted to the Reich Chancellor, 15 January 1915, appendix 63, p. 99. The '*White Book*' was the German official publication, *The Belgian People's War, a Violation of International Law/Die völkerrechtswidrige Führung*, to which reference is made below.

8. Anonymous letter of August 1914 in Delbrück, ed., *Der deutsche Krieg in Feldpostbriefen*, p. 106. The author excused the pillage by alleging that the French had behaved far worse in their own land.

9. 'The Sacking of Louvain', by Professor Leon van der Essen, cited in Charles Horne, ed., *Source Records of World War I*, vol. 2, pp. 153–8.

10. Michael and Eleanor Brock, eds., *Asquith. Letters to Venetia Stanley*, letter of 29 August 1914, p. 204.

11. *Kölnische Zeitung* 16 September 1914, 2nd morning edition.

12. Politisches Archiv des Auswärtigen Amts (PAAA) Berlin, R 20881, German translation fol. 39, original at fol 35: *Nieuwe Rotterdamsche Courant* 29 August 1914, evening edition C.

13. PAAA Berlin, R 20881, fol. 37, telegram German ambassador Rome to Foreign Ministry Berlin, 1 September 1914; 'L'Italie intellectuelle proteste contre l'incendie de Louvain', *Le Temps*, 2 September 1914.

14. The account of the events at Dinant is based on that in Horne and Kramer, *German Atrocities 1914*, pp. 42–52.

15. On the events in Andenne, see ibid., pp. 30–5.

16. BA Berlin, R 3003 ORA/RG bJ 594/20, fol. 28: post-war deposition Franz Worms, Guards Rifle Battalion.

17. *Kölnische Zeitung*, 21 September 1914, midday edition; 22 September, midday edition; 23 September, first morning edition.

18. Horne and Kramer, *German Atrocities 1914*, pp. 255–6. See *New York Times*, 22 September 1914, p. 10 (editorial). National Archives, Washington DC, State Department, 367.763 72116, memorandum on the 'Destruction of Historical Monuments in Europe 1914–15', 31 March 1915, listing the principal protests received. PAAA, Berlin, R 20886, fol. 148, [signature illegible] to Geheimer Rat Dr. Wilhelm von Bode, 6 October 1914.

19. Commission d'Enquête, *Rapports sur la violation du droit des gens* (1915–16), twentieth report (Tschoffen report), 3rd report, vol. 1, p. 56.

20. Mokveld, *The German Fury in Belgium*, pp. 121–2, 129; *Die völkerrechtswidrige Führung*, appendix D, summary memorandum, p. 236.

21. Horne and Kramer, *German Atrocities 1914*, p. 105.

22. Ibid., p. 41. Dupierreux referred to the destruction of the library of Alexandria by the Arabs in the 7th cent.

23. Cuvelier, *L'Invasion allemande*, p. 297.

24. Horne and Kramer, *German Atrocities 1914*, p. 41.

25. Cuvelier, *L'Invasion allemande*, pp. 287–9.

26. Cf. Horne and Kramer, *German Atrocities 1914*, p. 237.

27. Ibid., pp. 162–4.

28. [Germany] Auswärtiges Amt, *Die völkerrechtswidrige Führung des belgischen Volkskriegs*. An abbreviated version appeared in English translation as *The Belgian People's War, a Violation of International Law. Translations from the Official German White Book, Published by the Imperial Foreign Office* (New York, 1915). Translations into other languages included French, Swedish, and Spanish. The full text appeared in English only after the war (*The German Army in Belgium. The White Book of May 1915*). On the White Book, its relationship to the investigation by the Prussian Ministry of War, the editorial suppression of contrary evidence, distortions, and silences, in order to support the official thesis of a Belgian civilian insurrection, see Horne and Kramer, *German Atrocities 1914*, pp. 237–47.

29. *Die völkerrechtswidrige Führung des belgischen Volkskriegs*, p. 4; *The German Army in Belgium*, p. xvii.

30. *Die völkerrechtswidrige Führung des belgischen Volkskriegs*, p. 6; *The German Army in Belgium*, p. xviii; cf. appendix D and the attached evidence of German soldiers.

31. *The German Army in Belgium*, appendix D, p. 192.

32. Schöller, *Der Fall Löwen und das Weißbuch*, p. 70.

33. Horne and Kramer, *German Atrocities 1914*, pp. 237–8.

34. John Reed, 'German France', *Metropolitan Magazine*, New York, March 1915, p. xli, cited in Annette Becker, *Oubliés de la Grande Guerre*, pp. 50–1.

35. [Belgium], *The Case of Belgium in the Present War*, p. 44.

36. Ibid., p. xvi.

37. Hüppauf, 'Kriegsfotografie', in Michalka, ed., *Der Erste Weltkrieg*, p. 883.

38. Scott, ed., *Texts of the Peace Conferences at The Hague*, vol. 1, pp. 552–4.

39. [Prussian General Staff], *Kriegsbrauch im Landkriege*, translated into English as *The German War Book*.

40. Ibid., pp. 52–5.

41. [Germany], *Felddienst-Ordnung*, Appendix II, December 1911.

42. Horne and Kramer, *German Atrocities 1914*, pp. 149–50. On the war academy, Bucholz, *Moltke, Schlieffen, and Prussian War Planning*, pp. 185–91.

43. Philipp Zorn, 'Die beiden Haager Friedenskonferenzen von 1899 und 1907', in *Handbuch des Völkerrechts*, vol. 5 part 1, ed. Fritz Stier-Somlo, Stuttgart, 1915, cited in Hull, *Absolute Destruction*, p. 126.

44. Cf. Bourke, *An Intimate History of Killing*.

45. 'Die Kathedrale in Reims' 'The cathedral in Rheims', *Kunst und Künstler*, vol. 13 (1915), pp. 85–90, cited in Börsch-Supan, 'Die Reaktion der Zeitschriften "Kunst und Künstler" und "Die Kunst" auf den Ersten Weltkrieg', in Mommsen ed., *Kultur und Krieg*, p. 200.
46. Ibid.
47. Ernst Rump, private papers, Hamburg: Kriegsbriefe: Franz Nölken to Rump, 30 September 1914, emphasis in the original.
48. Herzog, *Ritter, Tod und Teufel*, pp. 44–5. Herzog had been invited to tour the war zones in Russia, Belgium, and France by General Litzmann, known for his Pan-German political sympathies; he was then attached to the army press office. In the elections of 1932 Herzog signed a pledge of support to Adolf Hitler. *Nationalblatt* 2 December 1939 (http://www.rheinbreitbach.net/heimatverein/herzog.htm, accessed on 28 June 2004).
49. Paul Dahms, 'Vor Soissons', *Tägliche Rundschau*, 9 March 1915, supplement, cited in Jannasch, *Untaten des preußisch-deutschen Militarismus*, pp. 55–6.
50. For a fine discussion of the broader debate and even divisions within the French intellectual community created by the 'Appeal to the World of Culture!' see Hanna, *The Mobilization of Intellect*, pp. 78–105 ('The *Kultur* War').
51. Horne and Kramer, *German Atrocities 1914*, pp. 285–7; Horne and Kramer, 'German "Atrocities" and Franco-German Opinion'.
52. Brocke, ' "Wissenschaft und Militarismus" ', pp. 677–8. The reference was to the sinking of the British passenger ship, the *Lusitania*, with the loss of 1,198 lives, including 127 US citizens.

2 THE RADICALIZATION OF WARFARE

1. Cited in Ludendorff, *Kriegführung und Politik*, p. 4.
2. Ibid.
3. Clausewitz, *On War*, pp. 84–5 (book 1, ch. 1). All emphases in the original.
4. Ibid., p. 102 (book 1, ch. 2).
5. Ibid., pp. 110–11 (book 1, ch. 2). I have added the word 'armed' because the German original, 'Streitkräfte', means precisely that.
6. Ibid., p. 106 (book 1, ch. 2).
7. Ibid., p. 110 (book 1, ch. 2).
8. Bucholz, *Moltke, Schlieffen, and Prussian War Planning*, p. 211.
9. Hanna, *The Mobilization of Intellect*, p. 24. Casualty figures from Stevenson, 'French strategy on the Western Front, 1914–1918', pp. 325–6.
10. Reichswehrministerium, *Sanitätsbericht*, pp. 31–436, passim. These figures do not include the IInd Army Corps in the 1st Army because the records were lost.
11. These figures are more useful in showing change over time than absolute totals of deaths, which the army medical service was not in a position to calculate. Since figures for the missing were often far higher than for those known to

have been killed, the actual death rates were at least double those shown here; the total of reported deaths in August and September 1914 was 54,064; the total missing was 81193. (Reichswehrministerium, *Sanitätsbericht*, vol. 3, p. 133*. Thus the total of 1,202,042 deaths from 1914 to 1918, as calculated by the German army medical service (ibid., p. 131*), is incomplete for two reasons: first, it leaves out August to November 1918, which were months of very high losses; second, it computes those missing at 771,659; the total was thus 1,973,701. (The medical service was presumably able to calculate separately the number of men taken prisoner from notifications via the International Red Cross.) The total of German military deaths in the Great War according to recent calculation was 2,037,000 men (including navy personnel and prisoners of war). See Hirschfeld, Krumeich, and Renz, eds., *Enzyklopädie Erster Weltkrieg*, 'Kriegsverluste', pp. 664–5. However, it remains unclear whether the large number of deaths in the heavy fighting August to November 1918 are included in this total.

12. Reichswehrministerium, *Sanitätsbericht*, vol. 3, p. 132*.
13. Ibid., pp. 36–7.
14. *Der Weltkrieg*, vol. 1, pp. 114–16.
15. Strachan, *The First World War*, vol. 1, p. 278.
16. Bundesarchiv (BA) Berlin, N 2089/1 fol. 329–30 (NL Gebsattel): Ludwig von Gebsattel to his brother Konstantin, 16 January 1915.
17. Kriegsarchiv (KA) Munich, HS 2309, war diary Rudolf Ritter von Xylander 1914–18, diary entry 25 August. Major von Xylander was member of the General Staff of the Sixth Army.
18. BA Berlin, N 2089/1 fol. 329–30 (NL Gebsattel): Lerchenfeld to Gebsattel, 15 December 1914.
19. Strachan, *The First World War*, vol. 1, p. 160.
20. BA Berlin, N2089/1, Nachlaß Konstantin Freiherr von Gebsattel, Ludwig von Gebsattel to Konstantin, 3 April 1915.
21. Ibid., Gebsattel to Major-General Keim (governor of Limburg province), 21 March 1916.
22. Ibid., Captain Theodor Frhr. v. Karg-Bebenburg, Péronne, to Gebsattel, 10 October 1914.
23. Ibid., Th. Pölnitz, to Gebsattel, 4 December 1914.
24. Fussell, *The Great War and Modern Memory*, pp. 131–4.
25. Becker, 'Guerre totale et troubles mentaux', p. 136.
26. Ibid., p. 147.
27. Robertson to Haig, 15 September 1917, cited in French, 'The strategy of unlimited warfare?' p. 295.
28. Sir Launcelot Kiggell, note on the Chantilly conference, November 1916, cited in Stevenson, 'French strategy on the Western Front', pp. 311–12.
29. Ibid., pp. 316, 322–3, 325–6.
30. Neitzel, 'Zum strategischen Mißerfolg verdammt?', p. 184.

31. Gat, *Fascist and Liberal Visions of War*, pp. 52–63.
32. Hanna, *The Mobilization of Intellect*, pp. 57, 62–3, and 255 fn. 32; 'Studenten', in Hirschfeld et al., eds., *Enzyklopädie Erster Weltkrieg*, pp. 910–12.
33. Cited in Hull, *Absolute Destruction*, p. 228.
34. BA Berlin, N2089/1, NL Konstantin Freiherr von Gebsattel, Captain Theodor Frhr. v. Karg-Bebenburg, Péronne, to Gebsattel, Aizecourt-le-Haut [8 km from Péronne] to Gebsattel, 17 January 1915.
35. Becker, *Oubliés de la Grande Guerre*, p. 44, also for both quotations.
36. Vanneste, 'Het eerste "IJzeren Gordijn"?', pp. 39–82. I am grateful to Guy Hoebeke, of Wachtebeke, for making this article available to me. The US ambassador, Brand Whitlock, mentioned the electrified fence several times in *Belgium under the German Occupation,* vol. 1, pp. 105, 395–6.
37. Föllmer, 'Der Feind im Salon', pp. 6–7.
38. Becker, *Oubliés de la Grande Guerre*, p. 49. The economic history of the German occupation still awaits its historian.
39. Centre for the Preservation of Historical-Documentary Collections (CPHDC) Moscow, 1280–2–24, undated study [probably of 1918/19] on a memorandum of 1916 on 'Die Industrie im besetzten Frankreich', Great General Staff, Information Department of the War Historical Department 2, Berlin, 11 March 1919.
40. BA Berlin, R/1501 119491, Bericht über die Tätigkeit der Politischen Abteilung bei dem General-Gouverneur in Belgien für die Zeit der Besetzung, von der Lancken, 30 June 1920, pp. 94–9.
41. Pirenne, *La Belgique et la guerre mondiale*, pp. 201–4.
42. De Schaepdrijver, *La Belgique et la Première Guerre mondiale*, p. 216.
43. Einem, *Ein Armeeführer erlebt den Weltkrieg*, diary entry 7 June 1918, p. 405.
44. Marks, *Innocent Abroad*, p. 180. In the end the Allies agreed on a sum of $500 million, which was in fact paid by 1925. Ibid., pp. 202–3.
45. Horne and Kramer, *German Atrocities 1914*, p. 166.
46. Becker, *Oubliés de la Grande Guerre*, pp. 55–6.
47. 3rd OHL to General Governors in Belgium and Warsaw, 13 September 1916, cited in Otto and Schmiedel, eds., *Der erste Weltkrieg*, p. 194; Köhler, *Die Staatsverwaltung der besetzten Gebiete*, p. 151.
48. Commission d'enquête, *Rapports sur les déportations,* vol. 2, pp. 24–5; see also de Schaepdrijver, *La Belgique et la Première Guerre mondiale*, pp. 220–31, who explains the development of the policy and the harsh exploitation.
49. Becker, *Oubliés de la Grande Guerre*, p. 63.
50. Gerard, *My Four Years in Germany*, p. 351.
51. BA Berlin, R/1501 119491, Bericht über die Tätigkeit der Politischen Abteilung bei dem General-Gouverneur in Belgien für die Zeit der Besetzung, von der Lancken, 30 June 1920, pp. 94–9; Pirenne, *La Belgique et la guerre mondiale*, p. 193.

52. Commission d'enquête, *Rapports sur les déportations*, vol. 2, pp. 24–5. Isabel Hull cites another Belgian official report which found that between 3 and 4 per cent of deportees had died. In addition, 35.8 per cent were ill when they returned home, and 5.2 per cent were maimed or invalided. These figures appear to include those deported to work behind the front in Belgium and France. Hull, *Absolute Destruction*, p. 240.

53. Cited in Becker, *Oubliés de la Grande Guerre*, pp. 355–6.

54. Gerard, *My Four Years in Germany*, pp. 339–40.

55. Horne and Kramer, *German Atrocities*, pp. 342–3.

56. Liulevicius, 'Von "Ober Ost" nach "Ostland"?', pp. 296–8.

57. Hull, *Absolute Destruction*, pp. 246–7.

58. Liulevicius, *War Land on the Eastern Front*. See my review in *German History*, 20, 2 (2002), 255–6.

59. Liulevicius, 'Von "Ober Ost" nach "Ostland"?', pp. 299–302 and 309.

60. BA Berlin, R/1501 119491, Bericht über die Tätigkeit der Politischen Abteilung bei dem General-Gouverneur in Belgien für die Zeit der Besetzung, von der Lancken, 30 June 1920, p. 107.

61. De Schaepdrijver, *La Belgique et la Première Guerre mondiale*, p. 248.

62. For the latter point: O'Brien, *Mussolini in the First World War*, p. 183.

63. Melograni, *Storia politica della Grande guerra*, p. 65.

64. Ibid., p. 44.

65. Quoted in ibid., p. 68.

66. Procacci, *Soldati e prigionieri italiani nella Grande guerra*, pp. 70–4.

67. Herwig, *The First World War*, p. 336.

68. Cadorna, *La Guerra alla fronte italiana*, vol. 2, pp. 116–17. On the losses: Herwig, *First World War*, p. 336, based on Austro-Hungarian figures; Isenghi and Rochat, *La Grande Guerra*, p. 205, give similar figures. Kiszling, *Österreich-Ungarns Anteil*, p. 64, puts Italian losses at 156,000 and Austrian losses at 100,000.

69. Stevenson, 'French strategy on the Western Front', pp. 325–6.

70. Ludendorff, *Meine Kriegserinnerungen*, pp. 383–4.

71. Giulio Douhet, *Diario critico di guerra*, vol. 1, *1915*, p. 262, quoted in Procacci, *Soldati*, p. 74.

72. Ibid., p. 70.

73. Cadorna, *La Guerra alla fronte italiana*, vol. 2, pp. 120–1, 125.

74. Kiszling, *Österreich-Ungarns Anteil*, p. 65.

75. Reichsarchiv, *Der Weltkrieg 1914 bis 1918*, vol. 13, pp. 249–50; Fadini, *Caporetto*, pp. 282–3.

76. Fadini, *Caporetto*, pp. 232–3.

77. Quoted in ibid., p. 241. It is not clear whether Krafft von Dellmensingen or General von Hofacker is cited here.

78. Isenghi and Rochat, *La Grande Guerra*, pp. 381–2. The figure is 600,000 if those fleeing cities like Treviso and Venice for fear of invasion are counted—ibid.,

p. 421. Cf. Herwig, *First World War*, pp. 339–42; Kiszling, *Österreich-Ungarns Anteil*, p. 68.

79. Fadini, *Caporetto*, p. 426, diary entry 29 December 1917.

80. *Relazioni della Reale Commissione*, vol. 1, p. 130.

81. Ibid., pp. 129–30.

82. *Relazioni della Reale Commissione*, vol. 2, pp. 330–1. Vol. 2 contains a precise list of the attacks, city by city, with numbers of victims, pp. 343–55, and following this there is a table of estimates of costs, presumably for submission to the Paris peace conference.

83. *Relazioni della Reale Commissione*, vol. 1, pp. 100, 109–10.

84. Ibid., pp. 144–7, 180.

85. *Verhandlungen des Reichstags. XIII. Legislaturperiode. 2. Session*, vol. 308, *Stenographische Berichte*, p. 1691; *Relazioni della Reale Commissione*, vol. 1, pp. 100–8. This was documented also by the capture of several German troops in 1915. A list of the captured Germans appears as appendix.

86. *Relazioni della Reale Commissione*, vol. 1, p. 100.

87. Ibid., p. 111.

88. Ibid., p. 115.

89. Kuhl, *Der Weltkrieg 1914–1918*, vol. 2, p. 218.

90. Herwig, *The First World War*, p. 344.

91. Corni, 'Die Bevölkerung von Venetien', pp. 316–19.

92. *Relazioni della Reale Commissione*, vol. 3, pp. 569–76.

93. Ibid., pp. 578–9, 591–2.

94. Ibid., pp. 592–3, 601.

95. Ibid., pp. 579–82.

96. Cf. note of 26 May 1918, by the commander of the district and city of Udine, in ibid., p. 583.

97. Ibid., pp. 583–8.

98. Memorandum by the chief of the general staff of the field army, Hindenburg, to the secretary of state in the foreign ministry, Kühlmann, 23 December 1917, in Otto and Schmiedel, *Der erste Weltkrieg*, pp. 276–7.

99. Ceschin, ' "L'estremo oltraggio" ', p. 14. I should like to express my gratitude to Dr Ceschin for making a copy of his paper available to me.

100. *Relazioni della Reale Commissione*, vol. 4, pp. 134–5. The source given is the *Commissione per la valutazione dei danni di guerra* presided over by the minister for the liberated territories, but no date etc. Presumably this includes the death-toll for the invasion, because there is no figure given separately.

101. *Relazioni della Reale Commissione*, vol. 4, p. 138.

102. Ibid., p. 140. On pp. 141–9 there are brief summaries of such killings in the context of requisitions or robbery.

103. Figures from 'Kriegsgefangene', in Hirschfeld et al., eds., *Enzyklopädie Erster Weltkrieg*, p. 641.

104. Cited in Afflerbach, *Falkenhayn*, p. 182.

105. BA-MA Freiburg, PH 5 II 185, 8. Armee, I. AOK, 1141 g, Erfahrungen des I. Reservekorps auf dem Gebiete des Gefangenenwesens, der Trophaen usw. Kortau, 31.8.14. I am grateful to my former research student Dr Heather Jones for this important reference.

106. Horne and Kramer, *German Atrocities 1914*, pp. 348–51.

107. Bourke, *An Intimate History of Killing*, p. 242.

108. ACS Rome, Presidenza del Consiglio dei Ministri 1915–1918, Busta 98, 19.4.6: unspecified press reports in Austria on 21 July 1918.

109. Bourke, *An Intimate History of Killing*, p. 182; for an example of such 'expediency' in 1917, see p. 189.

110. Selmar Blass, medical officer in Bavarian Infantry Regiment 4, report on his capture to German army, 7 December 1916, in Hirschfeld et al., eds., *Die Deutschen an der Somme*, pp. 135–8.

111. Ernst Rump, private papers, Hamburg: Kriegsbriefe: letters from Noyon to his wife, 23 September and 25 September 1914.

112. Jones, *The Enemy Disarmed.*

113. Wurzer, 'Die Erfahrung der Extreme', pp. 97 and 108. The figure in Herwig, *The First World War*, p. 358, is 500,000 deaths, which probably results from conflating these two categories. The figure given by Rachamimov is higher still: 2.77 million Habsburg prisoners. Alon Rachamimov, *POWs and the Great War: Captivity on the Eastern Front*, Oxford, 2002.

114. Andreas Hilger, review of Georg Wurzer, *Die Kriegsgefangenen der Mittelmächte in Russland im Ersten Weltkrieg*, Göttingen, 2005, in *sehepunkte.historicum.net/ 2006/03/9738.html*. Rüdiger Overmans estimates the number of German prisoners in Russia to be 170,000, and the death toll at 20 per cent: ' "Hunnen" und "Untermenschen" ', pp. 343 and 348.

115. Doegen, *Kriegsgefangene Völker*, p. 56.

116. Einem, *Ein Armeeführer erlebt den Weltkrieg*, letter to his wife, 3 March 1916, p. 196.

117. Procacci, *Soldati e prigionieri italiani*. The higher figure was given by an Italian NCO who had been employed in the statistical office of the Habsburg prisoner of war administration for all camps: ACS Roma, PCM Busta 98, 19.4.5, CS Servizio I Sezione U, to PCM, and Min Aff. Est. 4 June 1918. The total number of deaths could be much higher because Germany and Austria-Hungary were unable to provide figures for deaths in the labour companies, where the majority of prisoners worked. In addition there were many premature deaths among prisoners after their repatriation, above all from tuberculosis. Procacci, *Soldati e prigionieri italiani*, p. 171.

118. Doegen, *Kriegsgefangene Völker*, p. 56.

119. Wurzer, 'Die Erfahrung der Extreme'.

120. Procacci, *Soldati e prigionieri italiani*; Kramer, 'Italienische Kriegsgefangene im Ersten Weltkrieg'.

121. Procacci, *Soldati e prigionieri italiani,* pp. 174–5.

122. Spitzer, *Italienische Kriegsgefangenenbriefe*, pp. 192–3.
123. ACS Rome, PCM Busta 99 bis, Sub-file 85/4 Condizioni dei prigionieri italiani, high command information section R to prime minister, foreign minister, war minister, interior minister, and high command press office, 29 January 1918.
124. Cited in Becker, *Oubliés de la Grande Guerre*, pp. 102–3.
125. Spitzer, *Italienische Kriegsgefangenenbriefe*, p. 214.

3 THE WARRIORS

1. Gilbert, *The End of the European Era*, pp. 104–21.
2. Lloyd George, *War Memoirs*; Sidney Bradshaw Fay, *The Origins of the World War*, New York, 1934, both cited in Strachan, *To Arms*, p. 2; Henry Kissinger, *Diplomacy*, New York, 1994, cited in Herwig, *The First World War*, p. 23.
3. Cf. Hobsbawm, *Age of Empire*, pp. 312–14, 323–7. Cf. Lenin, *Imperialism*, pp. 744–5.
4. Kaiserliches Statistisches Amt, ed., *Statistisches Jahrbuch für das Deutsche Reich*, *1914*, pp. 257–8.
5. Lieven, *Russia and the Origins of the First World War*, p. 134; *Statistisches Jahrbuch für das Deutsche Reich*, *1914*, pp. 257–8.
6. Dülffer, 'Der Weg in den Krieg', p. 236.
7. Lenin, 'The War and Russian Social-Democracy', p. 652.
8. Mommsen, *Großmachtstellung und Weltpolitik*, p. 293.
9. Kennedy, *The Rise of the Anglo-German Antagonism*, p. 459; Lloyd George, *War Memoirs*, vol. 1, pp. 65–6.
10. This is argued by Jost Dülffer, linking the arms race with the nations' perception of potential enemies, but carefully distinguishing armaments budget increases from actual intentions to go to war: 'Der Weg in den Krieg'. It is argued at greater length by Herrmann, *The Arming of Europe*, *passim*, but esp. pp. 228–32.
11. Dülffer, 'Der Weg in den Krieg', p. 239.
12. Mommsen, *Großmachtstellung und Weltpolitik*, pp. 168–75.
13. Ibid., pp. 250–1.
14. Lieutenant-Commander J. M. Kenworthy (Lord Strabolgi), cited in Marder, *From the Dreadnought to Scapa Flow*, vol. 1, p. 429.
15. Offer, *The First World War: An Agrarian Interpretation*, p. 81.
16. Mommsen, *Großmachtstellung und Weltpolitik*, pp. 251–2.
17. Mombauer, *Moltke*, pp. 138–9; quotation from Bethmann Hollweg, letter of 20 December 1912, ibid.
18. Seligmann, ' "A barometer of national confidence" ', p. 338.
19. Crook, *Darwinism, War and History*, p. 30. On the 'unspoken assumptions' of pre-war Europe, see Joll, *The Origins of the First World War*. The debate about

social Darwinism is complex: the right-wing politicians and military men in Germany and Austria had no monopoly on social Darwinist thought, and many of its proponents in the late nineteenth and early twentieth centuries were politically on the Left. With good grounds Darwinism could be used by pacifists to condemn war because it ensured that the strongest were least likely to survive. See the stimulating article by Evans, 'In Search of German Social Darwinism'.

20. Bernhardi, *Deutschland und der nächste Krieg*, translated into English as *Germany and the Next War*.

21. On the influence of vulgarized Darwinism (via Haeckel) on Bethmann Hollweg, see Jarausch, *The Enigmatic Chancellor*, pp. 12–24: Haeckel and Darwin were Bethmann's first serious reading after school. Falkenhayn: Afflerbach, *Falkenhayn*, pp. 152, 170–1. On Conrad, see Strachan, *First World War*, vol. 1, pp. 68–9. On Moltke see Mombauer, *Moltke*, pp. 153, 176, 282, 285, 287.

22. Cited in Geiss, ed., *July 1914*, pp. 34–5; cf. Lindemann, *Les Doctrines Darwiniennes*, pp. 210–14.

23. Lindemann, *Les Doctrines Darwiniennes*, p. 211. On the pessimistic fatalism of Conrad, see Strachan, *First World War*, vol. 1, p. 69. On German leaders' racist conception of the inevitable conflict between Slavs and Germans, Lindemann, *Les Doctrines Darwiniennes*, pp. 224–48.

24. Moltke to Conrad, 10 February 1913, in Conrad von Hötzendorff, *Aus meiner Dienstzeit*, vol. 3, pp. 144–7; also cited in Kantorowicz, *Gutachten zur Kriegsschuldfrage*, p. 204.

25. Conrad von Hötzendorff, *Aus meiner Dienstzeit*, vol. 3, letter 15 February 1913, p. 149.

26. Quoted in Lieven, *Russia and the Origins of the First World War*, p. 44.

27. On social Darwinism in British intellectual life, see Crook, *Darwinism, War and History*, pp. 72–91, and *passim*. On British army officers, see Travers, 'Technology, tactics and morale', esp. pp. 282–4. On Fuller's social Darwinism before 1914 see Gat, *Fascist and Liberal Visions of War*, pp. 14–15.

28. Storz, *Kriegsbild und Rüstung vor 1914*, p. 229.

29. Travers, 'Technology, tactics and morale', p. 272.

30. Hamilton, writing in *Compulsory Service*, cited in ibid., p. 282. Hamilton, as Travers drily comments, 'was, however, to find out otherwise at Gallipoli'.

31. Bernhardi, *Taktik und Ausbildung der Infanterie*, p. 184.

32. Ibid., pp. 184–5.

33. Ibid., p. 194.

34. Bloch, *Der Krieg*, vol. 6, p. 35.

35. According to the Sanitätsbericht, the total size of German army, including officers, medics, etc., in August 1914 was 1,602,706. Reichswehrministerium, *Sanitätsbericht*, vol. 3, appendix, p. 5; Reichsarchiv, *Der Weltkrieg*, vol. 1, pp. 69, 646. Other estimates of the size of the army on mobilization are far higher: Strachan, *First World War*, vol. 1, p. 174, gives a figure of 3.8 million men.

Possibly the discrepancy arises from the successive call-up of reserves and the increase in the number of volunteers: not all could be immediately absorbed in August, but only over the subsequent months. The official war history, Reichsarchiv, *Der Weltkrieg 1914 bis 1918. Kriegsrüstung und Kriegswirtschaft, Anlagen zum ersten Band*, provides a figure of 725,000 NCOs and men, plus 29,000 as the peacetime strength of the army in 1914, and a wartime establishment of 3,823,000 men and officers, without colonial troops, including occupation troops (p. 510, table 19). For further information see the pull-out table after p. 508, and the text volume, p. 217. The reference to occupation troops indicates the figure of 3.8 million refers to the end of 1914.

36. 'Infanteriewaffen', in Hirschfeld et al., eds., *Enzyklopädie Erster Weltkrieg*, p. 576; Bourne, *Britain and the Great War*, p. 18.
37. Linnenkohl, *Vom Einzelschuß zur Feuerwalze*, pp. 16–26; 'Infanteriewaffen', in Hirschfeld et al., eds., *Enzyklopädie Erster Weltkrieg*, p. 577. Because of the shortage of the Hotchkiss gun the French also used the Puteaux 1905 and St Etienne 1907 which weighed 60 kg. and 57 kg. respectively.
38. Hutchison, *Machine Guns*, p. 129.
39. Storz, *Kriegsbild und Rüstung vor 1914*, pp. 31–2.
40. Cited in Hutchison, *Machine Guns*, p. 103.
41. Förster, *Der doppelte Militarismus*, p. 267; Strachan, *First World War*, vol. 1, p. 191.
42. Stevenson, *Armaments and the Coming of War*, table 4, p. 6. He writes: 'This measure is now accepted as the best economic indicator of the defence "burden" . . . It was not available to contemporaries, who used per capita figures . . .'
43. Storz, *Kriegsbild und Rüstung vor 1914*, p. 300; Smith et al., *France and the Great War*, p. 22.
44. Strachan, *First World War*, vol. 1, p. 194.
45. Lieven, *Russia and the Origins of the First World War*, p. 48.
46. Geyer, *Russian Imperialism*, pp. 261–4.
47. Keiger, *France and the Origins of the First World War*, pp. 88–102.
48. Cf. Kennedy, *The Rise of the Anglo-German Antagonism*; Stibbe, *German Anglophobia*, and see below, Ch. 5.
49. Strachan, *First World War*, vol. 1, pp. 198–200; Bourne, *Britain and the Great War*, p. 156.
50. Mommsen, 'Deutschland', in Hirschfeld et al., eds., *Enzyklopädie Erster Weltkrieg*, p. 15.
51. Ibid., p. 16; Herwig, *The First World War*, pp. 20–1.
52. Farrar, *The Short-War Illusion*.
53. Förster, 'Der deutsche Generalstab und die Illusion des kurzen Krieges', p. 66.
54. Goltz, *Denkwürdigkeiten*, p. 293.
55. Mombauer, *Moltke*, p. 118 n. 39.
56. Moltke to Bethmann Hollweg, 29 July 1914, in Geiss, ed., *July 1914*, pp. 282–4.
57. Afflerbach, *Falkenhayn*, pp. 161–7.

58. Seligmann, 'Germany and the origins of the First World War', p. 322.
59. Rauchensteiner, 'Österreich-Ungarn', in *Enzyklopädie Erster Weltkrieg*, pp. 64—5.
60. Lieven, *Russia and the Origins of the First World War*, pp. 36—40.
61. Strachan, *First World War*, vol. 1, p. 69.
62. Williamson, *Austria-Hungary and the Origins of the First World War*, pp. 48—9, 87—8.
63. Ibid., p. 194.
64. Kronenbitter, '*Krieg im Frieden*', pp. 449—51.
65. Ibid., pp. 386—7.
66. Ibid., pp. 386—7, 398—401.
67. Cited in ibid., p. 401.
68. Ibid., pp. 403, 412—13, 426.
69. Ibid., pp. 418—19; 427—8.
70. Cited in ibid., p. 451.
71. Ibid., pp. 436—46, 452—4.
72. *Österreich-Ungarns Außenpolitik*, vol. 8, the Hungarian prime minister Tisza to the Kaiser, 1 July 1914, p. 248. Emphasis added.
73. Cf. Kantorowicz, *Gutachten zur Kriegsschuldfrage*, p. 284.
74. *Österreich-Ungarns Außenpolitik*, vol. 8, p. 343.
75. Ibid., pp. 349—50.
76. Cited in Fellner, 'Austria-Hungary', p. 15
77. Cited in Kronenbitter, '*Krieg im Frieden*', p. 407.
78. Conrad von Hötzendorff, *Aus meiner Dienstzeit*, vol. 3, report by military attaché Baron Bienerth to Conrad on conversation with Moltke, 19 February 1913, p. 151.
79. Williamson, *Austria-Hungary and the Origins of the First World War*, p. 211.
80. Kronenbitter, '*Krieg im Frieden*', p. 468. Williamson was clearly incorrect to argue that Tisza's wishes were respected to take no further Slavs into the empire: *Austria-Hungary and the Origins of the First World War*, p. 204.
81. Fellner, 'Austria-Hungary', p. 13.
82. Cited in Kronenbitter, '*Krieg im Frieden*', pp. 485—6.
83. Williamson, *Austria-Hungary and the Origins of the First World War*, p. 204.
84. Circular of 23 July 1914, in Biwald, *Von Helden und Krüppeln*, vol. 1, p. 142.
85. ACS Rome, Salandra 32, telegram legation Belgrade 20 July 1914.
86. Cf. Kronenbitter, '*Krieg im Frieden*', p. 405.
87. Cited in ibid., p. 529.
88. Quoted in Fellner, 'Austria-Hungary', p. 14.
89. Fritz Fellner argues that Germany was entirely responsible for escalating what would have been a local war against Serbia, with Germany guaranteeing the safety of Austria-Hungary against attack by Russia, into a preventive, general European war, thus betraying the interests of Austria-Hungary. 'Austria-Hungary', pp. 19—23. In the light of the Habsburg leaders' awareness of the high risk of a European war, this argument appears to be overstated, and ignores the

decision-making process in Russia. Cf. Strachan, *The First World War*, vol. 1, pp. 75–70.

90. A useful discussion of the role of Germany in the July crisis can be found in Mombauer, *Moltke*, pp. 182–226.

91. Berghahn, *Sarajewo*, pp. 104–5. A similar opinion is expressed by Keiger, *France and the Origins of the First World War*, pp. 148–9.

92. Cited in Röhl, 'Germany', p. 44.

93. Fischer, *Krieg der Illusionen*, p. 584; this conversation is variously dated 19 May and 3 June, owing to the fact that the record of the conversation originates in a post-war memoir of Jagow; cf. Röhl, 'Germany', p. 46. The crucial point is unaffected, however: it was well before the assassination at Sarajevo.

94. Strachan, *The First World War*, vol. 1, p. 73; Röhl, 'Germany', p. 37.

95. Mombauer, *Moltke*, pp. 190–1.

96. Fischer, *Griff nach der Weltmacht* (Eng. edn., *Germany's Aims in the First World War*).

97. Fischer, *Griff nach der Weltmacht*, pp. 113–20.

98. BA Berlin, N2089/1, Nachlaß Konstantin Freiherr von Gebsattel, General-oberst v. Kessel, Berlin to Gebsattel, 14 November 1914, citing from a letter from Bethmann.

99. Cited in Kotowski, ' "Noch ist ja der Krieg gar nicht zu Ende" ', p. 425.

100. Fischer, *Krieg der Illusionen*, p. 671; cf. Mombauer, *Moltke*, p. 189.

101. Afflerbach, *Falkenhayn*, p. 170.

102. Mombauer, *Moltke*, pp. 212–27, esp. p. 227.

103. Wilson, 'Britain', pp. 183, 187.

104. Ibid., p. 195; the remark was made in a letter of 1 August.

105. Ibid., p. 179.

106. Bourne, *Britain and the Great War*, p. 3.

107. Quoted in Hamilton and Herwig, *Decisions for War, 1914–1917*, pp. 141, 143.

108. Bourne, *Britain and the Great War*, pp. 3–6; cf. Nasson, *The South African War*, pp. 286–7.

109. Bourne, *Britain and the Great War*, pp. 6–7; this argument is advanced primarily by Ferguson, *The Pity of War*.

110. Grey, *Twenty-Five Years*, vol. 2, p. 20; Steiner, *Britain and the Origins of the First World War*, p. 240. Grey wrote at the end of 1915 of his hatred of war: 'I hated it beforehand & I hate it now, though I do not see how it could have been avoided.' Steiner, 'The foreign office and the war', p. 517.

111. Philpott, 'Why the British Were Really on the Somme', p. 452. Haig, in August 1914 commander of the I Army Corps, shared Kitchener's views. See also the entries for Haig and Kitchener in *Dictionary of National Biography 1912–1921*, eds. H. W. C. Davis and J. R. H. Weaver (Oxford, 1927), and *DNB 1922–1930*.

112. Bourne, *Britain and the Great War*, p. 18; Strachan, *The First World War*, vol. 1, p. 206.

113. Kennedy, *The Rise of the Anglo-German Antagonism*, pp. 459–60, quotation p. 459.

114. Offer, *The First World War: An Agrarian Interpretation*, pp. 250–3, 278.

115. Stone, *The Eastern Front*, p. 218.

116. Müller, *Die Nation als Waffe und Vorstellung*, pp. 204–9; cf. Cornwall, *The Undermining of Austria-Hungary*, 2000.

117. French, ' "Had we known how bad things were in Germany" ', p. 69.

118. French, 'The strategy of unlimited warfare?' pp. 287–94.

119. Müller, *Die Nation als Waffe und Vorstellung*, p. 215.

120. Keiger, *France and the Origins of the First World War*, p. 75. Cf. Becker, *1914. Comment les Français sont entrés dans la Guerre*.

121. Keiger, *France and the Origins of the First World War*, pp. 97, 144, 167.

122. Duroselle, *La Grande Guerre des Français*, p. 37.

123. Becker, 'Frankreich', p. 32; Keiger, *France and the Origins of the First World War*, p. 72.

124. Horne, 'Der Schatten des Krieges', p. 146.

125. Keiger, 'France', pp. 142–5.

126. Smith et al., *France and the Great War*, pp. 29–30.

127. Keiger, 'Poincaré, Clemenceau, and the quest for total victory', p. 261.

128. Holquist, *Making War, Forging Revolution*, p. 15.

129. Geyer, *Russian Imperialism*, pp. 65–85.

130. Lieven, *Russia and the Origins of the First World War*, pp. 21, 27, 38, 51–7.

131. Report of the two chiefs of staff, 24 December 1906, cited in Geyer, *Russian Imperialism*, p. 252.

132. Lincoln, *In War's Dark Shadow*, p. 408.

133. Geyer, *Russian Imperialism*, pp. 256–7.

134. Kronenbitter, 'Krieg im Frieden', pp. 374, 381; Lincoln, *In War's Dark Shadow*, pp. 410–11.

135. Lieven, *Russia and the Origins of the First World War*, pp. 63–4.

136. Kronenbitter, 'Krieg im Frieden', pp. 382–3.

137. Fischer, *Krieg der Illusionen*, pp. 483–504; brief summary in Strachan, *The First World War*, vol. 1, pp. 60–1.

138. Lincoln, *In War's Dark Shadow*, pp. 416–19.

139. Lieven, *Russia and the Origins of the First World War*, p. 49.

140. Geiss, *German Foreign Policy*, p. 158.

141. Geyer, *Russian Imperialism*, pp. 274 and 312.

142. Kronenbitter, 'Krieg im Frieden', pp. 383, 390, 429, 449–52.

143. Lieven, *Russia and the Origins of the First World War*, p. 66; 72–4; 125; 137–8; cf. p. 116 for pan-Slavism in the officer corps.

144. Ibid., p. 139. For a detailed, balanced discussion of Russia's role in the July crisis, see ibid., pp. 139–54.

145. Joll, *The Origins of the First World War*, p. 66.

146. Geyer, *Russian Imperialism*, pp. 312–13.

147. Dahlmann, 'Rußland', p. 88; Strachan, *The First World War*, vol. 1, pp. 81–2.
148. Menning, *Bayonets Before Bullets*, pp. 211–12, 226.
149. Ibid., p. 216.
150. Lieven, *Russia and the Origins of the First World War*, p. 113.
151. Menning, *Bayonets Before Bullets*, pp. 227, 233–4; Strachan, *The First World War*, vol. 1, pp. 297–9.
152. Lieven, *Russia and the Origins of the First World War*, pp. 108–9.
153. Letter of 13 March 1914, Conrad, *Aus meiner Dienstzeit*, vol. 3, p. 611.
154. Kantorowicz, *Gutachten zur Kriegsschuldfrage*, p. 91; cf. [Kautsky], *Die Deutschen Dokumente zum Kriegsausbruch 1914*, vol. 2, document 445, p. 169.
155. Menning, *Bayonets Before Bullets*, pp. 242–6.
156. Lincoln, *Passage Through Armageddon*, pp. 44–7.
157. Pavlowitch, *Serbia*, pp. 87–8; cf. Dedijer, *The Road to Sarajevo*, pp. 160–284.
158. Dedijer, *The Road to Sarajevo*, pp. 202–3.
159. Ibid., pp. 175, 178, 197, 207–8.
160. Ibid., p. 288. I have modernized the translation.
161. Kellerhoff, *Attentäter*, p. 226; Berghahn, *Sarajewo*. See also Förster, 'Im Reich des Absurden'.
162. Cornwall, 'Serbia', p. 57.
163. Kronenbitter, *'Krieg im Frieden'*, pp. 456–7.
164. Malcolm, *Kosovo*, pp. 58–80, 310.
165. Boeckh, *Von den Balkankriegen zum Ersten Weltkrieg*, pp. 118–22.
166. *Österreich-Ungarns Außenpolitik*, vol. 7, report 26 January 1914, pp. 779–80.
167. Kronenbitter, *'Krieg im Frieden'*, pp. 435, 488.
168. Great Britain, War Office, *Armies of the Balkan States 1914–1918*, pp. 48–52. The estimate was made in 1915.
169. Cornwall, 'Serbia', pp. 56–71.
170. ACS Rome, Salandra 32, telegram legation Belgrade 20 July 1914.
171. Williamson, *Austria-Hungary and the Origins of the First World War*, p. 204.
172. Cornwall, 'Serbia', pp. 72–81, esp. p. 81; the Italian envoy also recorded that the Serbian government had been taken by surprise: ACS Rome, Salandra, 32, telegram legation Belgrade 24 July 1914.
173. Cornwall, 'Serbia', pp. 81–3. Cornwall carefully demolishes also the argument of Samuel Williamson that Serbia was encouraged throughout July by Russia to reject any Austrian demands. Serbia regarded itself as being isolated diplomatically, acted independently, and could not be certain even of Russian support until 26 July. Cf. Williamson, *Austria-Hungary and the Origins of the First World War*, p. 174.
174. Cf. Lincoln, *In War's Dark Shadow*, pp. 34–7, following Sidney Fay.
175. The Austro-Hungarian general staff stopped the bombardment of Belgrade on 31 July because it broke international law; the belated hope was to avoid provoking Russian intervention. Kronenbitter, *'Krieg im Frieden'*, p. 515.

4 GERMAN SINGULARITY?

1. This interpretation is to be found in Wehler, *The German Empire*; cf. also Ralf Dahrendorf, *Society and Democracy in Germany*, London, 1967.

2. Hull, *Absolute Destruction*, esp. p. 333. This does not, admittedly, do full justice to Isabel Hull's profoundly researched and carefully reasoned argument, a discussion of which is beyond the scope of this book. The main problem is the thesis of German singularity in the absence of a systematic comparison with other belligerents apart from some brief suggestive remarks, pp. 320–3.

3. Bosworth, *Italy and the Approach of the First World War*, pp. 82–3.

4. Albertini, *Venti anni di vita politica*, part 1, vol. 2, p. 117.

5. Ibid., p. 113.

6. Pierre Milza et Serge Berstein, *Dictionnaire Historique des Fascismes et du Nazisme*, Brussels: 1992: entry for Oriani, p. 510.

7. Albertini, *Venti anni di vita politica*, part 1, vol. 2, pp. 113, 116, 123, 126, 128–9, 186.

8. Moffa, 'I deportati libici della guerra 1911–12', p. 35.

9. Bosworth, *Mussolini's Italy*, pp. 50–1; Moffa, 'I deportati libici della guerra 1911–12', pp. 41–5.

10. Bosworth, *Italy and the Approach of the First World War*, pp. 90–1.

11. Christoph Dipper, report on paper by Katja Gerhartz at the conference of German historians of Italy, Berlin, June 2004, http://hsozkult.geschichte.hu-berlin.de/tagungsberichte/id=519, accessed July 2004.

12. Villari, in *Corriere della Sera*, 24 October 1912, cited in Albertini, *Venti anni di vita politica*, part 1, vol. 2, pp. 203–4.

13. Ibid., p. 204.

14. Bosworth, *Italy and the Approach of the First World War*, pp. 106–7, 125.

15. Quoted in Renzi, *In the Shadow of the Sword*, p. 30.

16. Bosworth, *Italy and the Approach of the First World War*, pp. 45, 58. Afflerbach, *Der Dreibund*, pp. 778–9, gives a full account of Pollio's suggestion.

17. Renzi, *In the Shadow of the Sword*, pp. 74–5; Procacci, *Dalla Rassegnazione alla Rivolta*, p. 254.

18. Renzi, *In the Shadow of the Sword*, p. 109.

19. Bosworth, *Italy and the Approach of the First World War*, p. 127.

20. Procacci, *Dalla Rassegnazione alla Rivolta*, p. 52.

21. Bosworth, *Italy and the Approach of the First World War*, p. 126.

22. Gibelli, 'La Grande Guerra tra consenso e rifiuto', p. 242.

23. Cf. Lyttelton, *The Seizure of Power*, p. 24.

24. Bosworth, *Italy and the Approach of the First World War*, p. 134.

25. Ibid., p. 34.

26. Report 20 April 1915, cited in Vigezzi, *Da Giolitti a Salandra*, pp. 383–4.

27. Renzi, *In the Shadow of the Sword*, p. 265.

28. Procacci, *Soldati e prigionieri italiani*, p. 24; Melograni, *Storia politica della Grande guerra*, pp. 10-11, citing Nitti's memoirs published in 1948.

29. Bosworth, *Italy and the Approach of the First World War*, p. 129.

30. Olindo Malagodi, *Conversazioni della guerra 1914-1919*, ed. Brunello Vigezzi, Milan and Naples: 1960, 2 vols, vol. 1, p. 32, cited in Isenghi and Rochat, *La Grande Guerra*, p. 90.

31. Melgrani, *Storia politica della Grande guerra*, pp. 10-11, citing Nitti's memoirs published in 1948.

32. Isenghi and Rochat, *La Grande Guerra*, pp. 142-3; Bosworth, *Italy and the Approach of the First World War*, pp. 124-5.

33. Cadorna, *La Guerra alla fronte italiana*, pp. 46-8.

34. Ibid., pp. 76-7.

35. Isenghi and Rochat, *La Grande Guerra*, pp. 64-7, 138-9, 145-6.

36. Cadorna, *La Guerra alla fronte italiana*, pp. 78-9.

37. Isenghi and Rochat, *La Grande Guerra*, pp. 138-9, 145-6.

38. Ibid., p. 142.

39. Cadorna, *La Guerra alla fronte italiana*, pp. 57-60.

40. Isenghi and Rochat, *La Grande Guerra*, pp. 145-7.

41. Ibid., p. 169; Rochat, *Gli Arditi*, p. 23.

42. Cadorna, *La Guerra alla fronte italiana*, p. 203.

43. Isenghi and Rochat, *La Grande Guerra*, pp. 176-83, 190, 197, 205.

44. Rochat, 'Lo Stato liberale e la Grande Guerra', p. 237.

45. Isenghi and Rochat, *La Grande Guerra*, pp. 155, 312-13.

46. Ibid., p. 248.

47. Procacci, *Soldati e prigionieri italiani*, pp. 42-53.

48. Ibid., pp. 54-6; 'Militärdiszplin', Hirschfeld et al., eds., *Enzyklopädie Erster Weltkrieg*, p. 716.

49. Isenghi and Rochat, *La Grande Guerra*, p. 446.

50. Rochat, *Gli Arditi*, pp. 28, 31-2, 65.

51. Ibid., pp. 36-7, 40.

52. Cited in Rochat, *Gli Arditi*, p. 52.

53. Gibelli, 'Nefaste meraviglie', p. 576-7.

54. Isenghi and Rochat, *La Grande Guerra*, pp. 301-2.

55. Procacci, *Dalla Rassegnazione alla Rivolta*, p. 36. Cf. Winter, 'Some paradoxes of the First World War'.

56. Isenghi and Rochat, *La Grande Guerra 1914-1918*, pp. 194-5.

57. Procacci, *Dalla Rassegnazione alla Rivolta*, p. 287, referring to *Popolo d'Italia*, 17 June 1917.

58. Ibid., pp. 287-307; Isenghi and Rochat, *La Grande Guerra*, pp. 319-20.

59. Procacci, *Dalla Rassegnazione alla Rivolta*, pp. 307-14.

60. Isenghi and Rochat, *La Grande Guerra*, p. 228; Gibelli, 'Nefaste meraviglie', p. 553. The figures given in Anglo-American histories tend to understate both

the Italian contribution to Allied victory and Italian losses. Thus Herwig, using German figures, cites Italian losses of 450,000 (*The First World War*, p. 446).

61. Jelavich, *The Establishment of the Balkan National States*, p. 141.
62. *Österreich-Ungarns Außenpolitik*, vol. 8, telegram Legation counsellor Wilhelm Ritter von Stock from Belgrad, 8 July 1914, pp. 352–3.
63. Jelavich, *The Establishment of the Balkan National States*, pp. 211–12.
64. Ibid., pp. 255–9.
65. Dedijer, *The Road to Sarajevo*, pp. 204–5.
66. *Report of the International Commission to Inquire into the Causes and Conduct of the Balkan Wars*, pp. 34–37.
67. Boeckh, *Von den Balkankriegen zum Ersten Weltkrieg*, p. 37.
68. Biwald, *Von Helden und Krüppeln*, vol. 1, pp. 43–4.
69. *Atrocités Bulgares en Macédoine*, pp. 8–9. This claimed (citing *Le Temps*, 15 July 1913) that correspondents of *The Times*, *Le Temps*, *Journal*, *Secolo*, *Reuters*, *Havas*, *Daily Telegraph*, *Frankfurter Zeitung*, *Neue Freie Presse*, and *Zeit*, sent a collective protest to the Ligue des droits de l'homme at the Bulgarian atrocities. However, no mention of such a protest could be found in the *Frankfurter Zeitung*. The Carnegie commission found that *Le Temps* uncritically accepted the grossly exaggerated Greek accounts of atrocities committed by the Bulgarians: *Report of the International Commission to Inquire into the Causes and Conduct of the Balkan Wars*, p. 78.
70. Biwald, *Von Helden und Krüppeln*, vol. 1, pp. 43–4.
71. Report by Heinrich Hoflehner from Niš, 18 February 1914, *Österreich-Ungarns Außenpolitik*, vol. 7, p. 891.
72. Report of vice-consul Rudolf Kohlruss from Prizren (Kosovo), 27 January 1914, *Österreich-Ungarns Außenpolitik,* vol. 7, pp. 784–6.
73. Report Baron Giesl to Vienna, 10 April 1914, *Österreich-Ungarns Außenpolitik*, vol. 7, pp. 1039–41.
74. *The Times* and the *Frankfurter Zeitung*, both 14 July 1913.
75. *The Times*, 24 July 1913.
76. *The Times,* 15 July 1913, pp. 8 and 7.
77. *Simplicissimus*, year 19 no. 18, 3 August 1914, p. 295.
78. Hall, *The Balkan Wars*, essentially follows the judgement of the Carnegie Commission on the atrocities. Boeckh, *Von den Balkankriegen zum Ersten Weltkrieg*, likewise regards it as an essential piece of research, but argues that the basis of samples encompassed too few persons to be truly representative; moreover, many of its witnesses were victims who offered their services to the Commission, which raised their desire to invent stories and reduced their reliability. Another difficulty was that in Serbia and Greece the state authorities hindered the work of the commission (p. 376). The Bulgarians thought the report was fair and objective, while not totally exculpating them; the Greeks found it biased towards the Bulgarians.

79. *Report of the International Commission to Inquire into the Causes and Conduct of the Balkan Wars*, pp. 72–95.
80. Ibid., pp. 106–8, 109–35, 155–7.
81. Ibid., pp. 151, 158–86.
82. Ibid., p. 267.
83. Kürsat-Ahlers, 'Über das Töten in Genoziden', p. 186.
84. *Report of the International Commission to Inquire into the Causes and Conduct of the Balkan Wars*, pp. 208–15.
85. Ibid., pp. 243–5, 257, 267, 268, 378.
86. Baron d'Estournelles de Constant, introduction to *Report of the International Commission to Inquire into the Causes and Conduct of the Balkan Wars*, p. 16.
87. Kieser and Schaller, 'Völkermord im historischen Raum', pp. 19–21. Cf. also *Persecutions of the Greeks in Turkey*. This concludes that a total of 1,500,000 Greeks had been deported or had fled, of whom half died in consequence (p. 71). It is not possible to resolve this in the scope of the present book.
88. First published 1945, first English translation London, 1959.
89. Dedijer, *The Road to Sarajevo*, p. 348.
90. ACS Rome, Salandra, 32, Telegram legation Niš, 24 September 1914.
91. Great Britain, War Office, *Armies of the Balkan States*, p. 41; Kronenbitter, 'Krieg im Frieden', p. 522.
92. Great Britain, War Office, *Armies of the Balkan States 1914–1918*, pp. 48–9, 52; 'Serbien', in Hirschfeld et al., eds., *Enzyklopädie Erster Weltkrieg*, p. 834.
93. Biwald, *Von Helden und Krüppeln*, vol. 2, pp. 368–70.
94. Procacci, *Soldati e prigionieri italiani*, p. 222 n. According to another study, a far higher number was involved: Of the 68,000 Austrian prisoners taken by the Serbs, 37,000 died during the march from Niš to Valona, from hunger, cold, disease, frostbite. Marcheggiano, *Diritto umanitario*, vol. 2, pp. 362–3, 366–71. The higher estimate of deaths on Asinara is from the Hungarian newspaper *Pester Lloyd*, 23 July 1918, extract in ACS Rome, PCM Guerra europea 1915–1918, busta 98, 19.4.6. sub-file 7.
95. ACS Rome, PCM Guerra europea 1915–18, busta 99, 19.4.6/20, letter from Austro-Hungarian medical officer Acrèl, prisoner of war at Asinara, 29 February 1916 to Isobel Meiklejohn, Chelsea, London.
96. Guttmann, *Schattenriß einer Generation*, p. 146. Guttmann drew his knowledge from a conversation with the German foreign minister Kühlmann on 20 November 1917; the latter made a remark about the Bulgarians taking Serbs to delousing facilities and 'eliminating' them by poison gas.
97. 'Serbien', in Hirschfeld et al., eds., *Enzyklopädie Erster Weltkrieg*, pp. 835–6; 'Kriegsverluste', in ibid., pp. 664–5.
98. Biwald, *Von Helden und Krüppeln*, vol. 2, p. 371.
99. Emin, *Turkey in the World War*, pp. 48–9.
100. An echo of this paranoid view is found in Emin's book: cf. pp. 36–7.

101. Hans-Lukas Kieser, review of Yusuf Halaçoglu, *Facts on the Relocation of Armenians 1914–1918 [Ermeni tehciri ve gerçekler (1914–1918)]*, Ankara, 2002. In H-Soz-u-Kult, accessed 21.07.2005, http://hsozkult.geschichte.hu-berlin.de/rezensionen/2005-3-048.

102. *Persecutions of the Greeks in Turkey*, pp. 13–21.

103. Ibid., pp. 22–5.

104. Emin, *Turkey in the World War*, p. 210.

105. Naimark, *Fires of Hatred*, pp. 42–4.

106. Ibid., pp. 52–6.

107. Bartrop, 'The relationship between war and genocide', pp. 519–32, here p. 523.

108. Trumpener, *Germany and the Ottoman Empire*, p. 201.

109. Emin, *Turkey in the World War*, p. 50.

110. Liman von Sanders, *Fünf Jahre Türkei*, pp. 17–19.

111. Naimark, *Fires of Hatred*, pp. 25–8.

112. Strachan, *The First World War*, vol. 1, pp. 743–4; on Kaiser Wilhelm's invocation to Turkey to launch Islamic world revolution against British rule in late July 1914, and in general on Germany's far-fetched hopes of fomenting revolution, see Kröger, 'Revolution als Programm', pp. 371–2.

113. Hans-Lukas Kieser, review of Sükrü Hanioglu, *Preparation for a Revolution. The Young Turks, 1902–1908*, Studies in Middle Eastern History, Oxford, 2000. In H-Soz-U-Kult, http://hsozkult.geschichte.hu-berlin.de/ 16 October 2002.

114. Naimark, *Fires of Hatred*, pp. 28–9.

115. Hagen, 'The Great War and the mobilization of ethnicity in the Russian Empire', pp. 40–1.

116. Emin, *Turkey in the World War*, pp. 216–21; Emin also alleges Armenian massacres of Turkish Muslims at Zeitun in February 1915 and at Kara-Hissar in June. Trumpener, *Germany and the Ottoman Empire*, pp. 202–3.

117. Trumpener, *Germany and the Ottoman Empire*, pp. 202–3.

118. Naimark, *Fires of Hatred*, p. 37.

119. Cited in Akçam, *Armenien und der Völkermord*, p. 59; see ibid., pp. 59–60 for further evidence of the decision taken by the central committee in March. The government was thus not formally involved.

120. Trumpener, *Germany and the Ottoman Empire*, pp. 217–18.

121. Anon, *Die armenischen Greuel und Deutschland*, pp. 9–10.

122. Lepsius, *Deutschland und Armenien*, pp. xiv–xx.

123. Akçam, *Armenien und der Völkermord*, p. 63. On Zeitun: Ambassador Wangenheim in Constantinople to Berlin, 26 March 1915, and Ambassador Wangenheim to Berlin, 8 May 1915, plus later documents available in English translation at www.armenocide.de, accessed on 6 January 2006.

124. Naimark, *Fires of Hatred*, pp. 29–34; Akçam, *Armenien und der Völkermord*.

125. Cited in Akçam, *Armenien und der Völkermord*, p. 75.

126. 'Armenien', in Hirschfeld et al., eds., *Enzyklopädie Erster Weltkrieg*, p. 344.

127. Golan, 'The Politics of Wartime Demolition and Human Landscape Trans-formation', p. 431.

128. Kieser and Schaller, 'Völkermord im historischen Raum', p. 34.

129. Hans-Lukas Kieser, review of Yusuf Halaçoglu, *Facts on the Relocation of Armenians 1914–1918 [Ermeni tehciri ve gerçekler (1914–1918)]*, Ankara 2002, and Yusuf Halaçoglu, Ramazan Çalik, Kemal Çiçek, Hikmet Özdemir, and Ömer Turan (eds.), *The Armenians: Banishment and migration [Ermeniler: Sürgün ve göç]*, Ankara, 2004. Both in H-Soz-u-Kult, 21.07.2005, <http://hsozkult.geschich-te.hu-berlin.de/rezensionen/2005-3-048> (accessed on 23.06.2005).

130. Conze, *Polnische Nation und deutsche Politik im Ersten Weltkrieg*, pp. 83–90.

131. Lohr, 'The Russian army and the Jews', pp. 2–3.

132. Hagen, 'The Great War and the mobilization of ethnicity in the Russian Empire', pp. 43–5. On antisemitism see also Levene, 'Frontiers of genocide'.

133. Jorg Baberowski, review of Victor Dönninghaus, *Die Deutschen in der Mos-kauer Gesellschaft. Symbiose und Konflikte (1494–1941)*, Munich, 2002; id. *Revo-lution, Reform und Krieg. Die Deutschen an der Wolga in ausgehenden Zarenreich*, Essen, 2002, in *Neue Politische Literatur* 48 (2003), pp. 347–9, here p. 347.

134. Ullrich, *Kriegsalltag. Hamburg im ersten Weltkrieg*, pp. 39–43, 51–6, 63–4, 68–72.

135. Ibid., p. 81; cf. Davis, *Home Fires Burning*, p. 180.

136. Cf. Davis, *Home Fires Burning*, p. 186.

137. Ziemann, *Front und Heimat*, p. 142 n. 496.

138. Davis, *Home Fires Burning,* p. 184, uncritically cites this figure. Ferguson, *The Pity of War*, p. 277, ridicules it as 'fantastic'. He may well be correct, but does not provide an alternative estimate.

139. Offer, *The First World War: An Agrarian Interpretation*, pp. 46–53.

140. Marder, *From the Dreadnought to Scapa Flow*, vol. 2, p. 376.

141. Winter, 'Surviving the war', p. 517 footnote 34. It is not altogether clear that the death rate was higher than in France: over the period 1914–18, the standardized death rate for females in Berlin was 15.08 per thousand; in Paris it was 16.09. Ibid., pp. 494–7, esp. Table 16.2. A full comparison can only be made by including the mortality rate among civilians in the occupied zone of France.

142. Marder, *From the Dreadnought to Scapa Flow,* vol. 2, p. 376; Vincent, *The Politics of Hunger*, p. 20. Vincent writes that 'the vast increase in civilian mortality after 1914 was largely attributable to the blockade' (p. 145).

143. Faulstich, *Hungersterben in der Psychiatrie*, p. 25.

144. Offer, *The First World War: An Agrarian Interpretation*, p. 335.

145. Cf. Strachan, *The First World War*, vol. 1, p. 442.

146. Figes, *A People's Tragedy,* p. 300.

147. Healy, *Vienna and the Fall of the Habsburg Empire*, p. 37.

148. *Meyers Conversations-Lexikon* 1906: Österreich.

149. Hanisch, *Der lange Schatten des Staates*, pp. 200–3; Berend and Ránki, 'Ungarns wirtschaftliche Entwicklung 1848–1918', pp. 523–4. Matis, 'Leitlinien der österreichischen Wirtschaftspolitik 1848–1918', p. 60.

150. Arz von Straussenburg, *Zur Geschichte des Großen Krieges*, p. 222.
151. Ibid., pp. 222–3.
152. Herwig, *The First World War*, pp. 434–5.
153. *Österreich-Ungarns letzter Krieg,* vol. 6, p. 67.
154. Schindling, 'Austria-Hungary', p. 137; 'Kriegsverluste', in Hirschfeld et al., eds., *Enzyklopädie Erster Weltkrieg*, pp. 664–5.
155. Narskij, 'Kriegswirklichkeit und Kriegserfahrung russischer Soldaten' p. 252; Stone, *The Eastern Front*, p. 168.
156. Stone, *The Eastern Front*, pp. 113–14.
157. Hussein Hussnu Emir, *Yildirim 1917–1918* (With the Yildirim Army 1917–1918), Istanbul, 1920, cited in Emin, *Turkey in the World War*, p. 251.
158. Ibid., pp. 252–3, citing the unpublished *Sanitary History of the War*, edited by the medical department of the ministry of war; 'Kriegsverluste', in Hirschfeld et al., eds., *Enzyklopädie Erster Weltkrieg*, pp. 664–5.

5 CULTURE AND WAR

1. Travers, 'Technology, tactics and morale', pp. 278–81.
2. Schubert-Weller, *'Kein schönrer Tod . . . '*, pp. 127–50.
3. *Der Feldmeister,* 8/1914, p. 62, cited in ibid., p. 151.
4. *Der Feldmeister,* 8/1914, p. 59, cited in ibid, p. 152.
5. Lange, ' " . . . da schreibt ein Volk seine Annalen" ', pp. 108–10. On the war veterans' associations, see Rohkrämer, *Der Militarismus der 'kleinen Leute'*, 1990.
6. Börsch-Supan, 'Die Reaktion der Zeitschriften "Kunst und Künstler" und "Die Kunst" ', p. 200.
7. Sombart, *Händler und Helden*, pp. 106–7.
8. Ibid., p. 117.
9. Mann, 'Gedanken im Kriege' ('Thoughts in Wartime'), pp. 84–5.
10. Falk, ' "Heil mir, daß ich Ergriffene sehe." pp. 242–3, and 255.
11. Mann, 'Gedanken im Kriege', p. 90.
12. Isnenghi, *Il mito della grande guerra*, pp. 11, 13. Mussolini expressed admiration of Pareto and his theory of elites as early as 1908: Sternhell et al., *Die Entstehung der faschistischen Ideologie*, p. 249.
13. Quoted in Clark, *Modern Italy*, p. 183.
14. Cited in O'Brien, *Mussolini in the First World Wa*, p. 12, emphasis in the original.
15. Facsimile of *Il Popolo d'Italia*, 21 January 1915, in Accame and Strinati eds., *A 90 anni dalla Grande Guerra*, p. 97.
16. Gat, *Fascist and Liberal Visions of War*, pp. 43–5.
17. Gibelli, 'Nefaste meraviglie', pp. 563–4.
18. Cited in Piero Palumbo, 'D'Annunzio: da Quarto al volo su Vienna', in Accame and Strinati, eds., *A 90 anni dalla Grande Guerra,* p. 107.

19. G. D'Annunzio, *Per la più grande Italia*, Milan, 1915, cited in O'Brien, *Mussolini in the First World War*, p. 54. Mussolini's speech taking responsibility for the murder of the Socialist deputy Matteottti in 1925, a key event in the consolidation of Fascist rule, contains a striking echo of D'Annunzio's speech.

20. Piero Palumbo, 'D'Annunzio: da Quarto al volo su Vienna', in Accame and Strinati, eds., *A 90 anni dalla Grande Guerra,* pp. 107–12. A summary of D'Annunzio's aerial exploits is in Gat, *Fascist and Liberal Visions of War,* pp. 49–52.

21. Cited in O'Brien, *Mussolini in the First World War*, p. 55, emphasis in the original.

22. Coli, 'Croce e Gentile', pp. 101–6.

23. Marinetti, 'Fondazione e Manifesto del Futurismo', pp. 11, 10.

24. Sternhell et al., *Die Entstehung der faschistischen Ideologie*, pp. 298–9.

25. Both cited in Cork, *A Bitter Truth*, p. 74. Apollinaire was strictly speaking a friend of the Futurists rather than being a Futurist himself.

26. Cork, *A Bitter Truth*, pp. 77 (for quotation), 168–9, and 208.

27. Demetz, *Worte in Freiheit*, pp. 17–19, 228–35.

28. Anz, 'Vitalismus und Kriegsdichtung', p. 237.

29. Demetz, *Worte in Freiheit*, pp. 99–113, 326, 332.

30. Ibid., pp. 114–32.

31. Anz, 'Vitalismus und Kriegsdichtung', pp. 236–7.

32. Cork, *A Bitter Truth,* p. 48.

33. Jahn, *Patriotic Culture in Russia during World War I*, p. 16. A colour image may be found at <http://www.nga.gov.au/RevolutionaryRussians/sun.cfm>, accessed on 21 September 2006.

34. Riese, *Malevitsch*, pp. 34–80.

35. Cited in anon. [F. C. Endres], *Die Tragödie Deutschlands*, p. 276.

36. Pressel, *Die Kriegspredigt 1914–1918*, p. 110.

37. [Endres], *Die Tragödie Deutschlands*, p. 276.

38. Quoted in Pressel, *Die Kriegspredigt 1914–1918*, p. 108.

39. Pressel, *Die Kriegspredigt 1914–1918*, pp. 108–20.

40. Ibid., p. 116. The article earned him a rebuke from the moderate Kiel theologian Otto Baumgarten.

41. Pressel, *Die Kriegspredigt,* pp. 131–2, 142, 169–71.

42. [Endres], *Die Tragödie Deutschlands*, p. 277.

43. Pressel, *Die Kriegspredigt,* pp. 140–1, 163.

44. [Endres], *Die Tragödie Deutschlands*, p. 279.

45. Melograni, *Storia politica della Grande guerra*, p. 139.

46. Becker, *War and Faith*, p. 57.

47. Smith et al., *France and the Great War*, p. 58.

48. Péladan, *L'Allemagne devant L'humanité*, p. 8.

49. Becker, *War and Faith,* pp. 13 and 15.

50. Péladan, *L'Allemagne devant L'humanité*, preface, p. vi. On Péladan see http://www.bc.edu/bc_org/avp/cas/artmuseum/exhibitions/archive/khnopff/glossary.html, accessed on 25 August 2005.

51. Péladan, *L'Allemagne devant L'humanité*, pp. ix–x, 2, 3, 6, 210.

52. Ibid., pp. 203–05. Emphasis in the original.

53. Cf. Cruickshank, *Variations on Catastrophe*, p. 11.

54. Ken Inglis, 'Foreword' to Becker, *War and Faith*, p. xi.

55. Becker, *War and Faith*, pp. 8–9, 16.

56. H. Lavedan in *L'Illustration*, 14 November 1914, cited in Jeismann, *Das Vaterland der Feinde*, p. 364.

57. Marwick, *The Deluge*, p. 48.

58. Jahn, *Patriotic Culture in Russia during World War I*, pp. 24–9, 165–6.

59. Ulrich von Wilamowitz-Moellendorff, 'Krieges Anfang' 'The beginning of the war', speech given on 27 August 1914 at the University of Berlin, in *Deutsche Reden in schwerer Zeit,* pp. 6–8 and 12–13.

60. Adolf Lasson, 'Deutsche Art und deutsche Bildung' 'The German way and German education', speech given on 25 September 1914 at the University of Berlin, in ibid., pp. 105–6.

61. Gustav Roethe, 'Wir Deutschen und der Krieg' 'We Germans and the war', speech given on 3 September 1914 at the University of Berlin, in ibid., pp. 32–3.

62. Otto von Gierke, 'Krieg und Kultur' 'War and culture', speech given on 18 September 1914 at the University of Berlin, in ibid., p. 100.

63. Adolf Lasson, 'Deutsche Art und deutsche Bildung' 'The German way and German education', speech given on 25 September 1914 at the University of Berlin, in ibid., p. 112. Yet Lasson, a Protestant who had converted from Judaism, was no racist: he wrote that it was wrong to consider only those German who had blond hair and blue eyes, and were tall and well proportioned. The Germans were just like all historically great people a mixed people. 'The Germans are not a race...He who in his heart respects that which is sacred to Germans and who has grown up in German decency so that he is capable of reproducing it for the coming generations is a German.' Ibid., p. 120.

64. Ernest Lavisse's lecture to open the first war semester at the Sorbonne, 5 November 1914, published as 'La Guerre' in the *Revue de Paris*, November 1914, cited in Krumeich, 'Ernest Lavisse', p. 148.

65. Hanna, *The Mobilization of Intellect*, pp. 10, 35–6, 144–5.

66. Émile Boutroux, *L'Allemagne et la guerre*, Paris, 1915, cited in Joas, 'Sozialwissenschaften und der Erste Weltkrieg', p. 22.

67. Lavisse, *Pourquoi nous nous battons*, Paris, 1917, cited in Krumeich, 'Ernest Lavisse', pp. 152–3.

68. Lavisse, 'Seconde lettre "à une normalienne', *Revue de Paris,* 1 January 1918, cited in Krumeich, 'Ernest Lavisse', p. 154.

69. Cited in vom Brocke, ' "Wissenschaft und Militarismus" '. p. 665.

70. Jeismann, *Das Vaterland der Feinde*, p. 346.

71. Ibid., pp. 350–4. The article in the *Revue de psychothérapie* was reported on at length in *Le Temps,* 11 September 1915.

72. 7 April 1917, cited in ibid., p. 358.

73. Smith et al., *France and the Great War,* pp. 59, 142–5.

74. Jeismann, *Das Vaterland der Feinde*, pp. 364–73.

75. Harel, ed., *Les Affiches de la Grande Guerre*, pp. 67, 95.

76. Lieven, *Russia and the Origins of the First World War*, p. 17.

77. Cited in Lincoln, *Passage Through Armageddon*, p. 44.

78. Jahn, *Patriotic Culture in Russia during World War I*, pp. 12–29.

79. Sombart, *Händler und Helden*, p. 93.

80. Ibid., pp. 85–92.

81. Ibid., p. 62. Citations from *Thus Spoke Zarathustra*, translated with an introduction by R. J. Hollingdale, Harmondsworth: Penguin, 1961, pp. 138 and 90. Sombart excerpted part-sentences and made big changes in the order of the original.

82. Sombart, *Händler und Helden*, pp. 63–4.

83. Ibid., pp. 84–5. Sombart was in fact not among the signatories.

84. Safranski, *Nietzsche. Biographie seines Denkens*, pp. 60–3.

85. Sombart, *Händler und Helden*, pp. 85, 88.

86. Ibid., p. 89, citing a poem of 1914.

87. Ibid., pp. 135, 142.

88. Ibid., pp. v–vi.

89. Cf. Reuveni, 'The "Crisis of the Book" and German Society after the First World War', esp. pp. 449–56.

90. Triebel, *Kultur und Kalkül. Der Eugen Diederichs Verlag*, p. 6.
    It should be added that Hans Zehrer did not become a Nazi; after the Second World War he re-emerged as a successful and influential publicist, becoming the editor of the daily *Die Welt* and adviser of the newspaper proprietor Axel Springer.

91. Wilhelm Kahl 'Vom Recht zum Kriege und vom Siegespreis' ('On the right to war and the prize of victory'), speech given on 9 October 1914 at the University of Berlin, in *Deutsche Reden in schwerer Zeit*, p. 173.

92. Cited in Mommsen, 'German artists, writers and intellectuals', p. 25.

93. Karl Scheffler, 'Der Krieg' ('The war'), *Kunst und Künstler* vol. 13 (1915), pp. 1–4, cited in Börsch-Supan, 'Die Reaktion der Zeitschriften "Kunst und Künstler" und "Die Kunst" ', p. 197.

94. Börsch-Supan, 'Die Reaktion der Zeitschriften "Kunst und Künstler" und "Die Kunst" ', p. 198.

95. Mommsen, *Bürgerliche Kultur und künstlerische Avantgarde*, p. 134, 136.

96. Schumann, ' "Der Künstler an die Krieger" ', pp. 226, 227.

97. *Simplicissimus*, year 19, no. 21, 25 August 1914.

98. Ibid., and year 20 no 5, 4 May 1915.

99. Mommsen, *Bürgerliche Kultur*, pp. 114, 132–3; Schumann, ' "Der Künstler an die Krieger" ', p. 228.

100. The best-known representative of the 'ideas of 1914' was the economist Johann Plenge with his publication *1789 und 1914: Die symbolischen Jahre in der Geschichte des politischen Geistes*, Berlin, 1916.

101. Rürup, 'Der "Geist von 1914" in Deutschland', p. 20.

102. Ibid.

103. Börsch-Supan, 'Die Reaktion der Zeitschriften "Kunst und Künstler" und "Die Kunst" ', pp. 201–2.

104. Schumann, ' "Der Künstler an die Krieger" ', pp. 231–3.

105. E.g. 'Lied an Alle' and 'Predigt ans deutsche Volk in Waffen', in *1914. Der Deutsche Krieg im Deutschen Gedicht*, selected by Julius Bab vol. 2, cf. afterword by Bab, written in autumn 1919, pp. 25 and 37.

106. Julius Bab, afterword, in *1914. Der Deutsche Krieg im Deutschen Gedicht*, pp. 389–90. Bab chose only poems that had been published in newspapers or books during the war.

107. Friedrich Meinecke, 'Grundzüge unserer nationalen Enwicklung bis zur Reichsgründung Bismarcks', published 1916, cited by Meineke, 'Friedrich Meinecke und der "Krieg der Geister" ', p. 115.

108. Letter to Paul Amann, 1 October 1915, in Mann, ed., *Das Thomas Mann-Buch*, p. 96.

109. Mann, *Betrachtungen eines Unpolitischen*, p. 32.

110. Nicolai, *Die Biologie des Krieges*; the text of Nicolai's appeal and useful editorial notes are in *The Collected Papers of Albert Einstein*, vol. 6, pp. 69–71.

111. *The Collected Papers of Albert Einstein*, vol. 8, p. 103.

112. Ibid., p. 170: Einstein to Rolland, 15 September 1915.

113. Ibid., pp. 341–3: Einstein to Weisbach, 14 October 1916.

114. Stern, 'Together and Apart: Fritz Haber and Albert Einstein', p. 116; the original reference is *The Collected Papers of Albert Einstein*, vol. 6, pp. 211–13, 'Meine Meinung über den Krieg', in *Das Land Goethes 1914–1916. Ein vaterländisches Gedenkbuch. Herausgegeben vom Goethebund*, Stuttgart, Berlin, 1916, p. 30.

115. *The Collected Papers of Albert Einstein*, vol. 6, pp. 532–3, n. 3.

116. Ungern-Sternberg and Ungern-Sternberg, *Der Aufruf 'An die Kulturwelt!'*, pp. 61–73.

117. Anz, 'Vitalismus und Kriegsdichtung', p. 244.

118. Demetz, *Worte in Freiheit*, pp. 90–5; 'Dadaismus', in Hirschfeld et al., eds., *Enzyklopädie Erster Weltkrieg*, p. 422.

119. Mommsen, *Max Weber in German Politics*.

120. Craig, *The Politics of the Prussian Army*, p. 337.

121. Pellegrini, 'L'influenza delle corazze nel Futurismo', pp. 366–72. Richard Cork believes Severini painted it from his room in Paris with the view of a suburban station (*A Bitter Truth*, p. 70), a claim convincingly refuted by Pellegrini.

122. Bovio, 'Gli Arditi', pp. 222–4.

123. *Manifesti illustrati della Grande Guerra*, ed. Marzia Miele and Cesarina Vighy, pl. 53, p. 68. I am grateful to Dr Maria Pia Critelli at the Biblioteca di Storia moderna e contemporanea, Rome, for pointing out this publication to me.

124. Gibelli, 'Nefaste meraviglie', p. 581.

125. Marinetti, *Taccuini,* editor's note, pp. 3, 43–4. The lack of commas was typical of Marinetti's notion of Futurist language, 'words in liberty'.

126. Marinetti, 'Manifesto agli Studenti' (Milan, 29 November 1914), in id., *Futurismo e Fascismo*, pp. 90, 94–5. Emphasis in the original.

127. Ibid., p. 97.

128. Marinetti, 'L'orgoglio italiano' (December 1915), in id., *Futurismo e Fascismo*, pp. 100–1.

129. Marinetti, *Taccuini*, diary entries 9 April 1917, p. 69, and 29 April 1917, p. 83.

130. Marinetti, 'Discorso agli Arditi' (published September 1918), in id., *Futurismo e Fascismo*, p. 103.

131. Marinetti, 'Discorso agli Arditi', pp. 104–6.

132. Marinetti, *Taccuini*, diary entry 3 March 1917, p. 57.

133. Ibid., diary entry 1 November 1918, p. 377.

134. Ibid., diary entries 28 February and 1 March 1917, p. 56.

135. Umberto Boccioni, *Gli scritti editi e inediti,* ed. Zeno Birolli, Milan, 1971, pp. 385–6, cited in Marinetti, *Taccuini*, p. 546 n. 4. It may be noted that the Italian 20-cent coin in circulation throughout Europe since 2002 features a sculpture by Boccioni.

136. Ibid., diary entry 24 April 1917, p. 77. A part was used in an article he published in 1919, 'Ideologie sfasciate dalla conflagrazione'.

137. Ibid., diary entry 19 April 1917, p. 71.

138. Theweleit, *Male Fantasies*.

139. Marinetti, *Taccuini*, diary entries 27 April 1917, p. 79, and 23 May 1917, p. 105.

140. Quoted in Isnenghi and Rochat, *La Grande Guerra*, p. 437.

141. Marinetti, *Taccuini*, diary entry 10 July 1918, p. 278.

142. Ibid., diary entry 13 March 1917, p. 62.

143. Isnenghi and Rochat, *La Grande Guerra*, pp. 311–12.

144. Marinetti, *Taccuini*, diary entry 20 April 1918, p. 222; cf. 30 April 1918, pp. 232–3. Marinetti's own contempt for the ordinary soldier occasionally reveals itself in his diaries, despite the rhetoric of the 'superior race', e.g. diary entry 7 January 1918, p. 179.

145. Ibid., editor's note 120, p. 582.

146. Ibid., diary entry 19 July 1918, p. 286.

147. Procacci, *Dalla Rassegnazione alla Rivolta*, p. 288.

148. Ibid., pp. 321–9.

149. Ward, 'Intellectuals, culture and power in modern Italy', pp. 84–8.
150. *Dizionario Storico Politico Italiano*, ed. Ernesto Sestan, Florence, 1971, entry 'Alfredo Rocco'.
151. Mussolini, *Mein Kriegstagebuch*, p. 188.
152. Cited in O'Brien, *Mussolini in the First World War*, p. 171. Emphasis in the original.
153. Mosse, *Fallen Soldiers*, pp. 10, 33; Eksteins, *Rites of Spring*, pp. 64–70. For further discussion on these points see Historiographical Note at the end of this book.

6 TRENCH WARFARE AND ITS CONSEQUENCES

1. Both cited in Ellis, *The Social History of the Machine Gun*, p. 135. One classic account of the Somme is in Keegan, *The Face of Battle*, pp. 204–84. Its focus is on the British experience; the Germans and the French are discussed only briefly.
2. Cited in Winter, *Haig's Command*, p. 46.
3. General Rawlinson, in a lecture in September 1915, and Foch, both cited in Winter, *Haig's Command*, p. 58.
4. Hirschfeld, 'Die Somme-Schlacht von 1916', p. 83. Cf. Robin Prior and Trevor Wilson, *The Somme*, New Haven and London, 2005.
5. Herwig, *The First World War*, pp. 244–5; Winter, *The Experience of World War I*, pp. 129–35. See also Jünger, *Storm of Steel*, pp. 40–2.
6. Sheffield, *Forgotten Victory*, p. 165.
7. Herwig, *The First World War*, pp. 199–204; Wilson, *The Myriad Faces of War*, 1986, p. 349, puts German losses at 500,000 and notes that the British official history of the war put German losses at 680,000. Martin Gilbert puts total British dead over four months July to October at 95,675, French 50,729 (Allied total 146,404), and German 164,055 (*First World War*, p. 299).
8. On the use of poison gas by the British, see report by Sergeant Karl Eisler, Reserve Field Artillery Regiment 29, August 1916, cited in Hirschfeld et al., eds., *Die Deutschen an der Somme 1914–1918*, pp. 99–106; use of gas by the French: report by Colonel Riebensahm, commander of Infantry Regiment 15, 26 September 1916, cited in ibid., p. 141.
9. Sheffield, *Forgotten Victory*, pp. 168–9.
10. One confirmation of the accurate and well-coordinated French artillery is in the report by Colonel Riebensahm, 26 September 1916, cited in Hirschfeld et al., eds., *Die Deutschen an der Somme 1914–1918*, p. 141.
11. Brown, *The Imperial War Museum Book of the Somme*, pp. xxiv–xxv.
12. Sheffield, *Forgotten Victory*, p. 186.
13. Cited in Reimann, 'Die heile Welt im Stahlgewitter', p. 141.

14. Ziemann, *Front und Heimat*, pp. 183–4.
15. Einem, *Ein Armeeführer erlebt den Weltkrieg*, letter to his wife, 4 July 1916, p. 239.
16. Cited in Otto and Schmiedel, eds., *Der erste Weltkrieg*, p. 188.
17. Cited in ibid, pp. 200–1.
18. Ziemann, *Front und Heimat*, p. 184.
19. Hugo Natt, cited in Hirschfeld, 'Die Somme-Schlacht von 1916', p. 86.
20. Cited in ibid., p. 87.
21. Afflerbach, *Falkenhayn*, p. 419; Sheffield, *Forgotten Victory*, p. 184.
22. Afflerbach, *Falkenhayn*, p. 423.
23. Duroselle, *La grande guerre des Français*, pp. 110–11; Krumeich, 'Verdun'; 'Verdun', in Hirschfeld et al. eds., *Enzyklopädie Erster Weltkrieg*, pp. 942–5.
24. Falkenhayn, letter to General von Einem, 7 February 1916, cited in Reichsarchiv, *Der Weltkrieg*, vol. 10, p. 36. Emphasis in the original.
25. Reichsarchiv, *Der Weltkrieg*, vol. 10, p. 41.
26. Afflerbach, *Falkenhayn*, pp. 407–9.
27. Krumeich, 'Verdun', p. 305.
28. Antoine Prost, cited in ibid., p. 302.
29. Archive of the Library of Contemporary History, Stuttgart, The papers of Pechtold-Peters: Walter Pechtold. Autobiographisches. 'Die Erinnerungen des Soldaten Walter Pechtold (1898–1977) aus den Jahren 1913–1919', transcription, pp. 12–13.
30. Ibid., pp. 13–21.
31. Ibid., letter to his father, 1 May 1916, pp. 27–9.
32. Ibid., pp. 31–41.
33. Ibid., letter to his father, 31 May 1916, p. 45.
34. Cited in Duroselle, *La grande guerre des Français*, p. 116.
35. Cork, *A Bitter Truth*, p. 154.
36. Cited in Stevenson, *French War Aims Against Germany*, p. 209.
37. Smith, *Between Mutiny and Obedience*.
38. Afflerbach, *Falkenhayn*, pp. 406, 445, 452.
39. The classic text on this remains Feldman, *Army, Industry, and Labor*. However, see the important corrections by Holger Herwig, who shows that its successes in raising production were largely 'smoke and mirrors', *The First World War*, 263–5.
40. Smith et al., *France and the Great War*, p. 49.
41. McPhail, *The Long Silence*, p. 184.
42. Herwig, *The First World War*, pp. 246–8.
43. Herwig, *The First World War*, pp. 249–51. On French civilian labour, McPhail, *The Long Silence*, pp. 158–85, esp. pp. 163–4 and 174–5. Michael Geyer arrives at far lower figures for forced labour: about 26,000 prisoners of war, plus 9,000 Belgian and French labourers, and 6,000 voluntary workers from Germany and Belgium; a large number of soldiers were also deployed as workers, but the number is not clear. 'Rückzug und Zerstörung 1917', p. 168.

44. Jünger, *Storm of Steel*, p. 128 (with minor alterations to the translation).
45. Geyer, 'Rückzug und Zerstörung 1917', pp. 175–7.
46. Cited in Gilbert, *First World War*, p. 280.
47. Herwig, *The First World War*, pp. 252–4.
48. Ibid., pp. 311–18.
49. Hurd, *History of the Great War. The Merchant Navy*, vol. 3, p. 379.
50. Herwig, *The First World War*, p. 325.
51. 'Artillerie', in Hirschfeld et al., eds., *Enzyklopädie Erster Weltkrieg*, p. 347.
52. Sheffield, *Forgotten Victory*, pp. 204–16; others put the losses of the British attackers somewhat higher: Herwig, *First World War*, p. 332, estimates it at 271,000 against 217,000 German casualties.
53. Diary entry 28 September 1917, in Otto and Schmiedel, eds., *Der erste Weltkrieg*, pp. 262–3.

7 WAR, BODIES, AND MINDS

1. Fiedler, ed., *Das Oxforder Buch Deutscher Dichtung*, p. 19.
2. Greim, ' "50 Fahrten mit dem Lazarettzuge nach der Westfront" ', pp. 337–9. Greim's article is based on Alfred Ihne and Alexander Perlyn, *50 Fahrten mit dem Lazarettzuge nach der Westfront*, Darmstadt: Hessischer Landesverein vom Roten Kreuz, 1917.
3. Jünger, *Der Kampf als inneres Erlebnis*, pp. 72–3, cited in the translation in Kaes et al., eds., *The Weimar Republic Sourcebook*, pp. 18–19.
4. Jünger, *Storm of Steel*, p. 215.
5. Cited in Roberts, *Minds at War*, p. 84.
6. Cited in ibid., p. 70. (This is the first of two stanzas.)
7. Ibid., pp. 73–7.
8. Cited in Marder, *From the Dreadnought to Scapa Flow*, vol. 2, p. 413.
9. Thellier de Poncheville, *Dix mois à Verdun*, cited in Duroselle, *La Grande Guerre des Français*, p. 116.
10. Greim, ' "50 Fahrten mit dem Lazarettzuge nach der Westfront" ', pp. 343–7. The argument that the cult of technology and progress was particularly German is put forward by Modris Eksteins in his suggestive book *Rites of Spring*. The idea that the worship of industrialized destruction was also particularly German has been floated by Isabel Hull, in *Absolute Destruction*, but the empirical basis for a comparison is absent.
11. Dewitz, *'So wird bei uns der Krieg geführt!'*, p. 230.
12. Schauwecker, *So war der Krieg*, p. 31.
13. *Zwischen Arras und Péronne. 311 Lichtbilder zur Erinnerung an die Zeit des Stellungskampfes und der Abwehr der englischen Offensive*, ed. 'by a German Reserve Corps', Bapaume, 1916; Joseph Sauer, *Die Zerstörung von Kirchen und Kunst-*

denkmälern an der Westfront, Freiburg, 1917. Cf. Krumeich, 'Die deutsche Erinnerung an die Somme', p. 233.

14. Mosse, *Fallen Soldiers*, p. 150.

15. Cf. Vondung, 'Propaganda oder Sinndeutung', pp. 11–37, here p. 12.

16. Mosse, *Fallen Soldiers*, p. 59.

17. Bloch's wartime writings and his photographs have recently been published by Annette Becker: *Marc Bloch. L'Histoire, la Guerre, la Résistance*, Paris, 2006.

18. Dewitz, *'So wird bei uns der Krieg geführt!'*, pp. 251–5; Barbusse, letter of 14 October 1915, cited in ibid., p. 79.

19. Caizergues, ed., *Jean Cocteau. Photographies et dessins de guerre.*

20. Undated entry in Louis-Jean Mairet, *Carnet d'un combattant*, Paris, 1919, cited in Smith et al., *France and the Great War*, p. 108.

21. Smith et al., *France and the Great War*, pp. 108–9.

22. Reimann, 'Die heile Welt im Stahlgewitter', p. 140.

23. Mussolini, *Mein Kriegstagebuch*, pp. 128–30.

24. Isnenghi and Rochat, *La Grande Guerra*, pp. 273–6. Cf. Melograni, *Storia politica della Grande guerra*, p. 138.

25. Narskij, 'Kriegswirklichkeit und Kriegserfahrung russischer Soldaten', p. 257; Norman Stone exaggerates somewhat the generosity of the soldiers' rations: *The Eastern Front*, p. 170.

26. Narskij, 'Kriegswirklichkeit und Kriegserfahrung russischer Soldaten', p. 256; Allan K. Wildman, *The End of the Russian Imperial Army. The Old Army and the Soldiers' Revolt (March–April 1917)*, Princeton, 1980, p. 106.

27. Wildman, *The End of the Russian Imperial Army*, pp. 335–9.

28. Henri Massis, *Le Sacrifice*, Paris, 1917, pp. 204–6, cited in Becker, *War and Faith*, p. 22.

29. Pierre Teilhard de Chardin, *Écrits du temps de guerre*, pp. 229–39, cited in Becker, *War and Faith*, p. 23.

30. Becker, *War and Faith*, pp. 31, 42, 64.

31. Reimann, 'Die heile Welt im Stahlgewitter', pp. 133–8, quotations p. 134.

32. Greim, ' "50 Fahrten mit dem Lazarettzuge nach der Westfront" ', pp. 342–3.

33. Smith et al., *France and the Great War*, p. 55; cf. the detailed account in Becker, *War and Faith*, p. 112. The phrase was quoted approvingly at several points by Joséphin Péladan in *L'Allemagne devant L'humanité* (1916).

34. Jünger, *In Stahlgewittern*, pp. 92–3. I have provided my own translation here.

35. Cf. Griffin, *The Nature of Fascism*, pp. 32–6, 38–40. At another point Jünger saw German steel helmets which 'seemed to sprout from the fire-harrowed soil like some iron harvest'. *Storm of Steel*, p. 235.

36. Mussolini, *Mein Kriegstagebuch*, p. 160. Entry apparently written in autumn 1916.

37. Brittain, *Testament of Youth*, pp. 414–16.

38. Cited in Kramer, ' "Greueltaten" ', p. 109.

39. Cited in Reimann, 'Die heile Welt im Stahlgewitter', p. 139.

40. Fussell, *The Great War and Modern Memory*, pp. 77–8; the quotations are from Stanley Casson, *Steady Drummer*, 1935.

41. Cited in Kruse, *Krieg und nationale Integration*, p. 126.

42. Verhey, *The Spirit of 1914*, p. 91.

43. Cited in Robb, *British Culture and the First World War*, p. 36.

44. Ibid., p. 102.

45. Marinetti, *Taccuini*, diary entry 13 October 1917, p. 148.

46. Ibid., diary entry 23 April 1918, p. 226; the context suggests it was a battalion of Alpini. It seems that in April 1918 he was on a speaking tour of front-line troops, perhaps sent by the high command, in order to prepare and re-mobilize men for a grand counter-offensive: diary entries April–May 1918.

47. Ibid., diary entry 27 April 1918, p. 231.

48. Horne and Kramer, *German Atrocities 1914*, pp. 196–9. On the relationship between rape, male imagination, and propaganda, see ibid., pp. 199–202.

49. Ibid., pp. 303–7; Harris, 'The "Child of the Barbarian"', pp. 170–206.

50. Ceschin, ' "L'estremo oltraggio" '.

51. Marinetti, *Taccuini*, passim.

52. Isnenghi and Rochat, *La Grande Guerra*, pp. 331–4.

53. Klemperer, *Curriculum vitae. Erinnerungen*, vol. 2, p. 387. Ernst Jünger made occasional reference to soldiers, possibly including himself, visiting prostitutes in France: *Der Kampf als inneres Erlebnis*, pp. 34, 68.

54. Heinrich Wandt, *Etappe Gent*, Vienna and Berlin (2nd edn.), 1926, pp. 155–6, cited in Ulrich and Ziemann, eds., *Frontalltag im Ersten Weltkrieg*, p. 138.

55. Majerus, 'La prostitution à Bruxelles pendant la Grande Guerre', pp. 16 (quotation), 26–7.

56. Robb, *British Culture*, p. 55; Ute Daniel, 'Frauen', p. 123.

57. William Orpen, *An Onlooker in France*, London, 1921, cited in Upstone 'Love and Beauty', p. 38.

58. Liulevicius, *War Land on the Eastern Front*, pp. 80, 133, 186, 188; Richert, *Beste Gelegenheit zum Sterben*, pp. 278–82; Ullrich, *Kriegsalltag*, p. 102. For the German measures for the social and medical control of prostitution and venereal disease, see Majerus, 'La prostitution à Bruxelles pendant la Grande Guerre'.

59. E.g. in the village Schweinitz near the army exercise range at Altengrabow near Magdeburg: Richert, *Beste Gelegenheit zum Sterben*, p. 291.

60. Rollet, 'The "other war" II: setbacks in public health', p. 459.

61. *Common Cause*, 28 August 1914, 9 October, 23 October, 27 November, cited in Kent, 'Love and death. War and gender in Britain', pp. 159–60.

62. Ziemann, *Front und Heimat*, p. 300.

63. Although this was certainly not true for all, as Vera Brittain showed with her faithfulness to her fiancé before and after his death, and her suggestion that promiscuity was not general. *Testament of Youth*.

64. Bourne, *Britain and the Great War*, p. 235.

65. Majerus, 'La prostitution à Bruxelles pendant la Grande Guerre', p. 35.

66. Smith et al., *France and the Great War*, p. 96.

67. Sheffield, *Forgotten Victory*, p. 111.

68. 'Sanitätswesen', in Hirschfeld et al., eds., *Enzyklopädie Erster Weltkrieg*, p. 812.

69. 'Sozialpolitik', in ibid., p. 857.

70. Sheffield, *Forgotten Victory*, p. 111.

71. Cited in Keegan, *The Face of Battle*, p. 264.

72. Smith et al., *France and the Great War*, p. 93; 'Soldaten', in Hirschfeld et al., *Enzyklopädie Erster Weltkrieg*, p. 157. Cf. Bourke, *An Intimate History of Killing*.

73. Biwald, *Von Helden und Krüppeln*, vol. 2, pp. 470–1; for additional insights thanks to MacGregor Knox.

74. Klemperer, *Curriculum vitae*, vol. 2, p. 609.

75. On the fate of the 'gueles cassées' in France, see Winter, 'Forms of kinship and remembrance', pp. 48–51.

76. Ernst Friedrich, *Krieg dem Kriege! Guerre à la guerre! War against war! Oorlog aan den oorlog!* Berlin, 1924; many subsequent German and international editions.

77. Ulrich, ' "... als wenn nichts geschehen wäre". Anmerkungen zur Behandlung der Kriegsopfer', p. 120; 'Invalidität', in Hirschfeld et al., eds., *Enzyklopädie Erster Weltkrieg*, pp. 584–6.

78. The women of Berlin were undoubtedly under-nourished, but there is no reference to this symptom in the thorough study by Davis, *Home Fires Burning*.

79. Becker, 'Guerre totale et troubles mentaux', pp. 140–1.

80. Smith et al., *France and the Great War*, pp. 90–1.

81. Wilfred Owen, letter to his brother, Colin, 14 May 1917, cited in Roberts, *Minds at War*, p. 119.

82. Vaughan, *Some Desperate Glory*, diary entry 27 August 1917, pp. 221–2.

83. Cited in Greim, ' "50 Fahrten mit dem Lazarettzuge" ', pp. 352–3.

84. Ernst Rump, private papers, Hamburg: Kriegsbriefe: letter to Nölken, 29 October 1914.

85. Freud, 'Vergänglichkeit' (On Transience), in Anna Freud, ed., Sigmund Freud, *Gesammelte Werke*, Frankfurt, 1946/49, vol. 10, p. 360. The translation based on that in *The Standard Edition of the Complete Psychological Works of Sigmund Freud*, vol. 14, but I have changed the English word 'civilization' to 'culture' reflect the original German 'Kultur'.

86. *Zeitgemässes über Krieg und Tod* (1915), in Alexander Mitscherlich, Angela Richards and James Strachey, eds., Sigmund Freud, *Studienausgabe*, Frankfurt, 1969–75, vol. 9, p. 35. English translation *Thoughts for the Times on War and Death*, in ibid., vol. 14, pp. 275–300.

87. *Zeitgemässes über Krieg und Tod* (1915), pp. 38–9.

88. Ibid., p. 57.

89. Cited in Gay, *Freud, Juden und andere Deutsche*, p. 91.

90. Hynes, 'Personal narratives and commemoration', p. 215. Hynes relates in the same context how Sassoon, after a failed attack on German trenches in May 1916, went out alone into no man's land to bring in a wounded man who died on the way back. Sassoon was awarded the Military Cross for his bravery. Hynes commented that Sassoon's narrative commemorated 'the brave individual rush into danger', 'heroic and pointless' adventures, expressing a kind of protest at modern mass war. This is undoubtedly valid, but only for the later act. Bringing back a wounded man, on the other hand, was an act of small-group solidarity which helped to ensure combat motivation. Cf. Smith et al., *France and the Great War*, p. 99.

91. Robb, *British Culture*, p. 47.

92. Robert Gaupp, *Die Nervenkranken des Krieges, ihre Beurteilung und Behandlung: Ein Wort zur Aufklärung und Mahnung an weite Kreise unseres Volkes: Vortrag*, Stuttgart, 1917, cited in Eckart, ' "The most extensive experiment that the imagination can conceive" ', p. 140.

93. Cited in Becker, 'Guerre totale et troubles mentaux', p. 138.

94. Letter of Franz Müller, 21 January 1915, cited by Ulrich and Ziemann, eds., *Frontalltag im Ersten Weltkrieg*, p. 102.

95. Ulrich, *Die Augenzeugen*, p. 213. See the suggestive discussion of mental illness, war psychiatry, and the discourse of 'nerves' in ibid., pp. 191–226.

96. Horne, 'L'invasion de 1914 dans la mémoire', p. 115.

97. Becker, 'Guerre totale et troubles mentaux', pp. 151, with reference to her article: 'Dadaïsme, surréalisme, guerre, choc traumatique', *14–18 Aujourd'hui / Today / Heute* 3, 2000.

98. Cited in Lenz, 'Kirchner—Meidner—Beckmann', p. 175.

99. Max Beckmann, letter of 4 May 1915, cited in ibid. p. 176.

100. Max Beckmann, letter of 18 April 1915, cited in Mommsen, *Bürgerliche Kultur und künstlerische Avantgarde*, p. 144.

101. Ibid., p. 186.

102. Cobb, *The Red Glutton*, p. 317.

103. Schubert, 'Otto Dix zeichnet im Ersten Weltkrieg'.

104. Barron, *Entartete Kunst*, pp. 224–30.

105. Winter, *The Experience of World War I*, p. 230. The Tate Gallery, London, holds a collection of his war work.

106. Rother, ed., *Der Weltkrieg 1914–1918*, p. 344.

8 VICTORY, TRAUMA, AND POST-WAR DISORDER

1. Lieutenant-General von Seeckt, the German chief of the Turkish general staff, letter 2 May 1918, in Otto and Schmiedel, eds., *Der erste Weltkrieg*, p. 296.

2. From a speech by Lieutenant-General Wilhelm Groener, chief of staff of the army group Kiev, to the education and press officers of the army group, late August or early September 1918, in ibid., pp. 314–16.

3. Herwig, *The First World War*, pp. 433–8; Isnenghi and Rochat, *La Grande Guerra*, pp. 460–4.

4. Herwig, *The First World War*, pp. 400–16; Bourne, *Britain and the Great War*, pp. 82–90; Sheffield, *Forgotten Victory*, pp. 221–37.

5. Cited in Deist, 'Verdeckter Militärstreik im Kriegsjahr 1918?', p. 148. Emphasis in the original.

6. Herwig, *First World War*, p. 410.

7. Einem, *Ein Armeeführer erlebt den Weltkrieg*, diary 23 June 1918, p. 410.

8. Herwig, *First World War*, p. 414; Smith et al., *France and the Great War*, p. 151.

9. ACS Rome, PCM Busta 98, 19.4.5, Comando Supremo, Ufficio Operazioni, report on the conditions of the population and prisoners in the invaded Italian territories, 24 February 1918.

10. Diary entry Albrecht von Thaer, 26/27 April 1918, in Otto and Schmiedel, eds., *Der erste Weltkrieg*, p. 289.

11. Herwig, *First World War*, pp. 416–22; 'Marne', in Hirschfeld et al., eds., *Enzyklopädie Erster Weltkrieg*, p. 699; Sheffield, *Forgotten Victory*, pp. 237–42.

12. Einem, *Ein Armeeführer erlebt den Weltkrieg*, editor's note to letter 9 August 1918, p. 423. Cf. Deist, 'Verdeckter Militärstreik im Kriegsjahr 1918?', pp. 146–67.

13. Otto, 'Die Kriegstagebücher im Weltkriege', p. 658.

14. Report by the commanders of the Weser Estuary Fortifications, 14 August 1918, in Berlin, ed., *Die deutsche Revolution 1918/19*, p. 110.

15. Archive of the Library of Contemporary History, Stuttgart, The papers of Pechtold-Peters: Walter Pechtold. Autobiographisches. 'Die Erinnerungen des Soldaten Walter Pechtold (1898–1977) aus den Jahren 1913–1919', pp. 180–4 and 194.

16. Hull, *Absolute Destruction*, pp. 260–2.

17. Einem, *Ein Armeeführer erlebt den Weltkrieg*, diary entry 20 August 1918, p. 427.

18. Ibid., diary entries and letters 23, 24, 28, 29 August and 14 September 1918, pp. 428–9, 434.

19. Ibid., letter 31 August 1918, p. 430.

20. Diary entry 1 October 1918, cited in Herwig, *The First World War*, p. 433.

21. Einem, *Ein Armeeführer erlebt den Weltkrieg*, letter 6 September 1918; p. 432, letter 9 September 1918, p. 433.

22. Ibid., diary entries 25, 27, 28 September 1918, pp. 438–40.

23. Ibid., diary entry 8 October 1918, p. 447.

24. Deist, 'Verdeckter Militärstreik im Kriegsjahr 1918?', pp. 151, 159.

25. Einem, *Ein Armeeführer erlebt den Weltkrieg*, diary entries 1, 2, 3 and letter 6 November 1918, pp. 458–62, 464.

26. Winter, *Haig's Command*, pp. 211–12. Winter's claim that German morale and strength were still 'high along the whole front' in the last three months of war is

not credible. It is not based on German sources or literature, but entirely on a selective reading of pessimistic Allied accounts. The Allies' surprise at the armistice is explained by their expectation of and desire for an unambiguous military defeat of the German army in battle, including a push to the Rhine.

27. French, ' "Had we known how bad things were in Germany, we might have got stiffer terms" ', p. 86.
28. Stone, *The Eastern Front*, pp. 232–55.
29. Ibid., pp. 124–7.
30. Cf. Rauchensteiner, 'Österreich-Ungarn', pp. 64–86.
31. Sanborn, *Drafting the Russian Nation*, p. 36.
32. Schumann, 'Europa, der Erste Weltkrieg und die Nachkriegszeit: eine Kontinuität der Gewalt?', pp. 30–1. He refers to Theodor Schieder, 'Typologie und Erscheinungsformen des Nationalstaats in Europa', *Historische Zeitschrift* 202 (1966), pp. 58–81.
33. Mosse, *Fallen Soldiers*, esp. ch. 8; Nolte, *Der europäische Bürgerkrieg*. Cf. for the brutalization thesis also Hobsbawm, *Age of Extremes*, pp. 26, 49.
34. Einem, *Ein Armeeführer erlebt den Weltkrieg*, letter 30 September, diary entry and letter 4 October 1918, pp. 441, 444–5.
35. Einem, *Ein Armeeführer erlebt den Weltkrieg*, letter 18 October 1918, p. 450.
36. Cf. Ziemann, *Front und Heimat*, pp. 178–82.
37. Herwig, *The First World War*, p. 445.
38. Mai, *Das Ende des Kaiserreichs*, p. 152.
39. Hoffmann, 'Between integration and rejection: the Jewish community in Germany, 1914–1918'; Angress, 'Die Ausbreitung des Antisemitismus'; in Werner Mosse and Arnold Paucker, eds., *Deutsches Judentum in Krieg und Revolution, 1916–1923* (Tübingen, 1971), pp. 409–510.
40. Stegmann, 'Vom Neokonservatismus zum Protofaschismus', pp. 223–4.
41. Einem, *Ein Armeeführer erlebt den Weltkrieg*, diary entry 9 November 1918, p. 465.
42. Foster, *Modern Ireland*, pp. 477–511.
43. Cf. Gregory, 'Peculiarities of the English? War, violence and politics: 1900–1939', pp. 44–59.
44. Cf. Lawrence, 'Forging a peaceable kingdom', pp. 557–89.
45. Sayer, 'British reaction to the Amritsar Massacre, 1919–1920', pp. 130–64.
46. *La Vie ouvrière*, 22 June 1919, cited in Wirsching, 'Political violence in France and Italy after 1918', p. 65.
47. Ibid., pp. 66–7.
48. Cf. Mosse, *Fallen Soldiers*, pp. 167–8, 177.
49. Bartov, *Mirrors of Destruction*, p. 16. Cf. Winter, *Sites of Memory, Sites of Mourning*, pp. 27–8, 102–5.
50. Bosworth, *Mussolini's Italy*, pp. 12–13, 36.
51. Ackermann, 'La vision allemande du Soldat inconnu', p. 389.

52. Bartov, *Mirrors of Destruction*, pp. 16–17; 'Denkmäler', in Hirschfeld et al., eds., *Enzyklopädie Erster Weltkrieg*, pp. 430–3.

53. Bartov, *Mirrors of Destruction*, p. 21.

54. Cited in Beyrau, 'Der Erste Weltkrieg als Bewährungsprobe. Bolshewistische Lernprozesse aus dem "imperialistischen" Krieg', p. 102. 'Barons and colonists' referred to the fact that the landowners in Baltic region were often originally German colonists. But the same sentiment was ubiquitous across Russia.

55. Figes, *A People's Tragedy*, pp. 597–603; quotation p. 603.

56. Robert C. Tucker, cited in Fitzpatrick, *The Russian Revolution*, p. 64.

57. Beyrau, 'Der Erste Weltkrieg als Bewährungsprobe. Bolshewistische Lernprozesse aus dem "imperialistischen" Krieg', pp. 114–15.

58. Holquist, *Making War, Forging Revolution*, pp. 143–4.

59. Beyrau, 'Der Erste Weltkrieg als Bewährungsprobe. Bolshewistische Lernprozesse aus dem "imperialistischen" Krieg', pp. 104–5.

60. Cited in Figes, *A People's Tragedy*, p. 618.

61. *Krasnaia gazeta,* 1 September 1918, cited in ibid., p. 630.

62. Ibid., pp. 642–9. Cf. Fitzpatrick, *The Russian Revolution*, p. 69.

63. Figes, *A People's Tragedy*, pp. 520–36.

64. Holquist, *Making War, Forging Revolution*, pp. 144–9.

65. Ibid., pp. 164–5.

66. Ibid., pp. 178–84, citing a circular of the Organizational Bureau of the Bolshevik Party Central Committee, 24 January 1919.

67. Ibid., pp. 187–96, 200.

68. Ibid., pp. 278–9.

69. Beyrau, 'Der Erste Weltkrieg als Bewährungsprobe. Bolshewistische Lernprozesse aus dem "imperialistischen" Krieg', p. 106. On the political section's train, see Babel, *1920 Diary*, editor's notes, pp. 110–11.

70. Holquist, *Making War, Forging Revolution,* p. 203. Holquist goes on to argue that Stalinist suppression had its roots in this early Soviet violence.

71. Babel, *1920 Diary*. References to destruction of (Catholic) churches: diary entry 29 July 1920, pp. 41–2, referring to Galicia in general; 7 August 1920, p. 58. References to destruction of synagogues by Cossacks and/or Poles, 30 July 1920, pp. 43–4; reference to atrocities committed by Polish forces on the Jews of Komarów, diary entry 28 August 1920, pp. 83–4; looting of synagogue by Bolshevik Cossacks in Komarów, diary entry 29 August 1920, p. 85.

72. Ibid., editor's introduction, pp. xlv–xlvi; diary entry 18 July 1920, p. 22; 18 August 1920, p. 76; cf. diary entry 10 August 1920, p. 63, where Babel records Apanasenko's 'deadly hatred of the aristocracy, the priests and, above all, the intelligentsia, whose presence in the army he can't stomach'.

73. Attempt to prevent looting: ibid., diary entry 10 August 1920, pp. 62–3; example of failed attempt to prevent the slaughter of Polish prisoners, 18 August 1920, p. 73. Cf. also 30 August, p. 87.

74. Ibid., entries 28 July 1920, p. 40; 3 August 1920, p. 50.

75. Ibid., entry 8 August 1920, p. 60.

76. Figes, *A People's Tragedy*, pp. 676–9.

77. Levene, 'Frontiers of genocide', pp. 101–2. This essay contains an incisive discussion of the dynamic of violence against the Jews in the Russian Civil War. On Zhitomir, Babel, *1920 Diary*, editor's notes, pp. 110–11.

78. Beyrau, 'Russische Intelligenzija und Revolution', pp. 562, 575, 581.

79. Plaggenborg, 'Grundprobleme der Kulturgeschichte der sowjetischen Zwischenkriegszeit', pp. 112–13.

80. Beyrau, 'Broken identities: The intelligentsia in revolutionary Russia', pp. 148–9.

81. Holquist, *Making War, Forging Revolution,* p. 282; Figes, *A People's Tragedy*, p. 773; Dietrich Beyrau cites a recent Russian estimate of a population loss on Soviet territory of 11.7 million from 1918 to 1921; military losses in the war are estimated at 1.8 million ('Kriegsverluste', in Hirschfeld et al., eds., *Enzyklopädie Erster Weltkrieg*, p. 665).

82. Cited in Horne, 'Socialism, peace, and revolution, 1917–1918', p. 231.

83. Ibid., pp. 232–3.

84. Procacci, *Dalla Rassegnazione alla Rivolta*, pp. 143–4.

85. Ibid., p. 145.

86. Bosworth, *Mussolini's Italy*, pp. 96–7.

87. Burgwyn, *Italian Foreign Policy in the Interwar Period,* pp. 13–14. Maier, *Recasting Bourgeois Europe*, pp. 111–14, in my opinion overstates the crisis in Italy in April 1919. Certainly there was a polarized, heated political atmosphere, with serious newspapers like Albertini's *Corriere della Sera* warning that plots were being hatched for Leninist revolution and asking Orlando to return from Paris for fear of civil war, while moderate voices counselling acceptance of a compromise peace settlement were shouted down by intemperate nationalists.

88. Bosworth, *Mussolini's Italy*, pp. 101–5.

89. Reichardt, *Faschistische Kampfbünde*, p. 71.

90. Cited in Isnenghi and Rochat, *La Grande Guerra*, p. 416.

91. Rochat, *Gli Arditi*, pp. 16, 118–19.

92. Ibid., pp. 16, 119–20, 123.

93. Ibid., pp. 121, 142–50.

94. Bosworth, *Mussolini's Italy*, p. 117.

95. Petersen, 'Das Problem der Gewalt im italienischen Faschismus, 1919–1925', pp. 329–30.

96. Ibid., p. 326, quoting Wolfgang Schieder on the Fascist will to destroy. Emphasis in the original.

97. Bosworth, *Mussolini's Italy*, pp. 79, 151, 180.

98. Reichardt, *Faschistische Kampfbünde*, p. 82.

99. Marinetti, 'Ideologie sfasciate dalla conflagrazione' (Dal giornale *L'Ardito*, febbraio 1919), in id., *Futurismo e Fascismo*, pp. 109–12.

100. Marinetti's political statements on diet were also hardly likely to endear him to the Italian masses. In 1930 he launched a great campaign against traditional

Italian cooking, particularly against pasta. 'Futurist cooking will be liberated from the ancient obsession of weight and volume, and one of its principal aims will be the abolition of *pastasciutta*. *Pastasciutta*, however grateful to the palate, is an obsolete food; it is heavy, brutalizing, and gross; . . . it induces scepticism, sloth, and pessimism . . . Spaghetti is no food for fighters . . . *Pastasciutta* is anti-virile . . . A weighty and encumbered stomach cannot be favourable to physical enthusiasm towards women.' The right Futurist food was meat. Cited from his *La Cucina Futurista*, 1932, in Elizabeth David, *Italian Food*, Harmondsworth, 1969, pp. 93–4.

101. Sternhell et al., *Die Entstehung der faschistischen Ideologie*, p. 271.
102. Bosworth, *Mussolini's Italy*, pp. 154–8.
103. Reichardt, *Faschistische Kampfbünde*, pp. 85, 101–2, 200.
104. Bosworth, *Mussolini's Italy*, p. 85.
105. Lyttelton, *The Seizure of Power*, p. 22.
106. Reichardt, *Faschistische Kampfbünde*, p. 71.
107. Petersen, 'Das Problem der Gewalt im italienischen Faschismus, 1919–1925', *passim*; Bologna province: Bosworth, *Mussolini's Italy*, p. 134.
108. Petersen, 'Das Problem der Gewalt im italienischen Faschismus, 1919–1925', pp. 339–40.
109. Maier, *Recasting Bourgeois Europe*, pp. 46–7.
110. Bosworth, *Mussolini's Italy*, p. 180; quotation with emphasis in the original, p. 182. For a superlative account of the Fascist seizure of power see MacGregor Knox, *War and Revolution. Origins and Dynamics of the Fascist and National Socialist Dictatorships*, vol. 1: *To the Threshold of Power, 1922/1933*, forthcoming, Cambridge, 2007.
111. Gugliemo Ferrero, *Problems of Peace: From the Holy Alliance to the League of Nations*, New York, 1919, cited in Mayer, *Politics and Diplomacy of Peacemaking*, p. 6.
112. Both cited in ibid., p. 6.
113. Charles de Gaulle, 'La limitation des armaments', October 1918, *Lettres, notes et carnets, 1905–1918*, Paris, 1980, p. 536, cited in Smith et al., *France and the Great War, 1914–1918*, p. 181.
114. Cited in Ullrich, *Kriegsalltag. Hamburg im ersten Weltkrieg*, p. 156.
115. Ibid., pp. 157–60.
116. Berlin, ed., *Die deutsche Revolution*, pp. 135–6.
117. Mendelssohn-Bartholdy, *The War and German Society*, pp. 171–3, quotation p. 173.
118. Volkmann, 'Gesellschaft und Militär am Ende des Ersten und des Zweiten Weltkrieges', p. 842.
119. Cited in Liulevicius, 'Von "Ober Ost" nach "Ostland"?', p. 306.
120. Bessel, *Germany after the First World War*, p. 258.
121. Cited in ibid., p. 85.
122. Volkmann, 'Gesellschaft und Militär am Ende des Ersten und des Zweiten Weltkrieges', p. 843; Krumeich and Hirschfeld, 'Die Geschichtsschreibung zum Ersten Weltkrieg', p. 305.

123. Cited in Kotowski, ' "Noch ist ja der Krieg gar nicht zu Ende" ', p. 433.
124. Schumann, *Politische Gewalt in der Weimarer Republik*. Sven Reichardt argues that it is incorrect to describe political violence in the Weimar Republic as a civil war, for a civil war is fought between military-type organizations against each other or the state. *Faschistische Kampfbünde*, p. 54.
125. Mosse, *Fallen Soldiers*.
126. Klemperer, *Curriculum vitae,* vol. 2, p. 558.
127. Brüning, *Memoiren*, p. 96.
128. Wette, *Gustav Noske*, pp. 416–24.
129. Ibid., pp. 418–22.
130. Cf. Weisbrod, 'Gewalt in der Politik. Zur politischen Kultur in Deutschland zwischen den beiden Weltkriegen', p. 395; cf. Schumann, *Politische Gewalt in der Weimarer Republik*, pp. 45–142.
131. Count Brockdorff-Rantzau, confidential letter to People's Commissar Scheidemann, 9 December 1918, in id., *Dokumente und Gedanken um Versailles*, p. 30.
132. Cited in Klein, 'Between Compiègne and Versailles', p. 203.
133. *Akten der Reichskanzlei,* vol. 1, note of the First Quartermaster-General, Groener, on the days in Weimar, 18 to 20 June 1919, pp. 484–5; Schwabe, 'Germany's peace aims and the domestic and international constraints', pp. 55–6.
134. Cited in Horne, 'Der Schatten des Krieges: Französische Politik in den zwanziger Jahren', p. 149.
135. Stevenson, 'French war aims and peace planning', pp. 93–4.
136. 'Kriegsschäden', in Hirschfeld et al. eds., *Enzyklopädie Erster Weltkrieg*, pp. 658–61, here p. 660.
137. Cited in Goldstein, 'Great Britain: the home front', p. 151.
138. Ibid., pp. 148–57.
139. Marks, 'The myths of reparations'; Ritschl, *Deutschlands Krise und Konjunktur 1924–1934*.
140. See Marks, 'Smoke and mirrors: in smoke-filled rooms and the Galerie des Glaces', p. 357; cf. Stephen A. Schuker, *The End of French Predominance in Europe: The Financial Crisis of 1924 and the Adoption of the Dawes Plan*, Chapel Hill, NC, 1976. The argument is summarized in McNeil, 'Could Germany pay?'.
141. Glaser, 'The making of the economic peace', esp. pp. 469–71.
142. Count Brockdorff-Rantzau, appendix to the cover note to the German counter-proposals to the draft treaty, 29 May 1919, in id., *Dokumente und Gedanken um Versailles*, pp. 102–3.
143. Count Brockdorff-Rantzau, memoir of Versailles, 1 January 1922, in ibid., p. 207.
144. Jeannesson, 'Übergriffe der französischen Besatzungsmacht und deutsche Beschwerden', p. 214.
145. Krumeich, 'Der "Ruhrkampf" als Krieg', pp. 20 and 24.

146. Cf. Soutou, 'Vom Rhein zur Ruhr: Absichten und Planungen der französischen Regierung'; Horne, 'Der Schatten des Krieges: Französische Politik in den zwanziger Jahren', p. 151.

147. Cited in Cepl-Kaufmann, 'Zwischen "Ruhrbesetzung" und "Ruhrkampf". Schriftsteller im Spannungsfeld der Politik', p. 60.

148. Schieder, 'Das italienische Experiment', pp. 76 and 122.

149. Interview with Leo Negrelli, published in *Corriere Italiano* (Rome), 16 October 1923, in Jäckel, ed., *Hitler. Sämtliche Aufzeichnungen*, pp. 1035–7.

150. Cited in Ulrich, *Die Augenzeugen*, p. 256.

151. General Hans von Seeckt, memorandum on the international situation, 11 September 1922, Michalka and Niedhart eds., *Die ungeliebte Republik*, pp. 143–4.

152. Prost, *In the Wake of War. 'Les anciens combattants'*.

153. Horne, 'Der Schatten des Krieges', p. 148.

154. Archives Nationales, Paris: Fonds Millerand—AP/470, Carton 43 Elections 1919.

155. Hanna, *The Mobilization of Intellect*, p. 220.

156. Cited in Fischer, *Krieg der Illusionen*, p. 670.

157. Kantorowicz to Ministerialdirektor de Haas, Auswärtiges Amt, 23 June 1929, in the Kantorowicz papers, cited in Geiss, foreword to Kantorowicz, *Gutachten zur Krieggschuldfrage 1914*, p. 35.

158. Geiss, ibid., p. 36 n. 68.

159. The Treaty of Versailles laid down the drastic limitation of Germany's army, the prohibition of an air force, the reduction of its navy to the level of a coastal force; Germany agreed to surrender most of its merchant fleet, deliver coal free to France, Belgium, and Italy for ten years, the loss of 13 per cent of its territory containing 10 per cent of its population including the loss of Alsace-Lorraine to France and large parts of Silesia, Posen, and West Prussia to Poland, and all its colonial territories. The German offer of 100 billion marks: Count Brockdorff-Rantzau, cover note to the German counter-proposals to the draft treaty, 29 May 1919, in id., *Dokumente und Gedanken um Versailles*, p. 85. In fact, the offer of 100 billion marks was without interest, and hedged around with so many conditions that it was actually worth far less—30 billion, on the estimate of Keynes. See Marks, 'Smoke and mirrors', p. 355.

160. Kershaw, *Hitler, 1889–1936: Hubris*, pp. 90–7.

161. Cited in ibid., p. 102.

162. Köpf, 'Hitlers psychogene Erblindung. Geschichte einer Krankenakte', pp. 783–90.

163. Recently discovered by Paul O'Brien, *Mussolini in the First World War*.

164. Binding and Hoche, *Die Freigabe der Vernichtung lebensunwerten Lebens*, pp. 24, 27, 32, and *passim*.

165. Burleigh, *Death and Deliverance*, p. 160, and pp. 93–161, *passim*.

166. Blasius, 'Ambivalenzen des Fortschritts. Psychiatrie und psychisch Kranke in der Geschichte der Moderne', pp. 261–3.
167. Burleigh, *Death and Deliverance*, p. 11.
168. Cited in Fest, *Hitler. Eine Biographie*, p. 735.
169. Hitler, *Mein Kampf*, p. 290.
170. Evans, *The Coming of the Third Reich*, p. 197.
171. Cited in Kershaw, *Hitler 1889–1936: Hubris*, p. 249.

CONCLUSION

1. Wehler, *Deutsche Gesellschaftsgeschichte*, vol. 3, p. 1168. In fact, even contemporaries perceived it thus. Cf. Churchill, *The Second World War*, vol. 1, p. ix; Hobsbawm, *Age of Extremes*.
2. Petra Terhoeven, review article of Aram Mattioli, *Experimentierfeld der Gewalt. Der Abessinienkrieg und seine internationale Bedeutung 1935–1941*, Zürich 2005, and Giulia Brogini Künzi, *Italien und der Abessinienkrieg 1935/36. Kolonialkrieg oder Totaler Krieg?* Paderborn 2005. In H-Soz-u-Kult, accessed 06.09.2006, <http://hsozkult.geschichte.hu-berlin.de/rezensionen/2006-3-166>.
3. Cf. Thoß, 'Die Zeit der Weltkriege—Epochen als Erfahrungseinheit?', p. 17.
4. Hoeres, 'Ein dreißigjähriger Krieg der deutschen Philosophie?'. On theologians see Greschat, 'Begleitung und Deutung der beiden Weltkriege durch evangelische Theologen'.
5. Förster, 'Einführende Bemerkungen', p. 37.
6. *Hitler's Willing Executioners*.
7. Kershaw, 'Antisemitismus und die NS-Bewegung vor 1933', p. 29.
8. The Allies did succeed in having the Turkish government prosecute some of the perpetrators, mainly of lower ranks. On this first series of war crimes trials in history see Kramer, 'The First Wave of International War Crimes Trials: Istanbul and Leipzig'; Akçam, *Armenien und der Völkermord*.
9. Mark Levene has pointed to this relationship (except for Turkey) in 'Frontiers of genocide', especially pp. 104 and 115–17. Recent research on the development of the decision to murder all the Jews of Europe increasingly points to the connection between the failure of 'Blitzkrieg' in the invasion of the Soviet Union and the realization in late 1941 that this entailed a long war of attrition for which Germany was not prepared, together with the entry of the USA into the war in December 1941, and a probable decision of Hitler and the Nazi elite to carry out systematic mass murder of the Jews. Cf. the summary of the research in Bergmann and Wetzel, 'Antisemitismus im Ersten und Zweiten Weltkrieg. Ein Forschungsüberblick'. For a comprehensive study, see Browning, *The Origins of the Final Solution*.

10. Kershaw, 'War and political violence in twentieth-century Europe', p. 110. I am grateful to Ian Kershaw for making available to me his stimulating and wide-ranging article.

11. *Documents on German Foreign Policy 1918–1945*, Series D, vol. 7, p. 205.

12. Vejas Gabriel Liulevicius, 'Von "Ober Ost" nach "Ostland"?', in *Die vergessene Front. Der Osten 1914/15. Ereignis, Wirkung, Nachwirkung,* ed. Gerhard P. Groß, Paderborn, etc: Schöningh, 2006, pp. 295–310, here pp. 303–5.

13. Böhler, 'Tragische Verstrickung oder Auftakt zum Vernichtungskrieg?', p. 50; cf. Jochen Böhler, *Auftakt zum Vernichtungskrieg. Die Wehrmacht in Polen 1939,* Frankfurt, 2006.

14. Overmans, ' "Hunnen" und "Untermenschen"—deutsche und russisch/sowjetische Kriegsgefangenschaftserfahrungen im Zeitalter der Weltkriege'.

HISTORIOGRAPHICAL NOTE

1. For a recent survey see Jay Winter and Antoine Prost, *The Great War in History. Debates and Controversies, 1914 to the Present,* Cambridge, 2005. The best guide to the historiography of Germany (as well as to almost every other imaginable country and theme) is the excellent *Enzyklopädie Erster Weltkrieg,* edited by Gerhard Hirschfeld, Gerd Krumeich, and Irina Renz; although it contains only two very brief historiographical articles, most essays and encyclopaedia entries contain references to the historiography.

2. Cork, *A Bitter Truth,* pp. 8, 10.

3. Ibid., p. 149. The only exception to the rule was American art, which remained resolutely pro-war and anti-German: see ibid., pp. 189–94.

4. Ferguson, *The Pity of War,* p. 360.

5. Eksteins, *Rites of Spring,* p. 156.

6. The term 'modern militarism' is not used by Eksteins; see Förster, *Der doppelte Militarismus.*

7. Eksteins, *Rites of Spring,* pp. 64–70.

8. Hull, *Absolute Destruction,* pp. 1–2.

9. Ferguson, *The Pity of War,* pp. 282–317.

10. Hull concedes this point, saying the ' "cult of the offensive" was a European phenomenon that gripped all the Continental armies before 1914', but immediately relativizes it by claiming 'nowhere [was it] more assiduously cultivated or more thoroughly adopted as the single foundation for all military training and planning than in Germany'. *Absolute Destruction,* p. 167.

11. Ibid., p. 165.

12. Ibid., pp. 96–7.

13. Ibid., p. 3.

14. Wolfgang Sofsky, *Traktat über die Gewalt,* pp. 225–6 A selection of Sofsky's writings in English can be found in his edited collection: *Violence: Terrorism, Genocide, War,* London, 2003.

15. Cited in Pick, *War Machine*, p. 11.

16. Joseph A. Schumpeter, *Imperialism and Social Classes*, [1919 and 1927], Oxford, 1951, cited in Pick, *War Machine*, p. 163.

17. Ibid., p. 11.

18. Zygmunt Bauman, *Modernity and the Holocaust*, Cambridge, 1989, cited in Pick, *War Machine*, pp. 186–7.

19. Mosse, *Fallen Soldiers*, pp. 10, 33.

20. Mosse, *The Nationalization of the Masses*, p. 2.

21. Mosse, *Fallen Soldiers*, pp. 53–5; 70. Mosse was aware of this defect in his argument, conceding that the elite was probably not representative of all youth, especially in relation to 'war enthusiasm' in 1914. However, his focus was on the memory of war, and he claims with some justification that because that elite group of youth published widely on its war experience, their views dominated after the war. Ibid., p. 68.

22. Mosse, *Fallen Soldiers*, ch. 8; quotations p. 163.

23. Winter, *The Experience of World War I*, pp. 140 and 213–14.

Bibliography

SOURCES, OFFICIAL PUBLICATIONS, AND MEMOIRS

Akçam, Taner, *Armenien und der Völkermord. Die Istanbuler Prozesse und die türkische Nationalbewegung* (Hamburg, 1996)

Akten der Reichskanzlei, vol. 1: Hagen Schulze, ed., *Das Kabinett Scheidemann: 13. Februar bis 20. Juni 1919* (Boppard am Rhein, 1971)

Albertini, Luigi, *Venti anni di vita politica*, part 1: *L'Esperienza democratica italiana dal 1898 al 1914*, vol. 2: *1909–1914* (Bologna, 1951)

Anon, *Die armenischen Greuel und Deutschland. Urkundliche Belege* (no place, 1917)

Atrocités Bulgares en Macédoine (Faits et Documents). Exposé soumis par le recteur des Universités d'Athènes aux recteurs des Universités d'Europe et d'Amérique [by Théodore Zaïmis, recteur de l'Université Nationale et de l'Université Capodistrienne] (Athens, 1913)

[Austria] Glaise von Horstenau, Edmund, ed., *Österreich-Ungarns letzter Krieg, 1914–1918*, for the Österreichisches Bundesministerium für Landesverteidigung und das Kriegsarchiv, 7 vols. (Vienna 1929–38), vol. 6: *Das Kriegsjahr 1917* (1936).

Bab, Julius ed., *1914. Der Deutsche Krieg im Deutschen Gedicht*, 2 vols. (Berlin, n.d., probably 1919)

Babel, Isaac, *1920 Diary,* edited and with an Introduction and Notes by Carol J. Avins. Trans. from Russian (New Haven and London, 2002; 1995)

Becker, Annette, ed., *Marc Bloch. L'Histoire, la Guerre, la Résistance* (Paris, 2006)

[Belgium], *The Case of Belgium in the Present War. An Account of the Violation of the Neutrality of Belgium and of the Laws of War on Belgian Territory*, published for the Belgian Delegates to the United States (New York, London, etc., 1914)

Berlin, Jörg, ed., *Die deutsche Revolution 1918/19. Quellen und Dokumente* (Cologne, 1979)

Bernhardi, Friedrich von, *Taktik und Ausbildung der Infanterie. Gedanken und Erwägungen in Geiste des modernen Gefechts* (Berlin, 1910)

—— *Deutschland und der nächste Krieg* (Stuttgart and Berlin, 1912), trans. into English as *Germany and the Next War* (London, 1912)

Binding, Karl and Alfred Hoche, *Die Freigabe der Vernichtung lebensunwerten Lebens. Ihr Maß und ihre Form* (Leipzig, 1922; 1920)

Bloch, Johann von, *Der Krieg*, 6 vols., vol. 6: *Der Mechanismus des Krieges und seine Wirkungen. Die Frage vom internationalen Schiedsgericht* (Berlin, 1899)

Brittain, Vera, *Testament of Youth. An Autobiographical Study of the Years 1900–1925* (London, 1979; 1933)

Brock, Michael and Eleanor Brock, eds., *H. H. Asquith. Letters to Venetia Stanley* (Oxford, 1985)

Brockdorff-Rantzau, Count, *Dokumente und Gedanken um Versailles*, Berlin: Verlag für Kulturpolitik (3rd edn., 1925; 1920)

Brüning, Heinrich, *Memoiren 1918–1934* (Stuttgart, 1970)

Cadorna, Luigi, *La Guerra alla fronte italiana. Fino all'arresto sulla linea del Piave e del Grappa (24 maggio 1915–9 novembre 1917)*, 2 vols. (Milan, 1921)

Caizergues, Pierre, *Jean Cocteau. Photographies et dessins de guerre* (Paris, 2000)

Clausewitz, Carl von, *On War*, ed. and trans. Michael Howard and Peter Paret (London, 1993; 1976)

Cobb, Irvin S., *The Red Glutton. Impressions of War Written at and near the Front* (London, New York, Toronto, 1915)

Commission d'Enquête sur la violation des règles du droit des gens, des lois et des coutumes de la guerre, *Rapports sur la violation du droit des gens en Belgique*, 2 vols. (Paris and Nancy, 1915–16)

—— 4 vols. (Brussels, 1921–3): vol. 1 (2 parts), *Rapports sur les attentats commis par les troupes allemandes pendant l'invasion et l'occupation de la Belgique* (Brussels, 1922); vol. 2, *Rapports sur les déportations des ouvriers belges et sur les traitements infligés aux prisonniers de guerre et aux prisonniers civils belges*, 2 vols. (Brussels and Liège, 1923)

Conrad von Hötzendorff, Franz, *Aus meiner Dienstzeit 1906–1918*, 5 vols. (Vienna, 1921–5)

Delbrück, Joachim, ed., *Der deutsche Krieg in Feldpostbriefen*, vol. 1: *Lüttich/Namur/ Antwerpen* (5th edn., Munich, 1915)

Deutsche Reden in schwerer Zeit [subtitle: gehalten von den Professoren an der Universität Berlin v. Wilamowitz-Moellendorff etc.], eds., Zentralstelle für Volkswohlfahrt und . . . Verein für volkstümliche Kurse von Berliner Hochschullehrern (Berlin, 1914)

Documents on German Foreign Policy 1918–1945, Series D, vol. 7, *The Last Days of Peace. August 9–September 3, 1939* (London and Washington, 1956)

Einem, Karl von, *Ein Armeeführer erlebt den Weltkrieg. Persönliche Aufzeichnungen des Generalobsteren v. Einem*, ed. Junius Alter (Leipzig, 1938)

The Collected Papers of Albert Einstein, vol. 6, *The Berlin Years: Writings, 1914–1917*, ed. A. J. Kox, Martin J. Klein, and Robert Schulmann (Princeton, 1996); vol. 8, *The Berlin Years: Correspondence, 1914–1918*, Part A: *1914–1917*, ed. Robert Schulmann, A. J. Kox, Michel Jansen, and József Illy (Princeton, 1998)

Fadini, Francesco, *Caporetto dalla parte del vincitore. La biografia del generale Otto von Below e il suo diario inedito sulla campagna d'Italia del 1917* (Florence, 1974)

Fiedler, H. G., ed., *Das Oxforder Buch Deutscher Dichtung vom 12ten bis zum 20sten Jahrhundert* (Oxford, 1920)

Freud, Sigmund, 'On Transience' (1915); *Thoughts for the Times on War and Death* (1915); in *The Standard Edition of the Complete Psychological Works of Sigmund Freud*, vol. 14 (London, 1957)

Geiss, Imanuel, ed., *July 1914. The Outbreak of the First World War: Selected Documents* (London, 1967)

Gerard, James W., *My Four Years in Germany* (New York, 1917)

[Germany] Auswärtiges Amt, *Die völkerrechtswidrige Führung des belgischen Volkskriegs* (Berlin, 1915); English edition: *The German Army in Belgium. The White Book of May 1915*, trans. E. N. Bennett (London, 1921)

[Germany] *Felddienst-Ordnung*, Berlin, 1908

[Germany] Kaiserliches Statistisches Amt. *Statistisches Jahrbuch für das Deutsche Reich, 1914*

[Germany] *Verhandlungen des Reichstags. XIII. Legislaturperiode. 2. Session*, vol. 308, *Stenographische Berichte.*

Goltz, Generalfeldmarschall Colmar von der, *Denkwürdigkeiten*, ed. Friedrich Freiherr von der Goltz and Wolfgang Foerster (Berlin 1929)

Great Britain, War Office, *Armies of the Balkan States 1914–1918. The Military Forces of Bulgaria, Greece, Montenegro, Rumania, and Servia* (Nashville, Tenn. 1996)

Greim, Andreas, ' "50 Fahrten mit dem Lazarettzuge nach der Westfront". Die Kriegserlebnisse und -erfahrungen der Darmstädter Sanitäter Alfred Ihne und Alexander Perlyn auf dem Vereinslazarettzug 03 "Großherzogin von Hessen" ', in Ute Schneider and Thomas Lange, eds., *Kriegsalltage. Darmstadt und die Technische Hochschule im Ersten Weltkrieg* (Darmstadt, 2002), pp. 311–56

Grey of Falloden, Viscount, *Twenty-Five Years, 1892–1916*, 2 vols. (London, 1925)

Guttmann, Bernhard, *Schattenriß einer Generation, 1888–1918* (Stuttgart, 1950)

Harel, Véronique, ed., *Les Affiches de la Grande Guerre* (Péronne, 1998)

Herzog, Rudolf, *Ritter, Tod und Teufel: Kriegsgedichte* (Leipzig, 1916)

Hitler, Adolf, *Mein Kampf*, trans. Ralph Mannheim (London, 1992; 1969)

Horne, Charles F., ed., *Source Records of World War I*, 7 vols. (Lewiston, New York; Queenstown, Ontario; Lampeter, Wales, 1998); Originally published as *The Great Events of the Great War* (New York, 1923)

Hurd, Archibald, *History of the Great War Based on Official Documents. The Merchant Navy*, 3 vols. (London, 1920–1924)

Jäckel, Eberhard, with Axel Kuhn, eds., *Hitler. Sämtliche Aufzeichnungen 1905–1924* (Stuttgart, 1980)

Jannasch, Lilli, *Untaten des preußisch-deutschen Militarismus* (Wiesbaden, 1924)

Jünger, Ernst, *Der Kampf als inneres Erlebnis* (Berlin, 1922)

—— *In Stahlgewittern. Aus dem Tagebuch eines Stoßtruppführers*, 6th edn. (Berlin, 1925); English ed. *Storm of Steel*, trans. Michael Hofmann (London, 2003)

Kaes, Anton, Martin Jay, and Edward Dimendberg, eds., *The Weimar Republic Sourcebook* (Berkeley, Los Angeles, and London, 1994)

[Kautsky] *Die Deutschen Dokumente zum Kriegsausbruch 1914*, published by Karl Kautsky for the German Foreign Ministry, ed. Walter Schücking and Max Montgelas (Berlin, 1922), 2nd edn.; 4 vols. in 2 parts

Klemperer, Victor, *Curriculum vitae. Erinnerungen 1881–1918*, ed. Walter Nowojski, 2 vols. (Berlin, 1996)

Kuhl, Hermann von, *Der Weltkrieg 1914–1918* (Berlin, 1929)

Lenin, Vladimir I., 'The War and Russian Social-Democracy', in *Sotsial-Demokrat*, 1 November 1914, in *Selected Works*, 3 vols. (Moscow, 1963) vol. 1

—— *Imperialism, the Highest Stage of Capitalism* (1917), in *Selected Works*, 3 vols. (Moscow, 1963) vol. 1

Lepsius, Johannes, *Deutschland und Armenien 1914–1918. Sammlung Diplomatischer Aktenstücke* (Potsdam, 1919)

Liman von Sanders, Otto, *Fünf Jahre Türkei* (Berlin, 1920)

Lloyd George, David, *War Memoirs*, 6 vols. (London, 1933)

Ludendorff, Erich, *Meine Kriegserinnerungen 1914–1918* (Berlin, 1919)

—— *Kriegführung und Politik* (Berlin, 1922; 1921)

Manifesti illustrati della Grande Guerra, ed. on behalf of the Biblioteca di Storia moderna e contemporanea by Marzia Miele and Cesarina Vighy (Rome, 1996)

Mann, Thomas, 'Gedanken im Kriege' first published in November 1914, in Michael Mann, ed., *Das Thomas Mann-Buch. Eine innere Biographie in Selbstzeugnissen* (Frankfurt, 1965), pp. 80–95

Mann, Thomas, *Betrachtungen eines Unpolitischen*, in *Gesammelte Werke*, vol. 12, *Reden und Aufsätze* (Berlin, 1960; 1918)

Marinetti, Filippo Tommaso, 'Fondazione e Manifesto del futurismo' (first published in *Le Figaro*, 20 February 1909), in id., *Teoria e invenzione futurista*, ed. Luciano De Maria, pp. 7–14

—— *Futurismo e Fascismo* (Foligno, 1924)

—— *Taccuini 1915–1921*, ed. Alberto Bertoni (Bologna, 1987)

—— *Teoria e invenzione futurista*, ed. Luciano De Maria (Milan, 1998; 1968)

Michalka, Wolfgang and Gottfried Niedhart, eds., *Die ungeliebte Republik: Dokumente zur Innen-und Außenpolitik Weimars 1918–1933* (Munich, 1980)

Mokveld, L., *The German Fury in Belgium* (London, 1917)

Mussolini, Benito, *Mein Kriegstagebuch* (Zürich, Leipzig, Vienna, 1930; Ital. edn. 1923)

Nicolai, Georg Friedrich, *Die Biologie des Krieges. Betrachtungen eines deutschen Naturforschers* (Zürich, 1917)

Österreich-Ungarns Außenpolitik von der bosnischen Krise 1908 bis zum Kriegsausbruch 1914. Diplomatische Aktenstücke des österreichisch-ungarischen Ministeriums des Äußern, selected by Ludwig Bittner, Alfred Francis Pribram, Heinrich Srbik, and Hans Uebersberger, 8 vols. (Vienna and Leipzig, 1930)

Oszwald, Robert P., *Der Streit um den belgischen Franktireurkrieg. Eine kritische Untersuchung der Ereignisse in den Augusttagen 1914 und der darüber bis 1930 erschienenen Literatur, unter Benutzung bisher nicht veröffentlichten Materials* (Cologne, 1931)

Otto, Ernst, 'Die Kriegstagbücher im Weltkriege', *Archiv für Politik und Geschichte*, 5 (1925)

Otto, Helmut and Karl Schmiedel, eds., *Der erste Weltkrieg. Dokumente* (Berlin, 1983; 1977)

Péladan, Joséphin, *L'Allemagne devant L'humanité et Le Devoir des Civilisés* (Paris, 1916)

Persecutions of the Greeks in Turkey since the Beginning of the European War. Trans. from official Greek Documents by Carrol N. Brown and Thedore P. Ion (New York, 1918)

[Prussian General Staff] *Kriegsbrauch im Landkriege* (*Kriegsgeschichtliche Einzelschriften*, 31), (Berlin, 1902); Eng. trans., *The German War Book. Being 'The Usages of War on Land' issued by the Great General Staff of the German Army*, with a critical introduction by J. H. Morgan (London, 1915)

Reichsarchiv, *Der Weltkrieg 1914 bis 1918. Die militärischen Operationen zu Lande*, 14 vols. (Berlin, 1925–44), vol. 1, *Die Grenzschlachten im Westen* (1925); vol. 10, *Die Operationen des Jahres 1916 bis zum Wechsel in der Obersten Heeresleitung* (1936); vol. 13: *Die Kriegführung im Sommer und Herbst 1917. Die Ereignisse außerhalb der Westfront bis November 1918* (1942)

Reichsarchiv, *Der Weltkrieg 1914 bis 1918. Kriegsrüstung und Kriegswirtschaft, Anlagen zum ersten Band* (Berlin, 1930)

Reichswehrministerium, *Sanitätsbericht über das deutsche Heer [. . .] im Weltkrieg, 1914–1918*, 3 vols. (Berlin, 1934–8); vol. 2, *Der Sanitätsdienst im Gefechts- und Schlachtenverlauf im Weltkriege 1914/1918* (1938); vol. 3, *Die Krankenbewegung bei dem Deutschen Feld- und Besatzungsheer* (1934)

Relazioni della Reale Commissione D'Inchiesta sulle Violazioni del Diritto delle Genti Commesse dal Nemico. 8 vols., Milan and Rome, n.d. [1919 et seq.], vol. 1: *La Partecipazione della Germania. Danni ai Monumenti*; vol. 2: *Mezzi illeciti di guerra*; vol. 3: *Trattamento dei Prigionieri di Guerra e degli Internati Civili*; vol. 4: *L'occupazione delle provincie invase*

Report of the International Commission to Inquire into the Causes and Conduct of the Balkan Wars, 1914 (Carnegie Endowment for International Peace. Division of Intercourse and Education, Publication No. 4, 1914)

Richert, Dominik, *Beste Gelegenheit zum Sterben. Meine Erlebnisse im Kriege 1914–1918*, ed. Angelika Tramitz and Bernd Ulrich (Munich, 1989)

Roberts, David, *Minds at War. The Poetry and Experience of the First World War* (Burgess Hill, West Sussex, 1998)

Sauer, Joseph, *Die Zerstörung von Kirchen und Kunstdenkmälern an der Westfront* (Freiburg, 1917)

Schauwecker, Franz, *So war der Krieg. 200 Kampfaufnahmen aus der Front* (2nd edn., Berlin, 1927)

Schmitz, Jean, and Norbert Nieuwland, *Documents pour servir à l'histoire de l'invasion allemande dans les provinces de Namur et de Luxembourg*, 8 vols. (Brussels and Paris, 1919–24)

Scott, James Brown, ed., *Texts of the Peace Conferences at The Hague, 1899 and 1907* (Boston and London, 1908)

Sombart, Werner, *Händler und Helden. Patriotische Besinnungen* (Munich and Leipzig, 1915)

Ulrich, Bernd and Benjamin Ziemann, eds., *Frontalltag im Ersten Weltkrieg. Wahn und Wirklichkeit* (Frankfurt, 1994)

Vaughan, Edwin Campion, *Some Desperate Glory. The Diary of a Young Officer* ([London], 1981)

Whitlock, Brand, *Belgium under the German Occupation. A Personal Narrative*, vol. 1 (London, 1919)

Zwischen Arras und Péronne. 311 Lichtbilder zur Erinnerung an die Zeit des Stellungskampfes und der Abwehr der englischen Offensive, ed. 'by a German Reserve Corps' (Bapaume, 1916)

LITERATURE

Accame, Giano, and Claudio Strinati, eds., *A 90 anni dalla Grande Guerra. Arte e Memoria* (Rome, 2005)

Ackermann, Volker, 'La vision allemande du Soldat inconnu: débats politiques, réflexion philosophique et artistique', in Jean-Jacques Becker et al., eds., *Guerre et Cultures 1914–1918* (Paris, 1994), pp. 385–96

Afflerbach, Holger, *Falkenhayn. Politisches Denken und Handeln im Kaiserreich* (Munich, 1994)

—— *Der Dreibund. Europäische Großmacht- und Allianzpolitik vor dem Ersten Weltkrieg* (Vienna, 2002)

Andrić, Ivo, *The Bridge over the Drina* (London, 1959; 1945)

Angress, Werner T., 'Die Ausbreitung des Antisemitismus', in Werner Mosse and Arnold Paucker, eds., *Deutsches Judentum in Krieg und Revolution, 1916–1923* (Tübingen, 1971), pp. 409–510

anon. [F. C. Endres], *Die Tragödie Deutschlands. Im Banne des Machtgedankens bis zum Zusammenbruch des Reiches* (3rd rev. edn., Stuttgart, 1924)

Anz, Thomas, 'Vitalismus und Kriegsdichtung', in Mommsen ed., *Kultur und Krieg*, pp. 235–47

Arz von Straussenburg, Artur, *Zur Geschichte des Großen Krieges 1914–1918* (Vienna, Leipzig, and Munich, 1924)

Barron, Stephanie, *Entartete Kunst. Das Schicksal der Avantgarde im Nazi-Deutschland* (Munich, 1992; Los Angeles, 1991)

Bartov, Omer, *Mirrors of Destruction. War, Genocide, and Modern Memory* (New York and Oxford, 2000)

Bartrop, Paul, 'The relationship between war and genocide in the twentieth century: a consideration', *Journal of Genocide Research*, 4 (2002), pp. 519–32

Becker, Annette, *War and Faith. The Religious Imagination in France, 1914–1930* (Oxford and New York, 1998); (*La Guerre et la foi. De la mort à la mémoire (1914–1930)* Paris, 1994)

—— *Oubliés de la Grande Guerre. Humanitaire et culture de guerre* (Paris, 1998)

Becker, Annette, 'Guerre totale et troubles mentaux', *Annales* 55 (2000), pp. 135–51

Becker, Jean-Jacques, *1914. Comment les Français sont entrés dans la Guerre* (Paris, 1977)

—— 'Frankreich', in Hirschfeld et al., eds., *Enzyklopädie Erster Weltkrieg*, pp. 31–43

Berend, Iván T. and György Ránki, 'Ungarns wirtschaftliche Entwicklung 1848–1918', in Adam Wandruszka and Peter Urbanitsch, eds., *Die Habsburgermonarchie 1848–1918*, 8 vols. (Vienna, 1973–2006), vol. 1, Alois Brusatti, ed., *Die wirtschaftliche Entwicklung* (Vienna, 1973), pp. 462–527

Berghahn, Volker, *Sarajewo, 28. Juni 1914: der Untergang des alten Europa* (Munich, 1999; 1997)

Bergmann, Werner, and Juliane Wetzel, 'Antisemitismus im Ersten und Zweiten Weltkrieg. Ein Forschungsüberblick', in Thoß and Volkmann, eds., *Erster Weltkrieg. Zweiter Weltkrieg*, pp. 437–69

Bessel, Richard, *Germany after the First World War* (Oxford, 1993)

Beyrau, Dietrich, 'Russische Intelligenzija und Revolution', *Historische Zeitschrift*, 252 (1991), pp. 559–86

—— 'Broken identities: The intelligentsia in revolutionary Russia', in *Social Identities in Revolutionary Russia*, ed. Madhavan K. Palat (Houndmills, 2001), pp. 134–60

—— 'Der Erste Weltkrieg als Bewährungsprobe. Bolshewistische Lernprozesse aus dem "imperialistischen" Krieg', *Journal of Modern European History*, 1 (2003), pp. 96–123

Biwald, Brigitte, *Von Helden und Krüppeln. Das österreichisch-ungarische Militärsanitätswesen im Ersten Weltkrieg*, 2 vols. (Vienna, 2002)

Blasius, Dirk, 'Ambivalenzen des Fortschritts. Psychiatrie und psychisch Kranke in der Geschichte der Moderne', in Frank Bajohr, Werner Johe and Uwe Lohalm, eds., *Zivilisation und Barbarei. Die widersprüchlichen Potentiale der Moderne. Detlev Peukert zum Gedenken* (Hamburg, 1991), pp. 253–68

Boeckh, Katrin, *Von den Balkankriegen zum Ersten Weltkrieg. Kleinstaatenpolitik und ethnische Selbstbestimmung auf dem Balkan* (Munich, 1996)

Boemeke, Manfred F., Gerald D. Feldman, and Elisabeth Glaser, eds., *The Treaty of Versailles. A Reassessment after 75 Years* (Washington and Cambridge, 1998)

Böhler, Jochen, 'Tragische Verstrickung oder Auftakt zum Vernichtungskrieg?', in Klaus-Michael Mallmann and Bogdan Musial, eds., *Genesis des Genozids. Polen 1939–1941* (Darmstadt, 2004), pp. 36–56

Börsch-Supan, Helmut, 'Die Reaktion der Zeitschriften "Kunst und Künstler" und "Die Kunst" auf den Ersten Weltkrieg', in Wolfgang J. Mommsen with Elisabeth Müller-Luckner, eds., *Kultur und Krieg: Die Rolle der Intellektuellen, Künstler und Schriftsteller im Ersten Weltkrieg* (Munich, 1996), pp. 195–207

Bosworth, Richard J. B., *Italy and the Approach of the First World War* (London and Basingstoke, 1983)

—— *Mussolini's Italy. Life under the Dictatorship 1915–1945* (London, 2005)

Bourke, Joanna, *An Intimate History of Killing. Face-to-Face Killing in Twentieth-Century Warfare* (London, 1999)

Bourne, John M., *Britain and the Great War 1914–1918* (London, 1989)

Bovio, Oreste, 'Gli Arditi', in Accame and Strinati, eds., *A 90 anni dalla Grande Guerra*, pp. 222–4

Brocke, Bernhard vom, ' "Wissenschaft und Militarismus." Der Aufruf der 93 "An die Kulturwelt!" und der Zusammenbruch der internationalen Gelehrtenrepublik im Ersten Weltkrieg', in William M. Calder III, Helmut Flashar, and Theodor Linken, eds., *Wilamowitz nach 50 Jahren* (Darmstadt, 1985), pp. 649–719

Brown, Malcolm, *The Imperial War Museum Book of the Somme* (London, 1996)

Browning, Christopher R., *The Origins of the Final Solution: The Evolution of Nazi Jewish Policy, September 1939–March 1942* (London, 2004)

Brüning, Heinrich, *Memoiren 1918–1934* (Stuttgart, 1970)

Bucholz, Arden, *Moltke, Schlieffen, and Prussian War Planning* (Providence and Oxford, 1991)

Burleigh, Michael, *Death and Deliverance. 'Euthanasia' in Germany c. 1900–1945* (Cambridge, 1994)

Burgwyn, H. James, *Italian Foreign Policy in the Interwar Period 1918–1940* (Westport, Conn. and London, 1997)

Cepl-Kaufmann, Gertrude, 'Zwischen "Ruhrbesetzung" und "Ruhrkampf". Schriftsteller im Spannungsfeld der Politik', in Krumeich and Schröder, eds., *Der Schatten des Weltkrieges,* pp. 47–61

Ceschin, Daniele, ' "L'estremo oltraggio": la violenza alle donne durante l'occupazione austro-germanica (1917–1918). Studi, fonti, prospettive di ricerca', paper presented to the 3rd Congress of the Società Italiana delle Storiche, Florence, November 2003

Chickering, Roger, and Stig Förster, eds., *Great War, Total War. Combat and Mobilization on the Western Front, 1914–1918* (Cambridge, 2000)

Churchill, Winston S., *The Second World War*, vol. 1, *The Gathering Storm* (London, 1949; 1948)

Clark, Martin, *Modern Italy 1871–1982* (Harlow, 1984)

Coli, Daniele, 'Croce e Gentile. I filosofi tra neutralità e intervento', in Accame and Strinati, eds., *A 90 anni dalla Grande Guerra*, pp. 101–6

Conze, Werner, *Polnische Nation und deutsche Politik im Ersten Weltkrieg* (Cologne and Graz, 1958)

Cork, Richard, *A Bitter Truth: Avant-Garde Art and the Great War* (New Haven and London, 1994)

Corni, Gustavo, 'Die Bevölkerung von Venetien unter der österreichisch-ungarischen Besetzung 1917/1918', *Zeitgeschichte* (1990), pp. 311–28

Cornwall, Mark, 'Serbia', in Keith Wilson ed., *Decisions for War 1914* (London, 1995), pp. 55–96

—— *The Undermining of Austria-Hungary: The Battle for Hearts and Minds* (Basingstoke, 2000)

Craig, Gordon A., *The Politics of the Prussian Army, 1640–1945* (Oxford, 1964; 1955)

Crook, Paul, *Darwinism, War and History. The Debate over the Biology of War from the 'Origin of the Species' to the First World War* (Cambridge, 1994)

Cruickshank, John, *Variations on Catastrophe. Some French Responses to the Great War* (Oxford, 1982)

Cuvelier, Jacques, *L'Invasion allemande, (La Belgique et la guerre*, vol. 2) (Brussels, 1926; 1920)

Dahlmann, Dittmar, 'Rußland', in Hirschfeld et al., eds., *Enzyklopädie Erster Weltkrieg*, pp. 87–96

Daniel, Ute, 'Frauen', in Hirschfeld et al., eds., *Enzyklopädie Erster Weltkrieg*, pp. 116–34

Davis, Belinda J., *Home Fires Burning. Food, Politics, and Everyday Life in World War I Berlin* (Chapel Hill and London, 2000)

Dedijer, Vladimir, *The Road to Sarajevo* (London, 1967; 1966)

Deist, Wilhelm, 'Verdeckter Militärstreik im Kriegsjahr 1918?', in Wolfram Wette, ed., *Der Krieg des kleinen Mannes. Eine Militärgeschichte von unten* (Munich, 1992), pp. 146–67

Demetz, Peter, *Worte in Freiheit. Der italienische Futurismus und die deutsche literarische Avantgarde (1912–1934)* (Munich and Zürich, 1990)

de Schaepdrijver, Sophie, *La Belgique et la Première Guerre mondiale* (Brussels, Berne, etc., 2004; first published Amsterdam and Antwerp, 1997)

Dewitz, Bodo von, *'So wird bei uns der Krieg geführt!' Amateurphotographie im Ersten Weltkrieg* (Munich, 1989)

Doegen, Wilhelm, *Kriegsgefangene Völker*, vol. 1: *Der Kriegsgefangenen Haltung und Schicksal in Deutschland* (Berlin, 1921)

Dülffer, Jost, 'Der Weg in den Krieg', in Hirschfeld et al., eds., *Enzyklopädie Erster Weltkrieg*, pp. 233–41

Duroselle, Jean-Baptiste, *La Grande Guerre des Français. L'Incompréhensible* (Paris, 1994)

Eckart, Wolfgang U., ' "The most extensive experiment that the imagination can conceive". War, emotional stress, and German medicine, 1914–1918', in Chickering and Förster, eds., *Great War, Total War*, pp. 133–49

Eksteins, Modris, *Rites of Spring. The Great War and the Birth of the Modern Age* (London, New York, etc., 1989)

Ellis, John, *The Social History of the Machine Gun* (London, 1993; 1976)

Emin, Ahmed, *Turkey in the World War* (New Haven and London, 1930), for the Carnegie Endowment for International Peace: Division of Economics and History. Economic and Social History of the War, ed. James T. Shotwell. Turkish Series

Evans, Richard J., *The Coming of the Third Reich* (New York, 2004)

—— 'In Search of German Social Darwinism', in Manfred Berg and Geoffrey Cocks, eds., *Medicine and Modernity. Public Health and Medical Care in Nineteenth- and Twentieth-Century Germany* (Washington and Cambridge, 1997), pp. 55–79

Falk, Walter, ' "Heil mir, daß ich Ergriffene sehe." Literatur vor dem Ersten Weltkrieg', in August Nitschke, Gerhard A. Ritter, Detlev J. K. Peukert, Rüdiger vom Bruch, eds., *Jahrhundertwende. Der Aufbruch in die Moderne, 1880–1930*, 2 vols. (Reinbek bei Hamburg, 1990), vol. 1, pp. 230–57

Farrar, Lancelot L., *The Short-War Illusion: German Policy, Strategy, & Domestic Affairs August–December 1914* (Santa Barbara and Oxford, 1973)

Faulstich, Heinz, *Hungersterben in der Psychiatrie 1914–19. Mit einer Topographie der NS-Psychiatrie* (Freiburg im Breisgau, 1998)

Feldman, Gerald D., *Army, Industry, and Labor in Germany, 1914–1918* (Princeton, 1966)

Fellner, Fritz, 'Austria-Hungary', in Keith Wilson, ed., *Decisions for War 1914* (London, 1995), pp. 9–25

Ferguson, Niall, *The Pity of War* (London, 1998)

Fest, Joachim C., *Hitler. Eine Biographie* (Frankfurt, 1973)

Figes, Orlando, *A People's Tragedy. A History of the Russian Revolution* (New York, 1997; 1996)

Fischer, Fritz, *Griff nach der Weltmacht. Die Kriegszielpolitik des kaiserlichen Deutschland 1914/18* (Düsseldorf, 1961); Eng. trans. *Germany's Aims in the First World War* (London, 1969)

—— *Krieg der Illusionen. Die deutsche Politik von 1911 bis 1914* (Düsseldorf, 1969); Eng. trans. *War of Illusions. German Policies from 1911 to 1914* (London, 1975)

Fitzpatrick, Sheila, *The Russian Revolution* (Oxford, 1982)

Föllmer, Moritz, 'Der Feind im Salon. Eliten, Besatzung und nationale Identität in Nordfrankreich und Westdeutschland 1914–1930', *Militärgeschichtliche Zeitschrift*, 61 (2002), pp. 1–24

Förster, Stig, *Der doppelte Militarismus. Die deutsche Heeresrüstungspolitik zwischen Status-Quo-Sicherung und Aggression 1890–1913* (Stuttgart, 1985)

—— 'Der deutsche Generalstab und die Illusion des kurzen Krieges, 1871–1914 Metakritik eines Mythos', *Militärgeschichtliche Mitteilungen* 54 (1995), pp. 61–95

—— 'Im Reich des Absurden: Die Ursachen des Ersten Weltkrieges', in Bernd Wegner, ed., *Wie Kriege entstehen. Zum historischen Hintergrund von Staatenkonflikten* (Paderborn, 2000), pp. 211–52

—— 'Einführende Bemerkungen', in Thoß and Volkmann, eds., *Erster Weltkrieg. Zweiter Weltkrieg*, pp. 33–42

Foster, Roy F., *Modern Ireland 1600–1972* (Harmondsworth, 1988)

French, David, ' "Had we known how bad things were in Germany, we might have got stiffer terms": Great Britain and the German armistice', in Boemeke et al., eds., *The Treaty of Versailles*, pp. 69–86

—— 'The strategy of unlimited warfare? Kitchener, Robertson, and Haig', in Chickering and Förster, eds., *Great War, Total War*, pp. 281–95

Friedrich, Ernst, *Krieg dem Kriege! Guerre à la guerre! War against war! Oorlog an den oorlog!* (Berlin, 1924; many subsequent edns.).

Fussell, Paul, *The Great War and Modern Memory* (Oxford, 1977; 1975)

Gat, Azar, *Fascist and Liberal Visions of War. Fuller, Liddell Hart, Douhet, and Other Modernists* (Oxford, 1998)

Gay, Peter, *Freud, Jews and Other Germans* (New York and Oxford, 1978)

Geiss, Imanuel, *German Foreign Policy, 1871–1914* (London, 1976)

Geyer, Dietrich, *Russian Imperialism. The Interaction of Domestic and Foreign Policy 1860–1914* (Leamington Spa, etc., 1987; German 1st edn. 1977)

Geyer, Michael, 'Vom massenhaften Tötungshandeln, oder: Wie die Deutschen das Krieg-Machen lernten', in Peter Gleichmann and Thomas Kühne, eds., *Massenhaftes Töten. Kriege und Genozide im 20. Jahrhundert* (Essen, 2004), pp. 105–42

—— 'Rückzug und Zerstörung 1917', in Hirschfeld et al., eds, *Die Deutschen an der Somme*, pp. 163–79

Gibelli, Antonio, 'La Grande Guerra tra consenso e rifiuto', *Storia e Memoria* (Rivista Semestrale. Istituto Ligure per la storia della Resistenza e dell'età contemporanea) 7 (1998), pp. 241–6

—— 'Nefaste meraviglie. Grande Guerra e apoteosi della modernità', in *Storia d'Italia*, eds. Ruggiero Romano and Corrado Vivanti. Vol. 18: *Guerra e pace*, ed. Walter Barberis (Turin, 2002), pp. 549–89

Gilbert, Felix, with David Clay Large, *The End of the European Era, 1890 to the Present*, 4th edn. (New York and London, 1991; 1970)

Gilbert, Martin, *First World War* (London, 1994)

Glaser, Elisabeth, 'The making of the economic peace', in Boemeke et al., eds., *The Treaty of Versailles*, pp. 371–99

Golan, Arnon, 'The Politics of Wartime Demolition and Human Landscape Transformation', *War in History* 9 (2002), pp. 431–45

Goldhagen, Daniel J., *Hitler's Willing Executioners. Ordinary Germans and the Holocaust* (New York, 1996)

Goldstein, Erik, 'Great Britain: the home front', in Boemeke et al., eds., *The Treaty of Versailles*, pp. 147–66

Gregory, Adrian, 'Peculiarities of the English? War, violence and politics: 1900–1939', *Journal of Modern European History*, 1 (2003), pp. 44–59

Greschat, Martin, 'Begleitung und Deutung der beiden Weltkriege durch evangelische Theologen', in Thoß and Volkmann eds., *Erster Weltkrieg. Zweiter Weltkrieg*, pp. 497–518

Griffin, Roger, *The Nature of Fascism* (London, 1993; 1991)

Groß, Gerhard P., ed., *Die vergessene Front. Der Osten 1914/15. Ereignis, Wirkung, Nachwirkung* (Paderborn, etc., 2006)

Hagen, Mark von, 'The Great War and the mobilization of ethnicity in the Russian Empire', in Barnett R. Rubin and Jack Snyder, eds., *Post-Soviet Political Order. Conflict and State Building* (London and New York, 1998), pp. 34–57

Hall, Richard C., *The Balkan Wars 1912–1913. Prelude to the First World War* (London and New York, 2000)

Hamilton, Richard F. and Holger H. Herwig, *Decisions for War, 1914–1917* (Cambridge, 2004)

Hanisch, Ernst, *Der lange Schatten des Staates. Österreichische Gesellschaftsgeschichte im 20. Jahrhundert* (Vienna, 1994)

Hanna, Martha, *The Mobilization of Intellect. French Scholars and Writers during the Great War* (Cambridge, Mass., and London, 1996)

Harris, Ruth, 'The "Child of the Barbarian". Rape, Race and Nationalism in World War I', *Past and Present* 141 (1993), pp. 170–206

Healy, Maureen, *Vienna and the Fall of the Habsburg Empire. Total War and Everyday Life in World War I* (Cambridge, 2004)

Herrmann, David G., *The Arming of Europe and the Making of the First World War* (Princeton, 1996)

Herwig, Holger, *The First World War. Germany and Austria-Hungary 1914–1918* (London, 1997)

Hirschfeld, Gerhard, 'Die Somme-Schlacht von 1916', in id. et al., eds., *Die Deutschen an der Somme 1914–1918*, pp. 79–89

Hirschfeld, Gerhard, Gerd Krumeich and Irina Renz, eds., *Keiner fühlt sich hier mehr als Mensch . . . Erlebnis und Wirkung des Ersten Weltkriegs* (Essen, 1993)

—— —— —— eds., *Enzyklopädie Erster Weltkrieg*, Paderborn, etc., 2003

—— —— —— eds., *Die Deutschen an der Somme 1914–1918. Krieg, Besatzung, Verbrannte Erde* (Essen, 2006)

—— —— Dieter Langewiesche, and Hans-Peter Ullmann, eds., *Kriegserfahrungen. Studien zur Sozial- und Mentalitätsgeschichte des Ersten Weltkriegs* (Essen, 1997)

Hobsbawm, Eric, *The Age of Empire, 1875–1914* (London, 1987)

—— *Age of Extremes. The Short Twentieth Century 1914–1991* (London, 1995; 1994)

Hoeres, Peter, 'Ein dreißigjähriger Krieg der deutschen Philosophie? Kriegsdeutungen im Ersten und Zweiten Weltkrieg', in Thoß and Volkmann, eds., *Erster Weltkrieg. Zweiter Weltkrieg*, pp. 471–95

Hoffmann, Christhard, 'Between integration and rejection: the Jewish community in Germany, 1914–1918', in Horne, ed., *State, Society and Mobilization*, pp. 89–104

Holquist, Peter, *Making War, Forging Revolution. Russia's Continuum of Crisis, 1914–1921* (Cambridge, Mass. and London, 2002)

Horne, John, ed., *State, Society and Mobilization in Europe during the First World War* (Cambridge, 1997)

—— 'L'invasion de 1914 dans la mémoire (France, Grande-Bretagne, Belgique, Allemagne)', in Sylvie Caucanas and Rémy Cazals, eds., *Traces de 14–18. Actes du colloque international tenu à Carcassonne . . . 1996* (Carcassonne, 1997), pp. 115–26

—— 'Socialism, peace, and revolution, 1917–1918', in Hew Strachan, ed., *The Oxford Illustrated History of the First World War* (Oxford, 1998), pp. 227–38

—— 'Der Schatten des Krieges: Französische Politik in den zwanziger Jahren', in Hans Mommsen, ed., *Der Erste Weltkrieg und die europäische Nachkriegsordnung. Sozialer Wandel und Formveränderung der Politik* (Cologne, 2000), pp. 145–64

Horne, John and Alan Kramer, 'German "Atrocities" and Franco-German Opin-
ion, 1914: The Evidence of German Soldiers' Diaries', *The Journal of Modern
History*, 66/1 (1994), pp. 1–33
────── *German Atrocities 1914. A History of Denial* (London and New Haven,
2001)
Hull, Isabel V., *Absolute Destruction. Military Culture and the Practices of War in
Imperial Germany* (Ithaca, NY, and London, 2005)
Hüppauf, Bernd, 'Kriegsfotografie', in Michalka, ed., *Der Erste Weltkrieg, pp.
875–909*
Hutchison, Graham Seton, *Machine Guns. Their History and Tactical Employment
(Being also a History of the Machine Gun Corps, 1916–1922)* (London, 1938)
Hynes, Samuel, 'Personal narratives and commemoration', in Jay Winter and
Emmanuel Sivan, eds., *War and Remembrance in the Twentieth Century* (Cam-
bridge, 1999), pp. 205–20
Isnenghi, Mario, *Il mito della grande guerra* (Bologna, 1997; 1970)
────── and Giorgio Rochat, *La Grande Guerra 1914–1918* (Milan, 2000)
Jahn, Hubertus F., *Patriotic Culture in Russia during World War I* (Ithaca, NY, and
London, 1995)
Jarausch, Konrad, *The Enigmatic Chancellor. Bethmann Hollweg and the Hubris of
Imperial Germany* (New Haven, Conn., and London, 1973)
Jeannesson, Stanislas, 'Übergriffe der französischen Besatzungsmacht und deutsche
Beschwerden', in Krumeich and Schröder, eds., *Der Schatten des Weltkriegs*,
pp. 207–31
Jeismann, Michael, *Das Vaterland der Feinde. Studien zum nationalen Feindbegriff und
Selbstverständnis in Deutschland und Frankreich 1792–1918* (Stuttgart, 1992)
Jelavich, Charles, and Barbara Jelavich, *The Establishment of the Balkan National
States, 1804–1920* (Seattle and London, 1977)
Joas, Hans, 'Sozialwissenschaften und der Erste Weltkrieg: Eine vergleichende
Analyse', in Mommsen, ed., *Kultur und Krieg, pp. 17–29*
Joll, James, *The Origins of the First World War* (London, 1992; 1984)
Jones, Heather, *The Enemy Disarmed. Prisoners of War and the Violence of Wartime,
Britain, France and Germany, 1914–1920*, Ph.D. University of Dublin, 2006
Kantorowicz, Hermann, *Gutachten zur Kriegsschuldfrage*, ed. Imanuel Geiss, (Frank-
furt, 1967)
Keegan, John, *The Face of Battle* (London, 1976)
Keiger, John F. V., *France and the Origins of the First World War* (London, 1983)
────── 'France', in Keith Wilson ed., *Decisions for War 1914*, pp. 121–49
────── 'Poincaré, Clemenceau, and the quest for total victory', in Roger Chickering
and Stig Förster, eds., *Great War, Total War*, pp. 247–63
Kellerhoff, Sven Felix, *Attentäter. Mit einer Kugel die Welt verändern* (Cologne etc.,
2003)
Kennedy, Paul, *The Rise of the Anglo-German Antagonism 1860–1914* (London,
1980)

Kent, Susan Kingsley, 'Love and death. War and gender in Britain, 1914–1918, in Frans Coetzee and Marilyn Shevin-Coetzee, eds., *Authority, Identity and the Social History of the Great War* (Oxford and Providence, 1995), pp. 153–74

Kershaw, Ian, *Hitler, 1889–1936: Hubris* (London, 1998)

—— 'Antisemitismus und die NS-Bewegung vor 1933' in Hermann Graml, Angelika Königseder and Juliane Wetzel, eds., *Vorurteil und Rassenhaß. Antisemitismus in den faschistischen Bewegungen Europas* (Berlin, 2001), pp. 29–48

—— 'War and political violence in twentieth-century Europe', *Journal of Contemporary European History*, 14 (2005), pp. 107–23

Keylor, William R., 'Versailles and international diplomacy', in Boemeke et al., eds., *The Treaty of Versailles*, pp. 469–505

Kieser, Hans-Lukas and Dominik J. Schaller, 'Völkermord im historischen Raum 1895–1945', in eidem, eds., *Der Völkermord an den Armeniern und die Shoah. The Armenian Genocide and the Shoah* (Zürich, 2002)

Kiszling, Rudolf, *Österreich-Ungarns Anteil am Ersten Weltkrieg* (Graz, 1958)

Klein, Fritz, 'Between Compiègne and Versailles: the Germans on the way from a misunderstood defeat to an unwanted peace', in Boemeke et al., eds, *The Treaty of Versailles*, pp. 203–20

Köhler, Ludwig von, *Die Staatsverwaltung der besetzten Gebiete*, vol. 1: *Belgien*, (Stuttgart and New Haven, 1927)

Köpf, Gerhard, 'Hitlers psychogene Erblindung. Geschichte einer Krankenakte', in *Nervenheilkunde. Zeitschrift für interdisziplinäre Fortbildung*, 24 (2005), pp. 783–90

Kotowski, Mathias, ' "Noch ist ja der Krieg gar nicht zu Ende": Weltkriegsgedenken der Universität Tübingen in der Weimarer Republik', in Hirschfeld et al., eds, *Kriegserfahrungen*, pp. 424–38

Kramer, Alan, ' "Greueltaten". Zum Problem der deutschen Kriegsverbrechen in Belgien und Frankreich 1914', in Hirschfeld et al., eds., *Keiner fühlt sich hier mehr als Mensch*, pp. 85–114

—— 'The War of Atrocities. Murderous scares and extreme combat', in: Alf Lüdtke and Bernd Weisbrod, eds., *No Man's Land of Violence. Extreme Wars in the 20th Century*, (Göttingen, 2006), pp. 11–33

—— 'The First Wave of International War Crimes Trials: Istanbul and Leipzig', *European Review*, 14 (2006), pp. 441–55

—— 'War crimes', in *Europe since 1914: Encyclopedia of the Age of War and Reconstruction*, John Merriman and Jay Winter, eds. (New York, 2006), 2671–81

—— 'Italienische Kriegsgefangene im Ersten Weltkrieg', in Hermann J. W. Kuprian and Oswald Überegger, eds., *Der Erste Weltkrieg im Alpenraum. Erfahrung, Deutung, Erinnerung. La Grande Guerra nell'arco alpino. Esperienze e memoria* (Innsbruck, 2006), pp. 247–58

Kröger, Martin, 'Revolution als Programm. Ziele und Realität deutscher Orientpolitik im Ersten Weltkrieg', in Michalka, ed., *Der Erste Weltkrieg*, pp. 366–91

Kronenbitter, Günther, *'Krieg im Frieden'. Die Führung der k.u.k. Armee und die Großmachtpolitik Österreich-Ungarns 1906–1914* (Munich, 2003)

Krumeich, Gerd, 'Ernest Lavisse und die Kritik an der deutschen "Kultur"', 1914–1918', in Mommsen, ed., *Kultur und Krieg*, pp. 143–54

—— 'Verdun, 21. Februar bis 9. September 1916', in Stig Förster, Markus Pöhlmann, and Dierk Walter, eds., *Schlachten der Weltgeschichte von Salamis bis Sinai* (Munich, 2001), pp. 295–305

—— 'Der "Ruhrkampf" als Krieg: Überlegungen zu einem verdrängten deutsch-französischen Konflikt', in Krumeich and Schröder, eds., *Der Schatten des Weltkriegs*, pp. 9–24

—— 'Die deutsche Erinnerung an die Somme', in Hirschfeld et al., eds., *Die Deutschen an der Somme*, pp. 231–45

—— and Gerhard Hirschfeld, 'Die Geschichtsschreibung zum Ersten Weltkrieg', in Hirschfeld et al., eds., *Enzyklopädie Erster Weltkrieg*, pp. 304–15

—— and Joachim Schröder, eds., *Der Schatten des Weltkriegs. Die Ruhrbesetzung 1923* (Essen, 2004)

Kruse, Wolfgang, *Krieg und nationale Integration. Eine Neuinterpretation des sozialdemokratischen Burgfriedensschlusses 1914–15* (Essen, 1993)

Kürsat-Ahlers, Elçin, 'Über das Töten in Genoziden. Eine Bilanz historisch-soziologischer Deutungen', in Peter Gleichmann and Thomas Kühne, eds., *Massenhaftes Töten. Kriege und Genozide im 20. Jahrhundert* (Essen, 2004), pp. 180–206

Lange, Thomas, ' "...da schreibt ein Volk seine Annalen". Die Darmstädter Weltkriegssammlungen im Kontext von Kriegsvorbereitung und Kriegsmentalität', in Ute Schneider and Thomas Lange, eds., *Kriegsalltage. Darmstadt und die Technische Hochschule im Ersten Weltkrieg* (Darmstadt, 2002)

Lawrence, Jon, 'Forging a peaceable kingdom: war, violence, and fear of brutalization in post-First World War Britain', *The Journal of Modern History*, 75 (2003), pp. 557–89

Lenz, Christian, 'Kirchner—Meidner—Beckmann. Drei deutsche Künstler im Ersten Weltkrieg', in Mommsen, ed., *Kultur und Krieg*, pp. 171–8

Levene, Mark, 'Frontiers of genocide: Jews in the eastern war zones, 1914–1920 and 1941', in Panikos Panayi, ed., *Minorities in Wartime. National and Racial Groupings in Europe, North America and Australia during the Two World Wars* (Oxford, 1993), pp. 83–117

Lieven, Dominic C. B., *Russia and the Origins of the First World War* (London, 1983)

Lincoln, W. Bruce, *In War's Dark Shadow. The Russians before the Great War* (New York and Oxford, 1994; 1983)

—— *Passage Through Armageddon. The Russians in War and Revolution 1914–1918* (New York and Oxford, 1994; 1986)

Lindemann, Thomas, *Les Doctrines Darwiniennes et la Guerre de 1914* (Paris, 2001)

Linnenkohl, Hans, *Vom Einzelschuß zur Feuerwalze. Der Wettlauf zwischen Technik und Taktik im Ersten Weltkrieg* (Koblenz, 1990)

Liulevicius, Vejas Gabriel, *War Land on the Eastern Front. Culture, National Identity, and German Occupation in World War I* (Cambridge, 2000)

—— 'Von "Ober Ost" nach "Ostland"?', in *Die vergessene Front. Der Osten 1914/ 15. Ereignis, Wirkung, Nachwirkung*, ed. Gerhard P. Groß (Paderborn, etc., 2006), pp. 295–310

Lohr, Eric, 'The Russian army and the Jews: mass deportation, hostages, and violence during World War I', *Russian Review*, 60 (July 2001), pp. 2–24

Lyttelton, Adrian, *The Seizure of Power. Fascism in Italy 1919–1929* (London, 1973)

McNeil, William C., 'Could Germany pay? Another look at the reparations problem of the 1920s', in Gerald D. Feldman et al., eds., *Consequences of Inflation/Konsequenzen der Inflation* (Berlin, 1989), pp. 109–23

McPhail, Helen, *The Long Silence. Civilian Life under the German Occupation of Northern France, 1914–1918* (London and New York, 2001; 1999)

Mai, Gunther, *Das Ende des Kaiserreichs. Politik und Kriegführung im Ersten Weltkrieg*, (3rd edn., Munich, 1997; 1987)

Maier, Charles S., *Recasting Bourgeois Europe. Stabilization in France, Germany, and Italy in the Decade after World War I* (Princeton, 1975)

Majerus, Benoît, 'La prostitution à Bruxelles pendant la Grande Guerre: contrôle et pratique', *Crime, Histoire & Sociétés/Crime, History & Societies*, 7 (2003), pp. 5–42

Malcolm, Noel, *Kosovo. A Short History* (London, 1998)

Marcheggiano, Arturo, *Diritto umanitario e sua introduzione nella regolamentazione dell'esercito italiano*, 2 vols., vol. 2: *La protezione delle vittime della guerra* (Rome, 1991)

Marder, Arthur, *From the Dreadnought to Scapa Flow. The Royal Navy in the Fisher Era, 1904–1919*, 5 vols. (London, 1961–70)

Marks, Sally, 'The myths of reparations', *Central European History*, 11 (1978), pp. 231–55

—— *Innocent Abroad. Belgium at the Paris Peace Conference of 1919* (Chapel Hill, 1981)

—— 'Smoke and mirrors: in smoke-filled rooms and the Galerie des Glaces', in Boemeke et al., eds., *The Treaty of Versailles*, pp. 337–70

Marwick, Arthur, *The Deluge. British Society and the First World War* (London, 1965)

Matis, Herbert, 'Leitlinien der österreichischen Wirtschaftspolitik 1848–1918', in Adam Wandruszka and Peter Urbanitsch, eds., *Die Habsburgermonarchie 1848–1918*, 8 vols. (Vienna, 1973–2006), vol. 1, Alois Brusatti, ed., *Die wirtschaftliche Entwicklung* (Vienna, 1973), pp. 29–67

Mayer, Arno, *Politics and Diplomacy of Peacemaking. Containment and Counterrevolution at Versailles, 1918–1919* (London, 1968; 1967)

Meineke, Stefan, 'Friedrich Meinecke und der "Krieg der Geister" ', in Mommsen, ed., *Kultur und Krieg*, pp. 97–117

Melograni, Piero, *Storia politica della Grande guerra 1915–1918*, (Milan, 1998)

Mendelssohn-Bartholdy, Albrecht, *The War and German Society. The Testament of a Liberal* (New Haven and London, 1937)

Menning, Bruce W., *Bayonets Before Bullets. The Imperial Russian Army, 1861–1914* (Bloomington and Indianapolis, 2000; 1992)

Michalka, Wolfgang, ed., *Der Erste Weltkrieg. Wirkung, Wahrnehmung, Analyse* (Munich, 1994)

Moffa, Claudio, 'I deportati libici della guerra 1911–12', *Rivista di Storia contemporanea*, 19 (1990), pp. 32–56

Mombauer, Annika, *Helmuth von Moltke and the Origins of the First World War* (Cambridge, 2001)

Mommsen, Wolfgang J., *Max Weber in German Politics, 1890–1920* (Chicago and London, 1984; 1974)

—— *Großmachtstellung und Weltpolitik. Die Außenpolitik des Deutschen Reiches 1870 bis 1914* (Frankfurt and Berlin, 1993)

—— *Bürgerliche Kultur und künstlerische Avantgarde 1870–1918. Kultur und Politik im deutschen Kaiserreich* (Frankfurt and Berlin, 1994)

—— with Elisabeth Müller-Luckner, ed., *Kultur und Krieg: Die Rolle der Intellektuellen, Künstler und Schriftsteller im Ersten Weltkrieg* (Munich, 1996)

—— 'German artists, writers and intellectuals and the meaning of the war, 1914–1918, in Horne, ed., *State, Society and Mobilization*, pp. 21–38

—— 'Deutschland', in Hirschfeld et al., eds., *Enzyklopädie Erster Weltkrieg*, pp. 15–30

Mosse, George L., *The Nationalization of the Masses: Political Symbolism and Mass Movements in Germany from the Napoleonic Wars through the Third Reich* (New York, 1975)

—— *Fallen Soldiers. Reshaping the Memory of the World Wars* (New York and Oxford, 1990)

Müller, Sven Oliver, *Die Nation als Waffe und Vorstellung. Nationalismus in Deutschland und Großbritannien im Ersten Weltkrieg* (Göttingen, 2002)

Naimark, Norman, *Fires of Hatred. Ethnic Cleansing in Twentieth-Century Europe* (Cambridge, Mass., and London, 2001)

Narskij, Igor, 'Kriegswirklichkeit und Kriegserfahrung russischer Soldaten an der russischen Westfront 1914/15', in Gerhard P. Groß, ed., *Die vergessene Front. Der Osten 1914/15. Ereignis, Wirkung, Nachwirkung* (Paderborn, etc., 2006), pp. 249–61

Nasson, Bill, *The South African War 1899–1902* (London, 1999)

Neitzel, Sönke, 'Zum strategischen Mißerfolg verdammt? Die deutschen Luftstreitkräfte in beiden Weltkriegen', in Thoß and Volkmann, eds., *Erster Weltkrieg, Zweiter Weltkrieg*, pp. 167–92

Nolte, Ernst, *Der europäische Bürgerkrieg 1917–1945: Nationalsozialismus und Bolschewismus* (Frankfurt, 1987)

O'Brien, Paul, *Mussolini in the First World War. The Journalist, the Soldier, the Fascist* (Oxford and New York, 2005)

Offer, Avner, *The First World War: An Agrarian Interpretation* (Oxford, 1991; 1989)

Overmans, Rüdiger, ' "Hunnen" und "Untermenschen"—deutsche und russisch/sowjetische Kriegsgefangenschaftserfahrungen im Zeitalter der Weltkriege', in Thoß and Volkmann, eds., *Erster Weltkrieg. Zweiter Weltkrieg,* pp. 335–65

Palumbo, Piero, 'D'Annunzio: da Quarto al volo su Vienna', in Accame and Strinati, eds., *A 90 anni dalla Grande Guerra*, pp. 107–12

Pavlowitch, Stevan K., *Serbia. The History Behind the Name* (London, 2002)

Pellegrini, Giorgio, 'L'influenza delle corazze nel Futurismo e del cubismo nella mimetizzazione', in Accame and Strinati eds., *A 90 anni dalla Grande Guerra*, pp. 366–72

Petersen, Jens, 'Das Problem der Gewalt im italienischen Faschismus, 1919–1925', in Wolfgang J. Mommsen and Gerhard Hirschfeld, eds., *Sozialprotest, Gewalt, Terror. Gewaltanwendung durch politische und gesellschaftliche Randgruppen im 19. und 20. Jahrhundert* (Stuttgart, 1982), pp. 325–48

Philpott, William 'Why the British were really on the Somme: A reply', in *War in History*, 9 (2002), no. 4, pp. 446–71

Pick, Daniel, *War Machine. The Rationalisation of Slaughter in the Modern Age* (New Haven and London, 1993)

Pirenne, Henri, *La Belgique et la guerre mondiale* (Paris, 1928)

Plaggenborg, Stefan, 'Grundprobleme der Kulturgeschichte der sowjetischen Zwischenkriegszeit', *Jahrbücher für Geschichte Osteuropas*, N.F. 48 (2000), pp. 109–18

Pressel, Wilhelm, *Die Kriegspredigt 1914–1918 in der evangelischen Kirche Deutschlands* (Göttingen, 1967)

Procacci, Giovanna, *Soldati e prigionieri italiani nella Grande guerra. Con una raccolta di lettere inedite* (Turin, 2000; 1993)

—— *Dalla Rassegnazione alla Rivolta. Mentalità e comportamenti popolari nella grande guerra* (Rome, 1999)

Prost, Antoine, *In the Wake of War. 'Les anciens combattants' and French Society 1914–1933* (Providence and Oxford, 1992)

Rauchensteiner, Manfred, 'Österreich-Ungarn', in Hirschfeld et al., eds., *Enzyklopädie Erster Weltkrieg*, pp. 64–86

Reichardt, Sven, *Faschistische Kampfbünde. Gewalt und Gemeinschaft im italienischen Squadrismus und in der deutschen SA* (Cologne, 2002)

Reimann, Aribert, 'Die heile Welt im Stahlgewitter: Deutsche und englische Feldpost aus dem Ersten Weltkrieg', in Hirschfeld et al., eds., *Kriegserfahrungen*, pp. 129–45

Renzi, William A., *In the Shadow of the Sword. Italy's Neutrality and Entrance into the Great War, 1914–1915* (New York, etc., 1987)

Reuveni, Gideon, 'The "Crisis of the Book" and German Society after the First World War', *German History*, 20 (2002), pp. 438–61

Riese, Hans-Peter, *Kasimir Sewerinowitsch Malewitsch* (Reinbek, 1999)

Ritschl, Albrecht, *Deutschlands Krise und Konjunktur 1924–1934. Binnenkonjunktur, Auslandsverschuldung und Reparationsproblem zwischen Dawes-Plan und Transfersperre* (Berlin, 2002)

Robb, George, *British Culture and the First World War* (Basingstoke, 2002)

Rochat, Giorgio, *Gli Arditi della Grande Guerra. Origine, battaglie e miti* (Gorizia, 1990; 1981)

—— 'Lo Stato liberale e la Grande Guerra', *Storia e Memoria* (Rivista Semestrale. Istituto Ligure per la storia della Resistenza e dell'età contemporanea), 7 (1998), pp. 235–9

Rohkrämer, Thomas, *Der Militarismus der 'kleinen Leute'. Die Kriegervereine im Deutschen Kaiserreich 1871–1914* (Munich, 1990)

Röhl, John C. G., 'Germany', in Keith Wilson, ed., *Decisions for War 1914* (London, 1995), pp. 27–54

Rollet, Catherine, 'The "other war" II: setbacks in public health', in Jay Winter and Jean-Louis Robert, eds., *Capital Cities at War. Paris, London, Berlin 1914–1919* (Cambridge, 1997), pp. 456–86

Rother, Rainer, ed. on behalf of the Deutsches Historisches Museum, *Der Weltkrieg 1914–1918. Ereignis und Erinnerung* (Berlin, 2004)

Rürup, Reinhard, 'Der "Geist von 1914" in Deutschland. Kriegsbegeisterung und Ideologisierung des Krieges im Ersten Weltkrieg', in Bernd Hüppauf, ed., *Ansichten vom Krieg. Vergleichende Studien zum Ersten Weltkrieg in Literatur und Gesellschaft* (Königstein/Ts., 1984), pp. 1–30

Safranski, Rüdiger, *Nietzsche. Biographie seines Denkens* (Frankfurt, 2002; 2000)

Sanborn, Joshua, *Drafting the Russian Nation. Military Conscription, Total War, and Mass Politics, 1905–1925* (DeKalb, Ill., 2003)

Sayer, Derek, 'British reaction to the Amritsar Massacre, 1919–1920', *Past and Present*, 131 (1991), pp. 130–64

Schieder, Wolfgang, 'Das italienische Experiment. Der Faschismus als Vorbild in der Krise der Weimarer Republik', *Historische Zeitschrift*, 262 (1996), pp. 73–125

Schindling, John, 'Austria-Hungary', in Robin Higham with Dennis E. Showalter, eds., *Researching World War I. A Handbook* (Westport, Conn., and London, 2003)

Schivelbusch, Wolfgang, *Eine Ruine im Krieg der Geister. Die Bibliothek von Löwen August 1914 bis Mai 1940* (Frankfurt, 1993; 1988)

Schöller, Peter, *Der Fall Löwen und das Weißbuch. Eine kritische Untersuchung der deutschen Dokumentation über die Vorgänge in Löwen von 25. bis 28. August 1914* (Cologne and Graz, 1958)

Schubert, Dietrich, 'Otto Dix zeichnet im Ersten Weltkrieg', in Mommsen, ed., *Kultur und Krieg*, pp. 179–93

Schubert-Weller, Christoph, *'Kein schönrer Tod . . .' Die Militarisierung der männlichen Jugend und ihr Einsatz im Ersten Weltkrieg 1890–1918* (Weinheim and Munich, 1998), (Materialien zur Historischen Jugendforschung)

Schumann, Andreas, ' "Der Künstler an die Krieger". Zur Kriegsliteratur kanonisierter Autoren', in Mommsen, ed., *Kultur und Krieg*, pp. 221–33

Schumann, Dirk, *Politische Gewalt in der Weimarer Republik 1918–1933. Kampf um die Straße und Furcht vor dem Bürgerkrieg* (Essen, 2001)

—— 'Europa, der Erste Weltkrieg und die Nachkriegszeit: eine Kontinuität der Gewalt?', *Journal of Modern European History*, 1 (2003), pp. 24–43

Schwabe, Klaus, 'Germany's peace aims and the domestic and international constraints', in Boemeke et al., eds., *The Treaty of Versailles*, pp. 37–67

Seligmann, Matthew, 'Germany and the origins of the First World War in the eyes of the American diplomatic establishment', *German History*, 15 (1997), pp. 307–32

Seligmann, Matthew, ' "A barometer of national confidence": a British assessment of the role of insecurity in the formulation of German military policy before the First World War', *English Historical Review*, 107 (2002), pp. 333–55

Sheffield, Gary, *Forgotten Victory. The First World War: Myths and Realities* (London, 2002; 2001)

Smith, Leonard V., *Between Mutiny and Obedience: the Case of the French Fifth Infantry Division during World War I* (Princeton, 1994)

—— Stéphane Audoin-Rouzeau, and Annette Becker, *France and the Great War, 1914–1918* (Cambridge, 2003)

Sofsky, Wolfgang, *Traktat über die Gewalt* (Frankfurt, 1996)

Soutou, Georges-Henri, 'Vom Rhein zur Ruhr: Absichten und Planungen der französischen Regierung', in Krumeich and Schröder, eds., *Der Schatten des Weltkriegs*, pp. 63–84

Spitzer, Leo, *Italienische Kriegsgefangenenbriefe. Materialien zu einer Charakteristik der volkstümlichen italienischen Korrespondenz* (Bonn, 1921)

Stegmann, Dirk, 'Vom Neokonservatismus zum Protofaschismus: Konservative Partei, Vereine und Verbände 1893–1920', in id., Bernd-Jürgen Wendt and Peter-Christian Witt, eds., *Deutscher Konservatismus im 19. und 20. Jahrhundert. Festschrift für Fritz Fischer zum 75. Geburtstag und zum 50. Doktorjubiläum* (Bonn, 1983), pp. 199–230

Steiner, Zara S., *Britain and the Origins of the First World War* (London, 1977)

—— 'The foreign office and the war', in Francis H. Hinsley, ed., *British Foreign Policy under Sir Edward Grey* (Cambridge, 1977), pp. 516–31

Stern, Fritz, 'Together and Apart: Fritz Haber and Albert Einstein', in id., *Einstein's German World* (London, 2001; Princeton, 1999)

Sternhell, Zeev, Mario Sznajder, and Maia Asheri, *Die Entstehung der faschistischen Ideologie. Von Sorel zu Mussolini* (Hamburg, 1999) (*Naissance de l'idéologie fasciste*, Paris, 1989)

Stevenson, David, *French War Aims Against Germany 1914–1919* (Oxford, 1982)

—— *Armaments and the Coming of War in Europe* (Oxford, 1996)

—— 'French war aims and peace planning', in Boemeke et al., eds., *The Treaty of Versailles*, pp. 87–109

—— 'French strategy on the Western Front, 1914–1918', in Chickering and Förster, eds., *Great War, Total War*, pp. 297–326

Stibbe, Matthew, *German Anglophobia and the Great War, 1914–1918* (Cambridge, 2001)

Stone, Norman, *The Eastern Front 1914–1917* (London, 1975)

Storz, Dieter, *Kriegsbild und Rüstung vor 1914. Europäische Landstreitkräfte vor dem Ersten Weltkrieg* (Herford, Berlin, and Bonn, 1992)

Strachan, Hew, *The First World War*, vol. 1, *To Arms* (Oxford, 2001)

Theweleit, Klaus, *Male Fantasies*, 2 vols. (Leamington Spa, 1987; German edn. 1977–78)

Thoß, Bruno, 'Die Zeit der Weltkriege—Epochen als Erfahrungseinheit?', in Thoß and Volkmann, eds., *Erster Weltkrieg. Zweiter Weltkrieg,* pp. 7–30

—— and Hans-Erich Volkmann, eds., *Erster Weltkrieg, Zweiter Weltkrieg. Ein Vergleich. Krieg, Kriegserlebnis, Kriegserfahrung in Deutschland* (Paderborn, 2002)

Travers, Tim H. E., 'Technology, tactics and morale: Jean de Bloch, the Boer War, and British military theory, 1900–1914', in *The Journal of Modern History,* 51 (1979), pp. 264–86

Triebel, Florian, *Kultur und Kalkül. Der Eugen Diederichs Verlag 1930–1949,* phil. Diss. Universität Konstanz, 2001, URL: http://www.ub.uni-konstanz.de/kops/volltexte/2003/1123/ (consulted on 16 August 2005). This was published as a book: (Munich, 2004)

Trumpener, Ulrich, *Germany and the Ottoman Empire 1914–1918* (Princeton, 1968)

Ullrich, Volker, *Kriegsalltag. Hamburg im ersten Weltkrieg* (Cologne, 1982)

Ulrich, Bernd, *Die Augenzeugen. Deutsche Feldpostbriefe in Kriegs- und Nachkriegszeit 1914–1933* (Essen, 1997)

—— ' " . . . als wenn nichts geschehen wäre". Anmerkungen zur Behandlung der Kriegsopfer während des Ersten Weltkriegs', in Hirschfeld et al., eds, *Keiner fühlt sich hier mehr als Mensch,* pp. 115–29

Ungern-Sternberg, Jürgen and Wolfgang von, *Der Aufruf 'An die Kulturwelt!' Das Manifest der 93 und die Anfänge der Kriegspropaganda im Ersten Weltkrieg* (Stuttgart, 1996)

Upstone, Robert, 'Love and Beauty in an Age of Extremes', in id., ed., *William Orpen. Politics, Sex, and Death* (London, 2005), pp. 7–51

Vanneste, Alex, 'Het eerste "IJzeren Gordijn"? De elektrische draadversperring aan de Belgisch-Nederlandse grens tijdens de Eerste Wereldoorlog', *Het Tijdschrift van Dexia Bank,* 54 (2000), pp. 39–82

Verhey, Jeffrey, *The Spirit of 1914. Militarism, Myth, and Mobilization in Germany* (Cambridge, 2000)

Vigezzi, Brunello, *Da Giolitti a Salandra* (Florence, 1969)

Vincent, C[harles] Paul, *The Politics of Hunger. The Allied Blockade of Germany, 1915–1919* (Athens, Oh., and London, 1985)

Volkmann, Hans-Erich, 'Gesellschaft und Militär am Ende des Ersten und des Zweiten Weltkrieges', in Thoß and Volkmann, eds., *Erster Weltkrieg, Zweiter Weltkrieg,* pp. 841–72

Vondung, Klaus, 'Propaganda oder Sinndeutung', in id., ed., *Kriegserlebnis. Der Erste Weltkrieg in der literarischen Gestaltung und symbolischen Deutung der Nationen* (Göttingen, 1980), pp. 11–37

Ward, David, 'Intellectuals, culture and power in modern Italy', in Zygmunt G. Barański and Rebecca J. West, eds., *The Cambridge Companion to Modern Italian Culture,* (Cambridge, 2001), pp. 81–96

Wehler, Hans-Ulrich, *The German Empire 1871–1918,* (Leamington Spa, 1985; German edn. 1973)

—— *Deutsche Gesellschaftsgeschichte*, 4 vols., vol. 3: *Von der 'Deutschen Doppelrevolution' bis zum Beginn des Ersten Weltkriegs 1949–1914* (Munich, 1995)

Weisbrod, Bernd, 'Gewalt in der Politik. Zur politischen Kultur in Deutschland zwischen den beiden Weltkriegen', *Geschichte in Wissenschaft und Unterricht*, 43 (1992), pp. 391–404

Wette, Wolfram, *Gustav Noske: eine politische Biographie* (Düsseldorf, 1987)

Williamson, Samuel R., *Austria-Hungary and the Origins of the First World War* (London, 1991)

Wilson, Keith, ed., *Decisions for War 1914* (London, 1995)

—— 'Britain', in id., ed., *Decisions for War 1914*, pp. 175–208

Wilson, Trevor, *The Myriad Faces of War. Britain and the Great War, 1914–1918* (Cambridge, 1986)

Winter, Denis, *Haig's Command. A Reassessment* (Harmondsworth, 1992; 1991)

Winter, Jay, 'Some paradoxes of the First World War', in Richard Wall and Jay Winter, *The Upheaval of War. Family, Work and Welfare in Europe, 1914–1918* (Cambridge, 1988), pp. 9–42

—— *The Experience of World War I* (London, 1989; 1988)

—— *Sites of Memory, Sites of Mourning. The Great War in European Cultural History* (Cambridge, 1995)

—— 'Surviving the war: life expectation, illness, and mortality rates in Paris, London, and Berlin, 1914–1919', in id. and Jean-Louis Robert, eds., *Capital Cities at War. Paris, London, Berlin 1914–1919* (Cambridge, 1997), pp. 487–523

—— 'Forms of kinship and remembrance in the aftermath of the Great War', in id. and Emmanuel Sivan, eds., *War and Remembrance in the Twentieth Century* (Cambridge, 1999), pp. 40–60

Wirsching, Andreas, 'Political violence in France and Italy after 1918', *Journal of Modern European History*, 1 (2003), pp. 60–79

Wurzer, Georg, 'Die Erfahrung der Extreme. Kriegsgefangene in Russland 1914–1918', in Jochen Oltmer, ed., *Kriegsgefangene im Europa des Ersten Weltkriegs* (Paderborn, etc., 2006) pp. 97–125

Ziemann, Benjamin, *Front und Heimat. Ländliche Kriegserfahrungen im südlichen Bayern 1914–1923* (Essen, 1997)

Sources and Acknowledgements for Illustrations

Figure 16. *L'Isola dei morti. Fagaré*, painting by Giulio Aristide Sartorio (Copyright holder not traced/photo courtesy of Ministerio degli Affari Esteri)

Figure 17. *Attaceo aereo di Venezia*, fresco by Giulio Aristide Sartorio (Copyright holder not traced/photo courtesy of Ministerio degli Affari Esteri)

Figure 18. Destruction caused by British artillery at Passchendaele (Bibliothek für Zeitgeschichte, Stuttgart/Archivalische Sammlungen)

Figure 19. Dixmuide after Allied shelling (Courtesy of Leuven University Archives)

Figure 20. Dixmuide, the main square (Courtesy of Leuven University Archives)

Figure 21. The deliberate demolition of a church by German forces—probably because it was being used as a target marker (The British Library)

Figure 22. Officers posing next to the destroyed fort of Loncin, near Liège (Courtesy of Leuven University Archives)

Figure 23. Officers posing next to the destroyed fort of Marchovelette, near Namur (Courtesy of Leuven University Archives)

Figure 24. Poster for a war loan (*Emprunt national*) by Chavanaz, 1918 (Photo courtesy of Historial de la Grande Guerre, Péronne (Somme)/© Yazid Medmoun)

Figure 25. German brothel in Belgium, from Ernst Friedrich, *War against War!* (Courtesy of Leuven University Archives)

Figure 26. *Changing Billets, Picardy*, painting by William Orpen, 1918 (Courtesy of Pyms Gallery, London)

Figure 27. Railwayman, mouth torn away and lower jaw gone (Courtesy of Leuven University Archives)

Figure 28. *Aufbrechender Mars und trauernde Frau 1914* ('Mars departing and woman mourning, 1914'), drawing by Max Beckmann (© DACS 2006/Courtesy of Max Beckmann Archiv)

Figure 29. *Die Granate* ('Shell', 1914), drawing by Max Beckmann (© DACS 2006/Sprengel Museum)

Figure 30. *Spielende Kinder* (Children Playing, 1918), by Max Beckmann. Sprengel Museum/©DACS 2007

Figure 31. *Auferstehung* ('Resurrection', 1918), unfinished painting by Max Beckmann (© DACS 2006/ Staatsgalerie Stuttgart)

Figure 32. *Mahlzeit in der Sappe* ('Meal in the Sap' [i.e. forward trench], 1924), etching by Otto Dix ((© DACS 2006/National Gallery of Australia, Canberra)

Figure 33. *Dead Germans in a Trench*, painting by William Orpen, 1918 (The Art Archive/Imperial War Museum)

Index